Springer Texts in Business and Economics

For further volumes:
http://www.springer.com/series/10099

V. Kumar • Werner Reinartz

Customer Relationship Management

Concept, Strategy, and Tools

 Springer

V. Kumar
Georgia State University
J. Mack Robinson College of Business
Center for Excellence in Brand and
Customer Management
Atlanta, Georgia
USA

Werner Reinartz
University of Cologne
Department of Retailing and
Customer Management
Köln
Germany

ISSN 2192-4333
ISBN 978-3-642-20109-7 (hardcover)
ISBN 978-3-642-20130-1 (softcover)
DOI 10.1007/978-3-642-20110-3
Springer Heidelberg New York Dordrecht London

ISSN 2192-4341 (electronic)
ISBN 978-3-642-20110-3   (eBook)

Library of Congress Control Number: 2012940215

Printed on acid-free paper

Springer is part of Springer Science+Business Media (www.springer.com)

Dedicated with Love
To my parents, Patta & Viswanathan and uncle Kannan, and
other family members – Prita, Anita, Rohan and Aparna
  - V. Kumar

To my family, Viktoria, Henry and Lily
  - Werner Reinartz

Preface

Customer relationship management (CRM) as a strategy and as a technology has gone through an amazing evolutionary journey. The initial technological approach has been followed by many disappointing initiatives only to see the maturing of the underlying concepts and applications in recent years. Today, CRM refers to a strategy, a set of tactics, and a technology that has become indispensible in the modern economy.

This book gives a unified treatment of the strategic and tactical aspects of customer relationship management as we know it today. It stresses developing an understanding of economic customer value as the guiding concept for marketing decisions. The goal of the book is to be a comprehensive and up-to-date learning companion for advanced undergraduate students, master students, and executives who want a detailed and conceptually sound insight into the field of CRM.

Aimed at students, teachers, and practitioners of CRM, this book offers a comprehensive treatment of CRM and database marketing, the approach to strategic CRM, implementing the CRM strategy and the various metrics to measure customer value. This book provides all the necessary steps in managing profitable customer relationships. It stresses on developing an understanding of Customer Value as the guiding concept for marketing decisions, and illustrates the importance of the Customer Lifetime Value metric as the guiding concept for profitable customer management. This book also analyzes the implementation of CRM strategies in the areas of loyalty programs, marketing campaigns, and channel management. Specifically, this book provides insights into several customer level marketing strategies that can be implemented by adopting a Customer Lifetime Value approach. The goal of this book is to be a useful learning companion to students, teachers, and practitioners of CRM.

The goal of this book is to be a useful learning companion to students, teachers, and practitioners of CRM. To summarize, with this book, you can:

- Obtain a comprehensive understanding of CRM strategy, concepts, and tools. This unified perspective would enable readers to see the forest AND the trees.
- Benefit from the numerous cases that show direct application of concepts thus making the material very accessible and applicable.
- Learn the latest developments in metrics, practices, and substantive domains (e.g. multi-channel management).

Objectives of this Text

This book captures the critical elements of managing customer relationships. The objectives in writing this text are to:

1. Outline the need for customer-centric marketing strategies.
2. Explore the science behind CRM and the effectiveness of various CRM techniques.
3. Explain the concepts, metrics, and techniques that form the backbone of CRM activities.
4. Learn and apply CRM tools and methodologies that aid customer-level analytics.
5. Provide clear examples and illustrations that tie concepts with real world scenarios.
6. Understand the relationship between CRM analytics and business performance.
7. Discuss the structure of databases, their uses and benefits from a marketing standpoint, rather than a technical one.
8. Understand the implications of CRM and marketing activities like loyalty programs, channel management, and planning promotional campaigns.
9. Learn the cutting-edge profitable customer-level strategies and how they have been implemented in companies with impressive bottom-line results.
10. Understand the potential for the growth of CRM as the dominant form of marketing strategy.

Highlights of this Book

The book offers a comprehensive treatment of CRM and database marketing. The highlights of the book are as follows:

1. An overview and summary at the beginning and the end of each chapter to help the reader stay focused.
2. Exhaustive cases to help readers appreciate how CRM is being carried out in the age of information.
3. Real world illustrations in various chapters under the title "CRM at Work."
4. Mini cases at the end of various chapters designed to address key managerial issues, stimulate thinking, and encourage a problem solving approach.
5. Illustrations and explanations of key traditional and new marketing metrics a clear and concise manner.
6. Clear explanations for the need for customer value metrics, such as the traditional past customer value, and the forward-looking customer lifetime value.

7. Procedures to follow when measuring past customer value and customer lifetime value.
8. Explanations of techniques like RFM, logistic regression, decision trees, and data mining in an easy to follow fashion.
9. Presentation of the latest advances in customer value management practices, which include implementation of several CRM related strategies.
10. Adoption of a non-technical viewpoint of CRM rather than a technical one.

Supplements to the Book

1. An online Instructor's Manual with Test Questions accompanies this text. This manual provides solutions to end-of-chapter Questions and Problems, and discusses all text cases in greater detail. Exam questions are arranged by chapters and include multiple-choice and true/false questions. An example of a course syllabus is presented, and many suggestions for the organization of the course are provided.
2. Web site support: The Web site will be updated periodically in order to supplement the text with new up-to-date examples. This site includes the cases and Web links cited in the text.
3. A computerized version of the test bank is available to instructors for customization of their exams.
4. Downloadable PowerPoint presentations are available for all chapters via the text Web site.

Organization of the Text

The book adopts a holistic approach towards CRM by providing the concepts, explaining the tools and developing relevant strategies. It introduces key concepts and metrics needed to understand and implement CRM strategies. It describes the process of successful CRM implementation. Finally, it presents techniques to aid in strategic marketing decisions using the concept of customer lifetime value. The book is divided into four parts as follows:

- *Part One: Introduction* consists of two chapters and introduces the concept of customer equity/value as a key aspect of customer relationship management (CRM). This part explains the role of CRM in the current business scenario and presents a comprehensive link that connects CRM, database marketing and customer value.
- *Part Two: Strategic CRM* consisting of Chaps. 3 and 4 introduces the concepts related to Strategic CRM. This part describes the difference between strategic and functional CRM and presents the case for developing a CRM strategy. It also elaborates on the elements of a CRM system and provides the implementation aspects of the customer management strategy.

- *Part Three: Analytical CRM* consisting of Chaps. 5–8 presents the tools pertaining to Analytical CRM. This part focuses on commonly used CRM metrics and techniques such as acquisition rate, retention rate, share of wallet, logistic regression, decision trees, RFM, past customer value, and customer lifetime value. This part also discusses the concepts relating to data mining and implementing database marketing. Types of databases and their uses and benefits are outlined. Guidelines to develop and plan marketing campaigns in order to maximize customer value are discussed. This section also addresses the technical aspects of CRM software tools and dashboards required to implement and manage CRM applications.

- *Part Four: Operational CRM* consisting of Chaps. 9–16 presents the strategies involved in Operational CRM. This part discusses loyalty programs and the characteristics that make up an effective loyalty program. This part also discusses the impact of CRM on marketing channels. Tracing recent advances in CRM applications, this section illustrates new and emerging techniques in customer value based CRM. Critical marketing issues like optimum resource allocation, purchase sequence, and the link between acquisition, retention, and profitability are examined on the basis of empirical findings. These applications are categorized on the basis of applicability for the B2B and B2C scenarios. The last chapter looks into the future and envisions the developments and changes that are likely to take CRM ahead.

Acknowledgments

We wish to thank Benedikt Berlemann, Vanessa Gartmeier, Monika Käuferle, Lara Lobschat, Bharath Rajan, Peter Saffert, and Barbara Unterbusch for their assistance and contribution in the preparation of this text. We would also like to thank our colleagues at various universities for giving valuable suggestions in developing this book. Special thanks owed to Michaela Bastian, Benjamin Leblois, Seul-Gi Lee, Amber McCain, Andrea Nickolay, and Sandra Scheer for their assistance in various aspects of the book. We owe additional thanks to Renu for copyediting the book.

V. Kumar and Werner Reinartz

Contents

List of Figures

List of Tables

List of Abbreviations

ABC	Activity Based Costing
AC	Acquisition Cost
ACS	Acquisition Cost Savings
AES	Asset Efficiency Services
AID	Automatic Interaction Detection
AIT	Average Inter-Purchase Time
AMC	Allowable Marketing Cost
APR	Annual Percentage Rate
aSCR	Aggregate Share of Category Requirement
aSW	Aggregate Share of Wallet
AVR	Automated Voice Recognition
B2B	Business-to-Business
BE	Breakeven Value
BEI	Breakeven Index
BYS	Big Yellow Square
CCO	Chief Customer Officers
CBV	Customer Brand Value
CE	Customer Equity
CEO	Chief Executive Officer
CES	Customer Equity Share
CHAID	Chi-Square Automatic Interaction Detection
CLV	Customer Lifetime Value
CM	Contribution Margin
CPE	Cost per Enquiry
CPM	Cost per Thousand
CPR	Cost per Response
CPS	Cost per Sale
CR	Conversion Rate
CRM	Customer Relationship Management
CRV	Customer Referral Value
CSR	Corporate Social Responsibility
CSS	Customer Service and Support
CTI	Computer Telephony Integration
DAP	Development Action Plans
DPWN	Deutsche Post World Net
DRR	Direct Response Radio
EDI	Electronic Data Interchange

EM	Expectation Maximization
EPIC	Electronic Privacy Information Center
ERP	Enterprise Resource Planning
ETL	Extract-Transform-Load
EU	European Union
FDI	Foreign Direct Investment
FMCG	Fast-Moving Consumer Goods
FTC	Federal Trade Commission
GCRM	Global Customer Relationship Management
GB	Gigabyte
GM	General Motors
H	Hypothesis
HBR	Harvard Business Review
HR	Human Resources
IaaS	Infrastructure as a Service
IBS	Information-Based Strategy
IM	Internal Marketing
IMC	Integrated Marketing Communications
iSCR	Individual Share of Category Requirement
iSW	Individual Share of Wallet
IT	Information Technology
KAM	Key Account Management
KPI	Key Performance Indicators
LP	Loyalty Program
LTV	Lifetime Value
M&A	Marketing and Analysis
MLE	Maximum Likelihood Estimation
MS	Market Share
NBD	Negative Binomial Distribution
NFC	Near Field Communication
NPV	Net Present Value
P&G	Procter & Gamble
PaaS	Platform as a Service
PCVB	Past Customer Value
PDS	Process Delegation Services
PLS	Product Lifecycle Services
PSS	Process Support Services
QA	Quality Assurance
R&D	Research & Development
Rc	Retention Rate Ceiling
RFID	Radio Frequency Identification
RFM	Recency, Frequency and Monetary
ROI	Return on Investment
ROP	Return on Promotion
SaaS	Software as a Service
SCR	Share of Category Requirement
SFA	Sales Force Automation

SFM	Sales Force Management
SME	Small and Medium-Sized Enterprises
SOW	Share of Wallet
SPC	Satisfaction-Loyalty-Profit Chain
SPG	Starwood Preferred Guest
SR	Survival Rate
SSN	Social Security Number
SW	Share of Wallet
USP	Unique Selling Proposition
V	Volume of Sales
VLC	Value of an average Lost Customer
VRU	Voice Response Units
VW	Volkswagen
WACC	Weighted Average Cost of Capital
WOM	Word-of-Mouth

Part I

CRM: Conceptual Foundation

Strategic Customer Relationship Management Today

1.1 Overview

Peter Drucker defined the marketing concept as "the business as seen from the customer's point of view." This definition has undergone further refinement, such that the marketing concept became a distinct organizational culture, represented by a fundamental shared set of beliefs and values that put the customer at the center of a firm's thinking about strategy and operations (Deshpande & Webster, 1989). These definitions emerged when the approach to marketing was predominantly about addressing the needs of customer segments, because distinguishing individual customers was far too difficult.

Thus traditional mass marketing approaches segmented customer populations according to consumer needs. Firms then designed standardized products and services to deliver to those segments. With mass marketing, the importance of the individual preferences of an individual consumer gets downgraded, for two main reasons. First, individual customer-level data were not available. Second, serving the needs of individual customers was expensive and, in some cases, impossible for firms.

Leaps in information technology and the ubiquity of the Internet have changed all that, together with vast improvements in flexible manufacturing and outsourcing practices. Today, understanding and meeting individual customer needs have become the key dimension on which firms forge their competitive advantage. With this shift, it is important to state clearly the underlying belief that can drive the success of firms: The marketing concept needs to make way for the customer concept.

> The customer concept is the conduct of all marketing activities with the belief that the individual customer is the central unit of analysis and action.

This definition emphasizes the analysis and measurement of marketing activities and consequences at the individual customer level. When marketing activities are directed at the individual, interactive relationships can be forged by the firm with individual customers.

In this chapter, we introduce two key terms: customer value and customer relationship management (CRM). We also discuss changes taking place with respect to (1) consumers, (2) marketplaces, (3) technology, and (4) marketing functions. Rapid changes related to these forces drive firms to be customer centric and market driven. Simultaneously, there is a visible shift from product-based to customer-based marketing. In other words, firms are updating their processes and practices to align with the customer concept, and marketing plays the important role of forging relationships with customers so that the firm can stay relevant to the customer and accountable to its stakeholders.

1.2 An Introduction to Strategic CRM

At one time, marketing campaigns aimed mainly to increase customer loyalty to a product or service. The thought was that more loyal customers would engage in more repeat business, develop a larger tolerance to price increases, and therefore be more profitable to the firm. However, this pathway does not always hold. A very loyal customer may repeatedly call customer service with questions and constantly hunt for the best price on a product, taking advantage of every rebate and sales offer. Ultimately, this customer actually costs the company money, rather than providing a source of profits. An important part of CRM is identifying the different types of customers and then developing specific strategies for interacting with each one. Examples of such strategies include developing better relationships with *profitable* customers, locating and enticing new customers who will be profitable, and finding appropriate strategies for unprofitable customers, which could mean terminating those relationships that cause a company to lose money.

The concept of *customer value* thus is critical to CRM. It refers to the economic value of the customer relationship to the firm, expressed as a contribution margin or net profit. As a marketing metric, customer value offers an important decision aid, beyond its ability to evaluate marketing effectiveness. A firm can both measure and optimize its marketing efforts by incorporating customer value at the core of its decision-making process.

In turn, the notion of CRM with customer value at its core enables us to define CRM from a customer value perspective:

> CRM is the practice of analyzing and using marketing databases and leveraging communication technologies to determine corporate practices and methods that maximize the lifetime value of each customer to the firm.

A customer value–based approach to CRM then can help answer the following questions:
- When does it pay to pursue customer loyalty?
- How does loyalty link to customer profitability?
- How can we compute the future profitability of a customer?
- What is a good measure of customer lifetime value?
- How can firms optimally allocate marketing resources to maximize customer value?
- How might firms maximize the return on marketing investments?

By answering these questions, it becomes possible to leverage the customer value–based approach for superior marketing decisions, because *benefits* accrue in the following forms:
- Decreased costs
- Maximized revenues
- Better profits and return on investment (ROI)
- Acquisition and retention of profitable customers
- Reactivation of dormant customers

Yet the field of CRM remains under development. Consulting firms and companies have created their own definitions and conceptualizations that continue to evolve, though they can be grouped into three types: functional level, customer-facing front-end level, and strategic level. These types of CRM are outlined briefly here, before we discuss them in detail in Chap. 2.

1. *Functional level:* Customer relationship management can be practiced on a very limited functional basis (e.g., sales force automation in the sales function, campaign management by the marketing function). Such CRM often combines with a strong technology orientation that arises when vendors need to position their particular product. For some vendors or buyers, functional CRM is nearly synonymous with technology.

2. *Customer-facing front-end level:* This type of CRM evolves from practitioners' need to describe a new business capability or new arrangement of capabilities that focuses on the total customer experience. The goal is to build a single view of the customer across all contact channels and to distribute customer intelligence to all customer-facing functions. This view stresses the importance of coordinating information across time and across contact channels to manage the entire customer relationship systematically. It also supports the notion of marketing to customers throughout their purchasing lifecycle.

3. *Strategic level:* The primary objective of strategy-centric definitions of CRM is to free the term "CRM" from any technology underpinnings and from specific customer

management techniques. These definitions describe CRM as a process to implement customer centricity in the market and build shareholder value. Here, knowledge about customers and their preferences has implications for the entire organization, such as for R&D or supply chain management.

This book defines CRM from a business strategy perspective. CRM aims to gain a long-term competitive advantage by optimally delivering value and satisfaction to the customer and extracting business value from the exchange. From this standpoint,

> CRM is the *strategic process* of *selecting* customers that a firm can most profitably serve and shaping *interactions* between a company and these *customers*. The ultimate goal is to optimize the *current and future value of customers* for the company.

The key components of this definition include:

- *Strategic process:* The CRM activities are initiated and managed from the very top of the organization. Strategic initiatives by definition span multiple, if not all, organizational functions. CRM does not belong to any single department but rather demands contributions and reinforcement from all corporate functions. There is no place for a *silo mentality* that discourages information sharing and condones the idea that one function "owns the customer." Furthermore, CRM is a continuing *process* that cannot be handled as just another software implementation project. It must be viewed as a continuous effort to become an ever more customer-centric company.
- *Selection:* When the economic value of a customer is the basis for resource allocation, firms focus on their most profitable or potentially profitable customers. It is not about denying services to certain customers but rather about recognizing a fit between the firm's offer and a customer's desires, behaviors, and characteristics.
- *Interactions:* The relationship between the customer and the firm takes the form of an interactive dialog. Information and goods are exchanged, and the exchange evolves as a

function of past exchanges. This is very different from a scenario in which firms sell one-off products and services to customers.

- *Customers:* The term is applied broadly here. Depending on the industry and company, a customer can be an individual account, one or several segments within a market, or an entire market. Customers include not only end users but also intermediaries, such as distributors, retailers, and so on. Generally, firms are moving away from single, all-purpose solutions and starting to satisfy smaller segments with better targeted products, services, and communication propositions. Although segmentation is nothing new, the degree of fine-tuning is considerably tighter for CRM, such that firms now expect to target individual customers with customized product offerings.
- *Current and future value of the customer:* Optimizing current and future value means that firms move away from extracting profit from single transactions and work to maximize profits over a series of transactions. Firms want to maximize customer equity— that is, the value of all customer relationships. In this process, traditional measures such as market share get replaced with new measures, as for example share of wallet and customer lifetime value.

Yet it also remains important for managers to manage fairness in the exchange process. Optimization of the current and future value of customers intrinsically recognizes that unless customers are treated with respect and fairness, it is impossible to manage and sustain a mutually profitable relationship.

Overall, marketing-driven customer relationship management is a relationship management concept based on established marketing principles that recognizes the need to balance organizational and customer interests carefully. Marketing-driven CRM is not a result primarily of technological solutions but is rather supported by them. These complex sets of activities together form the basis for a sustainable and hard to imitate competitive advantage: the customer-centric organization. CRM also involves automating and enhancing customer-centric business processes, including sales, marketing, and service. Instead of just automating these processes, CRM focuses on ensuring that front-office applications improve customer satisfaction, which results in increased customer loyalty and thus affects the company's bottom line. With CRM, a company creates an environment and flexible support system that can deal readily with issues surrounding product innovation, increasing customer expectations, acquisitions, globalization, deregulation, the convergence of traditional markets, emergence of new technologies, privacy issues, and new customer contact channels. In the following section, we describe these main reasons and trends that underlie the growing importance of a strategic customer management approach.

1.3 Why Managing Customers Is More Critical than Ever

The competitive landscape and the volatile economies that mark the modern world mean there is no way around the need to manage customers profitably in the long term. It is a more pressing issue than ever before. Data are easily available, so much that firms are overwhelmed, and the amount doubles every 18 months. New trends, such as the rise of social media and mobile devices, then arrive to create new CRM challenges for companies.

This section outlines the major factors that influence strategic CRM and have severe consequences for companies; it also introduces a customer-centric management approach and shows how the evolution of CRM points to a new understanding. Modern firms face gradual but still seismic changes with respect to four major forces: (1) consumers, (2) marketplaces, (3) technology, and (4) marketing functions. It is important to understand those changes to function successfully in the marketplace.

1.3.1 Changes with Respect to Consumers

There are nine major consumer trends, listed in Table 1.1, that are essential to understand the

growing importance of a strategic approach to CRM. They comprise two main subgroups: demographic and behavioral changes. Demographic changes relate mostly to current developments in the growing diversity of customers; behavioral changes describe shifts in the way consumers act and react to market offers.

1.3.1.1 Demographic Changes and Increasing Consumer Diversity

A key development is the diversity of customers whom vendors confront. On the most basic level, this diversity is triggered by the changing demographic composition of the population, as can be observed in all industrialized nations, from Western Europe to the United States and Japan. Changing demographics serve as a good indicator of the future marketplace, because providers must change their offerings when the demographic make-up, and thus the needs, of the marketplace change. Three important demographic trends are transforming the marketplace:

Aging populations in developed countries
The birth rate in most developed countries has been falling for more than two decades. This phenomenon has been described as *deyouthing*—an historically unprecedented event. Populations in many developed countries are actually shrinking. For example, between 1990 and 2030, the number of Japanese under the age of 50 years will decrease by some 24 million people, a net loss of 26%. The differences in median ages across countries thus can be quite dramatic. In the United States, the median age of adults is 43 and will reach 50 in less than two decades. Middle-age values and perspectives thus will increasingly dominate the national psyche—including older consumers' generally favorable responses to relationship marketing approaches.

Increasing diversity in ethnicity
The closer integration of countries in Western Europe has made it easier for people to move and establish lives abroad. Such migration often is driven by better economic conditions in highly industrialized countries, such that it leads to great increases in cultural and ethnic diversity in countries such as France, England, the

Table 1.1 Major consumer trends

Demographic changes and increasing consumer diversity	Behavioral changes
	Time scarcity
Aging populations, especially in developed countries	Value consciousness and intolerance for low service levels
Increasing diversity in terms of ethnicity	Information availability and technological aptitude
Increasing individualization	Decreased loyalty
	Rise of convenience and self-service
	Increased usage of social media

Netherlands, and Germany. The United States historically has been ethnically diverse, and that trend is on the rise: Hispanics are the fastest growing group, and in California and Texas, whites will soon become minority populations. As a result of the shifting ethnic make-up of U.S. society, several changes are underway. Markets are becoming more segmented. Vendors must cater to ethnically diverse needs in housing, clothing, and food. Marketing communications will reflect this diversity for companies to serve their customers effectively.

Increasing individualization

In many Western countries, approximately 60% of women work full time, a trend that places tremendous pressure on traditional notions of family. In the old model, women stopped working when they decided to have children. In the new model, they continue to work, regardless of whether or when they have kids. By losing an anchor, in the form of a full-time homemaker, the family is evolving as a unit of social and consumption analysis. Single-parent and dual-career households proliferate, and the need to define a separate existence or space encourages highly individualistic lifestyles and behaviors, even within family units. Firms must increasingly consider the individual behaviors of family members who spend more time apart, rather than assuming household homogeneity. This trend will increase the need for personalized attention to each household member, though without further increasing the already high degree of perceived loneliness in society. The marketplace will feel the impact of such demographic trends in the form of

consumer choices, such as outsourcing of activities due to time constraints, more consumption on demand (24/7), and more consumption on the basis of symbolism and social group values. Customers who are single also may seek out products and services that offer them social and emotional value.

1.3.1.2 Behavioral Changes

As these developments show, developing a customer-centric business strategy requires consideration of changes to the overall behavior of consumers. These shifts are closely linked to changes in media usage, availability of information, attitude toward service levels, and convenience.

Time Scarcity

Many households are technologically rich but time poor. When firms impose time or place constraints (e.g., stores open only from 8:00 AM to 5:00 PM), consumers react negatively. Time in particular is becoming a most precious commodity. As various activities compete for time, consumers redesign tasks that consume too much of it and embrace time-saving and time-shifting technologies. For example, cooking at home may become a special occasion, and the kitchen serves as a communication center rather than a food center. Another factor is time spent getting places: The number of vehicles on the road has risen six times faster than the population growth rate. According to Texas Transportation Institute, U.S. drivers spent an average of 300 h on road, which contributes to their lack of time.

Thus consumers increasingly engage in multitasking. For example, many people consider it normal to use the phone while driving or surf the web on a mobile device while watching television. In response, car manufacturers are building GPS, Internet, and e-mail functionalities into their cars. The sales of push lawn mowers are up dramatically too—not because people cannot afford a gardener but because they want to combine exercise time with tending their lawn.

Thus marketers must provide products and services on demand and pay careful attention to time value when interacting with customers. The success of Internet banking is largely due to its ability to increase customer convenience dramatically by eliminating the limitations of strict branch hours. Consumer time scarcity thus offers a terrific opportunity for the savvy marketer who can effectively bring relevant, value-added messages, products, and services to time-starved consumers.

Value Consciousness and Intolerance for Low Service Levels
Customers are more demanding. Their expectations of reliable products and responsive services are more extreme. They continuously demand more and are much less tolerant of failures. Customers also compare their experiences against best-in-class examples. As they become more educated about options available in the market, as they try new products and services, and as they develop new needs, their expectation levels just keep rising. And every time their expectations are met, they raise their bar, so what once delighted customers is likely to only satisfy them today (Fig. 1.1).

The phenomenon of increasing expectation levels is not going away. It is an inherent characteristic of doing business and cannot be avoided. Yet firms in industrialized economies are struggling to satisfy customers. Across a wide swath of industries, U.S. customer satisfaction has been generally flat with no significant upward tendencies. The experience in other countries, including Germany, Sweden, and New Zealand, appears similar. We can only speculate about the reasons, but one ironic explanation might realize that early, technology-focused CRM implementations contributed to customer malaise. As firms started using technology to reduce personal interactions and rely more on Internet or call-center–based transactions, customers experienced less quality in the exchange process.

Information Availability and Technological Aptitude
Changes to technology are perhaps the most dramatic form of change we see. Internet technology has enabled virtually any manufacturer or service provider to publish its information and perform transactions online. Powerful online search engines have dramatically decreased customers' search costs. Customers can access a tremendous amount of published information using any digital device connected to the Internet. In 2010 in the United States alone, 239.9 million people functioned online, and the number continues to increase every day (see www.internetworldstats.com).

The availability of information has made customers more knowledgeable when making purchase decisions, even at the point of sale. Mobile technologies built into smartphones allow shoppers to scan barcodes, get all the information they need about the product, and conduct a price comparison on the go. Customers increasingly appreciate the use of such technologies to gather information; for example, Barcoo, a company that produces smartphone applications that allow users to find independent, consumer-generated information on any product, has more than one million users in Germany alone. It is a new form of transparency, and companies must get accustomed to it.

Being aware of their options and how easy it is to perform comparisons of providers means customers have a much more powerful position when dealing with providers. This shift has both positive and negative impacts on the provider. On the positive side, the playing field is leveled for providers that make their information available to customers. On the negative side, a level playing field makes it harder for providers to differentiate their products and services from those of their competitors in a way that attracts attention and influences purchase decisions.

Increased Use of Social Media
Closely related to information availability is the rising trend of the interactive web, or Web 2.0, and its dramatic transformation of how

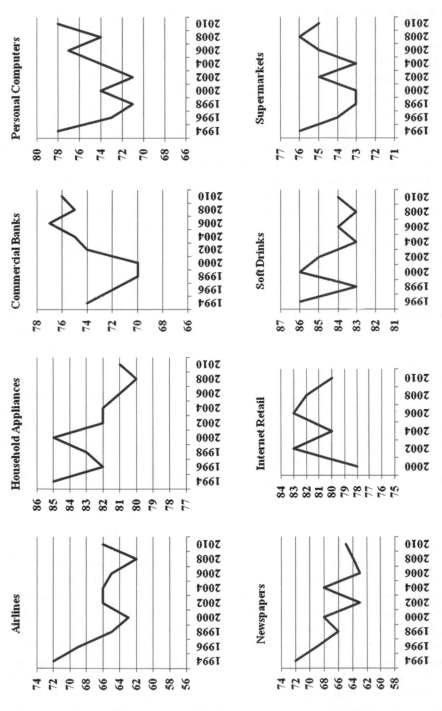

Fig. 1.1 Decreasing/stagnating overall satisfaction among U.S. consumers (Source: www.theacsi.org)

consumers act. People talk online about products, inform themselves, and engage in far more word of mouth, because information sharing is no longer limited to people they actually know. Companies must realize this fundamental shift in consumer behavior and act accordingly, especially to take advantage of at least three key opportunities for companies. First, they can learn by listening to consumers online. Online buzz helps companies understand what consumers really want, and they can use these insights for product development, communication strategies, and success measures. Second, social media offers ways to improve the timeliness of customer feedback. People who use social media to interact with companies, such as through Facebook or Twitter, expect to receive from customer immediate responses management. In 2011, more than 500 million active consumers on Facebook spent 700 billion minutes there each month, often browsing company-run Facebook pages. That means firms have great opportunities to interact with customers in channels that the customers themselves have chosen. Third, social media allow companies to execute new forms of communication strategies and advertising that integrate consumers. For example, Henkel used social media to excite people about a limited edition of detergent by letting consumers design the package and vote for the best option. The winning design appeared in stores as a limited edition. Consumers are not longer happy to be confronted with a message; they want to be an active part of it.

Decreased Loyalty

Increasingly selective consumers diversify their business as institutions implement more intensive cross-selling campaigns. Figure 1.2 shows the responses to the question, "Are you planning to change your landline phone provider?" asked in a 2010 survey of German customers by infas Market Research. Only 33% were truly loyal to their provider; more than 50% planned to switch. These data exemplify how difficult it is for companies to make their customers loyal.

Some brands (e.g., Apple) have a truly loyal fan base, but they represent the exception and not the rule. A 2011 AMP Agency study, "Inside the Buy," showed that only 4% of consumers between 25 and 49 years of age are loyal to a particular brand, meaning they never buy anything else. Thus 96% of consumers are eternally ready to switch, so companies must work hard to persuade customers each and every time. Loyalty is not something that most companies can count on.

Need for Convenience and the Rise of Self-Service

As their time poverty increases, consumers seek more and more convenience, which has impacts on all aspects of business. Small convenience stores, like the Tesco Express format, that offer a limited assortment can cater to daily needs; formats such as Marks & Spencer's Food boast a wide offer of prepared meals and ready-to-cook ingredients. In their relationship with a vendor, consumers demand a more active role by the company. It can no longer just answer questions; for example, many financial institutions now offer customized monthly reports of customers' financial activity.

At the same time, demands for convenience have led to the rise of self-service options. When they can, people want to take care of their own needs without hassle. Online banking platforms give consumers the means to buy stocks and search for information on their own. As these tools grow more sophisticated, consumers see no reason to interact with employees. In retailing for example, shoppers can use dedicated self-service checkouts, scan their basket items, and pay without further assistance. Even McDonald's offers self-service terminals: Customers place their order and pay without talking to any employee, then pick up their order from a dedicated express lane.

Other recent innovations in this field include home delivery and online shopping services offered by grocery stores such as Tesco and Walmart, though these examples have appeared in only a few countries so far (e.g., UK). Yet the

Fig. 1.2 German
consumer responses to
"Are you planning to
switch phone operators?"
(Source: Infas, 2010)

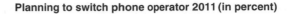

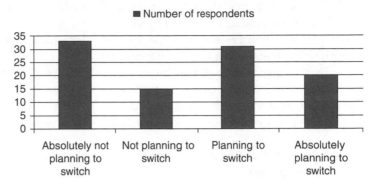

overall notion of online shopping, conducted outside regular store hours, has added significantly to the development of a stronger orientation toward convenient offers and 24/7 access to goods. For example, according to HDE, consumers in Germany bought 2.5 billion EUR worth of goods online in 2001, but that level rose to more than 23 billion EUR in 2011.

In summary, companies must do both: Empower consumers to perform minor services themselves by offering convenient self-service options but be consistently available when customer problems grow more complex.

1.3.1.3 Consequences

Changes in markets, demographics, and overall consumer lifestyles have powerful impacts on customer behavior. The overarching result is that consumers place greater demands on firms, in terms of high-value products and services provided at the right place at the right time and higher expectations for transparency and consumer focus. Marketers must be extremely wary of making heavy time demands of consumers. Generally speaking, customers have more power relative to vendors as their technological aptitude and product knowledge continue to increase. Diversification and time scarcity increase the pursuit of more personalized products and services that also offer the very best deal. This trend is well corroborated by the increasing inefficiency of traditional mass marketing approaches (which we discuss subsequently). Seemingly paradoxically, consumers' time scarcity and need for consumption-on-

demand make them good targets for *well-crafted* relationship strategies. Firms that can satisfy this demand will thrive in this new environment.

The reality of a changing customer environment is underscored by the results of an international top management survey by PWC. When asked, "What are the critical challenges that confront senior management today?" the most responses by far mentioned "meeting consumer demands" (67.5%) and "technological change and integration" (67.3%). Cost reduction (21.3%), once a major challenge for companies, fell from its top spot.

Another survey of top management executives regarding organizational challenges, conducted by McKinsey & Co. in 2007, offers similar results (McKinsey & Co., 2007). The ubiquitous access to information, importance of environmental aspects, and changing consumer landscape represent companies' top challenges. For example, 36% of respondents mentioned the need to manage complexity by tailoring products or services to different local conditions and preferences without diluting the brand.

Demographic and behavioral shifts mean that demand is becoming more and more heterogeneous, individualized, and fragmented. A mass marketing approach focused on pushing similar products to everyone thus has become a weak proposition.

1.3.2   Changes with Respect to the Marketplace

Until recently, business was characterized by its manufacturing. The focus on goods rather than services led to mass-market, product-focused marketing strategies, in which businesses tried to sell the same product to as many people as possible. This strategy increased the cost of acquiring new customers but lowered switching costs for customers. But globalization of the marketplace, the growth of services economies, and technology advances mean that business has undergone some key changes and developments.

1.3.2.1 Intensified Competition for Customers

As trade barriers fall and geographic boundaries are redefined, by both established and emergent trading blocs, the idea of a location advantage is being eroded for most companies. Access to markets is no longer localized, so demands for logistics management and distribution partnering are becoming more significant.

1.3.2.2 Fragmented Markets

In a developed market in which supply exceeds demand, customers have differentiated needs. To address customers' particular needs, the market must be broken down into multiple segments, which facilitates individualized marketing.

1.3.2.3 Difficult Differentiation

The quality of objective product attributes has risen substantially and is no longer a source of competitive advantage for most companies. Brand loyalty founded on a product differential is a relative, not an absolute, achievement. As products' quality differentials diminish, companies seek competitive advantages through their closer, service-focused relationships. A case in point is an example from the grocery industry, which continues to experience the rise of private labels. Private labels are growing worldwide (Institut d'Economie Industrielle [IDEI], 2011), such that approximately 25% of all grocery sales are now generated by private labels, whereas in 2003, this number was only 15%. Some forecasts suggest that by 2025, 50% of all sales will include private label. Even more conservative estimates still see room for growth: Planet Retail forecasts a 30% share of private label sales by 2020. The objective quality features of private-

label products in many cases are entirely comparable to national brands, and as consumers realize it, they find fewer reasons to pay a premium for national brand equity.

1.3.2.4 Consequences

A good product is not sufficient to compete in a world of very high product standards. As products and services improve and become similar in their objective performance, companies must question traditional marketing models. They start to shift away from a transaction-based model to focus instead on enduring commercial relationships. In turn, firms can learn about new and latent customer preferences by observing their purchase and behavioral histories and using social media to gather consumers' opinions. Developments in mass customization mean firms also can offer genuine value to customers through customized product and service propositions.

As these changes drive the marketplace to become more relationship-oriented, the primary way to maintain market share is to realign business strategies and become customer centric. Thus, CRM is critically strategically important in company positioning in today's market.

1.3.3   Changes with Respect to Data Storage Technology

The third field that features major shifts in recent years is data storage and processing. Both the supply of and demand for data storage technology have changed dramatically, leading to the collection and processing of ever-increasing amounts of transaction- and customer-related data. These shifts in turn offer new possibilities for companies to make strategic use of their collected data.

1.3.3.1 Data Storage Supply

On the supply side, technology is getting better and storage is getting far cheaper on a cost-per-bit basis. Units of storage are growing radically larger. Looking back at the mid-1990s, the whole Western economy had around 1 petabyte

(1,024 terabyte, where 1 terabyte equals 1 trillion bytes) of data storage available. Today, half of that amount is used to develop a single oil field. In the late 1990s, one gigabyte (GB) of hard disk memory would make PC users swoon. In 2011, most computers come with at least 100 GB of hard drive storage, and smartphones usually have 16–32 GB of storage. Prices for storage accordingly have dropped an average of 40% annually, and there is no foreseeable reason that such trends will halt. In addition, consumers and companies increasingly use online space to save even more data and gain convenient access to it from anywhere. Google thus offers webspace to consumers and companies; Apple has introduced the iCloud to make people's documents and music available everywhere they want it.

1.3.3.2 Data Storage Demand

On the demand side, since consumers discovered the Internet, the World Wide Web, and electronic business, the amount of data available has grown exponentially. It is not just industry verticals, such as energy exploration, where better technology, better instrumentation, and better mathematics have increased demand for data storage and analysis. With more than two billion people on the Web worldwide, every business must keep track of shoppers on its website. Along with web log files, other factors also drive demand for storage: packaged applications (CRM, sales force automation, data-marts), greater data warehousing applications, storage service providers, and storage-intensive consumer applications. Many companies must double their storage capacity every 6–12 months. Not surprisingly, worldwide disk storage capacity grew 33% in 2009—a trend not likely to change.

1.3.3.3 Consequences

Firms have never confronted a better situation for informing themselves about customer behavior and attitudes. If they do it correctly, firms can develop unprecedented insights into and information about customers' buying behavior. Yet having too much data can be challenging too. Misapplied, wrong-footed analyses are often the

consequences when a firm is overwhelmed with more data than it can handle.

1.3.4 Changes with Respect to the Marketing Function

Finally, changes in technology and society lead to shifts in understanding of the role of the marketing function. This aspect is strongly affected by changes in the usage and availability of classic and new media channels, as well as a dramatic reduction in the effectiveness and efficiency of marketing activities. But it remains crucially important to monitor these changes to develop matching solutions for new products and services.

1.3.4.1 Media Dilution and Channel Multiplication

The nature of marketing communications is undergoing significant shifts. Brand managers, service providers, and product manufacturers once used mass communication vehicles (print, TV, radio) as their prime carriers. The messages focused on product and price, with little regard to heterogeneity in customer needs or wants. Communication based on mass advertising is largely a thing of the past though. Customer needs and wants have simply become too diverse for marketers to satisfy them with a single, all-purpose approach.

The availability of new data collection and communication tools, such as loyalty programs, means there is less need to employ techniques that indiscriminately focus on price. Driven by technological advancements, the concept of commercial communication has been completely restructured. In Germany for example, usage of radio is slowly decreasing, television viewing continues to rise, and online channels have skyrocketed, with significant consequences for company marketing strategies (see Fig. 1.3).

When we also include the Internet, the amount of communications media focused on customers is staggering. In particular, direct-to-consumer channels (mail, e-mail, telephone) and interactive media (Internet, interactive TV, apps) are outpacing traditional media when it comes to firm spending.

Fig. 1.3 Daily media
usage behavior in Germany
(Source: ARD ZDF
Onlinestudie 2010)

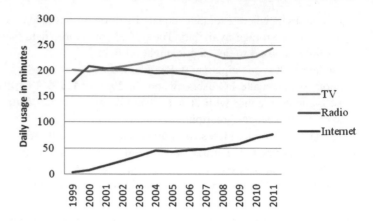

Fig. 1.4 Hybrid/smart
television household
penetration in Germany
(Source: Goldmedia, 2010)

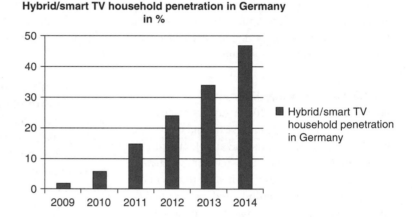

Technology is the key, in that it enables small-batch catalog production, catalog customization, cable TV proliferation, and pay-per-use channels. By 2014, an estimated 47% of households will have smart televisions that can connect to the Internet, as the growth chart in Fig. 1.4 shows.

In the United States for example, the Hulu service allows users to watch their favorite television shows, regardless of the network that aired them, at their convenience and on the device they choose (e.g., Apple's iPad). Clearly, firms can take great advantage of this modified media landscape, because direct-to-consumer communication fits perfectly with their objective of building two-way relationships and creating loyal customers.

1.3.4.2 Decreasing Marketing Efficiency and Effectiveness

Pressure has been growing on corporate marketers to revamp their departments to demonstrate how marketing investments improve the company's bottom line profits. The famous saying by John Wanemaker (1838–1922)—"I know that half of the money I spend on advertising is wasted, I just don't know which half"—has probably never been as true as it is today. We thus can understand the demands of shareholders and CFOs who want better accountability and documentation of the value added by the marketing function.

The problem stems in part from previous marketing practices that focused on acquisition rather than retention, price rather than added value, and short-term transactions rather than the development of lasting, profitable relationships. The proliferation of new contact channels contributes to decreasing efficiency and effectiveness as well. With the emergence of more sophisticated and knowledgeable customers, the existing situation includes flat or increasing costs of contact but decreasing consumer responses. The impact of advertising in any medium has lost some value; according to the Direct

Marketing Association, response rates for direct mail average only 1.4–3.4% in the United States (Direct Marketing Association [DMA], 2010). In many other countries, the rates are even lower; many direct campaigns simply fail to resonate with customers.

The phenomenon of media proliferation is paralleled by the difficulty of communicating meaningfully with customers. As more and more media channels become available, and firms use more of them, the challenge of channel coordination increases. The complexity associated with coordinating messages across greater numbers of channels thus increases exponentially.

1.3.4.3 Consequences

The pressure on the marketing function is intense. Marketers must be better about demonstrating their impact on the bottom line. Otherwise, they will take a back seat and effectively be restricted to advertising and media planning.

1.3.5   Implications

Given all these changes, the marketing scenario today makes greater demands to learn about customer preferences, value provision, and product and service customization. Product-centric strategies cannot address these advanced requirements, but customer-centric strategies are emerging in response. In exactly this environment, CRM, if executed correctly, represents a formidable competitive means to satisfy new demands. Marketers need a management approach that realizes increasing customer heterogeneity, addresses concerns about marketing accountability, puts available data to good use, and uses customer profitability as a key objective function. We term this approach customer value management.

1.4   The Benefits of the Customer Value Management Approach

A successful data-based CRM system, with customer value as its driving metric, empowers a company to perform ten actions that will lead to strategic advantages.

1. *Integrate and consolidate customer information.* With relevant customer information and client histories, the treatment of a customer remains consistent across contact and service channels.
2. *Provide consolidated information across all channels.* The entire company must assist in timely and relevant communication with customers, matching their needs with the most appropriate product.
3. *Manage customer cases.* This action provides the right person with management control in a planned and transparent manner, ensuring that appropriate responses occur at the proper time.
4. *Personalize.* If possible, personalization should span both the service and products offered to each customer to satisfy his or her special expectations.
5. *Automatically and manually generate new sales opportunities.* Measures of customer profiles can rely on predefined business rules or contact between a customer and an employee.
6. *Generate and manage campaigns.* Companies should provide sufficient flexibility to adapt to changes in customer information or behavior.
7. *Yield faster and more accurate follow-up.* Such efforts include sales leads, referrals, and customer inquiries.
8. *Manage all business processes.* The firm should introduce a central point of control to ensure all business processes are executed in accordance with predetermined, effective business rules.
9. *Give top managers a detailed and accurate picture.* All members of the top management team should be aware of all sales and marketing activities.
10. *Instantly react to changing market environments.*

To understand the development toward data-oriented customer value management, it is helpful to take a closer look at the evolution and growth stages of CRM in recent years.

1.5 Evolution and Growth of CRM

This section describes the stages of development of CRM, from the 1990s until today. It has grown from a tactical marketing tool to a strategic element in all marketing decisions. The growth of the Internet also has increased the adoption rate of CRM in many industries.

1.5.1 Timeline of CRM Evolution

Since the concept of customer relationship management came into vogue in the mid-1990s, CRM has undergone a substantial evolution. To provide a historical perspective, Fig. 1.5 depicts a timeline, and this section describes each of the phases in that timeline.

1.5.1.1 First Generation (Functional CRM)
The collection of activities that later took on the umbrella acronym CRM originally developed as two independent product offerings:

Sales force automation (SFA): These products addressed presales functions such as maintaining prospect and customer data, telemarketing, generating leads, creating sales quotes, and placing sales orders.

Customer service and support (CSS): This function addressed mainly after-sales activities, such as help desks, contact and call centers, and field service support. The CSS databases often worked with specific customer information, isolated from other systems.

Although fragmented and poorly integrated with the back office, early SFA/CSS applications delivered the promise of sales and service improvements, though their combined market niche remained small. The market for enterprise resource planning (ERP)—a tool designed to integrate all company departments and functions within a single computer system that served every department's needs—instead was growing.

1.5.1.2 Second Generation (Customer-Facing Front-End Approach)
Innovations in CRM during the 1990s matched those of ERP, including the integration of different independent subsystems into one package. CRM technology was expected to fill the gaps left by ERP functionality and address the business needs of the company's customer-facing front end.

The goal was to create a single view of all interactions with customers, independent of the purpose of that contact (e.g., pre-sales, sales transaction, post-sales service) or its means (e.g., telephone, e-mail, Internet). For the most part, this goal was not achieved during the 1990s, leading to increasing disillusionment with CRM technology and implementations. Customer expectations in this period far exceeded the realized benefits of CRM technology. Industry observers began talking about the demise of CRM. Even as the Internet fuelled new expectations, it became clear that revenue increases through technology were difficult to implement, realize, and measure, without a more strategic understanding of the process (Fig. 1.6).

1.5.1.3 Third Generation (Strategic Approach)
By the end of 2002, the CRM market had started to pick up, and the gap between customers' perceived value and value realized was closing. Organizations learned from experience and their failure to implement prior versions of CRM. The best organizations began to focus on integrating customer-facing front-end systems with back-end systems, as well as with the systems used by partners and suppliers (see Fig. 1.5).

The integration of the Internet technology helped to boost CRM. Many organizations realized that they could benefit by adopting a strategic CRM approach rather than blindly implementing technology-based solutions. Companies recognized the eventual goal of CRM: to grow revenue, not just control costs.

1.5.1.4 Fourth Generation (Agile and Flexible Strategic CRM)
At the end of the first decade of the twenty-first century, we face the start of the fourth generation

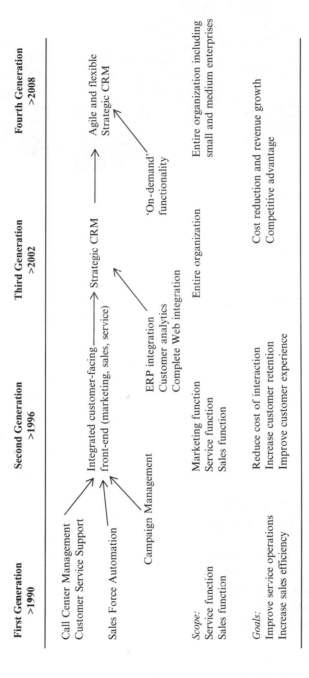

Fig. 1.5 Timeline of the CRM evolution

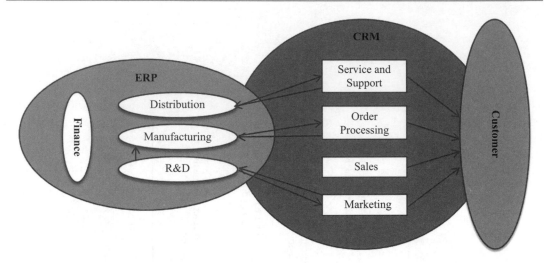

Fig. 1.6 Integration of front-end customers with back-end systems

of CRM. Strategic CRM is widely accepted and established as an essential element of the marketing strategy, and an ever-increasing number of small and medium-sized companies adopt this management tool and its corresponding technologies to drive their business. Agility, flexibility, and low fixed costs are key. The emergence of social media and increased self-service, as well as the growing prevalence of web-based services, mean that customer empowerment is an emerging topic. In particular, CRM technology on a pay-per-use basis can provide on-demand functionality.

1.6   CRM and the IT Revolution: The View from the Industry

Considering these major market and technology shifts and their contributions to the rapid development of CRM as a strategic management tool, we also want to shed light on what industry executives think of this evolution, in terms of how it appears in practice.

> In my discussions with senior executives around the world about the power of IT systems and networked computing, I consistently make the point that the real revolution isn't about the technology itself. The real revolution here has to do with institutional change—the fundamental transforma-

tion of time-honored ways of doing things. (Lou Gerstner, former CEO IBM)

Consider a comment from a CRM consultant:

> One of the reasons I prefer to deal with SMEs [small and medium-sized enterprises] in implementing CRM is that I always have direct *access* to the CEO of the business to ensure they understand what CRM is about. We always put the strategies together first, then find a technology solution that makes carrying out those strategies easier. I strongly believe the much-touted 70% failure rate of CRM projects has resulted from a too-heavy reliance on technology.
>
> There is still a major issue in CRM of people not understanding what it is all about—which is listening to the customer and communicating with them in a manner most likely to increase their satisfaction and win repeat and referral business. Unfortunately, I believe this reliance on technology has been driven by the big CRM information technology players. CEOs of major companies see it as something that they simply must do, without understanding what it is all about.

This view of CRM represents a substantial adjustment. Some managers initially became disillusioned with the process and results of implementing CRM solutions and systems. They felt that they reaped limited benefits from new IT systems, faced resentment among employees when implementing them, and gained little in terms of being able to offer added value to customers.

This negative reaction to CRM as it was practiced was based on an IT view of the world. Too often, the introduction of CRM has been regarded as a technological project and temporary activity. Managers simply believed that CRM equaled software or technology, though nothing could be further from the truth. With these misconceptions, it is no surprise that many CRM efforts never met the expectations of the companies implementing them.

For CRM to be implemented successfully, top management must integrate all corporate functions and focus them on customer value. The growth of CRM also should not be equated with the growth of what has been called the CRM industry, which consists mainly of IT vendors. Darrell Rigby, from Bain & Co., researches the use of management tools and finds that both CRM tool usage and satisfaction with CRM have been relatively high in recent years. This finding implies that companies may have learned to view CRM as a strategic marketing element; they are realizing its untapped potential. The future thus is bright for CRM, and with the aid of appropriate IT systems, CRM can become a preferred marketing approach for many firms.

1.7   Further Growth of the CRM Industry

Today the CRM industry represents a fast growing sector, with billions spent on CRM applications, consulting, and training every year. For example, the worldwide market for CRM software alone was nearly US$9 billion in 2008, and it appears likely to grow to more than US$13 billion by 2012 (Gartner, 2008).

1.7.1   Factors Driving the CRM Industry

As we have discussed, the emergence and development of CRM have been driven by a shift from transactional to relationship-based markets. Five further factors also are responsible for moving the CRM industry forward.

1. *Growing proof of profitable impacts of good customer relationships.* Continued investments in CRM practices have confirmed the belief that value exists in targeted customer relationships.
2. *Improved marketing communication effectiveness.* Integrated marketing agencies have made great progress in improving the effectiveness of their communication activity, with superior database technology, analysis tools, targeted communications, and performance measurement techniques.
3. *IT vendors and associated change management consultancies.* To IT vendors and change management consultancies concerned with the technology or process side of customer relationships, CRM represents a vast arena of untapped potential. Initial demand for stand-alone products—such as sales force automation, marketing campaign management, or call center management tools—has given way to requests for integrated, strategic CRM solutions.
4. *Falling costs of data capture and storage.* The economies of CRM improve as data capture and storage costs continue to drop. CRM solutions thus represent increasingly attractive investments.
5. *Customer value measurement.* Firms are aware that CRM investments must be based on accurate metrics that account for expected returns. Developments in the area of customer value measurement and use provide the needed assurance that CRM efforts will bear fruit.

1.8   Summary

The increasing availability of technology allows firms to collect and analyze customer-level data and interact with customers simultaneously. Yet rapid changes are taking place in the environment in which firms operate, which make the development of new market strategies and a shift from a product focus toward a customer-centric offer necessary. These changes, as introduced in this chapter, pertain to (1) consumers, (2) marketplaces, (3) technology, and (4) marketing functions.

On the consumer front, growing diversity reflects the changing demographic composition of market populations. Consumers are becoming more value conscious, less loyal, and intolerant of poor service; they also suffer increasing time pressures, exhibit more technology savvy, look for more convenience, and use social media. The marketplace is characterized by more intense competition, greater fragmentation, and increasing difficulties in terms of differentiation. These changes have driven the marketplace to become relationship-based and customer-centric. Data storage technology has become cheaper, leading to exponential growth in storage capacity. This favorable situation for firms means they can collect and analyze information about consumers, their needs, and their preferences, which has set the stage for CRM implementation.

That is, following years of relying on a transactional-based CRM approach, companies increasingly are choosing to apply a strategic CRM process that is strictly customer centric and relationship based.

Exercise Questions
1. What is customer value, and why is this term essential for CRM?
2. What makes CRM the preferred approach to marketing in the modern information age?
3. List some key changes in the business environment. How are these changes driving the shift from product-based marketing to customer-based marketing?

4. Which technologies influence strategic CRM, on both the consumer and the company sides?
5. How has CRM evolved in the past decade? List some primary changes and their effect.
6. Which factors drive CRM development forward?

References

ARD ZDF Onlinestudie (2010). http://www.ard-zdf-onlinestudiede/index.php?id=189
Deshpande, R., & Webster, F. E., Jr. (1989). Organizational culture and marketing: Defining the research. *Journal of Marketing, 53*(1), 3–15.
Direct Marketing Association (DMA). (2010). *DMA releases 2010 response rate trend report.* Accessed May 21, 2011, from http://www.the-dma.org/cgi/dispannouncements?article=1451
Gartner. (2008). *Gartner says worldwide CRM software market to grow 14 percent in 2008.* Accessed July 1, 2011, from http://www.gartner.com/it/page.jsp?id=653307
Goldmedia. (2010). Smart TV: Starker Wettbewerb im Fernsehmarkt der Zukunft. Accessed June 3, 2011, from http://www.goldmedia.com/presse/newsroom/smart-tv.html
Infas. (2010). Der Telekommunikationsmonitor- eine integrierte Mobilfunk und Festnetzstudie. Accessed June 2, 2011, from http://www.infas-geodaten.de/fileadmin/media/pdf/Aktuelles/Telekommunikations-monitor.pdf
Institut d'Economie Industrielle (IDEI). (2011). *Private label development continue worldwide.* Accessed June 3, 2011, from http://idei.fr/doc/conf/inra/2011/bonvallet.pdf
McKinsey & Co. (2007). The organizational challenges of global trends: A McKinsey Global Survey. Accessed June 2, 2011, from http://download.mckinseyquarterly.com/organizational_challenges.pdf

Relationship Marketing and the Concept of Customer Value

2.1 Overview

In the previous chapter, we discussed the concept of CRM and understood its role, evolution, and future. In this chapter, marketing takes on a more specific context when we enter the realm of relationship marketing due to the ability of the firm to differentiate between individual customers.

In a traditional mass-marketing approach, the customer population is segmented based on the needs of the consumers in those segments. The products and services are then designed and delivered to meet the general needs of the segments. However, with the leap in information technology and the improvement in flexible manufacturing practices, meeting individual customer needs has become an important dimension on which firms can differentiate their products and services and build competitive advantage. Marketers now need to recognize that relationships with individual customers are at the heart of decision-making. In this regard, there has been a visible shift from product-based marketing to customer-based marketing and in order to retain customers many firms have focused their attention on increasing customer satisfaction levels.

The degree of customer satisfaction is indeed a key measure. However to what extent customer satisfaction leads to loyalty and profitability is an important issue that needs to be examined. Traditionally, it is believed that customer satisfaction is expected to lead to greater retention or loyalty, which in turn, leads to greater profit. This is the Satisfaction-Loyalty-Profit chain (SPC).

Though customer satisfaction and loyalty are key indicators of profit, these measures cannot be taken as simple predictors of profit. From an organizational standpoint, what is more important is to identify and nurture the relationship with profitable customers. In this chapter, we relate the concept of CRM to database marketing and highlight the importance of customer value. Following this, we will look at the SPC and determine its relationship to CRM and relationship marketing.

In order to understand the SPC, we must first understand the importance of databases in providing information that will create and elevate the value of the customer and overall profitability of the firm in the long run.

2.2 The Link Between CRM and Database Marketing, and the Importance of Customer Value

Database marketing has traditionally allowed a company to identify and analyze segments of its customer population for valuable information that can be used to increase the impact of its marketing campaigns. The increasing availability of technology over the years made it possible for companies to gather and analyze large amounts of data on their customers and prospective customers and thereby develop rich customer databases.

Traditionally, customer databases helped identify groups of customers that were similar in identifiable ways. These groups of customers were then treated as segments and separate marketing campaigns were recommended for these different groups. Direct marketers would send different mailers at varying times and frequencies to theses different segments. However, technology now allows firms to not only capture customer data, but also interact with the customer simultaneously. This not only includes traditional 'snail mail' but extends to e-mail, SMS or text messaging, and social media. This provides the opportunity for firms to develop flexible customer level responses.

Over the years, the CRM concept has enabled organizations to leverage databases and modern communication technologies to "think and act" at the individual customer level. In other words, *CRM takes the practice of database marketing principles to increasingly disaggregated levels – ultimately to the individual customers.* Thus, CRM revolves around applying database marketing techniques at the customer level to develop strong company-to-customer, relationships. For instance, AAA Mid-Atlantic has been able to merge its customer database successfully with a new CRM system. AAA calls this program Member Relationship Management. As a result of these integrated efforts they have come to boast a 90% renewal rate for their 3.7 million members. Additionally, they have been able to determine unique ways to cross-sell and up-sell to an individual customer's needs (Martinez, 2010). The use of IT is critical to the success of implementing a good CRM plan. However, the overarching framework of CRM includes much more than just databases and IT systems.

In the past, one of the main goals of marketing campaigns has been to increase customer loyalty to a product or service. This goal was driven by the wisdom that more loyal customers will do more repeat business and will develop a larger tolerance to price increases and therefore are more profitable to the firm. However, this is not always the case. A very loyal customer may also be an individual who repeatedly calls customer service with questions and is constantly hunting for the best price on a product, taking advantage of every rebate and sale offer. Ultimately, such an individual could actually be costing the company money rather than providing a source of profits. An important part of CRM is identifying the different types of customers and then developing specific strategies for interacting with each customer. Examples of such strategies are developing better relationships with *profitable* customers, locating and enticing new customers who will be profitable, and finding appropriate strategies for unprofitable customers, which could mean eventually terminating the relationship with customers who are causing a company to lose money.

The concept of customer value is critical to CRM. We define customer value as the economic value of the customer relationship to the firm – expressed on the basis of contribution margin or net profit. Customer value is a marketing metric that is proving to be an important decision aid in addition to evaluating marketing effectiveness. A firm can both measure and optimize its marketing efforts by incorporating the concept of customer value at the core of its decision-making process. The adoption of CRM with customer value at the core of its strategy helps us define CRM from a customer value perspective as follows:

> CRM is the practice of analyzing and utilizing marketing databases and leveraging communication technologies to determine corporate practices and methods that will maximize the lifetime value of each individual customer to the firm.

A customer value-based approach to CRM can provide guidelines necessary to answer the following questions:

- When does it pay to go after customer loyalty?
- How do you link loyalty to customer profitability?
- How do you compute the future profitability of a customer?
- How do you measure customer lifetime value?
- How do you optimally allocate marketing resources to maximize customer value?
- How do you maximize the return on marketing investments?

The customer value-based approach can thus be leveraged for superior marketing decisions since *benefits* accrue in the form of the following:

- Decrease in costs
- Maximization of revenues
- Improvement in profits and ROI
- Acquisition and retention of profitable customers
- Reactivation of dormant customers

Consulting firms and companies have created their own definitions and conceptualizations of CRM. These conceptualizations have evolved over time, but they can still be grouped into three types: functional level, customer facing front-end level, and strategic level. These types of CRM are explained briefly here and are discussed in more detail in Chap. 3:

1. *Functional Level:* The CRM process can be practiced on a very limited functional basis (e.g., it could entail the practice of sales force automation in the sales function or the practice of campaign management within the marketing function). Often, this goes along with a strong technology orientation evolving out of the need for vendors to position their particular product. For some of the vendors or buyers, functional CRM is nearly synonymous with technology.

2. *Customer-facing front-end level:* This type of CRM evolves from the need for CRM practitioners to describe a new business capability, or a new arrangement of capabilities, that focuses on the total customer experience. The goal is to build a single view of the customer across all contact channels and to distribute customer intelligence to all customer-facing functions. This view stresses the importance of coordinating information across time and across contact channels in order to systematically manage the entire customer relationship. This view also supports the notion of marketing to customers throughout their purchasing lifecycle.

3. *Strategic level:* The primary objective of strategy-centric definitions of CRM is to free the term CRM from any technology underpinnings and from specific customer management techniques. These definitions describe CRM as a process to implement customer centricity in the market and build shareholder value. Here, knowledge about customers and their preferences has implications for the entire organization, such as for R&D or for supply chain management.

In this book, CRM will be defined from a business strategy perspective. The goal will be to gain long-term competitive advantage by optimally delivering value and satisfaction to the customer as well as extracting business value from the exchange. From this standpoint, CRM is the *strategic process* of *selecting* the customers a firm can most profitably serve and of shaping the *interactions* between a company and these *customers*. The goal is to optimize the *current and future value of the customers* for the company.

The key components of this definition include:

- **Strategic process:** This means that CRM activities are initiated and managed starting from the very top of the organization. For example, in order to maintain control of relationship management, companies such as Hershey's, Oracle, Samsung, Sears and United Airlines have created Chief Customer Officers (CCOs). These executives are responsible for the CRM processes and driving individual customer profitability. Strategic initiatives by definition span multiple, if not all, organizational functions (Rust, Moorman, & Bhalla, 2010). CRM does not belong to any single department but needs contributions and reinforcements from all corporate functions. There is no place for a *silo mentality* that discourages information sharing and that condones that one function "owns the customer". Furthermore, CRM is a continuing *process* that cannot be handled as just another software implementation project. It must be viewed as a continuous effort with the goal of becoming a more customer-centric company. Management at all levels must learn to view the business from the customers' perspective and better enable relationship building. However, a recent survey of 300 companies in North America reported that 42% have the CRM function managed by the IT department, with just 9% managed by the marketing department (Rust et al.). The finding from this survey indicates that companies still view CRM as more of an IT function, as opposed to a cross-functional effort.

- **Selection:** When the economic value of a customer is the basis for resource allocation, it is logical that firms focus on their most profitable or potentially profitable customers first. This is not about denying services to certain customers but about recognizing that there is a fit between a firm offering and a segment's desires, behaviors and characteristics. This fit can vastly differ between each customer.

- **Interactions:** This means that the relationship between the customer and firm takes the form of an interactive dialogue. Information and goods are exchanged and most importantly, the exchange evolves as a function of past exchanges. This is very different from the view that firms sell one-off products and services to the customer.

- **Customers:** The term 'customers' is applied broadly here. Depending on the industry and company, a customer can be an individual account, one or several segments within a market, or an entire market. Also, customers include not only end users but also intermediaries, like distributors, retailers etc. Generally, firms that are maximizing their CRM capabilities are starting to satisfy increasingly smaller segments with better-targeted products, services, and communication propositions. Clearly, while segmentation is nothing new to most marketing managers, the degree of fine-tuning is considerably larger in the case of CRM. In fact we now expect to be able to target *individual* customers with customized product offerings, as shown by the following industry example.

- **Current and future value of the customer:** Optimizing current and future value means that firms are moving away from extracting their profit from single transactions to maximizing profits over a series of transactions. Thus, firms are starting to maximize customer equity – that is the value of all their customer relationships to them. In this process, tradi-

tional measures such as market share are increasingly being replaced with newer measures such as share-of-wallet and customer lifetime value. Firms are also deriving new ways to maximize customer equity through customer collaboration. For instance, companies such as Mozilla and P&G create value through obtaining feedback and information from customers using their products Firefox and Swiffer, respectively, to create newer products or adjust features of existing products (Rust et al., 2010).

CRM AT WORK 2.1

Database and Direct Mail Marketing, Targeting the Right Customer

In 2009, Forrester Research Inc. released a survey about consumers and their attitudes towards direct marketing. The survey found that only 10% of consumers believe that the direct mail marketing they receive is relevant. Consider e-mail and the relevancy drops to 7%. Additionally, 62% and 66% of customers feel that they get too much direct mail and e-mail marketing, respectively. This disparity shows that there is a need to refine the process of targeting customers with offers. Studies have shown that when more directly targeted mailings are utilized, marketers get 5–10 times the response rate and a 20–30% increase in sales.

Prudent utilization the data collected from various marketing channels is a feat that few companies are accomplishing today. For example, fragrance and beauty supply company Sephora has been able to aggressively target its consumers based on their shopping channel (online or in-store) as well as the type of product they purchase. They use this knowledge to deliver relevant information to the customers based on their profile. Targeting marketing by Sephora has garnered increased response rates and market-share gains.

Source: Zmuda and Bush (2009).

Fig. 2.1 The satisfaction-loyalty-profit chain (*Source*: Anderson & Mittal, 2000, p. 107)

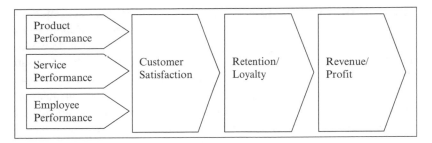

It is, however, important for managers to recognize the importance of managing fairness in the exchange process. Optimization of the current and future value of customers intrinsically recognizes that unless customers are treated with respect and fairness, it will be impossible to manage and sustain a mutually profitable relationship.

Overall, marketing-driven customer relationship management is the concept of relationship management that is based on established marketing principles and that recognizes the need to carefully balance organizational and customer interests. Marketing-driven CRM is not primarily driven by technological solutions but is supported by them. It is a complex set of activities that, together, form the basis for a sustainable and hard to imitate competitive advantage: the customer-centric organization. CRM also involves automating and enhancing the customer centric business processes of sales, marketing, and service. It not only deals with automating these processes, but also focuses on ensuring that the front office applications improve customer satisfaction, resulting in increased customer loyalty which directly affects the company's bottom line. With CRM, a company would have an environment and a flexible support system to readily deal with the issues of product innovation, increasing levels of customer expectations, acquisitions, globalization, deregulation, convergence of traditional markets, emergence of new technologies, privacy issues, and new customer contact channels.

Now that we have understood the importance and value of CRM in determining customer value, in the following section we will discuss how CRM plays a role in the satisfaction-loyalty-profit chain.

2.3   Satisfaction-Loyalty-Profit Chain

The satisfaction-loyalty-profit chain is a key concept requiring a thorough understanding because of its link to CRM (see Fig. 2.1). It has been popular since the early 1990s, when companies realized the importance of measuring and managing customer satisfaction (Heskett, Jones, Loveman, Sasser, & Schlesinger, 1994). The key underlying idea is that improving product and service attributes will lead to an improvement in customer satisfaction. Increased customer satisfaction is expected to lead to greater customer retention, which is often used as a proxy for customer loyalty, which then is expected to lead to greater profitability. Despite the almost self-evident nature of these positive links, the empirical evidence from a number of years of research shows only mixed support (Zeithaml, 2000). Likewise, translating the conceptual framework into practical reality has been problematic for many firms. For example, a firm may have improved its performance on a key attribute, only to discover that the overall satisfaction score did not noticeably increase. At other times, changes in overall satisfaction scores have failed to show a demonstrable impact on customer retention (Ittner & Larcker, 2003). We believe, therefore, that it is critical to have a complete understanding of the entire satisfaction-profit chain in order to manage customers in an efficient manner.

2.3.1 Issues to Consider

The Level of Analysis

When employing the SPC concept, it is worthwhile to consider the level of analysis. Most of the empirical studies have looked at aggregate, *firm-level* results. For example, a series of studies (Anderson, Fornell, & Rust, 1997; Anderson, Fornell, & Lehmann, 1994) looked at how firm-level customer satisfaction indices are linked to firm-level performance.

The finding from this and similar studies indicate a positive association between the company-wide satisfaction score and company's overall performance. However, in a world where resources are allocated on the individual customer level, the chain needs to be implemented at a *disaggregate level*. There is much less hard evidence of the nature of the SPC on the individual customer level. Although one would expect a correlation between firm-level and individual-level results, it is not clear how strong this correlation really is.

The Direct Link between Customer Satisfaction and Profits

The direct link between customer satisfaction and profits suggests that as customers experience greater satisfaction with a firm's offering, profits rise. For example, a recent study (Edvardsson, Johnson, Gustafsson, & Strandvik, 2000) found that the *stated sales satisfaction* of Volvo customers is significantly linked to *new car profitability* (e.g., through closing financing and insurance deals, Volvo card membership, and workshop loyalty). Many companies other than Volvo can attest to the benefit of SPC. For instance, Zappos Inc., an online shoe and apparel retailer has gone to great lengths to maintain its high level of customer satisfaction. The company's focus on customer service includes utmost customer satisfaction and, free return shipping in case of problems with the purchase. While excessive returns may eat into company profits, for Zappos this is an "acceptable risk" in return for increased profits through customer loyalty. This customer service selling point, in addition to special training

for their customer service representatives, has propelled Zappos to its success.

But, what do we know, in general, about this direct link between satisfaction and profitability? Although early proponents of the SPC argued customer satisfaction always has a positive bottom-line impact, we have a much more complete picture today. It is interesting to note research on the direct relationship between satisfaction and profits has shown both positive effects in a limited number of studies (Ittner & Larcker, 1998), and no effects in other studies (Zeithaml, 2000). In other words, while there is empirical evidence to suggest that a variety of quality strategies failed to deliver anticipated business performance, there is also contrasting evidence that indicates a positive correlation between customer satisfaction and return on assets.

What is important to understand and explains some of the seemingly contradictory findings, is that it is simply not enough to link satisfaction and revenues. Improving customer satisfaction comes at a cost, and once the cost of enhancing satisfaction is factored in, it may well be that offering "excessive satisfaction" does not pay. This is because the marginal gains in satisfaction decrease, while the marginal expenses to achieve the growth in satisfaction increase. This falls in line with what is said about the vastly improved product quality offered by many firms today. As the general level of quality reaches high levels, it becomes more and more costly to improve satisfaction with a further rise in quality. For example, is an investment in another ride justified for an amusement park, given the expected incremental traffic? Although the additional ride is likely to increase customer satisfaction, the question is whether it generates enough additional revenues to offset the investment. In addition, increasing customer satisfaction leads, in many cases, to an adaptation of expectation levels; consumers, quickly get used to a better service level without necessarily rewarding the firm with additional purchases. What this probably means is that there is an optimum satisfaction level for any firm, beyond which increasing satisfaction does not pay. To find such an optimum level,

Fig. 2.2 Illustration of the satisfaction-retention link (*Source*: Anderson & Mittal, 2000, p. 114)

Note: The dotted line represents a linear approximation of the nonlinear relationship shown.

firms need to conduct longitudinal satisfaction studies to investigate changes in customer satisfaction *over time* and link them to improvements in their offering.

The Link between Satisfaction and Retention
Given some of the difficulties associated with establishing unequivocal links between customer satisfaction and company performance, the 1990s witnessed many managers increasingly turning to customer retention as a long goal. By focusing on customer retention, managers moved closer to the ultimate dependent variable – profits. Figure 2.2 shows a typical shape confirmed by a number of studies (even though there can be considerable departures from this shape). The data are typically derived at the firm level, not the customer level.

The data show the link between satisfaction and retention is asymmetric: dissatisfaction has a greater impact on retention than satisfaction. A satisfied customer is influenced by many factors when making a purchase and has many options. Even if the level of satisfaction is high, retention is not guaranteed, as there may be another product that would satisfy the customer to the same extent. Conversely, if the customer is dissatisfied, then the other product becomes more enticing. The link is nonlinear; the impact of satisfaction on retention is greater at the extremes. The flat part of the curve in the middle has also been called the zone of indifference (Jones & Sasser, 1995). As seen in the industry-level databases (such as the ACSI from the University of Michigan), a number of factors-

including the aggressiveness of competition, degree of switching cost, and the level of perceived risk – influence the shape of the curve and the position of the elbows (the two points in the graph where there is a sharp change in the shape of the curve).

An example of the variable link between satisfaction and retention can be demonstrated. Figure 2.3 shows the variability in the relationship across industries. In Fig. 2.3, in the competitive automotive industry, very high levels of satisfaction are necessary for a customer to repurchase the same brand again. On the contrary, consumers may incur considerable switching costs when utilizing an airline. This cost might increase due to bonus-point build-up in frequent-flyer programs or limited airline choice at any given airport. Thus, consumers tend to re-patronize an airline even though satisfaction might only be moderate.

The same caveats that apply to the satisfaction-profit link also apply to the satisfaction-retention link. First, firms should thoroughly investigate the nature of the link for a specific industry, category, or segment. For example, two firms operating in two different industries might have identical satisfaction levels, yet the relationship between customer satisfaction and retention might be quite different for the two firms. To assess the impact of satisfaction on retention in a better manner, firms must account for the attractiveness of alternatives in addition to what they offer. Another aspect to consider is that the link might change, depending on the measurement employed for the loyalty measured. For example, a study (Mital &

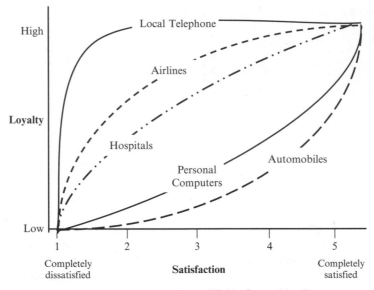

Noncompetitive Zone
- Regulated monopoly or few substitutes
- Dominant brand equity
- High cost of switching
- Powerful loyalty program
- Proprietary technology

Highly Competitive Zone
- Commoditization or low differentiation
- Consumer indifference
- May substitutes
- Low cost of switching

Note: Loyalty was measured as the customer's stated intent to repurchase.

Fig. 2.3 How the competitive environment affects the satisfaction-loyalty relationship (*Source*: Jones & Sasser, 1995, p. 5)

Kamakura, 2001) found that repurchase behavior is a better measure than repurchase intent. Finally, we know comparatively less about the link on an individual customer level as compared to a company or industry level analyses.

The Link Between Loyalty and Profits

Due to the complexity and specificity of the links, taking customer satisfaction as a proxy measure for customer loyalty or for customer profits is not a viable solution. Therefore, it is not surprising to see increasing interest in examining the direct link between customer retention and a firm's performance. The key proponent of looking at this link is Frederick F. Reichheld, who, in a series of writings, stresses the importance of managing customer retention (Reichheld, Markey, & Hopton, 2000).

Long-term customers supposedly do the following, according to the principal hypotheses of Reichheld:

- Spend more per period over time
- Cost less to serve per period over time

- Have greater propensity to generate word-of-mouth customers
- Pay a premium price when compared to that paid by short-term customers

The underlying argument is that customers are acquired at a cost, which then gets recovered over time, thus becoming more and more profitable over time. Although this might hold true in a contractual relationship (e.g., magazine subscription, cable TV contract) it hardly holds true in a noncontractual relationship (such as shopping in a department store). In a noncontractual relationship, the revenue stream must be balanced by the cost of constantly sustaining the relationship and fending off competitive attacks. However, managing these constant investments in customer relationships can be quite tricky. Obviously, a high retention rate is very desirable, but increasing the marginal retention comes at an increasing cost. Blindly increasing retention spending will eventually lead to overspending. Clearly, efforts at increasing customer satisfaction and retention not only consume a firm's resources, but are subject to diminishing returns. In addition, be aware that Reichheld's propositions are derived from *asking managers about what they believe* the benefits of relation are. Since managerial opinions can be biased and self-serving, it is important to consequently investigate actual customer behavior in order to investigate the true, more underlying, link.

Reichheld's propositions have been tested recently by Reinartz and Kumar, who investigated the profitability of a sample of more than 16,000 individual customers across four industries (Reinartz & Kumar, 2002). Their results bring out a different picture. Essentially, the researchers found the relationship between customer retention and customer profits is not as strong as anticipated. Reinartz and Kumar demonstrate, for example, that, across different firms, there is a segment of customers who are loyal but not very profitable (due to excessive resource allocation), and a segment that generates very high profits although it has only a short tenure. Since these short-term customers can be very profitable, it is clear that loyalty is not the only path to profitability. As the following figure illustrates, the overall trend shows a direct correlation between loyalty and profitability. However, outliers on the graph who generate high profits while not having high loyalty will outperform those customers with a high level of loyalty but low profitability (see Fig. 2.4).

The key implication of Reinartz and Kumar's finding is that caution must be exercised when equating customer retention with customer profitability. Firms ultimately have to make an effort to obtain information on individual or segment profitability (see Fig. 2.5).

2.3.2   What Does It All Mean?

Although the SPC is conceptually sound, measuring and managing customer satisfaction is not enough. By not understanding the exact nature (e.g., strength, symmetry, and nonlinearity) of the various links, many companies have seriously misallocated resources based on an incorrect understanding of the underlying mechanics.

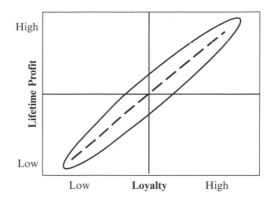

Fig.   2.4 Lifetime duration-profitability association (*Source*: Reinartz & Kumar, 2000)

The key conclusion from this section's discussion is the importance of moving to the ultimate end of the satisfaction-profit chain (SPC). Moving to the ultimate dependent variable, customer profits are ultimately required for making good marketing decisions. This does not mean that knowing the status of customer satisfaction or customer loyalty is no longer important. However, it is important to assess the various links in the SPC in a correct manner. As we know today, these links are almost always nonlinear, asymmetric, and certainly segment- and industry-specific. As such, taking customer satisfaction or customer loyalty as a simple proxy measure for customer profits is not sufficient, and we therefore need to make every effort to measure customer-level profitability. However, since firms cannot influence profits per se (but do so via product and service quality) the impact of customer satisfaction and customer loyalty as key mediators cannot be neglected.

2.4   Summary

Database and relationship marketing is a significant departure from the traditional forms of mass-media marketing. Rapid advances in technology have amassed a trove of data about customers that marketers can use to target spe Additionally, marketing is becom focused on the individual custome a product that meets custome

Fig. 2.5 Association of profitability and longevity of customers (*Source*: Reinartz & Kumar, 2002, p. 86)

High Profitability	*Percentage of Customers*		*Percentage of Customers*
Corporate service provider Grocery retail Mail-order Direct brokerage	20% 15% 19% 18%	Corporate service provider Grocery retail Mail-order Direct brokerage	30% 36% 31% 32%
Low Profitability	*Percentage of Customers*		*Percentage of Customers*
Corporate service provider Grocery retail Mail-order Direct brokerage	29% 34% 29% 33%	Corporate service provider Grocery retail Mail-order Direct brokerage	21% 15% 21% 17%
	Short-Term Customers		**Long-Term Customers**

particular moment. Businesses are focusing more on managing customers than managing products, becoming more customer-centric. Relationship marketing seeks to establish these individual relationships and monitor them over time, delivering specifically targeted marketing campaigns.

By using a customer-value based approach to CRM marketers are able to generate more profit for the company and increase the satisfaction of their customers in the long run. This leads to the satisfaction-profit chain. The key conclusion from the satisfaction profit chain discussion is the importance of moving it towards profitability. Moving to the dependent variable, customer profits are ultimately required for making good marketing decisions. This does not mean that knowing the status of customer satisfaction or customer loyalty is no longer important. However, it is important to assess the various links in the SPC in a correct manner. As we know today, these links are almost always nonlinear, asymmetric, and certainly segment- and industry-specific. As such, taking customer satisfaction or customer loyalty as a simple proxy measure for customer profits is not sufficient, and we therefore need to make every effort to measure customer-level profitability. However, since firms cannot influence profits per se, but do so via product and service quality, the impact of customer satisfaction and customer loyalty as key mediators cannot be neglected.

Exercise Questions

1. How do you define CRM?
2. How are CRM activities similar/different from marketing activities? Please discuss.
3. What makes CRM the preferred approach to marketing in the Information Age?
4. What is the distinction between traditional database marketing and a customer value-based approach toward database marketing?
5. Illustrate situations where you think companies are following CRM practices. Point out where they are going wrong.
6. Companies want relationships with customers, but do customers want relationships with companies? Please discuss.
7. Explain what we have learned in the last few years about the satisfaction-loyalty chain?

References

Anderson, E. W., Fornell, C., & Lehmann, D. R. (1994). Customer satisfaction, market share, and profitability: Findings from Sweden. *Journal of Marketing, 58*(3), 53–66.

Anderson, E. W., Fornell, C., & Rust, R. T. (1997). Customer satisfaction, productivity, and profitability: Differences between goods and services. *Marketing Science, 16*(2), 129–145.

Anderson, E. W., & Mittal, V. (2000). Strengthening the satisfaction-profit chain. *Journal of Service Research, 3*(2), 107.

Edvardsson, B., Johnson, M. D., Gustafsson, A., & Strandvik, T. (2000). The effects of satisfaction and loyalty on profits and growth: Products versus services. *Total Quality Management and Business Excellence, 11*(7), 917–927.

Heskett, J. L., Jones, T. O., Loveman, G. W., Sasser, W. E., Jr., & Schlesinger, L. A. (1994). Putting the service-profit chain to work. *Harvard Business Review, 72*(2), 164–172.

Ittner, C. D., & Larcker, D. F. (1998). Are nonfinancial measures leading indicators of financial performance? An analysis of customer satisfaction. *Journal of Accounting Research, 36*(1), 1–35.

Ittner, C. D., & Larcker, D. F. (2003). Coming up short on non-financial performance measurement. *Harvard Business Review, 81*(11), 88–95.

Jones, T. O., & Sasser, W. E., Jr. (1995). Why satisfied customers defect. *Harvard Business Review, 73*(6), 88–99.

Martinez, J. (2010). Driving results. *CRM Magazine.* Accessed July 6, 2011, from http://www.destinationcrm.com/Articles/Editorial/Magazine-Features/Driving-Results-68090.aspx

Mital, V., & Kamakura, W. A. (2001). Satisfaction, repurchase intent, and repurchase behavior: Investigating the moderating effect of customer characteristics. *Journal of Marketing Research, 38*(1), 131–142.

Reichheld, F. F., Markey, R. G., Jr., & Hopton, C. (2000). The loyalty effect-the relationship between loyalty and profits. *European Business Journal, 12*(3), 134–139.

Reinartz, W., & Kumar, V. (2000). On the profitability of long-life customers in a non-contractual setting: An empirical investigation and implications for marketing. *Journal of Marketing, 64*(4), 19.

Reinartz, W., & Kumar, V. (2002). The mismanagement of customer loyalty. *Harvard Business Review, 80*(7), 86–94.

Rust, R. T., Moorman, C., & Bhalla, G. (2010). Rethinking marketing. *Harvard Business Review, 88*(1–2), 94–101.

Zeithaml, V. A. (2000). Service quality, profitability, and the economic worth of customers: What we know and what we need to learn. *Journal of the Academy of Marketing Science, 28*(1), 67–85.

Zmuda, N., & Bush, M. (2009). Direct disconnect: Retailers neglect valuable data trove. *Advertising Age.* Accessed July 6, 2011, from http://adage.com/article/news/direct-mail-retailers-neglect-valuable-data-trove/139151/ *80*(31)

Part II
Strategic CRM

3.1 Overview

It is essential to understand that strategic CRM consists of multiple dimensions. Yet many companies instead think of CRM only in terms of technology, so they look for a software-based quick fix, without examining the key elements of successful CRM. That is why we can find so many CRM failures. Too many projects have been abandoned, with investments written off as wasted. But just as building a house requires an architectural plan, implementing CRM must be preceded by a sound strategy.

In this chapter, we therefore present CRM as a business strategy and company-level philosophy, such that knowledge about customers and their preferences have implications for the entire organization. In this customer-centric business philosophy, the customer is an asset, so the focus shifts away from the product and toward the customer as the source of wealth generation. The goal of strategic CRM is to deepen knowledge about customers actively, then use this knowledge to shape the interactions between a company and its customers and maximize the lifetime value of customers for the company.

We present four key components of a successful CRM strategy and explain each of them using real-life case studies. We then deal with ways to define and develop a CRM strategy, keeping its key components in mind. We stress the importance of the integration of various functions and an enterprise-wide commitment to the success of a CRM solution.

3.2 Strategic CRM

CRM encompasses three perspectives: the functional level, the customer-facing level, and the company-wide level, as illustrated in Fig. 3.1. If viewed from a functional perspective, CRM refers to the set of processes that must be in place to execute marketing functions, such as sales force automation or online campaign management.

In contrast, from the customer-facing perspective, CRM is a set of activities that provides a single view of the customer across all contact channels. This approach assumes that customer intelligence is available uniformly to all customer-facing functions. It also stresses the importance of coordinating information across time and contact channels to manage the entire customer relationship systematically. For example, a bank customer who owns a loan product and a savings product could interact with the bank through various channels for different reasons (e.g., transaction, information request, complaint). The nature of these interactions also might change over time.

Finally, the CRM process at the company level suggests that knowledge about customers and their preferences has implications for the entire organization, including functions such as

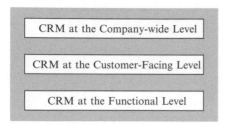

Fig. 3.1 CRM perspectives

R&D or supply chain management. When CRM is adopted by a firm at the company-wide level, it represents *strategic CRM*.

Strategic CRM stems from sound marketing principles. It recognizes the need to balance organizational with customer interests. The goal of strategic CRM is to shape the interactions between a company and its customers in a way that maximizes the lifetime value of customers for the company. This goal also reflects the philosophy that not all customers are created equally. They differ in their economic value to firms, as well as their expectations (e.g., willingness to engage in long-term relationships). The notion of shaping the customer–firm interaction through the attraction and retention of target customer groups is woven into the strategic and operational fabric of successful CRM adopters. A successful strategic CRM thus features a complex set of activities that together form the basis for a sustainable, hard-to-imitate competitive advantage. Specifically, a CRM strategy requires four components (see Fig. 3.2):

1. A customer management orientation
2. The integration and alignment of organizational processes
3. Information capture and the alignment of technology
4. CRM strategy implementation

3.2.1 Customer Management Orientation

Customer management orientation is the set of organizational values, beliefs, and strategic actions that enable the implementation of customer management principles. It is characterized by a top

management belief and commitment that the customer is the center of all activity (not the product, geography, etc.). A successful CRM strategy starts from the top, (see the CRM at work 3.1) as the Capital One case later in this chapter shows. Although this claim might sound obvious, the main reason many CRM efforts have failed is the lack of commitment from top management. If top management fails to create the appropriate structural design and reward system, the result could be insignificant, or even negative CRM outcomes. Customer management orientation recognizes that customers are heterogeneous in their needs and value, so the firm is ready to treat different customers differently. Finally, it recognizes that no single function can be equated with CRM; rather, corporate functions must be implemented, integrated, and aligned with this strategy, which in turn demands a longer-term view of customer revenues.

The following questions can reveal if the company has set a customer management-oriented strategy:

1. Does the top management subscribe to a customer-centric philosophy, and does it show?
2. Does the entire organization engage in the implementation of this philosophy?
3. Does the company attempt to establish win–win relationships with customers?
4. Does the company recognize that customers differ in their needs and in their value to the firm? Is that reflected in its interaction with customers?

CRM at Work 3.1
Capital One: CRM Business Model
To appreciate the key role of the top management in a customer-oriented strategy, consider the example of Capital One, headquartered in McLean, Virginia. One of the fastest growing financial corporations in the United States, Capital One was founded in 1988 and went public in 1994. From the moment of its IPO to 2000, its stock price increased by 1,000%, and the company grew at an average annual rate of 40% (excluding mergers and acquisitions). In 2001, it handled more than $24.2 billion in loans and 36 million customers

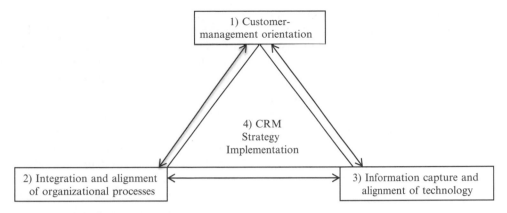

Fig. 3.2 The components of CRM strategy

worldwide, all serviced by more than 20,000 employees. How was such phenomenal growth possible?

The CEO Richard Fairbanks asserts that Capital One's business model is founded on a simple, crucial premise: Every customer carries a specific and unique credit risk and potential revenue profile, and those profiles determine the customer's risk–return profile, according to the company. The better the company can understand and assess a customer's specific risk, the better it can manage that risk and earn returns. Furthermore, as the company gains a better understanding of individual customers, it can tailor its products better to their needs. Low risk and high returns for the company, combined with high satisfaction for the customer, ideally go hand in hand.

Capital One has succeeded not only in subscribing to a customer management–based business model, which recognizes the heterogeneous needs of different customers, but in integrating and aligning its structure and functioning with its strategy. For example, it uses the extensive information it gathers to acquire the type of customers whom Capital One can serve most profitably. Managerial and employee evaluations thus are tied to customer retention and customer profitability measures. Overall, Capital One is a remarkable

example of a company that has implanted customer management principles into the mindsets of all its members.

3.2.2 Integration and Alignment of Organizational Processes

In the context of strategic CRM, the integration and alignment of organizational processes involve the organization-wide creation and synchronization of processes, systems, and reward systems that enable the implementation of customer management principles.

The notion that CRM affects only activities and processes in sales and customer services often prevails even today. But what a customer experiences when interacting with a company's sales or service staff also depends on internal activities, such as product development, IT support, and human resource management. Most firm departments and functions must be involved in a strategic CRM initiative. The notion that sales, marketing, or IT performs CRM is, quite simply, false. Rather, strategic CRM works best for organizations that adopt cross-functional processes rather than functional silos (see the CRM at Work 3.2).

Why are processes so important? They incorporate the needs of the customer and the goals of the firm together into product and service delivery. A process view forces managers to think more deeply about the purpose of activities and their expected outcomes, not the names of the activities or their individual, functionally oriented goals. Processes must cut through the internal barriers that hamper efforts to build effective customer relationships.

The integration and alignment of organizational processes also require the recognition that the value provided to target customers constitutes the driver of all processes. Outcomes can be used to define and design an organization's processes. Individual processes work in sync with the goal of attracting and retaining target customers. Then incentive-based schemes should reflect and reinforce the relationship approach to customer management processes and outcomes. Stated differently, customer management–compatible incentives drive employee and organizational goals simultaneously. The design of the processes should make feedback automatic, which encourages learning from customer management outcomes to improve functions and refine the process.

The following questions can help the firm assess the extent of integration and alignment in its organizational processes:

1. Does the company have a clear understanding of the desired value of the target customers? Do its processes produce this value?
2. Are its various processes in the value chain synchronized to maximize value to the customer?
3. Are the processes configured such that the learning from outcomes applies to make process improvements?

CRM at Work 3.2
Capital One: Interfunctional Management
Capital One entered the UK market in 1996 and quickly emerged as a major issuer of credit cards. By aligning its organizational process with its customer-focused strategy, Capital One built the backbone for its CRM success. In particular, Capital One demands close cooperation between its back-office and front-office departments' activities, all oriented toward customer service. Back-end activities such as account management, strategy, and product testing—which the customer never sees—contribute substantially to the performance of front-end activities and also incorporate front-end agents' feedback.

As an example, consider the cooperation between front-end service operations and the marketing and analysis department, which is responsible for new product development. Operations cooperates closely with marketing and analysis in the new product introduction process, such that the latter designs new products, develops marketing material, and follows up on customers' responses, while the former collects feedback from customers and makes improvement suggestions. Information from operations also improves the net present value models that provide sophisticated decision-making aids. Marketing and analysis then works closely with operations to see how products work—such as by listening to comments about online applications or identifying which questions in an application appear poorly understood.

The customer information used to craft strategy mostly comes from the front-end. Through their partnership, operations and marketing and analysis review Capital One's current risk profile and its future strategy. They also collaborate in permanent or ad hoc cross-functional teams, including a credit policy team that consists of members from both operations and marketing analysis defining credit policies for new products.

3.2.3 Information Capture and Alignment of Technology

In the context of strategic CRM, the capture of information and alignment of technology entail all the technology and processes needed to collect, store, and process relevant and timely customer information, which in turn enables the implementation of customer management principles. Information technology has made processes more efficient, transformed both processes and services, and supported entirely new processes, especially in terms of online activities.

Information capture and the alignment of technology also demand the capability to leverage data into actionable information—a process that may sound generic but is very hard to execute. Firms that can generate and act on intelligence derive competitive advantages. The recognition that technology is built around strategy, processes, and people, and not the other way around, thus is very important. Information capture and the alignment of technology can make customer management processes not only more efficient but also more effective, while creating new processes and channels based on online and wireless applications.

CRM at Work 3.3
Customer Profiling at a German Telephone Company

A German phone company confronted the following question:

How do we leverage the enormous amount of data we collect to provide a unique and valuable customer experience?

The answer was a combination of predictive behavior analysis and proactive proposal generation. This operator uses call detail data and demographic data to score each customer on key relationship dimensions. Profitability and behavior are cataloged to create a unique customer profile. These profiles then become the basis for proactively tailored, one-to-one marketing campaigns, delivered directly to customers' handsets. In turn, the operator has been able to reduce customer turnover significantly and increase the average profitability of its mobile customers.

Three questions can help reveal where a company stands with respect to information capture and alignment of technology:

1. Does your organization harness the enabling capabilities of IT systems in terms of customer management?
2. How timely and relevant is the available customer information?
3. Are you able to leverage data about customers into information that can be acted on?

3.2.4 CRM Implementation

Implementing CRM demands certain processes and activities, as captured in the *CRM Implementation Matrix*. This matrix spans the vast scope of potential activities and is structured along two key dimensions (Reinartz, Krafft, & Hoyer, 2004):

1. A *customer dimension*, pertaining to the changing phases of a customer–firm relationship (customer acquisition, growth, retention, exit)
2. A *management dimension*, or the activities and processes that constitute analytical CRM (i.e., to obtain a good understanding of customer needs, behaviors, and expectations) and operational CRM (to roll out and manage interactions with customers across all demands).

The implementation matrix (Fig. 3.3) lets us map a set of managerial activities and processes onto various phases of the customer–firm relationship. Each cell in the matrix corresponds to a specific implementation activity or process.

Marketing-driven CRM implementation thus is characterized by:

- Activities and processes that constitute analytical CRM and operational CRM. They might include customer data collection, satisfaction and loyalty metrics, customer needs analyses, relationship economics, or segmentation for example.
- Activities and processes that constitute operational CRM, such as value proposition management, campaign management, channel management, referral management, and loyalty management.

Customer Dimension

		Acquisition Stage	Growth and Retention Stage	Decline and Exit Stage
Management Dimension	Analytical CRM			
	Operational CRM			

Fig. 3.3 CRM implementation matrix: Specific CRM activities and processes

- The firm's ability to understand the value of the customer to the firm and varied needs of different customers (see the CRM at work 3.4).
- An acquisition and retention process that continuously aligns the offering with customer needs and values.
- An ability to improve the company's offerings continually by learning about its customers.

Thus three questions help assess where a company stands with respect to its CRM implementation:

1. Do you have systematic testing in place to rationalize product development and marketing spending?
2. Do processes continually align customer needs and customer value with the offer proposition?
3. Does your CRM system provide feedback and improve on the learning from past interactions?

CRM at Work 3.4
Capital One: Testing New Products
Capital One employs a unique process to improve its offerings constantly through learning about its customers. In the credit card business, individual customer risk is a key determinant of profits. To adjust its product offerings to customer risk, it uses an approach dubbed *poking the bear*. Poking a bear makes it move; incentives make customers react and reveal their characteristics and preferences. Many tests (pokes) administered by the company seek to determine what type of customer behavior will be associated with a certain level of credit risk. For example, offering a higher credit line might make customers with a higher default risk respond (because they need the money), which reveals their higher risk.

This method therefore provides a way to learn which customer characteristics might predict risk profiles.

In practical terms, hypotheses about customer characteristics appear in experiments that test which characteristics best correlate with various usage and risk profiles. For example, direct mailings with different texts, designs, and credit conditions go out to a limited group of customers. Their response rates are carefully monitored, as is their behavior during the first months after they receive a card. Capital One can then use this data to determine the value of each direct mail campaign.

Depending on the test, the results may be available after just a few weeks or take as long as several years. As soon as the test results are clear though, Capital One assesses the viability of new products and rolls out the ones with the best potential for success. Because the product development was based on customer data and feedback, its final products are truly mass customized. Test results integrated into the databases can be used again to initiate idea development and product design processes. This strategy has led to an innovative product portfolio with more than 600 credit card products, all very well aligned with their *diverse* customers' needs.

The four components taken together in an integrative form constitute the complete CRM strategy. They interact and reinforce one another, and each component plays an essential role, with none being sufficient in and of itself. To compete, a firm should at least match its competitors on all components and ensure positive interactions among them. The effects of these positive interactions help CRM champions truly excel.

3.3 Steps in Developing a CRM Strategy

Developing a CRM strategy consists of four steps (Fig. 3.4):
1. Gain enterprise-wide commitment.
2. Build a CRM project team.
3. Analyze business requirements.
4. Define the CRM strategy.

Step 1: Gain Enterprise-Wide Commitment
As we have discussed, strategic CRM involves multiple areas within a company. Therefore, it is important to get support from all departments involved (e.g., sales, marketing, finance, manufacturing, distribution) and use their valuable input when developing the company's CRM strategy. The involvement of multiple departments promotes both cooperation and wider acceptance of the new system by all segments. Generally, enterprise-wide commitment thus includes these attributes:
- Top-down management commitment
- Bottom-up buy-in from system users
- A dedicated full-time project team
- Budget allocation for the total solution

To get support from all relevant departments, CRM strategy developers should keep the departments informed of all progress during the development and implementation phases and emphasize the positive results of the CRM strategy.

Step 2: Build a CRM Project Team
Once enterprise-wide commitment has been secured, the next step should be to select the CRM project team, whose members will take responsibility for making key decisions and recommendations and communicating the details

and benefits of the CRM strategy to the entire company. The most effective CRM project team should contain active representatives from at least the following work groups, to ensure the groups' specific desires will be addressed by the CRM strategy:
- Management
- Information services/technical personnel
- Sales, marketing, and service groups
- Financial staff
- External CRM expert

Management
Management should provide leadership, motivation, and *supervision* of every step of the CRM strategy development, especially when it involves significant changes to business processes, organizational structures, or roles and responsibilities. Managers typically evaluate a CRM strategy according to basic criteria, such as
- Will the CRM strategy provide information required to make key decisions?
- Will the CRM strategy significantly impact and improve existing processes?
- Will it significantly reduce costs?
- Can the return justify the investment?

Information Services/Technical Personnel
The development of a CRM strategy must be based on a comprehensive analysis of the company's information, so information services should be deeply involved. The technical group must be actively involved too, because it can provide valuable input with respect to which CRM processes can be automated. Furthermore, they should ensure the CRM system is compatible with existing software applications.

Sales, Marketing, and Services Groups
These departments often are the final users of the CRM system, after the strategy has been developed and implemented. A CRM strategy is successful only if the users are satisfied and comfortable with the final CRM system. Involving sales and marketing groups in the

Fig. 3.4 Developing a CRM strategy

development of the CRM strategy helps members evaluate the potential system's usability, according to three criteria:

- *Effectiveness*. Users must be able to complete the tasks they wish to perform. An effective system is paramount, because it determines outcome quality.
- *Efficiency*. Efficiency measures the required input for completing any given task. In view of the many users of a final CRM system, minor efficiency improvements can have significant effects on the firm's overall productivity.
- *Satisfaction*. If the final CRM system is not user friendly, it will not be used widely by users, which means the investment in the CRM strategy cannot be justified. This problem is particularly prevalent in the CRM market, where many systems have failed because of users' resistance to new practices.

Financial Staff

A CRM strategy must also be evaluated from the financial point of view. Finance department members of the CRM project team can provide critical analyses of the proposed CRM strategy with respect to (1) increased sales productivity, (2) operating costs, (3) costs of system expansion, and (4) ROI projections.

External CRM Expert

In many cases, external CRM experts (business consultants, vendors) can be very helpful for developing a CRM strategy, if the company lacks sufficient CRM expertise, experience, or technology. A consultant's experience can provide a valuable source of objective information and feedback. In particular, an external observer can help analyze the company's real business needs, assist with the formation of the project team, and work with the team to review, amend, and approve functional specifications. Choosing this external expert and deciding when and how to integrate this source thus may be a critical element of the success or failure of the CRM project.

In addition to these work groups, the CRM project team may contain members from other internal or external parties (e.g., personnel responsible for managing relationships with suppliers, strategic partners, investors), if necessary, to ensure the CRM strategy addresses relationships with all important parties.

Step 3: Analyze Business Requirements

An effective CRM strategy must be based on the firm's business requirements. An analysis of business requirements, with the objective of gathering information on a company-wide basis, assesses the current business state and identifies problem areas. This process is absolutely critical to develop a good CRM strategy. Therefore, this step should feature a series of sessions and surveys to canvass top sales, marketing, and customer service managers to gather their expectations; a consensus should be formed as the result. Company-wide goals should be defined, along with objectives for each department and work group. Special care should be taken to acknowledge and evaluate all ideas so participants feel they are part of the process. Ideas that seem unnecessary or unrealistic may be eliminated later during the development of the CRM strategy.

At this juncture, information on specific problem areas must be gathered uniformly to identify particular goals and define objectives for the entire company. After gathering information, it should be able to take the following ten steps:

1. Identify the services and products being supported.
2. Map current workflows, interfaces, and interdependencies.
3. Review existing technologies, features, and capabilities.
4. Discuss the vision for the business and the operational plan.
5. Define business requirements.
6. Develop enhanced business workflows and processes.
7. Identify gaps in technology functionality.
8. Map functionality to business processes.
9. Develop a new technology and functionality framework.
10. Develop a conceptual design and prototype plan.

The following sample CRM survey questions are designed to gather crucial information from different departments for developing a CRM strategy:

- What functions do you perform?
- What types of data do you use?
- How do you interact with customers?

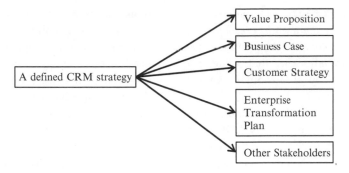

Fig. 3.5 Characteristics of a defined CRM strategy

- What data can be made available to help you better understand customers?
- How can you improve your communication with customers and management?
- How can you reduce administrative and scheduling requirements that detract from the time available to build relationships?
- How involved are you in outreach activities such as telemarketing and direct mail?
- What are your reporting needs and requirements?
- How are you involved in lead tracking, lead follow-up, data transfer, and other daily actions, and how can these processes be improved?

The survey results—including input from end users of the CRM system, such as the sales force, customer service representatives, marketing personnel, order fulfillment, and account management staff, or those who deal with customers on a daily basis—must be gathered carefully. These informants know what changes are necessary to develop and improve customer relationships. From an analysis of business needs, the firm can identify the functions that need to be automated, as well as discover the basis for determining which technological features are required.

Step 4: Define the CRM Strategy

After the business needs analysis (which means sufficient information has been gathered for the CRM strategy development), it is time to define the CRM strategy that can be implemented in the future. A good CRM strategy should address five

areas, though they are not necessarily five separate areas in our implementation (Fig. 3.5).

The Value Proposition

The goal of a CRM strategy is to retain strategically important customers, and the objective of customer retention is to develop, communicate, and deliver value propositions that meet or exceed customer expectations. The value proposition in turn is a multifaceted package of product, service, process, price, communication, and interaction that customers experience during their relationships with a company. It is the soul of the company's business, in that it differentiates the company from others. If the value proposition is not affected by an investment in CRM, the company is not as customer-centric as it needs to be or it lacks a basic understanding of what its customers value. The value proposition must address three areas:

1. What customers value
2. What the company says it offers the customers
3. What the company actually offers the customers

The company should strive to offer what customers value; if all three elements of value proposition are not aligned, the company likely cannot achieve customer centricity, because it is not delivering actual value to customers.

Business Case

The business case for CRM determines whether the company will meet its specific and measurable expectations from its investments. An effective business case should directly link the delivery of customer value with the creation of shareholder value, exhibit a good return on investment (ROI), and account for three areas:

1. *The planned increase in the economic value of the customers over the duration of their connection with the company.* The lifetime value, risk involved in unlocking that value, and growth potential by a customer segment should be considered.

2. *Reference and referral effects.* The preceding calculations alone cannot justify ROI. If the company is investing more to satisfy the needs of customers, there should be a significant impact in the form of increased customer acquisition through referral. Thus a value must be placed on new customers who have been acquired as a result of the investment.

3. *The impact of learning and innovation.* The enhanced learning and innovation resulting from CRM add more value by reducing the cost incurred by the company through higher marketing effectiveness and improved products and services delivered to customers.

Customer Strategy

A customer strategy defines how the company will build and manage a portfolio of customers. A portfolio likely consists of customer segments differentiated by the actual or perceived characteristics of those customers. An effective customer strategy covers at least these four areas:

1. *Customer understanding.* To develop, communicate, and deliver a satisfactory value proposition, the company must understand its customers' expectations. There are six distinct levels: *delight, excellent, should, will, minimally tolerable,* and *intolerable.* They form a hierarchy from highest to lowest. *Will* expectations are those that customers develop through previous experience. *Should* expectations rely on promises made or inferred by the company. Customers benchmark their expectations against their past experience and best-in-class standards. In most cases though, even the best companies cannot meet customers' *excellent* expectations all the time. Therefore, meeting expectations is a realistic goal for most companies' CRM strategies. *Delight* is not always desirable either, because it is costly and shifts customer expectations considerably. To understand customers' expectations, a company should have effective customer segmentation and obtain as much customer data as possible regarding their needs (active and passive) for products and services, then extract information from the data using specific analytical tools.

2. *Customer competitive context.* The company should be aware of how its competitors are servicing their customers and how it should retain and increase its share of customers in the competitive marketplace.

3. *Customer affiliation.* Customer affiliation is critical because it is a primary factor affecting a company's ability to retain and extract greater value from the customer through cross- and up-selling. Comparative assessments of the strength of customer affiliation affect strategies for customer retention.

4. *Customer management competencies.* The company must have a defined standard process about who should and how to manage customers. To retain its customer management competency, the company also needs to benchmark its management against that of its competitors and improve it continuously. The best way to meet customers' expectations may be to provide them with customized instead of generic offers. Customized offers should include not only customized products but also services, processes, distributions, communication, and even prices.

Enterprise Transformation Plan

The transformation required by a CRM strategy must cover these six areas:

1. *Business process.* All primary business processes should be assessed from the perspective of the customer strategy to determine whether the distinct needs of the customer are met and, if not, how to do so.

2. *Organization.* Most customer strategies result in organizational changes, which include cultural changes.

3. *Location and facilities.* Particular locations that customers visit have profound impacts on their perceptions of the company, so the physical assets of the company must be adjusted to match the customer-centric strategy.

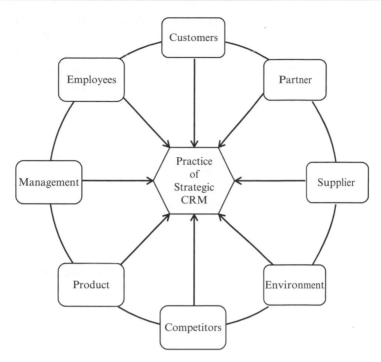

Fig. 3.6 Practice of strategic CRM: Framework

4. *Data flows.* CRM strategy should lay out a data strategy, covering the collection of more data, creating and deriving additional data from these data, and distributing the data to different users (staff and customers).
5. *Application architecture.* To implement a CRM strategy, the application architecture should be changed to feature new application software—or at least to integrate existing software in new ways.
6. *Technology infrastructure.* A CRM strategy definitely requires a change to the technology infrastructure, including new hardware, new operating software, and operations personnel.

A change strategy that manages the process in well-paced steps can mitigate the pain associated with change. It should ensure buy-in from employees, who must be prepared for the new paradigm through adequate and effective training.

Relationship Management of Other Stakeholders

Strategic CRM is a comprehensive practice involving all facets of an organization, as shown in Fig. 3.6.

Stakeholders of a company include *management, customers, employees, suppliers,* and *part-*ners, in addition to *owners/investors. Management* initiates CRM and takes the responsibility to ensure that in the comprehensive CRM strategy, the relationships with all stakeholders are effectively managed. Because strategic CRM is a top-down approach, it succeeds only if *management* is committed to the CRM strategy. Furthermore, because customers often evaluate the company according to the value of the goods/services provided, the *product* provides the link between the organization and the customer.

Apparently, the relative importance of individual stakeholders for a strategic CRM approach may differ across industries or businesses. For example, in industries in which customers derive satisfaction mostly by interacting with employees (e.g., hotels), employees are essential to achieve a high value proposition to the customer. Yet, *customers* are of course the major focus of a CRM strategy because customers are the only source of revenue whereas relationships with all other stakeholders generate costs.

Employees are involved in the execution of the CRM strategy. The employees' behaviors can have positive or negative effects on the customer's value perception. Only satisfied employees likely deliver exceptional service. As discussed in detail in Chap. 2, employee satisfaction is one important driver of customer satisfaction, especially for businesses in the service industry. Therefore, a company's CRM strategy must address employee satisfaction to increase customer satisfaction.

The quality of a product or service depends to a large degree on the *suppliers* who provide for example raw material, components, technological or business know-how (consultants), personnel (recruitment agencies), or money (creditors). With the evolvement of total quality management, the past decades have seen a dramatic change in the structure of supply chains. Relationship-orientation has entered supply-chain management and companies now tend to build strategic, long-term, and interactive relationships with fewer suppliers. The focus on fewer but closer relations to suppliers has two major advantages: (1) Drive efficiency, e.g., cost reduction (search as well as transaction costs), for example through electronic data interchange (EDI) to manage a lean and efficient supply chain. (2) Drive effectiveness, e. g. synergetic efforts in producing value for customers where both parties achieve more together than individually (1 + 1 = 3), for example in creating customer-oriented innovation.

Partnerships such as strategic alliances and joint ventures enable their participants to share technological know-how and customer data, develop new products more rapidly, and share costs as well as risks. As a result, these participants enjoy lower costs, better customer insights, and eventually a broader customer base, all of which enables them to provide additional value to their customers. As part of its CRM strategy, a company must have such a partnership strategy to identify the strategic area in which partnerships are necessary, determine the ideal partner profile, search for appropriate partners, enter a strategic alliance agreement, and manage its ongoing partnerships.

Competitors also play a major role, because any firm is always compared with the other players in the market. The key is to provide better value than competitors, as well as use them to benchmark the firm's own strategy and definition of success. Similarly, *external factors* always play a critical role in devising any strategy,

though firms have little to no control over them. Yet before developing its CRM strategy, the firm should perform its own SWOT (strength-weaknesses-opportunities-threats) analysis, so it is ready to exploit the opportunities and face the threats by relying on its own strengths or avoiding its weaknesses.

Finally, a successful CRM strategy also needs to create value for the company's *owners/investors*. If the value proposition offered to customers ultimately cannot reap benefits for investors, the strategy will lose its support. From this perspective, creating more value for customers goes hand-in-hand with ensuring owners' benefits. However, conflicts also occur: A CRM strategy focused on delivering higher value to owners in the long term sometimes requires sacrificing short-term benefits, which cannot satisfy owners who seek short-term ROI. Unfortunately, it appears this short-term focus is the more common reality: In many large companies, the carousel of CEO replacement is accelerating, such that between 1997 and 2000, 65% of *Fortune* 500 companies replaced their CEO (Bianco & Lavelle, 2000).

To develop a successful CRM strategy, a company needs owners with a long-term orientation. For most public companies, short-term profit seeking is common among investors, but three general approaches to increase the long-term orientation exist: (1) convince existing investors, (2) attract long-term oriented owners, and (3) take the company private.

If investors focus only on long-term returns, they are more likely to become advocates of a profound CRM strategy.

3.4 Case Study: CRM Implementation at IBM

IBM is the world's largest information technology company, with 2003 revenues of $89.14 billion.[1] Its portfolio of capabilities ranges from

---

[1] This case study is based on research by several INSEAD MBA students: Alper Aras, Natalia Boksha, Tatiana Kachalova, and Eyal Katzenstein.

sophisticated services, such as business transformation consulting, to product offerings including software, hardware, fundamental research, financing, and component technologies used to build larger systems.

In the 1990s, the landscape of the IT industry changed significantly. A narrow set of incumbents, including IBM, Hewlett-Packard, and Compaq, faced fierce competition from domestic and foreign invaders. Their products were virtually interchangeable and hard to differentiate. The environment was marked by tight margins and shrinking market share. To survive, companies had to minimize inefficiencies in their operations and develop the ability to deliver high-quality customer service. To increase customer satisfaction and loyalty, as well as reduce the costs of serving customers, IT companies began to implement CRM programs, which also created more transparency between customers and partners.

For IBM, implementing a CRM program involved streamlining client offerings and strengthening its brand image across all lines of business. The main goal was to be able to offer full-scale solutions for clients, instead of multiple, separate products. This goal meant moving away from the sale of boxes and toward real solutions for clients. In this implementation process, IBM also realized the need to manage the increasing complexity of web-based, multichannel business environments. Most companies in the market faced frustration in their efforts to combine a consistent, high-quality customer experience with better cost structures. But IBM found a way to use CRM to streamline and integrate its customer-facing operations (e.g., sales, marketing, customer service). In 2004, IBM initiated the world's largest CRM application, with 60,000 users. In 2005 more than 80,000 employees, thousands of business partners, and ns of IBM customers would use the system.

3.4.1 CRM Implementation Process Objectives

IBM's overall goal in its CRM implementation initiative was to ensure each and every customer interaction was handled with the same degree of excellence, using the same tools, and informed by data gathered across all IBM geographies and sales channels. This integration would help improve customer satisfaction, and encourage collaboration among employees and business units. Moreover, the CRM implementation enabled the company to reduce its internal IT systems, from about 800 in 1997 to fewer than 200 in 2006 through rigorous integration.

Furthermore, its CRM implementation sought to create a disciplined framework that enabled IBM to

- Share information and collaborate easily internally and across the entire value chain.
- Focus on core capabilities while shedding its less profitable or nonstrategic business activities.
- Build a fully integrated IT infrastructure to support the business vision and reduce the total cost of operations.

3.4.2 CRM Implementation Process Stages

IBM developed a six-step process for its CRM implementation:

1. *Establish a common CRM vision and strategy across the enterprise.* The strategy included the following key objectives: Decrease operating costs, drive incremental revenue, create market advantage, and reduce risk. At this stage, it was crucial to obtain senior management support and ensure the viability of necessary trade-offs to achieve enterprise-wide efficiency. One of the key factors was to predict how stated values could be implemented top-down throughout the organization. For example, IBM carefully adjusted incentive systems linked to balanced scorecard measures.

2. *Identify the required capabilities to execute the vision.* The company assessed its current situation according to several major blocks: organization (structure and corporate culture), business processes, and IT. In so doing, it also identified specific gaps in its desired capabilities.

3. *Develop a roadmap of prioritized initiatives.*
   This stage suggested the detailed design of the
   architecture, together with a master plan for
   closing gaps. Specific initiatives were prioritized according to their impact, constraints,
   risks, and dependencies, with the ultimate
   goal of creating customer value.
4. *Manage the end-to-end change process.* This
   stage required skillful change management
   implementations. The program needed to predict levels of end-user support across all
   implementation phases. User involvement
   and training were crucial.
5. *Implement in phases, with a broad initial
   deployment of each CRM application.* A phased
   approach decreased the time for deployment, as
   well as resistance and frustration within the
   organization. It also allowed for plan and
   scope revisions down the road.
6. *Adopt a comprehensive, end-to-end deployment methodology.* The framework ensured
   the coordination of different project teams to
   achieve a common goal.

3.4.3   CRM Implementation

**Initial Stages: Opportunity Management
(1993–2000)**
The CRM initiative at IBM started with the
development of an in-house application. The initial feature, implemented before 1995, was the
opportunity management element, used primarily by the sales organization during the customer
acquisition phase of a sales cycle. IBM selected
this area as a starting point for its implementation
because the company was looking for the biggest
possible initial ROI, as well as for a quick way to
demonstrate the positive impact of the initiative
to senior management. The initiative had cross-
organizational effects, spanning a large portion
of the members of the organization. Because
there was no application already available on
the market for this purpose, the company developed its *Virtual Machine,* a host-driven IBM
application.

This initiative was first designed to work for
customer acquisition in a particular geography.
The initial phase was followed by system implementation, rolled out across all offices. Customer
acquisition processes were reengineered to be
consistent across all products and geographies.
The opportunity management program also
included supportive processes for customer acquisition, including tools to help create solution
designs and delivery plans. In addition, the solution could be tested, checkpoints could be identified, and quality assurance could be performed
across all the involved individual products and
services. A newly created team pursued each
opportunity. The system could identify opportunities, track methods, and store information, such
as pricing, inventory, and customer master records
(i.e., name of the company, address, key contacts,
client financing options), provided by the marketing department. If a particular opportunity could
not be pursued, information about the customers'
requirements or needs that IBM could not fulfill
also was recorded.

Customer segmentation in the system followed two criteria: Size and needs. The size
criteria featured customers divided into either
large and small/mid-market segments. Furthermore, larger companies were segmented by
industry. The needs criteria provided segmentation based on customers' needs and geography.

The collected information then drove the marketing campaigns. Opportunity teams tracked
customer behavior and past revenues, then identified growth rates. Prospective clients were
added to marketing campaigns or forwarded to
telesales to contact. Each client was assigned a
code linked to planned revenues. This stage of
the implementation continued until 2000.

Motivation of Employees (1993–2000)
A CRM implementation strategy can be achieved
only with the full support, participation, and
commitment of employees. Accordingly, IBM
undertook substantial efforts to streamline its
organization according to lines of business.
Selected employees were identified as *change
champions* to drive others through the change
process. Although there was no direct incentive

link to the CRM initiative, the members who adapted well to the new requirements received a sense of appreciation. For example, employees received better laptops when they made significant contributions to the CRM implementation.

Encouragement also came from the CRM project members each time a module had been implemented successfully. Employees enrolled in required training programs, which typically lasted for 2–3 days, and they received support as needed during the implementations. These measures set the necessary organizational background and made it possible to start, in 2000, the full-scale CRM implementation across the entire organization.

Siebel Implementation (2000–2004)

Siebel Systems, "the world's leading provider of customer relationship management (CRM) solutions and a leading provider of applications for business intelligence and standards-based integration" (Siebel, 2005) was chosen as the first partner in IBM's CRM implementation. Through its extensive partnership with Siebel, IBM has been implementing various modules, then using its extensive technical and business process expertise to adapt the software for its customers.

The modules of Siebel's CRM software that IBM has implemented include Sales, Call Center, Marketing, Field Service, Service, e-Channel, e-Marketing, e-Service, and General e-Business (IBM, 2003a). Figure 3.7 illustrates several steps of the Siebel project at IBM, in terms of the scope of each implementation phase. That is, the implementation began with the launch of the *ibm.com call center*, a channel for contacting business partners, particularly dealers and solution vendors. The initial rollout of Siebel's call center package started with 26 ibm.com call centers. By October 2003, it had been deployed in 47 call centers in 32 countries.

This system supports information flow, mainly from IBM to the dealers. When a particular chance to acquire a new customer or initiate a new sales cycle appears, IBM informs dealers about this opportunity. After this notification, dealers must respond within 48 hours, specifying whether they want to pursue the opportunity. If the opportunity is rejected, the rejection

message returns to IBM. IBM then seeks other suitable dealers that are interested in this opportunity.

Even though the dealers were the main source and owners of customer data, they did not act as reliable sources of customer information for IBM. Confidentiality agreements with their multiple customers meant their customer records were closed. When dealers provided some customer data, the information often was not reliable. Because both IBM and the dealers came to recognize the benefits of seamlessly integrated and two-way data flows though, both parties joined efforts in marketing campaigns toward the end of 2003. The call center implementation also included telesales and telemarketing. These subordinate modules served mainly to manage simple product campaigns.

In 2001, the implementations of the service and support initiatives began. Within this functionality, *Service* refers to back-office operations; it supports exchanges with other applications, such as pricing and configuration. *Configuration* refers to the arrangement, customization, and preparation of a customer order, depending on the variation of product features in the order. Used for both hardware and software solutions, configuration is available only for internal and partners' use, not for customers. However, IBM foresees customer access to this functionality in the future, in which case it must determine whether customers are sufficiently technically literate to perform configuration on their own. Other challenges of this extension include finding ways to perform change management with each business customer. The implementation of the *support* module also is underway. As Fig. 3.7 portrays, business partners were included in all these initiatives in 2002.

IBM is now tackling the field sales initiative with the Siebel implementation. Field sales operations mainly refer to activity management processes, which enable efficient task allocation to sales personnel. This assignment is based on the specific availability of a sales opportunity, customer sales history data and requirements, order specifications, and so on. In 2004, IBM also implemented the marketing block, an

Fig. 3.7 Scope and timing of Siebel implementation at IBM

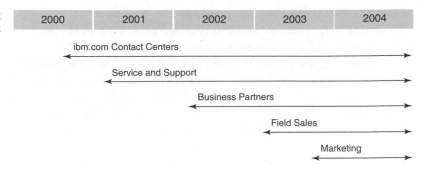

effective tool for facilitating its interactions with business partners, which has enhanced one-way communication processes to encourage bidirectional communication.

These initiatives have helped IBM respond increasingly well to customer requests in real time (or *On-Demand,* as IBM calls it). The company promises products, services, and information to its customers as they demand individual modules or components. This system also allows IBM to customize offerings for particular customer orders and requests. Such capabilities are greatly appreciated by customers, especially in the rapidly changing high-tech area. For example, on-demand services can provide customers access to CRM applications without having to implement an entire solution.

3.4.4 Case Summary

At a more specific level, several points illustrate the key strengths of the IBM CRM initiative that has enabled the company to generate competitive advantages:

- The On-Demand operating environment establishes an ability to provide customized solutions, available on an immediate and, if desired, piecemeal basis.
- Although some of IBM's competitors have been implementing Siebel solutions, none has a full-scale CRM implementation covering as many people and functions as IBM's system.
- Integrated process management through CRM provides instant updates about inventory levels, customer complaints, recommendations, and so on. In turn, sales and production strategies can be updated quickly and efficiently.

- The pricing and revenue data are integrated, which provides revenue analysis opportunities for IBM. Each customer gets a code in Siebel, describing its revenue-generation potential. When IBM seeks to sell a particular hardware or software solution, the codes provide potential customers in the next cycle.

With these competitive advantages, IBM has achieved the following positive outcomes:

- Improved sales productivity, effectiveness, and channel integration.
- Greater awareness of market dynamics and the elimination of integrated legacy applications.
- Higher customer satisfaction through better responsiveness and ease of doing business.
- Improved sales management effectiveness, reflected in tighter management controls and proactive sales coaching.
- Better forecast accuracy and reporting.
- Enhanced partnership management.
- A top-ranking position for IBM in the IT area, according to a recent survey by *Forbes.*
- Decreased time to complete the sales cycle and serve a customer. (These times also are lower than competitors', so IBM serves its customers faster.)
- Transformed contract management process to more efficient and simpler procedures.

As of today, IBM estimates its internal CRM implementation has provided it with $2 billion in cost reductions,[2] 22% productivity

_____

[2] A component of savings also comes from gaining efficiencies in the sales process, measured in the hours saved because sales personnel use the CRM system. These saved hours, multiplied by the cost per hour to employ that salesperson, equal the total savings value achieved through sales efficiency improvements (IBM Corporation, 2003a).

improvements, significant IT cost mitigation, reduced sales staff requirements, and improved management reporting (IBM Corporation, 2003b).

Key Lessons: Insights from IBM

The IBM case summarizes some lessons for implementing large-scale CRM initiatives:

- *Genuine top-level support within the organization is essential.* The lack of such support during the initial phases of the implementation caused significant bottlenecks and delays at IBM.
- *To deliver a truly enterprise-wide CRM solution, chief information officers must stand firm.* These top managers must have the willingness and power, to say no to requests for separate CRM solutions that are not fully integrated with other supporting IT systems within the organization.
- *CRM is not just an exercise for IT; without the cooperation of each business unit, an enterprise-wide implementation is not possible.* Data integration plays an essential role in this case.
- *Data are typically in much worse condition than one might think.* To acquire the full benefit of an investment in CRM, data cleansing at the initial stages of an implementation is crucial.
- *Front-line personnel cannot just be pulled off their posts and train for several weeks.* Business units within the enterprise cannot afford to lose these work hours. The CRM training time thus needs to be planned well in advance and managed carefully.
- *CRM implementations induce extensive business process reengineering and change management initiatives.* The potential difficulties, bottlenecks, and delays that might result from these initiatives likely cause much more severe impacts than initially foreseen. Moreover, an effective CRM implementation often requires that the organization's structure and philosophy radically change, including alterations in customer service values, incentive systems within the company, and critical success factors.

Conclusion

IBM, a global leader in implementing CRM solutions, both internally in business units and externally for customers, provides an excellent example of the effects of the CRM initiative on the entire organization. Implementing CRM goes far beyond implementing software. Achieving complete success requires the commitment of the entire organization, from the bottom to the top. Planning such an initiative also creates a wide range of business process reengineering and change management issues. Designing efficient processes, creating appropriate milestones, engaging business partners and customers at the right time, and effectively managing data are key elements of success in CRM implementations. It is vital that commitment and patience be embedded any CRM initiative.

3.5 Summary

In this chapter, we have looked at CRM from a strategic perspective. When CRM is viewed as a company-level philosophy, such that knowledge about customers has implications for the entire organization, it is *strategic CRM*. The goal of strategic CRM is to shape interactions between the firm and its customers in a way that maximizes the lifetime value of each customer to the firm. The four main components of CRM strategy are

1. Customer management orientation, which is the set of organizational values, beliefs, and strategic actions that enable the implementation of customer management principles, driven by a top-management belief that the customer is at the center of activity.
2. Integration and alignment of organizational processes, which consist of the creation and synchronization of processes and systems to enable the organization to implement customer management principles.
3. Information capture and alignment of technology, because an understanding of the value provided to target customers drives processes.

The processes also work in line with the goal of attracting and retaining target customers.

4. CRM strategy implementation. The processes and activities required for a successful CRM strategy are structured around two key dimensions in a CRM implementation matrix. The customer dimension captures the influence of the changing phase of a customer–firm relationship, and the management dimension comprises analytical and operational CRM.

In turn, developing a CRM strategy consists of (1) gaining enterprise-wide commitment (2), building a CRM project team, (3) analyzing business requirements, and (4) defining the CRM strategy according to its value proposition, business case, customer strategy, enterprise transformation plans, and other stakeholders.

The value proposition of each firm is a multifaceted package that customers experience, including the product, service, process, price, communication, and interaction. The business case determines whether an investment in CRM meets expectations by linking the delivery of customer value to the creation of shareholder value, or ROI. It should take into account not only the economic value of a customer but also the potential for increased customer acquisition through referrals and the impact of learning and innovation. A customer strategy helps build and maintain a portfolio of customers through an understanding of their expectations, competitor contexts, and customer affiliations. The CRM strategy also demands transformations in business processes, organizations, locations and facilities, data flows, application architecture, and technology infrastructure. Finally, strategic CRM covers all facets of an organization—customers, management, products, competitors, environment, employees, suppliers, and investors. In the next chapter, we will discuss how to carry out investment and operational decisions to implement these various elements of a firm's CRM strategy.

Leading into that discussion, we have illustrated the implementation of CRM in an industry through a case study. When IBM implemented its CRM, its main objective was to offer full-scale solutions for clients, instead of multiple products. The first step was establishing a common CRM vision and strategy across the enterprise. IBM also developed an in-house application for opportunity management, primarily designed for use by the sales organization in the customer acquisition phase. This initiative had cross-organizational impacts for many members of the organization, which helped IBM recognize the importance of employee motivation. IBM selected a group of *change champions* to encourage the change process and provided further encouragement on a firm-wide level. Training programs and other forms of support persisted throughout the implementation, which laid a necessary organizational foundation for a successful CRM implementation.

Once the stage was set, IBM installed Siebel CRM modules in phases, starting with the ibm.com call center. By improving communication between dealers and IBM, it involved business partners early on in the implementation. Then the service and support module supported back-office operations. IBM also continued to implement other modules, always in phases. This project has yielded significant results: $2 billion in cost reductions, 22% productivity improvements, significant IT cost reductions, lower sales staff requirements, and improved management reporting.

Exercise Questions

1. Are traditional marketing principles valid in the age of CRM? What are the fundamental differences between transaction-based marketing approaches and relationship-based marketing approaches?

2. What structural changes must an organization undertake to switch from a product to a customer orientation? Should companies start investing in such structural changes?

3. Can a heavily operations-oriented company (e.g., Walmart) benefit from practicing CRM?

4. Have you heard stories of companies that had difficulties implementing CRM? What was the nature of the problem, and how could it have been solved?

5. What are the key steps in implementing CRM?

References

Bianco, A., & Lavelle, L. (2000). The CEO Trap. *BusinessWeek*, December 11

IBM Corporation. (2003a). *Implementing Siebel e-business applications in IBM*. Internal paper, Copyright © IBM Corporation.

IBM Corporation. (2003b). *CRM: Transformation for an on-demand world: The road to successful customer relationship management*. IBM CRM executive brief, Copyright © IBM Corporation.

Reinartz, W., Krafft, M., & Hoyer, W. (2004). The customer relationship management process: Its measurement and impact on performance. *Journal of Marketing Research, 41*(3), 293–305.

Siebel. (2005). Siebels Customer Relationship Management (CRM) application. Accessed January 13, 2005, from http://www.siebel.com.

Implementing the CRM Strategy

4

4.1 Overview

Firms recognize that customers have a large degree of control over the firm customer relationship. However, it is the firm that must make investments in creating and managing the various points of interactions with a customer. From the customer's standpoint, CRM is about courteous service. Over a period of time, customers develop expectations from their interactions based on information gained from their experience with various touch points such as the salespersons, e-mail and mail messages, telephone, and so on. Every touch point is therefore critical in improving the firm-customer relationship. Touch-point efficiencies are maximized when integrated with the sales, marketing, and service functions of the organization. From the firm's perspective, managing customer expectation and maintaining ongoing relationship with customers has a cost. There are the costs of gathering and analyzing information about customers, providing customer support, and implementing customized strategies for customers. Companies need to balance these costs with the benefits to be profitable. In other words, they have to calculate the long-term ROI from CRM implementation before they invest in the customer interface elements and applications of CRM.

This chapter provides guidelines to identify the costs and benefits involved in implementing CRM. We not only look at the economic costs and benefits but also at the people costs and indirect benefits. A three-step process of arriving at ROI for a strategic CRM implementation is explained. We will begin by looking at the elements that are involved in creating an integrated CRM system. Once we have learned about these elements, we will look at the importance and value of computing the ROI for CRM activities as well as what elements should be considered for its calculation. Finally, we will look at the implementation of a CRM system within an organization and discuss the organizational behaviors that may be exhibited and how to control for those factors.

4.2 Elements of a CRM System

Before implementing a CRM system, we need to understand the various elements involved in it. One way to do this is by separating the CRM activities into front-and back-office activities (as done by many practitioners and software vendors). Figure 4.1 depicts the various elements in a composite CRM system.

To begin, the front-end customer interface and application components include:

- *Customer interface/touch points*. Customers interact with the company through a variety of touch points. The CRM system should be able to offer a consistent view of all customers regardless of the touch point being used by the

Fig. 4.1 Customer Interface and Application Components of CRM

customers. For example, a salesperson should have knowledge of the products that the customer browsed for recently on his mobile web site, before suggesting an appropriate upgrade in a face-to-face meeting. Touch points are the exact moment the firm can simultaneously gather and disseminate information. It is critical that the CRM system is able to provide current information about that customer's needs for maximum opportunity for a sale.

- *CRM applications.* CRM is implemented by a wide set of applications which enable the firm to deliver offers, generate orders, and respond to customer enquiries and feedback. These applications span the sales, marketing, and customer service functions in an organization. Additionally the applications can be useful for generating back-end information through dashboards, scorecards, and more traditional reports.
  - *Sales and sales management function.* Contact and quote management, account management (activities, order entry, proposal generation, etc.), pipeline analysis (forecasting, sales cycle analysis, win/loss analysis, territory alignment and assignment, roll-up, and drill-down reporting) are important sales functions that a CRM system needs to integrate. The sales process must be managed across many domains including other business units. Sales personnel are an essential source of information for the company and must have the tools to both access up-to-date field information and

provide this information to various domains of the business. The interaction of the sales force with the prospect, turning the prospect into a customer, and then maintaining a mutually profitable relationship, are key aspects of the business.

- *Marketing function.* Multichannel campaign management, opportunity management, market segmentation, and lead generations/enhancement/tracking are critical marketing functions that the CRM *system* should integrate. Today, initial mass-marketing activities are often used for the first contact, and are then followed up by more focused campaigns with specific target audiences or even an individual customer in mind. Personalization, where customers' preferences and buying habits are taken into account, is quickly becoming the expected norm of interactions. With the ability to utilize mobile-based touch points and e-mail, personalization based on the individual customer's current (and ever changing) tastes and preferences must be addressed. Content management, relationship marketing, and one-to-one marketing are now key aspects of conducting business.
- *Customer service function.* This includes incident assignment, escalation, field personnel tracking, reporting, problem management, resolution, order management, and warranty contract management. The customer service function is the key to a company's ability to maintain proactive

relations with customers and hence retain satisfied loyal customers. CRM systems can assist in managing the help desk and providing customer care across all types of customer queries, including product concerns, information needs, order requests, and quality field service. The following example shows how companies are using technology to connect with their customers.

CRM AT WORK 4.1
La Croissanterie, Paris, France: Enhancing Customer Interface using Technology

La Croissanterie, a Paris based fast-food chain was facing a problem because many of its customers had too many loyalty cards and were forgetting or losing their cards all together. Additionally, the company had an outdated system that collected only the basic information about the customers and rewarded only customers who purchased full meals. For instance, customers ordering only coffee were not rewarded thereby reducing the incentive for customers to use the loyalty card.

To resolve this, La Croissanterie updated its loyalty program with the introduction of Loyalty Pass in June 2010. The new system allowed customers to record purchases through any of the following three channels – a loyalty card, a mobile phone or a transit pass. Additionally, the company also used these three channels to track and offer product promotions. This advancement in customer data collection and usage was made possible using the Near Field Communication (NFC) technology.

The NFC technology is an extension of Radio Frequency Identification (RFID) and smartcard technology geared towards mobile phones. It is a wireless technology that allows the customers to store their unique IDs on the phone. When the customer arrives at the store, he/she simply taps a smart poster imbedded with another

NFC device to transmit their information. This device will instantly present him/her with promotions based on their specific profile. At the checkout, the customer taps again and his/her transaction is recorded for the loyalty rewards.

Additionally, La Croissanterie was able to immediately catalog all individual customer transactions across all locations, frequency and purchase type. This advancement in technology allows for a consistent interface with the customer and presents the company with more detailed view of the customer from all available touch points.

Source: Felding, M. (2010, September 15). C'est Delicieux. *Marketing News*, p. 6.

Now that we have learned the essential elements of a CRM system, the next section explores the value and importance of calculating ROI for CRM activities.

4.3   Return on Investment of CRM

Once a firm decides on the elements required for implementing a CRM system, it must ask one important question: Is the investment in CRM elements worth it? The practice of developing and implementing a CRM *system* should always measure the expected monetary benefits to *see* if the investment is likely to payoff. From 2008 and on companies have continued to tighten the marketing belt and the ROI has become more important than ever. Companies such as Proctor & Gamble, Coca-Cola, and HP have all implemented CRM programs to personalize the individual experience (Bush, 2008). The estimation of ROI of CRM determines many critical decisions, such as whether a CRM strategy is needed, what CRM strategy should be developed, and how it should be implemented. The formula for ROI is well known:

$$\text{Profits}/\text{Investment} * 100\% = \text{ROI}(\%)$$

Table 4.1 Key issues to consider in computing ROI for CRM activities

Business areas to be considered	Key issues to be asked
Consulting services	What will be the consulting cost for the project (business case, strategy, IT engineering, implementation, training)?
Business processes	To what degree is business process re-design necessary?
Information technology	What new IT software and hardware must be purchased to accommodate the new system?
Vendor management	Does the system need to be customized or will it work "out of the box"? How much customization is required and at what cost?
Procurement & maintenance	Can the system be easily configured and maintained by internal IT staff or is continuous external assistance required?
Staffing & training	What is the cost of training the company's staff to use the CRM system?
Implementation	What is the timeframe for implementation and what will happen to the current system processes during that time?
Costing	What are recurrent costs in the implementation?

While the formula is simple, a deeper understanding of the elements of CRM investments is warranted to accurately ascertain the ROI of CRM activities. Due to the cross-functional nature of strategic CRM, costs are incurred in many areas. Generally, the cost level is determined by several factors. Table 4.1 provides a list of areas and key issues to be considered in deciding the nature of the costs.

4.3.1 Costs Associated with a CRM Implementation

From Table 4.1, it can be determined that the elements of CRM investments can be divided into five major categories: organizational requirements, technology needs, database needs, human resource potential, and implementation factors. This section will explore each of these categories.

Organizational Requirements

The overall requirements of the organization interested in deploying the CRM initiative play a significant role in determining the final cost of CRM implementation. Managers and functional experts within the various departments of the organizations will contribute the business and department-specific requirements that will go into the overall framework of the CRM program to be implemented. In effect, the organizational requirements will depend on the nature of the

CRM project, such as campaign management, channel management, customer support, and product development, among others (Bohling et al., 2006). The organizational requirements will also be supplemented by business infrastructure needed to achieve the goal, and information about the customer segment(s) being served by this implementation. These requirements put together decide the final cost of the CRM program. The more complex the requirements are, higher is the cost of CRM implementation.

Technology Needs

To go along with the organizational requirements, the technology requirements play a vital role in seeing the CRM implementation through development and to fruition. The technology requirements typically include software and hardware components, database development and IT infrastructure. Each of the types of IT plays a part in the overall costs of CRM implementation. Typically, software can be purchased or licensed. For the typical CRM project, IT costs usually account for one-fifth to one-third of the total cost. This might remain an accurate prediction for future years too, because the savings associated with the falling costs of hardware and software are offset by the rising cost of hiring IT professionals.

An important element when dealing with CRM technology is in identifying and examining the role of relational information processes and how they aid in effective customer relationship management. The relational information processes are defined as encompassing the specific routines that a firm uses to manage customer information to establish long-term relationships with customers. These information processes help in the capture and use of customer information so that a firm's effort to build relationships is not rendered ineffective by poor communication, information loss and overload, and inappropriate information use. Research has shown that by moderating the influence of relational information processes on customer relationship performance, technology used for CRM performs an important and supportive role (Jayachandran et al., 2005). When firms adopt these insights into their implementation, they are bound to witness significant impact on the cost incurred on technology.

Database Needs

Based on the nature of the CRM project and the customer segment(s) that will be served, the database costs will vary. The customer database is at the heart of an IT-enabled CRM system. Customers often have multiple channels to communicate with a firm and could interact with numerous departments, such as sales, customer service, and marketing. The information from these interactions serves as the basis for future interactions in the context of CRM (Peppers & Rogers, 1997). Further, creating a single database by combining internal data from several channels and divisions, with relevant external data, is a huge challenge faced by many companies, particularly those who have grown through mergers and acquisitions. If the organization already maintains a robust database containing all relevant information, the database needs will add very little to the overall costs. However, if the organization will have to create a database or add a significant amount of information to their existing database, this requirement could become a significant addition to the overall costs.

Human Resource Potential

The human resource potential in an organization is a critical component, and perhaps even the most challenging one to manage, in the development and implementation of a CRM project. Getting the right people to helm the CRM projects makes all the difference in an implementation. For instance, Continental Airlines went from worst to first in customer satisfaction. This transformation clearly stresses the importance of firms having people issues under control before investing in expensive CRM technologies (Reitz, 2005). The human resource costs include the hiring of IT professional as well as the costs of training current employees. Operations researchers and statisticians may be required for developing and implementing a CRM system. The analytical side of CRM may require expertise in segmentation analysis, migration modeling, lifetime value estimations, customer acquisition planning, and customer churn analysis. Recruitment of CRM talent in direct marketing, campaign, management, and many other areas may also be required. Training costs also fall into this category. Current and future employees will need to be trained on how to properly query the CRM system.

Implementation Factors

Often when a new or different CRM strategy is employed, significant changes need to be made to a firm's current mode of operation. One of the key CRM implementation challenge is defining and communicating the need and use for the proposed changes to all members of the management. In other words, change management plays a crucial role in deciding the success (and cost) of CRM implementation (Kumar et al., 2004). One way to counter this challenge is to implement the entire project as a series of small projects, in which only a single activity is performed/achieved. The costs involved in such small projects not only require a lower cost outlay, but also enables easy tracking of costs for the entire project.

4.3.2   Financial Benefits from a CRM Implementation

While it is relatively easier to identify the costs involved in a CRM project, pinpointing the financial benefits from a CRM strategy implementation requires a firm grasp of the company's pre-CRM financials. Since CRM projects are vast and usually take place over a long period of time, they are implemented in stages. This step by step process allows a firm to judge the financial impact (whether or not it is a positive gain) of each stage as it is put in to place.

Since it is hard to compute concrete CRM profits, companies are also likely to count indirect future returns on CRM investment. Some of these indirect returns reflect CRM's direct impact on costs and revenues, including lower customer acquisition costs, lower costs-to-serve, higher average transaction margin, higher average customer value, and so on. Some other indirect returns reflect neither cost nor revenue, but the drivers of either or both. Among these are improvements in customer satisfaction, customer retention, customers acquired, customer attrition rates, cross-sell rates, up-sell rates, products owned per customer, inventory turns, average number of transactions, share of wallet, customer complaint rates, process costs, rework, employee satisfaction, and employee retention.

Companies in different industries face different CRM problems and emphasize different returns on CRM. For example, the biggest customer problem for companies in the telecom industry is *customer churn rate*, which can be up to 40% a year (Churn rate is the number of existing customers who have left by the end of a given period divided by the number of existing customers at the beginning of the respective period, 2999). Therefore, their most valued CRM return should be the retention of the most valuable customers and the opportunities of cross selling to them data and other communication services so as to build a multiproduct bond that is hard to break. In the financial services industry, the companies' major CRM concern could be to reduce transaction costs by shifting customers from branches to the phone or to the Web, and to cross-sell and up-sell to customers based on their past behavior and propensity to buy, thus earning a greater share of customer wallet.

Profits are what remain after costs are subtracted from revenues. As, we can see from the previous examples, CRM investments can lead to reduced costs and improved revenue for a company. Thus, the ultimate return on CRM investments is the improved long-term customer profitability. Since this return is long-term and indirect, recognizing it during the stage of developing the CRM strategy is critical, because it provides the decision makers correct judgment of whether a CRM strategy is really worth the cost.

4.3.3 Computing the ROI of CRM Initiatives

After determining the costs and related financial benefits associated with CRM investments, it becomes easier to compute the ROI of CRM activities. In evaluating the ROI of CRM activities, it is common for organizations to find that the many costs associated with the CRM activities are not recovered within the initial project cycle. Even though the initial results may look negative, it is important to project the return of the project over several time periods to ascertain the true ROI of the project. Such projections over future time periods should also consider the entire cycle of developing, implementing, and continuously improving the CRM strategy – a process that is long and complex. Additionally, an accurate calculation of ROI entails the understanding and development of measurable indexes of business outcomes in each of the stages of implementation. Such indexes make it easy for the management to in not only analyzing the impact of the project, but also in identifying the financial benefits arising out of the implementation (Rust et al., 2004).

So, what does it all mean? As, we can see, the ROI estimates vary according to the assumptions made by the firm's management. It is important, therefore, to get a dependable picture of the expected return from a CRM project. How do you ensure the figures are accepted by the business? This is about ownership as well as accuracy. Management must create a shared view of how the returns on a CRM project are to be computed, which results in a degree of shared belief in the numbers. These estimates are usually arrived at through a three-stage process, as shown in Table 4.2.

Before a consensus can be reached, there are likely to be iterations between stage 1 and stage 2. Estimating ROI for strategic CRM is by no means easy. Yet, if approached objectively,

Table 4.2 Stages of ROI estimation

Stage	Content	Questions to raise
1. Setting the target	Determine ROI goal of CRM project based on benchmarking, similar projects, external and internal knowledge	Is the goal sufficient?
		Is this goal achievable?
2. Reaching the target	Generate ideas of how to reach target through internal bottom-up participation, external views, consultants, benchmarks, etc.	What factors have to change and by how much to achieve the goal?
		Does it work from a technical perspective?
		Are the proposed benefits clear/unclear?
		Will customers and/or staff accept these measures?
3. Building consensus and commitment	Have executives and line staff agree on proposed ROI goals and ensure commitment on both sides	Are we collectively prepared to sign them off?

our discussion shows that a satisfactory measure of the ROI is not elusive.

So far in this chapter we have looked at the basic elements of a CRM system, the main cost drivers for implementation and maintenance, and finally how to arrive at a reasonable measurement of ROI. In the following section we will look at how exactly to implement the CRM system.

4.4 CRM Implementation

As mentioned earlier, the implementation of a CRM strategy is a process of developing and executing a series of small CRM projects. These projects are all aimed at the business needs and value propositions identified when the strategy is defined, and they normally fall into three categories:

1. Operational CRM projects that enable the company to meet the technical and functional requirements of the CRM strategy
2. Analytical projects, whose objective is to obtain a good understanding of the customer's needs, expectations, and behaviors
3. Implementation projects that deploy the operational and analytical outputs to improve marketing decision and customer relationships

The rest of this section will provide an in-depth look at each of these categories in order to understand their roles in CRM implementation.

CRM AT WORK 4.2
Giant Eagle: Fuel for Thought
The flexibility to adapt to the needs of the consumer is critical when implementing a CRM system. Grocery and convenience store chain Giant Eagle realized the importance of a customer relationship management program, especially during the recent economic slump. Discounts and promotions acquired by using a loyalty card is not a new concept. However, Giant Eagle added a creative idea to increase use of its customer loyalty program during the most recent economic slump – Fuel discounts.

The program was launched in all the 221 corporate and independently owned full locations as well as 150 GetGo outlets, which are convenience/fueling locations. Since the program's inception, Giant Eagle has successfully managed to crossover fuel discounts with a food discount loyalty card, allowing for increased cross buy between food and fuel purchases. This new initiative has led to significant gains in sales for the chain.

Source: Garry, M. (2009, October 19). The Fab Five. *Supermarket News*. Vol. 57, Issue 42, pp. 32–35.

4.4.1   Operational Projects

The objective of these projects is to construct an infrastructure that meets the technical and functional requirements of CRM. Examples of these projects include automation of functions such as a call center or an order-processing system, developing an online transaction Web site, changing the process of data collection and data management, selecting and installing appropriate hardware and software, upgrading or reconfiguring the IT infrastructure, setting up a customer database and or a data warehouse, and so on. On the surface, most of these projects do not create revenues directly, but, if successfully developed and completed, they provide the company the necessary resources to perform value-added CRM projects. From a technical perspective, a typical CRM infrastructure should have the components listed in Table 4.3.

In addition to the components listed in Table 4.3, many companies may want to develop a comprehensive data warehouse to store real-time data to facilitate marketing data intelligence analysis. The operational projects should, of course, have been conceived with the objective to maximize profitability, reduce support costs, and increase sales and customer loyalty.

4.4.2   Analytical Projects

Analytical projects are implemented to help the company understand its customers by using data analysis tools that mine the company's databases. This area of CRM is also called *data analytics*. Data analytics is the process of combining data-driven marketing and technology to increase the company's knowledge and understanding of customers, products, and transactional data to improve strategic decision making and tactical market activity. Analytical projects draw from the investments in the operational projects by leveraging the resources that the latter has created, and add value by enabling the firm to understand its customers. These projects create the ability for a firm to establish and

manage profitable relationship with its customers. Also, the results of these analyses provide critical information for determining a company's customer strategy and help develop an on-going CRM strategy. Data analytics projects include two major types of activities: customer data transformation and customer knowledge discovery.

Customer Data Transformation

This type of data analytics activity involves extracting and transforming raw data from a wide source of internal and external databases, marts, or warehouses, and then pooling the total data value and information into a place where it can be accessed and explored. To perform customer data transformation, the company needs to first build a data warehouse. Data warehousing involves getting all organizational data together under one roof making it accessible to the people who need it. Although the proportion of companies having implemented a data warehouse application is growing, many are planning to deploy one as part of their total CRM project. However, even where the data warehouse is up and running, accessing and analyzing the data is not as easy, fast, or as accessible as it should or could be. Unless the data are available in a useful format, in a timely fashion, and enable the train of thought analysis that marketers rely on, the data are of no value at all.

Second, a firm must enhance the data on a customer by integrating information from various internal sources. If the integrated customer data is incomplete, the company should enhance the data with externally available information. For example, geographic, lifestyle, and psychographic data can help in developing a complete image of a customer. All this information can be pulled together to a single source, and a historical perspective can be developed over time.

Customer Knowledge Discovery

This type of data analytics project provides marketers with the tools and processes to discover customer data, convert information into usable customer knowledge, and deploy it to enhance marketing decision making. However, accomplishing this requires two activities – analyzing the data using statistical tools to better

Table 4.3 Components of CRM infrastructure

Component	Description
Information Delivery/Online Catalogs	Capability to display and list the company's products and services online
Customer Database	Capability to capture, organize, present, and analyze customer-specific data, in order to identify sales opportunities and address product development and delivery requirements
Personalization and Content Management	Utilizing results of data analysis to create an individualized experience for the customers
	Enhance/modify service delivery vehicles to match the specific needs of customers (based on their user profiles)
Sales force Automation	The deployment and use of tools and services designed to automate the sales and marketing lifecycle
Partner Channel Automation	The deployment and use of tools and services designed to integrate a company's service vehicles with those of its provider and third-party partners
Customer Services	The deployment and use of technology and business processes designed to successfully support a company's products and services

understand customers, and predicting the future based on analytical results obtained from existing data. Successful analytical CRM should cover the following three major areas.

Capturing All Relevant Customer Information

An effective customer data analysis must be based on as complete a customer database as possible. Building a complete customer database requires capturing all relevant customer information, and this can be a significant challenge to many companies. However, it is a necessity for accurate and proper analysis that a complete database be constructed.

There are a few steps that should be taken to construct a complete database. First, before the CRM strategy is implemented, all customer information from any varying formats or data sources must be standardized from both the business and technical point of view. This is extremely important for analytical purposes.

Second, customers can interact with the company in a number of new ways over time, and this will generate a new range of data sources. Therefore, the analytical solution should also be able to flexibly and consistently integrate all the data across all the channels and all customer-company touch points. This will ensure that the customer information is updated in real time and that no important information is left out. This is no small task.

Third, external sources of information should also be incorporated to keep the company aware of the competitive situation. The following are examples of external sources:

- Competitors' data dealing with the company's customers
- Published survey results to supplement the customer information with details about customer satisfaction and customer preferences
- Data from communities or clubs with a common interest

Finally, the customer-related back office data related to billing and shipment should be evaluated from a financial perspective and should be consolidated into a coherent picture of financial success and customer profitability. Successful data intelligence solutions integrate customer data and ensure that useful analytical results are delivered.

Customer Demographic Analysis and Customer Behavior Modeling

With customer demographic analysis, the company will be able to know who its customers are: their name, gender; address, age, education, number of people in the household, and so on. By observing and modeling customers' behavior, the company can know how customers have behaved and then predict how they will behave. Therefore, the company should be able to define customer segments and use them as the basis for making differential decisions in marketing, sales, and customer services to different customer segments. For example, by analyzing customers' transaction history, the company can know the customers' recency, frequency, and monetary value of their purchases. Analyzing customer service records can also indicate customers' attitudes and their feedbacks. Based on this information, the company should be able to model a behavior pattern for specific customers and predict whether they will buy again, what they will probably buy, when they will buy, how much they will spend, and what additional services they may need.

Customer Value Assessment

After establishing the methods to model customer behavior and analyze customer demographic information, it is essential to assess customer value. It helps the company focus its limited resources most efficiently on the best and most valuable customer relationships. Subsequent chapters in this book deal extensively with the measurement and analysis of customer value and customer profiling and scoring processes that are based on these measures of customer value.

4.4.3 Deploying Operational and Analytical Outputs (To Improve Marketing Decisions and Customer Relationships)

Although an operational CRM project can put the CRM architecture into place, and an analytical CRM project can extract helpful information on customers' needs and expectations, no value will be created until this system and the information are utilized to improve the company's marketing decision making and the company's relationships with its customers.

Generally, the goal of these projects is to increase revenue and profit by improving relationships with customers. For example, automation of a call center will service customers more promptly and effectively, and on-line transaction processes will enable customers to transact through self-service. Using the analytical result of customer value assessment and customer profiling, marketing campaigns will target the customers or prospects most likely to respond. Also, customer calls would be directed to the appropriate, contact person in the call center depending on customer rating and customer value, to ensure that the most profitable customers get the greatest satisfaction. Products or service should be customized, or even personalized, based on customer behavior modeling and customer segmentation, to meet their unique expectations. The planning and forecasting of sales, marketing, and customer service will be improved based on customer life-cycle patterns (engage, transaction, fulfill, and service) to make the sales and marketing efforts more focused and efficient. All these will help the company acquire and retain more ideal customers and improve profitability of existing customers.

None of these projects are technical or analytical, but they are as important as the operational and analytical projects, because they cover the last few miles to the destination, the successful value delivery to both the company and the customers. They are even harder to define and execute because they often deal with people, where the most important and difficult change occurs.

Defining and executing these projects requires dealing with what is going on inside of people (the ones who use the system and information), their perceptions, feelings, and ability to adapt and accept external changes. No value can be realized from CRM without understanding and managing its impact on the people who live with it and make it work on a daily basis. The key to successfully dealing with the people aspects of change is to accept change and to deal with issues as and when they arise. If the management ignores the uncomfortable aspects of change, the entire CRM strategy will fail. It must be willing to prioritize human issues in order to ensure that the CRM strategy succeeds. Three major issues must be addressed here:

1. Resistance from employees
2. Motivation and training
3. Availability of information

Resistance from Employees

The first issue these projects have to address is resistance. People resist change, but there are two ways to positively work with resistance.

First, think of resistance as energy. If employees are resistant, then this shows that they do indeed care, and this is much better than total apathy. When the management recognizes resistance as energy and passion, its goal will be to channel that energy into positive commitment and behavior. Second, resistance is information that tells management what is and is not working in the change process. By paying attention to resistance and even encouraging it, management harnesses the energy of change and learns about the next steps it must take to make the change succeed.

There are some guidelines that companies can follow to overcome resistance and help people utilize the CRM system as well as the information:

- **Plan:** Be prepared, focus attention on the benefits of changing, the consequences of not changing, and the impact of these changes on the individual and group.
- **Communicate:** Hold regular meetings. Provide as much information as possible to clarify what is happening and how it will impact the people.
- **Listen:** Encourage people to talk about what is happening. Allow people to "grieve."
- **Support:** Understand that there are no quick fixes for these changes and managers who become champions of change should be supported.

Motivation and Training

To help handle resistance, the company should not only motivate employees to utilize the new system and analytical information, but also train them on how to use the new system and information. Internal marketing campaigns should be initiated to motivate the information users, such as sales reps, customer service reps, marketing analysts, and even decision-making executives, to use the analytical information to achieve obtain their objectives, improve their productivity, and affect the company's bottom line so that they can show their importance and their impact to the company.

Implementing CRM requires employees to change their work habits. The most effective way to do this is training. Users need to be trained on how to utilize the information. This process may include demonstrating to users how to access and utilize needed information, providing users

with frequently updated and understandable user documentation, offering online tutorials that can be customized for each user, providing a telephone help line to stand-by users, and training the "trainers" to ensure that new users can quickly be up and running the system.

Availability of Information

Another important issue here is the availability of information. The company should have an information system that makes the results of the analysis available to all relevant employees in marketing, sales, and customer service to support their decisions in real time. This will necessitate that a person or department take up the responsibility for overseeing this information system. Information sheets should be developed for the individual tasks involved and they must contain results of the analysis that is consistent throughout the company and across all customer touch-points. Furthermore, the processes must be supported so that the relevant information is readily accessible for transactions in operational CRM activities.

Figure 4.2 shows how investing in CRM by overcoming challenges ultimately results in the reduction of time and money resources. In the next section, we will look at Capital One and how it was able to successfully implement a CRM strategy.

Source: Adapted from *Essentials of CRM: A Guide to Customer Relationship Management*, Bryan Bergeron, 2002, John Wiley and Sons, Inc., New York.

4.5   CASE STUDY:

Customer Relationship Management at Capital One[1] (UNITED KINGDOM)
Source: Copyright © 2003 INSEAD, Fontainebleau, France.

Ian: "Customer Relationship Management is another buzzword to me, but what does it actually mean? It just seems like a nice concept. We don't talk about it

---

[1] This case was prepared by Ulrike Wiehr, the Boston Consulting Group MBA Fellow, under the supervision of Professor Werner J. Reinartz, at INSEAD.

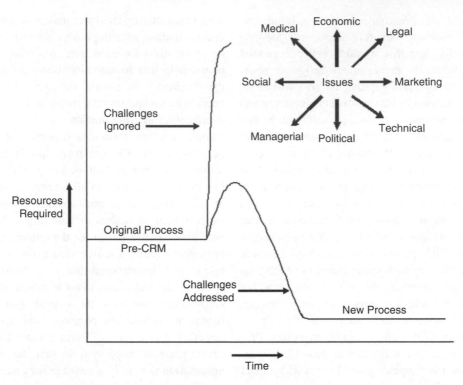

Fig. 4.2 Improving Profitability by Investing in CRM

internally – we have many buzzwords, but not this one."

Phil: "We've internalized it so much – that's why we don't talk about it."

Ian: "You're right, we don't do Customer Relationship Management – we just get on and manage Customer Relationships!"

- Conversation between Phil Marsland, director of Marketing and Analysis, and Ian Cornelius, account manager, Capital One, June 2002.

4.5.1   Case Background

Capital One's leaders, Richard Fairbank and Nigel Morris, had a vision of creating an information-based company rather than a financial services company when they worked in the consulting business in the late 1980s. They envisioned that the strategy for credit card providers

should be to deliver 'the right product to the right customer at the right time, at the right price'. While sounding obvious, their statement marked a revolution that would trigger huge changes in the credit card business. However, this revolution did not happen overnight.

As consultants, Fairbank and Morris could see the potential for improving the credit card business for both customers and shareholders alike through the application of their nascent strategy ideas. The US credit card market during the 1980s was characterized by the fact that the financial institutions were offering very similar products across the whole spectrum of their customer bases, charging a standard 19.8% interest rate and a US$20 annual fee. The market lacked a customization of offers, and one-to-one marketing was practically inexistent. The prevailing story was very much 'one size fits all'.

The journey began in late 1988, when Signet Bank, in Virginia, not only bought Fairbank and Morris' concept but also engaged them to execute the plan from within. In contrast to the prevailing attitude of the major players, Signet put a different understanding at the heart of its new strategy. According to Morris and Fairbank:

"Credit cards are not banking, they are information. It's all about collecting information on millions of people that you've never met, and, on the basis of that information, making a series of critical decisions about lending money to them and hoping they pay you back."

Therefore, Signet Bank rebuilt its credit card operations around information technology and sophisticated analytical techniques. This new adopted strategy, named *"Information Based Strategy" (IBS)* was to compile what was ultimately to become the world's largest Oracle database, allowing the company to understand its customers and to develop mass-customized products, which would ideally suit their needs and risk profile.

By early 1994, Signet made the decision to float the credit card business separately, and hence *Capital One Financial Corporation* was born in November 1994, with Richard Fairbank as Chairman and Chief Executive Officer, and Nigel Morris as President and Chief Operating Officer.

Since its IPO in 1994 to 2011, the stock price of the company has increased by almost 400% and the company has grown at an average annual rate of about 40%, excluding mergers and acquisitions. At the end of the first quarter in 2011, the company reported quarterly revenue of $4.082 billion and 43 million customers worldwide, serviced by more than 27,000 employees. (See Table 4.4 for awards given to the company).

Encouraged by its success in the US, Capital One decided to launch its first overseas operations in the UK. In July 1998, Capital One opened its operations centre in Nottingham. On day one, 250 associates were employed. By 2001, this number had grown to over 2,000, and Capital One associates in Nottingham now deal with application processing, customer service, product design and marketing, card issuing, collections, business development and database management. As early as 2002, the company reached profitability and became one of UK's top six credit card issuers.

Capital One's percentage of outstanding bad debt, a key performance measure in a risk-driven business, was significantly lower than that of key competitors. This is especially significant, given that the company, unlike most of its competitors, lends to customers across the whole credit risk spectrum. At year end, 2001, Capital One posted its 18th consecutive quarter of record earnings: annual earnings grew by more than 20% and delivered a yearly return on equity of more than 20%. Reaching this goal seven times in a row put Capital One in a league with only seven other publicly held US companies. From 2001 to 2007, Capital One's quarterly revenues fluctuated, but maintained a steady annual increase in revenues. In 2008, Capital One enjoyed a successful first quarter before succumbing to the economic climate and experiencing quarterly fluctuations with annual revenue losses during both 2008 and 2009. In response to this 2 year downturn, Capital One recorded its highest annual and quarterly revenues, a positive sign for what is to come. (See Figure 4.3 for the growth history of Capital One's revenues).

In early 2001, Fairbank and Morris could not help wondering about its success: while all their competitors were also embracing CRM (Customer Relationship Management), and most seemed to pursue the concept with significant investments in software and reorganization, Capital One's customer base was developing at a compound annual growth rate of 40%. It seemed as if Capital One could indeed be seen as creating industry best practice in developing valuable customer relationships and managing risk based on an intimate understanding of the customer. But what exactly was it that made Capital One's approach to CRM so unique? Was the company's success down to luck or was it based on a real competitive advantage – and, if so, would this be a sustainable advantage, in the light of competitors' efforts on CRM?

4.5.2   Industry Background

An overview of the UK Credit Card Market
In the early 1990s, the major British banks dominated the market (such as Barclays, Lloyds, The Midland, NatWest, and The Royal Bank of

Table 4.4 Capital one – selection of awards and accolades

2010	Capital One is ranked 232nd on the Forbes global 2000
	Capital One is the recipient of the Richmond Metropolitan Business League's 'Distinguished Service Award'
2008	Capital One is ranked #5 in Diversity Edge's 'Best companies for Diverse Graduates'.
	Capital One is the recipient of the U.S Department of Labor's 'Award for contributions to create a youth supply pipeline'.
2007	Capital One is name to The Dave Thomas Foundation for Adoption's '100 Best Adoption-Friendly Workplaces'
	Capital One is ranked 154th in the Fortune 500
2006	Capital One receives the U.S Chamber's 'Corporate citizenship award'
	Capital One receives the American Red Cross's 'Pennington Award'
2005	Capital One is named for the 5th year in a row in Forbes 400 list- Best Big Companies in America
2004	Capital One is ranked 200th in the Fortune 500
2003	Capital one is placed in the top half of Training's 'Top 125'
2002	Capital One is named the 12th 'Best Place to Work in the UK' by the Sunday Times
	Capital One is named in Fortune's list of '100 Best Places to Work in America' for the fourth consecutive year.
2001	Capital One is named the 3 rd 'Best Place to Work in the UK' by The Sunday Times.
	Capital One named in Forbes 400 list - Best Big Companies in America.
2000	Capital One is named in the Information Week 500 for innovation in IT.
	Capital One receives CIO 100 award for Customer Excellence (the second consecutive year of recognition from CIO).
1999	Business Week names Capital One Number 15 in its list of top 50 performers in the S&P 500.
	Computer World ranks Capital One Number 13 in its list of the '100 Best Places to Work in IT'.
1998	Rich Fairbank is named Executive of the Year by Credit Card Management magazine.
	Future Banker names Rich Fairbank and Nigel Morris "Future Bankers of the Year".
	Capital One is named in the Information Week 500 for innovation with information technology.
1997	Forbes names Capital One as one of the fastest-growing companies in its list of top 25 'Champs'.
	Beyond Computing presents Capital One with its Gold Award for successful integration of IT and business strategies.
1996	Capital One wins the Gartner Group 'Excellence in Technology' Award.
1995	Credit Card Management magazine names Capital One 'Issuer of the Year'.

Scotland). These banks would typically charge all customers interest rates of about 22% as well as an annual fee of £12. Products were barely differentiated and customers had little real choice. In the mid-1990s, the market was shaken up by the entrance of competitive US banks such as Capital One, Morgan Stanley Dean Witter and MBNA, that targeted the UK market to expand their own business. The Internet wave also prompted the emergence of new competitors such as the online banks Egg, Cahoot and IF.

The introductory offer of the new entrants revealed an aggressive pricing strategy. By offering lower interest rates and lower fees, they built sizeable customer bases. Working on the basis that around three quarters of the sums owed on credit cards are attracting interest, providers have begun to offer extremely low-cost balance transfer deals (see Table 4.5 for balance transfer rates). As a consequence, the credit card market today is highly competitive and the market share of the major UK banks (two thirds of credit cards in issue) is eroding (see Figure 4.4 for market shares). It is clear that the days of the 22.9% standard interest rate are truly over.

Credit Card Revenues

Credit card issuers have many sources of income from the use of credit cards as a payment device or as a form of credit. The most frequent are: interest charge paid by customers taking extended credit, annual card fees, interchange (a service

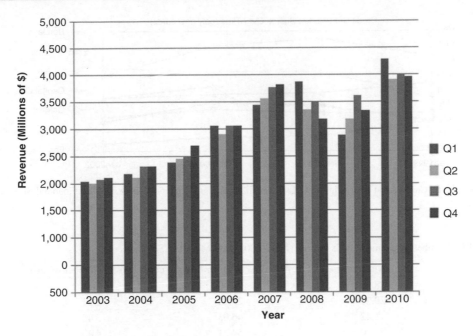

Fig. 4.3 Growth of Capital One's Revenue (Worldwide Operations)

Table 4.5 Capital one: comparisons of selected credit card rates and balance transfer offers (Source: Compiled from Moneyfacts.co.uk and Money.co.uk)

	Standard rate (%)	Balance transfer rate (%)
High street banks:		
Abbey national (santander)	16.9	3.00
Bank of Scotland	16.9	3.00
Barclaycard	16.9	2.99
HSBC	16.9	2.90
Lloyds TSB	15.9	3.00
NatWest	16.9	2.90
Royal bank of Scotland	16.9	2.90
Selected other providers:		
American express	17.9	3.00
Capital one	12.9	N/A
Egg	17.9	0.00
Goldfish	12.9	3.00
MBNA	16.9	3.00
Tesco	16.9	2.90

commission from the merchants accepting the card) and other fees, such as late or over-limit fees.

Another valuable source of income for credit card issuers is the revenue originated by cross-selling other financial products related to the cards, such as insurance against fraud, or personal loans and mortgages. However, the main source of profit for a card company is the Annual Percentage Rate (APR) on an outstanding balance, i.e., the use of the credit card requires that the customer pays a specific minimum proportion of their balance each month, and, in addition, an interest rate on the outstanding balance. The more outstanding balances customers have, the greater the

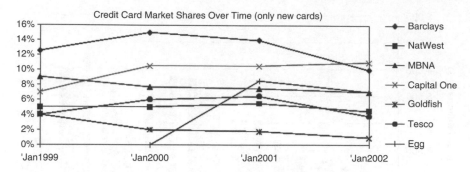

Fig. 4.4 Credit Card Brand Shares in the UK. Base: all credit card holders. *Source:* MORI Financial Services, June 2002

Table 4.6 Number of payment cards in issue: 1992-2001 (Source: APACS/Mintel)

	Number of credit cards (m)	Number of debit cards (m)	Number of charge cards (m)
1992	28.28	22.60	2.35
1995	28.27	28.44	2.51
1999	41.42	46.08	3.45
2001	51.70	54.31	4.43
% change 1992-2001	+96.8	+140.3	+88.1

company's revenues are, and the higher the APR, the higher the interest charges incurred.

Consumers

As mentioned, credit cards may be both a payment device and a form of revolving credit. Credit card customers can be divided into two main segments:

1. *Transactors:* clients who regularly repay their entire balance;
2. *Revolvers:* clients who pay less than their entire balance and usually benefit from an interest-free grace period, which may be up to 54 days.

Revolvers are the customers who provide the biggest source of revenue, since they are always revolving their credit and therefore always providing revenue as they pay their interests.

Relatively buoyant consumer confidence and low interest rates have combined to create an environment in which consumers are happy to take on extra debt. An example of this confident environment is the comparative strength of both credit and debit card markets, with charge cards

in issue trailing far behind (see Table 4.6 for the evolution of card issues). The growth in the number of credit cards in issue is, in part, a result of the increased market competition but also a consequence of the changing attitude of the British towards credit. The amount of total consumer credit increased by 96.7% from 1995-2001 (£89.1bn to £175.3bn). Credit cards represented 53.5% of this total credit in 1995, rising to 59.6% in 2001 (Source: Mintel). For many, consumer credit is simply another financial tool to be taken advantage of, in the same way as a current account or mortgage.

Also, consumers are increasingly happy to play credit card providers off against one another, switching from card to card in order to take advantage of introductory deals. While APR is clearly a key factor in customers' preferences for specific cards, there are other factors that influence their choices. These include, for example, the availability of a reward point system, the acceptance rate at stores, the size of the credit line, the card design, or the affiliation with a charitable organization.

4.5.3   Capital One Company Background

Business Model
The business model of Capital One is founded on the simple, yet crucial, premise that each customer requires a different product and service from its credit card provider. The company believes in the assertion that customers, if offered what they want and need, as opposed to what banks want to offer them, will choose the provider that gives them choice and individuality.

Each customer carries a specific and unique credit risk and potential revenue profile, based mainly on their previous credit history (or lack thereof). The better the company can understand and assess a customer's specific risk, the better it can manage it. And the better it understands the customer, the more it can tailor its products to his or her needs. Risk is a crucial factor in the credit card business. "We're in a risk-driven business where one bad debtor can easily wipe out the benefits from 20 average customers or 4.5 good ones – thus, it's vital to manage them carefully," explains Ian Cornelius. "It is one of our competitive advantages to understand and manage these different levels of risk."

Information-Based Strategy (IBS)
Capital One's goal is to use information to acquire the types of customers it can most profitably serve. In order to understand them, the company uses information technology to accumulate and manage large amounts of data on its customers. Alongside publicly available data on credit risk, the company supplements this with data on customer demographics and behavior collected internally during the application and account management process, where every transaction is carefully registered. None of this could be achieved without the entire company being completely aligned behind the whole process.

With the data accumulated, the company executes its proprietary "Test & Learn" strategy. Test & Learn is a scientific, hypothesis-driven approach to test any customer related activity in a controlled condition on a sample of customers before rolling it out on a large scale. Using this scientific process, Capital One's Marketing and Analysis teams develop ideas, design products, and select target customers. Real products are empirically tested with genuine customers: the number of tests run is impressive – 36,000 in 1999 and 45,000 in 2000. Figure 4.5 summarizes the principle behind the "Test & Learn" strategy. For example, mailings with different copy and/or letter design are sent out to potential customers. Their response rates are monitored, as is their behavior as new customers, so that Capital One can understand the relative value of different offers. All test results are then analyzed and integrated into databases that can be referenced later to initiate further ideas on development and product design. Similarly, by analyzing customer behavior, the view of risk can be refined, and the credit offer can be improved accordingly. Balance-building programs can be targeted at the low risk customer, thereby reducing the average loss rate of the portfolio.

As a result, the company continues to improve its portfolio of products and services, and it now offers more than 6,000 products, most of them variations of credit cards. Here are some key products:

- Credit cards with different conditions (APR, credit limit, fees) and designs
- Products directly related to the credit card such as card protection plans and payment protection insurance (cross-selling)
- Other financial services such as travel insurance

4.5.4   Customer Relationship Management Practices at Capital One (UK)

Managing its relationships with customers is at the heart of Capital One's strategy. CRM is not seen as a tactical or functional approach but as a key strategic process. This strategic CRM orientation expresses itself; for example, in the way the various corporate functions are interlinked. It is not only the way in which departments are structured but also the way they interact with one another. As Capital One managers usually

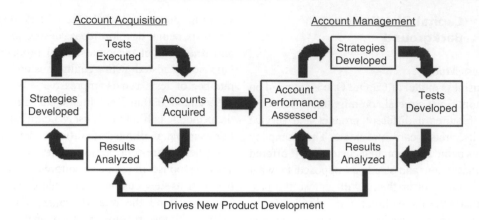

Fig. 4.5 Capital One's Test and Learn Strategy

say: "All departments work in an integrated fashion and there are no silos within the company." Internally, the company is grouped in four key activities.

1. *M&A:* Responsible for Capital One marketing strategy, product development, credit and risk management, pricing strategy, monitoring market trends and competition.
2. *Operations:* In charge of all front- and back-office operations and for all customer inter-processes (e.g., cross-selling, customer acquisition and retention, etc.).
3. *Information Technology (IT):* In charge of the development and maintenance of the systems infrastructure.
4. *Human Resources (HR):* Responsible for employee recruitment, training and development, the internal satisfaction survey and for nurturing the company's culture.

Marketing & Analysis (M&A)

Capital One's M&A department has, as its main functions: segmentation, testing and analyzing customer data in order to elaborate the company's marketing strategy, and the development of new products and services. To segment customers, Capital One uses analytical techniques and tests to identify groups of customers and to cluster them into segments according their risk profile and behavior.

Segmentation Strategy

Capital One's segmentation strategy focuses on a full spectrum approach (i.e., it targets all types of risk profiles, offering them different products and prices accordingly). The company's database has many types of customers, such as "transactors", with a low risk profile, and "revolvers". Capital One was able to further distinguish two sub-segments in the latter group: "high risk revolvers", with a high level of credit line utilization and high probability of default, and "low risk revolvers", who use their credit line extensively but pay back their balances. In order to identify this profitable low risk "revolvers" segment, Capital One carried out some tests that revealed that these customers could be targeted by making them a better interest rate offer. In fact, offering them a lower APR to encourage them to transfer their balances from other banks to Capital One proves to be an attractive offer, since these customers intend to repay the balance they have already created. Many other tests were conducted to fine-tune the solicitation of these customers in terms of contact channels, credit offers and mailing preferences.

The company's other large customer segment is composed of customers for whom the Capital One card is very often the first card. This segment also includes people who have had problems obtaining or handling credit in the past, people with limited or non-existent credit records and young people. Since this segment carries a relatively higher risk, these customers are usually not well served by products offered by the main high street banks. Capital One's strategy in this case is to offer these customers an initial higher APR with an annual fee and a lower credit line. While this is clearly higher than other Capital One offers, it usually compares very favorably with alternative credit offers on the market, and represents good value to these customers.

Account Manager, Cavendish Elithorn, explains why the offer is an attractive one for this segment: "Given their credit history, the Capital One card is still a better deal than other sources of credit – store cards where interest rates are 30%, brokers who charge 40-50%, or door-to-door lenders with 100% rates." The potential volume of this segment is significant, which is why Capital One has the potential to grow this customer base alongside the low risk segment. The challenges to identify this segment are the same as those of "low risk customers": identify the customers, their risk assessment and managing attrition. To evaluate the customer risk profile on application, the company rates them based on their credit scoring, information taken from the application forms and credit bureau data.

Retention Strategy

To attract "low risk revolvers" with balances in other banks, Capital One may offer them a card with an introductory low rate that expires after a few months, and no annual fee. However, when the introductory rate expires, Capital One may witness increasing attrition from these clients, as many price-sensitive customers tend to reduce their debt or leave Capital One, without notifying the company or closing their account. "This is a dangerous development as it's the best customers – those that are low risk – that tend to leave to get better credit deals elsewhere," explains an account manager. "Consequently, we have active strategies to keep these customers, and their balances."

Many of the account management activities seek to keep these customers from being *"dormant"* or becoming permanently inactive. These retention activities are designed to help retain customers when their introductory rate expires or when other accounts risk "dormancy". "If a customer's account is dormant for a while, there is an increasing risk of losing that customer," explains Ian Cornelius. "That's why we

have a number of activities in place to guard against this – by making a range of offers to reactivate their account."

Capital One's retention strategy with this type of low risk segment is basically to grow the low credit line they received at the beginning of their relationship. Furthermore, they may also receive increased benefits, different card designs and other incentives to stay with Capital One. The key strategy with these customers is to treat them as well as any other customer segment. Just because Capital One was the best available offer on the market when they joined, it does not mean it will always be the case. Consequently, Capital One works hard to retain these customers.

At various points in time in the customer lifecycle, Capital One analyses its customer database in order to fine-tune its offers and retain customers. The behavioral and performance data allows the company to make proactive rate or credit limit offers, whenever appropriate. IBS testing is also used to help identify low- and high-risk customer profiles. By making different offers to customers, the company learns more about customer behavior and therefore improves its targeting and retention.

Operations

In order to offer a wide variety of cards and services, Capital One aligns its Operations department with customer requirements. This strategy has proven to give Capital One a competitive advantage over other banks in the market. Rather than taking the "assembly line" approach, the company attempts to handle its customers in a personalized and flexible way.

The Operations department handles front-end customer relationships. There are over 1,000 people working in Capital One's call-centre, handling more than 10,000 incoming calls per day. Most call centre type operations are aligned managerially and operationally in order to achieve specific targets that often compete with one another: 1) low cost efficiency, 2) high quality customer service, 3) flexibility and 4) associate satisfaction. In fact, these four measures are the cornerstones of a model known as the "Big Yellow Square" (BYS). Each quarter, the management team rate themselves on these four "corners" to take a qualitative assessment of how "big" and "square" the BYS is at any time. This is a simple model, easy to buy into emotionally. The BYS indicates that Capital One's view on operating a call centre differs from most other organizations, particularly in the way it weights "associate satisfaction", which is equally important as "service quality" and "cost efficiency".

As mentioned, 'Flexibility' is one of the BYS corners. Because the company tests so many products in the marketplace on a regular basis, flexibility in the approach and attitude of the Operations staff is a key part of the business' success. Flexibility is also present in the way that Capital One deals with operational overloads. Many associates, even those who normally do not work with the Operations department, are trained in one or more disciplines. Also, when volumes exceed expectations in a particular area, managers take the decision to ask associates to temporarily move jobs to cope with the peaks. Eventually, this action is more likely to be taken when there is an unexpected surge in high value customer contacts, such as applications for new products.

Another important aspect of Capital One's strategy is the way it uses customer profitability analysis. Profitability is calculated on an individual basis to improve the product offer to each customer. However, the company does not normally differentiate customer service levels according to a customer's profitability. As Mitch Beres explains:

"We would not be comfortable matching up high-value customers with high-level service – every customer has a choice of whether to use us or go elsewhere, and our quality of service can be a reason for them to stay. We aim to offer high-quality service to all our customers, regardless of their profitability."

However, Phil Marsland reflects on the subject of differentiating customer service: "It is a real question to me whether the lower risk customers should cross-subsidize those with higher risk, or whether everyone should get the deal they deserve." Although Capital One does not currently follow this line of thinking, Marsland's

comment indicates that Capital One's management is constantly contemplating new ways of managing its business, and may even consider changing this current strategy.

Another element that differentiates Capital One's Operations department from others is its IT infrastructure. IT is used to route calls and provide associates with the necessary information to best handle specific calls. The systems are updated directly by call-centre associates. Therefore, as soon as each call is completed, associates enter information about the interaction in an encoded form into the system, which will then be available for the next contact with the customer. In some ways, this ensures a modern version of so-called 'old fashioned' personal service. More specifically, the Operations department is divided in four main areas:

- Operations Processing
- Customer Relations
- Sales
- Collections
- Cooperation between M&A and Operations

Operations Processing

Operations processing handles all back-office operations. Some examples of its key functions are: keying in credit card applications, scanning all incoming correspondence into a document management system, managing vendors such as card embossers and statement printers and handling payments from customers.

Customer Relations

Customer relations handle incoming calls. While it is primarily devoted to providing particular service requirements and receiving customer complaints, it also attempts to cross-sell when appropriate. 400 customer service associates receive about 8,000-10,000 calls a day. These associates use the sales system (called SALSA – also used in the Sales department) when attempting to cross-sell. This allows them to identify suitable products to the customer who is calling and to avoid offering the same product twice.

Customer service associates, as well as sales associates, work to an incentive scheme that encourages sales and quality service. This incentive scheme is characterized by the following criteria:

Table 4.7 Capital one's NPV-based cross-selling process

Customer ID	CPP	PPI	Loan	BT	Shopping
4324 1223 7874 3333	10	30	40	21	1
4324 1223 7874 3334	43	22	9	45	24
4324 1223 7874 3335	12	59	8	43	3
4324 1223 7874 3336	0	1	5	12	33

- *Average handling time of the call*, as measured by the number of calls routed per day and the average call length in seconds.
- *Sales points per contact.* A sale is encouraged by awarding points per product sold in order to reflect product profitability.
- *Quality*. This is measured by using a system that records ten random calls a month, per associate, to which managers listen and give feedback.

Associates receive a review of their performance weekly that shows how they rank against overall department targets and against their own past performance. The call listening program, introduced two years ago by senior management, is very rigorous. As one customer relation manager explains: "This feedback from senior management has served not only as an extra quality screen, but also as a visible signal to our frontline associates that they are important". Competition between individual associates and call-centre teams is also encouraged. On the call-centre walls, colorful charts track the performance of different teams. Awards are given to the best performing teams or individuals, and their pictures are displayed on internal notice boards or appear in in-house publications.

Sales

The Sales department is divided into the following units:

- *Inbound*. Customers call to activate their cards or to respond to a marketing offer.
- *Outbound*. Capital One associates call the customers to sell them a product or to provide a proactive service (e.g., customers who received a card but did not take out the payment protection insurance).
- *Retention*. Associates try to retain customers who intend to close their accounts.
- *New Business*. Sales are attempted with new customers.

Within all units, teams of 12-14 associates plus a supervisor and a manager are formed. While some specialization is encouraged, there is also cross-staffing and rotation to familiarize sales people with other tasks and teams, and to allow for flexibility in meeting peak demand.

Offering new products to customers is one of the key tasks of the Sales department. Given the variety of new products on offer every month, computer-based training modules are developed to familiarize sales personnel with the new offers. When cross selling, Capital One's cross-selling system determines the likelihood of customers to buy certain products based on the projected NPV of a product to a customer, and suggests different products to different customers, or even no selling attempt at all (see Table 4.7 for the model).

1. Customer 4324 1223 7874 3335 calls in
2. System checks whether any sale is permissible in this channel (e.g. have we tried a CSM approach recently)
3. Product priority is sourced from the NPV table:
4. System checks whether approaches are allowable on these products. E.g. excludes product if customer already holds it or where the product has been attempted recently
5. The list of products we are "happy to offer" is shown to the associate, with the primary product at the top of the list.

The SALSA sales system (see Figure 4.6 for screenshot) enables targeting cross-sell offers to specific customers likely to be interested in particular products. To avoid inundating the customer with offers, SALSA prevents Capital One associates from offering the same product twice within a short period of time. Associates are not encouraged to sell more than one product during a single call, even if SALSA suggests more than one product offer. As one sales associate explains, "the target time for a call is challenging – this means you really need your sales pitch honed and ready!"

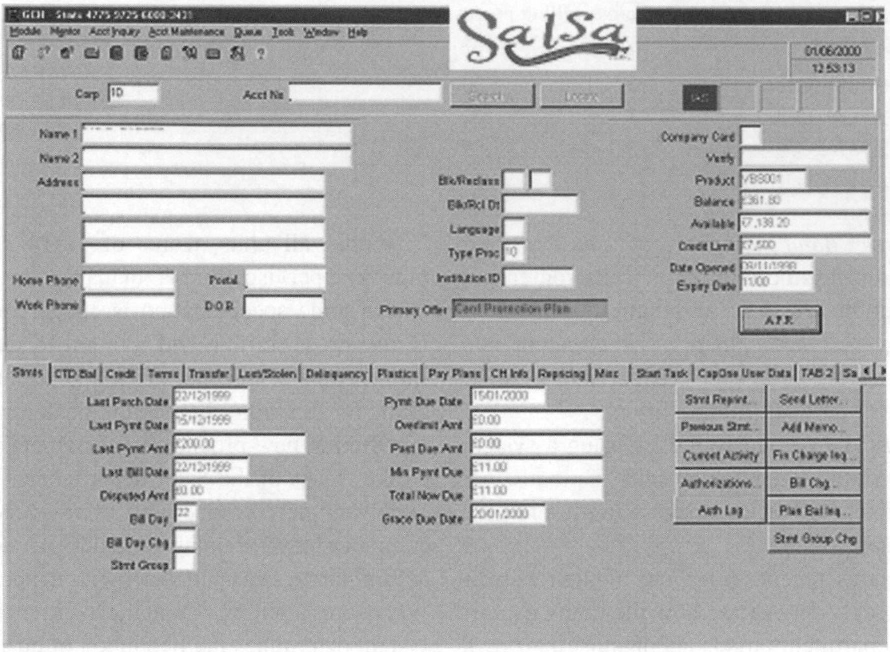

Fig. 4.6 Screenshot from Capital One's Customer-Service Screen (SALSA System)

This minimizes the chances of wasting the time of both customers and associates.

The SALSA system also uses accumulated data on customers to suggest how to react to specific customer requests. For example, if a customer asks for a credit line increase, a reduced APR or a cash advance, data on past behavior and risk assessment are used to decide whether to grant the request or not.

Collections

The Collections department deals with customers who have fallen behind with their payments or with accounts affected by fraud. The department is split into three main areas: payment assistance, recoveries and fraud.

In *payment assistance*, Capital One associates work with customers who are behind with their payments to try and help them recover their account. For example, if the customer cannot pay his bill because she is unemployed, payment assistance may put her in contact with a recruiting agency. If the customer is ill, payments may be temporarily suspended. In other circumstances, customers who are behind with their payments may be offered revised terms, enabling

them to make smaller, and regular payments. The overriding goal is to keep customers until they can pay and help them not to default. Elithorn explains:

"We believe we are better than most working with all customers to come to satisfactory solutions. For example, other card issuers might ask customers what they intend to do, in order to get out of debt, or give them few workable options. We might say that for a specific customer, based on our data, the best solution would be to lower its interest rate. We are still a long way away from individual solutions, but closer to it than most others in this field."

In *recoveries,* Capital One looks after those customers whose debt has been charged off and whose accounts are no longer open. The objective is to work with the customer to recover as much of the debt as possible.

Finally, the *fraud* team has two fundamental tasks: to help customers who have been victims of fraud and to prevent fraud itself. In the case of fraudulent activity, the team closes down the old account, writes off any fraudulent charges and transfers genuine transactions into a new account. Customers affected by fraud usually need a higher level of support, and the fraud team is trained to treat each case with sensitivity. A wide range of systems is in place to help prevent fraud, including real time transaction models and account behavior pattern systems. Very often, the fraud customer service team calls customers to let them know that they might have been victims of fraud, even before the customer realizes it. This is yet another strong selling point for Capital One from the customer relationship management perspective.

Co-operation between M&A and Operations

Given the large number of tests carried out and new products developed within Capital One each year, there clearly has to be a great deal of co-operation between these two major departments. For example, when introducing a new product, M&A and Operations work very closely together. While M&A designs the product, develops marketing material and follows up customer responses, Operations collect regular feedback from customers and make improvement suggestions. The information from Operations is also used to improve the NPV models that serve as decision-making mechanisms.

Much of the information on customers that is used to craft strategy is obtained from front-end associates, who are, of course, closest to the customer. There is a partnership between Operations and M&A to review the risk perspective of present as well as future strategies. Of course, such a tight link between Operations and M&A would not function without the enablement through IT. Furthermore, numerous permanent or *ad hoc* cross-functional teams, composed of members from Operations and M&A, exist to define, for example, the credit policies for new and existing products.

Information Technology (IT)

The IT department sits at Capital One's head table and reports directly to the board in its own right – it is highly valued as the enabler of business strategy. The IT division performs a broad function, ranging from pure business issues and decisions on how the company should deploy its resources and finances, through applications and software engineering, to detailed technical issues

of hardware, operating systems and networking. After Operations, IT is the company's second-largest division.

Against common practice in the financial industry, Capital One chose to *in-source* the majority of its IT capability, relying on the speed, management acumen and expertise of its in-house provision. Much of the IT intellectual property of the business is implemented internally, which proves that IT has become a core competence. This department offers a full-service capability to the business (Operations and M&A), covering the spectrum of products and processes through their genesis and complete life cycle. It houses the data, performs guardianship of the information, excels in data warehousing, and assures that the information can be readily accessed. All the terabytes of customer behavior data are kept indefinitely in-house for online or near-online access. Through query tools, batch updates and transactional data, IT provides the tools that enable IBS to work successfully. The IT department interacts with the company in the following domains:

- Prospect pool and solicitation management
- Account acquisition and management
- Account servicing and call-centre technologies
- Core systems

Prospect Pool and Solicitation Management

Capital One differentiates itself from the competition because of its internal prospect pool management and solicitation process. Rather than outsourcing the data on a prospect's behavior and lifestyle, Capital One runs an in-house database with this information, which targets and selects customer audiences and matches products according to the prospects' profiles. The information gathered over the years on Capital One customers has proved to be very useful in this perspective to tailor products to individuals.

Traditionally, Capital One has been using direct mail campaigns to target new customers. This approach has proved to be very beneficial since it allows the company to predict gross and net response rates to various offers, according to the product, customer type and creative process chosen. This allows an accurate prediction of its marketing effectiveness. Once the campaign results are received, data are introduced back into the Prospect and Solicitation Management system, to provide further data that will improve future acquisition programs.

Account Acquisition and Management
When a prospect becomes a customer, Capital One creates an account on the account management system, where all interactions with customers, from account detail changes to transactions and payments, are recorded. This information will create the customer profile, which allows the company to differentiate offers according to customer preferences. In fact, front-end customer acquisition processes rely upon sophisticated sets of credit models and automated decision algorithms to process the high volume of applications via the various channels (telephone, Internet, mail). Hardcopy applications are scanned and retained on optical disk. This information is subsequently communicated to credit bureau and external fraud prevention agencies that provide Capital One with up-to-date information about applicants. All the raw data are recycled to MIS on a daily basis. This consolidates the core of the IBS account management programs through which Capital One can develop reward schemes, change fees and products or make special offers to customers. In order to protect existing accounts against potential fraudulent card activities, expert real time neural network solutions are deployed to trigger the alarm at the earliest possible instant.

Account servicing and call-centre technologies
The call-centre is supported by automated call dialers, power dialers, voice response units (VRU) and local systems integrated with voice solutions. Many of the special systems for customer contact (cross-sales, balance transfer, retention and correspondence activities) are specifically designed to support the IBS approach. The system also stores information on customers' telephone numbers, which allows it to identify the origin of the call and route it to the most suitable associate. The sophisticated form of Computer Telephony Integration (CTI) ensures efficient customer handling and provides high quality service. (See Figure 4.7 for systems infrastructure description). When customers call in, they can choose to talk to an associate or to use the VRU system. The VRU, which currently handles about 7,500 calls every day, is used mainly for tasks such as balance enquiries.

In addition to the development of solutions to the Operations and M&A, IT also develops and maintains solutions in other departments of the company, such as the Finance or the HR departments. IT also develops the *Internet* system that allows customers to apply online, get real time information and manage their accounts. It also maintains the *Intranet* system, which provides accurate and accessible information to the company and functionality to all associates.

HR
The HR function is critical to Capital One's CRM strategy. Finding and keeping top quality associates is vital to the company's success. HR is responsible for two main activities: managing associate selection and, supporting and developing the company culture.

Associate Selection
Capital One considers the hiring process crucial and wants the selection process to be as science-driven as the overall customer strategy.

Hiring & Training: All associates are hired and evaluated based on the same criteria, which the company believes helps to prevent the formation of cliques. During the recruitment interviews, they test analytical and conceptual skills. The company also performs "behavior interviews" in order to access candidates' competency by asking them to provide examples of situations where they supported change, managed several tasks or made difficult decisions. According to one recruiter:

"We do not hire for specific experience, but for competencies. We try to find the best fit between a person and a role, and then train them. For example, we have a systems testing manager who used to test racing car engines before joining us – he had no direct experience, but certainly possessed all the competencies we were looking for."

Specific training, including some cultural induction, is offered for new "hires". Managers at all levels are offered a range of performance

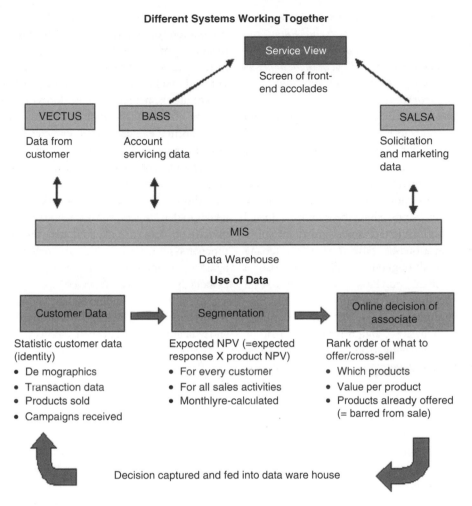

Fig. 4.7 Capital One's System Infrastructure

and skill enhancement classes that are carried out by either in-house trainers or external organizations. There is also a learning centre with books, videos and simulations, which are grouped around the core competencies that the company seeks to build. Career development is another important aspect. Capital One has a highly structured people management process which include 360° appraisals twice a year, personal Development Action Plans (DAP) to help employees prepare for their next job and a weekly one-to-one 10-minute meeting between each associate and their manager to discuss key issues. In fact, the company won a Training Magazine award in 2001 in the US and was featured as the '3rd Best Place to Work in the UK' in 2001 by *The Sunday Times* newspaper (Moskowitz & Levering, 2001).

Evaluation: All associates are evaluated every six months. Half of the evaluation is based on targeted achievements and the other half based on Capital One's defined core competencies. Several categories are used to evaluate the competencies of call-centre associates and team supervisors. Among the key elements are: communication, support of others, integrative decision-making, responsiveness to feedback and coaching, taking ownership and job specific knowledge. Evaluation is taken very seriously, and if metrics turn negative, managers spend time attempting to understand what went wrong. Says Mitch Beres:

"We see ourselves as coaches, rather than controllers or discipliners, nurturing talent and providing freedom. Even if our associates get it wrong, good coaching should help them improve – and we avoid getting the atrophy that often exists in other organizations."

Compensation: Incentives are an important part of the compensation package for all Capital One associates. For example, front-line associates can achieve a bonus of up to 14%, based on their results and competencies. Senior managers are awarded share options as well as cash bonuses. On several occasions, since the company floated in 1994, options have been awarded to junior associates on a one-off basis to share the feeling of ownership throughout the company. Also, a subsidized share purchase scheme allows all associates to purchase stock at a substantial discount on the market price. Take up is currently running at about 20%, and ownership behavior is very visible. According to one operations manager:

"People really watch the stock price – there is a refreshing clarity on the fact that what we do affects the share price, and, since we have share options, it makes a real difference to us."

Company Culture

As Capital One searched for suitable premises to house its operations centre in Nottingham, its main goal was to bring most activities in-house and under one roof, as well as creating a springboard for new products and businesses and a centre for recruitment. Combining all operations in one main location would also have the advantage that new employees could be more easily integrated.

Housing: A place with the potential to meet these goals was found in a huge, 1950s' building that matched not only Capital One's accommodation needs but also its culture of openness. They kept the two huge floor areas of 10,000 m^2 and a smaller second floor of 2,800 m^2. Call-centre and professional areas are not differentiated, allowing flexibility in use and reinforcing the company's open business culture. The open-plan spaces, in which most associates work, are arranged in team configurations, while a few glass-fronted offices and meeting rooms are separated from the main areas. The building

also has a convenience shop with refreshments, 'relaxation rooms', training rooms, a library and locker rooms with showers. Also, a large staff restaurant, with relaxed design elements, provides the feel of a trendy restaurant or bar.

The atmosphere of the huge floors of the Capital One building is busy and professional, yet relaxed and colorful. The associates' cubicles are personally decorated with photographs and nametags, cuddly toys sit on almost every computer, inflatable palm trees stand in the corridor and remote-control air balloons fly through the room. On the computers, 'Golden Nugget' stickers signify each sale of a priority product made by that associate. There are flipcharts showing how the different teams rank against one another. On the 'Wall of Greatness', associates who have received special company awards are shown alongside great people from American history, like Henry Ford, Thomas Edison and Muhammad Ali. As Scott Woolveridge, operations processing manager, sees it:

"What you see reflected in our decoration is that we try to avoid being a manufacturing shop. Our raw material is our people – so let them be themselves and have an environment to suit! If people are having fun, they do a better job – that's why we give them all these cuddly toys and stress balls. We want to make people feel they belong to something. And they do."

Culture of Involvement: Developing this strong culture of employee involvement was a conscious decision and part of the business plan. "If you do not treat the people who deal with customers as well as you want them to treat those customers then you are in trouble," continues Woolveridge. "People on the front-line need to be empowered – they *are* the company as far as customers are concerned. We try to take care of individual needs, so it is a natural step for this to be translated into customer treatment."

In line with its focus on associates, Capital One aims to create a culture of involvement and buy-in for all objectives. "We spend a lot of time explaining our objectives and ensuring that they are meaningful for everyone – where we are going and why – which is what creates a sense of excitement, of ownership, of understanding why we are making certain trade-offs," explains

Paul Hawker, Collections Manager. Trips, simulations and training programs are some of the other tools that Capital One uses with its managers to ensure that objectives are aligned, and to create a common language and methodology. Managers estimate that they spend about 10% of their time on creative activities. They comment that it greatly helps them in decision-making, as they tend to "assume positive intent on the other side of any discussion and know that we are all trying to do the right thing."

The company conducts an associate survey twice a year, containing more than 100 questions to "help the company remold itself for the future" as one manager puts it. The survey completion rate is well over 90% and the data obtained are carefully analyzed by managers. While some questions evaluate overall work satisfaction, others request more specific detail such as quality of management communications and stress levels. Using regression analysis, Capital One identifies the key drivers of employee satisfaction and devises action plans to improve weaknesses and exploit the opportunities identified.

Capital One is considered as one of the UK's top employers in 2001, and employee satisfaction is extremely high: 97% of staff regard the company as a friendly place; 96% report that people are willing to give that bit extra to get the job done; and 66% (20% above the market average) believe that they are getting a fair share of company profits. Associate turnover is extremely low – the attrition rate at Capital One's call-centre is around two thirds of the average figure of 35% at a standard call-centre. In Capital One's non-call-centre functions, turnover is even lower, and there has been virtually no senior management turnover.

Continuous Improvement: Improvement suggestions from front-line associates are highly encouraged. An example of an improvement suggestion made by call-centre associates is the 'APR indicator'. Call-centre staff noticed that customers often wanted to discuss their APR, so IT and M&A built in a quick access function that enabled them to view a customer's effective yearly APR without needing lengthy calculations. There are high levels of motivation and

co-operation for these initiatives. Those employees who contribute with particularly valuable ideas are given awards and highlighted on posters around the building.

There is also a high degree of co-operation among the various departments in the improvement process. As one operations manager explains:

> *"Our business is all about IBS, change and innovation – that is true for every department involved, and it is very liberating that there is no 'who's in charge' debate. There is an overall acceptance that we will change, and that we will launch new products – some will succeed, others will fail. We don't have conflicts of issues as regarding 'Marketing wanting to do this, but Operations not wanting to.'"*

4.5.5 Future Challenges

Building a Deeper Understanding of Customer Needs

While acknowledging the success of their approach, Capital One's Operations management is concerned with taking their understanding of customers and their behavior further. Today, Capital One knows which product a given customer holds, which financial transactions they have made and what interactions with the company have taken place. However, the company still knows relatively little about the customer as an individual, which would enable a deeper understanding of their behavior and needs. Mitch Beres envisions the following:

> *"If we could identify why customers call, we could segment them according to their needs – for example, if customer X calls mainly to check his balance, then he could immediately hear the message 'Mr. X, your balance is... if you have more questions, please press one."*

Increasingly, the company realizes that profitability is not necessarily driven by product ownership, but by customer characteristics (e.g., if they are working or studying, married or single, with or without children) and by product usage. Consequently, Capital One needs to ensure that it is able to address real customer needs at an individual level.

Managing Costs

In terms of cost structure (e.g., cost-per-customer account), Capital One's costs are currently higher than those of most of its competitors. The company views its heavy investment in IT and people as justified, but also seeks to keep costs within limits. David Farlow, Director of Operations Strategy, comments:

"We don't need to be more costly than our competitors. In fact, as IBS helps us to know our customers and their needs better, we should be well positioned to decide where to spend our resources. However, we are not yet at the part of the curve where increased spending on IBS does not add incremental value."

There is general agreement that associates are an expensive resource, and that they should be allocated to the highest value activities while lower value activities might be treated as a commodity, be outsourced, or at the limit, not serviced. It is debatable to what extent VRUs and the Internet can decrease operational costs.

Coordinating Channels

Capital One clearly sees a challenge in coordinating its customer interaction through all its different channels, which are currently coordinated, yet not fully aligned. "As every contact with the customer is precious, our next step will be to integrate our systems further so as to view customers through the same lens and align customer communications fully," explains Mark Sanders, Sales Manager. Sanders also believes that the company has to work to avoid giving conflicting messages to customers. "There is a clear degradation of responses when customers receive too many mailings, and we have to avoid an uncoordinated situation where Account Management contacts a customer to raise their credit line and then Sales contacts offer them a new product."

The fact that additional communication channels, such as websites and e-mail now exist, and others might be established in the future, creates future challenges. As Sanders continues: "Whenever we add a new channel, we witness an increase in demand also in the older channels because of the need for explanation. For example, customers telephone to make sure their Internet payment was processed okay." Furthermore, when information comes from new sources or when it is more frequently published, enquiries increase. For example, there are more customer enquiries now that balances are produced continuously on the Internet than when the traditional paper version was mailed once a month. Of course, this can be viewed either as a cost or an opportunity.

4.6   Summary

The key elements of CRM are touch points and the CRM applications that span the sales, marketing, and service functions. Touch points are means of interaction between the company and the customer. Once the elements of CRM are identified, it is important to calculate the ROI of CRM to see whether the investment is worthwhile. In calculating the ROI, care should be taken to identify the costs, gain or profit from CRM and the time period for assessing ROI. Three main categories of CRM costs are IT costs, people costs, and process costs. The investments in IT infrastructure, database development, and software are the main components of IT costs, and this may be usually one-fifth to one-third of total costs. The costs involved in recruitment of CRM talent and in redeployment and training of both the existing and new employees constitute the people costs. Process costs include investments in redesigning and reengineering of existing work practices. It is very difficult to compute concrete CRM profits because (1) the implementation takes two to five years to complete, during which the competitive environment might have been changed, (2) some CRM costs are necessary but do not generate revenue, and (3) the change or performance improvement cannot always be attributed to CRM investment. However indirect benefits of CRM in terms of lower customer acquisition costs, lower cost to serve, higher customer satisfaction and retention, and higher average customer value should be considered in arriving at the benefits of CRM.

The timeframe of ROI measurement varies, depending on the size of the project. The implementation of a CRM strategy is a process of developing and executing a series of small projects aimed at the business needs and value proposition of customers. These projects can be categorized as operational projects, analytical projects, and implementation projects. Operational projects construct infrastructure to enable companies to meet the technical and functional requirements of CRM. These include automation of functions, setting up a customer database, information delivery, and changing the process of data collection. Analytical projects, by contrast, are implemented to help a company understand its customers using data analysis tools. This is also called data analytics, and it combines data-driven marketing and technology to better understand customers. Data analytics projects include customer data transformation and customer knowledge discovery. Customer data transformation consists of pooling data from a number of sources to a data warehouse and enhancing the data with externally available information. Customer knowledge discovery is the stage when the data are analyzed using statistical tools and the future is predicted based on analytical results in order to enhance marketing decision making. Building a complete customer database incorporating all the relevant customer information from different departments and external sources is crucial for a successful analytical CRM project. This database is the basis for the customer demographic analysis, customer behavior modeling, and customer value assessment. The implementation projects deploy operational and analytical outputs to increase revenue and profits by improving marketing decisions and customer relationships. This is difficult to execute because this requires dealing with the perceptions and feelings of people and their ability to adapt to changes. Only a company that effectively handles the resistance from its employees and trains and motivates them can expect to see positive results from a CRM project.

The Capital One case study illustrates how the company successfully implemented a CRM strategy. Its business model was founded on the crucial premise that each customer requires a different product and service from a credit card provider. Following this business model, Capital One adopted an information-based strategy (IBS), which collects information about the customers. Test & Learn tests customer-related activity in a controlled condition before it is introduced in the market. This helps to develop ideas, design products, and select target customers. CRM is viewed as a key strategic process in Capital One, and different departments work in an integrated fashion toward understanding and satisfying customers and their needs. For example, there is a partnership between Marketing and Analysis (M&A) and Operations to review the risk perspective of present as well as future strategies. We can see that in Capital One all the departments implement the operational projects, analytical projects, and implementation projects in a coordinated way. This strategic approach to CRM has helped Capital One to be seen as creating industry-best practices in developing valuable customer relationships and managing risk based on an intimate understanding of the customer.

4.7 Exercise questions

1. What factors will you consider when measuring the ROI of CRM investments?
2. What are advantages and disadvantages when implementing CRM on an organizational basis versus on a limited functional basis (e. g., sales force only)?
3. What are the various components of the CRM architecture from an operational perspective?
4. What analysis is involved in assessing the value of a customer?
5. What customer backlashes can be expected when a company introduces CRM practices? What are the cautionary steps that you would advise companies to take to avoid these?

Minicase 4.1:
Implementing CRM in the Fast-Moving-Consumer-Goods Industry
Henkel is a globally operating group of companies, offering a wide range of consumer goods extending from detergents, household cleaners, cosmetics, toiletries and adhesives. In Europe, Henkel has held a leading position for decades in the detergents and household cleaners market

with brands such as Persil, Dixan, Vernel and Weißer Riese. In the US it is represented with the Dial brand. In the hyper-competitive European retail markets, many of the large manufacturers such as Henkel, P&G, and Unilever have focused on improving and managing supply chain efficiency.

Part of this ongoing activity is the concept of category management, where manufacturers and retailers collaborate to improve the profitability of the category at the store level. However, as an increasing number of firms are mastering the category management process, manufacturers like Henkel are looking how they can differentiate themselves further. This is where many of them have started to experiment with customer relationship management practices. The environment in which these companies operate is characterized by branded products, low absolute margins on a per product basis, and lack of direct consumer contact. In line with the general CRM idea, the goal of a CRM approach would be to identify and target high value customers and to then to devise a retention or growth strategy for them. In practice, this means to allocate disproportionate resources to these customers. Whereas CRM is strongly established in direct to consumer environments such as banking or telecommunications, the exact nature of CRM in the FMCG environment is less clear. Therefore, the challenge that lies in front of firms like Henkel is to define, conceptualize, and implement a suitable CRM approach.

Questions:

1. How would you define and measure customer value to Henkel? Should it define value on the individual level or on the segment level?
2. What is the look and feel of CRM in the FMCG environment?

3. Is there a necessity for manufacturers to partner up with retailers in order to implement an effective CRM strategy?

Minicase 4.2:
B-to-B   CRM   Implementation   at Deutsche Post World Net
Deutsche Post World Net (DPWN) is a fast growing international logistics service provider. Its portfolio of companies includes its European B to B parcel service EuroExpress, its express delivery service across the globe DHL, and its global logistics provider (air, sea, and road transportation) DANZAS. Revenues for the three divisions in 2001 were approximately €15.5bn with an increasing portion (45%) coming from outside its home market Germany. The central problem of DPWN was that the three companies served in many cases the same customers without knowing this. Each company has its own sales force and was calling simultaneously on many identical clients, for example virtually all of the large companies in Europe. As one would expect, the organizational structures and systems support (IT) was quite different for the three companies. DPWN felt that the group of individual companies could achieve much better results by coordinating their sales efforts, specifically, be being able to systematically cross-sell its various products and services to the many existing clients. Therefore, the company set out to leverage the entire customer base across the three companies and to build an integrated customer management approach. Specifically, DPWN wanted to first create a key account management system that allows the three companies to coordinate their offerings and sales communication to the most important business clients. Given that the three individual companies offered complementary services, the objective was to present "one-face to the customer" with the idea to provide complete logistics solutions for these clients regardless of the type of desired service. The

challenges that would lie ahead of DPWN were to (a) create transparency across customer relationships and customer potentials, (b) to design cooperation processes across the three companies, and to (c) develop sales support tools.

Questions:

1. How would one define and measure the potential for cross selling in this context?
2. If DPWN creates an integrated key account management system, which key processes need to be integrated across the three companies?
3. What are the barriers to increased cooperation between the companies?

References

Bush, M. (2008). More Marketers Want to Get to Know You: CRM Surges as Brands Demand Measurable Results. AdAge. http://adage.com/article/news/marketers/130497/. Accessed 6 July 2011.

Bohling, T., Bowman, D., LaValle, S., Mittal, V., Naryandas, D., Ramani, G., & Varadarajan, R. (2006). CRM Implementation: Effectiveness Issues and Insights. *Journal of Service Research, 9*(2), 184–194.

Jayachandran, S., Sharma, S., Kaufman, P., & Raman, P. (2005). The Role of Relational Information Processes and Technology Use in Customer Relationship Management. *Journal of Marketing, 69*(4), 177–192.

Peppers, D., & Rogers, M. (1997). *Enterprise One to One*. New York: Doubleday.

Reitz, B. (2005), Worst to First to Favorite: The Inside Story of Continental Airline's Business Turnaround. *Customer Management (MSI conference summary)*. Cambridge, MA: Marketing Science Institute, 4–5.

Kumar, V., Ramani, G., & Bohling, T. (2004). Customer Lifetime Value Approaches and Best Practice Applications. *Journal of Interactive Marketing, 18*(3), 60–72.

Churn rate is the number of existing customers who have left by the end of a given period divided by the number of existing customers at the beginning of the respective period.

Rust, R., Lemon, K., & Zeithaml, V. (2004). Return on Marketing: Using Customer Equity to Focus Marketing Strategy. *Journal of Marketing, 68*(1), 109–27.

Moskowitz, M. & Levering, R. (2001). The 50 Best Companies to Work For. *Sunday Times 9*.

Part III

Analytical CRM

Customer Analytics Part I

5

5.1 Overview

Customer value management rests on the idea of allocating resources differently to different customers. The basis of this differential resource allocation is the economic value of the customer to the firm. Thus, before one can start to manage customers, one must have a thorough understanding of how to compute the value contribution each customer makes to a firm. Various economic concepts and procedures have been developed that help us to achieve this. Some are based on simple notions, whereas others require the application of mathematical techniques. But as a precursor to understanding and applying these concepts, it is necessary to define measures or metrics of marketing activities and their outcomes. This chapter reviews traditional marketing metrics and introduces various primary customer-based metrics for acquisition and customer activity measurement, before it explains some popular customer-based metrics. The following chapter will then introduce surrogate metrics of customer value used in the industry.

It is important at this stage to note the difference between traditional marketing metrics and customer-based metrics. *Market share* and *sales growth* are popular traditional marketing metrics normally computed for the geographical area covered by a particular market. These metrics were developed when individual customer data were hard or impossible to obtain and therefore do not provide customer-level insight into the market. However, over the years, the increased availability of customer-level data has resulted in the development of a new set of metrics that reflect the need to evaluate managerial performance based on the value each individual buyer brings to the customer base of the firm. In order to arrive at some measure of customer value, various activities and their costs and returns need to be recorded and assessed. We denote such metrics primary customer based metrics which can be further subdivided into customer acquisition metrics and customer activity metrics. *Acquisition rate* and *acquisition cost* are two primary metrics measuring the customer-level success of marketing efforts aimed at acquiring new customers. Specific metrics have also been developed to track customer activities from the point of their acquisition until they cease to be customers. The customer activity measures comprise *average inter-purchase time, retention rate, survival rate, probability of a customer being active*—P(Active)—and *customer lifetime duration*. A third block of customer metrics are popular customer-based metrics: *Size of wallet* and *share of wallet* are popular metrics firms frequently apply to evaluate a customer's worth. In FMCG categories the *share of category requirement* is a commonly used popular customer-based metric to track consumer loyalty.

Thus, the various marketing metrics which will be discussed in the course of this chapter can be classified as follows (Table 5.1):

Table 5.1 Metrics used in customer analytics part 1

Metrics	
5.2 Traditional marketing metrics	**5.3 Customer acquisition metrics**
5.2.1 Market share	5.3.1 Acquisition rate
5.2.2 Sales growth	5.3.2 Acquisition cost
5.4 Customer activity metrics	**5.5 Popular customer-based value metrics**
5.4.1 Average inter-purchase time	5.5.1 Size of wallet
5.4.2 Retention & defection rate	5.5.2 Share of category requirement
5.4.3 Survival rate	5.5.3 Share of wallet
5.4.4 Lifetime duration	(5.5.4 Transition matrix)
5.4.5 P(Active)	

5.2 Traditional Marketing Metrics

Traditional marketing metrics have been used by marketing professionals for years and are helpful in measuring performance of brands, products, and firms in a given geographical region. These metrics were developed when individual customer data were hard or impossible to obtain. Traditional marketing metrics provide information about how products or brands perform in a market neglecting the individual customer-level. Historically, managerial rewards and incentives have been based on how well a manager is able to deliver on these metrics.

5.2.1 Market Share

Market Share (MS) is one of the most common metrics for measuring marketing performance. It is defined as the share of a firm's sales relative to the sales of all firms—across all customers in the given market. MS is an aggregate measure across customers. It can be calculated either on a monetary or a volumetric basis.

$$MS \ of \ firm \ j \ (\%) = 100 * \left[\frac{s_j}{\sum_{i=1}^{I} s_i} \right] \quad (5.1)$$

Where
j = focal firm
S_i = sales of firm i
I = all firms in the market

Where does the information come from?
- Numerator: Sales of the focal firm are readily available from internal records.
- Denominator: Category sales are available from market research reports or from competitive intelligence.

Evaluation

MS is one of the most common measures of marketing performance because it conveys an important piece of information and is readily computed. It is a typical measure of a product-focused marketing approach. However, it does not provide any information about how the sales are distributed across customers—it only gives an aggregate notion of category performance. For example, a given MS can be caused by selling large amounts to a small percentage of the customer base or by making small sales to a large proportion of the market.

5.2.2 Sales Growth

Sales growth of a brand, product, or a firm is a simple measure that compares the increase or decrease in sales volume or sales value in a given period to sales volume or value in the previous period. Hence, it is measured in percent. It indicates the degree of improvement in the sales performance between two or more time periods and acts as a flag for the management. A negative sales growth or sales growth lower than the rest of the market is normally a cause for concern.

$$\text{Sales growth in period } t\,(\%) = 100 * \left[\frac{\Delta S_{jt}}{S_{jt-1}}\right] \tag{5.2}$$

Where
j = focal firm,
t = time period
ΔS_{jt} = change in sales in period t from period t − 1
S_{jt-1} = sales of firm j in period t − 1

Where does the information come from?

- Both the numerator and denominator are available from internal records.

Evaluation

Sales growth is a quick indicator of the current health of a firm. If compared with the sales growth of the other players in the market, it also provides a relative measure of performance. However, it does not tell us which customers have grown and which ones have not. This information is necessary if we are to take customer-level marketing initiatives.

5.3 Customer Acquisition Metrics

One group of primary customer based metrics is customer acquisition metrics. The second are customer activity metrics which are discussed in Sect. 5.4. Customer acquisition metrics have been receiving increased attention recently. Managers have become more sensitive toward balancing customer acquisition and customer retention activities. In order to evaluate customer acquisition activities, we use two simple concepts—acquisition rate and acquisition cost.

5.3.1 Acquisition Rate

When firms attempt to acquire customers, they are typically targeting a specific group of prospects. For example, a European credit card issuer might target the student market in Italy. In order to describe the success of the acquisition campaign, a key performance indicator is the acquisition rate, i.e., the proportion of prospects converted to customers. It is calculated by dividing the fraction of prospects acquired by the total number of prospects targeted.

$$\text{Acquisition rate }(\%) = 100 * \frac{\#\ of\ prospects\ acquired}{\#\ of\ prospects\ targeted} \tag{5.3}$$

For example, the target market of the credit card issuer might have been two million students in Italy. Acquisition was measured in terms of new credit cards issued. The bank issued a total of 60,000 new credit cards. Thus, the acquisition rate was 100 * (60,000/2,000,000) = 3%.

The acquisition rate denotes an *average probability* of acquiring a customer from a population. Thus, the acquisition rate is always calculated for a *group* of customers (e.g., a segment), not for an individual customer. The equivalent measure for an individual is the acquisition probability. An acquisition rate for an individual customer does not exist.

Defining What Acquisition Is

Firms have different definitions for the term *acquisition*. In the credit card example, an acquisition was recorded when a new credit card was issued to the prospect. However, it is possible that the prospect signed up for the card only because she was interested in the promotional incentive and that she will never use the card. As a solution, the bank could define two different levels of acquisition—for issuing the credit card and issuing a statement (which depends on credit card activity). For example, although 60,000 credit cards have been issued to new customers, only 55,000 of them have received a statement, indicating activity on the card account. Thus, the level 1 acquisition rate is 3% and the level 2 acquisition rate is 2.75%.

In noncontractual contexts, acquisition is typically defined as the first purchase or purchasing in the first predefined period. For example, an outdoor direct-mail merchant received 110 first-time orders from a campaign based on a new mailing list of 5,000 prospects. Thus, the firm's acquisition rate is 2.2%.

It is important to note that acquisition rates are typically computed on a campaign-by-campaign basis. Since acquisition rates can vary tremendously within the same firm, an average (firm-wide) acquisition rate is mostly of limited value.

Where does the information come from?
- Numerator: Number of prospects acquired is determined from internal records.
- Denominator: Number of prospects targeted can be available from internal records or has to be estimated from market research data (e.g., for television campaigns).

Evaluation

Acquisition rate gives a first indication of the success of a marketing campaign by setting the number of new customers in relation to the number of targeted customers. However, it cannot be regarded in isolation. For example, it does not account for the costs of acquiring the customers. Other important factors that have an impact on the acquisition rate are the marketing strategy and the selection of target customers.

5.3.2   Acquisition Cost

The second key metric in customer acquisition is the acquisition cost (AC). The acquisition rate measures responsiveness to a campaign, but it does not say anything about the cost efficiency of a campaign. AC is defined as the acquisition campaign spending divided by the number of acquired prospects. AC is measured in monetary terms.

$$Acquisition\ cost\ (\$)\ per\ prospect\ acquired$$
$$= \frac{Acquisition\ spending\ (\$)}{Number\ of\ prospects\ acquired}$$

(5.4)

For example, the cost of the acquisition campaign of the Italian credit card issuer was \$3 million. Thus, the average cost of acquiring a single new customer for this campaign was \$3,000,000/60,000 = \$50. Depending on the exact definition of what constitutes acquisition, the cost can be calculated for different acquisition levels.

Delineating Acquisition Spending

It is not difficult to identify acquisition spending in an organization that (1) acquires prospects in distinct campaigns and (2) is able to pinpoint its acquisition efforts quite precisely to the prospect group. In this situation AC can be calculated with the highest accuracy. Any company targeting prospects through direct mail would fall into this category—it knows the precise target group and the acquisition spending directed toward that group. As soon as firms rely on broadcasted communication (e.g., advertising through television or print media), measurement of AC becomes less precise. For example, prospects can be persuaded by advertising that was originally not targeted at them but toward existing customers. Clearly, AC will seem lower if those customers enter the AC calculation—making the numbers look more attractive than they really are. Also, firms might not necessarily differentiate between acquisition advertising and retention advertising. Calculating the precise AC in such a case can become quite difficult.

Where does the information come from?
- Both the numerator and denominator are available from internal records.

Evaluation

AC is a very important metric that firms should strive to continuously monitor as it indicates how effective a customer acquisition investment is.

5.4   Customer Activity Metrics

Once a prospect has been converted into a customer, the main phase of the customer-firm relationship begins. The concept of measuring the activity status of this relationship deals with a very fundamental issue—whether a customer is a customer. On first sight, this might appear to be obvious. If a customer buys, then the customer is, in fact a customer—otherwise, she is not. However, digging a little bit deeper, it seems that we are uncovering a quite complicated matter. It is not at all clear what constitutes a living relationship. What is more, the meaning of an active relationship differs across industries. Clearly, one has to look at more than just purchasing acts executed by a customer. Customers interact with the firm in multiple ways (pre-purchase inquiry, post-purchase service, complaints, etc.), all of which contribute to the entirety of the customer-firm relationship. Even in a simple case such as grocery shopping where the purchase per se is of highest importance to both parties involved, a multitude of other nonpurchase interactions adds or detracts from the relationship quality (e.g., the interaction with service employees, the communication of the store toward the customer, and the shopping experience).

Thus, it becomes clear that the customer-firm interaction comprises many more elements that may contribute to the essence of the relationship. In most cases, however, the sequence of purchase is used to define whether a relationship exists. However, even if one uses this simplification, there still is the issue of customer dormancy. Dormancy occurs when an ongoing relationship is disrupted temporarily during a period without any observable purchase activity. To state an example, this might occur naturally when someone loses her job and therefore is forced to scale down consumption. Once the person finds a new position, she is likely to return to the old consumption pattern. Consequently, the person is not starting a new relationship but is continuing an existing relationship. (We admit this discussion becomes complex when the period of dormancy has been very long.)

The challenge from a managerial point of view is to establish whether a seemingly dormant relationship has ended or the customer will return. In practice, this is a very tough call to make. Dormancy will or will not be considered, depending on the specific measure used to estimate customer activity.

Objective of Customer Activity Measurement The reason we want to shed light on customer activity measurement is twofold. First, knowing the status of a customer's (or a segment's) activity is important for managing marketing interventions. A customer-oriented organization tries to align resource allocation with actual customer behavior. Instead of mass advertising or mass marketing, managerial action can gain tremendous efficiency by adjusting its interventions to the actual customer needs or activity status. The second reason for measuring customer activity is because it is a key input in customer valuation models such as net-present value (NPV) models like the lifetime value. The marketing function has come under increasing pressure to demonstrate how it adds to shareholder value. This demonstration typically involves the estimation of the evolving customer value over time. Thus, measuring customer activity is a critical intermediary step in this valuation process.

This section covers the following types of customer activity measures:
- Average inter-purchase time (AIT)
- Retention rate and defection rate
- Survival rate
- Lifetime duration
- P(Active)

Each metric has a purpose with its own set of strengths and weaknesses. Thus, the task of the manager will be to find the most suitable metric for a given situation.

5.4.1 Average Inter-Purchase Time

Average Inter-Purchase Time (AIT) is the average time elapsing between purchases. It is measured in terms of specific time periods (days, weeks, months, etc.). It is computed by taking the inverse of the number of purchase incidences per time period.

AIT of a customer

$$= \frac{1}{Number\ of\ purchases\ during\ a\ prespecified\ period}$$
(5.5)

Example: If a BINGO supermarket customer buys, on average, six times at BINGO during a month, then the AIT for that customer will be $1/6 = 0.1667$ months, or approximately 5 days $(0.1667 * 30)$.

Where does the information come from?

- Denominator: Sales records are used, assuming individual customer records are maintained and individual customers are identified.

Evaluation

AIT is an easy-to-calculate indicator which can be an important statistic of the customer's activity status, especially for those industries where customers buy on a frequent basis.

5.4.2 Retention and Defection Rate

Retention and defection are like two sides of the same coin. One can be inferred from the other, and, depending on the context, it is better to use one or the other metric. *Retention rate* in period t (Rr_t) is defined as the average likelihood that a customer purchases from the focal firm in a period (t), given that this customer has also purchased in the period before (t−1). The *defection rate* is defined as the average likelihood that a customer defects from the focal firm in a period (t), given that the customer was purchasing up to period (t−1).

(wherein a cohort refers to a batch of customers acquired within a specified period of time), proportionally fewer customers leave over time, thus forcing the average retention rate (for this cohort) to increase over time. One has to keep this in mind when extrapolating retention rates for one period to an entire time horizon for a cohort of customers.

Assuming that the retention rate is constant over time (i.e., $Rr_t = Rr$ for all t) allows a simple calculation of the average lifetime duration.[1]

$$Avg.life\ time\ duration = \frac{1}{(1-Rr)} \qquad (5.8)$$

How to assess lifetime duration in a more general setting will be discussed in Sect. 5.4.4.

Example: If the average customer lifetime duration of a group of customers is 4 years, then the average retention rate is 1−(1/4) = 0.75, or 75% per year. This means that on average, 75% of the customers remain customers in the next period. If we look at the effect for a cohort of customers

$$Rr_t(\%) = 100 * \left(\frac{\#\ of\ customers\ in\ cohort\ buying\ in\ (t)|customer\ in\ (t-1)}{Total\ \#\ of\ customers\ in\ cohort\ buying\ in\ (t-1)} \right) \qquad (5.6)$$

The resulting retention rate refers to the average retention rate of a cohort or segment of customers. Theoretically, the retention rate differs for each individual customer but is approximated by the average retention rate of a (homogeneous) customer group or segment. Most of the time, no distinction is made between the (individual level) retention rate and the average retention rate.

Average retention rate and average defection rate are directly related:

$$Rr_t(\%) = 100 - Avg.defection\ rate(\%) \qquad (5.7)$$

Although we use the case of an average retention rate, one has to be aware that retention rates are typically not equal across different periods. For example, if one deals with a single cohort

over time (see Table 5.2) we find that from 100 customers who are acquired in year 1, about 32 remain at the end of year 4.

Assuming constant retention rates, the number of retained customers in any arbitrary period $(t+n)$ can simply be calculated using (5.9):

$$\#\ of\ retained\ customers\ in\ period(t+n) =$$
$$\#\ of\ acquired\ customers\ in\ cohort\ at\ time\ (t) * Rr \qquad (5.9)$$

Where
n = Number of periods elapsed

---

[1] The terms lifetime duration, customer lifetime, and customer tenure are often used interchangeably.

Table 5.2 Example for customer lifetime calculation

Customers starting at the beginning of year 1:	100.00	
Customers remaining at the end of year 1:	75.00	(0.75 * 100)
Customers remaining at the end of year 2:	56.25	(0.75 * 75)
Customers remaining at the end of year 3:	42.18	(0.75 * 56.25)
Customers remaining at the end of year 4:	31.64	(0.75 * 42.18)

For the previous example, the number of retained customers at the end of year 4 is $100 * 0.75^4 = 31.64$. If we plot the entire series of customers who defect each period, we see the variation (or heterogeneity) around the average lifetime duration of 4 years (see Fig. 5.1).

Given an average retention rate of 75% (constant over time), many customers leave in the early years. However, a small number of customers continue to stay for a long duration. This pattern results in average lifetime duration of 4 years.

As already mentioned, the concepts of defection and retention are closely related. Defection rate is calculated as follows:

$$Avg.\ defection\ rate\ in\ t\,(\%) = 100 - Rr_t(\%)$$
$$(5.10)$$

Example: The average retention rate in the previous example is 75%. Thus, the average defection rate is:

$$100 - 75\% = 25\%.$$

Where does the information come from?
- Internal records and customer tracking (e.g., loyalty card programs or contractual information).

Evaluation

A key assumption of the retention rate concept is that once customers leave the relationship, they are gone forever. The concept of retention rate does not allow for temporary dormancies. Managers have to make a judgment whether the dormancy phenomenon plays a major or a minor role in their business. Using the retention rate is fine if it plays a minor role. If dormancy plays a major role, other concepts have to be used to assess customer activity. These concepts will be dealt with in Sects. 5.5 and 5.6.

Is Retention only about Buying?

Typically, retention refers to the fact that a customer continues to purchase goods or services from the company. This is not always the case.

Take, for example, Yahoo.com. Most of Yahoo's services, such as basic e-mail and weather forecasts, are free. Although most of Yahoo's customers do not have any transactions in the traditional sense, one would consider site visits as the critical activity, which then would be used to measure retention for Yahoo. Thus, in the case that the customer-firm relationship is not primarily about monetary transactions, it is important to define an appropriate basis in order to measure retention.

How Is Retention Different from Loyalty?

Retention is *not* the same as customer loyalty. Although retention is measured on a period-by-period basis and indicates whether customers are coming back, the loyalty construct has a much stronger theoretical meaning. If somebody is loyal toward a store or a brand, this person has a positive emotional or psychological disposition toward this brand. People might continue to purchase a particular brand or might patronize a particular store, but this may be purely out of convenience or inertia. In this case, someone might be retained, but the person is not loyal (see Chap. 9).

Projecting Retention Rates

Very often, we find ourselves in a situation where we would like to get an idea about future retention rates of a particular cohort of customers. To do so, we use information on past retention

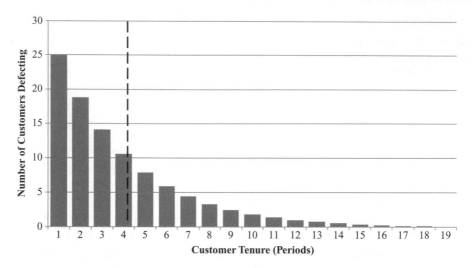

Fig. 5.1 Variation in defection with respect to customer tenure

rates to make a prediction of future retention rates. We have already discussed that retention rates tend to increase over time. As short-term customers drop out, the retention rate of the remaining (loyal) customers increases necessarily. This increase, however, is not linear. Almost always, retention rates tend to increase at a decreasing rate.

There is a simple method which allows us to forecast nonlinear retention rates—a simple exponential form. This approach models the retention rate as a function of time.

$$Rr_t = Rc * \left(1 - e^{-rt}\right) \qquad (5.11)$$

Where

Rr_t = predicted retention rate for a given period t in the future

Rc = retention (rate) ceiling

r = coefficient of retention

Rc is defined as the maximum attainable retention rate if unlimited resources were available. Clearly, a firm will not be able to retain all customers even if they spent unlimited advertising on them. Rc is typically estimated through managerial judgment. The parameter r is the coefficient of retention. This parameter determines how

quickly retention rates converge over time to the retention ceiling. It can easily be estimated through spreadsheet analysis based on past retention data.

Figure 5.2 shows actual retention rates for a credit card company (white bars). The time horizon is 20 quarters. Equation 5.10 was applied with Rc = 0.95, which means that managers believe that the maximum attainable retention rate is 95%. The parameter r = 0.2 is based on estimates that come from previous observations. Applying (5.10), the retention rates for periods 11–20 were estimated (grey bars). It can be seen that the method to approximate the actual retention rates was very close.

If past estimates of the parameter r are not available, one can use another method. The retention rate Rr_t is observed for a number of past periods. Equation 5.10 can be regrouped to form (5.11):

$$r = \left(\frac{1}{t}\right) * \left(ln(Rc - Rr_t)\right) \qquad (5.12)$$

For example, the known retention rate in period 9 is 80%, while the one in period 10 is 82%. Thus, the parameter r for period 9 is (1/9) * (ln(0.95)−ln (0.95−0.8)) = 0.205. The parameter r for period

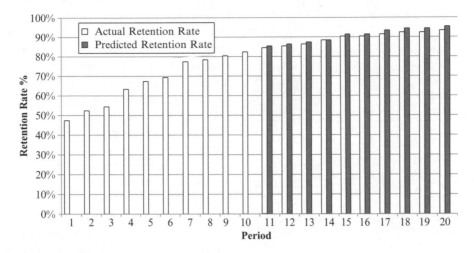

Fig. 5.2 Actual and predicted retention rate for a credit card company

10 is $(1/10) * (\ln(0.95) - \ln(0.95 - 0.82))$ 0.198. One can see that for both periods the parameter r is fairly close to the value 0.2.

5.4.3   Survival Rate

Another concept closely linked with retention and defection is survival. The survival rate (SR) indicates the proportion of customers who have *survived* (or, in other words, continued to remain as a customer) until a period *t* from the beginning of observing these customers. SR is measured for cohorts of customers, wherein a cohort refers to a group of customers acquired within a specified period of time.

Although retention rate and defection rate provide information for a given period, the SR gives a summary measure of how many customers survived between the start of the formation of a cohort and any point in time afterward. SR at time *t* is equal to the product of the retention rate at time *t* and the SR during the immediately preceding period $(t-1)$.

$$SR_t(\%) = 100 * Rr_t * SR_{t-1} \qquad (5.13)$$

In the initial period, SR_1 is, set to equal the retention rate$_1$.

Where does the information come from?
- Similarly to retention rate, information comes from internal records and customer tracking (e.g., loyalty card programs or contractual information).

Evaluation

The SR is of great interest, because one can conveniently calculate the absolute number of survivors in a given period t. One simply multiplies the SR, by the cohort size in the beginning.

Example: Number of customers starting at the beginning of year 1 is 1,000.

Computing the number of survivors:

Number of survivors for period 1 = Survival rate for period$_1$
  * Number of customers at the beginning

Therefore,

Number   of   survivors   for   period
$1 = 0.55 * 1,000 = 550$

Computing survival rate:

Survival rate$_t$ (%) = Retention rate$_t$ * Survival rate$_{t-1}$

In the table below (Table 5.3):

Table 5.3 Survival rate example

	Retention rate	Survival rate	Survivors
Period 1	0.55	0.55	550
Period 2	0.62	0.341	341
Period 3	0.68	0.231	231
Period 4	0.73	0.169	169

Survival rate$_2$ = Retention rate$_2$ * Survival rate$_1$
Survival rate$_2$ = 0.62 * 0.55 = 0.341, or 34.1%

CRM AT WORK 5.1
Amazon: Acquisition and Retention
Amazon.com is one of the leaders in implementing customer relationship management programs on the Web and operates with the vision of being the most customer-centric company offering everyone the possibility to discover anything they might want to buy online in mind. Because of its unique and sophisticated CRM program, the company has constantly been able to drive both customer acquisition and retention. Only 5 years after the company was founded, in 1999, Amazon acquired 11 million new customers nearly tripling its number of customers from 1998, but its greatest success in that year was not adding customers, but keeping those that it already had. Repeat customers during the year accounted for 71% of all sales.

Amazon has been able to acquire and retain customers at such a high rate by striving to learn about its customers and their needs and then using this information to offer them value-added features. This is done via numerous technological tools enabling the company to learn.

Source: Blattberg, Getz, and Thomas (2001)

5.4.4 Lifetime Duration

It is sometimes unclear how long a customer has been associated with a firm in a noncontractual setting, since there is no expiration date explicitly stated by the customer. In such situations, it is important to be able to predict the lifetime duration of a customer by observing buying patterns and other explanatory factors. Knowing for how long a customer remains a customer is a key ingredient in the calculation of the *customer lifetime value*—a key strategic metric. Furthermore, it has implications for churn management, customer replacement, and management of lifetime duration drivers.

The calculation of average lifetime duration for the case that the retention rate remains constant over time has already been presented (see Sect. 5.4.2). But since the retention rate usually changes over time (e.g., through customer self-selection) such a calculation would be misleading. We need to weigh in the number of survived periods. For one cohort of customer the avg. lifetime duration is defines as:

$$Avg.\,lifetime\,duration$$
$$= \frac{\sum_{t=1}^{T}(t * Number\ of\ retained\ customers\ in\ t)}{N}$$

$$(5.14)$$

Where
N = cohort size
t = time period
T = time horizon
(t * Number of retained customers in t) represents the number of active customer periods for the cohort at time t

Section 5.4.6 provides a comprehensive example of the calculation.

Limitations

If information is not complete, i.e., either the time of first purchase or the time of last purchase or both are unknown, the calculation of lifetime duration becomes more challenging. The case where either the time of first purchase, or the time of last purchase or both are unknown is illustrated in Fig. 5.3. The information for buyer 1 is complete. The data for buyer 2 is left-censored, i.e., the start of the relationship is not recorded. Buyer 3's information is right-censored. His relationship continued beyond the end of the observation window. Thus, it is not known to the firm at t_1 how much longer the customer will in fact be a customer. Finally Buyer 4's relationship started before the

Fig. 5.3 Customer lifetime duration when the information is incomplete

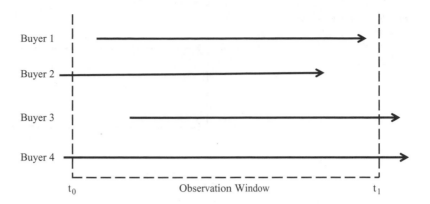

observation window and ends after the observation window. This observation is called left- and right-censored. Data that consists of right-censored observations require the use of survival analysis techniques (e.g., retention rate, P(Alive)).

Where does the information come from?

- Similarly to retention and SR, information comes from internal records and customer tracking (e.g., loyalty card programs or contractual information)

Evaluation

The average lifetime duration of a cohort of customers gives an indication of how fast the company needs to replace its customer base. When talking about the concept of a customer's lifetime duration, not all relationships are equal. We must take the type of product, which is subject to exchange into account. Here, we are specifying the following three cases:

1. Contractual
2. Noncontractual (or always-a-share)
3. One-off purchases

Contractual relationships are those where buyers engage in a specific commitment. This commitment may foresee duration and/or level of usage. A contractual relationship that defines length and level of usage is, for example, an apartment rental lease or a cable TV subscription. A contractual relationship, which defines only length, is, for example, a mobile phone contract. Finally, a contractual relationship which defines neither length nor usage level is a credit card. This category has also been labeled

lost-for-good because a company loses the entire customer relationship once a client terminates the contract.

Noncontractual relationships are those where buyers do not commit in any way, either in duration or level of usage. Purchasing with a department store, an airline, or a direct-mail company are examples. Since customers may use several suppliers at any given time (e.g., go to several different supermarkets), this category has been labeled *always-a-share*.

One-off purchases In case of One-off purchases there is no need to talk about a relationship between the exchange partners since it involves a once in a lifetime buy, such as a yacht or a vacation house.

5.4.5   P(Active)

In a noncontractual case, given a particular customer, it may be useful to know whether the customer is likely to transact in a particular time period. In other words we would like to know the probability of that customer being active in time t, P (Active). A simple approach for computing the probability of being active, P(Active), is via the following formula (Schmittlein & Morrison, 1985):

$$P(Active) = \tau^n \qquad (5.15)$$

Where

n = the number of purchases in a given period
τ = the time of the last purchase (expressed as a fraction of the observation period)

Fig. 5.4 Sample purchase patterns of two customers for the estimation of P(Active)

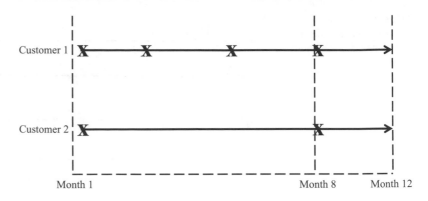

Month 1   Month 8   Month 12

Example: To compute the P(Active) of each of the two customers in the twelfth month of activity, where customer A bought four times within the first 8 out of the observed 12 months and customer B bought only two times within the first 8 out of the last 12 months (see Fig. 5.4).

Thus for Customer A: $\tau_A = (8/12) = 0.6667$
  and $n_A = 4$
P(Active)$_A = (0.6667)^4 = 0.197$
And for Customer B: $\tau_B = (8/12) = 0.6667$
  and $n_B = 2$
P(Active)$_B = (0.6667)^2 = 0.444$

It is interesting to observe that a customer who has bought four times in the first 8 months but has not bought in the last 4 months has a lower probability of buying in the 12 month over a customer who has bought only twice in the same window of 8 months. This is due to the assumption that customers do not change the frequency of buying. For an advanced application of further methods of calculating P(Active) see Reinartz and Kumar (2000, 2002).

Where does the information come from?
- Information comes from customer tracking, e.g., loyalty card programs

Evaluation

The probability of a customer being active in time t is a function of the duration since the last purchase and applicable in non-contractual cases. When calculating P(Active) it is assumed that customers pertain to their usual purchase patterns with respect to the frequency of buying.

5.4.6 Comprehensive Example of Customer Activity Measures

Looking at an actual retention pattern of a direct marketing firm, we want to illustrate the concepts of retention rate, defection rate, SR, and lifetime duration. A cohort of 7,500 customers was acquired at the outset of the analysis. Table 5.4 shows the actual retention pattern for ten periods in column 2. For example, after period 1, only 32% of the customers are retained into the second period. Thus, this company has a rather high defection rate. If we are at the end of period 10 and want to make an assessment of future retention rates, we need to make a customer activity forecast.

Column 3 shows the predicted retention pattern, based on (5.11) (p. 13). The underlying retention rate ceiling (Rc) for the example is 0.80, and the coefficient of retention (r) is 0.5 (estimated from past company data). Thus, retention rates approximate the maximum rate already at period 10. This means that after period 10, the company retains approximately 80% of its customer base from period to period. The defection rate in column 4 is simply calculated as (1−retention rate). Finally, the SR, calculated with (5.12), indicates the proportion of the original cohort that survives until period t. For example, only 1.2% of the original cohort survives until period 11. If the SR is multiplied by the original cohort size—in this case, 7,500—we obtain the number of customers surviving up to period t (column 6).

Another important measure which can be derived from the information is that of lifetime duration. A simple approach (as illustrated in (5.8), p. 11) would be to calculate the mean

Table 5.4 Actual retention pattern of a direct marketing firm

1	2	3	4	5	6	7
Period since acquisition	Actual retention rate (%)	Predicted retention rate (%)	Defection rate (%)	Survival rate (%)	Expected number of active customers	Number of active customer periods
1	32.0		68.0	32.0	2,400	2,400
2	49.1		50.9	15.7	1,178	2,357
3	63.2		36.8	9.9	745	2,234
4	69.0		31.0	6.9	514	2,056
5	72.6		27.4	5.0	373	1,865
6	76.7		23.3	3.8	286	1,717
7	77.9		22.1	3.0	223	1,560
8	78.5		21.5	2.3	175	1,400
9	79.0		21.0	1.8	138	1,244
10	80.0		20.0	1.5	111	1,106
11		79.7	20.3	1.2	88	969
12		79.8	20.2	0.9	70	844
13		79.9	20.1	0.7	56	730
14		79.9	20.1	0.6	45	628
15		80.0	20.0	0.5	36	538

lifetime duration from the average retention rate. The average retention rate across the 15 periods (column 2 and 3) is 71.8%, which results in an average lifetime duration of 3.54 periods. Since the retention rates change over time, we would have to compute an appropriate measure of average retention in order to compute average lifetime duration. More specifically, since many more customers are subject to a lower retention rate in the early periods as compared to higher retention rates in later periods, using a simple average of retention rates 1–15 would be misleading. In the computation of an average retention rate, the number of survived periods needs to be weighed accordingly (see (5.14), p. 17). The result of the weighing process is shown in column 7. Intuitively, it is the number of active customer periods for every period. For example, at the end of period 1 we have 2,400 (2,400 customers * 1 period) active periods, at the end of period 2 we have 2,357 (1,178 customers * 2 periods) active periods, and so on. If we add all active periods 1–15 and divide by the initial cohort size of 7,500, the average lifetime duration is 2.89 periods (= 21,648/ 7,500). Thus, the company needs to replace its customer base every 3 periods, and not every 3.5 periods, as indicated before.

5.5 Popular Customer-Based Value Metrics

Firms have adopted some popular surrogate measures of customer value which they anticipate to be reasonable indicators of the actual customer value. These metrics assist firms in prioritizing their customers in a manner that helps them assign a higher proportion of resources to the customers who they expect will generate greater profits in the future. We suggest managers attempt to correlate these surrogate measures on a selective basis with more rigorous customer value metrics. Only if these correlations yield satisfactory results (i.e., correlations are substantial) can and should the surrogate measures be used for decision making.

5.5.1 Size of Wallet

Size of wallet is the amount of a buyer's total spending in a given category—or, stated differently, the category sales of all firms to that customer. The size of wallet is measured in monetary terms.

Size of wallet (\$) *of customer i in a category*

$$= \sum_{j=1}^{J} S_{ij} \qquad (5.16)$$

Where
i = a particular customer
j = firm
J = all firms offering products in the considered category
S_{ij} = sales value (in category) to customer i by firm j, j = 1, ..., J

Example: A consumer might spend an average of \$400 every month on groceries, across several supermarkets. Thus, her size of wallet is \$400.
Where does the information come from?
Information about the size of wallet can be gathered in many ways. For existing customers, the information can be collected through primary market research (e.g., surveys). A typical question a firm might ask is, "On average, how much do you spend every month on category A?" For prospects, it is quite difficult to obtain the size-of-wallet information on an individual level. Instead, segment-level information is often used.

Evaluation
Size of wallet is a critical measure of the customer-centric organization. When firms attempt to establish and maintain profitable relationships, the customer's buying potential (i.e., size of wallet) is a critical piece of information. Firms are particularly interested in acquiring and retaining customers with large wallet sizes. The assumption firms make here is that large wallet customers will bring in more revenues and profits.

5.5.2 Share of Category Requirement

Share of Category Requirement (SCR) is defined as the proportion of category *volume* accounted for by a brand or focal firm within its base of buyers. This metric is often computed as an aggregate level metric, when individual purchase data are unavailable.

On an aggregate level the SCR is calculated as follows:

aSCR (%) *of firm* (*or brand*) j_0 *in a category*

$$= \frac{\sum_{i=1}^{I} V_{ij_0}}{\sum_{i=1}^{I} \sum_{j=1}^{J} V_{ij}} * 100 \qquad (5.17)$$

Where
j_0 = focal firm or brand
i = customer
I = all customers buying in focal category
J = all firms or brands available in focal category
V_{ij} = purchase volume of customer i from firm (or brand) j

Example: In this example, there are three customers in the category. The category consists of three brands—SAMA, SOMO, and SUMU. Table 5.5 shows the number of purchases during a 3-month period.

The category volume in the 3-month period is 24 units. Brand SAMA has a MS of 33% (i.e., 8 purchases out of a total of 24) and an aSCR of 42.1% (i.e., 8 purchases out of 19, made by its two buyers). This example shows that even though SAMA's MS is already substantial, its aSCR is even higher. The high aSCR for SAMA indicates that once consumers have purchased this brand, they tend to prefer it disproportionately more than its two competitors.

The aSCR ratio is sometimes calculated simply by using purchase occasions or product units as the unit of analysis. The computation discussed here is for the aggregated case. aSCR can also be calculated for individual customers.

Individual Share of Category Requirement (iSCR)
At the individual level, when such data are available, iSCR is computed by dividing the volume of sales (V) of the focal firm to a particular customer by the total category volume she buys. The metric thus indicates how much of the category requirements the focal firm satisfies of an individual customer.

Table 5.5 Calculation of aSCR—purchases during a 3-month period

	Brand SAMA	Brand SOMO	Brand SUMU	Total
Customer 1	2	8	0	10
Customer 2	6	0	3	9
Customer 3	0	4	1	5
Total	8	12	4	24

iSCR (%) *of customer* i_0 *that firm*
$\times$ *(or brand)* j_0 *satisfies*

$$= \frac{V_{i_0 j_0}}{\sum_{j=1}^{J} V_{i_0 j}} * 100 \qquad (5.18)$$

Where

j_0 = focal firm or brand
i_0 = focal customer
J = all firms or brands available in focal category
V_{ij} = purchase volume of customer i from firm (or brand) j

Example: Suppose a computer manufacturer, say PEAR Computers, has collected the following data about its annual customer purchases on Notebook Computers for the year 2010. Using Table 5.6 it can compute the iSCR ratio for each of its customers and identify those customers who have a higher iSCR ratio from those with a lower iSCR ratio. From Table 5.6, we can see that customer 3 has the highest iSCR. PEAR Computers should identify high iSCR customers such as customer 3, and target more of its marketing efforts (mailers, advertisements, etc.) toward such customers and their respective requirements. In addition, customer 3's size of wallet (column A) is the largest, making her even more attractive.

Where does the information come from?

- Numerator: Volumetric sales of the focal firm are readily available from internal records.
- Denominator: The total volumetric purchases of the focal firm's buyer base are typically obtained through market and distribution panels, which are quite common for certain industries (e.g., fast-moving consumer goods [FMCG]). Other industries use mainly primary market research (surveys). Since this information is costly to gather, it is typically collected for a representative sample and then

extrapolated to the entire buyer base. Qualitative managerial judgment is another potential low-cost alternative.

Evaluation

The aggregate level SCR (aSCR) is a general indicator of loyalty for a specific firm (or brand), whereas the individual level SCR (iSCR) is a measure of the importance of a particular firm (or brand) for a single customer. SCR is one of the most commonly accepted measures of customer loyalty, at least for FMCG categories. It separates the question, "whether anyone buys the brand" from the question, "how much they buy." An important characteristic of this measure is that it controls for the total volume of the segments/individuals category requirements. In other words, regardless of the total value of purchases per period, in terms of percentage of allocated purchases (loyalty), it puts all customers on the same metric. However, this metric does not necessarily indicate whether a high iSCR customer will generate substantial revenues or profits—this is only achieved by knowing something about the size of wallet of this customer.

5.5.3   Share of Wallet

Share of Wallet (SW) is defined as the proportion of category value accounted for by a focal brand or a focal firm within its base of buyers. It can be measured at the individual customer level or at an aggregate level (e.g., segment level or entire customer base).

Individual Share of Wallet (iSW)

Individual Share of Wallet (iSW) is defined as the proportion of category value accounted for by a focal brand or a focal firm for a buyer from all brands she purchases in that category. It indicates the degree to which a customer satisfies her needs

Table 5.6 Individual SCR-ratios

	A Total requirement of notebook computers per customer in 2010	B Total number of notebook computers purchased from PEAR computers per customer in 2010	B/A iSCR for PEAR computers per customer in 2010 (%)
Customer 1	100	20	0.20
Customer 2	1,000	200	0.20
Customer 3	2,000	500	0.25

in the category with a focal brand or firm. It is computed by dividing the value of sales (S) of the focal firm (j_0) to a buyer i in a category by the size of wallet of the same customer in a predefined time period.

$$iSW~(\%)~of~firm~j_0~to~customer~i$$

$$= \frac{S_{ij_0}}{\sum_{j=1}^{J} S_{ij}} * 100 \qquad (5.19)$$

Where
j = firm
i = customer
S_{ij} = sales of firm j to customer i
J = see below

Example: If a consumer spends $400 monthly on groceries, and $300 of her purchases are with Supermarket BINGO, then BINGO's iSW for that consumer is 75% in that month.

Aggregate Share of Wallet (aSW) (Brand or Firm Level)

Aggregate share of wallet (aSW) is defined as the proportion of category *value* accounted for by a focal brand or a focal firm *within its entire base of buyers*. It indicates the degree to which the customers of a focal firm satisfy their needs on average, in a category with a focal firm.

$$aSW~(\%)~of~firm~j_0 = \frac{\sum_{i=1}^{I} S_{ij_0}}{\sum_{j=1}^{J} \sum_{i=1}^{I} S_{ij}} * 100$$

$$(5.20)$$

Where
i = customer
j = firm
I = all customers

J = all firms who offer the category under consideration
S_{ij} = sales (value) of firm j to customer i

Example (continued): BINGO may calculate its aSW, using (5.20). The aSW is BINGO's sales (value) in period t ($750,000) divided by the total grocery expenditures of BINGO's customers in the same period ($1,250,000); thus, 750,000/1,250,000 = 60%.

Where does the information come from?
- Numerator: Typically, sales information comes from internal records. In case of the iSW that information has to be available on the individual customer level.
- Denominator: Sales value across all firms comes from primary market research (surveys), administered to individual customers. Since this information is costly to gather, it is often collected for a representative sample and then extrapolated to the entire buyer base. Sometimes, firms can infer the size, of wallet for a certain product, especially in certain business-to-business (B-to-B) contexts. For example, BASF, one of the few manufacturers of car paint, supplies its product to Mercedes-Benz. Based on its knowledge of how much paint it takes to paint an average sized car, it can infer Mercedes-Benz's size of wallet for car paint based on its worldwide production output—a figure easily derived from secondary sources.

Evaluation

Just like SCR, SW is a measure of customer loyalty and can be an important metric. The main difference is the focus on sales volume (SCR) and the focus on sales value (SW). The iSW sheds light on how important the firm is for an individual customer in terms of his

Table 5.7 Share of wallet and size of wallet

	Individual share of wallet (%)	Individual size of wallet ($)	Absolute expenses with firm ($)
Buyer 1	50	400	200
Buyer 2	50	50	25

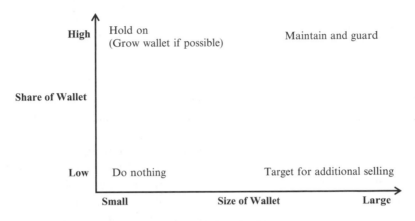

Fig. 5.5 Segmenting customers along share of wallet and size of wallet

expenditures in the category. The aSW indicates how important (value wise) a specific firm is for its customer base in terms of their expenditures in the category. However, SW is unable to provide a clear indication of future revenues and profits that can be expected from a customer.

When to Use SCR and When to Use SW

Information on SW is slightly more difficult to obtain than for SCR. SCR is, in most cases, the preferred measure. This is particularly true for

Share of Wallet and Size of Wallet Hold Important Pieces of Information

Even though two buyers might have the same SW, firms might find their attractiveness as customers to be different as illustrated in Table 5.7.

Depending on the size of wallet, the absolute attractiveness of buyer 1 is eight times higher, even though the SW is the same as for buyer 2. The example shows it is always important to consider SW and size of wallet simultaneously.

$$MS \; of \; firm \; j_0 (\%) = \frac{\sum_{i=1}^{I} \left(iSW \, of \; customer \; i \, to \, firm \, j_0 \, * \, Size \; of \; Wallet \; of \; customer \; i \right)}{\sum_{i=1}^{I} \sum_{j=1}^{J} S_{ij}} * 100 \quad (5.21)$$

categories where the variance of customer expenditures is relatively small (groceries, for example). If purchases are similar in volume, a customer's lifetime value is primarily driven by his frequency of purchases. Thus, SCR is a fairly appropriate measure of loyalty. However, if the variance of consumer expenditures is relatively high (furniture, cars, or other infrequent purchases), then SW is a better measure of loyalty than SCR. In the former case, the frequency is more easily remembered. In the latter case, the customer more easily remembers the expenditures.

The matrix presented in Fig. 5.5 illustrates this and shows the recommended strategies for the various segments. The firm makes optimal resource allocation decisions only by segmenting the customers along both dimensions simultaneously.

Difference of Share of Wallet to Market Share

It is important to recognize the difference between market share (MS) and share of wallet (SW). MS is calculated across buyers and non-buyers, whereas SW is calculated *only among actual buyers*. The MS of a firm is the SW across

Table 5.8 Transition matrix

		Brand purchased next time		
		A (%)	B (%)	C (%)
Brand currently purchased	A	**70**	20	10
	B	10	**80**	10
	C	25	15	**60**

Source: Rust, Zeithaml, and Lemon (2000)
Note: Customer retention probabilities are in bold

all its customers in the category divided by the sales across all firms in the category in period t. Where
i = customer
j = firm
I = all buyers of the category
J = all firms offering the category
S_{ij} = sales of company j to customer i

Example (continued): If BINGO has 5,000 customers with an average expense at BINGO of $150 per month (SW times size of wallet), and the total grocery sales in BINGO's trade area are $5,000,000 per month, then BINGO's MS is $(5,000 \times \$150)/\$5,000,000 = 0.15$, or 15%. The implication here is that although BINGO has an overall low MS, it has a high SW for those consumers buying at BINGO. This indicates that BINGO is a niche player with a very loyal clientele.

buyers; 70% of them will buy brand A next time, 20% will buy brand B, and 10% will buy brand C. The diagonals (in bold) are customer-retention probabilities computed by the company. However, we see that consumers can switch back and forth from brands. For example, the probability that a consumer of brand A will transition to brand B and then come back to brand A in the next two purchase occasions is 20 * 10% = 2%. If, on average, a customer purchases twice per period, the two purchases could be AA, AB, AC, BA, BB, BC, CA, CB, or CC. We can compute the probability of each of these outcomes. This process can be continued for as many purchase occasions as desired. Information for the matrix may come from routine surveys, with questions such as, "Which hotel did you stay in last time?" or "The next time you stay in a hotel, what is the probability that you will stay at each of the hotels that you consider as options?"

5.5.4   Transition Matrix

All of the previously discussed metrics describe only the current state and make no prediction about the future development. A simple idea to forecast SCR or SW is to use a transition matrix. A transition matrix is a convenient way to characterize a customer's likelihood to buy over time or a brand's likelihood to be bought. The assumption is that a customer moves over her lifetime through various stages of activity. Table 5.8 shows such a transition matrix.

In Table 5.8 the top row indicates the movements for customers who are currently brand A

5.6   Summary

Since customer value management involves allocating resources differently for individual customers based on their economic value, understanding value contribution from each of the customers to the firm is very important. In the absence of individual customer data, companies have relied on traditional marketing metrics such as market share and sales growth. Market share (MS) is defined as the share of a firm's sales relative to the sales of all firms—across all customers in the given market. It only gives an aggregate notion of category performance, but does not give any information about how the sales are distributed among customers. Sales growth provides a relative measure of performance but fails to indicate which customers contributed more and which contributed less.

The availability of customer-level data helps firms utilize a new set of metrics which enables the assignment of value to each individual customer. These so-called primary customer-based metrics can be subdivided into customer acquisition metrics and customer activity metrics. Customer acquisition metrics measure the customer level success of marketing efforts to acquire new customers. Two important metrics are the acquisition rate and acquisition cost (AC). Acquisition rate is the proportion of prospects converted to customers, and acquisition cost is the campaign spending per acquired customer. Customer activity metrics, by contrast, serve to track customer activities after the acquisition stage. Some critical customer activity metrics are average inter-purchase time (AIT), retention rate, survival rate (SR), customer lifetime duration, and probability of a customer being active, P(Active). These are important inputs for the calculation of customer value and for aligning resource allocation with customers' behavior. AIT is defined as the average time elapsed between purchases. The retention rate is the average likelihood a customer purchases from the focal firm in a period (t), given this customer has purchased in the last period (t−1). The defection rate expresses the average likelihood a customer defects from the focal firm in a period (t), given the customer was purchasing up to period (t−1). The survival rate (SR) is another preliminary customer metric, and indicates the proportion of customers that have "survived" (or, in other words, continued to remain as a customer) until a period t from the beginning of the relationship with these customers. SR is closely linked with retention rate. SR is a summary measure of how many customers survived between the start of the formation of a cohort and any point in time afterward, while retention rate reflects retention in a given period only. The SR can be measured as the product of the retention rate at time t and the SR during the

immediately preceding period (t−1). Lifetime duration is a key strategic metric in the calculation of the customer lifetime value. The calculation of lifetime duration is different in contractual and noncontractual situations. In a contractual case, this is the time from the start of the relationship until the end of the relationship. However, in a noncontractual situation, firms are interested in the likelihood the customer is active at a given point in time. If the likelihood is below a threshold value, the customer is considered inactive. An estimation of whether a customer is active is given by P(Active). A simple formula for P(Active) is $P(Active) = T^n$, where n is the number of purchases in a given period and T is the time of the last purchase expressed as a fraction of the observation period.

Firms use different surrogate measures of customer value to prioritize their customers and to differentially invest in them. Popular customer-based metrics comprise size of wallet, share of category requirement, and share of wallet. Size of wallet is the buyer's total spending in a category and usually firms are interested in acquiring and retaining customers with large wallet sizes. (Aggregate) Share of category requirement (aSCR) is an aggregate level measure of the proportion of the category volume accounted for by a brand or a focal firm. SCR is one of the most commonly accepted measures of customer loyalty for FMCG categories. On an individual level the iSCR indicates how much of the category requirement of an individual a firm satisfies. Although this is an overall indicator of customer loyalty, it does not necessarily indicate whether a high iSCR customer will generate substantial revenues or profits, for which the knowledge about the customer's size of wallet is necessary. Share of wallet (SW) is the proportion of category value accounted for by a focal brand or firm within its base of buyers. At an individual level, iSW is defined as the proportion of category value accounted for by a focal brand or firm for a buyer. It indicates the degree to which a customer satisfies her needs in the category with a focal brand or firm. Firms can use the information about size of wallet and share of wallet together for optimal allocation of resources. To forecast the

SCR or SW a transition matrix can be used. The transition matrix provides us with the probability a customer will purchase a particular brand if we know which brand she purchased previously.

5.7 Exercise Questions

1. How would you calculate the retention rate of your company's customer base? What assumptions do you need to make?
2. How will you calculate the acquisition cost per customer? Consider a mail-order catalog company, an IT services company, and a retail store. What are the underlying assumptions in each case? How precise are your calculations?
3. Try to predict retention rates using (5.13).
4. How will you determine if a customer is still your customer in noncontractual settings?
5. How would you implement the recommended strategies in Fig. 5.5? What are some specific marketing actions you would take in the four quadrants?

Catalina is changing supermarket shopper measurement

Catalina Inc. is a Florida-based company specializing in supermarket shopper tracking and coupon issuing. The company has about 1,200 employees and operates in the United States, as well as in major European countries. The company built its business model on issuing coupons to grocery shoppers online when they check out. The basis for this business model is that traditional print media has long production lead times, and the response to these media is not measurable on the individual customer level. Thus, supermarkets and manufacturers cannot run and track individualized campaigns with traditional media. Catalina's system consists of a printer connected to the cashier's scanner and a database. The information on each shopping basket that checks out via the scanner is then stored in the database. Using the person's credit card number or check number, the database links individual shopping baskets over time. If the person pays cash, the system cannot link the basket.

The system then allows both manufacturers and retailers to run individualized campaigns based on the information in the database. For example, Catalina could partner with the retailer to improve its cross-selling. A typical issue for any given retailer is that certain customers use the store as their primary shopping location, whereas others use it as their secondary store. To improve the SW with the latter group of customers, Catalina first investigates basket composition of the various buyers. It then finds that certain buyers buy, for example baby or children products (thus, there is apparently a family behind this shopping bask), yet the number of calories in that basket does not match that of an average family. One explanation for this might be that this shopper uses this outlet as a secondary store. Given this interpretation, the decision then is to allocate to this customer a gift of say $10, for shopping for 4 weeks in a row spending at least $40 per week in the store. The goal is to selectively target those shoppers of whom the store captures only a low SW, and to entice them to change their behavior.

Questions

1. Explain why Catalina's approach is superior from a retailer's perspective vis-a-vis the traditional mass media approach.
2. Discuss the role of traditional metrics (such as market share) in this new CRM environment. Should they be discarded?
3. Do you think Catalina's practice (which is entirely legal) is ethically acceptable?

Appendix

Notation Key

Notation	Explanation
a	Coefficient of acquisition
AC	Acquisition costs
ACS	Acquisition costs Savings
Ar	Acquisition rate

(*continued*)

Notation	Explanation
c	Category
CE	Customer Equity
Dr	Defection rate
GC	Gross contribution
i	Individual customer
I	Total number of buyers with a focal firm
j	Firm
J	Total number of firms in a market
LTV	Lifetime value
MC	Marketing costs
n	Customer in cohort
N	Cohort size
r	Coefficient of retention
Rr	Retention rate
Rr_c	Retention rate ceiling
S	Sales (value)
Sr	Survival rate
t	Time period
T	Length of time horizon
V	Sales (volume)
δ	Applicable discount rate

References

Blattberg, R. C., Getz, G., & Thomas, J. S. (2001). *Customer equity: Building and managing relationships as valuable assets*. Cambridge, MA: Harvard Business School Press.

Reinartz, W., & Kumar, V. (2000). On the profitability of long-life customers in a noncontractual setting: An empirical investigation and implications for marketing. *Journal of Marketing, 64*(4), 17–35.

Reinartz, W., & Kumar, V. (2002). The mismanagement of customer loyalty. *Harvard Business Review, 80*(7), 4–12.

Rust, R. T., Zeithaml, V. A., & Lemon, K. N. (2000). *Driving customer equity*. New York: The Free Press.

Schmittlein, D. C., & Morrison, D. G. (1985). Is the customer still active? *The American Statistician, 39*(4), 291–295.

Customer Analytics Part II

6

6.1 Overview

In the previous chapter, we examined some traditional marketing metrics, various primary customer-based metrics, and explained some popular customer-based value metrics used in industry. Some of the primary customer-based metrics introduced earlier form the inputs to derive customer value – the key metric that drives decision making in the age of data-based marketing.

This chapter proceeds to conceptualize strategic metrics of customer value and introduces popular customer selection strategies and techniques to evaluate these strategies. Strategic customer-based metrics such as *recency, frequency, monetary value (RFM), past customer value, lifetime value metrics*, and the *customer equity* are forward looking measures. *RFM* value is a frequently used metric to predict, e.g., purchase behavior. The past customer *value (PCV)* assumes that the results of past transactions are an indicator of the customer's future contributions. Evaluating the long-term economic value of a customer to the firm is the goal of *lifetime value metrics*, which also form the basis for the calculation of the *customer equity*.

In addition to these metrics, some customer selection strategies are explained in Sect. 6.3. These techniques help firms identify the right customers in order to optimally allocate the available marketing resources. The chapter introduces three popular customer selection strategies: profiling, binary decision trees, and logistic regression.

Finally, Sect. 6.4 discusses methods, such as misclassification rates and lift analysis, which companies can use to evaluate alternative selection strategies.

An overview of the metrics and methods discussed in this chapter is given in Table 6.1.

6.2 Strategic Customer-Based Value Metrics

Strategic customer based value metrics are forward looking and aim to guide company decisions with the goal to maximize long-term profitability of the customer base. In particular we will introduce recency, frequency, and monetary value (RFM), past customer value, the lifetime value of a customer, and customer equity.

6.2.1 RFM Method

RFM stands for recency, frequency, and monetary value. This technique utilizes these three metrics to evaluate customer behavior and customer value and is often used in practice.

1. *Recency* is a measure of how long it has been since a customer last placed an order with the company.
2. *Frequency* is a measure of how often a customer orders from the company in a certain defined period.
3. *Monetary value* is the amount that a customer spends on an average transaction.

V. Kumar and W. Reinartz, *Customer Relationship Management*, Springer Texts in Business and Economics, DOI 10.1007/978-3-642-20110-3_6, © Springer-Verlag Berlin Heidelberg 2012

Table 6.1 Metrics and methods used in customer analytics part 2

Metrics
6.2 Strategic customer-based value metrics
6.2.1 RFM value
6.2.2 Past customer value
6.2.3 Lifetime value metrics
6.2.4 Customer equity
Methods
6.3 Popular customer selection strategies
6.3.1 Profiling
6.3.2 Binary classification trees
6.3.3 Logistic regression
6.4 Techniques to evaluate alternative customer selection strategies
6.4.1 Misclassification rate
6.4.2 Lift analysis

The general idea of RFM is to classify customers based on their RFM measure. The resulting groups of customers are associated with purchase behavior, e.g., likelihood to respond to a marketing campaign. RFM is similar to the transition matrix approach in that it also tracks customer behavior over time in what is called a state-space. That is, customers move over time through space with certain defined activity states.

The RFM Method

For the following discussions about RFM coding, consider the example of a firm with a customer base of 400,000 customers. From this customer base, a sample of 40,000 customers is chosen. In other words, every tenth customer from the larger database of 400,000 customers was picked in order to form a test group of 40,000 customers who are representative of the whole customer base.

Also, assume this firm is planning to send a marketing mailer campaign of a $150 discount coupon to be mailed to its customers.[1]

Recency Coding

Assume this firm sends its $150 mailer campaign to the 40,000 customers in the test group, and assume that 808 customers (2.02% of 40,000)

responded. In order to determine if there is any correlation between those customers who responded to the mailer campaign and their corresponding historical recency, the following analysis is done.

The test group of 40,000 customers is sorted in descending order based on the criterion of *most recent purchase date*. The earliest purchasers are listed on the top and the oldest are listed at the bottom. The sorted data are further divided into five groups of equal size (20% in each group). The top-most group is assigned a recency code of 1, the next group is assigned a code of 2, and so on, until the bottom-most group is assigned a code of 5. An analysis of the customer response data from the mailer campaign and the recency-based grouping point out that the mailer campaign received the highest response from those customers grouped in recency code 1, followed by those grouped in code 2, and so on. Figure 6.1 depicts the distribution of relative frequencies of customers who responded across the recency groups coded 1 through 5. The highest response rate (4.5%) for the campaign was from those customers in the test group who had the highest recency quintile (recency code = 1). Note the average customer response rate computed for all five groups would be none other than the actual response rate of 2.02% achieved by the campaign, i.e., (4.50% + 2.80% + 1.50% + 1.05% + 0.25%)/5 = 2.02%.

At the end of this recency coding exercise we would assign recency values of r = 1 through 5 for groups of customers, depending on the quintile that they belong to.

Frequency Coding

The frequency coding process is the same as the recency coding process just discussed. However, to sort the test group of 40,000 customers based on the frequency metric, we need to know the average number of purchases made by a customer per month. Of course, the choice of the appropriate time period depends on the usual frequency of purchases (e.g., weeks, months, quarters, years, etc.). In this case, customers with the highest number of purchases per month are grouped at the top, while those with lower number of purchases per month were listed below. Here again, the sorted list is grouped

---

[1] All numerical figures mentioned in the discussions below are hypothetical data created for instructional purposes only. However, due care has been exercised to ensure these data are fairly close to real life experiences of many firms.

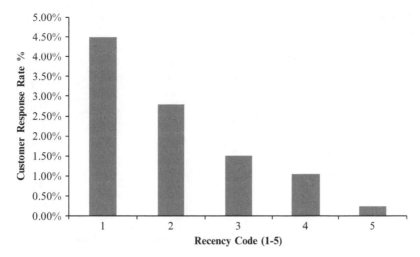

Fig. 6.1 Response and recency

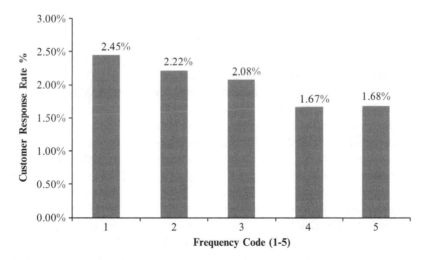

Fig. 6.2 Response and frequency

into five quintiles. Those in the top are assigned a code of 1 and those at the bottom a code of 5. The response rate of each of the frequency-based sorted quintiles is depicted in Fig. 6.2.

An analysis of the customer response data from the mailer campaign and the *frequency*-based grouping show that the mailer campaign received the highest response rate from those customers grouped in *frequency* code 1, followed by those grouped in code 2 (2.22%), and so on.

At the end of the *frequency* coding we would assign frequency values of f = 1 though 5 for groups of customers in the five frequency quintiles.

Monetary Value Coding

The *monetary value* coding process is exactly the same as the recency and frequency coding processes. However, to sort the test group of 40,000 customers based on the *monetary value* metric, we need to know the *average amount purchased per month*. As with *recency* and *frequency*, the customer data are sorted, grouped, and coded 1 to 5.

As can be seen in Fig. 6.3 the highest response rate (2.35%) for the campaign was from those customers in the test group who had the highest *monetary value* quintile (monetary value code = 1). Thus, indicating that the monetary

Fig. 6.3 Response and monetary value

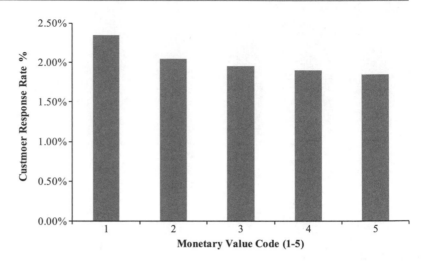

value is also an important metric for the analysis of customer behavior.

At the end of this *monetary value* coding exercise, we would assign a *monetary value* of $m = 1$ through 5 for groups of customers, depending on the quintile that they fall within.

After performing the three steps (R, F, and M) you will have individual R, F, and M scores for each customer. Each customer will be assigned to one of the 125 groups such as 111, 233, 432, . . . , 555, based on her respective RFM code. An overview of the RFM procedure is given in Fig. 6.4.

Limitations

This method independently links customer response data with R, F, and M values and then groups customers belonging to specific RFM codes. However, this method may not produce an equal number of customers under each RFM cell. This is because the individual metrics R, F, and M are likely to be correlated. For example, someone spending more (high M) is also likely, on average, to buy more frequently (high F). However, for practical purposes, it is desirable to have exactly the same number of individuals in each RFM cell. A sorting technique ensuring equal numbers in each RFM cell is described as follows.

RFM Cell Sorting Technique

An alternative approach to applying RFM sequentially to the initial dataset is the RFM cell sorting. This is a more sophisticated sorting technique which helps to arrive at an RFM code for each customer and ensures the grouping of

an equal number of customers under each RFM code. Figure 6.5 depicts a schematic diagram of the logic behind RFM cell sorting. Consider the list of 40,000 test group customers. The list is first sorted for recency and grouped into five equal groups of 8,000 customers. Therefore group 1 will have 8,000 customers, and so will the other groups through group 5. Now, take the 8,000 customers in each group and sort them based on frequency and divide them into five equal groups of 1,600 each. At the end of this stage, you will have RF codes starting from 11 through 55, with each group having 1,600 customers. In the last stage, each of the RF groups is further sorted based on monetary value and divided into five equal groups of 320 customers each. Again, we will have RFM codes starting from 111 through 555, each having 320 customers. Considering each RFM code as a cell, we will have 125 cells (5 recency divisions * 5 frequency divisions * 5 monetary value divisions = 125 RFM codes).

Breakeven Value (BE)

To arrive at a decision which customers (more precisely: which customer "cells") to target, it is necessary to determine a cutoff point for the marketing campaign. This cutoff point should be based on the profitability of the customer. The breakeven value (BE) provides a simple to calculate metric for this purpose. In marketing literature *breakeven* refers to the fact that the net profit from a marketing promotion equals the

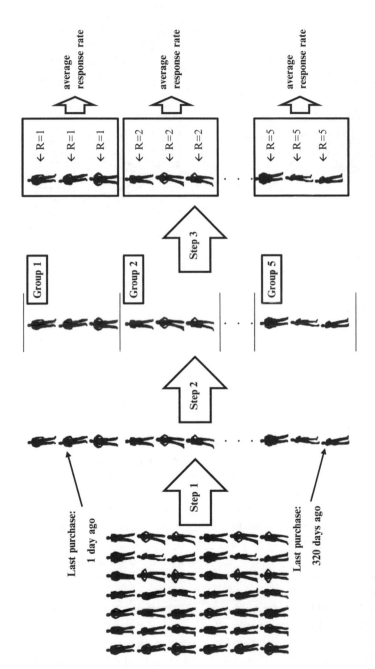

Fig. 6.4 RFM procedure

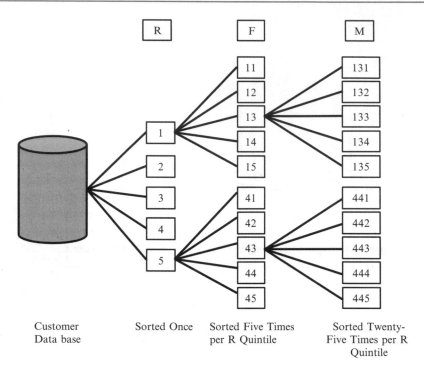

Fig. 6.5 RFM cell sorting

cost associated with conducting the promotion. The BE is defined as

$$BE = \frac{unit\,cost\,price}{unit\,net\,profit} \qquad (6.1)$$

If this ratio for a particular promotion is 1, then the promotion only broke even and did not generate any net profits. This ratio also computes the minimum response rates required in order to offset the promotional costs involved and thereby not incur any losses. Thus, we also refer to the BE as the *breakeven response rate*.

Example (continued): Consider the example of mailing $150 discount coupons. Suppose the cost to mail each piece is a dollar, and the net profit (after all costs) is $45, then the breakeven value or breakeven response rate required can be computed as BE = $1/$45 − 0.0222, or 2.22%. This value can be computed and then can be compared with the actual response rate of each RFM cell.

To simplify comparison, the breakeven response rate just computed could be used in computing a *breakeven index* (BEI) for every RFM cell. The BEI is calculated using the following formula.

$$BEI = \left(\frac{(Actual\,response\,rate - BE)}{BE} \right) \qquad (6.2)$$

A positive BEI value indicates that some profit was made from the transaction. A BEI value of 0 indicates that the transaction just broke even, and a negative BEI value indicates that the transaction resulted in a loss.

Example (continued): Therefore, in the above example, if the actual response rate of a particular RFM cell was 3.5%, then BEI = ([3.5%−2.22%]/2.22%) * 100 = 57.66.

Table 6.2 shows an excerpt from the BEI computations for 35 RFM cells. The complete table is available in Appendix III of this chapter. RFM cells with a corresponding positive BEI value are the groups of customers the marketing campaign should target, and all those RFM cells with corresponding negative BEI

Table 6.2 Combining RFM codes, breakeven codes, breakeven index

Cell #	RFM codes	Cost per mail ($)	Net profit per sale ($)	Breakeven (%)	Actual response (%)	Breakeven index
1	111	1	45.00	2.22	17.55	690
2	112	1	45.00	2.22	17.45	685
3	113	1	45.00	2.22	17.35	681
4	114	1	45.00	2.22	17.25	676
5	115	1	45.00	2.22	17.15	672
6	121	1	45.00	2.22	17.05	667
7	122	1	45.00	2.22	16.95	663
8	123	1	45.00	2.22	16.85	658
9	124	1	45.00	2.22	16.75	654
10	125	1	45.00	2.22	16.65	649
11	131	1	45.00	2.22	16.55	645
12	132	1	45.00	2.22	16.45	640
13	133	1	45.00	2.22	16.35	636
14	134	1	45.00	2.22	16.25	631
15	135	1	45.00	2.22	16.15	627
16	141	1	45.00	2.22	16.05	622
17	142	1	45.00	2.22	15.95	618
18	143	1	45.00	2.22	15.85	613
19	144	1	45.00	2.22	15.75	609
20	145	1	45.00	2.22	15.65	604
21	151	1	45.00	2.22	15.55	600
22	152	1	45.00	2.22	15.45	595
23	153	1	45.00	2.22	15.35	591
24	154	1	45.00	2.22	15.25	586
25	155	1	45.00	2.22	15.15	582
26	211	1	45.00	2.22	15.65	604
27	212	1	45.00	2.22	15.55	600
28	213	1	45.00	2.22	15.45	595
29	214	1	45.00	2.22	15.35	591
30	215	1	45.00	2.22	15.25	586
31	221	1	45.00	2.22	15.15	582
32	222	1	45.00	2.22	15.05	577
33	223	1	45.00	2.22	14.95	573
34	224	1	45.00	2.22	14.85	568
35	225	1	45.00	2.22	14.75	564

values are those customers to be avoided for this promotion.

It is interesting to note that of the 125 cells, only customers within 56 cells have a higher chance of offering profitability to the firm, and the rest do not! Therefore, it becomes clear that a firm can achieve significant savings by only focusing on potentially profitable customers and not targeting the rest.

Figure 6.6 plots the RFM cell codes and their corresponding BEI values. Customers with posi-tive BEI values are to be chosen and the rest are to be left unconsidered. Note that customers with higher RFM values tend to have higher BEI values. However, at the same time, customers with a lower recency value but relatively higher F and M values also tend to have positive BEI values and hence should be considered for target mailing.

Order of Importance of R, F, and M

Most often businesses use the RFM technique in the order of recency, frequency, and monetary

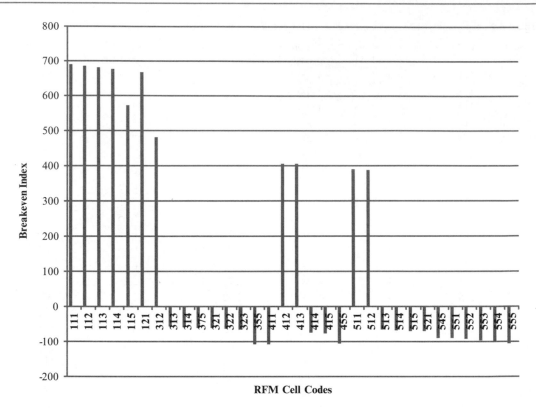

Fig. 6.6 RFM codes versus BEI

Table 6.3 Comparison of profits for targeting campaign test

	Test	Full customer base	RFM selection
Average response rate	2.02%	2.02%	15.25%
Number of responses	808	8,808	2,372.8
Average net profit/sale	$45	$45	$45
Net revenue	$36,360	$363,600	$122,976
Number of mailers sent	40,000	400,000	17,920
Cost per mailer	$1.00	$1.00	$1.00
Mailing cost	$40,000.00	$400,000.00	$17,920.00
Profits	(−$3,640.00)	(−$36,400.00)	$105,056.00

value. However, the order varies for different industry segments. Although the RFM order is normally acceptable, a more accurate order of coding would depend on the rapidity the customer response rate drops. The metric (R, F, or M) for which the customer response rates declines more quickly is likely to be the best predictor of future customer response and, hence, should be coded first. Once the metric of highest influence is determined, the same method of measurement can be used to determine the order of the remaining metrics.

Referring to Figs. 6.1, 6.2, and 6.3 it should be noticed that customer response rate drops more rapidly for the recency metric than the other two metrics. Similarly, the customer response rate for the frequency metric drops more rapidly than the monetary value metric. Therefore, the order of R, F, and M holds good in this case.

Table 6.4 Recency score

Customer	Purchase number	Recency (month)	Assigned points	Weighted points
John	1	2	20	100
	2	4	10	50
	3	9	3	15
Smith	1	6	5	25
Mags	1	2	20	100
	2	4	10	50
	3	6	5	25
	4	9	3	15

Points for recency: 20 points if within past 2 months, 10 points if within past 4 months, 5 points if within past 6 months, 3 points if within past 9 months, 1 point if within past 12 months, relative weight = 5

Table 6.6 Monetary value score

Customer	Purchase number	Value of purchase ($)	Assigned points	Weighted points
John	1	40	4	12
	2	120	12	36
	3	60	6	18
Smith	1	400	25	75
Mags	1	90	9	27
	2	70	7	21
	3	80	8	24
	4	40	4	12

Points for monetary value: 10% of the $-value of purchase within 12 months, maximum = 25 points, relative weight = 3

Table 6.5 Frequency score

Customer	Purchase number	Frequency	Assigned points	Weighted points
John	1	1	3	6
	2	1	3	6
	3	1	3	6
Smith	1	2	6	12
Mags	1	1	3	6
	2	1	3	6
	3	2	6	12
	4	1	3	6

Points for frequency: 3 points for each purchase within 12 months, maximum = 15 points, relative weight = 2

Table 6.7 RFM cumulative score

Customer	Purchase number	Total weighted points	Cumulative points
John	1	118	118
	2	92	210
	3	39	249
Smith	1	112	112
Mags	1	133	133
	2	77	210
	3	61	271
	4	37	308

Example (continued): Table 6.3 compares the profits made by targeting all customers vs. using RFM to target selected customers. It is clear the firm will benefit significantly more by sending the mailers to select customers within selected RFM cells, than by sending it to their entire customer base. The loss of $3,640 incurred in conducting the test is offset by the profits generated by sending mailers to the RFM select customers.

Relative Importance of R, F, and M

In the simplest case the RFM values are assigned for each customer by sequential sorting based on the RFM metrics. However, there is an alternative method which uses regression techniques to compute the relative weights of the R, F, and M metrics, and these relative weights are used to compute the cumulative points of each customer. The pre-computed weights for R, F, and M, based on a test sample, are used to assign RFM scores to each customer (see Appendix II). The higher the computed score, the more profitable the customer is likely to be in the future. This method, unlike the earlier one, is more flexible and can be tailored to each business situation.

Example (Aaker, Kumar, & Day, 2003): Three customers have a purchase history calculated over a 12-month period (see Tables 6.4–6.7). For every customer, numerical points have been assigned to each transaction according to a historically derived RFM formula. The relative weight based on the importance assigned to each of the three variables, R, F, and M on the basis of an analysis carried out on past customer transactions is as follows:

Recency = 5, Frequency = 2, Monetary = 3

The resulting cumulative scores, 249 for John, 112 for Smith, and 308 for Mags, indicate a potential preference for Mags. In this case, John seems to be a good prospect as well, but mailing to Smith might be a misdirected marketing effort. This example illustrates a simple application of the RFM technique. In practice, however, the number of customers to be analyzed can run into millions. Regression techniques are often employed to arrive at the relative weights for RFM. See Appendix II for an overview of a regression scoring model.

Evaluation

The RFM technique helps organizations significantly, not only in identifying and targeting valuable customers who have a very high chance of purchasing, but also in avoiding costly communications and campaigns to customers who have a lower probability of purchasing. Instead it helps to identify only those customers with high probabilities of purchase and to target the companies' marketing strategies and communications accordingly. A limitation is that the RFM technique can be applied only on historical customer data available and not on prospects data.

6.2.2 Past Customer Value

Past customer value (PCV) is a metric which assumes the results of past transactions are an indicator of the customer's future contributions. The value of a customer is determined based on the total contribution (toward profits) provided by the customer in the past. This modeling technique assumes that the past performance of the customer indicates the future level of profitability. Since products or services are bought at different points in time during the customer's lifetime, all transactions must be adjusted for the time value of money.

$$PCV\,of\,customer\,i = \sum_{t=0}^{T} GC_{i(t_0-t)} * (1+\delta)^t \quad (6.3)$$

Where
i = customer
t = time index

Table 6.8 Spending pattern of a customer

	January	February	March	April	May
Purchase amount ($)	800	50	50	30	20
GC	240	15	15	9	6

Gross contribution (GC) = purchase amount × contribution margin

δ = applicable discount rate (for example 1.25% per month)

t_0 = current time period

T = number of time periods prior to current period that should be considered

GC_{it} = gross contribution of transactions of customer i period t

Example: If we have data on the products purchased by a customer over a period of time, the value of the purchases, and the contribution margin, we can calculate the value generated by the customer by computing all transactions in terms of their present value. Assuming a contribution margin of 0.3, a monthly discount rate of r = 1.25%, and a spending pattern as illustrated in Table 6.8, the PCV is calculated as:

$$PCV_i = 6(1+0.0125)^0 + 9(1+0.0125)^1$$
$$+ 15(1+0.0125)^2 + 15(1+0.0125)^3$$
$$+ 240(1+0.0125)^4 = 302.01486$$

This customer is worth $302.01 expressed in net present value in May dollars.

Evaluation

By comparing the PCV of a set of customers, we arrive at a prioritization for directing future marketing efforts. The underlying assumption is that the past contribution of a customer is a good predictor of her future contributions. The customers with higher values are normally those deserving greater marketing resources. This method, while extremely useful, does not incorporate other information which could help refine the process of selecting profitable customers. For instance, it does not consider whether a customer is going to be active in the future. It also does not incorporate the expected cost of maintaining the

Fig. 6.7 Principles of LTV calculation

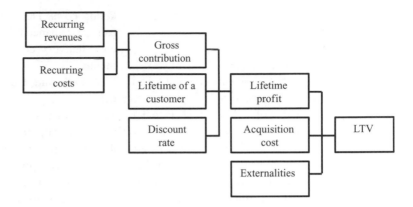

customer in the future. Concluding, it is still a backward-looking metric.

6.2.3 Lifetime Value Metrics

Evaluating the long-term economic value of a customer to the firm has seen a dramatic rise in interest. This is a direct outcome of the shift from transactional marketing to relational marketing. If a manager wants to evaluate marketing resource allocation plans targeted at improving the long-term value of customers, corresponding control measures must be put in place. Looking at profits on a per-transaction basis is not sufficient. Managers want to have an idea how the value of a client has evolved over time. The general term used to describe the long-term economic value of a customer is lifetime value (LTV), also referred to as the customer lifetime value (CLV). In very simple terms, it is a multi period evaluation of a customer's value to the firm in net present value. However, the term LTV is not without controversies. Although it is the Holy Grail for some, others call it "an elaborate fiction of presumed precision" (Jackson, 1992). In the following section we present some of the most common ways to calculate LTV. Nevertheless, the reader should be aware that there are many specific formulations.[2] It is important to present the principle in such a manner that read-

ers can adapt the calculation to their own requirements. Conceptually, the principle of calculating LTV is represented in Fig. 6.7.

As one can easily see, there is not a single way to arrive at each component. For example, are the recurring costs comprised only of direct product costs or also marketing, sales and service costs? Depending on many factors, such as nature of product, data availability and statistical capabilities, the inputs for the LTV calculation change. Is this problematic? It is not. First and foremost, it is important to understand the principle. Based on the general principle, one can then start to adjust the calculation to the available data. Also, one needs to adapt the formulation to the industry and company context. For example, having a defined finite lifetime duration (as for a contractual relationship such as cable subscription) makes for a different formulation as having a non-finite relationship (as for a noncontractual relationship such as buying from a supermarket).

After discussing the basic formulations, we will highlight key issues that should be considered when employing the models. In the following discussion, we will present different formulations of the same principle.

Basic LTV Model

In the most simple definition, the lifetime value of an individual customer i is the sum of her discounted gross contribution over the respective observation horizon T.

[2] For details on various forms of LTV models, see: Jain and Singh (2002), Berger and Nasr (1998).

$$LTV_i = \sum_{t=1}^{T} GC_{it} \left(\frac{1}{1+\delta} \right)^t \qquad (6.4)$$

Where

i = customer

t = time period

δ = interest (or discount) rate

GC_{it} = gross contribution of customer i at time t

T = observation time horizon

LTV_i = lifetime value of an individual customer i in net present value at time t = 0

The resulting LTV is a measure of a single customer's worth to the firm. The gross contribution (GC) may vary, of course, across customers and across time. This formulation is primarily used for pedagogical and conceptual purposes. It is typically based on past customer behavior and may have limited diagnostic value for future decision making.

> *Cautionary note* If the time unit is different from a yearly basis, the interest rate δ needs to be adjusted accordingly. For example, if the yearly interest rate is 15%, the quarterly interest rate is 3.56%.

LTV with Splitted Revenues and Costs

On the next level, one can break down the gross contribution into its constituting elements.

$$LTV_i = \sum_{t=1}^{T} \left((S_{it} - DC_{it}) - MC_{it} \right) \left(\frac{1}{1+\delta} \right)^t$$

(6.5)

Where

i = customer

t = time period

T = observation time horizon

δ = interest (or discount) rate

S_{it} = sales value to customer i at time t

DC_{it} = direct costs of products purchased by customer i at time t

MC_{it} = marketing costs directed at customer i at time t

LTV_i = lifetime value of an individual customer i in net present value at time t = 0

The cost element in this example is broken down into direct product-related costs and mar-

keting costs. Depending on data availability, it can be enhanced by including service-related cost, delivery cost, or other relevant cost elements.

LTV Including Customer Retention Probabilities

So far, an assumption was that all customers under investigation remain fully active during the period of interest. However, in reality, more and more customers stop their relationship with the firm over time. The next step is therefore to consider customer retention probabilities. This relates to the fact that customers tend to remain in the relationship only with a certain probability approximated by the average retention rate Rr. Also, the AC is now subtracted from the customer's value.

$$LTV_i = \left(\left(\sum_{t=1}^{T} \left(\prod_{k=1}^{K} Rr_k \right) GC_{it} \left(\frac{1}{1+\delta} \right)^t \right) \right) - AC_i$$

(6.6)

Where

i = customer

t = time period

T = time horizon under consideration

δ = interest (or discount) rate

Rr_t = average retention rate at time t (it is possible to use an individual level retention probability Rr_{it} but usually this is difficult to obtain; see discussion in Sect. 5.4.2)

GC_{it} = gross contribution of customer i at time t

AC_i = costs of acquiring customer i (acquisition costs)

Note that in this equation the term $\prod_{k=1}^{t} Rr_k$ is actually the survival rate SR_t (see Sect. 5.4.3).

It is also noteworthy, that if the retention rate is constant over time (i.e., it does not vary across time and thus $Rr_k = Rr$ for all k) and thus the expression can be simplified using the identity:

$$\prod_{k=1}^{t} Rr_k = (Rr)^t \qquad (6.7)$$

Although this is a common assumption, it is mostly not very realistic, as was previously discussed.

LTV with Constant Retention Rate and Gross Contribution

Under the assumption that $T \to \infty$, that the retention rate (Rr) is constant over time, and that the GC does not change over time, (6.6) can be simplified to the following formula:

$$LTV_i = GC_i \left(\frac{Rr}{1 - Rr + \delta} \right) - AC_i \qquad (6.8)$$

We call the term

$$\frac{Rr}{1 - Rr + \delta}$$

the margin multiplier.

This formulation is easy applicable for quick calculations and, unless the retention rate is very high, produces results very close to the more precise formulation. One only needs to multiply the GC with the margin multiplier ($Rr/[1-Rr + \delta]$) and subtract the acquisition cost.

How Long is Lifetime Duration?

The word *lifetime* must, in many circumstances, be taken with a grain of salt. Although the term makes little sense with one-off purchases (say, for example, a house), it also seems strange to talk about LTV of a grocery shopper. Clearly, there is an actual lifetime value of a grocery shopper. However, given the long time span, this actual value is not practical. For all practical purposes, the lifetime duration is a longer-term duration used managerially (see Sect. 5.4.4). For example, in a direct marketing general merchandise context, managers do not look beyond a 4-year time span. Beyond that, any calculation and prediction may become difficult due to so many uncontrollable factors (e.g., the customer moves, new competitors enter the market, and so on). It is therefore important to make an educated judgment regarding a sensible duration horizon in the context of making decisions.

Incorporating externalities in the LTV

The value a customer provides to a firm does not only consist of the revenue stream that results from her purchases of goods and services. In the era of modern telecommunication technology and the rapid growth of online social communities (e.g., Facebook), product rating websites, and weblogs, the passing on of personal opinions about a product or brand can contribute substantially to the lifetime value of a customer. Examples are customer referrals that result in new customer acquisitions or the posting of negative product reviews that detract potential customers from buying a product. We subsume all these activities under the term word-of-mouth (WOM).

Measuring and incorporating WOM

A first step at measuring WOM is to look at its effects on revenues and expenses. It can be expected that WOM has a direct effect on new customer acquisitions through reducing (or in case of negative WOM increasing) the AC. To incorporate the value of WOM in the LTV calculation we need to determine the savings in AC per customer due to a referral (AC savings: ACS) and the number of new customer acquisitions (n_i) that arise due to the referrals of customer i.

$$LTV_i = \left(\left(\sum_{t=1}^{T} \left(\prod_{k=1}^{T} Rr_k \right) (GC_{it} + n_{it}ACS_t) \right) \left(\frac{1}{1 + \delta} \right)^t \right) - AC_i \qquad (6.9)$$

Where
i = customer
t = time period
T = time horizon under consideration
δ = interest (or discount) rate
Rr_t = average retention rate at time t
GC_{it} = gross contribution of customer i at time t
n_{it} = number of new acquisitions at time t due to referrals of customer i
ACS_t = average acquisition cost savings per customer gained through referral of customer i at time t

Table 6.9 Customer value matrix

		Average CRV after 1 year	
		Low	High
Average LTV after 1 year	High	Affluents	Champions
	Low	Misers	Advocates

Source: This table is adapted from Kumar, Petersen, and Leone (2007)

AC_i = costs of acquiring customer i (acquisition costs)

Equation 6.9 accounts for the fact that there are opinion leaders who have a stronger influence on their peers and the differences in the size of the social network of customers through an individual level n_{it}. The downside is that this number is difficult to obtain. Surveys and questionnaires may be used but are costly, time consuming, and often not reliable. Instead network centrality metrics such as degree centrality or betweenness can help to approximate the number of referrals.[3] Still, it neglects the differences in GC of the customers that were acquired through referrals.

Alternative ways to account for externalities

The situation becomes even more complex, when acknowledging that WOM not only reduces AC but also impacts the purchase frequency, purchase volume, and cross-buying and thus the LTV of the customer that was acquired because of a referral. A major problem is to whom to account the additional value of a customer j if his GC rises due to WOM by customer i. To avoid this question, the value of a customer's referrals can be separated from the LTV, for example by calculating a separate customer referral value (CRV) for each customer. A joined evaluation of both metrics helps the management to select and determine how to develop its customers (see Table 6.9). A separate calculation of a CRV from the LTV also allows acknowledging for the fact that the customers you acquire due to referrals have different GC.[4]

---

[3] For a discussion of degree centrality and betweenness see for example Lee, Catte, and Noseworthy (2010) or Kiss and Bichler (2008).

[4] Further illustrations and a practical application of the concept of CRV can be found in Kumar et al. (2007)

How to spur positive referrals

WOM agent campaigns, viral marketing, opinion leader programs, or referral reward programs are activities that companies can initiate to encourage its customers to make more referrals. But companies need to bear in mind that investments in these initiatives can only pay off if customers are satisfied with the product or service offering encountered.

Where does the information come from?

The information on GC, sales, direct cost, and marketing cost comes from internal company records. The key issue is that this information must be known on a per-customer basis. This knowledge is not necessarily common among many firms. An increasing number of firms are installing activity-based costing (ABC) schemes. ABC methods are used to arrive at appropriate allocations of customer and process-specific costs. The observation horizon (duration of customer relationship) T are derived either from managerial judgment or come from actual purchase data (see Sect. 5.4.6). The retention rates can be calculated from internal records and customer tracking (see Sect. 5.4.2). The interest rate is a function of a firm's cost of capital and can be obtained from the financial accounting department. Information on externalities such as number of referrals or WOM can be derived from social network analyses or customer surveys.

Evaluation

LTV (or CLV) is a forward looking metric that allows for long-term decision making. It is a flexible measure that has to be adapted to the specific business context of an industry. Each individual customer is evaluated on his expected contributions to the company. Yet, one has to bear in mind that all forecasts are subject to uncertainty. Being aware of the assumptions (especially for the prediction of the retention rate and GC) is important for the correct interpretation of LTV and in implementing the right actions. LTV is useful in a variety of situations as for example, to evaluate the effect of a loyalty program (or an investment in customer satisfaction) on the bottom line. Other applications comprise price discrimination of customers with low LTV, better treatment of high LTV customers (e.

g., Lufthansa Gold Card Members) or the decision on how much to pay for a click-through from an internet banner advertisement for new customer acquisition.

6.2.4 Customer Equity

Building on the definition of LTV, we can aggregate the LTV measure across customers. The resulting quantity is the customer equity (CE). This metric is an indicator of how much the firm is worth at a particular point in time as a result of the firm's customer management efforts.

$$CE = \sum_{i=1}^{I} LTV_i \qquad (6.10)$$

Where

i = customer

I = all customers of a firm (or a specified customer cohort or segment)

LTV_i = lifetime value of customer i

The CE is the sum of individual lifetime values of the customer base in net present value. In this case, the CE measure gives the economic value of an entire cohort or segment of customers. As CE is based on LTV this metric requires the allocation of revenues and costs on an individual customer level. One can relax this constraint by calculating the LTV of an average customer and take the sum of these average LTVs. This is further illustrated in the comprehensive example in Sect. 6.2.5.

Customer Equity Share (CES)

An alternative metric to MS that takes the lifetime value of customers into account is the customer equity share (CES). The CES for a brand j can be calculated using the following formula:

$$CES_j = \frac{CE_j}{\sum_{K=1}^{K} CE_k} \qquad (6.11)$$

Where

j = focal brand

K = all brands a firm offers

CE_j = customer equity of brand j

Where does the information come from?

- Basically the same information as for the LTV is required

Evaluation

The CE represents the value of the customer base to a company. This metric therefore can be seen as a link to the shareholder value of a firm. Besides the core elements of LTV (retention rate and GC), an important influencing factor for the CE is the proportion of profitable to unprofitable customers. In order to increase the CE management efforts should focus on increasing the number of highly profitable customers while reducing the number of unprofitable ones.

The CES is a relative measure of the value of a brand within a firm.

6.2.5 Comprehensive Example

The following example illustrates some aspects of the previously introduced LTV and customer equity models (see Table 6.10). The observation horizon for this example is 5 years (column 1). A company targets a list of 10,000 purchased addresses with an acquisition campaign. The company acquires 1,000 customers through the target mailing; thus, the acquisition rate is 10%. At the end of the first period only 400 of the 1,000 customers remain. Once acquired, a customer generates on average $120 in sales (column 2). For simplicity's sake, this level of sales is assumed to be constant over the lifetime of the customers. The margin of the firm is 30% (column 3), resulting in a constant gross margin (column 4). Marketing and service cost while alive are constant as well (column 5). The retention rate in the first period is 40% and then increases over time, as the loyal customers remain. The resulting number of remaining customers in each period is shown in column 8. The profit per customer (column 9) is computed by subtracting the marketing and service cost from the gross margin. This per-period contribution is discounted to present value with a yearly rate of 15% (column 10). Finally, the yearly discounted profit is multiplied with the number of remaining

Table 6.10 Customer equity calculation example

Year from acquisition	Sales per customer	Manufacturer margin	Manufacturer gross contribution	Marketing and servicing costs	Actual retention rate	Survival rate	Expected number of active customers	Profit per customer per period to manufacturer	Discounted profit per customer per period to manufacturer	Total discounted profits per period to manufacturer
0	120	0.3	36	20	0.4	0.4	400	16	16	6,400
1	120	0.3	36	20	0.63	0.25	250	16	14	3,500
2	120	0.3	36	20	0.75	0.187	187	16	12	2,244
3	120	0.3	36	20	0.82	0.153	153	16	11	1,683
4	120	0.3	36	20	0.85	0.131	131	16	9	1,179
Total customer equity										**15,006**

customers in each year. Then these values are summed up to the total customer equity of this group or cohort of customers (column 11).

6.3 Popular Customer Selection Strategies

Customer selection strategies are applied when firms want to target individual customers or groups of customers. The reason for targeting these customers can be manifold, for example, for sending out a promotion or inviting them to a special event. Finding the right targets for marketing resource allocation is at the heart of any CRM strategy. Smart targeting allows firms to spend resources judiciously and allows customers to receive messages relevant to them. Inconsiderate targeting actions destroy value by over- or under spending from the firm's perspective and by providing undesirable messages (junk mail). One step in the successful implementation of CRM is the smart deployment of targeting methodologies to maximize the benefits to firm and customer.

In particular we will discuss the techniques of *profiling*, *binary classification trees*, and *logistic regression* which can all be applied to binary (i. e., 0/1) outcome variables. To check the performance of each of these models, typically, two thirds of the available data are used to calculate the model and the remaining third is used as a hold-out sample for validation. At the end of this chapter we introduce the *misclassification rate* and *lift analysis*, which are simple techniques to compare the performance of two or more alternative models.

CRM at Work 6.1

Tesco

Tesco, the British supermarket chain has a very successful loyalty program in place, the Tesco Clubcard. In addition, the company has built up distinct analysis and targeting capabilities, which allow Tesco to customize its promotions to a large number of different segments. Consider the following case: Using the loyalty program, Tesco builds a market basket history for each cardholder. It can then analyze basket content, and, based, on the current basket, can propose certain items via its promotions. Tesco observed that a certain group of customers never buy meat from Tesco. The underlying hypothesis could be that these customers buy their meat from the local butcher because they believe its quality is superior to Tesco's. This would mean Tesco could send them coupons in order to entice them to buy Tesco's meat. However, a completely different interpretation could be that these customers are vegetarians. This, then, would mean if Tesco were to send them coupons, the company would basically show it doesn't really understand its customer. In reality, Tesco plays it safe and doesn't send any coupons for meat. They might forgo some purchases from those who do buy from the local butcher, but Tesco prefers to not harm the relationships with those who are vegetarian.

This is an example where a company combines analytical skills, judicious judgment, knowledge about consumer behavior, and careful targeting of customers. It also shows that targeting always happens in a business context and is not a mechanic activity.

6.3.1 Profiling

An intuitive approach to customer selection is to assume that the most profitable customers share common characteristics (i.e., profitable customers are similar to one-another). Based on this assumption the company should try to target customers with similar profiles to the currently most profitable ones. Depending on the intended goal (e.g., customer acquisition or direct-mail promotion to

existing customers) "most profitable" can have different meanings, e.g., the customers who are most likely to respond to a direct-mail promotion. In the latter case RFM (see Sect. 6.2.1) is widely used in practice for profiling. An alternative is to use available demographics instead of recency, frequency, or monetary value to sort and group the customer base. For the identification of variables that best characterize profitable customers classification trees or regression models can be used. A disadvantage of profiling is that only customers are considered for targeting that are similar to the existing ones. Profitable customer segments that do not match the current customer base might be missed.

Example: Consider the case of a bank which wants to acquire new, profitable customers. Profiling consists of identifying profitable customers in the bank's current mass-market segment and then to target similar profiles in the prospect pool.

Since the objective is to acquire prospects likely to be high-value customers, the bank must rely on customer characteristics common to both current customers (the basis for establishing the critical profile) and the prospects (scored on the basis of their profile). The process is shown in the Fig. 6.8.

Let's say the response variable for current customers is the GC (field A). The company sorted customers by GC and chose to profile the top 20% of customers. Transaction information (field B) is not available for prospects. This is why the bank has to rely on information available for both existing customers and prospects. One type of information is geodemographic data, such as socioeconomic status of a region, average age, type of housing, and so on. These data are provided from direct marketing agencies that specialize in the collection of geodemographics. They can be purchased and then appended to individual records of existing customers. That is, depending on name or ZIP code, geodemographic data are added to existing customer records. The model attempts to predict GC as the dependent variable with geodemographic information as the independent

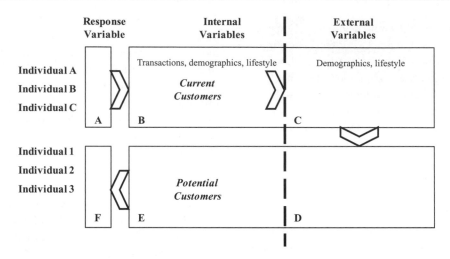

Fig. 6.8 Using profiling for new customer acquisition

Table 6.11 Classification of potential hockey equipment buyers

	Male		Female		Total	
	Bought hockey	Did not buy hockey	Bought hockey	Did not buy hockey	Bought hockey	Did not buy hockey
Bought scuba	60	1,140	50	1,550	110	2,690
Did not buy scuba	1,540	2,860	80	1,320	1,620	4,180
Total	1,600	4,000	130	2,870	1,730	6,870

variables. The rationale behind this process is to find the profile that best characterizes high-value clients, which is subsequently applied to prospects' information. Finally, prospects with a high expected GC are targeted for the acquisition campaign.

6.3.2 Binary Classification Trees

Using classification (or decision) trees is a methodology that can be used for finding the best predictors of a 0/1 dependent variable. For example, a company wants to know the differential demographic characteristics of loyalty program members versus nonmembers. Classification trees are especially useful when there is a large set of potential predictors for a model. In such a case, it may be difficult to determine which predictors are the most important or what the relationships between the predictors and the target (dependent) variable are.

Classification tree algorithms can be used to iteratively search through the data to find out which predictor best separates the two categories of a binary (or more generally categorical) target variable.

Classification Tree Algorithm

Assume that Y is a binary outcome variable, i.e., $Y \in \{0,1\}$, explained by a set of explanatory variables $X_1, \ldots, X_p$ which are also binary.[5] The algorithm proceeds as follows: (1) To find out which of the explanatory variables X_i best explains the outcome Y, calculate the number of misclassifications (i.e., the number of not correctly predicted outcomes, for example if you want to predict credit card ownership and use

---

[5] If X_i is not binary one can find an optimal (in the sense that it best separates Y on the basis of classification of X_i) cutoff point to divide the domain of X_i in two parts and thus reduce X_i to a binary variable. For a further discussion see Hastie, Tibshirani, and Friedman (2009)

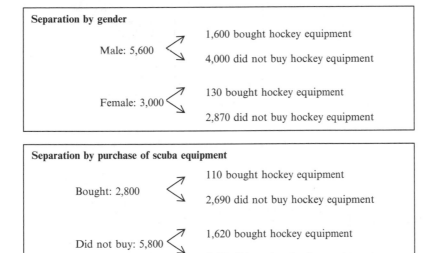

Fig. 6.9 Possible separations of potential hockey equipment buyers

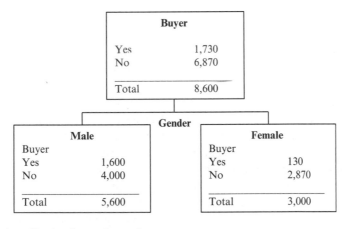

Fig. 6.10 Classification of hockey buyers by gender

gender as the predictor variable the misclassification rate is the number of male persons that do not own a credit card plus the number of female persons that do own a credit card) for each predictor variable X_i. (2) Use the variable X_i with the lowest misclassification rate[6] to separate the customer base. (3) This process can be repeated for each sub segment, until the misclassification rate drops below a tolerable threshold or all of the predictors have been applied to the model.

Example: Consider customer data for purchases of hockey equipment from a sporting goods catalog. For simplicity, there are only two predictor variables given, gender and whether a customer has previously bought scuba equipment (see Table 6.11). There are 8,600 customers in total. 1,730 bought the hockey equipment, 3,000 are female and 5,600 are male. It is also known that of the 8,600 customers 2,800 have bought scuba equipment in the past and 5,800 have not bought scuba equipment.

Step 1. To determine the optimum approach how to separate the customers, we calculate the number of misclassifications for both predictor variables (gender and scuba equipment;

---

[6] A discussion of further optimal splitting rules can be found in Blattberg, Kim, and Neslin (2008).

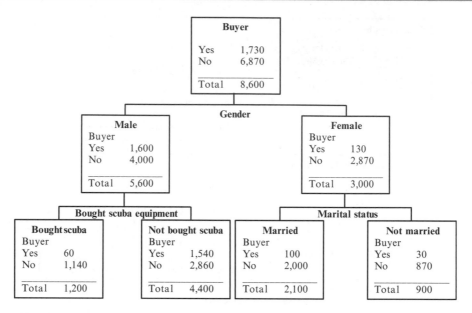

Fig. 6.11 Classification tree for hockey equipment buyers

see Fig. 6.9). Using gender as predictor of hockey sales we assume that all male persons buy hockey equipment, whereas no female buys. For the predictor variable gender we get a misclassification rate of (4,000 + 130)/ 8,600 = 0.48. When using the scuba equipment predictor variable (everyone who bought scuba is going to buy hockey equipment) we obtain (2,690 + 1,620)/8,600 = 0.50. Thus, separating the customers based on gender is the optimal first step.

Step 2. We split the customer base by gender to obtain the classification tree as depicted in Fig. 6.10.

Step 3. If further predictor variables were available besides the scuba indicator, we could continue to identify the optimal predictor for separation in each subsegment and restart with step 1. For example, we could find that it is best to separate female customers by marital status and male customers by whether they have bought scuba equipment. The resulting tree could look like Fig. 6.11.

When this process is complete, a tree has developed in which segments are nested within segments. The profitable segments can then be identified for use as target markets.

Evaluation

One problem with the decision tree approach is that it is prone to overfitting, whereby segments are tailored to very small segments, (based upon the dataset that was used to create the tree) and as a result, the model developed will not perform nearly as well on a separate dataset. A hold out sample (typically 1/3 of the data set, not used for model calibration) can be used for model validation (see Sect. 6.4). If the results show a large discrepancy with what was expected, then the model will need to be reevaluated. If the results are within the range of what is predicted from the model, it is likely that the model is a good fit.

6.3.3 Logistic Regression

Linear regression starts with the specification of the dependent variable and the independent variable. For example the number of people entering a store on a Saturday is the dependent variable of interest and the amount of money the store spent on advertising on Friday is the independent variable. We expect to see a linear relationship between the two variables. A regression analysis

Fig. 6.12 Comparison of linear and logistic regression

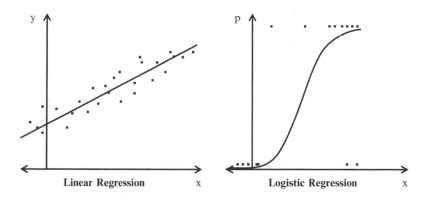

Linear Regression   x   Logistic Regression   x

creates an estimate of the coefficient that represents the effect of advertising on store traffic. In this situation we note that store traffic (the dependent variable) can take on a large range of values. However, in marketing we often encounter situations where the dependent variable is binary. For example, in a situation where we are interested in whether a customer bought a product or not, we assign the value 0 to this variable when the customer does not buy, and the value 1 when the customer buys. Regression models that allow for such a data structure are linear probability models, probit models, and logit models. Logit models also referred to as *logistic regression* are the most frequently applied method when the dependent variable is binary and assumes only two discrete values. For example:

- Whether a customer responded to a marketing campaign or not
- Whether a person bought a car or not

These observed values for the dependent variable take on only two values and are usually represented using a 0–1 dummy variable. The mean of a 0–1 dummy variable is equal to the proportion of observations with a value of 1, and can be interpreted as a probability. Furthermore, the predicted values in a logistic regression fall between 0 and 1 and are also interpreted as probabilities. For example, home ownership as a function of income can be modeled whereby ownership is delineated by a 1 and non ownership by 0. The predicted value based on the model is interpreted as the probability that the individual is a home-owner. With a positive correlation between increasing income and increas-

ing probability of ownership, we can expect to see results where the predicted probability of ownership is, for example, 0.22 for a person with an income of \$35,000, and 0.95 for a person with a \$250,000 income.

Example: Consider the upgrade of a credit card. Logistic regression can be used to identify potential targets for marketing credit card offers to existing customers of a bank.

- Dependent variable – whether or not the customer signed up for a gold card offer
- Predictor variables – other bank services the customer used plus financial and demographic customer information

The goal is to estimate the logistic regression on a sample of customers that were offered a gold card. Inputting values of the predictor variables for each potential target customer, the logistic model will yield a predicted probability for the target customer to sign up for the gold card offer. Customers with high predicted probabilities may be chosen to receive the offer because they seem more likely to respond positively.

Dots represent observations of the dependent variable y. In case of linear regression y can take any value whereas in case of logistic regression y is either 0 or 1. The logistic regression curve reflects the predicted probability p of the event y at given levels of x.

Mathematically, linear regression takes the form

$$y = \alpha + \beta x + \varepsilon$$

Where
y = dependent variable
x = predictor variable
α = constant (which is estimated by linear regression and often called intercept)
β = the effect of x on y (also estimated by linear regression)
ε = error term

In this sort of regression, y can take on any value between negative infinity and positive infinity. However, as we noted earlier, in many instances we observe only binary activity represented by 0 or 1. Sample plots of observations with fitted linear and logistic regression curves are illustrated in Fig. 6.12. Hence, if the actually observed dependent variable has to be constrained between 0 and 1 to indicate the probability of an event occurring, a transformation is necessary. This transformation is the basis of logistic regression. The steps of the transformation are given as follows:

Step 1. If p represents the probability of an event occurring, consider the ratio $\frac{p}{1-p}$. Since p is a positive quantity less than 1, the range of this expression is 0 to infinity.

Step 2. Take the logarithm of this ratio

$$log\left(\frac{p}{1-p}\right)$$

This transformation allows the range of values for this expression to lie between negative infinity and positive infinity.

Step 3. The value

$$z = log\left(\frac{p}{1-p}\right)$$

can now be considered as the dependent variable. A linear relationship of this value with predictor variables in the form $z = \alpha + \beta x + \varepsilon$ can be written out. The α and β coefficients can be estimated by maximum likelihood implemented in standard software packages.

Step 4. In order to obtain the predicted probability p, the following back transformation is necessary:

Table 6.12 Sample data for contract extension and sales

Contract extension	Number of sales calls
1	2
1	4
0	6
0	2
1	4
1	8
0	3
0	0
0	2
0	5
0	0
1	2
1	8
1	4

Table 6.13 Odds of logistic regression example

	Sales calls = 0	Sales calls = 1
Odds (exp($\alpha + \beta$*sales calls))	0.253	0.375
Probability of contract extension	0.202	0.273
Difference in probabilities	0.071	

Since

$$log\left(\frac{p}{1-p}\right) = z = \alpha + \beta x + \varepsilon$$

we can write

$$\left(\frac{p}{1-p}\right) = e^z$$

This allows us to calculate the probability p of an event occurring, the variable of interest, as

$$p = \left(\frac{e^z}{1+e^z}\right) = \left(\frac{1}{1+e^{-z}}\right) \quad (6.12)$$

Interpretation of coefficients
Care has to be taken when interpreting the coefficients. The interpretation of coefficients differs

from simple linear regression. If the logit regression coefficient $\beta = 2.303$ then the log odds ratio is

$$e^{\beta} = e^{2.303} = 10,$$

which says that when the independent variable x increases one unit, the odds that the dependent variable equals 1 increases by a factor of 10, keeping all other variables constant. Usually, besides the coefficients, "odds" are reported, i.e.,

$$\left(\frac{p}{1-p}\right) = e^{z}$$

is called the "odds" and represents the chance of an event occurring to the chance of the event not occurring, where p is the probability of the event.

Example: Consider the extension of a service contract in a B2B setting. The service company wants to know the probability that a client extends his existing contract. Therefore, it tracks the number of sales calls and whether a client extends his contract (see Table 6.12).

It expects that the sales calls impact the probability of contract extension. Thus, it estimates the model:

$$Prob\,(contract\;extension)$$

$$= \frac{1}{1 + e^{-\alpha - \beta(sales\,calls)}} \quad (6.13)$$

The resulting estimates are $\alpha = -1.37$ and $\beta = 0.39$. The odds and the probability of extension are illustrated in Table 6.13. In this example the odds represent the relative likelihood that a customer will extend his contract to not extending his contract. If no sales calls are made the odds are 0.253 and in case of a sales call the odds are 0.375. The log-odds are $e^{0.39} = 1.477$ meaning that for each additional sales call the odds for contract extension change by a factor of 1.477. The probabilities of contract extension are 0.202 and 0.273 for no and for one sales call, respectively. Thus, the difference in probabilities for a contract extension of making one sales call over not making a call is 0.07. Note that the difference of an additional sales call is not constant. For

example making four instead of three sales calls changes the probability for a contract extension by 0.098.

Evaluation

Unlike in linear regression where the effect of one unit change in the independent variable on the dependent variable is assumed to be a constant represented by the slope of a straight line, for logistic regression the effect of a one-unit increase in the predictor variable varies along an s-shaped curve (see Fig. 6.12). This means that at the extremes, a one-unit change has very little effect, but in the center a one-unit change has a fairly large effect. In the case of the income versus home ownership example, the difference in the likelihood that an individual owns a home may not change much as income increases from $10,000 to $30,000 or from $1,000,000 to $1,020,000, but may increase considerably if income increases from $50,000 to $70,000.

6.4 Techniques to Evaluate Alternative Customer Selection Strategies

A critical step to decide which model to use to select and target potential customers is to evaluate alternative selection strategies. When several alternative models are available for customer selection, we need to compare their relative quality of prediction. To compare the predictive capabilities of models, we typically divide the data into a training (calibration) dataset (2/3 of the data) and a holdout (test) sample (1/3 of the data). The models are estimated based on the training dataset. Using these estimates predictions are made for the holdout data. We can then compare the predictive performance of the models. Some models will have more predictive power than others, and we will select the model that generalizes best from the training to the test data.

The most common way to assess a model's performance is by comparing their respective misclassification rates obtained on the test set. An alternative method for getting an idea about model performance is lift analysis.

6.4.1   Misclassification Rate

To obtain the misclassification rate, we estimate the different models on two thirds of the available data and calculate the misclassification rate on the remaining third to check the model performance. The misclassification rate is the number of false predictions divided by the total number of predictions made.

A misclassification error rate or confusion matrix could look like Table 6.14. The number of false predictions is the sum of the off-diagonal entries (56 + 173 = 229). Thus, the misclassification rate in this example is 229/1,459 = 15.7%.

6.4.2   LIFT Analysis

A lift chart shows how much better the current model performs against the results expected if no model was used (base model). This gives a baseline measure of how good the model is. As an example, consider 1,000 prospects, of which 100 have purchased. A good predictive model helps increase the relative amount of purchasers in the selected group: a random-based selection of 100 prospects would contain about 10 purchasers, whereas a model-based selection of 100 prospects could result in 30 purchasers. This is what lift charts help to visualize. The models with the highest lift are candidates for final selection.

Lifts can be used to compare two or more alternative models, track a model's performance over time, or to compare a model's performance on different samples. To calculate lifts for different deciles of data, we need the following information about a model with regard to the set of customer data.

Table 6.14 Confusion matrix

		Predicted		
		1	0	Totals
Observed	1	726	56	782
	0	173	504	677
Totals		899	560	1,459

- Cumulative number of customers: The number of total customers up to and including that decile
- Cumulative percentage of customers: The percent of total customers up to and including that decile
- Cumulative number of buyers: The number of buyers up to and including that decile
- Actual response rate for each decile: computed by dividing the number of buyers by the number of customers for each decile
- OR predicted response rate based on the model for each decile: computed by dividing the predicted number of buyers by the number of customers for each decile

With this information we can calculate:

$$Lift\% = (\text{Response rate for each decile}) \div (\text{Overall response rate})^* 100$$

and

$$Cumulative\ lift\% = (\text{Cumulative response rate}) \div (\text{Overall response rate})^* 100$$

Where

$$Cumulative\ response\ rate = \text{Cumulative number of buyers} \div \text{Number of customers per decile.}$$

A comprehensive example is given in Table 6.15.

Lift Performance Illustration

Initially, the model (such as RFM, or logistic regression) which one wants to evaluate needs to be run and the customer base should be sorted accordingly. On the basis of the sorted customer list, customers are distributed into 10 equal-sized groups (see Table 6.15). In a model that performs well, customers in the first decile exhibit the highest response rate and the response rate continuously drops as we proceed along the deciles. (see Fig. 6.13)

For the top decile in this case, the lift is 3.09 (see Fig. 6.14). This indicates that by targeting

Table 6.15 Lift and cumulative lift

Number of decile	Number of customers	Number of buyers	Response rate (%)	Lift	Cumulative lift
1	5,000	1,759	35.18	3.09	3.09
2	5,000	1,126	22.52	1.98	5.07
3	5,000	998	19.96	1.75	6.82
4	5,000	554	11.08	0.97	7.80
5	5,000	449	8.98	0.79	8.59
6	5,000	337	6.74	0.59	9.18
7	5,000	221	4.42	0.39	9.57
8	5,000	113	2.26	0.20	9.76
9	5,000	89	1.78	0.16	9.92
10	5,000	45	0.90	0.08	10.00
Total	50,000	5,691	11.38		

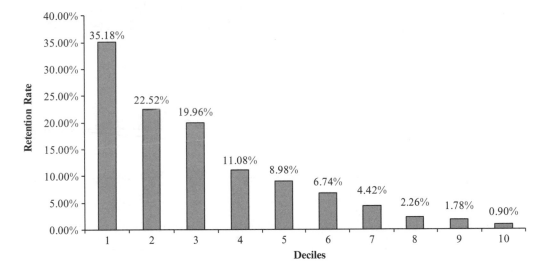

Fig. 6.13 Decile analysis

only these customers we would expect to yield 3.09 times the number of buyers found by randomly mailing the same number of customers. In contrast, the last decile (decile 10) attracts only 0.08 times the number of buyers as one would expect in a random sample of the same size. Lifts that exceed 1 indicate better than average performance of that particular decile, and those that are less than 1 indicate a poorer than average performance. Also keep in mind that lift is a relative index to a baseline measure, in this case the average response rate for the entire sample.

The cumulative lifts for the model in Fig. 6.15 reveal the proportion of responders we can expect to gain from targeting a specific percent of customers using the model. If we choose the customers from the top three deciles (i.e., the top 30% of the customers), we will obtain 68% of the total responders. The larger the distance between the model and no model lines, the stronger or more powerful is the model. The slope of the cumulative lift curve reflects the lift. In a nutshell, lifts can be used to compare two or more alternative models, track a model's performance

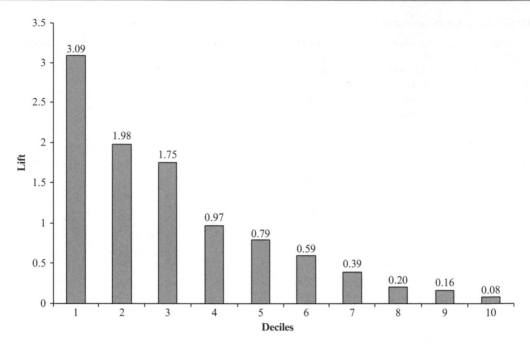

Fig. 6.14 Lift analysis

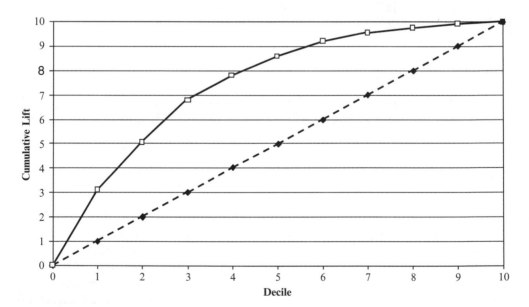

Fig. 6.15 Cumulative lift analysis

over time, or to compare a model's performance on different samples.

Past experience shows that logistic models tend to provide the best lift performance when used as a tool for customer selection. This is seen from the topmost curve in the lift chart in Fig. 6.16. The model is better able to identify the best customers and group them in the first few deciles. The past customer value approach provides the next best performance, whereas the

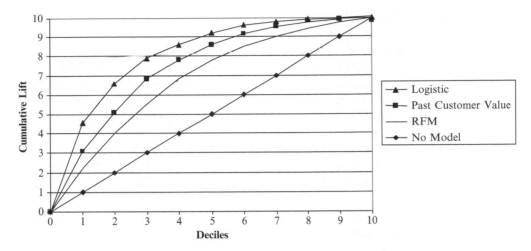

Fig. 6.16 Model comparison using lift analysis

traditional RFM approach, though by no means redundant, exhibits the poorest performance.

6.5 Summary

Since customer value management involves allocating resources differently for individual customers based on their economic value, understanding value contribution from each of the customers to the firm is very important. The availability of customer-level data helps firms utilize a new set of metrics beyond traditional and popular marketing metrics introduced in Chap. 5. These strategic customer-based metrics enable the assignment of value to each individual customer.

Popular strategic customer-based value metrics are RFM, past customer value, lifetime value, and customer equity. RFM is a composite score of recency, frequency, and monetary value. Two methods used for computing and applying RFM are sorting techniques and calculation of relative weights for R, F, and M. In the sorting technique the RFM values are assigned for each customer by sequential sorting based on the RFM metrics and then used to group customers, belonging to specific RFM codes. However, this method might not produce an equal number of customers under each RFM cell. A hierarchical sorting technique ensures equal numbers in each RFM cell. This is done by first sorting the list of customers by

recency and dividing them into equal groups. Each of these groups is then sorted based on frequency and divided into groups of equal size. Each of these subgroups is sorted on monetary value and divided into groups of equal size. This way, each RFM cell will have an equal number of customers. An alternate method for RFM metric uses linear regression to arrive at the relative weights of the R, F, and M metrics, and these relative weights are used to compute the RFM score of each customer. The higher the computed RFM score, the more profitable the customer is likely to be in the future. This method has the advantage of being flexible, so that it can be tailored to each business situation. In order to decide which RFM cells to target the breakeven value (BE) and break even index (BEI) can be calculated for each RFM cell. With respect to a promotion, breakeven refers to the fact that the net profit from a marketing promotion equals the cost associated with conducting the promotion. The BE can be used in computing a BEI, calculated as Breakeven index (BEI) = ([Actual response rate − BE]/BE) × 100. A positive BEI indicates some profit was made from the transaction. A BEI value of 0 indicates the transaction only broke even, and a negative BEI value indicates the transaction resulted in a loss.

Another important customer-based metric is past customer value (PCV), in which the value of a customer is determined based on the total contribution (toward profits) provided by the customer in the past after adjusting for the time value of money. The lifetime value (LTV), in contrast, reflects the long-term economic value of a customer and is calculated as the sum of the discounted expected contribution margins over the respective observation horizon. The contribution margin can be computed knowing the values of sales, direct costs, and marketing costs. The sum of the lifetime value of all the customers of a firm represents the customer equity (CE) of a firm. It is an indicator of how much the firm is worth at a particular point in time as a result of the firm's customer management efforts. This metric therefore can be seen as a link to the shareholder value of a firm.

Firms employ different customer selection strategies to target the right customers. Some of the popular customer selection strategies are profiling, binary classification trees, and logistic regression. Profiling rests on the assumption that profitable customers share common characteristics. Profiling consists of identifying profitable customers in the existing customer base and then to target similar customers from the prospect pool. The construction of binary classification trees relies on a recursive partitioning algorithm used for finding the predictors which best separate the two categories of a binary (0/1) dependent variable. To avoid over fitting, this search is performed on two thirds of the available data with one third of the data reserved for testing the eventual model that will be developed. Logistic regression is a statistical tool to predict the probability of a binary outcome using predictor variables.

To evaluate alternative selection strategies, firms can use techniques such as misclassification rates and lift analysis. The misclassification rate is the number of false predictions divided by the total number of predictions made. Lifts indicate how much better a model performs than no model or average performance, and are calculated as (Response rate for each decile) ÷ (Overall response rate) × 100. Based on lifts we can perform a decile analysis. Therefore, customers are sorted based on the model to be evaluated and grouped into deciles. For a good model, customers in the first deciles have a significantly higher response rate. Cumulative lift is calculated as (Cumulative response rate) ÷ (Overall response rate) * 100. It reveals the proportion of responders we can expect to gain from targeting a specific percent of customers using the model.

6.6 Exercise Questions

1. A hotel chain wants to analyze its customer base with RFM. Describe the data fields (variables) in the database necessary to do this.
2. Whatever RFM analysis can do, regression analysis can do as well. Evaluate this statement.
3. How will you use lift charts to determine future marketing action?
4. Describe three business situations where you would consider using logistic regression as the preferred technique for analysis and decision making.
5. What is the link between customer lifetime value and the profitability of an organization?

Differentiating Customer Service According to Customer Value at Akzo Nobel NL

Akzo Nobel, headquartered in Arnhem, Netherlands, is one of the worlds largest chemical manufacturers and also one of the world's largest paint makers. Its chemical unit produces pulp and paper chemicals, functional chemicals (including flame retardants and animal feed additives), surfactants (used in detergents and personal care products), polymers, and catalysts. The polymer division, which serves exclusively the B-to-B market, established a tiered customer-service policy in the early 2000s. The necessity to introduce this policy came out of the recognition that customers are becoming more and more demanding when it comes to asking for additional services around the purchase of polymer products. For example, customers became increasingly aware that Akzo

Nobel offers product disposal services, delivers nonstandard pallet sizes, and offers negotiable delivery times. On the one hand, Akzo Nobel did not typically charge for these services, and on the other hand, while extended services were typically offered only to medium- to high-volume clients, the relationship between service offerings and client profitability was not clear. When Akzo Nobel investigated more closely who received the service offerings, it found the correlation with client profitability (i.e., contribution margin) was very low. This finding led to the development of a formal *tiered service-level framework* within the polymer division.

In the first step, the company developed a thorough list of all possible service activities the company currently offers. Interestingly, the sales force provided a significant number of these services with little further consideration. Since the sales force was compensated on the sales volume it generated, it had all the incentive to lure in clients with little consideration for bottom-line results. Concurrently, to formalize customer service activities, the company implemented a customer scorecard mechanism. The scorecard allowed it to measure and document contribution margins per individual customer. Based on these two pieces of information, the organization then specified which customer type should be eligible for which type of service. In terms of service allocation, it designated certain services would be free for all types of customers, certain services would be subject to negotiation for lower-level customer groups, another set of services would be subject to fees for lower-level customers, and finally, certain services would not be available for the least valuable set of customers. Although the sales force was not very happy at first with these new measures, the new policy had a dramatic impact on the sales force understanding of the drivers of customer profitability.

Questions

1. How can an organization compute client-level profitability?
2. What types of systems and processes are needed to document client profitability in a systematic and ongoing fashion?
3. Is there a way to move established clients accustomed to receiving a large number of ancillary services for free to paying for these services?

Appendix I

Notation Key

Notation	Explanation
a	Coefficient of acquisition
AC	Acquisition costs
ACS	Acquisition costs savings
Ar	Acquisition rate
c	Category
CE	Customer equity
Dr	Defection rate
GC	Gross contribution
i	Individual customer
I	Total number of buyers with a focal firm
j	Firm
J	Total number of firms in a market
LTV	Lifetime value
MC	Marketing costs
n	Customer in cohort
N	Cohort size
r	Coefficient of retention
Rr	Retention rate
Rr_c	Retention rate ceiling
S	Sales (value)
Sr	Survival rate
t	Time period
T	Length of time horizon
V	Sales (volume)
δ	Applicable discount rate

Appendix II

Regression Scoring Models

Scoring models is the process of evaluating potential customer behavior on the basis of test results. Typically, a test is conducted in a limited market or in an experimental set up on a small subset of customers. This subset of customers is exposed to a marketing campaign and a product offering. The purpose of this test is to assign to each of the remaining customers a value which is extrapolated from the results of this test. These values typically reflect the prospective customer's likelihood of purchasing the test marketed product. The process of regression scoring can be represented in the following steps:

1. Draw a random sample from the overall population of prospective customers.
2. Obtain data from the sample that profiles individual consumer characteristics. The R, F, and M scores are variables which profile behavioral characteristics of a customer and are

typically used in this procedure, along with other relevant variables.

3. Initiate a marketing campaign directed at the random sample, and record the individuals who become customers.
4. With that information, develop a regression scoring model to obtain a series of weighted variables that either predict which prospects are more likely to become customers or the value of profits that each customer is likely to provide, based on their individual characteristics.
5. By applying these weights to individual characteristics of prospective customers, we can arrive at a value for each customer which indicates how likely it is that the customer will purchase a product, or how much profit the customer will generate, if exposed to the tested marketing campaign.

Appendix III

Cell #	RFM codes	Cost per mail ($)	Net profit per sale ($)	Breakeven (%)	Actual response (%)	Breakeven index
1	111	1	45	2.22	17.55	690
2	112	1	45	2.22	17.45	685
3	113	1	45	2.22	17.35	681
4	114	1	45	2.22	17.25	676
5	115	1	45	2.22	17.15	572
6	121	1	45	2.22	17.05	667
...						
52	312	1	45	2.22	12.91	481
53	313	1	45	2.22	0.98	−56
54	314	1	45	2.22	0.94	−58
55	375	1	45	2.22	0.90	−60
56	321	1	45	2.22	0.136	−61
57	322	1	45	2.22	0.82	−63
58	323	1	45	2.22	0.78	−65
...						
75	355	1	45	2.22	−0.15	−107
76	411	1	45	2.22	11.25	−107
77	412	1	45	2.22	11.22	406
78	413	1	45	2.22	0.55	405
79	414	1	45	2.22	0.52	−75
80	415	1	45	2.22	0.49	−77

(continued)

Cell #	RFM codes	Cost per mail ($)	Net profit per sale ($)	Breakeven (%)	Actual response (%)	Breakeven index
. . .						
100	455	1	45	2.22	−0.11	−105
101	511	1	45	2.22	10.88	390
102	512	1	45	2.22	10.85	388
103	513	1	45	2.22	0.78	−65
104	514	1	45	2.22	0.73	−67
105	515	1	45	2.22	0.70	−69
106	521	1	45	2.22	0.67	−70
. . .						
120	545	1	45	2.22	0.25	−89
121	551	1	45	2.22	0.22	−90
122	552	1	45	2.22	0.19	−91
123	553	1	45	2.22	0.10	−96
124	554	1	45	2.22	0.01	−100
125	555	1	45	2.22	−0.08	−104

References

Aaker, D. A., Kumar, V., & Day, G. S. (2003). *Marketing research* (8th ed.). New York: John Wiley & Sons.

Berger, P. D., & Nasr, N. (1998). Customer lifetime value: Marketing models and applications. *Journal of Interactive Marketing, 12*(1), 17–30.

Blattberg, R., Kim, B. D., & Neslin, S. A. (2008). *Database marketing – Analyzing and managing customers.* New York: Springer. 427ff.

Hastie, T., Tibshirani, R., & Friedman, J. (2009). *Elements of statistical learning – Data mining, inference, and prediction* (2nd ed.). Stanford: Springer.

Jackson, D. R. (1992). In quest of the grail: Breaking the barriers to customer valuation. *Direct Marketing, 54* (11), 44 48.

Jain, D., & Singh, S. (2002). Customer lifetime value research in marketing: A review and future directions. *Journal of Interactive Marketing, 16*(2), 34–46.

Kiss, C., & Bichler, M. (2008). Identification of influencer – Measuring influence in customer networks. *Decision Support Systems, 46*(1), 233–253.

Kumar, V., Petersen, J. A., & Leone, R. P. (2007). How valuable is word of mouth. *Harvard Business Review, 85*(10), 139–146.

Lee, S. H., Catte, J., & Noseworthy, T. J. (2010). The role of network centrality in the flow of consumer influence. *Journal of Consumer Psychology, 20*(1), 66–77.

Data Mining

7.1 Overview

The way in which companies interact with their customers has changed dramatically over the past few years. Customers' expectations have risen, and it is becoming increasingly difficult to satisfy them. Customers have access to an array of alternative products to choose from and their loyalty is difficult to gain. At the same time, companies need to retain the profitable customers to succeed in a competitive and dynamic marketplace. As a result, companies have found they need to understand their customers better, and to respond to their wants and needs faster. The time frame in which these responses need to be made has been shrinking. More customers, more products, more competitors, and less time to react means understanding the customers is now much harder to do.

To succeed, companies must be proactive and anticipate customer desires. Many firms have realized this and are collecting information about their customers and their preferences. Firms collect, store, and process vast amounts of highly detailed information about customers, markets, products, and processes through different programs. Data mining this information gives businesses the ability to make knowledge-driven strategic business decisions to help predict future trends and behaviors and create new opportunities. Data mining can assist in selecting the right target customers or in identifying (previously unknown) customer segments with similar behaviors and needs.

This chapter describes the importance and benefits of data mining and gives a detailed overview of the underlying process. The data-mining procedure breaks down into five subsections: defining the business objectives, getting the raw data, identifying relevant variables, gaining customer insight, and acting. The discussion of these steps will help the reader understand the overall process of data mining. The process steps are illustrated with the case study of Credite Est (name disguised), a French mid-tier bank. Finally, the case study, "Yapi Kredi—Predictive Model–Based cross-sell Campaign," shows a comprehensive application of data mining.

7.1.1 The Need for Data Mining

Today, most companies do not suffer from lack of data about their customers, products, transactions, and markets. To the contrary, *data deluge* is a problem in many companies. This is especially challenging for information-intensive businesses, such as banking, telecommunication, and e-commerce, where large amounts of data can easily be recorded. The sheer amount of raw data is, for many, an obstacle to using it for extracting knowledge and for making critical business decisions. By default, educated guessing becomes the primary decision-making tool. It does not have to be that way.

Availability of computers and mass storage, statistical and data analysis methods, sophisticated reporting platforms, and online touch

V. Kumar and W. Reinartz, *Customer Relationship Management*, Springer Texts in Business and Economics, DOI 10.1007/978-3-642-20110-3_7, © Springer-Verlag Berlin Heidelberg 2012

points with customers, now give companies access to a powerful asset: information. Data have become a company's most important—and in many cases, untapped—asset. To extract customer intelligence and value from that data, companies must implement a standardized data-mining procedure. A successful data-mining infrastructure consists of technology, human skills, and tight integration with enterprise operations to allow transforming new knowledge into business action and value. It is important to standardize the data-mining process to assure the required quality of results, make it a repeatable process, better maintain and keep the knowledge inside the company, as well as training new employees more quickly.

7.1.2 The Business Value of Data Mining

In the context of customer management, data mining can help to gain a better understanding of customers and their needs. Marketing is still frequently associated only with creative and soft skills. But by scientifically enhancing targeting, we can obtain more impressive cost reductions and revenue growth than by working only with the creative aspects of marketing. Data mining can assist in selecting the right target customers or in identifying (previously unknown) customer segments with similar behaviors and needs. A good target list developed by using data-mining techniques is likely to increase purchase rates and have a positive impact on revenue.

Applications of data mining include the following:

- Reducing churn with the help of predictive models (see Sect. 7.3), which enable early identification of those customers likely to stop doing business with your company
- Increasing customer profitability by identifying customers with a high growth potential
- Reducing marketing costs by more selective targeting

This chapter introduces a systematic approach to data-mining projects.

7.2 The Data-Mining Process

A complete data-mining process does not *only* consist of building analytical models using techniques such as logistic regression (see Sect. 7.3.3). It includes assessing and specifying the business objectives, data sourcing, transformation, creation of analytical variables, selecting relevant variables, training predictive models, selecting the best suited model, and acting on the basis of the findings. These activities can be grouped into five process steps of defining the business objectives, getting raw data, indentifying relevant variables, gaining customer insight, and acting. Figure 7.1 presents an overview of the data-mining process.

In many instances of current data-mining projects we find data preparation steps easily take from 60% to 70% of the total project time. This is not due to the weaknesses of any specific data-mining methodology. It is due to issues regarding unavailability of relevant variables describing customer behavior. An example of which is the difficult access to legacy data source systems managed by different departments which do not possess the customer centric views required for data mining projects. These departments are more likely geared towards transaction, product, contract, or other type of views more suited to fulfill the needs of their current operational systems. The graph shown in Fig. 7.2 helps to understand the timeframe of the individual steps of the data-mining process.

It is important to automate the time-consuming data extraction and manipulation, as well as the data quality monitoring and enhancement steps. To achieve this goal, it is necessary to sequentially and systematically code data knowledge into programs that can be executed, for instance, in batch mode. This will free up time of highly qualified quantitative data analysts (data miners) to concentrate on the value-generating tasks such as the precise definition of business objectives, extraction of customer insight, and effective actions based on gained knowledge.

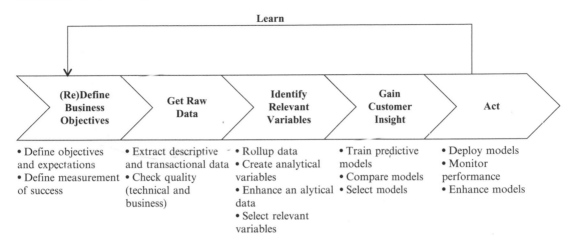

Fig. 7.1 Overview of the data-mining process

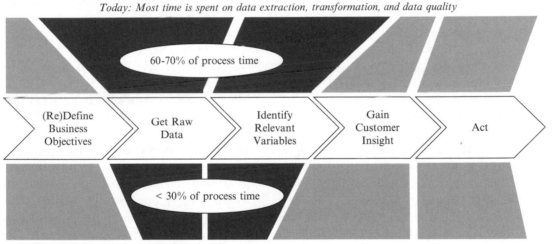

Tomorrow: Most time is spent on business objectives and customer insight

Fig. 7.2 Allocation of time for the steps in the data-mining process

Involvement of Resources

Usually, different functional departments are involved in data mining projects. The main groups are the business group (e.g., marketing, product management), data mining, and IT. The business group is primarily involved in defining business objectives, and takes the lead when it comes to deploying the new insights into corporate action. The data-mining group must understand the business objectives and support the business group in refining and sometimes correcting the scope of the project and aligning their expectations to fit the limitations posed by the available data. The data-mining group is most active during the variable selection and modeling phase. It will share the obtained customer insights with the business group, who are strongly involved at this point to check the plausibility and soundness of the solution in business terms. IT resources are required for the sourcing and extraction of the required data used for modeling. Figure 7.3 shows the extent of involvement of the three main groups participating in a data-mining project—business, data mining, and IT—during the different process steps.

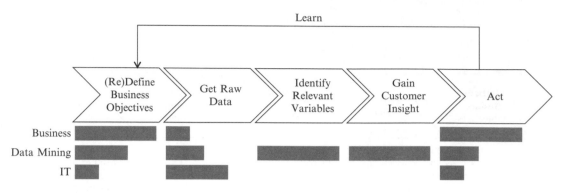

Fig. 7.3 Level of involvement of business, data mining, and IT resources in a typical data-mining project

Data Manipulation

As we move through the data-mining process, the dimensionality of the data used may change dramatically. In a simple, two-dimensional data table we think of the columns as being the descriptive variables and the rows as being single observations, each pertaining to a collection of variables about the same primary object (e.g., customer identification number, transaction identification number).

Manipulations on columns can take several forms:

- *Transformation*. Transform birth date to age.
- *Derivation*. Create new variables based on existing ones (e.g., compute monthly profits from sales and cost information).
- *Elimination*. A whole variable may be excluded from further processing due to a variety of possible reasons (e.g., a variable that does not help in predicting or a variable that is correlated to one or more variables already in the model could be eliminated).

The number of variables used changes drastically during the data-mining process. Figure 7.4 illustrates a typical example of the changes in the number of variables used at each step.

If we also take into consideration that we usually work with up to several millions of rows it becomes obvious that scalability and good sampling methods are essential for any data mining environment.

There are also several types of row manipulations, the most common ones can be classified into:

- *Aggregation*. Examples include counts, mean, and standard deviation of the number of transactions of a specific type over a given time period, for a specific customer, product type and many more.
- *Change detection*. This is used to detect when and if certain variables change their value such as ZIP code of customers domicile, or her credit rating.
- *Missing value detection*. It is common that raw data come with many data fields either totally missing or with some missing values. The reasons for this may be nonmandatory input fields in front-office systems, incomplete data migration from one system to another, and so on. There are various ways of treating a variable with missing values, including eliminating the whole row from further processing when a missing value is detected, replacing the missing value with a constant value, or replacing it with a randomly generated value based on the distribution of this data field's nonmissing values or based on correlations with: other data fields.[1]
- *Outlier detection*. In some cases observations may contain variables with extreme values, meaning values far away from the bulk of other values for the distinct variable.

---

[1] An example would be the expectation maximization algorithm (EM) that takes into account the correlation of the data field for which a nonmissing value is to be generated with other data fields.

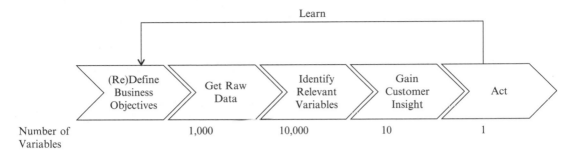

Fig. 7.4 Number of variables at different process steps

Sometimes these outliers are real; sometimes they are the consequence of bad data quality. Outlier detection is in its simple form univariate: we just look at one variable and try to find values that stand out. In its more sophisticated form we look at many variables at the same time and watch out for multivariate outliers (a data point might look like an outlier in the univariate case but not in the multivariate case). Outliers can be mapped to other values or the corresponding rows and be excluded from further processing.

When preparing the data for modeling, it is common to sample and split the incoming data into various streams for different purposes:

- *Train set.* Used to build the models.
- *Test set.* Used for out-of-sample tests of the model quality and to select the final model candidate.
- *Scoring data.* Used for model-based prediction. Typically, this data set is large as compared to the previous ones.

The data sets must be carefully examined and designed to assure statistical significance of the results obtained.

7.2.1 Define Business Objectives

Data mining finds application in many situations. Profitable customer acquisition requires modeling of expected customer potential, in order to target the acquisition of those customers who will be profitable over the lifetime of the business relationship (they might be unprofitable in the beginning and turn into very profitable customers later—e.g., a medicine student). In a cross-selling or up-selling model, we model the customer's affinity with a set of products or services translated into her purchase likelihood. In churn management, it is crucial to correctly model a customer's likelihood to defect based on past behavior. Some applications require predicting not only who will purchase which product or service, but also the expected amount spent on the transactions (Fig. 7.5).

Once it has been identified which customer behavior has to be predicted, we need to mathematically define this target variable (dependent variable). For example, while up-selling platinum credit cards to customers already owning a standard credit card, we might find several types of standard and platinum cards exist. The business objective might, in fact, only be to up-sell platinum cards of types P2 and P3 to customers not owning a card yet, or those already owning standard cards of type S1, S3, and S4. The target variable has to reflect these conditions when calculated. This has a later direct impact on the modeling process.

To prepare the modeling data sets we will look for two types of customers in the customer database and set the value of the target variable accordingly:

- For all customers who (first purchased a standard card of type S1, S3 or S4 and then purchased a platinum card of type P2 or P3) or (purchased a platinum card of type P2 or P3 immediately) set target variable = 1.
- For all other customers set target variable = 0.
- Once these restrictions and considerations have been applied to the data, the model will

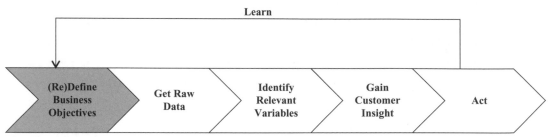

Fig. 7.5 Data-mining process: define business objectives

be trained to distinguish between customers with a target variable equal to zero and customers with a target variable equal to one (for example using logistic regression, see Sect. 6.3.3) After training, the model will be applied to predict if a given customer is likely to buy the platinum cards. The business group must establish likelihood threshold levels above which they think a prospect should be included in the marketing campaign.

Another aspect of the campaign which should be defined during this project phase is the set of business or selection rules for a campaign. Rules define the customers that should be excluded from or included in the target groups: certain products or services might not be available for specific customer groups. Suppose that in certain countries only customers over 18 years are eligible to purchase a credit card. Credit products in general have restrictions with respect to the customer's credit rating. Companies have "blacklists" containing customers who should not receive any new offerings, either due to bad debt indicators (they do not have a good credit rating) or persons explicitly asking not to be contacted for marketing purposes. Some countries have centrally managed lists with all persons not wanting to receive unauthorized direct mails or calls. By contrast, there might also be customer groups that should be included at any price in the campaign—for instance, due

to strategic issues such as need to gain market share in a specific region or otherwise defined group. In those cases, it is not relevant if members of that group get high model scores; they are included anyway.

To ensure a successful project, we need to define at this point the details of its execution. Therefore, we should create a project plan specifying, for instance, the start and delivery dates of the data-mining process, as well as the responsible resources for each task. For the final model selection the business group must be available for reviewing the data-mining results, perform consistency checks with the data-mining group, and make the final decision about the model selected for deployment. Delivery dates for the final model or scores also need to be defined, along with dates for start and end of the supported campaign.

We need to carefully define the chosen experimental setup for the campaign; this is critical for correctly evaluating its success later. It is highly recommended to spend a significant amount of time getting this right. Usually, we split the target group into various cells. In the simplest case there will be only two cells:

1. *The control group contains only randomly selected customers.* This group will be needed to measure the baseline effect (i.e., what would have been the normal customer behavior without the influence of the campaign).

Table 7.1 Cost/revenue matrix

Cost/revenue matrix	Prospect did not purchase		Prospect did purchase	
Model predicts prospect will not purchase (not contacted)	Cost:	$0	Lost business opportunity of + $895	
	First year revenue:	$0		
	Total:	$0		
Model predicts prospect will purchase (contacted)	Cost:	−$5	Cost:	−$105
	First year revenue:	$0	First year revenue:	+$1,000
	Total:	−$5	Total:	+$895

2. *The other cell will contain only the best customers according to the model used.* This simple setup allows measuring how the model-based selection is doing with respect to the average customer behavior.

More refined setups may generate more than two cells. As an example, take the control group and two target groups to which we communicate different content about the same offering during the campaign. This will show the impact of the communication content on the purchase behavior.

To get the business context into the data-mining project, describe the nature of the business involving the data-mining project, and the cost and revenue drivers of the business. This knowledge will affect the final model and target group selections. It is helpful to define a cost/revenue matrix describing how the business mechanics will work in the supported campaign and how it will affect the data-mining process. As an example, consider a call center campaign to sell a mobile phone contract. Table 7.1 shows an example of the associated cost/revenue matrix.

Here, we assume the average cost per call is $5. Each positive responder (purchaser) will generate additional cost including administration work required to register him as a new customer and the cost of the delivered phone handset of, say, $100. Customers who respond positively will generate average revenue of $1,000 a year. Putting all these factors together defines the cost/revenue decision matrix, which will subsequently have an impact, on the choice of model parameters such as the cut-off point for the selected model scores. It will also give business users an immediately interpretable table.

Finally, we need to establish the criteria for evaluating the success of the campaign. This is a key aspect for the success or failure of the whole project. Often there is a misunderstanding on both sides—business and modelers—with respect to what is feasible from a business and statistical perspective. Clearly defining the expectations helps. If, for example, gaining market share is more important than obtaining high purchase rates, the measure of success changes from "percentage of sold cards per contacted customer" to "absolute number of cards sold during the campaign." In this context, it is crucial to specify how the campaign results will be tracked and analyzed. Depending on the type of business, how it is structured into customer segments, regions, products, and others, we could be interested in measuring purchase rates per region, per sales channels, per product type, and so on as a function of time. When we consider a situation where we have defined various target groups for different communication contents or product offers in one campaign, it is worth measuring the purchase rates for each group.

Sometimes it is useful to look for a benchmark to compare results obtained in the past for the same or similar campaign setups using traditional targeting methods and not predictive models. We have to be careful when comparing the result of the old and new methods because there could be hidden differences due to different business (market) conditions, changes in the products or services, etc. In this chapter, we examine the French company Credite Est, a regional bank that implemented a data-mining process. The following example looks at how Credite Est defined its business objectives.

7.2.2 Get Raw Data

Now that we have gained a clear understanding of the business objectives, we need to translate them into data requirements (i.e., which data are available that appropriately and accurately describe the problem thereby allowing us to model the targeted behavior?) Once the required data has been identified, it has to be extracted and consolidated in a database (often called analytical data mart) so it is readily available for subsequent data manipulation and data-mining steps. Another important step is to check the quality of the analytical raw data. This includes technical checks as well as ensuring the data make sense in the given business context and that correct deductions can be obtained.

During this phase of the project (see Fig. 7.6), database administrators and IT professionals with knowledge of the data source systems will be asked to extract and provide all the data fields required for the data-mining project. This is done in close cooperation with the data miners to ensure the extracted data corresponds to the initial requirements. Then, we also need to involve business resources to ensure and cross-check data quality.

Step 1: Looking for Data Sources

To start the acquisition of raw data, we look into data sourcing, a mixed top-down and bottom-up process driven by business requirements (top) and technical restrictions (bottom). Its main objective consists of searching for available data sources in your company (or externally) which describe the problem at hand. The availability of a data warehouse can sometimes speed up this process. Conflicting and bad quality of addresses and other demographic information is quite common. For example, you might find the same or similar information field resides in various source systems, but with contradictory content (e.g., in one database the gender code for a given customer is "male" and in another database it is "female" for the same customer). Data warehouse infrastructures with advanced data cleansing processes can help ensure you are working with high-quality data. It is also a good idea to ask for small sample data extractions from the sources to examine if the information represents what you thought it would. Make sure that you talk to many people from business and data management to understand which data sources are commonly used in certain contexts, but also to detect possible new sources that may contain valuable information. Collect all metadata

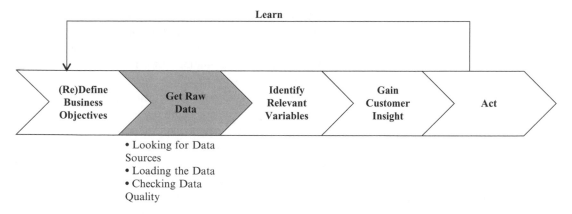

Fig. 7.6 Data-mining process: get raw data

available to fully understand data types, value ranges, and the primary/foreign key structures.

Once there is a better understanding of the data sources that need to be loaded, build a (simple) relational data model onto which the source data will be mapped. This model should be kept as simple and as close to a business data model as possible. Even though this data model might not be perfectly suited for data mining and analysis, it is important that all involved groups have a clear understanding of the data. Later in the process we will *denormalize* (flatten) the model to enable easier data analysis and predictive modeling.

Step 2: Loading the Data

After specifying where and how the required data will be extracted, we still need to define further query restrictions because we might want to model only subsets of the full data (e.g., specific customer segments, geographical regions, time periods, etc.). Then it is time to request data management (IT) to deliver the specified data needs.[2] IT teams will prepare the necessary data queries, which will be executed during predefined time windows in batch mode (such as each night at midnight or each Sunday after completion of the accounting batch process).

Depending on the data miner's needs they might also get direct *asynchronous* access to the data so they can run extractions when necessary. The extracted data are then delivered to the data-mining environment in a predefined format such as database tables in native format, or simply flat files in ASCII or XML (text) format with fixed or variable record lengths. In fact, flat files are still the most commonly used format for data mining due to their simplicity, enhanced definition of system boundaries, and interfaces. Data miners define how the data will be imported into the data-mining environment. Delivery using an ftp protocol is common, or data may also be put onto a common file server to be accessed directly through the network. If a DB-link is preferred, a direct database connection from the data-mining system to the source systems (or vice versa) will be established. After the data have been delivered to a defined landing area, they will be further processed and used to fill the previously defined data model in the data mining environment. The involved steps are part of the *ETL process* (Extract-Transform-Load) supported by dedicated software packages. Some data-mining tools also offer quite advanced and comprehensive utilities for ETL.

Step 3: Checking Data Quality

It is often underestimated how seriously bad data quality may affect business decisions. According to Olson (2003) the costs of poor data quality are estimated at 15–25% of operating profit, for example through wrong inferences on customer

---

[2] Sometimes, obstacles such as lacking authorization of the data mining team for accessing the required data might emerge. Data miners frequently work with data which other business departments do not have access to. There is a high level of secrecy and trust involved.

attitudes, lost customers through poor services, or delays in delivering data to decision makers. We need to ensure that once the data for the data-mining project have been loaded, we assess and understand their limitations resulting from their inherent quality (good or bad) aspects. We have to create an analytical database that all involved parties (business, data mining, IT) feel comfortable with, as it is the basis for subsequent analyses. Only then can the generated customer insights be trusted and applied in practice with maximum confidence regarding their effect on the organization.

Data quality crucially depends on the intended use and the data itself. Relevant aspects of data quality are:

- Accuracy (consistency and validity)
- Relevance
- Completeness
- Reliability

I.e., when checking data quality, we focus not only on technical aspects of the data (primary keys, duplicate records, missing values, etc.) but also on quality issues related to the business context (a customer should not be 200 years old or have a future birth date, customers should not be purchasing nonexisting or expired products, etc.).

A preliminary data quality assessment is carried out to ensure an acceptable level of quality of the delivered data and to ensure the data mining team has a clear understanding of how to interpret the data in business terms. All parties—business, data mining, and IT—are involved in this important task. Thus, the data available for the mining project must be analyzed to answer to the following questions: (1) Does the data correspond to the original sourcing requirements? (2) Is the quality sufficient? and (3) Do we understand the data?

Several iterations of data extractions may be necessary to satisfy the data requirements. The data miner represents the link between business and IT demands. Miscommunication between business and IT can lead to incorrect data extractions.

As already mentioned, data should have sufficient quality for achieving the project's objectives. A data field does not always have a clearly defined meaning (although available metadata might initially give you that impression). Sometimes the information it carries is different from its official description. This is a consequence of the accumulation of undocumented system changes over many years. Another common issue is missing data, which means that in some cases (i.e., for some records) a data field is not filled. We might also find wrong or contradictory information in a data field.

Finally, data miners must demonstrate they understand the data. To this end, it is useful to have them carry out some basic data interpretation and aggregation exercises where two things can be shown: (1) the data quality and (2) the ability to correctly interpret the data. As simple data interpretation examples, consider correctly counting the number of customers per region, customer segment, product ownership, total transaction volume per time periods, etc. Choose to include aggregations familiar to the business group and that can be easily cross-checked. We see an example of getting and combining data in CRM at Work 7.2 a further study of Credite Est.

Since the objective is to acquire prospects likely to be high-value customers, Credite Est must rely on customer characteristics common to both customers (the basis for establishing the critical profile) and the prospects (scored on the basis of their profile). For a more detailed description of the profiling process see Sect. 6.3.1.

CRM at Work 7.2
Gathering Raw Data at Credite Est
The response variable for current customers is customer contribution margin. The company sorted customers by operating contribution and chose to profile the top 20% of them. Transaction information is not available for prospects. This is why the bank has to rely on information available for both existing customers and prospects. One type of information is geodemographic data, such as socioeconomic status of a region, average age, type of housing, and so on. They can be purchased from direct marketing agencies and then appended to individual records of existing customers. That is, depending on

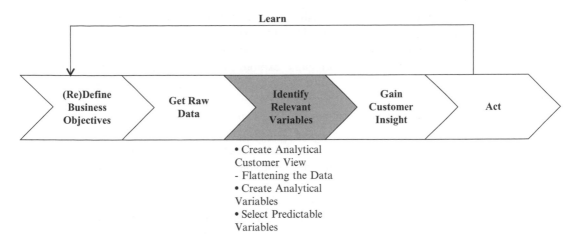

Fig. 7.7 Identify relevant variables

ZIP code, geodemographic information is added to existing customer records. The model attempts to predict customer operating margin as the dependent variable with geodemographic information as the independent variables. The rationale behind this process is to find the profile that best characterizes high-value clients, which is subsequently applied to prospects' information. Credite Est appended a total of 65 variables to existing customer records. They were procured from the French list manager CIFEA, as well as from Claritas.

7.2.3   Identify Relevant Predictive Variables

The raw data, now available for analysis, is not yet in a format suited to powerful predictive modeling. This is due to data formatting aspects, since the sourced data are still in a relational format, and do not yet represent a customer-centric view. During this step (see Fig. 7.7), we will (1) create a flattened view of the extracted raw data aggregating all facts about the customer behavior over time in a single observation (also called record or row). Also, it is a good practice to include a priori business knowledge by (2) creating new analytical variables which might have

predictive power. This part will require imagination and participation from the business group. As a result, we might end up with thousands of variables describing each customer. Further analysis is likely to reveal that most variables do not possess predictive power at all. Therefore, we will (3) identify and select only those few variables with sufficient explanatory power for the modeled target behavior.

Step 1: Create Analytical Customer View— Flattening the Data

In the context of CRM, very often the individual customer is the central object analyzed by means of data mining. All data available for an individual customer must be gathered and consolidated because the individual customer constitutes an observational unit for data analysis and predictive modeling. The historical behavior of customers is obtained from the corresponding data queries in a time series–oriented relational transaction database.

Usually, we choose a simple, flat data model as the basis for predictive modeling. In this representation all data pertaining to an individual customer are contained in one observation (row, record). Individual columns (variables, fields) represent the conditions at specific points in time or a summary over a whole period. Creating such a customer view requires denormalizing the original relational data structures *(flattening).*

This task will involve data miners to define the details of the flattening process and use IT resources to obtain the targeted form of data.

The business objectives for the data mining project determine which features of the customer's record need to be aggregated from the analytical raw data and how. The detail levels for calculating grouped sums (e.g., sum of monthly cash withdrawals from a bank account) and counts (e.g., number of address changes within a certain year) need to be defined. This includes specification of the temporal granularity of the time series in the flattened data table. Descriptive statistics such as sums, mean, median, and standard deviation will be employed to capture features of the related time series. As an example, consider raw data describing 1 year of customer transactions and create four new variables containing the average transaction volume per quarter. Different kinds of global transformations, combinations, or arithmetical operations can also be applied to selected variables such as currency exchange calculations, scaling factors, logarithmic transforms, and so on. Many new variables will be created through these types of operations, leading to very wide data tables. Later, we will use the newly created variables in addition to the raw data variables as predictors during the predictive modeling step.

Another key variable to be created during this step is the target or dependent variable. Its correct definition is extremely important for predictive modeling. In the example of modeling customer defection, a target value of zero is assigned if the customer was still maintaining a business relationship and a target value of one if the customer already terminated the business relationship. The definition of the target variable is not always as straightforward as it might seem. In the previous examples, we could also think about a customer who is inactive since a defined time period as a *lost* customer. There might be a multitude of business rules specifying the conditions under which the target variable is either one or zero. Once we've found a satisfactory definition of the target variable, its values should be generated for all customers and added to the existing data tables.

Step 2: Create Analytical Variables

The basic set of variables resulting from the previous flattening might not be enough to fully explore the data potential for predictive modeling. We might want to introduce additional variables derived from the original ones. For example, consider a variable resulting from the product of customer age and salary. This is often referred to as an *interaction term.* Transforming variables is another operation that might lead to new and more predictive variables. We could transform customer birth date into age, or use the number of days between two customer transactions instead of the absolute dates of each transaction. Variable *binning* (or categorization) is also often encountered. Here we take highly skewed variables (such as salary) and map the distribution to a few discrete classes such as low, medium, and high salary, each defined by its boundary values. More refined methods help to increase normality of variable distributions, which in turn help the predictive model training process. Many data-mining tools provide support for increasing normality of the analytical variables. Finally, missing value management is key for enhancing the quality of the data set. Numerous methods are available, including deleting each row with at least one missing value (the least preferred strategy), replacing a missing field with a constant value, randomly generating a value based on the variable's distribution, and randomly generating a value based on the variable's correlation with the other variables (such as the expectation maximization algorithm).

Step 3: Select Predictive Variables

At this point, we have a wealth of variables describing customer behavior; probably too many to enter the subsequent modeling phase of the data-mining project. We now need to reduce the dimensionality (i.e., exclude variables) to get a more parsimonious model. Presenting all predictor variables to a neural network, for instance, might make the modeling phase extremely time consuming and sometimes results in *overfitting*, i.e., the model gives good results on the training data (in sample) but fails to be generally applicable to previously unseen data (out of sample). Exclusion of variables is usually possible without deteriorating the predictive power of the obtained models since many variables have no predictive power at all. To this end we inspect the descriptive statistics of all univariate distributions associated to all available variables. We can immediately exclude those variables, which take on only one value (i.e., the variable is a constant), since they will certainly not have any predictive power. We might also exclude variables with mostly missing values. A threshold missing value count level should be defined above which the field would be excluded from further analysis.

Variables directly or indirectly identifying an individual customer represent another type of candidate for exclusion. Examples are primary keys such as the customer ID number or name and address fields. Later, when deploying predictive models (i.e., when scoring customers), identifiers will usually be required. Otherwise you would not know whom to address with an offering. In some cases, collinear predictive variables can have a negative impact on the convergence and performance of the estimation process of certain types of models such as logistic regression. These collinearities must be identified and the respective variables excluded before proceeding. Finally, we also exclude variables showing little correlation with the target variable. To identify them we may carry out pair-wise chi-square tests, linear correlation analyses, or pairwise simple linear regressions. Other frequently used techniques to support the variable selection process are histograms, scatter plots, box plots, and frequency tables.

Also notice that excluding variables from further processing does not automatically imply that the respective columns are deleted from the data sets. It could only mean flagging the respective columns to be temporarily ignored for further analysis. The exclusion should be easily reversible to readily test other variable scenario selections.

Before concluding the variable selection step, we should carefully check if all variables have been mapped to the appropriate data types. Some data fields might represent the data in an inappropriate format (e.g., ZIP codes stored as

numerical integer variables should rather be categorical (or nominal) for the purpose of data mining, unless you have a ZIP code-based distance measure associated for your analysis). The following example examines this issue.

CRM at Work 7.3
Identifying Relevant Variables at Credite Est
Upon creating a single data file including all appended information, the next step is to start with exploratory analyses. A key concern with appended data is the amount of potentially missing information. All appended variables had almost 50% missing data. The next step was to assess whether the missing data could be meaningfully replaced. These operations improved the overall rate of missing values from 42% to 21%. The next step was to investigate univariate statistics (means, standard deviations, frequencies, outliers) for all variables to ensure the included variables have sufficient integrity. This step brought a reduction in variables from 65 to 54. The next step was to calculate all bivariate correlations (or mean analyses in case of categorical variables) of the existing independent variables with the dependent variable—customer value. This was an iterative process where independent variables were subjected to transformations and where new variables were created. For example, there were three variables which indicated whether a household has children in age brackets 0–4, 5–11, and 12–18. From that, a new variable was created that was a simple dummy indicator: children versus no children. In the end, this data evaluation process resulted in a total of 17 variables that had a reasonable correlation with the dependent variable. These were retained for the next step, the response model.

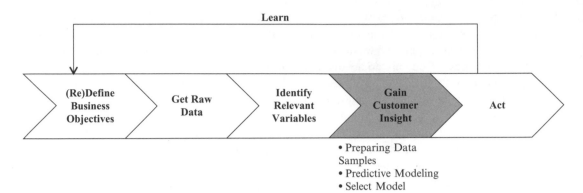

Fig. 7.8 Data-mining process: gain customer insight

7.2.4   Gain Customer Insight

Once we have obtained a credible, good-quality set of descriptive data (i.e., we have prepared the data samples), the next step is to extract the knowledge about customer behavior and/or other properties needed for carrying out the planned campaign through predictive modeling (see Fig. 7.8).

Frequently, we distinguish between different types of predictive models obtained through different modeling paradigms: supervised and unsupervised modeling. In the case where we want to predict the likelihood of a customer purchasing a certain product, we would build a predictive model on a predefined test set containing customers who already purchased the product and customers who did not. In this case, we are applying the supervised learning paradigm, because for each customer in the modeling data set we know the correct answer to the question, i.e., did the customer purchase or not?

Building a model means finding the right relationships between the variables describing the customers to predict their respective group membership likelihood: purchaser or non-purchaser. This is usually also referred to as scoring (e.g., between 0 and 1). Since we know the purchase behavior for each customer in the train set, we can also measure the model's prediction quality, i.e., its misclassification rate (see Sect. 6.4.1). A different situation arises in the context, for instance, of a customer segmentation problem. Suppose you want to identify groups of custo-

mers having a similar general behavior, not only with respect to purchase behavior. In the beginning you don't know which groups will be identified. It is a process purely driven by the data and relationships between variables. Here, we would apply unsupervised modeling where group membership is not known beforehand. We're looking for new and unexpected patterns. Typical examples of statistical models in this context are self-organizing neural networks (Kohonen networks) and clustering algorithms.[3]

The output of this project phase can either consist in the predictive model itself, which is later applied in an online production environment (i.e., to predict next product recommendations for customers calling a call center), or directly in the customer score values (e.g., to select all customers with a score value above 90% purchase likelihood and send them a direct mail).

---

[3] Kohonen networks belong to the family of neural network techniques. These are powerful data modeling tools able to capture and represent complex input/output relationships for example in target marketing, financial forecasting, or process control. In particular, the objective of a Kohonen network is to generate, out of complex input patterns of arbitrary dimension, a simplified (discrete) map with very few dimensions, say 1 or 2. Thus, the Kohonen network is an approach to quickly understand complex data as a result of a simplification of the structure. For a good overview of neural networks and Kohonen networks please refer to: Principe, Euliano and Lefebvre (2000).

Step 1: Preparing Data Samples

Before we start building (or training) the models, it is necessary to analyze if sufficient data are available to obtain statistically significant results. There are cases where there is only very little data available such as when modeling purchase behavior for a recently introduced product, with only very few customers having bought the product until now. If we have enough data available we split the data into two samples: the train set to fit the models and the test set to check the model's performance on observations that have not been used to build it. This will give an objective assessment of the model's generalization capability—a critical requirement before launching a product or campaign.

Step 2: Predictive Modeling

There are two steps of predictive modeling:

1. The rules (or linear/nonlinear analytical models) are built based on a training set.
2. These rules are then applied to a new dataset for generating the answers needed for the campaign.

Based on the training set, we develop predictive models that should minimize the prediction error. In the course of this process a set of optimal model parameters are obtained. Usually, several alternative models are trained together, applying different statistical methodologies such as neural networks, linear or logistic regression, survival analysis, principal component analysis, factor analysis, decision trees, or clustering.

Step 3: Select Model

When all alternative models have been trained, we start comparing their relative quality of prediction by comparing their respective misclassification rates (see Sect. 6.4.1) obtained on the test set or by performing a lift analysis (see Sect. 6.4.2). Some models will have more predictive power than others, and we will select the model we think generalizes best from the train to the test data.

We will also include the economic implications of a model by applying the previously defined cost/revenue matrix. Predictive models, for instance, deliver a score value, or likelihood, for each customer to show the modeled target behavior (e.g., purchase of a credit card). Nevertheless, determin-

ing the threshold level score to use for a given campaign is a business decision. It could be that you want to set it to the break-even point (see Sect. 6.2.1), or you may have a fixed budget for the campaign you want to fully use. This might lead to lowering the threshold until the point where your costs equal the budget. We continue to look at this issue in the following example.

CRM at Work 7.4

Gaining Customer Insight at Credite Est

The methodology chosen by the modelers was logistic regression. Since the goal was to either target or not target a certain individual in the prospect pool, classifying the dependent variable as 0/1 was appropriate. In the previous step, only those variables were retained with a minimum level of bivariate correlation. However, now the issue of multicollinearity came into play. Multicollinearity occurs when two variables convey essentially the same information, making one of them redundant. Thus, an important step was to make a theory-based elimination of those highly collinear variables. The final model was chosen on grounds of predictive ability while containing a low number of missing values. It contained five predictors of customer value: bourgeois cluster, technology cluster, children index, house value index, and managerial job position. The ability of the model to correctly classify was 75.5% in the estimation sample and 69.8% in the holdout sample, i.e., roughly 20% points higher than based on chance alone. This result was deemed successful, and thus it was decided to utilize this model for a prospecting campaign.

7.2.5   Act

The final objective of a data-mining project should be to act on its results (see Fig. 7.9). Sometimes we also refer to this as deployment

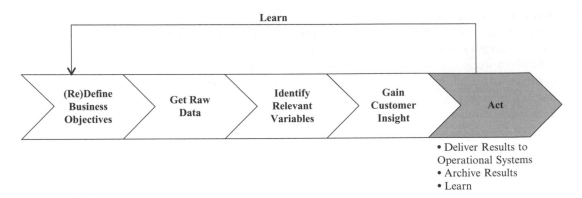

Fig. 7.9 Data-mining process: act

of the results. This is crucial to the success of the whole project. The planning phase of the project must have addressed the issue of implementing the project's results into the respective business processes. The project plan must foresee involvement and availability of IT resources required to feed data-mining results back into the process supporting IT systems (databases, Web sites, call centers, etc.). In practice, deployment can have numerous applications: score-based selection of customers to be addressed through a direct mailing campaign, score-based next-product recommendation on an e-commerce Web site, optimization of marketing spending according to the model-based customer lifetime value prediction, choice of the appropriate communication channel for each customer, and so on.

In particular, acting can be subdivided into delivering results to operational systems, archiving the results, and learning.

Step 1: Deliver Results to Operational Systems

The final goal of prognostic modeling within the context of CRM is to select a subset of customers for a campaign to determine which customers are more likely to be responsive than others. To identify this subset, we apply the selected model to the entire customer base (unless restrictions have been previously defined limiting the total universe of modeled and targeted customers, such as geographical regions, a subset of customer segments, etc.). The obtained score value for each customer and the defined threshold value will determine whether the corresponding customer qualifies to participate in the campaign. We can either deploy the customer scores or, alternately, the scoring model itself, which implies that it is applied on demand—for example, when a customer calls the call center or visits the company's Web site.

Before scoring customers we need to prepare the score data set containing the most recent information available for each customer with the variables required by the model. This implies that the score set variables go through exactly the same variable transformation, derivation, and selection process as did the train and test data sets used for building the model. Data recency is an important requirement because otherwise we are scoring customers based on old information, which may, in turn, lead to wrong conclusions.

Imagine we are scoring customers for a direct mail campaign to sell a credit card to all those customers not yet owning one. If the scoring data are not reasonably current, we might be scoring customers although they have recently purchased a credit card and potentially (if the model works well) include them in your target group. As a result, we end up offering these customers a product they have just purchased, giving a rather poor image of how much our company knows about its customers.

Finally, when delivering the results to the operational systems, make sure to also provide the necessary customer identifiers required by those systems to unambiguously link the models score information to the correct customer.

Step 2: Archive Results

The data-mining group is responsible for archiving all information related to each data-mining project it executes. This is an important and often neglected or poorly followed piece of advice. Companies that do not archive their models cannot expect to learn from past experience as fast as those who do.

Each data-mining project will produce a huge amount of information:

- Raw data used
- Transformations for each variable
- Formulas for creating derived variables
- Train, test, and score data sets
- Target variable calculation
- Models and their parameterizations
- Score threshold levels
- Final customer target selections

Knowing this information and having it readily available helps in understanding anomalies in model performance, and in learning what worked well and what did not (and why). It is also useful to preserve the details of the model when scoring has been done. The same model might be used to score different data sets obtained at different times.

Step 3: Learn

Learning from a data-mining project is an integral part of the process. This is also sometimes referred to as *closing the loop*. It means learning from the actions you have executed to improve performance the next time. To learn from the data-mining project, we must first obtain the facts describing its performance and business impact. In the ideal case, we would provide return on investment figures for the data-mining project at hand.

Usually these facts are obtained by monitoring the campaign performance while it is running and from the final campaign performance analysis after the campaign has ended. Campaign monitoring is an important capability the data-mining group must provide, since it avoids blind piloting of the campaign until its end, without any intermediate performance feedback. In rapidly changing environments, it is also required for detecting when a model should be retrained. Usually, monitoring provides some key performance indicators, such as the response and/or purchase rates by region, customer segment, product, and so on. These parameters will give early indication of undesired irregularities in model performance and enable early intervention. The final campaign performance analysis will produce similar performance indicators as the monitoring function. The main difference is that it is more complete and has a determined final time horizon of influence. This is required to ensure a correct measurement of the cause and effect of a campaign. It would, for instance, be unrealistic to positively attribute advertising to a customer's behavior when the customer purchases a product 1 year after seeing the advertisement of a direct mail campaign.

Sample learnings from campaign evaluation could be:

- Revealing that purchase rates depend on the choice of the communication channel
- Discovering that a direct mail with a colorful and detailed product brochure sells less than one with a black and white one-page flyer

Thus, the learning step requires data miners to generate the facts about campaign performance, and business resources to put them in context for correct interpretation. Our study of Credite Est concludes with the following example, showing how the company acted on the information it gleaned in the data-mining process.

CRM at Work 7.5

Acting on the Information at Credite Est

The final model was rolled out in a sequential fashion to the target prospect audience. The goal was to iteratively refine the model in future rounds. As a first step, Credite Est purchased addresses from list brokers that had nonmissing values for at least three out of five variables in the final model. The prospects were scored with the model and then ranked by likelihood of being a high-value customer. From the resulting pool of 10,000 prospects, half were targeted with a money-market product, and half with a lending product. The objective was to assess the receptivity of the two samples for the respective products. In addition, a baseline scenario was conducted whereby the same prospecting campaigns were conducted for a random sample of households. Although both target mailings were significantly more successful than the baseline scenario, this was only the first step in a further refinement of the model and the offer. In particular, besides assessing response rate, it was now important to track and document the value of the acquired customers—the original goal of the project.

A comprehensive example of an application of data mining is given in the case study, which is taking a look at Yapi Kredi, a company that put the data-mining tools to use to create a cross-selling campaign.

CRM at Work 7.6
Yapi Kredi—Predictive Model-Based Cross-Selling Campain
Established in 1944 as the first private bank in Turkey, Yapi Kredi has always been a pioneer in the Turkish financial sector. The bank has more than 860 domestic branches and various other subsidiaries, as well as affiliated companies active in leasing, factoring, investment banking insurance, brokerage and new economy companies. Yapi Kredi is positioned as the fourth largest privately owned commercial bank by asset size in Turkey, with leading positions in credit cards, assets under management, factoring, private pension funds, and life- and non-life insurances. As of 2010 it serves approximately six million customers.
The Challenge
To continue Yapi Kredi's development as the fastest-growing retail bank in Turkey, in terms of assets under management and

retail profitability, it targets to maintain anintimate banking relationship with the top customer segment to fully explore the potential of its 5+ million customer base, and to increase the contract per customer ratio to five.

To this end, Yapi Kredi introduced a modern retail banking approach to enable serving all customers according to their specific needs through individual product packages. The capabilities required to achieve these goals were as follows:
• Advanced analytical customer segmentation
• Segment-specific offering of product bundles
• Conversion of customers to more profitable segments via targeted campaigns using advanced CRM tools such as predictive modeling

Solution
To increase the product per customer ratio, to attract new money from customers, and to demonstrate the efficacy of the new analytical CRM methods, Yapi Kredi decided to carry out a set of pilot projects for cross-selling of consumer banking products. A reduced selection of target customers with a high propensity to positively respond would be included in a multichannel, two-step campaign. To illustrate the methodology we briefly describe the outcomes of the various project phases.
Define Business Objectives
Various cross-departmental workshops were held to define the business objectives, operational aspects of campaign execution, the basics of relevant data availability, and to measure the success of the campaign.

The first step was to find which product would be best suited for cross selling from a customer and bank perspective. After a deep analysis of potential products to be offered during this first predictive model based cross-selling campaign, it was decided to choose Yapi Kredi's B-type mutual funds, characterized by being low risk investment instruments based on fixed income securities. These funds can be easily purchased via the ATM, Web, and telephone channels.

Cross selling these mutual funds was considered to have a twofold positive business impact. It served the purpose of acquiring new money from customers, and even those customers transferring their existing investments from other Yapi Kredi products into mutual funds (*cannibalization effect*) was still considered beneficial to the bank. It was decided to offer this product to both customer groups:

- Customers already having invested into B-type mutual funds to stimulate an increase of the assets
- Customers not yet owning any B-type fund to help increase product ratio and attract new money

After fixing the product details, it had to be defined how the campaign would be carried out. The workshops helped define the start and end date of the campaign: a total duration of 5 weeks was considered appropriate. Communication channels for offering the product were agreed upon. A two-channel approach was deemed feasible since Yapi Kredi had just finished the implementation of a project integrating the call center and the bank's branch network. These were considered the right channels for the campaign.

Given the pilot project character of the campaign and the available resources, it had been decided to contact 3,000 customers based on out-bound calls and active marketing during customer branch visits. A total of 16 branches in the Istanbul area were selected for participation in the campaign. Additionally, 1,200 target customers were to be contacted by the call center.

It was decided to run a two-step campaign, where customers were first contacted with the B-type mutual fund offer. Then, positive responders received a follow-up call if they had not purchased 1 week after their initial positive response.

Response and purchase rates by contact channel (branch or call centre) were chosen as measures of the campaign's success.

Get Raw Data

A data mart was developed for supporting the activities of the CRM department. To this end, data were extracted from more than 50 source system tables. About 20 database tables were produced with 30 gigabytes of disk space for the initial project phase. The data mart included data most urgently needed for high-priority business activities (such as the pilot campaign) and assured that the data are readily available in a short time frame for subsequent data manipulation and data-mining steps.

Identify Relevant Variables

Various aggregations and transformations were required to obtain the right customer-centric data format as needed for analysis and predictive modeling. Basic data-quality crosschecks were performed to assure the validity of the data and its suitability for further data-mining activities.

Different types of attributes were found to be relevant and used to obtain a complete picture of customer behavior and preferences. These included the following customer attributes:

- *Demographics* Age, gender, marital status, group memberships, address, profession, and other identifying characteristics belong in this category,
- *Product ownership* This relates to product portfolio held by each customer, opening/closing dates, derived variables related to customer's tenure such as maximum tenure of owned products, and so on.
- *Product usage* Variables are related to a customer's frequency of usage such as the average number of banking transactions.
- *Channel usage* Variables are related to customer's automatic payment behavior,

average amount of automatic payments, ratios of different channels' usage, and so on.

• *Assets* Variables are related to savings and investment products such as the average balance invested in securities, time deposits, demand deposits, and so on.

• *Liabilities* Variables are related to loan usage such as average balance on loans, average balance on credit cards, and so on.

• *Profitability* For the pilot project, a profitability index was created, since profitability was not available for all customers at that time. The index was used for ranking customers according to their profitability without giving its absolute value.

Gain Customer insight

Based on 6 months of historical customer data, five different predictive models were developed to estimate a customer's propensity to invest in a B-type mutual fund during the following 3-month period. The best model was found to be a logistic regression yielding a lift value of 2.9 for the top customer decile. The lift value measures the effect of the predictive model (see Sect. 6.4.2), and expresses the fact that in this case the logistic regression reaches 2.9 times more responders for the top customer decile than a random selection of the same size.

All customers were then scored using this model, and a set of 4,200 customers with the highest propensity to purchase was selected as the target group for the pilot campaign.

Act

To roll out the campaign through the call center and the branches, each channel had to know exactly which customer to contact. Each channel needed a clear assignment of their respective target customers. A subset of 3,000 customers was assigned to the 16

branches holding the responsibility for the respective relationships. The remaining 1,200 customers were assigned to the call center. The target list with the corresponding channel assignment was then made available to the campaign management system. After preparing call scripts and training the staff involved in its execution, the campaign could start.

The following table summarizes the results. Impressive response rates of 6.5% and 12.2%, respectively, were obtained with the branch-based and call-center-based part of the campaign. The pilot campaign could acquire more than €1 million into B-type mutual funds.

	Response rate (%)	Amount of funds sold (€)
Branches	6.5	582,000
Call center	12.2	452,000
Total	8.2	1,034,000

It is interesting to observe that although the branches obtained a lower response rate than the call center, they still acquired significantly more investment into the funds. This reflects the advantages of the more personal branch-based customer relationship. As a consequence of this successful pilot campaign, a large-scale rollout to a larger part of Yapi Kredi's customers looked very promising.

7.3   Summary

Data mining can assist in selecting the right target customers or in identifying previously unknown customers with similar behavior and needs. A good target list is likely to increase purchase rates and have a positive impact on revenue. A complete data-mining process comprises assessing and specifying the business objectives, data sourcing, transformation and creation of analytical variables, as well as building analytical models using techniques such as logistic regression or neural networks. The number of variables used changes drastically during the data-mining process. Types of row manipulation include aggregation, change, missing value, and outlier detection. Profitable customer acquisition requires modeling of expected customer potential over the lifetime of the business relationship. In a cross-selling or up-selling model, we try to predict the customer's affinity with a set of products or services translated into the customer's purchase likelihood.

Another aspect of the campaign that should be defined is the set of business or selection rules for a campaign, which specifies the customers who should be excluded from or included in the target groups. To measure how the model based selection is performing with respect to the average customer behavior, the target group can be split into various cells like the control group— containing only randomly selected customers and another cell containing only the best customers according to the implemented model. It is helpful to define a cost/revenue matrix describing how the business mechanics will work in the supported campaign and how it will impact the data-mining process.

Once, the required data have been identified, extracted and consolidated, so that the data in a database (often also called *analytical data mart*) are readily available for subsequent data manipulation and data-mining steps. Another important step is to check the quality of the analytical raw data. Data warehouse infrastructures with advanced data cleansing processes can help ensure you are working with high-quality data. Missing value management is a key element for enhancing the data quality. A preliminary data quality assessment is carried out to assure a good level of quality of the delivered data, and that the data-mining team has a clear understanding of how to interpret the data in business terms.

It is important to identify and select only those variables with good explanatory power (relevant predictive power) for the modeled target behavior. Different methods are employed for selecting the predictor variables. These methods help us

drop collinear variables and those with very low correlation with the target variable. In the context of Customer Management, very often the individual customer is the central object analyzed by means of data mining methods. Usually a very simple, flat data model is chosen as the basis for predictive modeling. In this representation, all data pertaining to an individual customer is contained in one observation (row). Individual columns (variables, fields) represent the conditions at specific points in time or a summary over a whole period. Descriptive statistics such as sums, mean, median, and standard deviation will be employed to capture features of the related time series. Another key variable to be created during this step is the target or dependent variable, needed for predictive modeling. Once a satisfactory definition of the target variable is achieved, its values will be generated for all customers and added to the existing data tables. Many data-mining tools provide support for increasing normality of the analytical variables.

The next step is to select the best model to predict the dependent variable. The performance of different competing models is compared using classification tables and lift analysis (see Sect. 6.4). The final step in the data-mining project is acting based on final results. In this step, customers and prospects are scored and ranked to identify the right customers and prospects to target. Archiving and comparing the business results with the objectives initially set for the project are important activities of the data-mining process in order to derive learnings for future data mining projects.

Acknowledgments We thank Frank Block, Ph.D., of FinScore Corporation (Switzerland) for his collaboration on this chapter.

References

Olson, J. (2003). *Data quality – The accuracy dimension.* Amsterdam: Kaufmann.

Principe, J. C., Euliano, N. R., & Lefebvre, W. C. (2000). *Neural and adaptive systems: Fundamentals through simulations.* New York: Wiley.

Using Databases

8.1 Overview

Stephen Spielberg's 2002 blockbuster movie Minority Report shows a future in which marketing is instantaneous and remarkably personalized. In one of the most indelible sequences of the movie, Tom Cruise's character is walking through a shopping mall where the advertisements address him by name and flaunt products specific to his individual preference (CRM Technology in Minority Report movie). Though we are decades away from such interactivity in marketing, the premise is the basis for Customer Relationship Management – being able to accurately predict customer's purchase behavior and utilize that information to create efficiencies in marketing expenditure. The great leap forward that has made previously unimaginable scenarios, such as this, even remotely possible has been the ever-expanding capabilities of databases and their extensive analytical power. Today, companies gather information about their customers, store it in databases, analyze the data, make marketing decisions, and implement marketing programs based on the results of the data analysis on scales previously only possible in science fiction.

While this edition was being written an IBM super computer, Watson, defeated the two most celebrated Jeopardy champions in a 3 day cumulative event. The significance of this feat lies in its relevance to database management. Imagine a person who could retain a virtually infinite amount of data, retain it in perpetuity and recall it instantaneously. The applications are staggering in virtually every industry where databases are used. The companies that utilize technologies such as Watson will find a tremendous source of competitive advantage, vis-à-vis their competitors that fail to adopt such technologies. With ever expanding databases, efficient data mining and analysis will continue be the catalyst of competitive advantage.

In this chapter, we provide an overview of different types of databases and how they differ in terms of their function, information included, and technology. We also illustrate how companies use different types of databases and how they benefit from using different databases effectively.

8.2 Types of Databases

The types and nature of databases depend on the criteria we use to group databases. If we do not limit the discussion to marketing or customer database, databases used in companies can first be categorized using their main business functions. By doing so we would have the following:

- Databases managing business operations (e.g., account payable database, cost accounting database, order processing database, payroll database)
- Databases supporting decision-making activities (e.g., marketing databases, product development database, advertisement/promotion databases)

V. Kumar and W. Reinartz, *Customer Relationship Management*, Springer Texts in Business and Economics, DOI 10.1007/978-3-642-20110-3_8, © Springer-Verlag Berlin Heidelberg 2012

Databases can also be categorized according to the following criteria:

- The information included in the databases
- The nature of the underlying marketing activities
- Database technology

8.2.1 Categorization Based on the Information Included in the Databases

There are four types of databases:

1. Customer databases
2. Prospect databases
3. Cluster databases
4. Enhancement databases.

Let's look at each of these in turn.

8.2.1.1 Customer Database

The customer database is the core of any marketing database and an invaluable asset for any firm. Marketers typically use customer databases to identify and profile the most valuable customers and communicate with them in ways likely to elicit a customer response. Think about this the next time you use a loyalty card at a grocery store. Your purchases are stored in a large database and that information is used to target coupons that are printed on the back of your receipt! In general, the following information may be included in customer databases:

- *Basic information*: name, address, ZIP code, and telephone number
- *Demographic information*: age, gender, marital status, education, number of people in household, income, and so on
- *Psychographic information*: values, activities, interests, preferences, etc.
- *Transaction history*: What transactions have the customers conducted? How frequently do they purchase? How much did they spend? How were they acquired?
- *Other relevant information*: inquiries and referrals, satisfaction, loyalty

In addition to firms collecting data at the point-of-purchase, some companies buy large amounts of data from third party affiliates.

Several companies gather and sell data from public and private sources across the United States. These data allow the companies (buying them) to market their products to specific customer segments to achieve higher net marketing contribution. Some companies selling databases and database solutions are Acxiorn, D&B, and Prizm. The following examples of customer databases provide an insight into how businesses in the real world use data:

- *D&B's U.S. Marketing File*. This customer database comprises of telemarketing, direct mail, competitor analysis, and other types of data that emerge out of a global database of more than 130 million companies. This database covers businesses in more than 190 countries.
- *InfoBase eProducts*. E-mail marketing is the most inexpensive profit generating marketing tool to augment companies' direct mail or other channels of communication with their customers. E-mail marketing is used today in cross-selling and customer retention initiatives. Newsletters, discount offers, sneak previews, and so on are common inducements communicated through e-mails. InfoBase® eProducts from Acxiom provides the user companies with the e-mail addresses of their customers thereby enabling the companies to
  - Target personalized offers,
  - Reduce direct mail costs and therefore increase net marketing contribution,
  - Gain additional customer touch points, and
  - Acquire more visitors to the company's Web site.

The following example highlights the effective use of email marketing.

CRM AT WORK 8.1

Email Campaigns: When to Send an Email

Email stands as the most financially efficient form of direct communications between firms and their customers. The ability to effectively communicate with a potential consumer can depend on the day of the week they are contacted.

In the "Q2 2006 Email Statistic" study administered by eROI, they found that the there are days of the week where the receiver of an email is more apt to read and address it. The study suggests that for business-to-customer (B2C) firms the best days to send an email are Wednesday and Friday. Wednesday email allows recipients to incorporate the information into their weekend plans, whereas Friday email gives top-of-mind presence to the emailed information; both lead to an increased likelihood of weekend consumption. Saturdays and Sundays are the low points for receiving Business-to-business (B2C).

The B2B e-mail is earlier in the week. B2B e-mail received on Monday or Tuesday allows the recipient to address the email before tending to their other businesses. 33% of survey respondents said they prefer to receive e-mail on Monday, and 36% on Tuesday. Preference for the remainder of the week declines sharply each day.

Source: http://www.clickz.com/clickz/ stats/1707798/clarity-best-day-email

We should note that not only active customers, but also inactive customers should be included in customer databases. Data from active customers help marketers learn what has been done well in the past, and data from inactive customers help to identify what needs to be improved. For inactive customers, the following additional information would be important to document:

- How long have the customers been inactive?
- How long have they been active?
- What was their purchasing pattern when they were active?
- How much did they spend?
- How they were initially acquired?
- Why are they inactive?

8.2.1.2 Prospect Database
Prospects are noncustomers with profiles similar to those of existing customers. The prospect database should include as much information about prospects as the customer database does about customers. For obvious reasons, however, the prospect database does not contain any transaction history data. Marketers can use a prospect database to design marketing campaigns to target prospects with the intent of acquiring them as new customers. Marketers should carefully analyze the channels through which the prospects prefer to receive information-whether they are newspaper/magazine readers, TV viewers, radio listeners, or catalog purchasers. By doing this, marketers can effectively utilize all advertising media to achieve a higher response rate.

In order to achieve the best response rate, marketers also need to segment prospects just as they segment customers, so that they can position the company's differentiated products to the prospects' specific needs. Large-scale promotions to all the prospects should be implemented only after the prospect list has been tested on an experimental basis and has proved to be promising.

Examples of some prospect databases used in the industry follow:

- *InfoBase List*. Companies interested in marketing their products to new prospective customers would find this useful. The InfoBase list offers a collection of U.S. consumer data available in one source for list rentals covering 126 million households and 190 million individuals.
- *Harris Selectory Online*. This is a prospect database from D&B that helps companies find new customers. Such a database allows companies to
  - Qualify developing sales leads,
  - Contact the decision maker best suited to hear their sales pitch, and
  - Research potential opportunities

8.2.1.3 Cluster Database
Cluster databases include information about relatively small *clusters*. These clusters could be defined based on geographic reference groups (such as a ZIP code area), affinity groups (e.g., clubs and associations), and lifestyle reference groups. People in the same cluster tend to have common or similar interests, attitudes, purchasing habits, and preferences. Based on the

proportion of existing customers in each of these clusters, companies can identify the clusters to which prospective customers belong. Also, depending on the membership of prospective customers in specific clusters, firms can customize their marketing communications, thereby increasing the efficiency of marketing efforts. Prizm is a good example of cluster databases.

The Prizm database segments every U.S. neighborhood into 62 distinct areas. Companies can use these databases to identify their potential future customers, locate them, and determine how to reach them in the most effective way. Every Prizm database is categorized into groups, each group having several clusters. Some of thegroups in the Prizm databases follow:

- *S1 (Elite Suburbs).* The five clusters in group SI are the nation's most affluent Social people.
- *UI (Urban uptown).* These clusters include high concentration of executives and professionals.
- *CI (City Society).* The three clusters of group Cl make the upper crust of America's second and satellite cities.
- *T1 (Landed Gentry).* The clusters in this group are made of multi-income families having school-age kids and are headed by well-educated executives and professionals. This is the fourth most affluent group in the United States.

The following example highlights the use of cluster databases.

CRM AT WORK 8.2

American Express and Database Clustering

erican Express is a good example for database clustering. Take a moment to think about the types of data collected by your credit card company. Your purchase behavior spread across many different products, aggregated into a single database creates a great opportunity for clustering with the use of efficient database slicing techniques.

For instance, consider the case of Brian – an avid traveler. He has used his American Express Gold Card to purchase all his airline tickets. All his tickets have been for round trips, and in coach class. Based on his demographic information and other purchase-related attributes, American Express has categorized Brian into the "budget traveler" cluster. After a few years, Brian's income increases and he decides to purchase a first class ticket. Soon after this purchase, American Express revisits his customer information and determines that his behavior could be on the verge of change. Therefore, they offer him with an invitation to apply for a Platinum Card. The outcome of this invitation would help American Express determine if his behavior is related to a transition in behavior or merely a one-off purchase. If Brian signs up for the platinum card, American Express determines that he has changed from the "budget traveler" cluster to the "premium traveler" cluster. Having transitioned to this new cluster, Brian is likely to be provided with several cross-selling offers for other premium services from American Express.

Accurate database clustering is one-part information assimilation and one-part information adaption. It is important for marketers to understand that customer databases evolve over time, and that customers will move between the various clusters as determined by their purchase behavior. Those who believe that customer cluster exists in static isolation will undoubtedly misuse database clustering. Rather an evolving and moving clustering system allows customers to move freely in and out of clusters as is warranted by their purchase behavior.

Source: Rust, Moorman and Bhalla (2010).

8.2.1.4 Enhancement Database

An enhancement database is used to transfer additional information about customers and prospects. An overlaying process is used that eliminates duplications. Enhancements may include

Fig. 8.1 Passive database

demographic and psychographic data, transaction history, changes in address, changes in income levels, privacy status, and new product categories bought recently.

For instance, InfoBase^R Enhanced-InfoBase^R provides a large collection of U.S. customer information such as telephone and address data, mailing lists including hotline files, e-mail data, and so on in one single source. The InfoBase^R Enhanced provides the ability to append the latest demographics, socioeconomic and lifestyle data to your existing in-house customer database. A consumer goods company could use this data to better target its advertising and marketing campaigns, expand brand reach, improve acquisition and retention rates, and increase profitability. The following example highlights the use of enhancement databases.

CRM AT WORK 8.3

County Drain's Enhancement Database

County Drains is a rapidly expanding drainage services company that has built its business model around the strengths of its customer relationships and looks to strengthen those relationships, providing the bedrock of growth for future growth.

While County Drains has always prided its self on its exemplary customer service, its customer base was expanding at such a rate that its system of spreadsheets and manual processes were beginning to be squeezed into antiquity. County Drain needed an adaptive database that would allow it to continue its premium customer service even with the tremendous growth the firm was experiencing. The objectives for the database system were:

- Create a centralized source of data
- An easy, logical system that the staff would quickly adopt

- Improvement of all data; historic, current and new

The CRM program chosen for the project was GoldMine Premium Edition, which allowed them to accomplish each of their three stated goals. The system not only allowed County Drain to continue with its premium customer service, it allowed the firm to be more proactive with its customers providing even more relevant services while also increasing their revenues; a win-win for the customer and the firm.

Source: http://www.concentrix.co. uk/software/crm/case-studies/goldmine-premium-county-drains/

8.2.2 Categorization Based on the Nature of the Underlying Marketing Activities

There are two types of marketing databases – Passive and Active.

Passive Marketing Database
A passive marketing database involves generating a customer list and then storing this list in the database. Future marketing efforts target the same customers in the list. The database is only a mailing list passively storing information about acquired customers, and has no active influence on the company's strategic marketing decisions. Passive databases are often used in smaller companies that lack the resources to actively track customers and update databases. Rather, these firms periodically purchase third party mailing lists from data vendors. Figure 8.1 illustrates a layout of a passive database.

As Fig. 8.1 shows, the database uses the same customer list for different marketing campaigns. Any of the customer databases can be used as a passive database wherein a company keeps

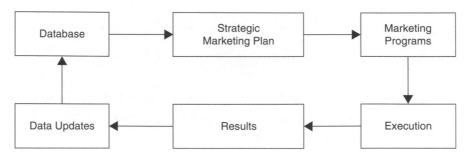

Fig. 8.2 Active database

buying a new and updated customer database every time it needs customer information for campaigns. The campaign results from a past campaign hold no significance in this case.

Active Marketing Database

In contrast, marketers can use an active database to develop strategic marketing plans. Every individual marketing program designed to carry out the plan will then be data-driven. After marketing programs are executed, the results are used to update the database. The updated database can then be used to help marketers adjust or redesign the strategic marketing plan. Figure 8.2 illustrates a layout of an active database. Active databases allow for customer segmentation and clustering due to constant updating. The following example highlights the use of an active database.

CRM AT WORK 8.4

Harrah's Casino and the Active database

Harrah's Casino has found the value of using an active database. By collecting huge volumes of data on customer touch points, Harrah's is able to not only encourage its customers to spend more per visit but also add value to the customer experience through rewards.

From their active database, Harrah's learned that 26% of their gamblers accounted for 82% of their revenues. Surprisingly this small segment was not the high rolling "Whales" that casinos histori-

cally covet. Rather it was the small scale gamblers that typically flock around the slot machines. The data on these customers was constantly updated through their use of a loyalty card, allowing Harrah's to create a rewards system, which could be specifically tailored to these players. A testament to the success of this program can be seen in Harrah's expansion and profitability. In 2003, Harrah's operated 26 casinos in 13 states and in 2002 posted more than $4 billion in revenue and $235 million in net income.

Source: Loveman (2003).

8.2.3 Categorization Based on the Database Technology

Databases can also be categorized according to their underlying technology. Please note that the term *database,* in this context does not refer only to marketing databases.

Hierarchical Database

A hierarchical database is useful when search queries are standard and routine, but require high-speed processing. Hierarchical databases are preferred in the banking, airline, and hotel industries. In hierarchical databases, all information pertaining to a customer will be in a master record. Hence, cross-referencing from other data sources is not needed.

A hierarchical database is organized in a tree-like structure, similar to that of a family tree. In fact, the different levels of the hierarchy are even

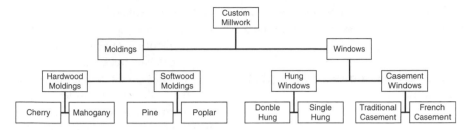

Fig. 8.3   Example of a hierarchical database

referred to as a *parent/child relationship*. Figure 8.3 provides a visualization of this concept for a custom millwork business.

As Fig. 8.3 illustrates, a custom millwork business may choose to design and maintain their database according to their product offerings. In this case, the millwork business has designed their database with three levels in their hierarchy. The first level is about the nature of the millwork – moldings or window work. The second level is about type of molding or window work. The last level is about the choice of wood and design in their millwork. Here, a search query such as "mahogany hardwood moldings" or "French casement windows" is likely to return the customer records pertaining to these products with very little processing time. Depending on the nature, size and scope of the business, the millwork business can choose to add more levels to the hierarchy to accurately capture information regarding their customers.

Databases used in mainframe technology typically are hierarchical databases. They are huge in size and are still used as databases supporting critical applications in some medium- to big-sized corporations.

Inverted Database

Inverted databases are suited for direct marketing applications because they have the speed of a hierarchical database and also the flexibility to respond to unanticipated questions. It is also easy to add new elements to an inverted database as and when updated information is acquired. Some of the commonly used inverted file systems are Model 204, Adabas, and Computer Associates' Datacom/DB. These vary in their processing speeds and flexibility in the implementation environments.

Relational Database

Relational databases are composed of many simple tables. Users can create queries to extract information from these tables and recombine it. This capability means that when compared to other types of databases, relational databases have the greatest flexibility. However, this flexibility also means the speed of processing is somewhat slower. Databases like Oracle, SQL Server, and Microsoft Access are all relational databases. Each one of these has different interfaces and capacities. Its use in organizations today depends on the size of the database marketing initiative. Oracle and SQL Server are capable of handling medium- to large-sized companywide marketing programs while Microsoft Access is used for smaller-sized database marketing initiatives.

8.3   The Benefits of Marketing Databases

Companies that efficiently use their marketing databases can expect the following benefits.

8.3.1   The Ability to Carry Out Profitable Segmentation

Customers can be classified into different groups, depending on their buying behaviors. Frequent buyers need to be treated differently than occasional buyers. First-time users should be approached differently than repeat buyers. Marketing databases allow us to analyze customers and classify them into different groups. Different marketing programs can then be executed and implemented for different groups or segments.

8.3.2 Retained Customers and Repeat Business

Retaining existing customers has become one of the important goals of many companies' marketing practices. Marketing databases enable marketers to determine the critical factors which influence the degree of customer satisfaction; and to develop effective campaigns accordingly to retain as many existing customers as possible at the lowest possible cost

8.3.3 The Ability to Spot Potentially Profitable Customers

With marketing databases, the company can profile its own customers, and then use lists and media surveys to locate potential customers with the same profile, and are therefore expected to contribute significantly to the company's revenues because of their higher response rates and willingness to buy premium products.

8.4 The Uses of Marketing Databases (Jackson and Wang 1994)

8.4.1 Uses that Directly Influence the Customer Relationship

- *Identify and profile the best customers.* By tracking customer transaction data, marketers can conduct recency, frequency, and monetary value (RFM) analysis or develop sophisticated models to identify customers who are of greatest value to the company.
- *Develop new customers.* Armed with the profile of the company's best customers, the company can find new customers with the characteristics of the best customers. Marketers could target not only the new users of the product/service but also competitors' existing customers.

- *Deliver customized messages consistent with product/service usage.* With customer transaction history data and customer service data, marketers can track customers' feedback to the specific products and services, and find out what pleased or displeased them. Then, the company can design specially customized marketing messages consistent with the product/service to promote their products and or services.
- *Send follow-up messages to customers for post-purchase reinforcement.*
- *Cross-sell* products/services. The company can identify customers' other needs based on their demographic, lifestyle, and behavioral characteristics, and then sell them other products/services that satisfy their needs.
- *Ensure cost-effective communication with customers.* A marketing database enables marketers to classify customers into high potential, medium potential, and low potential groups. After evaluating the monetary value of these customers' potential, marketers will be able to determine how much the company should invest on communicating with these customers.
- *Improve promotion result.* Marketers: can achieve better promotion results by targeting the customer groups who are most likely to respond (e.g., loyalists, prospects with best customer profiles).
- *Personalize customer service.* Knowing when, where, and what the customers purchased, the company can communicate with the customers to get their feedback, and then personalize the customer service delivered to them.
- *Stealth communication with customers.* Marketing databases provide the opportunity for one-on-one communications with each customer without the competitors' knowledge.

8.4.2 Uses that Directly Influence Other Business Operations

- *Evaluate and refine existing marketing practices.* By analyzing customer data, marketers can assess the effectiveness of all the aspects of the existing marketing practice, including strategy, planning, budgeting, campaign design, implementation, customer communication, and so on to identify shortcomings and suggest improvements.

- *Maintain brand equity.* Match brands with customers who fit the brand profile and keep communicating with those customers using specially designed brand-building messages.
- *Increase effectiveness of distribution channels.* Customers' transaction data and customer service data can tell how existing distribution channels work and how to make them more effective.
- *Conduct product and market research.* In a customer-centric company, product, and market research must focus on customer needs. Marketing databases provide a unique resource of information on customer needs.
- *Integrating the marketing program.* A complete and integral marketing database can track all marketing efforts toward a customer. Marketers will be able to avoid duplicate, supplemental, and misdirected communications. It also helps marketers determine any overlapping between marketing programs targeted at different customer groups.
- *Create a new valuable management resource.* A marketing database could be used to support not only the traditional marketing practices, but also a wide range of other business functions such as advertising, product R&D, distribution, customer service, and so on.

8.5   Summary

Effective database analysis is important for successful CRM. Databases can be categorized based on their main business function-databases managing business and databases supporting decision-making activities. In addition, databases can also be categorized based on the information included in the databases, the nature of the underlying marketing activities, and database technology. Based on the information included in the databases, databases can be classified as customer, prospect, cluster, and enhancement databases.

Customer databases identify and profile the best customers and communicate with these customers to elicit a response. These data allow the companies to market their products to specific customer segments to achieve higher net marketing contribution. Data from active and inactive customers are important to ensure efficient marketing function. The prospect database includes information on noncustomers with profiles similar to those of existing customers. It can be used by marketers to design marketing campaigns to target prospects with the intent of acquiring them as new customers. This is done after carefully analyzing the channels through which the prospects like to receive information. Cluster databases include information about small clusters based on geographic reference groups, affinity groups, and lifestyle reference groups. An enhancement database is used to transfer additional information on customers and prospects avoiding duplications.

Based on the nature of the underlying marketing activities, marketing databases are categorized into active and passive. A passive database is a customer mailing list that passively stores information about acquired customers for targeting future marketing efforts, and has no active influence on the company's strategic marketing decisions. An active database is used by marketers to develop strategic marketing plans. After marketing programs are executed, the results are used to update the database. The updated database can be used to help marketers adjust or redesign the strategic marketing plan.

Databases can also be categorized into hierarchical, inverted, and relational databases. A hierarchical database is useful for routine and standard queries which need high-speed processing. These have all the information pertaining to a customer in a master record and are typically used in mainframe technology. Inverted databases are suited for direct marketing applications on account of their speed, flexibility, and ease of updating. Relational databases have the greatest flexibility but lower speed of processing. Marketing databases allow marketers to analyze customers and classify them into different groups and, accordingly, implement different marketing programs for each group. These databases also enable marketers to determine the critical factors influencing customer satisfaction and take measures to retain existing customers at lowest cost. They also help marketers in identifying potentially profitable customers using lists and media surveys. Using marketing databases, marketers can identify individual customers of greatest value to the company. Other uses of marketing databases include developing new customers, delivering customized messages consistent with product/service usage, and effectively communicating with customers in the form of feedbacks on purchases, promotions, stealth communications, and so on. Maintaining brand equity, increasing effectiveness of distribution channels, as well as conducting product and market research are other uses of marketing databases that directly influence business operations.

Exercise Questions

1. What are the various ways to categorize databases?
2. How are databases classified based on the information they contain? Are these different classes of databases complements or substitutes?

3. Assume you are the marketing manager for a local US bank in Texas. Your assignment is to target prospects in Oklahoma (small to medium sized businesses). Go to the website of Axciom (http://www.acxiom.com) or Dun&Bradstreet (http://www.dnb.com) and determine the cost of obtaining ten variables of firmographic information on these firms.
4. List some of the key uses of marketing databases. Provide an example for each of those.

References

CRM Technology in Minority Report movie (2002). CIO. Accessed September 15, 2011, from, http://www.cio.com/article/31319/CRM_Technology_in_Minority_Report_movie

Jackson, R., & Wang, P. (1994). *Strategic database marketing* (pp. 40–53). McGraw-Hill Education, Framingham, MA.

Loveman, G. (2003). Diamonds in the data mine. *Harvard Business Review, 81*(5), 109–113.

Rust, R. T., Moorman, C., & Bhalla, G. (2010). Rethinking marketing. *Harvard Business Review, 88*(1–2), 94–101.

Part IV

Operational CRM

Software Tools and Dashboards

9

9.1 Introduction

Expectations are inevitably high when a company decides to implement a CRM system. Why shouldn't they be? CRM has been lauded as the next revolution in customer management, giving firms the ability to manage their customers on an individual level. This level of individualized marketing is said to decrease overall marketing spend while increasing marketing's overall effectiveness. These expectations are, indeed, feasible, but companies are often concerned about the implementation of the CRM system. There have been many cases of failed CRM implementation that have had adverse impacts on companies, their managements, and their stakeholders.

While failed CRM implementations are a reality, a careful examination of options as a precursor to implementation can negate much of the risk inherent in a CRM implementation. Firms have different requirements and different competencies and must ensure that their implementation method satisfies their requirements and highlights their competencies. With patience and careful examination of expectations and competencies, management can select a CRM system and associated implementation strategy that best suits their needs, leading to an invaluable customer management tool.

9.2 CRM Implementation Options

Companies can opt for any one or a combination of three different ways to implement a CRM solution: developing software in house, buying licensed software, or outsourcing creation of software.

9.2.1 Developing Software In-House

Building and managing a CRM solution in-house requires the company to define all its requirements, pay for software development, and bear all the R&D costs internally. Companies choosing to develop software in-house must invest heavily in storage, application software and hardware, all of which add considerably to the overhead costs. The initial hardware and software expenses constitute only a small portion of the total cost, which is largely shaped by maintenance demands, especially those arising from changing requirements inside the organization. This can be done with or without external consulting help, although it is useful to have external help because collecting data, managing related systems, and driving value from data is not a core competence of most businesses.

A good analogy for this route is building a professional sports franchise with young or

V. Kumar and W. Reinartz, *Customer Relationship Management*, Springer Texts in Business and Economics, DOI 10.1007/978-3-642-20110-3_9, © Springer-Verlag Berlin Heidelberg 2012

unknown players. The young players are able to fit into the scheme you develop but will lack the experience of more seasoned veterans. Because of this, much more oversight, training and management will be needed to ensure the success of the team that bears upfront costs and long-term costs as well. While the upfront cost of this choice may not be as much as acquiring seasoned veterans, the opportunity costs and long-term costs almost certainly are greater.

9.2.1.1 Advantages

Companies develop a tailor-made solution adapted to their needs and structure. They develop internal resources and skills that allow them to develop the system each time the company requirements change. By doing do, they can avoid dependence on CRM software vendors and on new software releases or developments. Since the solution is tailor-made to fit their current business practices, firms that choose this route are not required to adapt their business practices to any particular software. This independence of not relying too much on software often leads to a smoother transition for the majority of employees using the system.

9.2.1.2 Disadvantages

This is usually the most expensive option because the company has to maintain, operate, and improve the system on its own. Usually, it is very difficult to attract and retain the employees needed to solve data warehousing challenges. The typical time commitment is 1–2 years, which might be long when compared to other out-of-the box solutions in the market.

9.2.2   Buying Licensed CRM Software

Companies that choose to buy licensed CRM software will also need extensive IT resources. Even with a licensed CRM software solution, companies still need to develop the IT infrastructure and integrate the new software with existing applications. This solution can be sold as a block (it may be composed of different modules adapted to each. front-office application) or it can be sold as independent modules (e.g., the company just buys the sales automation module or the contact management module).

Although the CRM vendor should provide knowledge and training for the new system, considerable effort still needs to be invested in order to develop internal expertise and skills to effectively run the new CRM solution. Also, each time the CRM vendor releases a new or an upgraded version of the software, the company needs to go through the process of upgrading the systems, buying additional modules, and resolving other associated problems.

9.2.2.1 Advantages

Many of these software packages have a proven record of success, and the company can feel reassured that this solution has worked for other companies. Typically, the software packages are developed using a set of "best practices" and continually updated as the practices evolve. This ensures that the CRM system will function properly. The IT concept and developments will be implemented with the help of the CRM vendor and the company will only need to adapt its IT structure to integrate the new solution.

9.2.2.2 Disadvantages

This is also an expensive option and may take several months to be integrated with the company's operations. The initial fees and the licensing costs are usually high. Companies are often charged to renew the license each year. Maintenance costs are required over the life of the software, and each time a new version comes out, companies have to pay for it. If the company chooses to customize the solution to its needs, it will have to pay for consulting services, which are generally very expensive. In situations when companies change to a new CRM software package, they may also face resistance from employees in terms of adapting to the new system/process. Even programs that can save employees time and effort can be regarded as intrusive and complicated in the short run, if the new software package is a significant detour from the previously used CRM software. In this regard, a careful examination of the company's human capital

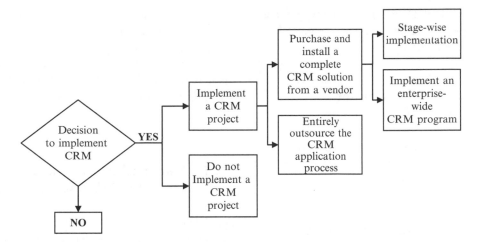

Fig. 9.1   The decision process for implementation

would be critical in making a decision on the choice of CRM software package.

9.2.3   Outsourcing a Managed Service

Companies can outsource the CRM solution from a third-party company. The outsourcing company provides the hardware, software, and human resources in exchange for a monthly fee. Implementation takes less time because applications are already built and operational and the outsourcing company has an incentive to get the system running so that it can initiate service and fees.

9.2.3.1 Advantages
The upfront costs are lower than in the other two approaches. Companies do not need to pay for software licenses and hardware systems. The firm does not need to recruit or develop internal IT skills to manage the new CRM solution. The company can adopt a pay-as-you-go approach, meaning that it can start the process of paying as the CRM results are visible, instead of paying upfront costs and licensing and maintenance costs. Especially pertinent for smaller companies or those with limited marketing and IT budgets, this approach allows these firms to take advantage of CRM programs which would otherwise be unavailable due to high costs. This approach is often referred to as Software as a Service (Dubey

& Wagle, 2007) (SaaS) or Software on Demand. An example of this type of software is Salesforce.com, which provides sales force automation without expensive licensing or software development.

9.2.3.2 Disadvantages
Each time the company needs to adapt the solution to new requirements it has to contact the outsourcing company and pay for the developments. The firm does not possess the necessary skills and knowledge to manage the CRM solution, and it risks losing the CRM solution investments if the outsourcing company goes out of business. The implementing firm is entirely dependent on the outsourcing company, placing even greater importance on platform selection. This option may not be viable for very large or specialized firms who require specific requirements in their CRM package.

9.2.3.3 The Decision Process for Implementation
When deciding about implementing the CRM project, the organization follows a structured hierarchical process (Fig. 9.1).

In the particular case that the company opts to buy a CRM solution, integration middleware suppliers and consulting services at the management, technical, and information systems levels are often employed, even though they are not always required. Depending on the type of application, these services may be included in the original contract.

9.3 CRM Software and Applications

In this section we will focus on the option where the company chooses to buy licensed CRM software or to outsource the CRM solution.

9.3.1 Stage-Wise Implementation Versus an Enterprise Wide CRM Solution

The CRM industry offers different types of solutions based on the company needs and processes. CRM software solutions can be looked at in two different ways:

1. CRM software is offered in different, independent modules, which are adapted to a specific department's needs (e.g., the company buys the sales automation software and the contact management module from different providers).
2. The enterprise wide CRM solution is composed of different modules from the same provider. These modules may be adapted to each department's needs, yet they are implemented as a whole by connecting the different modules and the existing databases. Individual components may be weaker than best-of-breed products; however, the organization knows the different components are fully compatible.

Sometimes the enterprise wide CRM solutions are not customized to specific needs. This could lead to further consulting costs in the future. Current market conditions and competition have resulted in CRM vendors now customizing individual modules to company needs.

Ideally, all CRM software solutions should integrate information and databases from marketing, sales, customer service, e-business, call-center, and other sources. The total CRM solution comprises a series of many different hardware devices and software components.

These components may or may not come from different suppliers and may run on different platforms. It is the company's decision, based on the precedent requirements, to choose between a stage-wise implementation of CRM modules or an enterprise wide CRM solution.

9.3.2 Relationships and Flows Between CRM Modules

As stated earlier, CRM modules can be implemented independently in phases or together in a global solution. In both cases, the important thing is to integrate the modules so that the company can have an integrated view of the customer. All the information obtained from the customer is stored in a data warehouse which will be used to perform analysis, modeling, and data mining. Consequently the analysis information will be used in different ways by each department to interface with the customer in the future, via the available channels of communication. To illustrate this adaptation, Fig. 9.2 a pictorial representation of an integrated CRM solution at work. This represents a generic implementation with room for customization as per the requirements of each industry.

A new trend emerging in the CRM industry is that of strategic supplier partnerships. These consist of a partnership between the company that implements CRM and the supplier of the software and services. The goal is not only to customize the CRM offer to the company's needs, but also to ensure that the supplying company takes part in the implementation processes. This is in response to buyers increasingly demanding a risk-sharing proposition from the supplier. This means that the seller of the tool has an interesting delivering the impact that was promised at the time of sale.

9.4 Summary

CRM has a curious duality. On one hand it can provide the capabilities for firms to optimize their marketing budgets and, increase revenues.

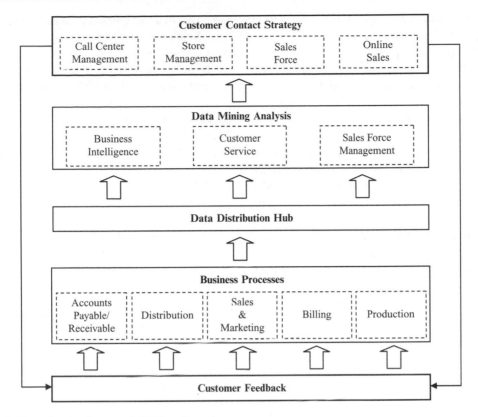

Fig. 9.2 Example of an integrated CRM configuration

However, poor planning in the implementation stage can cause confusion in operations and cost the firm millions, or worse, alienate its customers. This chapter discussed strategies associated with CRM implementations, although there are varying degrees of customization that are possible with each strategy.

The first strategy is to develop in-house software. This is the most expensive option and should only be undertaken by firms that have a competency in software development. Since the software is being developed in-house, it allows for customizations and permits the firm to tailor the system to its current business processes and culture.

The second strategy is to purchase licensed software from a third party vendor. This strategy is often less expensive than developing the in-house software, but can run up exorbitant costs in its associated implementation and pushback. Customization is possible in this strategy, but incurs additional costs when upgrading to newer software. The default practices and controls in the system are considered to be "best practices" as they are a product of research across a large number of firms. While these practices and controls are considered to be industry leading, they may not coincide with the implementing firm's culture and could result in considerable hesitancy from employees to adopt such a system.

The final option is outsourcing to a managed service. Companies such as Salesforce.com have made CRM capabilities available even to small and mid-sized businesses and have taken much of the anxiety out of implementation, since none is involved. This service is provided on a pay-for-play system, which equates to lower costs than the other two options. Outsourcing CRM is increasingly becoming popular with companies of all sizes. However, a prime concern with outsourcing CRM is limited control for the implementing firm from the provider. In addition, little or no customization options from the service provider are likely to create a cause for concern for the implementing firms.

Within each strategy lies the question of how to implement. There are two options: stage-wise and enterprise-wise implementation. Stage wise implementation often takes longer, but allows for firms to take the implementation "one step at a time" and learn from their mistakes as they progress. This is often considered as a safer approach. An enterprise-wide implementation is considerably more risky, but allows the firm to begin taking advantage of all of the system's benefits much sooner since the system rolls out over all business units simultaneously.

CRM is a valuable resource for any company that wishes to gain insight into customer behavior. It can cut costs, increase revenues and make a significant impact on the productivity of a company. While implementing a CRM system can prove to a mine field of danger, with careful consideration of available options and conscientious management of the problem, the minefield can be safely negotiated, leading to the successful implementation of a CRM system.

Exercise Questions

1. Practicing CRM without technology is not possible. Do you agree with this statement?
2. What are the various ways to deploy CRM? What are their advantages and disadvantages?
3. Describe some of the key CRM software applications and their functions.

Reference

Dubey, A., &. Wagle, D. (2007, May). Delivering software as a service. *The McKinsey Quarterly*, p. 1–12.

Loyalty Programs: Design and Effectiveness

10

10.1 Overview

To retain customers, many firms focus on increasing customer satisfaction levels. And the degree of customer satisfaction is a key measure. But the extent to which customer satisfaction leads to loyalty and thus profitability remains an important issue to be examined. Traditionally, customer satisfaction has been expected to increase retention or loyalty, thus leading to greater profits, as we introduced in Chap. 2. Although customer satisfaction and loyalty are key mediators of profit, they cannot be taken as simple predictors of it. From a business standpoint, it is more important to identify and nurture relationships specifically with *profitable* customers.

This is where loyalty programs come in. Loyalty programs (LP) represent an important CRM tool that can identify, reward, and successfully retain profitable customers. We discuss the objectives and design of various loyalty programs in Sects. 10.2 to 10.6. We also illustrate LP failures to offer insights into what distinguishes a successful program from unsuccessful ones. By reviewing LP characteristics, we also can systematically investigate outcomes and determinants of LP success and provide guidelines for designing optimal programs. The key dimensions of LP design, such as reward and sponsorship, are explained in detail and illustrated using relevant case studies.

The second part of this chapter then deals with the effectiveness of loyalty programs. In the past two decades, many firms have established some type of customer LP. Typically, these programs offer financial and/or relationship rewards to customers. In most cases, the aim is to increase sales revenue by increasing usage/purchase levels or engaging in up- and cross-selling. Loyalty programs also promise stronger relationships with customers. But they are not costless for the provider. Before any firm establishes an LP, it must ask: What is the cost effectiveness of this program? What differentiates an effective LP from an ineffective one? What key drivers ensure the effectiveness of loyalty programs? Understanding goals and design characteristics are critical means to develop and implement effective loyalty programs. It is equally, if not more, important to understand and monitor the features that make an LP effective; we suggest four such drivers. Therefore, after we present some empirical evidence about the performance of LPs across various industry segments, we use two case studies to reveal how firms can create competitive advantages through loyalty programs that are geared to attaining profits and value alignment. With this information, we derive a seven-point checklist for the successful design and implementation of loyalty programs.

V. Kumar and W. Reinartz, *Customer Relationship Management*, Springer Texts in Business and Economics, DOI 10.1007/978-3-642-20110-3_10, © Springer-Verlag Berlin Heidelberg 2012

10.2 What Is Loyalty? Behavioral Versus Attitudinal Loyalty

Loyal customers generate more repeat business, develop a larger tolerance to price increases, and are more profitable to the firm. This conventional wisdom has long been accepted, but as we have shown, it is not always true. A very loyal customer may consume an inordinate amount of firm resources by demanding services and discounts. But marketers want to locate and entice new customers who are *profitable*, while also finding appropriate strategies to identify and possibly release unprofitable customers.

In Chap. 1, we noted the concept of *customer value*, defined as the economic value ($-metric) of the customer relationship to the firm, expressed as a contribution margin or net profit. As a marketing metric, customer value provides an important decision aid, beyond its capability to evaluate marketing effectiveness. A firm can both measure and optimize its marketing efforts by incorporating the concept of customer value in the core of its decision-making processes.

Although customer loyalty to a product or service, manifested as repeat purchases, may be due to natural satisfaction and preference for the products' features and benefits, loyalty also can be induced through marketing plans and programs. For example, wireless cellular phone service requires a 1–2-year contractual relationship with the customer – an indirect way of ensuring repetitive and profitable transactions for a predictable period of time.

Whether contractual or motivated through incentives, the success or failure of a LP depends ultimately on the profitability of the customer. The longevity of the relationship also does not automatically translate into tangible profitability. Rather, various customer loyalty programs work to identify, reward, and retain specifically profitable customers.

Before reviewing the structure of these various loyalty programs, it is important to understand the significant difference between behavioral and attitudinal loyalty. Broadly speaking, *behavioral loyalty* refers to the observed actions that customers have demonstrated toward a particular product or service. *Attitudinal loyalty* instead refers to a customer's perceptions and attitudes toward a particular product or service. Ideally, there should be a strong correlation between a customers' attitudes and behaviors, though in some instances, customer behaviors differ radically from their attitudinal perceptions about the product or service.

A Case in Point

A frequent flyer member of ABC airlines might continue the relationship only because she has accrued many points and wants to redeem her miles. Although her attitudinal preference is to travel with XYZ airlines, because of its superior quality of service and experience, she feels compelled to continue transacting with ABC. In this situation, her relationship with ABC reflects strong behavioral loyalty, while her negative perceptions of it reflect poor attitudinal loyalty. Attitudinal loyalty is extremely important; customers who are not attitudinally loyal likely terminate the relationship at the earliest available opportunity. As we will find, not all loyalty programs are interested in creating attitudinal loyalty with the target customers.

10.3 What Is a Loyalty Program? Definition and Key Objectives

In recent years, many companies have introduced loyalty programs (LPs), frequent reward programs, or customer clubs. An LP comprises a marketing process that generates rewards for customers, based on their repeat purchases. As we use it, the term LP subsumes the many different forms of reward programs. Therefore, we recognize that consumers who enter an LP likely transact more with the focal company and give up some of the free choice they possess otherwise. In exchange for concentrating their purchases with the focal firm, they accumulate assets (e.g., points), which they may exchange for products and services, usually those associated with the focal firm. Because of these characteristics, LPs offer an important CRM tool that marketers use to identify, award, and retain profitable customers.

This is not to suggest that they are new additions in the relationship marketer's toolkit. Sainsbury (UK) archives show that in the 1970s, its managers wrote to customers who had not made their usual shopping trips, in an effort to encourage and maintain their patronage. Later, the store used a Green Stamps initiative, which customers enjoyed, despite the demand that they paste the stamps into many books before receiving any reward (Passingham, 1998).

Overall, the *key objectives* of introducing LPs consist of four categories:

1. Building true (attitudinal and behavioral) loyalty
2. Efficiency profits
3. Effectiveness profits
4. Value alignment

Any loyalty program implemented by a firm may pursue all or only some of these goals at the same time.

10.3.1 Building True Loyalty

An LP aims to build greater customer commitment to the product or organization by garnering true loyalty, which combines elements of both attitudinal and behavioral loyalty. According to this logic, customers exhibit behavioral loyalty (i.e., purchase a product repeatedly) for several reasons, including convenience or price, as well as a sense of loyalty. Behavioral loyalty may result from attitudinal loyalty, but it can be driven by other factors too.

Furthermore, though many LPs have the goal of "making customers more loyal," the outcomes of true loyalty – greater commitment, greater word of mouth, and so on – are difficult to observe. Enforcing loyalty by enticing customers with rewards and bonuses is unlikely to create true loyalty, because true loyalty instead is a

function of the value provided to customers. It encompasses various factors: degree of involvement in the product category, visibility of product usage, or the value expressive nature of the product, to name a few. None of these aspects can be controlled by the firm.

Take, for example, a low-involvement category – grocery shopping. Inducing true loyalty for grocery shoppers is a tough proposition, because their purchases are nearly always driven by tangible considerations, such as value for money.

10.3.2 Efficiency Profits

Efficiency profits result from a change in the customer's buying behavior, induced by the LP. This change in behavior can be measured in several ways:

- Basket size
- Purchase frequency acceleration
- Price sensitivity
- Share of category requirements (SCR) or share of wallet
- Retention
- Lifetime duration

The most widely used measure of behavioral loyalty is SCR, which describes the extent of purchases in a category that are served by the focal brand or retailer. Efficiency profits are net of LP cost. An LP that attempts to generate efficiency profits works on the assumption that customers build up switching costs when they accumulate loyalty-based assets. This accumulation encourages them to forgo their free choice, because the expected reward makes this reduction appear worthwhile.

There are two key criticisms of this viewpoint. First, for a customer to engage in an LP, the overall utility of being in the LP must be higher than the utility of not being in the LP. The cost for the firm to entice the customer to change behavior accordingly may be higher than it would be without the LP. Carlos Criado-Perez, the one-time CEO of Safeway (1999–2004), thus traded off the benefits: "Scrapping Safeway's (UK) ABC loyalty card scheme saves it £50 million this year, money that will be invested in cutting prices."[1]

Second, a goal of efficiency profits implies that the customer segment most likely to join the LP consists of those who are truly loyal anyway, so their business is already likely. In this case, the question arises about whether LPs actually change buying behavior. Perhaps they do not change behavior as much as they reinforce existing behavior, but at a much higher cost to the firm. For example, loyalty cards have been criticized for rewarding heavy spending rather than true loyalty. The segments most interested in these plans tend to be affluent groups who can afford to build up points, even if they hold cards from more than one store.[2]

Yet, despite the difficulty associated with achieving efficiency profits, many LPs are introduced with just this goal in mind.

10.3.3 Effectiveness Profits

Effectiveness profits refer to the medium- to long-term profit consequences realized through the development of better knowledge about customer preferences. The LP is designed to gather information about individuals, their behavior, and their preferences and then to derive knowledge from this information. This process of learning allows the firm to improve its knowledge of customer preferences and to offer increasingly better-tailored value propositions to various customers. The improvement in the value proposition comes through effective product and communication offerings. Effectiveness profits – more than any other type of LP outcome – are likely to generate sustainable competitive advantages and yield the highest profits in the long run.

**Achieving Effectiveness Profits
in a Grocery Store**

Effectiveness profits require an information-based strategy that gathers and analyzes information about every transaction. For example, in grocery retailing, the system must collect information about every item purchased, down to the color of ink in a pen, along with the time of day, weather, and even the checkout operator's name. Such *data mining* can generate personalized promotions and recommendations so that a vegetarian never receives a promotion for steaks. The knowledge that a customer is a vegetarian might come from either surveys or previous buying behavior. If the store's computer recognizes that a customer never buys meat, it can predict that the customer is a vegetarian, and not that she is buying her meat elsewhere. Although this assumption could be wrong, a store would rather not bother a customer with costly promotions for categories from which that customer has never bought anything.

Promotions of new products rely on an *ideas list*, populated by both new launches and existing products that the data mining algorithms suggest specific customers might desire. For example, if a customer buys a lot of California Chardonnay, the list might suggest that he is likely to try a white Burgundy on special promotion, because it is made from the same grape. The strategy of using an LP to *learn about customer preferences* thus can result in value, as well as impressive gains, for both customers and organizations. Customers get more of what they truly want; firms avoid costly, mass marketing exercises. However, a learning strategy demands a relatively high process sophistication for its implementation. The collection of massive amounts of data may have grown easier, but analyzing, learning about, and implementing the conclusions obtained is much more difficult. Few companies have mastered this strategic capability to a satisfactory extent.

10.3.4 Value Alignment

Finally, value alignment aims to match the cost to serve a particular customer with the value that

---

[1] Interview with Carlos Criado-Perez, CEO Safeway (UK), on BBC News (May 4, 2000).

[2] Interview with Richard Gaines, Retail Consultant with Mintel Research UK (Spring 2001).

Fig. 10.1 Revenue and profitability of customers

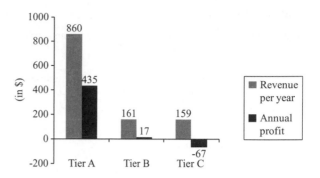

the person brings to the firm. The underlying concept states that for any industry, customers have differential monetary value to firms, and they also are differentially expensive to serve. For example, if a provider of wireless services were to arrange its customers from highest to lowest value, it might discover that its business users generate higher phone bills than casual, occasional users. Likewise, if it were to arrange the same customers according to the costs of serving them, it would find some customers easy to satisfy, whereas others exploit the customer service function constantly. If a firm pursues value alignment, it simply attempts to align the profits it receives from a given customer with the cost incurred to serve that customer. Clearly, not every customer is treated equally – a notion some managers find discomforting. However, this differentiation allows firms to ensure that their best customers get their best service. The goal of value alignment is particularly critical when there is great heterogeneity in customers' value and costs to serve, such as in the airline, hospitality, or financial services industries.

Example
Figure 10.1 illustrates an example of a firm with a highly heterogeneous customer base. It indicates the profitability of a bank, derived from three very different customer profiles: Tier A represents 31% of the customer base, whereas Tier B makes up 42%, and Tier C makes up the remaining 27% of the customer base. More than one-quarter of these customers are unprofitable and must be subsidized by the highly profitable ones – a condition not uncommon in banks.

If this bank were to institute an LP, it might pursue the four different LP goals. If it chooses a particular goal, how can it achieve that outcome most effectively? Such an assessment requires a more detailed understanding of the impact of the drivers of LP success. That is, to reach the goals of an LP, it seems useful to understand some of their characteristics, including the suitability of the goal, cost structures, challenges involved, and the degree of competitive advantage created, as summarized in Table 10.1.

10.4 Loyalty Programs: Increasing in Popularity

Interest in loyalty programs exploded in the late 1990s. Building mainly on the premise that it is cheaper to market to existing customers than to acquire new ones, firms across a multitude of industries raced to implement some form of loyalty schemes. Thus the growth in LP usage has been staggering. In 2006, U.S. loyalty programs counted 1.34 billion members. Just 2 years later, the number had risen to 1.81 billion members – and it continues to increase (Odell, 2009).

Some quantitative examples and the summaries attest to this growth:

- In 2010, "PAYBACK", Germany's largest loyalty program, documented 18.5 million membership accounts, 13.5 million of which represented active users. Holding on average two cards per account, it accounts for about 32% of Germany's population (Lebensmittelzeitung, 2011) and reaches about 42% of German households (Wyndham Worldwide, 2009).

Table 10.1 Key characteristics of loyalty programs

Goal of LP	Commitment, WOM, building communities (true loyalty)	Efficiency profits	Effectiveness profits	Value alignment
Most suited for …	All branded products (though larger brands have more difficulty uniquely differentiating their brand and managing customer interactions)	Many industries	▪ Firms with access to much information ▪ Firms that communicate directly with end users	All industries with skewed customer value distributions. Within this class, industries with product perishability (airlines, hospitality, rental cars) are particularly well suited.
Cost of LP may be mitigated by	—	Contributions from manufacturers (promotions)	Contributions from manufacturers (promotions)	Low marginal cost of rewards
Key challenges	▪ Providing meaningful value to create differentiation in consumers' minds	▪ Providing acceptable incentives to customers while also controlling costs	Capability to handle, analyze, learn from, and deploy knowledge from large databases	▪ Implementing the customer differentiation scheme (deployment automation)
	▪ Brand building	▪ Program differentiation		▪ Having fair and equitable relationships but ensuring that best customers are treated best
Degree of competitive advantage	*High* (a truly loyal customer base is hard and costly to replicate, because it can only be built over time)	*Low* (it is easy to replicate benefits, and program costs create major challenges)	*High* (capability of learning from customer behavior and using it is very difficult to copy and unique to a company's context)	*Low-medium* (LPs have become standard industry practice)

- By 2002, there were more than 120 million airline frequent flyers worldwide, with most residing in the United States (74 million), Europe (24 million), and Asia (21 million) (Webflyer, 2011).
- "American Advantage" is the largest frequent flyer program in the world. As of December 2009, its membership rolls boasted more than 64 million members (AMR Corporation, 2009).

- With 56 million members globally, who contribute $6.5 billion in room revenue, IHG's (InterContinental Hotels Group) "Priority Club" Rewards is one of the first, largest, and fastest growing guest loyalty program in the hotel industry. The program adds 600,000 members monthly and offers points for stays in 4,300 hotels in nearly 100 countries worldwide. Members can redeem points for future hotel stays, airline miles on more than 40 partner airlines, car rentals, gift certificates, or hundreds of products available in a rewards catalog (IHG, 2010).

- In the highly competitive U.K. retail industry, Tesco has managed to double its earnings by taking market share from rivals such as Sains-bury's. Its success has been credited to its popular customer loyalty program, which enables shoppers to earn points and redeem them on future visits or with airlines (ABC, 2003).
- The French retailer E. Leclerc spends approximately $23.5 million each year for LP marketing and management (Meyer-Waarden, 2007).[3]
- According to VSS Communications Industry Forecast, U.S. companies devoted $2.18 billion to loyalty programs in 2008 (Odell, 2009). Just a few years ago, in 2003, Gartner analyst Adam Sarner declared that U.S. companies spent more than $1.2 billion on customer loyalty programs (Young & Stepanek, 2003). This enormous growth reflects the great popularity of loyalty programs.

The most well-known examples of loyalty programs remain frequent flyer programs. American Airlines was the first, establishing its "Advantage" program in 1981. During the 1990s, supermarket chains and general merchandise retailers followed suit and established loyalty programs, such as the "Carte de Fidélité" program offered by the French retail chain Carrefour or the "Club-Card" at Tesco. The latest form of loyalty programs involves point collection schemes initiated by third parties (e.g., Webmiles, PAYBACK), where users collect points across a network of member companies.

Although LPs have become immensely popular, it is far from clear whether they actually help firms engender greater customer loyalty and higher profits, partly because of the considerable cost associated with managing an LP, and partly because their management can be so complex.

[3] Based on a conversion rate of 1 Euro = 1.305 USD, as of February 1, 2005.

CRM AT WORK 10.1
Frequent-Flyer Programs

In the airline industry, five main factors drive customers' choices of providers: market coverage, price, schedule, frequent flyer programs, and product attributes. For many years, the common belief in the airline industry was that loyal customers were more profitable, so by rewarding customers based on the miles they flew, the airline could increase their loyalty. But there were some serious shortcomings in this approach. By rewarding all passengers equally, the airline failed to maximize the value for its most profitable customers. Seat class and fare types were ignored in the reward system. When it realized this flaw, the airline industry moved away from basing rewards on miles flown; Airlines, United, Continental, and USAir all multiply the miles flown by a customer by a coefficient derived from the type of seat class the customer paid to receive.

Passengers willing to pay to upgrade to business or first class thus earn more miles and get rewarded sooner and more often. In contrast, customers who hunt for bargains and purchase deeply discounted tickets far in advance or at the last minute earn far fewer miles than those who pay the full fare. This practice makes sense conceptually: bargain-hunting customers tend to be loyal to finding a bargain than to a reward card program or a specific airline. By increasing the rewards granted to passengers who are willing to pay more per seat than the average passenger, the airlines maximize the benefits for their most profitable customers while minimizing rewards for bargain hunters.

Consider Southwest Airline's reward program. It initially was based on the number of flights each passenger took, and eight round-trip flights earned the person a free round-trip flight. In terms of rewards, a flight from Providence, Rhode Island, to

Baltimore, Maryland, was worth the same as a flight from Baltimore to Las Vegas, Nevada – despite the great difference in distance. On a conceptual level, it might make sense, because the cost of operating a plane is largely independent of the distance flown; flight crew, airport desks, and luggage handling costs are all constant. But customers who fly longer distances tend to pay more, because fares reflect distances. This extra revenue gets offset by the cost of the extra fuel used during the flight and the fewer per-day flights for a plane on a longer route.

But the conceptual argument was not sufficiently convincing. Therefore, Southwest relaunched its frequent flyer program as the "All-New Rapid Rewards" in March 2011, basing the rewards on dollars spent on flights by customers. Similar to other airline programs, this LP takes different fare types into account. It also allows passengers to earn points with partners in the retailing, lodging, dining, rental car, and banking industries.

Finally, the new program features a four-tier system that distinguishes Standard, A-List, A-List Preferred, and Companion Status customers. To reach A-List Status, a flyer must take 25 qualifying one-way flights or earn 35,000 Tier Qualifying Points in a calendar year. These members then enjoy benefits such as priority boarding, 25% earning bonus, and an A-List dedicated phone line for customer service. Companion Status (reached with 100 qualifying one-way flights or 110,000 Tier Qualifying Points in a calendar year) allows the member to designate a companion and receive a free ticket for that companion on every flight the member takes during the year. With this revision, Southwest attracts the business of high-value customers who tend to fly at least once a week (Southwest, 2011).

Examples of Loyalty Programs

- *Frequent buyer programs.* The simplest initiatives are based on punch-cards that offer a free complimentary product. City Bagels, a sandwich retail chain, offers customers a tenth sandwich free, after they garner nine stamps from previous purchases. The purpose is to increase both sandwich consumption and customer retention. Stores such as BigY, Kroger, and CVS offer discounts on certain store merchandise to cardholders, to ensure their loyalty and retention.
- *Volkswagen Club and Card.* The Volkswagen Club and Card concept attempts to establish a direct relationship with end customers. Customers collect points when Volkswagen (VW) services their car or if they buy VW accessories, as well as from partners, such as car rental companies and tour operators. The points can be redeemed for dealer services, price reductions on car purchases, or catalog merchandise. The purpose is to establish a better communication between VW dealers and customers, to bind them more closely to the brand.
- *Star Alliance Frequent Flyer Program.* The Star Alliance is a group of 27 airlines across all continents that cross-list flights, share facilities, and recognize their respective frequent flyer programs. Any flight on any Star Alliance airline counts toward a member's frequent flyer program. With 1,160 airports in 181 countries worldwide, the Star Alliance has become the largest airline network in the world.
- *Webmiles.de.* Webmiles.de, founded in 1999, claims to be the largest Internet-based loyalty program. It operates an LP that allows members to collect and redeem assets with a network of more than 470 retail partners. Thus, the retailers become members in Webmiles' partner network. Webmiles manages the program and communication with more than 2.6 million active members in Germany, Austria, and Switzerland.
- *Neiman Marcus.* A luxury retailer based in Dallas, Texas, Neiman Marcus offers its

"InCircle" LP to all its customers. Using a shopping card, customers accumulate points that can be redeemed for exclusive rewards.

10.5   Problems with Loyalty Programs

Although LPs have become widespread and popular, the benefits are not always clear. Many companies, such as ANZ Bank, invest millions of dollars into this CRM tool, only to find that it sucks up great resources without any obvious return.

CRM AT WORK 10.2

Example: ANZ Bank
In May 2003, ANZ Bank (Australia's third-largest bank) increased its annual fees by $50 on credit cards linked to its reward programs. This increase was primarily due to the increased point acquisition by frequent flyers and the potential fee reduction for inter-bank credit card transactions (Moneymanager, 2011). Specifically, ANZ Bank planned to raise fees on credit card holders who paid their balance monthly (taking advantage of the interest-free period). This was a wake-up call for corporations that had invested their marketing dollars in LPs (Kjellerup, 2003), because the primary reason for the price hikes was to stem losses incurred by the cost of running credit card related reward programs. The costs had risen to the point that the programs no longer were sustainable. Therefore, the bank needed to choose: reduce reward program benefits or increase annual fees to pass some of the costs on to customers.

Examples such as this may mark the beginning of a trend, in which large corporations that have spent millions of marketing dollars on LPs closely evaluate their costs and tailor reward programs more accurately to achieve better profitability.

Most companies need to revisit their business model, not only to reflect on the impact of loyalty programs on their bottom line, but also to determine how customer service initiatives add value and ensure future revenue streams. For some companies, this reassessment leads to the decision to eliminate any further investments in loyalty programs:

The LP test run by the U.K. chain ASDA Supermarkets (purchased by Walmart in 1999) cost £8 million in 1 year. The company chose not to invest in a full rollout, which would have cost £60 million (Direct Marketing, 2011). According to a spokesperson for ASDA, "We decided we didn't have to invest in points and plastic to make our customers loyal." And this assessment seems accurate: At the time it tested its pilot LP, ASDA's market share was 17.2%. A year later, it had risen to 17.6%.

Safeway terminated its LP in April 2000, which saved the company approximately $85 million in annual LP costs.[4] This chain's rationale was that "People have lost interest in (loyalty card) points and don't think they give value. What they really appreciate are straightforward product offers at great prices," according to the CEO Carlos Criado-Perez in May 2000.

A few years ago, Continental Airlines downgraded its liberal upgrading policy because it was too expensive. The company estimated a $100 million loss in revenue from upset frequent flyers. A class action suit also followed. What initially was designed to be a customer LP turned out to be a disappointing failure.

Despite their immense popularity, the aspects that distinguish a successful LP from an unsuccessful one remain unclear. Our discussion in the next section therefore reviews several LP characteristics to investigate the outcomes and determinants of LP success systematically, and thus to provide guidelines for designing optimal programs.

---

[4] Based on 1 British Pound = 1.7 USD, as of November 25, 2003.

10.6 Design Characteristics of Loyalty Programs

The multitudes of LPs attest to the various discretionary choices that arise for designers of such programs. Furthermore, LPs differ substantially both within and across industries. Managers can exercise discretion regarding the composition and the choice of dimensions to include in their LP design, as well as the corresponding weights assigned to each dimension. In this sense, we characterize LPs along the following key dimensions, which must be defined when designing a program:
- Reward structure
  - Hard versus soft rewards
  - Product proposition support (choice of rewards)
  - Aspirational value of reward
  - Rate of rewards
  - Tiering of rewards
  - Timing of rewards
  - Rewards based on specific criteria
- Participation requirements
  - Voluntary or automatic enrollment
  - Open versus closed LP
  - Automatic or manual point accumulation
- Payment function
- Sponsorship (existence of partner network, network externalities)
  - Single versus multiform LP
  - Within- versus across-sector LP
  - Ownership (focal firm versus other firm)
- Cost and revenues of LPs

10.6.1 Reward Structure

The principal motivation for consumers to enroll in LPs is to accrue benefits from rewards from their purchase transactions over time. From a consumer's perspective, the rewards attained through an LP membership are the key design benefit.

Hard versus Soft Rewards

Financial or tangible rewards (hard) differ from those based on psychological or emotional benefits (soft). Hard rewards run the gamut from price reductions to promotions and free products to preferred treatment. For example, a member of KLM's "Flying Dutchman" frequent flyer program may receive a free airline ticket for travel within Europe after collecting 20,000 miles – a hard reward. Soft rewards instead are linked to special recognition of the buyer, which offers the psychological benefit of being treated in a special way or having special status. For example, many frequent travelers with Silver or Gold status consider their membership in the category something special (often called the *badge effect*). Of course, the psychological recognition of loyalty status often comes with tangible benefits, such as preferred customer service (e.g., special service phone number).

Product Proposition Support

The rewards from a loyalty program may be linked to the company's product offering or be entirely unrelated. The U.S. bagel franchise Finagle-A-Bagel operates an LP that allows participants to redeem their accumulated bonus points only for the firm's own products – sandwiches and drinks. The reward thus directly supports the firm's product proposition. Other LPs allow members to redeem points for products completely unrelated to the focal firm's offering, such as BP's program, in which users can redeem points earned from gasoline-related purchases for merchandise such as first-aid kits, coffee mugs, or Barbie dolls.

Aspirational Value of Reward

From time to time, consumers engage in *hedonic consumption* of products that are mainly associated with pleasure and fun. Research in consumer psychology reveals that consumers prefer hedonic goods rather than utilitarian ones when receiving a gift. Consumers indulge more easily in luxury consumption when they get "something for nothing," as in the case of a gift or LP reward.

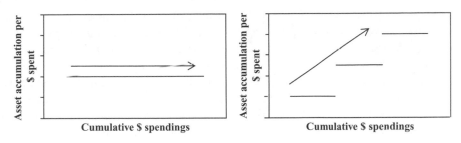

Fig. 10.2 Change in cumulative spending for two response functions

A free flight to an exotic destination thus might be worth more to a buyer (at least perceptually) than vouchers for the local supermarket, even if they have the same face value. Companies try to differentiate their LPs by highlighting the inspirational or hedonic value of their rewards. For example, the German TV channel PRO7 maintains the "PRO7 Club", one of whose most popular rewards is VIP service, which offers preferred access to talk show visitors or the chance to meet actors backstage. Mercedes-Benz's LP makes it possible to transform points into a flight in a MIG 29 combat aircraft. The luxury retailer Neiman Marcus catalogs a list of "wow and cool" rewards each year – such as having a world-famous photographer visit the customer's home to take family pictures.

Rate of Rewards
The *rate of rewards* refers to the ratio of reward value to transaction volume (both in monetary terms). In other words, it tells you how much a consumer gets in return for concentrating his or her purchases. Consumers prefer higher reward rates, but reward redemptions are a key cost factor for firms that run LPs. Rate of rewards is one of the, if not the primary, drivers of LP enrollment and active usage.

Tiering of Rewards
Rewards follow an asset accumulation response function, which describes how assets or rewards get accumulated as a function of spending behavior. Tiered rewards programs might follow constant, hierarchical, offer-related, or cyclical functions. With constant rewards, customers receive enduring, stable incentives (see case 1),

but hierarchical or graded rewards increase with greater spending levels (case 2). In the case of offer-related assets, customers receive rewards that are exclusive to a particular special offer, such as PAYBACK's 10-times points coupons that can be used only during a specific time period. Finally, cyclical rewards encourage a certain consistency in behavior, such as when LP providers use special occasions such as Christmas or the customer's birthday to express appreciation in the form of a reward.

Figure 10.2 depicts two different response functions. In case 1 on the left, the buyer receives the same amount of rewards per dollar spent regardless of spending level. In case 2 on the right, the buyer receives more rewards per dollar spent as his or her spending level increases. The program in case 2 thus is relatively more attractive for high spenders; many airline programs, as well as Bloomingdale's, follow this pattern.

CRM AT WORK 10.3

Bloomingdale's Rewards Plus Program
Bloomingdale's Rewards Plus program consists of three tiers whose levels of rewards to customers vary according to their annual spending level. Regardless of spending levels, all members with a Bloomingdale's credit card receive the benefits of the "Premier Insider" program: access to exclusive travel and entertainment offers, preview days before sales begin, and extra savings for using their cards during membership days. Women's shoe purchases by Premier Insider members also are

automatically tracked, and members receive 25% off their sixth pair of full-priced women's shoes.

The second tier, "Premier Plus Insider", is reserved for members who spend more than $1,000 annually. These customers receive the same rewards as Premier Insiders, as well as a host of other benefits. They can achieve certificates toward future Bloomingdale's purchases, earned at a rate of 3% for all purchases made at Bloomingdale's and 1% for all purchases made elsewhere with that credit card. During special double- and triple-reward events, the rebate increases to 6% or 9%. Premier Plus members also receive 12 free gift-wraps each year.

The pinnacle is the "Ultimate Premier Insider". These customers spend more than $2,500 each year and thus are exclusively offered some of the very best rewards, including unlimited free gift-wrapping and free local delivery of their purchases. Ultimate Insiders also have access to a customer service line reserved solely for their use, exclusive events, and offers.

By offering this differentiated rewards program, Bloomingdale's seeks to distribute the most rewards to its best customers. The rebate system effectively pays for itself by generating revenue from customers who carry a balance on their card. However, some of the other benefits, such as free delivery, can prove costly to the retailer.

Timing of Rewards

The timing of reward redemption is an important design feature. It is more attractive for the firm to create redemption rules that favor long accumulation periods, to ensure customer retention over time. This effect is also called *lock-in*. Customers build up assets over time, which function as switching costs for them. Customers instead favor immediate rewards or short accumulation periods. Managers must determine how long it takes to accumulate assets for a representative reward, given a certain buying pattern (e.g., average interpurchase time). The timing of rewards should be determined by the minimum redemption rules, type of reward given, and reward rate. The longer it takes to build up a certain reward level, the greater the *breakage*, or the amount of rewards never redeemed.

Rewards Based on Specific Criteria

Rewards can be designed to fit certain parameters, such as the time period, person, categories/brands, and distribution channels. When rewards refer to a specific time period, retailers pursue two main goals: generating additional revenue and increasing sales during weak sales periods. Offering rewards targeted to a specific group of card holders, such as customers whose last transaction was long ago, can help to activate "sleeping" customers. Furthermore, some companies tie rewards to specific categories, brands, or distribution channels to boost sales in these areas.

10.6.2 Participation Requirements

Another important characteristic of LPs are the requirements for becoming a member and the way points get collected.

Voluntary or Automatic Enrollment

When designing a loyalty program, companies must choose between voluntary and automatic enrollment. With automatic enrollment, the company deliberately enrolls all of its customers in the LP without differentiation. Voluntary programs are more common, because they allow consumers to self-select if they want to join. However, automatic enrollment is an appealing option if the company wants to track all consumers' transaction data (e.g., banks, credit cards).

Open versus Closed Loyalty Programs

Open LPs are accessible to anyone; closed LPs are deliberately restricted to a particular group of users, usually through the requirement of a membership fee. Both types of programs offer several advantages, as listed in Table 10.2:

Table 10.2 Open versus closed loyalty programs

Open loyalty program	Closed loyalty program
Reach critical numbers in the loyalty program faster	Concentrated target group due to access restrictions
More comprehensive database	Database mainly holds members with high interest in the assortment
Simplified acquisition/address of potential new customers and customers of competitors	Allows for more effective communication due to clearly defined member group
Greater efficiency of the LP due to larger customer base	Membership conditions (e.g., fee) limit number of members and associated costs
	Conveys feeling of exclusivity to program members

Automatic or Manual Point Accumulation

Most loyalty programs automatically record points, once the issued loyalty card is offered at checkout or the card number is entered in Internet transactions. Some programs such as "My Coke Rewards" or the German "Genusspunkte-Programm" (Nescafé Dolce Gusto Club) instead require online consumers to enter a code that can be found on products. Although consumers generally prefer automatic point accumulations, for companies, a manual system can be more cost effective.

10.6.3 Payment Function

For some LP providers, it has become common practice to endow loyalty cards with a payment function. Paying with a loyalty card can facilitate a comfortable purchase process for customers, and companies benefit as well because it is easier to generate purchase statistics at the individual customer level. In the United States, approximately 60% of all consumers own reward-based credit cards. The relevance of combining rewards with credit cards offered by retailers is strongly evidenced by Visa Claims reward cards, which now make up more than half of all credit cards and about 80% of money spent on credit (Credit Cards, 2011).

Retailers offer two types of loyalty cards that include payment functions. If the transactions aim to debit the customer's account and credit the retailer's account, the card must involve a banking partner (open loop). If instead the transactions do not actually pay for the purchase but rather grant the retailer access to an existing customer account (e.g., automatic debit transfer systems), no banking partner has to participate. The latter form is called a closed loop.

10.6.4 Sponsorship

The sponsorship function refers to supply-side features that describe the LP owner.

Single- versus Multi-Firm LP

Organizations may establish LPs that include only transactions with their own customers. For example, BP France accepts only transactions by members made at BP stations in France. In contrast, members of Tesco's "ClubCard" accumulate points by purchasing from the energy provider E. on. Such alliances with partners are a major growth axis in LP design. The advantage of bringing in partners is the increased attraction of LP members, who have additional opportunities to accumulate assets. However, the focal company also runs the risk that its LP loses meaning if it includes too many partners. In this case, customer transactions with the focal vendor and asset accumulation may become completely unrelated.

Within/Across Sectors

Another supply-side dimension that is specific to multi-firm LP designs is the degree of cross-sector partners. That is, do customers accumulate assets within the same sector or across different sectors? For example, the Star Alliance includes SAS, Lufthansa, United Airlines, Varig, and various other airlines, so this LP structure covers the same sector. However, the LP maintained by

AOL and American Airlines, with more than 2,000 partners, spans many industries.

Ownership

In multi-firm LPs, the ownership dimension reveals who owns the LP in the network. Is it the focal firm, a partner firm, or a firm whose sole purpose is to manage the LP? An example of the latter case is Webmiles, an organization that draws together a network of partners across many industries, with the sole purpose of LP management.

10.6.5 Cost and Revenues of LPs

In an empirical study, Leenheer, Bijmolt, Van Heerde, and Smidts (2002) show that the costs related to four of the seven loyalty programs they analyze are higher than the returns generated. Thus, any evaluation of the benefits of LPs must consider the various sources of both costs and revenues.

Cost factors include set-up/implementation, operating, and variable costs. The implementation costs accrue during the phases dedicated to planning and introducing a loyalty program (e.g., buying hard- and software, external consultancy, personnel training, initial promotions). After the LP has been launched, several expenses persist: maintenance of a service center, administration of the customer database, and (if applicable) inventory costs for the rewards themselves. Finally, variable expenses include discounts, rewards, sales costs (packaging, shipping), and communication, which determine the total cost of a loyalty program.

Compared with the evaluation of costs, the calculation of revenues turns out to be far more difficult. Two sources of revenues (indirect and direct) exist. Assessments of direct revenues (e.g., membership fees, sales of special editions) are rather straightforward, but indirect revenues, which consist of the retention and development of existing customer relationships and the acqui-

sition of new customers, prove very complex and difficult to estimate.

CRM AT WORK 10.4

Tesco's Green ClubCard Points: Sustainability in Loyalty Programs
Companies reward their customers not only for purchasing but also for not purchasing. What do we mean? Since August 2006, Tesco has granted customers one ClubCard point for every new carrier bag that they do NOT use. This incentive aims to encourage shoppers to reuse their plastic shopping bags. As a result, more than 9.5 million ClubCard customers now reuse their bags. These Green ClubCard points can be spent the same way as any other ClubCard points. Then Tesco began to reward shoppers with points when they recycled their cell phones and printer inkjet cartridges. The launch of recycling machines at Tesco stores, which issued the Green ClubCard points to customers who used them, doubled the recycling rates at sites featuring the machines.

But in March 2009, Tesco stopped issuing Green ClubCard points for recycled plastic and glass items, due to widespread misuse of the system. The grocer realized that customers were cutting up their plastic bottles and inserting the separate pieces in the machines to get more points. Currently recycling machines issue points only for aluminum cans. The recycling units, installed at more than 40 stores across England since their launch in 2005, take in more than a million items per week, according to Tesco.

10.7 Drivers of Loyalty Program Effectiveness

The factors that drive the effectiveness of a loyalty program can be structured into three main categories:

1. LP design characteristics
2. Customer characteristics
3. Firm characteristics

The configuration and interaction of these drivers determine whether an LP achieves its desired objective(s).

10.7.1 Loyalty Program Design Characteristics

The LP design characteristics, as we have noted, can be classified according to their:

- Reward structure
- Participation requirements
- Payment function
- Sponsorship (existence of partner network, network externalities)
- Cost and revenues

Thus three key questions must be answered to determine if a LP is effective:

1. From the consumer's perspective, are rewards attainable?
2. From the consumer's perspective, are rewards relevant?
3. From the firm's perspective, is the LP design aligned with desired goal(s)?

The first question asks how attractive the payoff is to the consumer. If the LP does not provide sufficient value (e.g., timing, rate of rewards), the customer cannot justify concentrating purchases, and no change in behavior will follow. For example, a traveler can redeem miles for a free flight after attaining the minimum mileage necessary. The level at which the airline sets this minimum mileage determines how many less frequent customers enroll in the program.

The second question pertains to whether the LP is relevant, regardless of attainability of rewards. It thus considers the degree to which an accumulation of assets in the program is relevant in terms of type of rewards (hard/soft, aspirational). If a consumer cares little for recognition and only wants hard rewards, an LP program that offers few hard rewards will not be relevant. The firm then must decide whether it wants to design its program to align

with the desired benefits of a particular target segment.

Finally, is the LP's design aligned sufficiently with the firm's goals? For example, if an LP offers hard rewards and promotions that focus on changing short-term behavior, the LP likely will have a greater impact on behavioral loyalty and less of an influence on attitudinal loyalty. If effectiveness profits are the declared goal, the LP instead must be designed to allow the firm to collect as much information as possible about the customer.

10.7.2 Customer Characteristics

The key customer characteristic relevant to the effectiveness of LPs is the skewness of the customer value distribution (or value heterogeneity). This skewness varies greatly across industries. In some industries, the value of individual customers or accounts is widely similar, whereas in others, these values diverge greatly. For example, in the gasoline industry, the average driver's monthly consumption of gasoline varies only moderately. However, in the financial services or telecom industries, usage patterns and customer profitability are widely varied.

How does this skewness determine the effectiveness of LPs? If an LP is designed to achieve value alignment, it can succeed best in an environment where customers exhibit high value heterogeneity. Thus, a value alignment goal is feasible in industries such as airlines, hotels, rental cars, pharmacies, telecom, and financial services.

10.7.3 Firm Characteristics

Factors relevant to LP effectiveness in terms of organizational characteristics include the:

- Perishability of a product
- Breadth and depth of the firm offering the product at the store/retail level

That is, the success of LPs depends on the characteristics of the product that the firm sells – and particularly whether that product is perishable. This point is why LPs are so widespread in

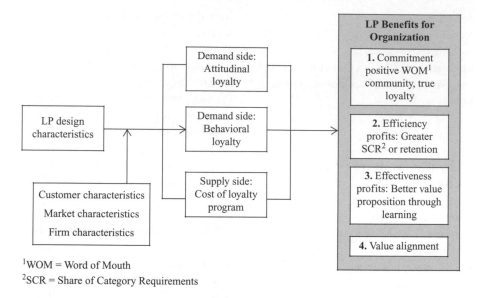

¹WOM = Word of Mouth
²SCR = Share of Category Requirements

Fig. 10.3 Drivers of effectiveness

the airline and hospitality industries. Thus a crucial feature of hotel LPs is that frequent users can get upgrades to "better" rooms when those offerings are not already taken up by paying customers.

In terms of the variety of products and brands offered at the retail level, an effective LP attains more opportunities for efficiency profits with greater breadth and depth at the store level, for several reasons:

- Buyers are more likely to be able to fulfill their needs.
- Buyers encounter more opportunities for one-stop shopping (which increases time savings).
- Buyers have more opportunities for behavioral loyalty (through more purchase occasions).

Thus, LPs generally should be more effective in terms of behavioral loyalty when the buying environment features greater choice. In addition, there should be opportunities for effectiveness profits with greater breadth and depth of offerings at the store level, because the latitude of purchases grants the firm more opportunities for learning about customer preferences and cross-selling products. Figure 10.3 summarizes how the drivers of LP effectiveness affect its outcomes.

10.7.4 Achieving a Competitive Advantage

Any firm develops its LP to create competitive advantage, or the ability to operate more profitably over a sustained period of time. In a 1999 survey conducted by McKinsey & Co. with 1,200 customers across 16 product categories, the effect of LPs varied depending on the industry category. First, a highly frequented category, like grocery stores, is more likely to attract members to its LP than less frequent purchase categories, such as casual apparel stores. Second, a far larger percentage of customers admitted to spending more as a result of the LP in the grocery stores than in casual apparel stores.

The evidence we have seen so far indicates that LPs that aim to create efficiency profits actually provide the smallest basis for competitive advantage. Once every major firm in the market matches the first mover, all firms are back to square one, *except that every firm now has higher costs*.

Thus, the key challenge when pursuing efficiency profits is to keep the costs of the LP under control. For the supermarket industry, which operates on razor-thin margins, this is a huge challenge, and perhaps the reason that most grocery LPs include manufacturer partners. Without manufacturers' funding, such as promotions and rebates, a supermarket LP could not offer decent or appealing rewards. Clearly then, organizations must be ingenious to keep LP costs under control. But still, the value of participating in an LP must be greater than the value of not participating for customers – otherwise, there is no reason for customers to be interested.

In contrast, LPs designed to create effectiveness profits have a good chance of creating competitive advantages. Effectiveness profits probably have the greatest appeal to large firms, and the continuous developments in IT make information-based strategies possible and even easy in some cases. The capability of learning from customer behavior through continuous monitoring, analyzing this information appropriately, and using newly found insights for designing and deploying LPs remains challenging though. Even with widely available, sophisticated technology, we still find great differences in firms' abilities to implement LPs that improve their effectiveness profits.

Finally, the goal of value alignment might yield low-to-medium competitive advantages. In certain industries (e.g., airline, hotel), value alignment is a necessary, standard industry practice. Little competitive advantage comes from the program itself. However, industries such as financial services or telecom services can expect to reap competitive advantages if they pursue this goal, because execution matters, and firms differ in their ability to execute such programs.

CRM AT WORK 10.5

Tesco: From Price Promotions to Marketing Efficiency

The British supermarket chain Tesco successfully implemented an LP aimed at achieving effectiveness profits. In 1997, Tesco was ranked third among grocery retailers in the United Kingdom, operating on a traditional model of promotion- and price-based competition. Data about customers' purchase behavior were, in principle, available from scanner checkout data, but the data were collected only at the store level, not for individual customers. In February 1995, Tesco had launched the first LP in the British supermarket industry, initially relying mainly on its incentive aspect. In time Tesco realized that it could capture both market share and share-of-category, though some debate continues about whether these gains came from the expansion of its sales areas, improved service, or its LP.

U.K. Supermarket Market Share in Percentages

	1996	2000	2006	2010
Tesco	20.9	25.0	30.6	30.8
Sainsbury	19.0	17.9	16.3	16.1
ASDA (Walmart)	12.1	14.1	16.6	16.9
Safeway's (Morrisons)	9.5	10.4	11.1	11.6

Source: TNS Worldpanel, Kantar Worldpanel

Over time, Tesco made more use of its sales data to target benefits and steer customers into new consumption areas. In addition, Tesco established a segmentation scheme to determine which customers it should aim to serve primarily. The LP reflects this segmentation; it offers specific cards to students, families, top customers, and seniors. Within its LP, Tesco also found ways to provide value for special groups, such as families with babies. In Tesco's Baby Club, parents can meet, obtain information about infant health and food, enroll in courses, and get special rebates on baby-related products. Thus, Tesco tries to align its LP offerings with each member's needs, as opposed to offering general incentives.

Its knowledge about individual customers' and segments' preferences comes from its extensive analyses of the data gathered within the LP. In addition, Tesco merges customer transaction information gleaned from its website with point-of-sale data (e.g., products, which store, time of the day, basket size). Thus Tesco can customize its product offerings and communications based on specific customer needs, as well as each customer's economic value. Tesco's segmentation is so precise that it sends 80 different versions of its promotion mailings to members and publishes four versions of its ClubCard magazine.

As a result, Tesco's loyalty program now displays few of the incentive scheme characteristics it offered when the idea started. Today, it is all about increasing the efficiency of Tesco's marketing efforts – which leads to happier consumers and more profitability for the grocer.

10.8 Empirical Evidence on Loyalty Program Effectiveness

More and more empirical evidence in markets indicates how successful LPs really are in achieving their stated goals. But limited empirical evidence details the success or failure of specific loyalty programs. It is particularly difficult to get unbiased information about the performance of firm-specific LPs, because proper metrics rarely are in place, and few firms are likely to admit to their poor performance. Appendix I lists a few studies that have examined LP outcomes, each of which covers only selected industries. In addition, the small number of studies limits our ability to make strong empirical generalizations. However, we can draw a few conclusions from these published studies:

- Published evidence that LPs create attitudinal loyalty is rare, though firms might have more proprietary information on this point.
- The evidence regarding the relationship between loyalty programs and behavioral loyalty measures, such as share-of-wallet, is mixed. Some studies attest to a positive effect of LPs on behavioral loyalty (to varying degrees), but other empirical research fails to identify such an impact.
- There is very little information on the cost efficiency of LPs. Companies may not have

the knowledge themselves, due to a lack of proper accounting or a reluctance to reveal it. Individual cases (e.g., Safeway, ASDA) suggest the great expense of managing LPs.

- Using LPs as a value alignment tool seems viable.

10.9 Loyalty Programs, Shackle or Reward: And to Whom?

Convincing evidence indicates that loyalty programs, as they exist today, fall short in terms of creating attitudinal loyalty. The name *LP* is a misnomer in that sense. Furthermore, programs that focus on incentives, deals, and promotions are often costly for the firm – unless it can offer mainly underutilized, perishable assets, such as unbooked hotel rooms or unrented cars. Costly rewards, on top of the razor-thin margins in the grocery industry, hardly seem sustainable in the medium to long run. Surviving LPs thus will be those that save companies money by replacing other communication tools, rather than just draining their resources. Designed properly, an LP can gather data that ultimately improve the efficiency and effectiveness of the marketing function.

The LPs that are most likely to provide sustainable competitive advantages are those that leverage data obtained from consumers into more effective marketing decisions, such that they result in true value creation for customers and thus the company. Loyalty is likely to follow in these cases (Reinartz, 2002). Furthermore, firms with admirable levels of true customer loyalty, such as Harley-Davidson, offer no loyalty programs. For them, LPs and being loyal do not go hand in hand, because true loyalty does not need hard incentives; it is based on attitudes.

10.10 The Seven-Point Checklist for Successful LP Design and Implementation

We offer a checklist for developing, designing, and implementing a successful LP, with seven key points:

- *Clearly determine your LP's goals.* Is its goal compatible with your marketing strategy and the positioning of your organization in the market?
- *Align the design of your LP with the characteristics of your market, your customer base, and your firm.* Knowing the customer base is important, because segments' preferences for LP benefits vary. For example, senior citizens may not value the long-term accumulation of redeemable points as much as immediate price discounts on a product.
- *Manage the costs of LPs.* LPs are expensive, so cost management will always be a critical component. Consider all the costs involved (e.g., opportunity cost of the time of the managers involved). Can these costs be mitigated by marginal cost rewards or contributions from manufacturers?
- *Measure the predicted benefits of the LP for your organization.* Although it is difficult to specify these benefits accurately, you should attempt to conduct a trade-off analysis between the cost and gains of the LP. Also consider the time horizon (short versus long term).
- *Avoid withdrawing an existing LP, which can have negative consequences in the form of customer dissatisfaction and defection.* Customers do not like it when LPs are withdrawn, once they have grown accustomed to the benefits. Thus, design faults will not only result in losses but haunt you later, in the form of customer dissatisfaction.
- *Design the LP to achieve maximum effectiveness in marketing operations.* This goal can be achieved by learning customer preferences and responding to these preferences with the offering.
- *Ensure that your firm has the necessary capabilities to manage its LP effectively.* These capabilities include data storage, data analysis, and empowerment of employees, among others.

10.11 Summary

The satisfaction–profit chain (SPC) is based on the idea that improving product and service attributes leads to better customer satisfaction, which then produces greater customer loyalty, which means increased profitability. Although empirical studies concentrate on aggregate, firm-level results, this chain needs to be implemented at a disaggregated or individual level.

Improving customer satisfaction comes at a cost, and it may not even deliver the anticipated business results. There is an optimum satisfaction level for any firm, beyond which increasing satisfaction does not pay off. To find this level, firms must conduct longitudinal satisfaction studies and find changes in customer satisfaction over time, linking them to improvements in their offering. By focusing on customer retention, managers can move closer to the ultimate dependent variable: profits. Graphical representations of data reveal that the link between satisfaction and retention is asymmetric (i.e., dissatisfaction has a greater impact on retention than does satisfaction). It is also nonlinear, such that the impact of satisfaction on retention is greater at the extremes, with a flat part in the middle of the curve called the zone of indifference.

According to a hypothesis proposed by Frederick F. Reichheld (2000), long-term customers spend more per period over time, cost less to serve, have greater propensity to generate word-of-mouth, and pay a premium price compared with that paid by short-term customers. However, Reinartz and Kumar (2002) have tested this hypothesis and demonstrated that across firms, a segment of customers is loyal but not very profitable (because they use up excessive firm resources), and another segment generates very high profits despite its short tenure with the firm. Considering that these short-term customers can be very profitable, loyalty cannot be the only path to profitability. This finding points to the importance of remembering the ultimate end of the satisfaction–profit chain: Customer profits ultimately are required to demonstrate the value of good marketing decisions.

The findings also suggest the need to understand different forms of loyalty. Behavioral loyalty refers to observed actions by customers; attitudinal loyalty entails their perceptions and attitudes. Customers who are not attitudinally loyal are likely to end the relationship at the earliest available opportunity, but a loyalty program aims to keep them by offering rewards to customers for their repeat purchasing. In exchange for concentrating their purchases with the focal firm, customers can accumulate assets (e.g., points) and exchange them for products or services. The success or failure of a loyalty program, whether contractual or incentive-based, depends on the profitability gained from the customers. Furthermore, LPs offer an important CRM tool that marketers can use to identify, award, and retain profitable customers.

The key objectives of introducing LPs include building true (attitudinal and behavioral) loyalty, efficiency profits, effectiveness profits, and value alignment. True loyalty is a function of the true value provided to the customers. Efficiency profits, which are net of LP cost, are the profits that result from a change in customers' buying behavior due to the LP. The most widely used measure of behavioral loyalty is share of category requirements or share of wallet, though LPs might not change behavior as much as they reinforce existing behavior – at a much higher cost to the firm. Effectiveness profits are the medium- to long-term consequences realized through better learning about customer preferences, which are more likely to generate sustainable competitive advantages and produce higher profits in the long run. Value alignment aims to match the cost to serve a particular customer with the value he or she provides the firm. It becomes particularly critical when there is great heterogeneity in customers' value and costs to serve. Across these goals, LPs may not be truly effective in helping firms engender greater customer loyalty and higher profits, con-

sidering the costs and special challenges posed by managing an LP. Most companies need to revisit their business model, not only to reflect on the impact of LPs on their bottom line but also to determine how customer service initiatives add value to future revenue streams.

From customers' perspective, rewards are the key design benefit of LPs. Hard rewards offer price reductions, promotions, free products, or preferred treatment, whereas soft rewards provide psychological recognition. Regardless of their type, rewards can be directly or indirectly linked to the company's product offering. Consumers also prefer hedonic goods over utilitarian goods when receiving a gift, so companies work to differentiate their LPs on the basis of their inspirational or hedonic value. The rate of rewards (i.e., ratio of reward value to transaction volume) is a key driver of LP enrollment and use; it depends on the chosen asset accumulation response function. For example, a tiered structure offers different levels of rewards and privileges to customers in differing tiers. The timing of reward redemption instead is determined by the minimum redemption rules, type of reward, and reward rate.

Sponsorship refers to supply-side features, such as the introduction of partners – a growing trend in LP designs. If LP members can accumulate assets at organizations associated with the focal firm, the design also must consider the degree of cross-sector partnerships. Do customers want to accumulate assets within the same sector, or across divergent, different sectors?

These design factors drive the effectiveness of an LP, together with customer and firm characteristics. The configuration and interaction of these drivers determine whether an LP achieves its desired objective(s). This effectiveness thus depends on the attractiveness of the LP from the consumer's perspective, the degree to which asset accumulation is relevant to the consumer, and whether the LP design aligns with the firm's goals. It also reflects the skewness of customer value distribution (value heterogeneity). Finally, on the organizational level, the perishability of the product and the breadth and depth of the firm offering influence LP effectiveness. When a firm cannot capitalize on the perishability of its products, the reward expenses come directly from its bottom line, which reduces the economic viability of an LP. Greater breadth and depth of offerings at the store level means the latitude of purchases allows the firm more opportunities for learning customer preferences and cross-selling products.

No published evidence shows that LPs create attitudinal loyalty, though there is evidence of an impact of LPs on behavioral loyalty. Moreover, we find very little information about the cost efficiency of LPs, though using LPs as a value alignment tool seems viable.

A firm develops an LP to create a competitive advantage and operate more profitably over a sustained period of time. Thus a key challenge is keeping the costs of managing the LP under control. The LPs designed to create effectiveness profits have the highest chance of creating competitive advantage; the effectiveness profit goal thus has great appeal for most (large) firms. Value alignment instead should yield low to medium competitive advantages. It may be necessary in certain industries such as the airline or hotel industry, where value alignment has become a standard industry practice. However, industries such as financial services or telecom can expect to reap competitive advantage when pursuing this goal since execution matters and firms differ in their ability to execute the programs well.

Loyalty programs, as they exist today, appear to be falling short in terms of creating attitudinal loyalty. Instead, perhaps LP managers need to emphasize its promise as a method to gather data to improve the efficiency and effectiveness of the marketing function.

Exercise Questions

1. Explain the difference between behavioral and attitudinal loyalty. Provide an example of each.
2. What are the key objectives of loyalty programs? Which of these objectives provide the strongest competitive advantages?
3. You are a consultant to a credit card organization that wants to establish a loyalty program. The CEO has just read about how most loyalty programs result in money-losing propositions. How do you alleviate the CEO's concerns?
4. Do companies profit by introducing loyalty programs? Is the success of a company's loyalty program dependent on its industry category?
5. How can you measure loyalty? How does loyalty relate to the profitability of a company?
6. Would low-ticket items (coffee, candy, sodas) benefit from loyalty programs? What kind of incentives might work best?
7. Design a loyalty program for your neighborhood gas station. Describe the incentives. Determine the cost structure. Set benchmarks, and evaluate the profitability of the program across possible scenarios.
8. What are the ethical issues that surround loyalty programs? Should the gaming industry be allowed to use loyalty instruments for example?

Minicase 10.1

Loyalty Program Management at Starwood Hotels

Starwood is one of the world's largest hotel and leisure companies. The company's services range from exclusive hotels, such as the St. Regis and the Luxury Collection, to five-star Sheraton and Westin hotels, down to the moderately priced Four Points hotel chain. With approximately 1,000 properties, Starwood functions in most major markets worldwide. The company also operates a customer loyalty program, "Starwood Preferred Guest" (SPG), which allows customers to accumulate points for staying and spending with Starwood. The program is unique in the industry, in that its points never expire, and Starwood does not impose any so-called black-out dates (i.e., dates when customers cannot use their points for redemption).

Despite these program advantages compared with major competitors, the company is struggling to exploit the full potential of the program and address several challenges. First, though it collects information on individual customer behavior (movie watching, minibar use, room service use, restaurant use), it is not clear how it can use that information. Some customers like that the company learns about their preferences, but many others remain concerned about possible privacy invasions and simply want to be left alone – or at least have control over the kind of information the company uses. Second, though roughly seven million Starwood customers are members of the loyalty program, another six million customers are not. Thus, the company has very little knowledge about nearly half of its customer base. Third, the company targets existing program members with customized offerings and communications, but it yet has to figure out how much customers are willing to be bothered by such communications. Although Starwood wants to maximize its cross-selling and up-selling opportunities, it recognizes that some customers will react negatively if they get too many offerings.

Questions

1. How can a large company such as Starwood exploit customer data while still safeguarding and respecting customer privacy?
2. What should Starwood do to attract loyalty program nonusers into the program or find out more about the behavior and preferences of this large group?
3. How far should Starwood push its direct offerings to its program members? How can it discover the boundary?

Appendix I. Key Studies of LPs with Notable Empirical Findings

No.	Organization details	Industry	Findings
1	Six partner companies of the FlyBuy program in Australia	General retail	LP has hardly any effect on repeat purchase patterns (behavioral loyalty) (Bolto et al., 2000)
2	Credit card firms (single firms) in three European countries	Credit cards	LP members are more likely to overlook negative experiences with the focal company
			LP members have higher usage levels and higher retention (Deighton/Shoemaker, 2000)
3	Single firm	Hospitality	20% of member stays are because of LP
			Strategy of using LP as a value alignment tool is successful
			LP is profitable (Crié et al., 2000)
4	—	Grocery industry in France	Being a LP member does not modify purchase behavior
			Events and promotions associated with LP seem to have clear effects on purchase
			The effects of LP are mostly short rather than long term. Thus, they seem to work as promotional tools rather than a means to induce loyalty (Reinartz/Kumar, 2003)
5	U.S. direct marketing firm	General merchandise	LP membership is associated with the longer duration of customer–firm relationships
			No information on cost-efficiency (Rajiv, 2001)

(continued)

No.	Organization details	Industry	Findings
6	—	U.S. grocery industry	LP is operationalized as a shocker program (e.g., turkey bucks), not a traditional long-term card program, so it can better be described as a long promotion There is significant increase in spending (market basket)
			LPs seem to affect "cherry-pickers" most
			Program is profitable (Meyer-Waarden/Benavent, 2001)
7	—	Cross-sector sample of 7 LPs	LPs are classified according to their objectives and characteristics
			The two main purposes of LPs are customer heterogeneity management or creating switching costs (behavioral loyalty)
8	—	U. S. grocery	LP increases sales through "point pressure" (short-term) and "rewarded behavior" (long-term) (Taylor/Neslin, 2005)
9	—	Coffee and music on Internet	LP induces purchase acceleration through the progress toward a goal (Kivetz et al., 2006)
10	Spanish supermarket chain	Grocery	LP members are more behavioral and affectively loyal than other participants
			Few customers change purchase behavior after joining the program (García Gómez et al., 2006)
11	Convenience store chain	Retailing	Positive influence of LP on consumers' purchase frequency and transaction size holds only for light and moderate buyers (Liu, 2007)
12	—	Airline industry	Only high-share firms experienced sales lifts from their loyalty programs
			Because high-share firms tend to possess complementary product and customer resources, they are more likely to gain from their loyalty programs than firms with a smaller market share (Liu/Yang, 2009)
13	Albert Heijn, Super de Boer, Edah, Integro, Konmar, COOP, Jan Linders	Dutch supermarket industry	Small positive, yet significant effect of loyalty program membership on share-of-wallet
			In terms of profitability, each program generates more additional revenues than additional costs in terms of saving and discount rewards (Leenheer et al., 2007)
14	—	Grocery industry	Customers satisfied with the rewards of LPs are more loyal to the store and allocate a higher proportion of their budget and patronage frequency to the store than unsatisfied customers (Demoulina/Ziddab, 2008)
15	Health and beauty provider	Retailing	LP was a significant predictor of store loyalty, in support of the contention that loyalty programs are capable of engendering loyalty (Bridson et al., 2008)

References

ABC. (2003). Accessed July 18, 2011, from http://www. abc.net.au/businessbreakfast/content/2003/s883133. htm

AMR Corporation. (2009). *Annual report 2009*. Accessed July 29, 2011, from http://phx.corporate-ir.net/External. File?item=UGFyZW50SUQ9MzgwNjA1fENoaWxkS UQ9Mzg0Nzc2fFR5cGU9MQ==&t=1

Bolton, R. N., Kannan, P. K., & Bramlett, M. D. (2000). Implications of loyalty program membership and service experience for customer retention and value. *Journal of the Academy of Marketing Science, 28*(1), 95–108.

Bridson, K., Evans, J., & Hickman, M. (2008). Assessing the relationship between loyalty program attributes, store satisfaction and store loyalty. *Journal of Retailing and Consumer Services, 15*(5), 364–374.

Crié, D., Meyer-Waarden, L., & Benavent, C. (2000). *Analysis of the efficiency of loyalty programs*. Working paper, University of Pau, France.

Deighton, J., & Shoemaker, S. (2000, October). Hilton HHonors worldwide: Loyalty wars. *Harvard Business* (online).

Demoulina, N. T. M., & Ziddab, P. (2008). On the impact of loyalty cards on store loyalty: Does customers' satisfaction with the reward scheme matter? *Journal of Retailing and Consumer Services, 15*(5), 386–398.

García Gómez, G., Gutiérrez Arranz, A., & Gutiérrez Cilián, J. (2006). The role of loyalty programs in behavioral and affective loyalty. *Journal of Consumer Marketing, 23*(7), 387–396.

IHG. (2010). *IHG annual report and financial statements 2010*. Accessed April 2011, from http://www.ihgplc. com/files/reports/ar2010/docs/ihg_annual_report_2010. pdf

Kivetz, R., Urminsky, O., & Zheng, Y. (2006). The goal-gradient hypothesis resurrected: Purchase acceleration, illusionary goal progress, and customer retention. *Journal of Marketing Research, 43*(1), 39–58.

Kjellerup, N. (2003). *The myth of customer loyalty programs and customer retention*. Accessed May 25, 2003, from http://www.callcentres.com.au/Ashgrove

Lebensmittelzeitung. (2011). *Payback: Coupons per app*. Accessed February 24, 2011, from http://www.lebens mittelzeitung.net/business/marketing/protected/Online-Werbung_2162_6890.html

Leenheer, J., Bijmolt, T. H., Van Heerde, H. J., & Smidts, A. (2002). *Do loyalty programs enhance behavioral loyalty? An empirical analysis accounting for program design and competitive effects*. Discussion paper 65, University of Tilburg, Netherlands

Leenheer, J., van Heerde, H. J., Bijmolt, T. A. H., & Smidts, A. (2007). Do loyalty programs really enhance behavioral loyalty? An empirical analysis accounting for self-selecting members.

International Journal of Research in Marketing, 24(1), 31–47.

Liu, Y. (2007). The long-term impact of loyalty programs on consumer purchase behavior and loyalty. *Journal of Marketing, 71*(4), 19–35.

Liu, Y., & Yang, R. (2009). Competing loyalty programs: Impact of market saturation, market share and category expandability. *Journal of Marketing, 73*(1), 93–108.

Meyer-Waarden, L. (2007). The effect of loyalty programs on customer lifetime duration and share of wallet. *Journal of Retailing, 80*(2), 223–236.

Meyer-Waarden, L., & Benavent, C. (2001). *Loyalty programs: Strategies and practice*. Working paper, University of Pau, France.

Moneymanager (2011). Accessed July 29, 2011. http:// moneymanager.smh.com.au/banking/guides/articles/ cc07.html

Odell, P. (2009). Faithful following. *Promo Magazine*. Accessed July 29, 2011, from http://promomagazine. com/incentives/marketing_faithful_following/

Passingham, J. (1998). Grocery retailing and the loyalty card. *Journal of the Market Research Society, 40*(1), 55–67.

Rajiv, L. (2001, July). *Retail loyalty programs: Do they work?* Marketing Science Conference, Wiesbaden, Germany.

Reichheld, F. F., Markey, R. G., Jr., & Hopton, C. (2000). The loyalty effect-the relationship between loyalty and profits. *European Business Journal, 12*(3), 134–139.

Reinartz, W. (2002)

Reinartz, W., & Kumar, V. (2002). The mismanagement of customer loyalty. *Harvard Business Review, 80*(7), 86–94.

Reinartz, W., & Kumar, V. (2003). The impact of customer relationship characteristics on profitable lifetime duration. *Journal of Marketing, 67*(1), 77–99.

Southwest. (2011). *Rapid rewards*. Accessed April 2011, from http://www.southwest.com/rapidrewards

Taylor, G. A., & Neslin, S. A. (2005). The current and future sales impact of a retail frequency reward program. *Journal of Retailing, 81*(4), 293–305.

Webflyer. (2011). Accessed July 29, 2011, from http:// www.webflyer.com

Woolsey, B., & Schulz, M. (2011). *Credit card statistics, industry facts, debt statistics*. Accessed July 29, 2011, from http://www.creditcards.com/credit-card-news/credit-card-industry-facts-personal-debt-statistics-1276.php#Card-ownership

Wyndham Worldwide. (2009). *Wyndham rewards enhances offerings with PAYBACK program and promotion*. Accessed July 29, 2011, from http:// www.wyndhamworldwide.com/media_center/pr/show_ release.cfm?id=547

Young, M. L., & Stepanek, M. (2003). *Trends: Loyalty programs*. Accessed December 1, 2003, from http://www.cioinsight.com/article2/0,3959,1458960,00. asp

Campaign Management

11.1 Overview

One important goal of customer value management is to profile the existing customers on the basis of their value and use this information to identify and acquire prospects matching this profile. A marketing campaign can be thought of as a series of activities used to market/promote a new or existing product/service using online and offline marketing channels. Marketing campaigns can be used by firms to

• Identify prospective customers,
• Acquire customers, and
• Retain and reward existing customers.

For many prospects, the campaign is the first opportunity for engaging in a dialogue with the firm. A dialogue between the firm and customers can effectively change customers' attitudes and behavior towards the firm. Hence it is very important for the firms to develop and plan with a specific end result in mind, and execute these campaigns effectively and analyze the campaign results carefully. There may be many desired results for a marketing campaign but they all begin with increasing the awareness of a firm, its products and/or its services. Marketing campaigns may be developed and executed within the company or in conjunction with a third party such as an advertising agency.

A marketing campaign may be executed through one or more channels of customer interaction: phone, direct mail, the Web, wireless devices, email, direct sales and partner network.

The success of a campaign involves reaching out to the right customer with the right offer at the right time and through the right channel. The campaign acts as a rich source of information and once the campaign is completed, both the marketing manager and sales manager should evaluate the effectiveness of the campaign and use what they have learned for future planning. An example of a recent marketing campaign is provided in the following example.

CRM AT WORK 11.1

The "All Adidas" Global Marketing Campaign
In March of 2011, Adidas, the world's second largest sporting goods brand, launched its largest marketing campaign ever entitled "All Adidas". The main focus of the campaign was to increase awareness of Adidas' entrenchment into diverse fields of interest, such as culture, sports and music.

Purpose
The purpose of this campaign is to unite each of Adidas' three distinctive sub-brands (Adidas Sport Performance, Adidas Originals and Adidas Sports Style) under the umbrella brand Adidas, in an effort to project a holistic and global Adidas brand. The campaign features the tagline "Adidas is All In" which further solidifies their goals of unification of brands.

Brand Ambassadors

Adidas has enlisted several well known public figures from the sports, music, and fashion arenas to become ambassadors for the "All Adidas" campaign, in an effort to merge cultural, sports and lifestyle sub-brands.

Channels

The primary medium being used to deliver "All Adidas" campaign messages is television and internet. Adidas enlisted the Sid Lee advertising agency to manage the campaign. The Sid Lee agency created 30- and 60-s commercials to be shown on TV and cinema as well as an extended 2-min version available online.

Viewers and fans of the brand (also current and potential customers) are able to engage with the firm via various social media platforms, where as a part of the campaign Adidas provides daily updates and exclusive content having to do with the brand (i.e. contests and info on new product releases).

In addition to television and social media, Adidas is engaging their fan and customer bases in a complete through-the-line offering, including mobile applications, presence in retail outlets, activation events and print.

Desired Outcome

The firm's intention is to showcase the breadth and depth of the Adidas brand in one global brand campaign. Perceived credibility and authenticity in Adidas seamless transition from the playing field to lifestyle wear.

Source: The Adidas Group http://www.adidas-group.com/en/pressroom/archive/2011/14March2011.aspx

In this chapter, we explain the different phases of Campaign Management processes such as Campaign Planning and development, Campaign execution, and Analysis and Control. The subphases in each of these main phases are shown in Fig. 11.1. In the discussion about Campaign planning and Development phase, we include issues such as identifying customers, developing communication strategies and media mix, developing an offer, and testing. The campaign execution phase involves actual implementation and subsequent fine tuning of the campaign. The last phase consists of measurement of campaign results, profile and response analysis.

11.2 Campaign Management

A campaign is a series of interconnected promotional efforts designed to achieve precise marketing goals. Managing a campaign encompasses planning, developing, executing, and finally analyzing the campaign results. A campaign is composed of one or more promotions, each of which is an initiative or a device designed to attract the customers' interest. It can be aimed at prospects or existing customers and usually is undertaken within a defined timeframe (such as a season, and generally not exceeding a calendar year). Marketers could use the customer value metric as a means to profitably target campaigns.

As a general rule, a successful campaign management process comprises four connected stages:

- *Planning*. Strategic process by which decisions are taken. The purposes and objectives of the campaign should be defined and rationalized at this stage.
- *Development*. Tactical process that takes care of creating the offer, choosing the support and design, choosing the media, and selecting the customer names.
- *Execution*. Operational process of running the campaign in the media chosen and controlling all related aspects.
- *Analysis*. Evaluation process of the campaign results in light of the original, objectives.

In practice, these stages do not have well-defined boundaries between them and are performed at the same time. Very often, planning and development go together. In the next few

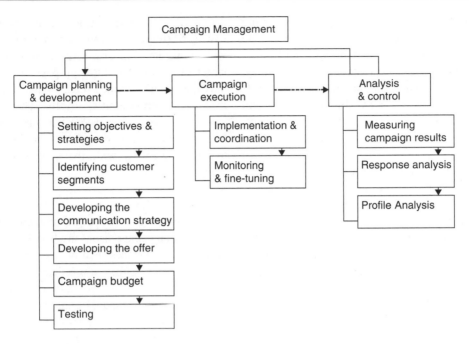

Fig. 11.1 The campaign management process

sections, we will take a closer look at how each stage is managed.

11.3   Campaign Planning and Development

At the campaign planning stage, marketers make strategic decisions that help define the overall objectives of the campaign, the best communication message, and the best target audience. Once these strategic issues are defined, the development phase starts.

11.3.1   Setting Objectives and Strategies

Campaigns have a central role in annual marketing plans, so campaign objectives should be in line with overall marketing and corporate objectives. These objectives are often from the four following categories: market penetration (increase usage or market share); market extension (find new user groups or enter new segments); product development (new products or services); and diversification (new markets and products, new strategies).

The different marketing strategies already in place should be examined. Questions asked should pertain to the product strategy (What is the product mix?), the pricing strategy (Is price important for market positioning?), the distribution strategy (Which channels does the firm use?), and the promotion strategy (Is the creative strategy consistent with product positioning?).

When defining the campaign strategy, marketers should be able to answer the following additional questions:

1. Who do you want to target? (i.e., Who are the targeted customer segments?)
2. Where should you target? (i.e., What are the channels, and points of contact?)
3. How do you get to them? (i.e., What is the communication strategy and offer?)
4. When is the best time? (i.e., When should you schedule the campaign?)

Who Do You Want to Target?
To answer this question, the company has three options: focusing on existing customers (retention strategy), concentrating on getting new

customers (acquisition strategy), or targeting existing and new customers at the same time (mixed strategy between retention-acquisition).

When pursuing a customer retention strategy, ideally the company should target its most profitable customers via LTV (lifetime value) and RFM (recency, frequency, and monetary) analysis. Here are some approaches to target these segments:

- Develop loyalty from the existing customers, via a strong relationship or superior quality or service (e.g., loyalty programs, one-to-one relationships)
- Develop tailor-made products adequate for the needs of the existing customer profiles
- Sell additional products to existing customers also known as cross-selling (e.g., selling an insurance policy to an existing bank customer)
- Sell a superior product (with more features or additional services) to customers who already use similar products, also called up-selling (e.g., selling a gold credit card to a regular credit-card holder)
- Merchandise different brands from different categories to the same customer, also known as cross-merchandising (e.g., sell the gold credit card with the best interest rate).

If the company pursues a customer acquisition strategy, it has two options: If it wants to sell the same product to new customers, it should target prospects based on the profile and behavior model of existing customers; if it wants to offer different products to new customers, it should develop new markets.

Where Should You Target?
The company either chooses to act in the markets it already knows (pursue market penetration or extension) or it can choose new markets (market diversification or new product development). It may choose a multichannel strategy (selling the same product in multiple channels like internet, store, phone, etc.) or a single-channel strategy (selling products in a single channel, like in a store).

How Do You Get to Them?
Getting your customers' and prospects' attention will be one of the goals of the company's communication strategy. Choosing the most effective media (for retention and acquisition strategies) will allow the company to efficiently reach its target segments. The offer proposition will also have a predominant role. What kind of incentives-coupons, gifts, loyalty schemes, and so on-suit a particular customer group? The company should develop the offer according to customer preferences, with the campaign budget being a constraint.

When Is the Best Time?
When preparing a campaign, marketers should be aware that some seasons are better to promote products and services than others. For example, new computer games are released and campaigned during November and December just before Christmas season. Retail banks may campaign for credit cards or personal loans in January, because people are expected to be short on money due to Christmas and New Year expenses. In addition to these examples, the product itself can be seasonable or it can have a short life cycle. For example, sunscreen lotions are sold during summer. Similarly, outdoor sports equipment is advertised before summer time. Figure 11.2 highlights the core market and product decisions for customer retention and/or customer acquisition strategies.

11.3.2 Identifying Customer Segments

Once the campaign objectives are established, the next step involves identifying the customer segments the campaign will target. Customer segments are homogenous groups of individuals that have similar tastes, wants, and needs with respect to the company's products or services, Lifetime segmentation and profiling should guide in targeting the specific customer segments most likely to respond to the company's offer.

Customer segments can be identified in two ways: purchase behavior and profile data. Purchase behavior is recorded in the CRM database and will allow the marketer to segment by product need and by LTV. Profile data will relate the individual customer to his or her response to past campaigns, allowing the implementation of an

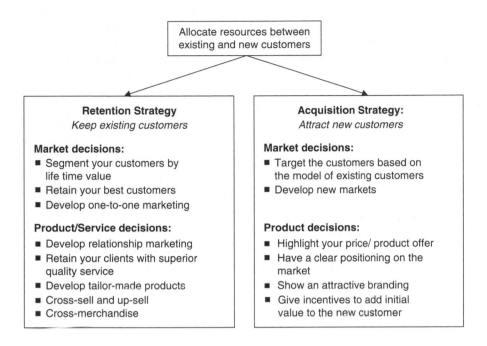

Fig. 11.2 Customer retention and acquisition strategies

ROI-driven marketing campaign, Profile data also identify tastes, needs, and preferences of customers, and therefore can be used to target new customers accurately.

Obtaining a successful campaign involves a careful choice of customer segments. Marketers can focus on a strategy-mix of three types of customer groups: the existing customers, the prospects, and the defectors. The existing customers are an important source of information. They provide information about their purchasing behavior, attitudes, and tastes. Their interests, motivations, multi-channel usage, and profile can be used to target prospect clients who exhibit a similar profile. The CRM database should record all the information from transactions, surveys, focus groups, complaint records, loyalty card data, web traffic analysis, and other external sources. Identifying profiles of existing customers will help identify new customers on the market. Defecting customers also provide enlightening information. When defecting, these clients have a reason to do so. Customers can be dissatisfied with the product itself, with the quality of the service offered, or with the company channel management. Paying attention to these customers will help the company learn from past errors, This information is very useful because it allows product improvement and development; better targeting, and better service, If the company listens to what its customers are saying, then it will be able to better satisfy their needs and consequently be profitable in the long run.

How Are Customer Segments Targeted?

Segmentation, as obvious as it sounds, is in many cases not straightforward. The CRM database plays a central role in this step of the campaign process. Effective use of the information on customer behaviors and profiles, channel preferences, and brand awareness will allow the accurate definition of the target segments. Of course, the segmentation can only be as good as the quality of the underlying data.

If the campaign is aimed at retaining existing clients, the firm's CRM system is central to analyzing the recorded purchase behaviors and profiles which will help the marketer adjust the offer to meet the unsatisfied needs of customers. Several analyses could be performed at this stage (e.g., lifetime value segmentation, profiling and RPM).

11.3.3 Developing the Communication Strategy

Marketing communications (marcom) are targeted interactions between the company and its customers and prospects, using one or more media, such as direct mail, newspapers and magazines, television, radio, telemarketing, and the Internet. A *marcom campaign* may use a single approach (e.g., direct mail) or it can combine several approaches (e.g., direct mail with advertising in television, radio, and newspapers).

When defining the communication strategy, the company identifies and defines to whom the campaign is directed (the target audience), what the campaign message is (content), and which are the best contact channels or media to deliver the content. The marketing team frequently develops the marketing communication plan, but a marketing communication agency (such as an advertising agency or a direct marketing agency) may help in its preparation. If the company chooses to outsource, it hires an agency to execute the marketing communications plan.

The campaign communication strategy will be more effective if planned in an integrated manner. Integrated marketing communications (IMC) is a process that involves the management and organization of the marketing communication tools (media, messages, promotions, and channels) in a way that delivers a dear and consistent message about the company and about the product. The CRM database system allows the effective use of IMC because it stores informa-

tion about customer and prospect preferences and allows the firm to focus marketing activities toward specific targets.

Marketing communication activities can vary from very small discrete pieces of promotion (such as a mailer), to the development of a larger campaign, which involves many promotional tools (direct mail, press inserts, TV spots), and to the coordination of multiple campaigns to achieve a global objective (increasing the level of cross-selling, customer retention, etc.) It is important to build one or more interlinked databases of each medium as part of the CRM database.

Which Communication Strategy?
Generally, marketers use hybrid combinations of strategies when developing the communication strategy. Some of these strategic approaches are enumerated in Table 11.1.

Prioritizing the target segments that provide a higher potential yield is one objective of the marcom strategy. Targeting the customers in an effective way should maximize the marketing communications ROI. Naturally, some media are more effective at targeting certain groups of customers than others. The challenge is to choose those media that are both effective in achieving the campaign objective and cost-efficient.

The choice of media depends in part on whether existing customers or prospects are targeted. If customers are nonaddressable, broadcast media are used for acquisition. If the prospects addresses are known, direct-to-customer media may be more effective. In the case of retention, the firm may spend more on personalized contacts (salesperson, telephone) with high-value clients. For low-value relationships, companies might opt for lower-cost contact channels such as the internet or mail. In practice, customer acquisition and retention strategies are often mixed. If a company is launching a new product directed at existing customers and new customers, it will use both kinds of media. A brief description of these media is available in Table 11.2. The effect of

Table 11.1 Communication strategy

Strategy	Description	
Generic strategy	No distinction is made between brands. The emphasis is placed upon category need rather than brand awareness (example: Promotions for a product category)	
Pre-emptive strategy	A generic claim is made about the superiority of the company's brand (example: promoting a product that is protected by a patent)	
Unique selling proposition (USP)	It emphasizes the superiority of the brand based on a unique feature or benefit. (e.g. promoting a product with a new feature)	
Brand image strategy	It relies on the development of mental or psychological associations through the use of signs, symbols and images	
Resonance Strategy	It attempts to recall events or feelings by evoking meanings, experiences, thoughts or aspirations that are relevant to target audiences	
Affective or emotional strategy	It attempts to invoke involvement and emotion, with a powerful message	
Informational strategy	It is based on the view that an important element of the creative theme is to convey information (example, an educational campaign)	
Push Promotional strategy	To focus a promotional effort in manufacturers of goods and services to encourage the trade channel members to stock, promote and sell its products	
Pull promotional strategy	To focus a promotional effort in encouraging end customers and consumers to demand goods and services	
Positioning strategies	Positioning by attribute, product characteristic, or consumer benefit	The brand is perceived to be better than others in a particular way. Marketing communications emphasize these features
	Positioning by price/quality	Positioning can be sought in high price/high quality, prestige positions, low price/acceptable quality positions
	Positioning by use or application	Segmentation and targeting can be carried out based on usage occasion. (Example: fast- food is for people who have little time to eat)
	Positioning by product user	It focuses on the requirements of target customers and consumers
	Positioning with respect to product category	Rather than competing with another brand, a brand or product category might be positioned against another product category. The competitive focus is placed on substitutes
	Positioning against a competitor	Brands are promoted with a full understanding of their relative competitive position in the minds of the target audience
	Cultural positioning	Positioning by cultural reference, where the brand is clearly associated with a particular culture, country, religion, ethnic group or sense of heritage or tradition

Source: Pickton and Broderick (2001)

Table 11.2 Retention and acquisition media

Retention media	Acquisition media
Direct mail:	*TV*:
Mailings:	Direct response TV (DRTV)
Single-product	TV spots
Multi-product	Home shopping channels
Miscellaneous:	Digital TV
Birthday cards	*Radio*:
Thank-you notes	Direct response radio (DRR);
Invitations	Radio spots
Enclosures:	*Telemarketing*:
Statements	Outbound
Parcels	Inbound
Telemarketing:	*Print media*:
Outbound	Press/newspapers
Inbound	Magazines
Catalogues	Inserts
Newspapers/ bulletins	*Direct mail*:
	Mailings
	Inserts
	Internet
	Exhibitions/field marketing

using media-mix in acquisition and retention strategies can be seen in the following example.

CRM AT WORK 11.2

Barack Obama's 2008 Presidential Campaign

A mixture of radio, television and internet was used to expose Obama's political views and garner supporters. Interpersonal communication allowed Barack Obama to build a political constituency (purchasing community) and get to know potential voters (customers).

Recruiting Support
Radio and Television

A number of television and radio commercials were created to both promote Obama and combat negative press from rival candidates. Radio commercials were aired nationally, while television commercials were both aired nationally as well as uploaded to Obama's official YouTube page.

Email

In his 2008 campaign, president–elect Barack Obama was able to use the power of the internet to amass a database of millions of potential voters and supporters. Throughout the campaign process the Obama team collected over 13 million email addresses from individuals who visited his official website (www.barackobama.com). Over 7,000 different "call to action" email messages were sent out, each including a request for donation. During and immediately following the election cycle, Obama's aides had sent over one billion emails, which raised over $500 million in donations.

Social Media

Social media has been hailed as a game changing tool in CRM. During this time President Obama had official profiles registered with over 15 social media outlets; including Twitter, Facebook and YouTube. Along with verified accounts, several unofficial support pages that were created during the campaign helped spread the word about rallies, appearances and speeches happening around the country. Immediately following his win, President Obama's social media stats read 134,000 YouTube subscriptions, over 3 million Facebook supporters and 3.5 million friends on the social network created specifically for his campaign (www.my.barackobama.com).

Continued Interaction

President Obama has continued his social media campaign in office. He uses YouTube sponsored Q&A Live Stream sessions to engage the country and uses YouTube to publish his weekly presidential address. As of May 4, 2011, Barack Obama's online statistics stand at 7,765,454 Twitter followers (3rd most followed Twitter page); 19,887,186 Facebook followers (33rd most followed Facebook page); and 204,862 YouTube subscribers (over 160.5 million content views) and counting.

Source: Compiled from "Obama's Wide Web" http://www.washingtonpost.com/wp-dyn/content/story/2008/08/19/ ST2008081903613.html; and "Obama Raised Half A Billion Online" http://voices. washingtonpost.com/44/2008/11/obama-raised-half-a-billion-on.html

Marketing Media Tools Most of the media referred in the earlier sections are known as direct marketing media tools. Table 11.3 gives a brief description of what they are and how they are used, together with their advantages and disadvantages. It provides a snapshot of different advertising mediums and their principal characteristics.

11.3.4 Developing the Offer

Developing the offer consists of offering the customer some kind of incentive which will induce him to buy or to ask the company for more information. This offer may range from a free product sample (e.g., getting a free sample of a shampoo in the mail) to price-related incentives (e.g., buying two CDs for the price of one), or an item providing information on the firm (e.g., a free promotion video about the firm's new products).

When developing the offer, the company must keep in mind the established objectives. Some examples of these objectives may be to attract new customers or members, obtain repeated business from existing customers, reactivate lapsed customers, produce sales leads, or acquire new customers. The offer planning should develop upon the required elements.

- What is the product positioning?
- What is the price?
- What is the length of commitment?
- What are the payment terms?
- What are the risk reduction mechanisms?

At the same time as marketers look at these elements, they should also be seeking answers to the following questions:

- How much can they afford to spend on the incentive? For example, what is the allowable marketing cost?
- Which promotion type should be used as an incentive? (price-incentives, free samples, coupons, etc.)
- What should be the promotional package? (creative message, design, materials, etc.)
- Which promotional media should be used? (television, radio, directs mail, etc.)
- Does it involve one-stage or several stages?

Answers to these questions will help estimate campaign costs and profitability. These answers should be recorded in the CRM system. They will be used as a model to fine-tune the campaign results.

Table 11.4 provides a list and a brief description of what kind of options a company can offer its customers and prospects. The example of MetLife gives an example of a company that used a successful retention strategy to do repeat business with its existing customers.

CRM AT WORK 11.3

Metropolitan Life Insurance Company (MetLife)

MetLife Insurance Company is one of the world's largest insurance providers, with customers in more than 60 countries. In 2008, the firm decided to launch a retention campaign for existing customers in Massachusetts, since the state made up a large portion of its business and rate deregulation was causing increased competition among insurance providers.

When designing the campaign, MetLife segmented its customers based on their profitability, duration of their relationship with the company, products purchased, and the channel through which they purchased insurance policies. Control groups were also created to measure the program's overall success.

MetLife subsequently sent out postcards, letters, and custom publications to all existing customers in Massachusetts to remind them of the value and benefits that their insurance policies and products provided. This campaign was conducted over the course of 1 year, and resulted in a .87% increase in customer retention. The campaign proved highly successful, as a .25% increase was MetLife's initial goal and would have sufficiently covered the overall campaign costs.

Source: Bell (2009)

11.3.5 Campaign Budget

The campaign budget allocates resources and coordinates expenditures across the marketing activities associated with the campaign (advertising fees, testing costs, list rentals, etc.). When calculating the campaign budget, the marketer will use a mix of estimates for both directly measurable and less easily measured activities (e.g., the long-term effect of advertising). In reality; the estimates for these less measurable activities come from similar past experiences, benchmarking, or plain guesswork. Although this might look unconventional, it is still better to make an educated guess than to neglect these estimates. In general; allocating the optimum financial resource level to each activity is a difficult task, and that is why arriving at a campaign budget should be a balance between measurement, financial calculations, competitive analysis, and good judgment.

There are many ways to calculate a budget. Some companies think of the campaign budget as a percentage of turnover derived from the sales forecast of a particular product or service (e.g., the general management establishes a sales objective of $2 million and states that the marketing department can only afford $500,000 on marketing activities with this product). Other firms may look at the previous year's budget and adjust it for the campaigns for the current year (e.g., the company spent $500,000. on last year's marketing activities and this year is going

to adjust it for the price increase of advertisement fees, inflation, etc.)

While there are no right or wrong ways to calculate a budget, we will present seven common methods to calculate a budget and present their main advantages and disadvantages:

1. Preset budgeting
2. Budgeting for an allowable marketing cost
3. Budgeting with the competitive parity method
4. Budgeting with the objective and task method
5. Budgeting with the percentage of sales method
6. Budgeting with key performance indicators
7. Budgeting using the lifetime value method

Preset Budgeting

Most companies determine a given year's marketing expenditure on the basis of what they spent the year before, by applying a ratio that adjusts media cost inflation, projected sales increase or decrease, market conditions, and so on.

Advantages: The campaign budget won't be drastically cut over the years, so it will follow a more or less steady expenditure flow.

Disadvantages: Working with a preset budget that doesn't take into account last year's sales is the least effective way of calculating a budget. Companies treat marketing as an expenditure instead of as an investment to boost future sales. As a consequence, working with this kind of budget planning may be hazardous for the firm, rendering its business less competitive and slower to change.

Although this is the least effective way to establish a budget, it is, in fact, one of the most commonly adopted.

Budgeting for an Allowable Marketing Cost

Budgeting for an allowable marketing cost (AMC) consists of determining the amount that can be spent on campaign marketing activities, while preserving the required profit margin. Each potential expenditure is given priority according

Table 11.3   Media characteristics

Medium	Principal characteristics	
Direct mail (letters, catalogues, price lists, brochures, leaflets, booklets, circulars, newsletters, cards, samples, etc.)	Direct mail consists of mailing pieces that can range from a postcard to a sophisticated package. A classic direct mail package is composed of an envelope, a letter, a brochure, a reply device and/or other inserts	
	Advantages	Disadvantages
	Accurate targeting	High cost per contact
	Unique capacity to involve the recipient	Long start-up time
	Creative flexibility/unlimited formats	Demands a large variety of knowledge and skills
	Discrete	Limited potential
	Ease of reply	
	No direct competition	
	Highly testable	
	Most controllable	
Direct mail catalogues	Direct mail also includes catalogues, which are small booklets that give a complete enumeration and description of the company's products and services	
	Advantages	Disadvantages
	Summarizes the company product range	Hazard acquisition of new names
	Distinctive positioning	Associated with "junk mail"
	Creative flexibility	
	Timeliness	
	Cost controllable	
	Has a repurchase cycle	
	Database construction and manipulation	
Telemarketing	Telemarketing is approaching customers via telephone. Its use originated the creation of call centers as a distribution channel. Telemarketing can be used in two ways: outbound and inbound. In the outbound version the company contacts the customers with a special motive (a promotion, a survey, or a follow-up). In the inbound mode it is the customer that is induced to initiate the contact	
	Advantages	Disadvantages
	Highly targeted	Expensive
	Efficient and direct	Number of prospects reached is limited
	Immediate feedback	Difficult to retain good employees
	Fast response time	No visual appeal
	Easily tested	Intrusive
	Builds and maintains customer relationships	Associated to "cheap selling"
	Incremental effectiveness	
	Increased levels of customer service	
Print media	Print media consists of advertisements or inserts in written communication media, such as newspapers and magazines. This media focus on media reach, i.e. in reaching as many readers as possible. Classical uses in print media are: advertisements in magazines, newspapers or newspaper supplements and freestanding inserts	
Newspapers (local, regional, international, daily, weekly, weekend)	Advantages	Disadvantages
	Low cost per 1,000 circulation	Often poor color
	Rapid, predictable response	Poor selectivity
	Moderate lead time, late deadlines	No personalization
	Wide variety of formats	Newspaper rates vary
	Broad local coverage	Sometimes affected by local conditions
	Inexpensive testing	Less selectivity than mail or phone
	Frequency, immediacy and reach	
	Year-round availability	

(continued)

Table 11.3 (continued)

Medium	Principal characteristics	
Magazines (local, regional, national international, weekly, monthly, annual, consumer, business, trade, technical, professional, etc.)	Advantages	Disadvantages
	Low cost per 1,000 circulation	Slower response
	Easily controlled costs	Less space to tell story
	Moderate lead time, late deadlines	Less personal
	Excellent research data on readers	Less selectivity than mail or phone
	Wide coverage of all markets	
	Wide choice of readers profiles	
	Good color reproduction	
	Long ad life	
	Test inexpensively	
	Advertising in a trust environment	
	Frequency, immediacy and reach	
	Year-round availability	
Inserts	Advantages	Disadvantages
	High volumes	Reduced flexibility
	Cost efficient	Not very popular
	Flexible design	No proof on insertion
	Impact	
	Informative	
	Testable	
Broadcast media (analogue/digital)	TV media methods are: direct-response television (DRTV) (interacts with the viewer inviting him to buy), infomercials (TV spots) that inform or describe the products and home shopping channels	
TV (terrestrial, satellite, cable, local, regional, national, international)	Advantages	Disadvantages
	Powerful demonstration capability	Limited copy time
	Fast response	Limited response options
	Wide choice of time buys	Difficult to perform split tests
	Total market coverage	Expensive (production costs and airtime cost)
	Strong support medium	Can take a long time to produce
	Brand awareness and differentiation	Information content limited
Radio (local, regional, national, international)	Radio can either use direct response radio (DRR) or radio spots that merely describe and advertise the product or service	
	Advantages	Disadvantages
	Excellent targeting	No response device
	Cost efficient	Limited copy time
	High frequency	No visual appeal
	Involvement, friendliness and loyalty	Creative treatment and quality often very mixed/poor
	Short start-up times	Audience passive receivers of information
	Powerful support medium	
Internet (www, web page, e-mail)	Advertisement on the web can be done via: banner ads, button ads, sponsorships or co-branded ads, keyword ads and affiliate marketing	
	Advantages	Disadvantages
	Attracts customers and prospects to the site	Diminishing returns
	Engaging and interactive	Involves web site maintenance
	Personalized	Involves investment in IT
	Builds database on customer preferences	Audience not guaranteed

(continued)

Table 11.3 (continued)

Medium	Principal characteristics	
	Cost efficient	Relies on browsers to find pages
	Interactivity possible	Hits may not represent interest (casual browsers)
	Message can be quickly and easily changed	
Door-to-door	Advertising door-to-door consists in selecting a residential area to promote or sell a product. Usually is delivered in each household with the normal mail by the postal services or in the form of insert in a local free newspaper	
	Advantages	Disadvantages
	Targeted	Poor personalization
	High penetration	Diminishing returns
	No duplication of coverage	Insufficient customer knowledge
	Versatile/no format restrictions	
	Test possibilities	
	Low cost	
	Ideal primary medium	
Posters (outdoors-boards, outdoor-transports, inside)	Posters can be placed on boards in the streets, in railway stations, in buses or taxis or even in shopping centers and underground trains	
	Advantages	Disadvantages
	Reaches broad audience	Creative limitations
	High repeated exposure	Short exposure time
	Relative low cost	Limited audience selectivity
	Strong impact	Message must be simple
	High geographic selection	
	High visibility	
Cinema	Advertising in cinemas can be made via advertising spots before the movie and during the breaks. It's usage varies across countries	
	Advantages	Disadvantages
	High quality production	High cost of production
	Captive audience	Limited audience size
	High selectivity via the movie and the cinema choice	Limited response options
	High creative flexibility	

to its forecast for return on investment, and each investment is given equal consideration. Its objective is to achieve the optimum revenue per customer and maximize sale profits. The AMC is obtained by subtracting the costs (cost of goods + distribution costs) and the required profit margin from the total sales value.

Advantages: When using the AMC there is no preset limit to the campaign budget unless a cash-flow constraint is imposed. By using this method the company controls costs.

Disadvantages: Many activities are hard to accurately forecast, and some activities may not pay back in a given year. These intricacies lead to

a degree of conservatism that inhibits the aggressive pursuit of an AMC marketing policy.

Example: One of the main sources of revenue for "Old Books Limited" comes from the subscription fees of its monthly magazine, *Rare Books*. In order to preserve this source of revenue, it has two choices: either put in place a cold mailing to obtain new subscribers or a mailing-to existing subscribers, inviting them to renew their subscription. It calculated the allowable marginal cost of each activity and discovered that sending four invitations (i.e., four direct mailings) to existing customers had a lower marginal cost than doing a cold mailing.

Table 11.4 Offer options

Offer option	Description
Price incentives	The customer gets a discount off the regular purchase price (a specific dollar amount or a percentage discount)
Payment options	Making it easier for customers to buy from you. These can be company's credit cards, easy pay plans, etc.
"You have been specially chosen"	Recognition is a motivating factor for customers. If they feel special they are more willing to buy. Offering something special to regular customers or inviting them to be part of a special club are some variations of this offer type
Premiums	A premium is usually a free item or a nominal fee offered as an incentive to purchase a particular product or service (free information, gifts, etc.)
Samples	Offer samples of the product or service you are selling
Free trial	Offer the customers a free-trial period to try the product
Automatic shipment	Keep sending out merchandise to customers until they cancel their order. Many publishing companies do this in order to renew subscriptions
"Member gets member"	One effective way of getting new customers is offering regular customers a gift or a dollar incentive to introduce others the company's product or service
Early bird offer	If the customer buys before the deadline he will pay a special low price
Contests and sweepstakes	Customers are given the chance to win a prize if they purchase something
Multiple discount offers	Customers who spend a lot of money with the company like to receive special treatment, so companies offer discount on big volume purchases, for example
Multiple product offer	Companies group related products under one price and entice customers to buy the whole package
Deluxe edition	The company offers the regular product at a specific price and then it offers the deluxe edition or the enhanced version of the product at a promotional cost
Bounce-back	When a customer puts an order, the company includes another offer in the package it sends
Money back guarantee	Offering a guarantee or warranty is an oral or written promise by a manufacturer or retailer that they will stand behind a product or service

Source: De Bonis and Peterson (1997)

Budgeting with the Competitive Parity Method

Competitive parity tries to equate budget allocation with those of competitors. Organizations in competitive environments may opt for this budget technique.

Advantages: In this method, emphasis is on competitor intelligence. By checking out what the competition is doing, the company is adapting itself to the market conditions.

Disadvantages: It is difficult to be precise as to who your competitors are. It is also difficult to estimate the relative size of competitors, because a company's nearest competitor may be significantly bigger or smaller than your company. Next, marketing communication strategies are certainly different for market leaders and for market followers and budgeting based on parity

may thus not be very wise. This method cannot satisfactorily take into account sudden changes in the competitive activity or objectives. It does not take into account the company's own objectives.

Budgeting with the Objective and Task Method

This method focuses on, first, determining the marketing objectives, and then deciding on the marketing communication tasks needed to achieve those objectives. By calculating the costs of these tasks, a budget can be set.

Advantages: This method focuses on marketing objectives. The resources are expended according to the objectives.

Disadvantages: Implementing this method is a difficult task because it is not always easy to define the objectives and to quantify their implementation costs. This method also makes an important presumption: It assumes that the relationship between objectives and tasks is well known and understood.

Budgeting with the Percentage of Sales Method

A fixed percentage of turnover is allocated to marketing communications. The marketing communication expenditure is directly linked to sales level. In order to determine the exact percentage to be allocated, the company looks at competitor allocations and industry averages. To define the turnover, the company can look at historic sales.

Advantages: This method incorporates a series of alternatives, and it allocates costs to the objectives.

Disadvantages: It may be difficult to determine the percentage of sales that must be allocated. Competitors may have a small advertising budget and concentrate their budgets on the sales force, and this would be a deceiving benchmark.

Budgeting with Key Performance Indicators

Determining the campaign budget via some key performance indicators is a process that allows the company to figure out, in a quick way, how much it can afford to spend on a special promotion. Sometimes this analysis is called *front-end analysis*. This analysis is done with simple performance measures such as the cost per sale, the conversion rate, the cost per inquiry, the marketing cost ratio, or the *return on investment*. These performance indicators are summarized in Table 11.5.

E-mail presents itself as an effective way to engage customers in a dialogue. As a flexible and consumer-preferred communication vehicle, e-mail has applications across acquisition, retention, and customer service. Messages can be tailored to each customer based on her/his stage of the buying process. E-mail also allows customers to opt-in with their own preferences.

Tables 11.6 and 11.7 show the key performance indicators from a study performed by Forrester research, "the e-mail marketing dialogue,"

which shows that in 1999, e-mail was the second most effective technique for driving traffic to a Website (Nail, 2000). Retention e-mail generated 10% click-through rates on in-house lists. But, using e-mail as a customer acquisition tool is expensive because rented lists are also expensive.

Budgeting with the Lifetime Value Method

Budgeting in the most effective and efficient way would imply reducing expenditures to a unit cost basis in order to focus on the value of individual customers and on the different values per customer. Given the data recorded in the CRM database, the company may predict ongoing customer value rather than only the individual sales revenue. Knowing the lifetime value of each customer will allow the company to compare returns on alternative marketing expenditures and to compare return on expenditure from obtaining business from existing customers or from new ones. This gives the opportunity to efficiently allocate the budget using the most profitable strategies.

Advantages: Using the CRM database information allows the company to predict, in a more accurate way, the cost of the campaign. At the same time, it efficiently allocates resources between strategies because it allows a comparison between the returns of alternative marketing campaigns.

Disadvantages: It is very difficult to keep track of customer values because most companies lack transactional data from customers. Forecasting the customer LTV as a budgeting measure is still in its infancy. Also, if the company doesn't keep track of the performance results of past campaigns, it won't be able to compare these results with similar campaigns and learn from past errors. Sometimes the strategy that produces the highest ROI does not provide the fastest return and therefore, it can be replaced by faster strategies with lower ROI.

Ideally, budgeting should use LTV forecasts to determine the cost of a campaign. In practice, this may be hard to implement. So in this case, the marketer should proceed with both

Table 11.5 Key performance indicators

Performance measure	Formula	Definition	Example case of a direct mail to 10,000 customers that costs $12,395
Cost per thousand (CPM)	CPM = (Total promotion expense/ Total quantity) × 1,000	Relates the total cost of a promotion with the quantity produced	The CPM is (12,395/ 10,000) × 1,000 = $1,239.50
Cost per response (CPR)	CPR = (Total promotion expense/ number of responses)	Ratio between total campaign costs and the number of responses obtained	The number of responses to the mailing was 340. Therefore the CPR was $36.50
Cost per enquiry (CPE)	CPE = (Total promotion expense/ total orders)	Ratio of the total campaign costs by the total enquiries	If the number of orders was 252, then the CPE was $49.20
Cost per sale (CPS)	CPS = [Total promotion expense/ (total orders- Returns and bad debts)]	Ratio between the total costs and the enquiries that were converted into sales, net of returns and bad debts	From the 252 enquiries or orders received, the company had 16 returns and 3 cases of bad debt, therefore the CPS was $12,395/ (252 − 16 − 3) = $53.20
Conversion rate (CR)	CR (%) = (number of buyers/number of responders) × 100	Calculated by comparing the number of buyers with the number of responders to the campaign.	In this case the CR would be (233/ 252) × 100 = 92%, which means that the company converts 9 of 10 customers with this campaign.
Return on investment (ROI)	ROI = sales revenue/ total promotion expense	Ratio between sales revenue and the campaign cost	Each sale represents $75 and since the company made 233 sales, the ROI will be a ration of 7/5 (1.4), which means that for each $5 spent in the campaign you obtain $7 from your customers.

Table 11.6 Email key performance indicators

	CPM	Click-through rate(%)	Purchase rate (%)	CPS
Rented lists	$200	3.5	2.0	$286
Sponsored email	$93	2.5	0.8	$465
In-house lists	$5	10.%	2.5	$2

Table 11.7 E-Mail campaign and customer acquisition and retention parameters

CPM (cost per thousand)	Customer acquisition			Customer retention	
	Direct mail to rented list	Banner advertising	Email to rented list	Direct mail to house list	Email to house list
Production	$462	N/A	N/A	$462	N/A
Media	$118	$15	$200	N/A	N/A
Delivery	$270	$1	N/A*	$270	$5
Total	$850	$16	$200	$686	$5
Click through rate	N/A	0.8%	3.5%	N/A	10%
Purchase Rate	1.2%	2.0%	2.0%	3.9%	2.5%
Cost per sale	$71	$100	$286	$18	$2

* Delivery costs for rented lists are incorporated into media costs.

front-end analysis and with the allowable marketing cost analysis. Keep in mind that no budget should be done without estimation of the return of marketing investment (ROI rates). Unfortunately, the preset budgeting is still a very common practice among companies, but it should ideally be replaced by the other methods discussed.

11.3.6 Testing

Testing involves conducting a comparison between different ways of proceeding with a campaign. In general, it is performed under a simple rule: You test individual campaign elements, other elements remaining constant, and you measure the resultant change in the performance of the campaign. Testing should concentrate first and foremost on the most important variables and parameters. More importantly, one should aim to test all the key parameters, not just one of them.

Testing is based on a basic principle. Take the current set-up of the campaign and use it as the *control* for the test. Then select the element you want to test and change it. Next, select a sample of your target customers and run a test with the changed element. Comparing the performance results of the test version with the control will illustrate the impact of this variable on the overall campaign objectives.

What Are the Benefits of Testing?
Testing has value-added benefits that can improve your campaign success and performance. Some of the most important ones are listed as follows:
- Testing shows real behavior, because it provides a (close to) real environment in which behavior is validated.
- Testing augments and validates research.
- Testing also stimulates creativity, since it not only provides healthy internal competition but also presents a challenge to the creative team to find ways to beat the control campaign.
- Tests protect the company's greatest asset (the customers): By using only small samples with each test you will finally give your customers the proven offer.
- Tests minimize financial risk and avoid costly errors.
- Tests uncover ways to reduce costs.

In general, tests help maximize the performance of the campaign. They are low cost (when compared with the overall campaign costs) and fast in providing results. They are reliable (as you resort to quantitative analyses),

simple to execute, and easy to prepare (as there are less customers involved). It is important that tests be done on an ongoing basis, and not be looked at as a one-time task.

What Should You Test?
We can test almost everything in a campaign. A key variable is the target audience, which is in the form of a list of targeted customers and prospects. We can also test the offer variables (prices, incentives, proposition), the format (physical shape, the *feel* and the size), the creative element (the appeal, the tone, and the message), the media, and/or the timing.

When determining the budget, the company should consider the importance it wants to give to testing, since this has a cost. If the marketing campaign is based on a well-known process (e.g., the company uses past designs of campaigns to promote similar products or services), then testing could be carried out with one or two tests, in order to make minor improvements. If the campaign aims at something new, like product or market development then testing should be more exhaustive. The following case provides an example of testing the media.

CRM AT WORK 11.4

Testing the Media before the Roll-Out

The Executive Corner, Limited produces executive accessories such as leather briefcases, business card cases, binoculars, golf scope, desktop accessories, leather mouse pads, and other corporate gifts.

The company is launching a campaign to promote a cigar case to new customers. The campaign customer objective is to acquire 1,000 customers. The company can afford $30 per customer (AMC = $30) and the gross margin per sale will be $50. The campaign budget for this program is $30,000 ($30 × 1,000).

The proposed campaign strategy is to run in four types of media: internet, direct mail (a mailing), telemarketing and magazine advertisement. The company will run a test with some customers (test target audience) to assess the most effective media. The firm has acquired customer lists for the different media and will conduct the test using a 5% sample for each, as shown in Table 11.8. For testing, the firm decided to send promotion emails to 3,000 and a mailing to 3,000 prospects. Telephone calls will be made to 500 prospects from a rental list. It also opted to insert an ad in the magazine *Top Management* whose readers are mostly top executives. The test campaign is an actual campaign resulting in effective sales, but conducted in a smaller scale with respect to the final campaign.

The first step is to determine the test budget and its size relative to the total campaign budget. Multiplying the cost per medium by the audience size gives the total test budget cost, which is $10,800. This figure represents 36% of the campaign budget (calculations are shown in Table 11.9).

Break-even target response rates can be obtained which quantify the number of customers needed to cover the testing costs. This is calculated as the ratio between test costs ($10,800) and the AMC ($30) for each medium (for example, 40 customers would be needed to respond to the cold mailing, representing 1.3% of the 3,000 target audience size, to cover the mailing costs).

Having run the test, the firm gets actual response rates. These will help estimate the effectiveness of each medium, by comparing the target response rates (needed to break-even on campaign costs) and the actual test response rate (which is an estimate for the campaign roll-out results). Table 11.9 presents the results.

Next, with the actual test response rate, the firm can calculate the total gross margin of having run the test, which is obtained by multiplying the actual number of customers that made a purchase by the gross margin per sale ($50). The net profit

margin will consist of subtracting the test costs from the total gross margin. At this stage the firm has all the necessary elements to determine the ROI of each medium. The ROI is the ratio between the net profit margin and the test cost, expressed as a percentage. Table 11.10 shows the results.

Given these results, the firm should run the campaign with the media that presented the highest ROI: email to prospective customers.

After the test campaign, there is a remaining budget of $19,200 of the original $30,000. This will be used to send emails to the remaining 57,000 email addresses not used by the test. Total cost for the email campaign will be $17,100, which leaves $2,100 for the next best ROI-medium: an ad in *Top Management* magazine. However, the cheapest ad insertion available in this magazine costs $5,000, well over the remaining budget. It is still possible to use the third-best ROI medium: direct mail using a rental list. A total of 5,250 promotional letters can be sent.

Does Testing Predict the Future?

Testing allows you to do a small-scale measurement of the potential campaign results. It can accurately give you the performance results for the overall campaign, through the testing of the following performance measures:

- *Response to the campaign, in percentage.* Running a test campaign will generate results from the customers selected to participate in it. The number of responses obtained (e.g., customer subjects who responded positively to the incentive), divided by the total number of customers selected, will give the response rate, in percentage. This number will serve as an indicator of the success that the particular campaign being tested can achieve.
- *Campaign profitability.* The performance results of the test allow you to do an estimate

Table 11.8 Test audience size per medium

Medium	Customer lists held (total target audience)	Test target audience
Internet	60,000 prospects	3,000 prospects
Mailing	60,000 prospects	3,000 prospects
Telephone	10,000 prospects	500 prospects
Magazine advertisement	2,000,000 prospects	100,000 prospects

Table 11.9 Costs of testing, break-even target responses and test results

Medium	Cost ($) per 1,000	Target audience size	Test cost ($)	No. of customers needed to break even	Target response rate (%)	Actual no. of test respondents	Actual response rate (%)
Mail using a rental list	300	3,000	900	30	1.0	33	1.1
Direct mail using a rental list	400	3,000	1,200	40	1.3	40	1.3
Telemarketing to existing customers	6,200	500	3,100	103	20.7	61	12.2
Top management magazine	56	100,000	5,600	187	0.2	200	0.2
Total			10,800	360		334	

Table 11.10 Net profit margin and ROI per medium of test

Medium	Actual response rate (%)	Actual no. of customers	(A) Total gross margin ($)	(B) Test cost ($)	(C) = (A) − (B) Net profit margin ($)	(D) = (C)/(B) Return on investment (%)
Email using a rental list	1.1	33	1,650	900	750	83
Direct mail using a rental list	1.3	40	2,000	1,200	800	67
Telemarketing to existing customers	12.2	61	3,050	3,100	−50	−2
Top management magazine	0.2	200	10,000	5,600	4,400	79
Total		334	16,700	10,800	5,900	

of the revenues of the real campaign. From this, you should deduct the total campaign costs (expenses of preparing the campaign, testing costs plus those of running the campaign). This gives you a prediction for the profitability of the campaign.

Testing in Different Media

Direct Mail: Just about any element in the direct mail is testable, ranging from the format and the package, the message, the creativity concept, the distribution lists to the offer itself. This is possible for direct mail because the direct marketer controls every aspect of the campaign, including the timing and the budget.

Telemarketing: In one call session, the telephone operators can promote a particular product or service, can test a different script, or can test a promotion. In a single day direct marketers can have enough responses to obtain a fairly good indication about the success of the offer. The time of response to a phone call is one of the unquestionable advantages of telemarketing.[1]

Press and Inserts: When testing in print advertisement, the direct marketer can test almost everything about the editorial fit: the audience composition, the magazine/newspaper circulation, the ad placement cost, the timing of the ad placement, its frequency, and the position of the ad or its color. Although testing is possible, it is not as easy and inexpensive as telemarketing or direct mail. The most used tests are split-run testing, A/B splits, and cross-over testing.

Split-Run Testing: Split-run testing is usually used for inserts. It compares the same title or message in two different insert formats, by alternating them in the print run. Basically, you insert a different code or a different phone number in each format so as to track which version has the best response rate.

Example of a Split-Run Test:

A company that produces crystal glasses for different types of wine is going to test four different ads (B, C, D, and E) against a control ad A to find out which ad performs better. This test will be performed in four different wine magazines with different audiences.

Analyzing the test results, ads B, C and E reveal a greater lift than ad A. In this particular test, ad C will be chosen to run the campaign because it presents the greatest lift of all the ads tested.

A/B splits: You run two versions of the print run (A and B) in alternative copies of the same publication. Usually, creative or color changes are tested this way. As in split-run testing you should devise a mechanism for tracking response.

Cross-Over Testing: You run two versions of the same advertisement: one version changes the creative message (A), the other changes the color (B). Then you insert version A in the first issue of magazine 1 and in the second issue of magazine 2. You then insert version B in the second issue of magazine 1 and in the first issue of magazine 2. This enables you to compare the response improvement when creative elements or color were changed. The response change in magazine 1 assesses the creative elements change, while response change in magazine 2 evaluates the color effect.

Example of a Cross-Over Test: Following the preceding example, imagine that the company wants to cross-over test ad A with ad B in two wine magazines.

In this case it is possible to compare the results of each issue of both magazines and compare creative concepts. Ad A performed better in the first issue of *World Wine* than in the second issue of *Food and Wine*. Ad B performed better in the first issue of *Food and Wine* than in the second issue of *World Wine*. If we compare the creative concepts, we realize that ad A always obtains higher responses than ad B. The test conclusion would be, always roll out with ad A.

How Reliable Are the Test Predictions?

Testing is meant to allow the marketer to make inferences using established methods of analysis. It is beyond the scope of this book to explain in detail the statistical models used to analyze test results. Some of the statistical techniques that can be used for this purpose are hypothesis testing, confidence intervals, and analysis of variance. For more on these techniques, readers can refer to *Marketing Research* by Aaker, Kumar, and Day (2004).

What Are the Potential Problems in Testing?

For testing to support profitable campaigns, one should be aware of the following potential errors:

---

[1] However, the federal do-not-call implementation has made it mandatory for telemarketers to scrub their contact lists against the national do-not-call registry 31 days.

Magazines	Cost $	Control	Control response	CPR control	Test	Test response	CPR test	Lift[a] (%)
World wine	1,736	A	331	29.6	B	396	24.7	20
Wine magazine	2,756	A	277	35.4	C	356	27.5	29
Wine enthusiast	2,960	A	308	31.8	D	282	34.8	−8
Food and wine	2,348	A	325	30.2	E	400	24.5	23
Total	**9,800**		**1,241**	**7.9**		**1,434**	**6.8**	

[a]Lift is the variation, in percent, between the CPR control and the CPR test

	World wine				Food and wine	
	Control	Control response			Control	Control response
First issue	A	331	⤬		B	308
Second issue	B	277			A	325

- *The marketer should avoid performing several tests with the same set of customers.* If you keep using the same group of customers for several runs of one campaign test, you should expect lower response rates. The same thing happens if you use the same fixed group for several campaigns in a short period of time. You must be aware of the extent to which there are diminishing returns. Therefore, you should plan the ideal frequency with which a customer is approached (i.e., the point where the marginal cost of testing exceeds the marginal revenue generated by the test).
- *Testing results have limited time validity.* Since customer preferences change over periods of time, conclusions drawn from tests are sometimes short-lived. Ongoing tests may provide adequate responses which reflect these changes.
- *Don't test the same things all over again.* As testing means only changing one or few variables, other things equal, change the analysis variable so you can see what changes in the results.
- *Overall marketing objectives should drive your testing. More* important than optimizing a particular campaign is to have a successful marketing program.

11.4 Campaign Execution

The campaign execution stage is the operational process by which a campaign is implemented. There are two important aspects at this stage: implementation and monitoring.

11.4.1 Implementation and Coordination

A thin line separates the development from the implementation stage. This difference arises from the fact that implementation summarizes everything that was developed and identifies all that has to be done before actually running the campaign. In order to implement the campaign, an action plan should be prepared to guide this process and all the resources involved. This plan should be divided into three sub-plans:

1. The campaign program
2. The campaign schedule
3. The activity schedule

Campaign Program

The campaign program is a summary of everything that has to be executed to run the campaign. It should lay out the list of tasks to be accomplished. These are to be assigned to a list of team members. It should contain the campaign briefing forms designed for members of the team and outside suppliers (e.g. advertising agency, merchandise suppliers, etc.). In order to coordinate the tasks between all persons involved, each task should be defined a deadline for completion. The summary of all these deadlines should result in the campaign timetable. Once the media and the promotion offer are chosen, the marketing team should do a description of all materials to be produced (the format, the color, the creative message) and events to take place (if it is a one-stage or a two-stage campaign).

Campaign Schedule

The campaign schedule lists the events that are planned and their respective timing. If this campaign is planned to coincide with other marketing activity a clash schedule should be done in order to identify potential conflicts of resources, timing and customer targets.

There are two key differences between the campaign and the activity schedule. The first one is directly related to the campaign components and the second one relates with the operational activity of the company itself.

Activity Schedule

It is very important to organize your company's activity during a campaign. Interdependent actions should be identified and time should be efficiently allocated for the completion of activities. It is at this stage that the critical path method can be applied. The critical path technique involves placing a time factor in each phase of the campaign, figuring what are the necessary precedent activities for each one and sequencing all the campaign phases (basically it works as a backward timetable). One advantage of this method is that it identifies potential bottlenecks and allows revision of allowed timings.

One important feature of activity scheduling is that not only does it allow sufficient time for completion and approval of the tasks but it also keeps the information up-to-date. Even when the campaign is running, its status will continue to be reported. The example of a Gantt chart[2] is shown in Fig. 11.3.

11.4.2 Monitoring, and Fine-Tuning

Monitoring is an ongoing process. When waiting until the end of the campaign one cannot make adjustments, such as schedule modifications. Nevertheless, the full effect of the campaign cannot be totally known until all the results have been received and analyzed. If the company is running an integrated campaign where results can be tracked through response, then the first status report will show the preliminary results that should be compared with the forecast results in order to show progress. Acting on the first results will allow a timely corrective action and the more up-to-date is the report, the more useful the corrections will be.

One question that should arise is "How can this process be fine-tuned?" Depending on the first measurable effects of a campaign, fine-tuning can be done in the following cases:

- The planning may be revised based on enquiry or orders performance alone. This adjustment is done based on the assumption that the conversion rate stays close to the forecasted level.
- The media selection may be adjusted. The first media results will determine if the advertising space in a specific media is profitable and if the media booking or cost should be cancelled or renegotiated.

---

[2] Gantt chart is a graphical representation of the duration of tasks against the progression of time.

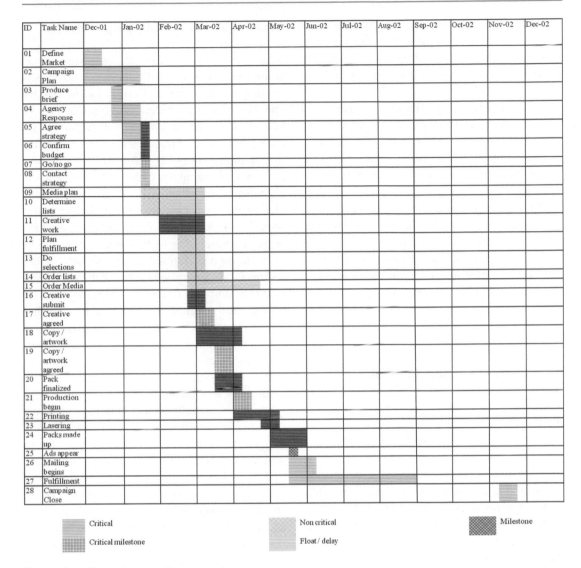

Fig. 11.3 A Gantt chart in a direct campaign

- If the campaign included a first sequence of creative and offer testing, then corrective action should be undertaken as quickly as possible.

11.4.3 Problems to Take into Account

Campaign management and particularly campaign execution involves the marketing team, other departments (sales force, call center, operations department, etc.), top management and outside suppliers. Many things can go wrong during the process. If the marketer runs a direct mail to customers requiring them to call the company's call-center and if the telemarketing team is not adequately informed about the campaign features, then the most probable outcome is that the campaign will be a failure On the other hand, suppliers should be briefed on the campaign program (the delivery dates, paper quality, color process, package dimensions, the script, etc.) in order to avoid rush work or imperfections. Then again, briefing every actor involved in this process is fundamental to the campaigns' success.

We have identified some causes of campaign failures:

- When the marketing planning is undertaken at a functional level and does not integrate with other functional areas of the company, then the campaign will be largely ineffective.
- Separating the responsibilities of operational marketing and strategic marketing planning will lead to a divergence of short and long term objectives. Concern over short-term results at the operational level will make the company less competitive in the long term.
- If top management doesn't take an active role in marketing planning then it will probably not be an effective system.
- If the degree of formalization of campaign management is not adapted to the diversity of operations within the company and its size, then campaign execution process won't be effective.

11.5   Analysis and Control

Analysis and control end the campaign management cycle. In this phase, marketers should be able to draw some conclusions about the campaign success and use these results not only to improve their customer knowledge but also to improve future campaigns. This is an important stage because it evaluates campaign results in light of the original objectives and determines the campaign level of success or failure. Features that run well should be used as "best practices" for other campaigns. For features that didn't perform well, marketers should search the reasons why this has happened. This research should be recorded in the CRM database to serve as a *learning lesson* to future campaigns.

Campaign analysis can be done in many ways. Marketers can use campaign key performance indicators (KPI) and compare them with budgeted KPI's and campaign objectives. They can also perform back end performance analysis to determine the purchase behavior of campaign respondents. Finally, more elaborated analysis can be performed, such as profile and response analysis, to link profiles and behavior with the campaign.

11.5.1 Measuring Campaign Results

Marketers can start measuring campaign results while the campaign is still running. As discussed in the previous section, as soon the results are known and analyzed the sooner action can be taken to fine-tune the campaign execution. Standard performance measures are the key performance indicators (KPI) discussed in the budget section. Comparing the CPM, CPS, ROI, and the CR with the budgeted KIP will give an intuitive idea about the campaign results. But marketers should look deeper and try to understand which target segment is driving the campaign success or what medium performed better and why. Back-end performance analysis is one of the answers to evaluate campaign results. It relates the behavior of a group of respondents with sales, contribution, and profit achieved in the campaign. It also relates this group of respondents with the advertising medium that converted them into customers.

In order to measure back-end performance it is necessary to maintain a system in which each customer is identified as coming from a specific advertising medium. Only then it is possible to analyze the behavior of all customers coming from the same initial source medium and calculate average sales, contribution and profits. Back-end performance will vary significantly from one advertising medium to another. For example, results from some direct marketing campaigns show that buyers acquired from direct mail buy more often than customers acquired through a magazine or newspaper insertion. Then it becomes vital to track customer performance in terms of its original medium source group, so that the decision to reinvest in a particular medium can be made on the basis of proven performance.

Back-end performance can be measured in many ways. For example, in a direct mailing, the measurement of back-end performance is simply the statement of profit or loss for the campaign promotion. For a loyalty program, this measurement should be done in terms of the allowable marketing cost and the breakeven. These two indicators will then be compared with the customer acquisition cost to determine customer contribution. Contribution is a formula that deducts from the gross margin the campaign costs and then divides the resulting value by the number of new customers. In the case of loyalty campaigns it is more adequate to calculate contribution in terms of the new customer lifetime value, because it can forecast future sales and profits from the new comers. Another measure to take into account is the attrition rate. This measure is used to determine the rate at which customers defect. When evaluating the profitability, for example, of a newspaper or magazine campaign to increase subscriptions or renewals, the KPI to take into account are the conversion rate, the renewal rates and the response rate to promotions.

In all cases, when running a promotions campaign, marketers should always calculate the *return on promotion* (ROP). ROP is a way of calculating the return on investment of a particular promotion:

$$ROP = [(\text{Contribution} - \text{Cost per order}) \\ /\text{Cost per order}] \times 100$$

The return is measured by the difference between the contribution that results from all the purchases that occur due to the promotion and the cost of acquiring the purchase.

11.5.2   Response Analysis

Response analysis calculates the campaign results up-to-date, projects its final results, such as responses, inquiries and leads, and analyzes these results. Response analyzes can be performed with customer and market segments, product lines, campaigns, offers and promotions, media or advertising agencies. To be able to perform this type of analysis, responses should be summarized by time—that is, by arrival date. Each response should be recorded at the CRM database and should have the calendar date it arrived. Results can then be analyzed as soon as the first campaign

responses are known and eventually they can correct the campaign progression. Response analysis uses statistical models such as regression analysis models to determine the impact of several variables of interest (age, gender, level of income, etc.) on probability of response.

11.5.3   Profile Analysis

Profile analysis is used to define and compare the profile of campaign responders with the actual profile of the company's customers and prospects. This comparison will allow marketers to verify if the initial targeted profile actually corresponds with the responder's profiles, i.e., if the customer segments were well targeted. Profile analyses can and should be performed at different stages of the campaign. It should be performed at the campaign planning stage, when defining the target segments; as part of the designing tests, as campaign results are received and after a campaign is completed to verify attrition.

The profile characteristics are recorded in the CRM database and they are used in this type of analysis if they can be related to the customer or prospect name. These characteristics may be fundamental (birth date, gender) or derived (age, score). Profile analysis considers the input (generally geographic, demographic or psychographic) and clusters names into groups with similar tastes and preferences. Two other statistical techniques used in profiles *analysis are automatic interaction detection* (AID) and *chi-square automatic interaction detection* (CHAID). These are not discussed in this text6; for more information on these techniques, see *Marketing Research* by Aaker et al. (2004).

By predicting the actions of customers or prospects by using these analyses, the company is refining and improving its marketing strategy.

11.6   Campaign Feedback

Everyday practice shows that it is far more valuable to have a reliable assessment of the measurable effects of marketing campaigns upfront. The effective registration of past marketing activities and their results, combined with modeling methods, different media and customer segments, enable the marketer to support campaign decisions in advance and to optimize them at the implementation stage. Information on successes, failures and the circumstances under which the campaigns were carried out should be stored. Patterns can be found and correlation between historical successes and campaign elements can be used as learning to ensure future success.

Companies should compile detailed information about the main aspects of campaigns, such as concepts, target groups, media used and campaign performance, into their CRM database. This way models can be designed to describe causal relationships between the variables under the marketer's control and criteria for success. The use of this stored information supports informed future action because it allows the prediction of the market environment in which certain campaigns will succeed. Recording and analyzing the success and failures of past campaigns improves the profitability of future campaigns. Deviations between achieved and desired results are minimized through the correct use of this compiled knowledge.

Keep in mind that three steps should be implemented in order to ensure successful campaigns and to enhance knowledge for the company:
1. Record all relevant data about campaign planning, implementation and results.
2. Model relationships between the data gathered, the controllable variables and the campaign results.
3. Apply this knowledge to future campaigns. If information is not sufficient, test the important variables to fill the gaps in knowledge.

11.7 Summary

A campaign is a series of interconnected promotional efforts usually undertaken within a defined timeframe, designed to capture customer's interest, and thereby achieve precise marketing goals.

A successful campaign management process comprises of planning, development, execution and analysis. At the campaign planning stage, marketers make strategic decisions that define the overall objectives of the campaign, the best communication message and the best target audience. The objectives often are market penetration, market extension, product development or diversification. When pursuing a customer retention strategy, ideally the company should target its most profitable customers via LTV (lifetime value) and RFM (recency, frequency, and monetary) analyses. The company can choose to pursue market penetration or extension, market diversification or new product development. Communication strategy involves choosing the most effective message and media (for retention and acquisition strategies) to efficiently reach its target segments.

Identification of the customer segments (homogenous groups of individuals that have similar tastes, wants and needs regarding the company's products or services) that the campaign will target can be done using lifetime segmentation and profiling, and on the basis of purchase behavior and profile data. The CRM database plays a central role in the segmentation process by providing information on customer behaviors and profiles, channel preferences and brand awareness. Marketing communications (marcom) are targeted interactions between the company and its customers and prospects using one or more media. Integrated marketing communications (IMC) involves the management and organization of all the marketing communication tools to deliver a clear and consistent message about the company and the product. Targeting the customers that provide a higher potential yield should be done in a way that maximizes the marketing communications ROI. Developing the offer consists of offering the customer some kind of incentive that will induce him/her to buy or to ask the company for more information.

The campaign budget allocates resources and coordinates expenditures across the marketing activities associated with the campaign. Making a campaign budget should be a balance between measurement, financial calculations, competitive analysis and good judgment. There are several methods to calculate a budget. Pre-set budgeting determines a given year's marketing expenditure on the basis of what they spent the year before, by applying a ratio that adjusts media cost inflation, projected sales increase or decrease, market conditions, etc. Budgeting for an allowable marketing cost (AMC) consists of determining the amount that can be spent on campaign marketing activities, while preserving the required profit margin. The AMC is obtained by subtracting the costs (cost of goods + distribution costs) and the required profit margin from the total sales value. Competitive parity method tries to equate budget allocation with those of competitors. Budgeting with the objective and task method focuses on determining the marketing objectives and then deciding on the marketing communications tasks that are needed to achieve those objectives. In the percentage of sales method, the company looks at the competitor allocations and on the industry averages, to determine the exact percentage that should be allocated. *Front-end analysis* allows the company to figure out, in a quick way, how much it can afford to spend on a special promotion.

Pre-set budgeting should ideally be replaced by LTV forecasts, front-end analysis, allowable marketing cost analysis and estimation of the return of marketing investment (ROI rates) because this will allow the company to compare returns on alternative marketing expenditures.

Tests help maximize the performance of the campaign. Key variables in testing are the target audience, the offer, the format, the creative element, the media and/or the timing. Testing can accurately predict performance measures like response to the campaign in percentage and campaign profitability.

Campaign implementation plan should be divided into three sub-plans: the campaign program, the campaign schedule and the activity schedule. In the analysis and control stage, marketers should be able to draw conclusions about the campaign success and use these results not only to improve their customer knowledge but also to improve future campaigns. Campaign

analysis can be done using campaign key performance indicators (KPI) and comparing them with budgeted KPI's and campaign objectives, by using back end performance analysis, or even profile and response analysis, to link profiles and behavior with the campaign. When running a promotions campaign, marketers should always calculate the return on promotion (ROP). While response analysis calculates the campaign results up-to-date, projects its final results, such as responses, inquiries and leads, and analyzes these results, profile analysis is used to define and compare the profile of campaign responders with the actual profile of the company's customers and prospects. Recording and analyzing the success and failures of past campaigns improves the profitability of future campaigns.

Exercise Questions

1. Explain the three key steps in the management of campaigns.
2. Imagine you are the manager of a chain of 25 seafood restaurants in Virginia. The restaurant has a mainstream positioning. You are planning a campaign to attract new clients and your available budget is $30.000. Describe how you would go about implementing this campaign.
3. Explain the ideas around the concept of campaign testing? Do you think that testing in general will become more important in the future? Why or why not?
4. Give examples for key performance indicators for the evaluation of campaign success.
5. Explain the advantages and disadvantages of the various campaign budget setting methods.

MINI CASE 11.1

Z4 Launch Campaign at BMW

BMW, the Munich-based luxury carmaker is a strong believer in CRM practices across dealers and end customers. Traditionally, customers communicated with dealers and dealers with the BMW Group. Today, many end customers expect to communicate directly with the BMW Group. The challenge therefore for BMW (and any carmaker) is to establish the relationship between BMW Group and end customers and yet strengthen the traditional relationship between end customers and dealers. BMW Group's CRM approach is therefore very integrated in nature, both in terms of spanning dealers and end customers, as well as in terms of customer service, new customer attraction, and loyalization.

The launch of the Z4 roadster in 2002/2003 is a prototypical example for BMW Group's approach. The objectives were to position the car in the premium segment, to conquer new customers, and to loyalize owners of the previous model Z3. An integrated communications campaign was launched that coordinated TV and print campaigns, direct marketing, preview events, electronic media as well as dealer marketing. The goal of the entire campaign was to select relevant prospects for the actual launch in March 2003. In practice, this meant that the addresses of the most interested set of prospects were known at launch and that these individuals were then invited for closed room and preview events. The selection was made based on prospects' reaction to the mailings, emails, Short Message Service (SMS), and Internet offers. The activities started with bulk mail activities, followed by TV and print inserts. These initial teasers set off a second wave where interested parties would call or email a service center that then forwarded information material to these qualified prospects. These address data and email addresses formed a key part of the prospect database. Prospects could then also sign up for preview events where the actual car was shown. Using feedback from these preview events, information on the hottest prospects was then given to the dealers who followed up on the prospects for landing the sales. The effectiveness of the pre-launch activities was measured in terms of number and quality of prospects, response rate of activities, and cost per contact. Overall, the campaign was extremely successful in not only achieving the desired premium positioning but also in terms of leading sales in the segment of premium roadsters.

Questions

1. Explain the likely issues (as discussed in the chapter) that may come up during the Z4 campaign management process.
2. Should the campaign stop here? Are there opportunities for BMW to proceed campaigning with the new owners of the Z4? What are some of those opportunities?

References

Aaker, D. A., Kumar, V., & Day, G. (2004). *Marketing research* (8th ed.). Hoboken, NJ: Wiley.

Bell, L. (2009). MetLife retention campaign boosts loyalty. *Direct marketing news*. Date retrieved July 26, 2011. http://www.dmnews.com/metlife-retention-campaign-boosts-loyalty/article/137350/.

De Bonis, J. N., & Peterson, R. S. (1997). *The AMA handbook for managing business to business marketing communications*. Chicago/Lincolnwood: NTC Business/American Marketing Association.

Nail, J (2000). *The email marketing dialogue. White paper* of *the forrester report*. Cambridge, MA: Forrester Research.

Pickton, D., & Broderick, A. (2001). *Integrated marketing communication*. Englewood Cliffs, NJ: Prentice-Hall.

Impact of CRM on Marketing Channels 12

12.1 Overview

Marketing channels move goods and services from firms to consumers and other businesses. From a customer management point of view, firms also use channels to interact with customers. These different channels vary not only in their cost structures but also in their ability to attract, bind, and serve customers. Each customer has distinct preferences for distribution or contact channels. To meet the needs of various customers, businesses must provide the right blend of direct (websites, e-commerce, stores, call centers, and enterprise sales representatives) and indirect (distributors, retailers, solution providers, and online resellers) channels. In other words, companies should adopt a multichannel strategy.

From the consumer's perspective, multichannel offers and communication imply greater choice and more convenient access to products and services. From the retailer's perspective, a multichannel system poses new implementation challenges, from delivering consistent experiences across all channels to fully exploiting the strengths of each channel.

Multichannel marketing also poses challenges for customer relationship management (CRM). Because focal firms interact with the end user through channel intermediaries, such as retailers, it is difficult for the firm to build and nurture an effective customer relationship program directed at the end customer that will lead to a good working relationship and ultimately create loyalty. Loyal customers have greater value to the firm; they

contribute to the firm's profits for a long time, whereas non-loyal customers merely generate short-term profits. The firm thus needs to ensure that its CRM messages and offerings reach its target consumers without dilution or digression. But such reach is especially difficult when the channel intermediaries have conflicting CRM programs in place, which often means that the focal firm only has indirect control over CRM implementation. Also, multichannel marketing establishes the challenge of eliciting customer information from multiple channels for central processing.

This chapter deals with the challenges of channel management in the context of CRM implementation. We point out current multichannel issues that firms are nowadays facing and provide insights into the management of the respective challenges.

Thus we start by presenting the role of channels in creating and maintaining customer relationships. We discuss emerging trends with regard to traditional and electronic channels and shed light on related chances and challenges for the implementation and maintenance of CRM. We leave the main part of this chapter for capturing attributes of multichannel design, including worthwhile insights into the management of multichannel systems (Fig. 12.1).

12.2 CRM and Marketing Channels

The effectiveness of CRM depends to a considerable extent on firms' channel strategies.

V. Kumar and W. Reinartz, *Customer Relationship Management*, Springer Texts in Business and Economics, DOI 10.1007/978-3-642-20110-3_12, © Springer-Verlag Berlin Heidelberg 2012

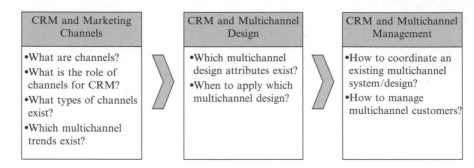

Fig. 12.1 Content structure of this chapter

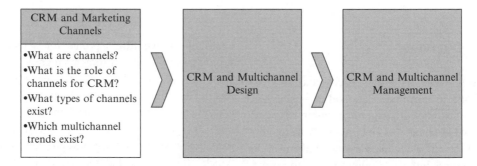

Fig. 12.2 Content structure of this chapter: CRM and marketing channels

Because marketing interactions with customers occur primarily through channels, conventionally, customer relationships are created and sustained through marketing channels. Thus, marketing channels are the primary vehicle of relationship building. In the following section we explain the basic channel terminology we use throughout this chapter, and then outline the role of channels with regard to CRM and multichannel trends that firms currently face (Fig. 12.2).

What Are Channels?

A channel is basically a "format" for accessing a customer base. Each format (or route) combines a package of different service outputs, i.e., functions that reduce the end user's search, waiting time, storage, and other costs (Coughlan, Anderson, Stern, & El-Ansary, 2006). An Internet channel thus is a spatially convenient way to purchase from a connected home at any time. However, the time required to receive the product is greater than it would be if the purchase occurred in a store channel, which itself offers minimal spatial convenience but also minimizes waiting time, in that the product may be taken home immediately. The term "channel" then can be used mainly in two ways.

First, a channel refers to the flow of the organization's offerings (e.g., physical goods, information) to ultimate end users (e.g., end customers), as well as of sales proceeds from the customer back to the focal firm. Marketing or distribution channels then indicate all entities (e.g., distributors, wholesalers, retailers, broker, agents) that perform functions for the marketing firm, such as stocking inventory, conducting sales transactions, conducting payments, providing point-of-purchase information, or offering upfront liquidity to the manufacturers.

Second, a channel refers to the mode of communication between a firm and its customers. These communication or contact channels convey information to customers to raise their awareness about the firm's products and services and persuade them to make purchases. Furthermore,

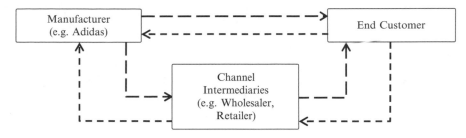

Fig. 12.3 Contact channels

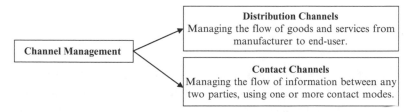

Fig. 12.4 Channel management

a distribution channel often encompasses several organizations in a single term, whereas a contact channel typically includes only two parties.

For example, the distribution channel of the sportswear manufacturer Adidas includes two distinct types of channels: wholesalers and retailers. By the implementation and the specific catering of these two intermediaries, the group can respond better to the needs of multiple types of customers and become more responsive to market developments. The contact channels between Adidas and its end customers refer to the modes of communication, such as Internet, direct mail, and SMS or wireless text messaging. Of course, different skill sets are required to manage distinctive channels effectively (Fig. 12.3).

Although distribution channels and contact channels are not always cleanly separated (remember that information exchange is a core task of distribution channels), we differentiate the terms here because the management of contact channels is a very important aspect of CRM. In addition, the term "channel management" often refers only to contact channels, even if this may not be technically precise (Fig. 12.4).

Conventionally, in a given geographical market, firms set up a single distribution channel that

performs all channel functions except advertising. For example, the German car manufacturer BMW uses its network of licensed dealers to sell cars to the market while also engaging in direct-to-consumer communication (beyond dealer communications) through mass and direct advertising.

Before the advent of the Internet, a direct sales channel between the marketing firm and the customer was often too costly and/or arduous to implement. Direct interaction was limited mainly to trade fairs and test marketing; third-party agencies usually performed the various channel functions. Thus, the customer interacted with the marketing firm indirectly through the channels, which mediated their communication. Only in the case of B2B marketing did manufacturers typically get to know the end users and interact directly with them.

12.2.1 The Role of Channels in Customer Relationships

Because channels are basically gatekeepers between the manufacturer and the end user, any channel must be managed and coordinated carefully to guarantee the effective reach and

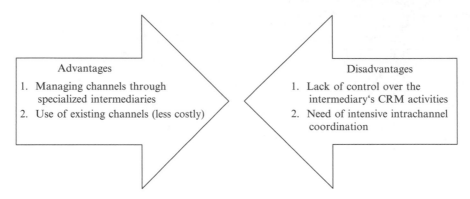

Fig. 12.5 Advantages and disadvantages of indirect channels

the attractiveness of the manufacturer's products (Coughlan et al., 2006). Various channel settings in any market likely include a diverse grouping of involved intermediaries and channel types. However, customer relationships can be created and maintained through various channel systems—as long as those channels are deployed and managed appropriately. This chapter notes the role of various channel types in the process of managing customer relationships and reveals the advantages and disadvantages of these different channel settings for CRM.

Managing Customer Relationships Through Indirect Channels

Indirect customer relationship management requires the use of an intermediary to manage the end-customer relationship indirectly. E.g., selling own products through supermarkets, the consumer goods manufacturer Henkel uses indirect channels intensively and is therefore confronted with the task of managing customer relationships indirectly. Because different skill sets are required to manage different channels and customer segments, firms benefit from distribution efforts that pass through specialized intermediaries. Furthermore, setting up a new direct channel demands profound investments, which can be avoided by the use of intermediaries' existing channel structures.

In this setting, the CRM process also involves (indirect) gathering and processing of customer and sales or transaction information, whether by the channel member or the focal firm. Accordingly, the goals and interests of all involved channel members must be coordinated. The indirect customer contact scenario means the focal firm lacks control over the intermediary's CRM activities. Thus, the focus of customer relationship management in an indirect channel structure is typically on (1) building a good working relationship with the channel member and (2) providing incentives for building strong relationships with end customers.

For example, incentives might encourage the channel member to gather and process sales and customer information and share this information with the marketing firm. Large consumer, nondurable marketing firms, such as Henkel or Procter & Gamble (P&G), traditionally had significant power over their distribution channels and could thus control the channels' activities to such an extent that the channels conformed absolutely to their customer relationship agenda. However, the arrival of private-label products on supermarket shelves and the increasing power of retail giants has meant that P&G's ability to control retail CRM activities has greatly decreased (Fig. 12.5).

The decision to deploy an indirect channel also involves the concrete choice of which channel type to use, such as selling the products through an intermediary's store or using an indirect web portal like Amazon.

(1) CRM and Indirect (Traditional) Offline Channels

The indirect management of customer relationships typically entails traditional, offline channels (i.e., stores, sales forces, catalogs). This tactic can enhance customer satisfaction and loyalty if its challenges are addressed effectively, and achieving loyalty creates an important asset for firms. Loyal customers are willing to pay higher prices than non-loyal customers, and they are more likely to recommend a firm, its products, and its services to other consumers (Wallace, Giese, & Johnson, 2004; Zeithaml, Berry, & Parasuraman, 1996), resulting in greater customer value. However, as noted previously, these traditional indirect channel structures leave the relationship with the end customer solely in the hands of the intermediary, which creates several challenges for the focal firm.

a) Dilution of CRM Strategies

Traditional intermediary structures make continuous, direct interactions with the end customer very difficult—if not impossible—such that it is no trivial task to build and nurture an effective customer relationship program. Firms must ensure that their CRM messages and offerings reach their target consumers, without dilution or digression. European retailers such as Carrefour, Dia, and Sainsbury's all sell high-quality, private-label brands that compete directly with the established brands of renowned manufacturers though. In a clear conflict of interest, private-label promotions often diametrically oppose the customer relationship programs of the national brands carried in the store.

b) Indirect Control of CRM Through Channels

The primary methods of CRM implementation include direct control and monitoring at the channel level by manipulating the upstream relationship with the channel partners, through incentives for them, to manage the downstream relationship in a way that aligns with the firm's overall CRM.

c) Eliciting Customer Information from All Channels for Central Processing

The lack of precise information about individual customers complicates the implementation of CRM. Distribution channel partners often provide only an approximation of customer preferences, such that customers remain largely anonymous to the firm, and the firm's offers represent merely estimations of customers' tastes and preferences. Effective CRM therefore needs customer information from different contact channels that gets centrally processed to provide critical input to the planning and execution of the physical distribution of goods. Because retailers compete with one another, it is difficult for firms to convince them to share critical sales information for central processing. Therefore, sophisticated information systems appear to be the key to the implementation of any CRM program.

Thus distribution through indirect offline channels may reduce basic channel investments, but it also requires enormous intrachannel coordination efforts to secure adequate customer relationship management.

(2) CRM and Indirect Online Channels

Deploying an indirect online channel, e.g. distributing through Amazon, is a low-cost alternative that offers great coverage and can exploit existing channel structures. Online shopping also has been widely adopted due to the channel's continuous availability and convenience for consumers (Sultan & Rohm, 2004). Yet such channels also entail certain challenges, because their focus is often on price comparisons among suppliers instead of product quality. Through a customer self-selection process, indirect websites often attract non-loyal customers, searching for the cheapest offer. These customers are willing to switch supplier if the product/service of interest is offered at a lower price. Thus, indirect online channels are an efficient means to create product awareness and increase coverage but not to

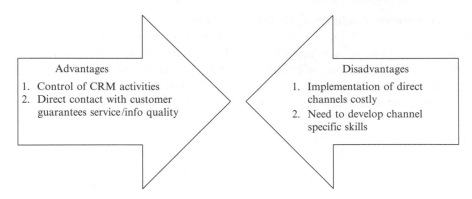

Fig. 12.6 Advantages and disadvantages of direct channels

access customers with high potential customer value—namely, loyal customers with promising long-term profit potential.

Managing Customer Relationships Through Direct Channels

Traditionally, a direct channel between the firm and the consumer took the form of a communication or contact channel. Firms communicated product information directly to consumers through television and print, to persuade the consumer to find the most readily accessible sales or distribution channel. Point-of-purchase advertising and promotions at the intermediary's outlet (e.g., retail store) further persuaded the consumer to purchase. However, consumer information moved indirectly to the firm through sales data.

The advent of new, direct, electronic channels and the increasing trend toward opening dedicated shops make two-way direct communication increasingly possible, such that firms can collect customer data through direct channels, too. In 2006 the international cosmetics brand Nivea opened its first company-owned store in Hamburg, Germany, to get direct access to customer data and benefit from direct interactions with its end customers.

Although the implementation of a direct channel requires channel-specific investments and the development of channel-specific skills, the direct contact with the customer enables the firm to establish and maintain valuable customer relationships, based on first-hand knowledge. The direct customer contact also reduces the need for excessive intrachannel coordination efforts and grants the firm comprehensive control over its planned CRM activities.

Combining all mentioned aspects, we derive the key advantages and disadvantages of managing customer relationships through direct channels in Fig. 12.6.

Finally, the decision to deploy a direct channel involves a second step: which specific channel type to use, such as a firm-specific store or website, as we discuss next.

(1) CRM and Direct Offline Channels

To implement directly operated offline channels (e.g., sales force, dedicated shops), a firm incurs extremely high costs due to channel implementation and maintenance (e.g., employee training, technical endowments, implementation of information systems). Nevertheless, traditional direct channels allow for personal and individual contact and thus typically create more loyalty than other channels because of their ability to create social and economic bonds with the customer.

The focus in these channels is typically on enhancing brand images or service quality perceptions, not price, which further explains their ability to attract loyal customers. However, based on this argumentation, loyal customers could be attracted by less costly mass media channels too, such as mail, if those channels provide brand-related instead of simply price information

(Verhoef & Donkers, 2005; Bolton, Lemon, & Verhoef, 2004). Because of the very high costs for many traditional channels, it is appealing for firms to switch to electronic channels and/or to develop customer self-service strategies to reduce their costs (Payne & Frow, 2004).

Through self-service offers for example, customers might place their order for products, collect the necessary pre- and/or post-sales information, and solve problems by themselves. Self-service is becoming more and more widespread in various contexts; one quite prominent example appears in movie theaters that host point-of-sale ticket kiosks. With these ticketing system kiosks, customers select a movie, choose their seating, process the payment, receive a printed ticket and a receipt, and, if applicable, have points credited to their loyalty program cards, without any assistance from a salesperson or service rep. Another familiar example has changed the face of retail banking, where less expensive self-service channels such as ATMs have helped reduce average transaction costs by nearly 15% since 1990 (Myers, Pickersgill, & Van Metre, 2004).

(2) CRM and Direct Online Channels

The implementation of direct online channels, such as a manufacturer's website, has become quite common. These channels offer a low cost alternative and can achieve great coverage, which makes them a key route to value chain efficiencies (Sultan & Rohm, 2004). Customers have adopted online channels nearly universally, due to their continuous availability and convenience (Sultan & Rohm, 2004), so they have become great sources of precise customer information for firms. Detailed customer information, easily available through electronic channels, arms the marketer with a constantly updated ability to forecast the shopping behaviors and needs of individual customers.

However, questions persist about whether impersonal, online, relatively anonymous channels can really develop customer retention or loyalty. On the one hand, customer retention and loyalty should result whenever a channel avoids a price focus and supports social and economic bonds, criteria that seem difficult to meet online. It is always easy for customers to compare prices across online sites, so firms must promise low prices to be able to compete. Thus, online channels inherently tend to induce a price focus, which leads to reduced customer loyalty (Ansari, Mela, & Neslin, 2008; Sinha, 2000). On the other hand, unlike the offline environment, it is quite easy to create personalized marketing messages through the Internet, which can nurture social bonds with customers. Once a customer has learned how to find information on a firm's website, switching to a competitor also creates switching costs (Ansari, Mela, & Neslin, 2008; Reichheld & Schefter, 2000; Chen & Hitt, 2002). Moreover, the channel's convenience and flexibility often increases customer satisfaction that can encourage customer loyalty (Srinivasan, Anderson, & Ponnavolu, 2002; Boehm, 2008). Thus it appears perhaps more difficult but nevertheless possible to achieve loyalty through electronic channels—if they are used adequately.

A current trend in electronic channels makes it even easier to collect data and personalize CRM efforts. The advent of Web 2.0, including its two-way communication between the firm and the customer, proved to be an important and successful tool for creating customer assets over time. Recent technological advances allow consumers to use the Internet interactively, which means firms can use the Internet not only to send information to their customers but also to receive direct feedback from them. This possibility creates a more complex, fruitful dialogue with the customer base, including easy access to customer feedback and demand, and companies then can use this data to refine and improve their CRM strategies (Payne & Frow, 2004).

Generally speaking then, there exists no single best channel type; each channel choice entails certain advantages and disadvantages. A firm does not necessarily need to choose just one channel but can also combine different channels in a multichannel system, to benefit from various advantages. Firms mostly combine online and offline channels in their multichannel system, though there are some differences with regard to the use of direct and indirect channels, as depicted in Fig. 12.7.

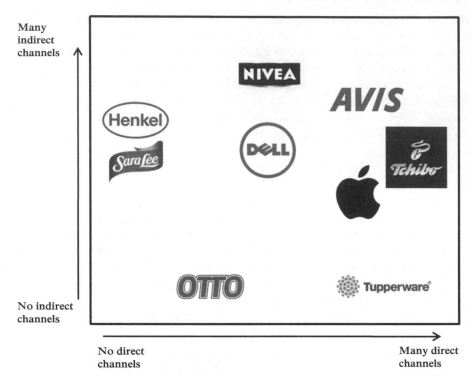

Fig. 12.7 Industry examples of channel combinations

To build and maintain their brands, firms like Apple choose to sell their products mainly through direct channels: their own stores, own websites, and by phone. This method creates exclusivity and builds customer relationships through the creation of brand equity. In contrast, firms such as Avis or Nivea try to achieve maximum coverage and brand awareness and thus implement far more channels, both indirect and direct (see Fig. 12.7), which obviously demands greater coordination effort.

Overall, the choice of a distribution or marketing channel (indirect/direct, online/offline, etc.) always involves a trade-off for the firm between certain advantages and disadvantages, such as the level of control, available CRM activities, costs, or market coverage. Using the preceding analyses, Table 12.1 summarizes the key issues (advantages/disadvantages) that characterize typical multichannel systems, from the firm's perspective.

12.2.2 Multichannel Trends and CRM

As illustrated in Fig. 12.8, four major trends with regard to multichannel systems demand further detailed discussion.

1. The proliferation of direct channels

The ubiquitous presence of the Internet, and especially of new electronic channels in business and daily life has had a tremendous impact on firms' channel options. Whether through a website, a mobile device, or sophisticated voice response systems, consumers take advantage of this great variety to seek information and transact directly with the firm. Computers, travel, books, music—the list of products that customers are familiar with and even prefer to purchase electronically is getting longer. Firms thus have direct access to end customers and also can recognize, in every interaction, whether the customer has bought from them before. When the

Table 12.1 Characteristics of different multichannel systems

	Few channels (indirect, offline)	Many channels (indirect, offline)	Few channels (indirect, online)	Many channels (indirect, online)	Few channels (mixed)	Many channels (mixed)	Few channels (direct, offline)	Many channels (direct, offline)	Few channels (direct, online)	Many channels (direct, online)
Need for intra-channel coordination	Med	High	Med	High	High	High	Low	Med	Low	Med
Implementation costs	Low	Low	Low	Low	Med	High	Med	High	Low	High
Need for channel-specific investments	Low	Low	Low	Low	Med	High	Low–med	High	Low–med	High
Coverage	Low	Med	Med	High	Med	High	Low	Med	Med	High

interaction occurs through a technology-enabled channel, the firm can record and store all relevant information about this customer, without having to negotiate with, provide incentives to, or train a third-party channel member, such as a retailer.

2. Multichannel as the norm

Recent times have witnessed a virtual explosion in the number of media channels that seek consumers' attention; multichannel strategies become more and more attractive, because they can be adapted individually to fit customers, the firm's products, and its overall CRM strategy perfectly. Firms adopt more and more channels due to two effects:

First, firms are actually pushed (*push effect*) toward a multichannel strategy by customers and competitors. Consumers continuously expand their experiences beyond traditional channels and thus are willing to use any given channel if it meets their service output demands. The growing number of channels also increases the possible combinations of service outputs. When he or she feels comfortable with these routes, the consumer expects all companies to be present in the preferred channels. The resulting push effect demands that firms comply with their customers' preferences, to keep up with their competitors (Rosenbloom, 2007).

Second, a continuous *pull effect* arises because a multichannel system provides potential improvements in terms of customer loyalty, sales growth, and efficiency. Channels differ in their attributes and thus the portfolio of service outputs (i.e., functions that reduce the end user's search, waiting time, storage, or other costs) they provide (Wallace, Giese, & Johnson, 2004). For example, Fig. 12.9 describes differences in the service outputs provided by a store, a catalog, and the Internet. Stores typically provide a good assortment to choose from and high levels of in-store (e.g., product demonstrations) and after-sales (e.g., product installation) service; the Internet instead offers great search convenience as it is possible to research and easily compare information across several suppliers quickly from home.

A complementary set of service outputs offered through various channels is more likely

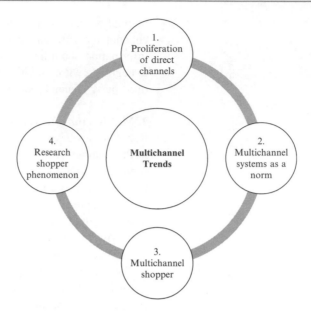

Fig. 12.8 Major multichannel trends

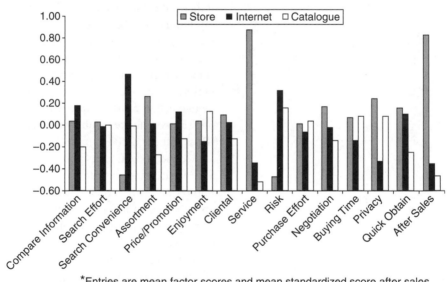

*Entries are mean factor scores and mean standardized score after sales

Fig. 12.9 Channel characteristics (Source: Verhoef, Neslin, & Vroomen, 2007, p. 139)

to meet the demands of consumers than is a single channel, so a multichannel system should achieve greater customer satisfaction and increase loyalty (Blattberg, Kim, & Neslin, 2008).

3. Multichannel shoppers
In response to the continuing increases in existing media and distribution channels and the implementation of multichannel systems, modern customers tend to change their habit, i.e., to use one specific channel for purchase, as they derive differing benefits from different channels. Depending on the desired product and the time available for the purchase, a consumer will choose the most convenient distribution channel. Thus many customers buy music online, because

haptics do not provide any additional benefit for purchasing. The same consumers may prefer to purchase a sweatshirt in a store though, to be able to touch the material and try on the item before buying it.

Customers who buy in more than one channel within a specific period of time are multichannel shoppers, and they are very attractive to selling firms, because they typically shop more frequently and spend more money—20 to 30% more on average—than single-channel shoppers (Myers, Pickersgill, & Van Metre, 2004; Kumar & Venkatesan, 2005; Thomas & Sullivan, 2005; Venkatesan, Kumar, & Ravishanker, 2007). The drivers of multichannel shopping and managing these types of shoppers are critical factors for firm success, as discussed in more detail in Section 12.4.2.

4. Research shoppers

With the proliferation of direct channels, multichannel systems become more and more attractive for consumers, who can easily pick the most convenient channel for purchase or to find information. In an emerging phenomenon, half of all consumers research the product in one channel (e.g., Internet), but purchase it in another channel (e.g., store). Such "research shopping" constitutes a massive challenge for the firm, namely, not losing the customer in the course of his or her shopping process (Nunes & Cespedes, 2003).

Each channel seeks to attract different consumers and obtains only limited attention from the firm's overall customer base. The emergence of new channels leads consumers to change their channel habits though, to derive the new and differing benefits across the different stages of their buying processes. For example, one consumer might search the Web for the best price quotes to be better informed about prices and negotiate a better deal. But for various reasons (e.g., uncertainty about the security and privacy of web transactions, perceived risk regarding the quality of web-based offers), the same consumer might plan eventually to purchase from a local retailer. In the vacation industry for example, 30% of consumers use one channel for search and a different channel for purchase (Verhoef, Neslin, & Vroomen, 2007). In this context, a firm

must provide sufficient information on the web but also ensure it hosts a corresponding outlet close by, to secure the deal.

The emergence of more and more direct channels (trend 1), implemented by firms to achieve a multichannel system (trend 2), combined with the customers' willingness to use these offers (trend 3 and 4), thus open a vast new range of opportunities for CRM activities.

Opportunities Due to Multichannel Trends

(1) Widening Coverage of the Consumer Population

The most immediate impact of distribution channel and contact channel proliferation is the increase in coverage of the population of potential consumers by firms' extensive channel networks. If people have more choice among different communication and transaction channels, they will choose those channels that best fit their preferences and habits. Potential customers who previously did not buy because they lacked access to the firm's products through traditional channels now may consider buying. Thus the firm's potential customer base grows and for example includes busy executives who are hard pressed for time, who once would travel only to the nearest outlet to shop but now can use the Internet or mobile offers to obtain products from anywhere.

(2) Improved Availability of Customer Information for the Firm

Multiple channels open the floodgates to multiple sources of consumer and demand information. Companies now have essentially unlimited access to multiple sources of the same information, which allows them to verify and cross-validate the reliability of longitudinal information. More important, they increasingly can turn to direct channels to reach customers. Through direct channels, firms acquire unfiltered information about individual customers' preferences and needs, independent of any mediating dealer. The need to exchange customer information across channels also makes central customer databases imperative at the firm level, which means the firm gains additional leverage effects from interacting directly with end customers.

Smart firms will leverage this information to produce detailed customer databases across channels and multiple shopping instances. Such databases improve forecasting ability and understanding of the behavior and needs of individual customers. Moreover, customer identification in each channel makes it possible to customize marketing mixes (including products and services) for each customer and opens up opportunities to sell complementary products—opportunities that competing firms may fail to recognize or be unable to offer.

(3) Less Dependence on Channel Partners
Channel proliferation also increases the firm's power vis-à-vis its channel partners. Channel exclusivity no longer exists, and channel partners grow more dependent on the firm to ensure the cross-channel coordination of customer information, marketing communications, and physical distribution. Different channels owned by different agencies may compete for sales volume and margins, but they still must be coordinated to address customers who keep switching between them. Therefore firms' CRM strategies cannot be overly channel-specific; rather, they should ensure uniform customer satisfaction across shopping instances and channels. That is, channel coordination is an essential ingredient of a multichannel strategy.

Along with these opportunities, new challenges arise. Recent technological developments may promise a more effective CRM strategy, but they also add to the complexity of the task, as explained in the following.

Challenges Due to Multichannel Trends
(1) Media Planning is Increasingly Difficult
As noted previously, the proliferation of channels changes customer behavior, including how customers obtain information. The great expansion of channels creates strong competition for customers' attention, and a communication strategy that relies on fewer channels becomes a rather limiting choice. Companies face the challenge of integrating inbound and outbound approaches for communicating with customers, all of which is even more difficult in the face of

shrinking budgets, and an explosion of new technologies which enable new ways of customer interaction.

In their media planning, firms must realize that different contact channels are proficient for different channel functions. Selecting a channel that is appropriate for performing a particular marketing function entails recognizing not only the customer's contact channel preference and the amount of exposure to the customer, but also to the ability of the channel to deliver the service output that supports the particular marketing purpose. For example, though product demonstrations at the International Consumer Electronics Show contribute significantly to product awareness and understanding, actual transactions may rather be achieved through the Internet or retail outlets.

(2) Channel Conflict and Differentiation
Companies can not only communicate through e-mail, the web, wireless, mobile devices, sales forces, customer contact centers, and enterprise portals but also transact business with more consumers through these various routes. Consumers in turn have started deriving different benefits from channels, which then adds to the complexity and difficulty of effective CRM. Conflicts of interest may arise among different members of a distribution channel, which invariably attenuates the marketing efforts of the focal firm. Interchannel competition for share of wallet from the same customer increases the challenge of ensuring a seamless interchange of information across channels, without harming channel members' interests. The firm walks a tightrope, between meeting the conflicting interests of different channel partners and fulfilling its own objective to address the customer's needs, all while maintaining equity.

But channel competition might not become as fierce as these dire predictions suggest. As channels grow more specialized, the implementation of CRM has become less vulnerable to channel conflict. For example, the Internet seems proficient in prospecting for and attracting new customers, rather than transacting. People may learn about the firm's offers through the Internet and

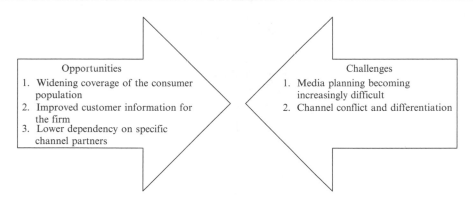

Fig. 12.10 Multichannel trends: opportunities and challenges

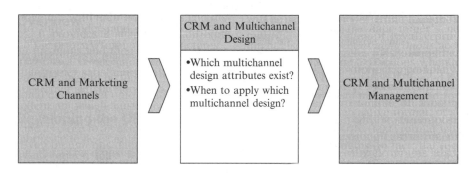

Fig. 12.11 Content structure of this chapter: CRM and multichannel design

make purchase decisions based on this information, and many consumers still prefer to visit a local departmental store or showroom for the final transaction. By actively managing a portfolio of specialized channels (e.g., website for prospecting, showroom for harvesting), the firm can nurture its relationship with the customer while also rendering issues such as channel conflict less contentious than what they would have been without channel specification (Fig. 12.10).

12.3   CRM and Multichannel Design

As already discussed, multichannel distribution and marketing is the norm today, rather than the exception, in virtually all industries. Moreover, one of the most challenging and important tasks a firm must undertake is the process of identifying, implementing (design decisions), and managing optimal channel systems (management decisions).

Even when it is aware of the various advantages and disadvantages of different channel types, a firm still must make concrete decisions about which channel system to implement and which channels to combine, considering its own individual situation. In the following section, we discuss key decisions for the firm with regard to the design of a multichannel strategy (design attributes) and the conditions in which different channel designs represent an efficient route to market (Fig. 12.11).

12.3.1 Attributes of Multichannel Designs

Three critical questions arise for a firm when deciding on channels to be implemented in its multichannel distribution or marketing system (Fig. 12.12):

1. How broad the offered variety of routes should be,

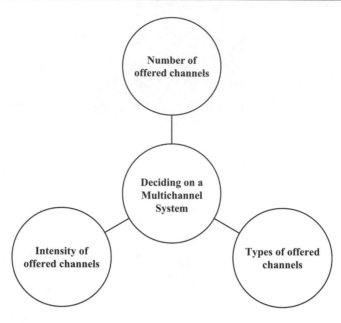

Fig. 12.12 Decision factors for multichannel design

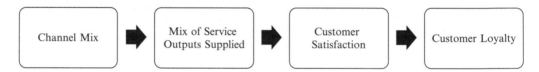

Fig. 12.13 Effects of channel mix decisions

2. which types of channels to implement and combine, and
3. how intensively to use each route (i.e., store density).

Great discrepancy exists between the firm's and customers' idea of the optimal *number of channels* and *channel intensity*, i.e. the number of stores in which a product should be available.

Using several different routes to market and/or pursuing a strategy of intensive distribution means that a firm achieves high market coverage but also runs the risk of escalating intrabrand competition. Competition for potential end users causes pressure on the product price, which leads to diminished margins. Trying to compensate for the loss of profit, intermediaries tend to reduce their service output or even refuse to offer the product or service, which might damage the brand image and reduce the firm's market share. Therefore, a firm might prefer to use a limited variety of routes to the market and minimal intensity to avoid unhealthy

intrabrand competition. But still the firm needs to challenge its competitors, so it must obtain long-term customer satisfaction.

In contrast, customers prefer a broader variety of routes and intensive distribution, demanding wider availability (i.e., greater coverage), greater purchase convenience, and a wider range of service outputs at the point of purchase (Jindal, Reinartz, Krafft, & Hoyer, 2007). For the firm to challenge its competitors, it needs to meet these demands for service outputs to ensure long-term customer satisfaction and customer loyalty (Fig. 12.13).

Another important issue pertains to the *types of channels* firms implement in their multichannel systems. As discussed in the previous section, each channel entails different levels of service outputs, so integrating different types of channels into a channel system, provides customers with access to a complementary mix of offerings. Because multiple channels meet more of their service output needs, customers express more satisfaction in multichannel settings, as well as more retailer loyalty (Wallace, Giese, & Johnson, 2004).

12.3.2 Designing Optimal Multichannel Offers

Now that we know which parameters must be modified to adapt a multichannel system, we need to develop a strategy that guides a manager when determining his or her own perfect channel strategy. In which conditions should specific types and number of channels, with which intensity, be implemented?

Two main inputs determine the appropriate design of a multichannel system
1. The channel system should fit the firm's overall business strategy and environment, and
2. the combination of channels should maximize synergies and minimize cannibalization.

(1) Fit multichannel systems to the business strategy and environmental conditions
Multichannel systems are most successful, in terms of their contribution to a firm's performance, if their structure aligns perfectly with the firm's business strategy and its surrounding environmental conditions (Kabadayi, Eyuboglu, & Thomas, 2007). In this case, *environmental conditions* refer to the
- Level of available resources (needed for innovation and differentiation)
- Complexity of an environment (i.e., number and diversity of competitors and buyers)
- Dynamism in the environment (i.e., frequency of environmental changes)

A *business strategy* instead refers to the manner in which firms compete in a specific industry or market. A firm can develop a competitive advantage through
- a differentiation strategy or
- a cost-leadership strategy (Kabadayi, Eyuboglu, & Thomas, 2007).

Overall then, there is no single best distribution or communication strategy that a firm can apply successfully, which seems quite intuitive. The multichannel system Apple has adopted

(focus on direct channels) thus would not fit Henkel (focus on indirect channels), because while Apple operates in a technologically turbulent environment, thriving due to its prompt responses to environmental changes and ability to differentiate itself from competitors, Henkel works in a rather stable environment and aims to achieve greater market coverage. Thus, their multichannel systems fit both their business strategies and their environmental conditions.

If the environment is dynamic and complex, the firm needs to be extremely flexible and react quickly to unexpected environmental changes. This ability to react properly to environmental changes demands a greater number of more specialized channels (Anderson, 1985; Moriarty & Moran, 1990; Kabadayi, Eyuboglu, & Thomas, 2007). In this case, firms that pursue a differentiation strategy and have sufficient resources available should distribute through a large number of mostly direct channels—as exemplified by Apple, the second-biggest company in the world by market value (Satariano, 2010). With its sales of consumer electronics, computer software, and personal computers, Apple functions in a competitive (complex) and technologically turbulent (dynamic) environment. Its multichannel system incorporates a mixture of many direct and selected indirect channel types, which guarantees distribution through specialized dealers, and is in line with the firm's differentiation strategy.

In contrast, a firm that can predict customer demands and raw material requirements accurately in stable and less complex environments can pursue a cost-leadership strategy, i.e. keep its costs at a minimum using a limited number of mostly indirect channels (Kabadayi, Eyuboglu, & Thomas, 2007). One successful example is Sara Lee, a global consumer goods company that operates in more than 40 countries. Focusing on distribution through a limited variety of indirect channels (mostly retail stores) in a stable environment, it is possible to keep costs at a minimum while achieving great market coverage.

Figures 12.14 and 12.15 depict two extreme environmental and strategic conditions, though in truth, there is a continuum of conditions, in

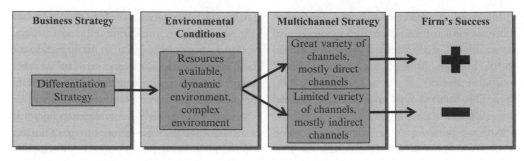

Fig. 12.14 Strategy and multichannel operations: differentiation

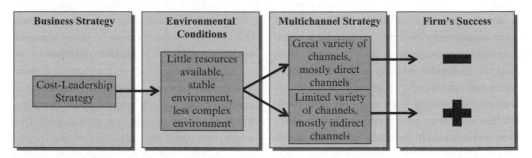

Fig. 12.15 Strategy and multichannel operations: cost leadership

between which lies the ideal distribution strategy, though finding it may be a challenge. Firms need to decide whether to implement more or fewer indirect or direct channels, but also which channel types to implement. The combination of various channel types requires care, as there exist both more and less harmonious sets of channels, as we discuss in the next section.

(2) Maximize positive and minimize negative cross-channel effects
Decisions about implemented channel combinations have huge impacts on the firm's performance. The use of multiple channels creates cross-effects among them, which can be either positive or negative, that is, synergetic or cannibalistic. Imagine, for example, that a telecommunication network provider observes that it acquires most customers through brick-and-mortar stores, but few customers sign contracts on its website. Should the provider reduce its online activities or shut down the online channel and focus on stores to maximize profits? This question cannot be answered by just looking at the number of customers acquired through each channel, because many potential customers likely

search and inform themselves about different offers online before purchasing in a store (Bakos, 1997; Morton, Zettelmeyer, & Silva-Risso, 2001; Verhoef, Neslin, & Vroomen, 2007)—that is, the research shopper phenomenon we discussed previously. Those shoppers prefer suppliers that offer a channel bundle that eases their search and purchase process, because the set of channels is organized in such a way that they complete each other in terms of product and service provision. This scenario helps the customer identify a good deal while also creating "smart shopper feelings" from the psychological perspective, which reduces perceived purchase uncertainty. These complementary channel bundles thus result in not only higher online acquisitions but also an increase in offline sales and loyalty, which represent positive cross-channel effects (Bucklin, Ramaswamy, & Majumdar, 1996; Wallace, Giese, & Johnson, 2004).

In contrast, channels within a bundle that are concrete substitutes from a functional perspective (i.e., search and purchase functions are similar in both channels) may steal sales volume from each other, because customers find no additional value offered through the second channel and

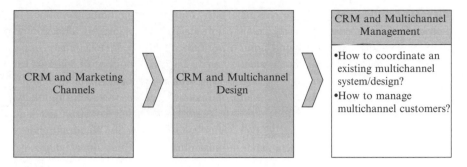

Fig. 12.16 Content structure of this chapter: CRM and multichannel management

thus use one or the other. This negative cross-channel effect implies channel cannibalization: Increased returns in one channel lead to decreased returns in a very similar channel offered by the firm, because no additional benefit is being provided to customers.

A firm that deploys a dedicated store channel thus may experience limited benefit from opening franchise stores, because searching and purchasing in both channels is similar, from a customer's perspective. The firm might enjoy a basic increase in sales volume due to the greater market coverage by the franchise stores, but existing customers will be indifferent between purchasing in either store. Shifting sales volume from the dedicated store channel to the franchise store channel also leads to an increase in sales volume in the franchise store but a decrease of sales volume, or cannibalization, in its own stores.

This discussion highlights the dimensions to be considered when choosing a multichannel system (i.e., appropriate types and number of channels). In summary, the two main prerequisites of a successful multichannel strategy implementation are
1. Fit between the channel system and the firm's business strategy and environment, and
2. A combination of complementary channels that achieves positive cross-channel effects.

Having successfully composed a multichannel system, a new challenge now arises for the firm: managing the multichannel system, the various specific customer types and the integration of different channel offers and functions.

12.4   CRM and Multichannel Management

Existing multichannel systems must be managed properly to exploit all opportunities and handle the respective challenges. Having implemented a multichannel system, a firm needs to determine its degree of channel integration, i.e. the coordination of channel functions, which requires great effort but also offers the potential to increase the firm's attractiveness to customers (Fig. 12.16).

As mentioned in the context of channel trends, the offer of multiple channels also attracts certain kinds of customers: multichannel and research shoppers. Both types have great potential for the firm—if it manages its multichannel system properly.

12.4.1 Managing Multichannel Systems: Integration Versus Separation

In a multichannel environment, it becomes challenging for the firm to achieve customer loyalty, because the possibility of comparing prices and offers across retailers through various channels decreases the customer's search costs but increases competition and price wars.

Furthermore, as the customer's switching costs decrease, his or her motivation to switch increases, which implies decreasing customer loyalty. Of course, this threat does not mean

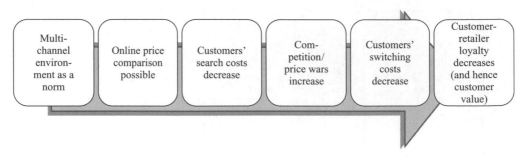

Fig. 12.17 Effects of multichannel environment on customer loyalty

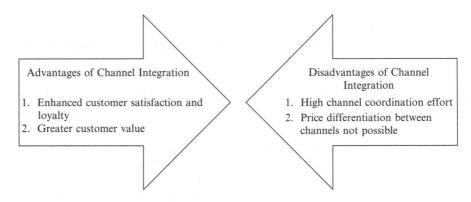

Fig. 12.18 Advantages and disadvantages of channel integration

that firms can just refrain from offering multiple channels, but it does suggest that they should manage multichannel systems carefully (Fig. 12.17).

A firm can handle this situation in two ways:
1. Integrate channel functions to enhance customer loyalty and long-term profits.
2. Separate channel functions and differentiate prices to increase short-term profits.

(1) Integrate channel functions to enhance customer loyalty and long-term profits
Trying to improve CRM to enhance the customer's retailer loyalty and bind that customer means a firm needs to make its overall multichannel offer valuable to the customer, instead of focusing on selected channels of its own portfolio. One possible means to achieve this overall appraisal of a complete channel system is the integration of functions across channels to enhance loyalty. For example, H&M, the Swedish fashion retailer, allows customers to return their online purchases in any stores. Besides, customers can try on clothes in the store and purchase those items later online, for the same price.

Combining the service outputs of complementary channels thus increases customer value for the firm, because customer satisfaction increases, and with it, loyalty (Wallace, Giese, & Johnson, 2004). The firm also gains access to more customer data through a wider set of channels, which makes it easier to derive further lessons from the recorded customer behavior. Of course, the integration of channel functions requires extensive coordination efforts, which increase with the number of integrated channels included in the multichannel system. In addition, the supplier must unify prices across channels to allow for channel integration (Fig. 12.18).

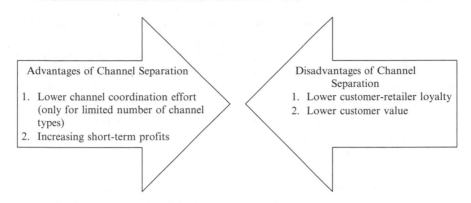

Fig. 12.19 Advantages and disadvantages of channel separation

(2) Separate channel functions and differentiate prices to increase short-term profits
The opposite of channel integration is a channel mix, which involves various independent channels combined in a multichannel offer which is less expensive with regard to channel implementation and maintenance tactic. Each channel provides a certain package of services, attracting different types of customers in different situations instead of making existing customers more valuable for the firm. This strategy harms long-term customer loyalty, and as the channels cannot be combined, a self-selection process arises. Different customers use different channels. Therefore, the firm can charge different prices across its channels to skim the market most efficiently. If managed successfully, between-channel price differentiation can increase short-term profits; Avis, the car rental agency, successfully charges different prices online and in branch offices for the same car.

To ensure cross-channel price differentiation does not confuse or irritate customers, but rather increase the firm's profits, certain fundamental success factors need to be considered:

(a) Price differentiation will succeed if online competition is low.
The Internet is an easy and transparent means to compare prices. In this channel, the motivation to compare prices is high, and switching costs are quite low, so the likelihood of customers switching to competitors is great.

(b) Price differentiation is profitable if the number of offered channels is low.
The greater the number of channels implemented by a firm, the more complex and costly is their coordination (price differentiation) in a multichannel system.

(c) Price differentiation is especially successful for one-time products.
If a product can be resold, the selling firm faces competition not only from other retailers but also from its own customers. If it is possible to resell a product to other consumers for a cheaper price, a price differentiation strategy will fail.

Overall, nondurable products and services are less appropriate for resale and less subject to online price comparisons, so price differentiation is a more promising means for increasing short-term profits in a channel system with a limited number of channel types (Wolk & Ebling, 2010) (Fig. 12.19).

12.4.2 Managing Multichannel Shoppers

Offering multiple channels for purchase and information attracts shoppers who are willing to use various channel types and choose different channels for transactions in various situations. These so-called multichannel shoppers tend to be more profitable than single-channel shoppers. The potential explanations for this phenomenon all may apply to a certain extent, as the following sections detail.

(1) Multichannel shoppers are more loyal than single-channel shoppers.
Using various channels for transactions means that customers can achieve their service output demands more easily than if they only used a single channel. In contrast with single-channel shoppers, multichannel shoppers choose the most appropriate and convenient channel for each transaction, using different channels for different transactions if it provides them with additional value. Single-channel shoppers instead repeatedly use the same channel for each step in the purchase process and ignore other channels. As a consequence, they evaluate the firm's multichannel system solely on the basis of this one channel, and if it does not meet their demands, they become dissatisfied and even may switch suppliers. Because multichannel shoppers consider all existing channels potential sites for their transactions, they take them all into account in their evaluations. If one channel does not meet the customer's service output demands, she will just switch to a more appealing channel, instead of immediately switching suppliers.

Imagine a multichannel shopper plans to order a product from a suppliers' call center, but the telephone fee exceeds the level she is willing to pay. She then might be willing to switch to the same supplier's website to purchase the product. With their greater satisfaction with the firm's overall offer, multichannel customers tend to be quite loyal, with greater value than single-channel shoppers.

(2) Multichannel shoppers spend more money because they see advertisements more frequently than single-channel shoppers.
Customers who consider each type of channel for their purchases actually receive advertising communications in all types of channels as well. Thus, compared with single-channel shoppers, they confront the latest offers more frequently and are more likely to purchase a product, which makes them more prone to spend more

money. Consider a single-channel shopper who only purchases in physical stores. He may see advertisements in the stores but not the banner ads on the firm's website. Multichannel shoppers check the website from time to time though, as well as the store to see the latest offers and may be more likely to purchase.

(3) Multichannel shoppers purchase more frequently than single-channel shoppers because shopping is possible in every situation.
With their willingness to purchase in various types of channels, multichannel shoppers have access to offers, regardless of when or where they are, such that they may decide to purchase a product spontaneously. These customers can purchase online late at night, use their mobile device to purchase while traveling by train, or just stop by a store when being downtown during the day.

In contrast, single-channel shoppers wait until they have access to their channel of choice. If they prefer the store channel, their shopping is necessarily less spontaneous, such that they make more deliberate purchase decisions. If they lack access to the product of interest at the moment they need it, they likely postpone their purchase intent or do not purchase, especially if an untimely purchase fails to provide value anymore.

(4) Only customers who typically shop frequently and spend much money actually use multiple channels for purchase (customer self-selection).
Another possible but contrary explanation for the profitability of multichannel customers reflects the idea of customer self-selection. In this case, it is not the multichannel offer that makes some customers more profitable, but rather, more profitable heavy users of a product decide to purchase from various channels (Neslin et al., 2006).

Regardless of which explanation is true—whether multichannel offers make customers more valuable for a firm or if they just attract more valuable customers—it is obviously important for firms to identify multichannel shoppers to increase their profits. The next section outlines key factors that drive multichannel shopping, which a firm must be aware of to manage its CRM efforts profitably.

Fig. 12.20 Drivers of
multichannel shopping

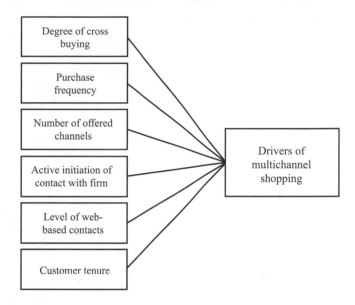

Drivers of Multichannel Shopping

Several factors determine the likelihood that a customer is a multichannel shopper (Venkatesan, Kumar, & Ravishankar, 2007) (Fig. 12.20).

- Customers who exhibit a *higher degree of cross-buying* typically use more channels to place their orders. Cross-buying refers to the number of different product categories that a customer has bought from the firm. We can reasonably expect customers who exhibit a high degree of cross-buying to be more familiar with the firm; this familiarity should reduce the perceived purchase risk and lead to a greater degree of multichannel shopping.
- Customers who *actively initiate contact with a firm* also should have a higher degree of familiarity with the firm and its channels and exhibit a greater degree of multichannel shopping than customers whom the firm proactively contacts.
- In addition, a *higher level of web-based contacts* plays a role in motivating customers to transact through multiple channels, because awareness of a supplier's website implies the customer's willingness to employ new technologies.
- *Customer tenure* is positively associated with multichannel buying, due to the high level of

familiarity with the firm and the firm's channels. Customers who have been transacting with a firm for longer tend to use multiple channels more.

- Also, customers who *buy more frequently* tend to migrate toward multichannel shopping, because they want to improve the efficiency of their transactions by using the ideal channel for each transaction.
- Finally, the *number of channels* that a firm uses to contact the customer is positively correlated with multichannel buying. In other words, firm-induced exposure to multiple channels leads customers to try multiple channel options.

The key drivers of multichannel shopping thus consistently reflect the notions of *familiarity* and *awareness*. If a firm wants to enhance multichannel shopping by its customers, it should increase their awareness of all existing channels and their features, as well as increase their familiarity with the firm and its channels to minimize their perceptions of the risk of using those channels for transactions. Accordingly, a firm should actively employ all types of channels to contact customers and provide incentives for using new channels, to encourage customers to increase their familiarity (e.g., promoting a new channel with price reductions).

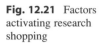

Fig. 12.21 Factors
activating research
shopping

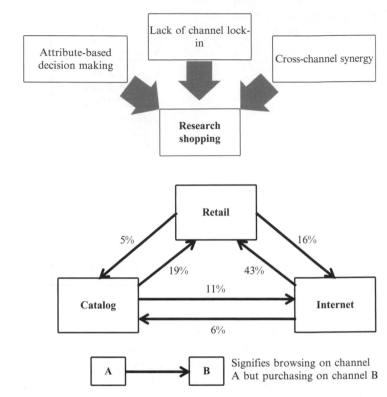

Fig. 12.22 Purchasing
behavior of research
shoppers (Source: Adapted
from Verhoef, Neslin, &
Vroomen, 2007, p. 130)

12.4.3 Managing Research Shoppers

Research shoppers benefit the firm by being loyal
and enjoying their perception of themselves as
smart, information-based shoppers. If the pre-
purchase information they gather applies to multiple firms and is not supplier-specific though, a
company faces a serious risk. It might invest in
attracting the customer but then lose him or her
during the purchasing process, especially if the
customer uses one firm's channel for search but
another supplier's channel for purchase. Managing research shoppers thus requires profound
knowledge about the factors that explain research
shopping, to be able to attract and bind them to
the firm.

Prior literature suggests three factors that activate research-shopping: attribute-based decision-
making, lack of channel lock-in, and cross-
channel synergy (Verhoef, Neslin, & Vroomen,
2007) (Fig. 12.21).

As we have established, channels differ in
their attributes and thus the service outputs they

provide (Wallace, Giese, & Johnson, 2004) (e.g.,
an online channel offers great spatial convenience, whereas the store channel is typically
famous for its high level of customer service).
If a customer perceives some channels as especially convenient for search but other channels as
preferable for transactions (*attribute-based decision-making*), the basic mechanism for research
shopping is set. The Internet often appears as a
convenient search channel, especially in terms of
price and product comparisons, even across suppliers. However, some customers still perceive
the Internet as a risky channel for purchase and
prefer to visit the store for the actual transaction.
Research even shows that 43% of the existing
research shoppers search for information online
before making their final purchase at a brick-and-
mortar retail store. In contrast, only 16% search
for information in retail stores and then purchase
from the Internet (Fig. 12.22).

A second factor that enhances research shopping is the *lack of channel lock-in*. If a channel
has a high lock-in, searching in one channel

increases the likelihood of purchasing in that channel. If it is easy to switch to another channel for purchase, then the channel lock-in is low, which encourages research shopping. For example, the channel lock-in of a website clearly is lower than that of a store, because switching to a different website is far easier than walking out of a store to purchase somewhere else.

The third factor that enhances research shopping is the existence of *cross-channel synergy*. If searching in one channel increases the economic benefit of purchasing in another, consumers tend to pursue research shopping. A consumer thus might gather price information online, which helps her negotiate a better price in the store later; such cross-channel synergies lead to research shopping (Verhoef, Neslin, & Vroomen, 2007). This phenomenon also appears in Fig. 12.22. This effect is rare in some channel combinations though; only 11% of customers search for information in a catalog and then purchase online, and only 6% search on the Internet and then purchase from a catalog. This channel combination obviously provides less additional benefit than the store–Internet combination.

This analysis suggests some approaches to enhance research shopping and reduce customer loss during the purchasing process. To encourage research shopping, a firm might reduce its channels' functions to key attributes, emphasizing their search or purchase advantages compared with other channels. For example, a firm can offer an information-only website that is tightly integrated with the store (Bendoly et al., 2005). However, this approach can be risky in very competitive environments if competitors combine all attributes into one channel (Neslin et al., 2006).

Moreover, to bind the customer to the store and prevent losing him or her during the purchasing process, the firm needs to generate customer loyalty through customer satisfaction. Satisfaction with one channel reinforces satisfaction with other channels of the same supplier (Teerling & Huizingh, 2005). The more satisfied a customer is with a firm's channels, the greater that customer's loyalty and the lower the likelihood of losing the customer during the purchasing process. Greater loyalty also translates into greater sales volume, because loyal customers are willing to pay higher prices than non-loyal customers and also recommend a firm, its products, and its services to other consumers (Wallace, Giese, & Johnson, 2004).

The management of a multichannel system thus confronts a firm with new challenges. Although these challenges, such as the coordination of various channel types, new customer types, and varying customer behaviors, requires additional management effort, their proper management provides the chance for the firm to achieve greater profitability through enhanced customer satisfaction and loyalty.

12.5 Summary

In the course of this chapter, we have outlined the role of channels in creating and maintaining customer relationships. We also have discussed the role of channels as gatekeepers for communication and interaction with the customer, which offers the possibility of working on the relationship to increase loyalty and customer value to the firm. The channel further functions as a route to market for products and services. With regard to CRM, choosing the right channel is a fundamental means for creating customer loyalty, which increases the value of customers to a firm and thus long-term profitability.

Channel types can be divided basically, into indirect and direct ones. Both types offer various advantages and disadvantages for the firm with respect to implementation and maintenance costs, the need to develop channel-specific skills, the guarantee of service and information quality, and the level of control over the intended CRM activities. These factors should be evaluated carefully when choosing channels for a firm's distribution system.

In this context, we also have presented current channel trends, such as the proliferation of direct channels and the emergence of multichannel distribution as a new norm, which have prompted customer-level trends, including the arrival of multichannel shoppers and research shoppers.

Multichannel systems cannot work efficiently if each decision about every channel type implemented in the channel system occurs independently. All channels implemented in a multichannel system must fit together, align with the firm's business strategy, and reflect the environmental conditions.

Having decided on the channel design, including the types and numbers of channels to be implemented in the multichannel system, there is still one major challenge left for the firm: the management of the channel system to maximize profits. Should channel functions and prices be integrated or separated? Determining the right level of multichannel integration requires the firm to evaluate whether it rather wants to work on its customer relationships, which means greater investments today and greater profits in the long run, or if it prefers to reduce current costs to attain short-term profits, at the expense of building strong, long-term customer relationships.

Finally, we have discussed how a firm should manage multichannel shoppers and research shoppers to maximize its profits. We presented customer, channel, and environmental conditions that activate these emerging shopper types, which should help firms identify these customers and thereby manage them appropriately, so that the firm can profit from their indisputable benefit potential.

Exercise Questions
1. Discuss, with regard to a firm's CRM strategy, whether the proliferation of direct channels is just a current trend or if online channels will someday replace traditional channels completely.
2. Obi, a German DIY supplier, initially sold through franchise stores, but it just opened an online shop in November 2010. The implementation of this additional channel resulted in an unhealthy conflict between Obi and its franchisees, leading to a battle in court. The focal issue was the cannibalization by the website of sales in the franchise stores, especially due to the low prices charged online. Discuss Obi's multichannel design and management. What went wrong?

3. Manufacturers such as Henkel or Procter & Gamble are very detached from end customers. Given the increasing power of retailers, how might they reestablish closer contact with these ultimate customers?

Mini Case 12.1.

Otto Versand

Otto Versand, in Hamburg, Germany, runs the world's largest mail-order business, with subsidiaries on all continents. The mail-order and specialty divisions form the core business area of the Otto Group, with a particularly strong presence in Europe through the French company, 3 Suisses France S.C.S., the market leader in France, Belgium, and Spain. Otto also owns a majority stake in Crate & Barrel, a chain of home furnishing stores that is a major supplier of housewares, furniture, and accessories. A well-defined customer orientation has helped the company build a continually expanding product range and reputation for quality. Within the overall group, Otto issues 62 catalogs each season, distributing more than 109 million copies.

Originally a pure mail-order operation, the Otto Group in Germany increasingly has been adding communication and delivery channels, in response to increased demand for more customized access to the company and technological developments, such as e-commerce. Today the company operates in the following distribution and communication channels: catalog, call centers, television shopping, mass advertising, Internet, and store pick-up. Multiple challenges arise in this multichannel environment.

First, the company must create a single view of the customer. This task might sound easy for a company that does not sell through intermediaries, but it is challenging in practice. The operational and IT systems behind each channel have very specific characteristics, so it is not straightforward to create a meta-database that integrates the entire multitude of customer contacts in a standardized, scalable fashion. Second, if it finds a way to integrate information seamlessly across several channels, Otto needs to discover how to leverage that information to make better, more tailored marketing decisions. For example, a customer might receive a catalog by mail and buy an item of interest through the Internet channel. In this case, did the catalog really create the purchase impulse, or would the customer have bought even without the catalog, via the Internet? Stated differently, customers may not appear to react to catalogs, but the catalog still may have an important trigger function. Teasing out these channel interactions is important for Otto in its quest to economize on its acquisition cost while maximizing its acquisition results. The reality in a multichannel environment, such as the one in use at Otto, is an ongoing struggle to understand the interactions of contact channels and contact channel allocations to customers to maximize customers' lifetime value.

Questions

1. Can you think of experiments that would allow Otto to make inferences about whether one channel functions as a lead in to another channel?

2. Would you expect customers who access the company through different channels to have differential values for the company? Why?

References

Anderson, E. (1985). The salesperson as outside agent or employee: A transaction cost analysis. *Marketing Science, 4*(3), 234–254.

Ansari, A., Mela, C., & Neslin, S. (2008). Customer channel migration. *Journal of Marketing Research, 45*(1), 60–76.

Bakos, J. Y. (1997). Reducing buyer search costs: Implications for electronics marketplaces. *Management Science, 43*(12), 1676–1692.

Bendoly, E., Blocher, J. D., Bretthauer, K. M., Krishnan, S., & Venkataramanan, M. A. (2005). Online/in-store integration and customer retention. *Journal of Service Research, 7*(4), 313–327.

Blattberg, R. C., Kim, B. D., & Neslin, S. A. (2008). *Database marketing, analyzing and managing customers*. New York: Springer.

Boehm, M. (2008). Determining the impact of Internet channel use on a customer's lifetime. *Journal of Interactive Marketing, 22*(3), 2–22.

Bolton, R. N., Lemon, K. N., & Verhoef, P. C. (2004). The theoretical underpinnings of customer asset management: A framework and propositions for future research. *Journal of the Academy of Marketing Science, 32*(3), 271–292.

Bucklin, L. P., Ramaswamy, V., & Majumdar, S. K. (1996). Analyzing channel structures of business markets via the structure-output paradigm. *International Journal of Research in Marketing, 13*(1), 73–87.

Chen, P. Y., & Hitt, L. (2002). Measuring switching costs and the determinants of customer retention in Internet-enabled businesses: A study of the online brokerage industry. *Information Systems Research, 13*(3), 255–276.

Coughlan, A. T., Anderson, E., Stern, L. W., & El-Ansary, A. I. (2006). *Marketing channels*. Upper Saddle River, NJ: Pearson Prentice Hall.

Jindal, R., Reinartz, W., Krafft, M., & Hoyer, W. D. (2007). Determinants of the variety of routes to market. *International Journal of Research in Marketing, 24*(1), 17–29.

Kabadayi, S., Eyuboglu, N., & Thomas, G. P. (2007). The performance implications of designing multiple channels to fit with strategy and environment. *Journal of Marketing, 71*(4), 195–211.

Kumar, V., & Venkatesan, R. (2005). Who are the multichannel shoppers and how do they perform? Correlates of multichannel shopping behavior. *Journal of Interactive Marketing, 19*(2), 44–62.

Moriarty, R. T., & Moran, U. (1990). Managing hybrid marketing systems. *Harvard Business Review, 68*(6), 146–155.

Morton, F. S., Zettelmeyer, F., & Silva-Risso, J. (2001). Internet car retailing. *The Journal of Industrial Economics, 49*(4), 501–519.

Myers, J. B., Pickersgill, A. D., & Van Metre, E. S. (2004). Steering customers to the right channels. *The McKinsey Quarterly, 4*(October), 36–47.

Neslin, S. A., Grewal, D., Leghorn, R., Shankar, V., Teerling, M. L., Thomas, J. S., & Verhoef, P. C. (2006). Challenges and opportunities in multichannel customer management. *Journal of Service Research, 9*(2), 95–112.

Nunes, P. F., & Cespedes, F. V. (2003). The customer has escaped. *Harvard Business Review, 81*(11), 96–105.

Payne, A., & Frow, P. (2004). The role of multichannel integration in customer relationship management. *Industrial Marketing Management, 33*(6), 527–538.

Reichheld, F. F., & Schefter, P. (2000). E-loyalty: Your secret weapon on the web. *Harvard Business Review, 78*(4), 105–113.

Rosenbloom, B. (2007). Multi-channel strategy in business-to-business markets: Prospects and problems. *Industrial Marketing Management, 36*(1), 4–9.

Satariano, A. (2010). Apple passes PetroChina to become second-largest stock. Bloomberg. http://www.bloomberg.com/news/2010-09-23/apple-passes-petrochina-to-become-world-s-second-largest-stock.html. Accessed on July 10, 2011.

Sinha, I. (2000). Cost transparency: The net's real threat to prices and brands. *Harvard Business Review, 78*(2), 43–50.

Srinivasan, S., Anderson, R., & Ponnavolu, K. (2002). Customer loyalty in e-commerce: An exploration of its antecedents and consequences. *Journal of Retailing, 78*(1), 41–50.

Sultan, F., & Rohm, A. (2004). The evolving role of the Internet in marketing strategy: An exploratory study. *Journal of Interactive Marketing, 18*(2), 6–19.

Teerling, M. L., & Huizingh, E. K. R. E. (2005). *The complementarity between online and offline consumer attitudes and behaviour* (Working paper). Groningen, The Netherlands: University of Groningen.

Thomas, J. S., & Sullivan, U. Y. (2005). Managing marketing communications with multichannel customers. *Journal of Marketing, 69*(4), 239–251.

Venkatesan, R., Kumar, V., & Ravishanker, N. (2007). Multichannel shopping: Causes and consequences. *Journal of Marketing, 71*(2), 114–132.

Verhoef, P. C., & Donkers, B. (2005). The effect of acquisition channels on customer loyalty and cross-buying. *Journal of Interactive Marketing, 19*(2), 31–42.

Verhoef, P. C., Neslin, S. A., & Vroomen, B. (2007). Multichannel customer management: Understanding the research-shopper phenomenon. *International Journal of Research in Marketing, 24*(2), 129–148.

Wallace, D. W., Giese, J. L., & Johnson, J. L. (2004). Customer retailer loyalty in the context of multiple channel strategies. *Journal of Retailing, 80*(4), 249–263.

Wolk, A., & Ebling, C. (2010). Multi-channel price differentiation: An empirical investigation of existence and causes. *International Journal of Research in Marketing, 27*(2), 142–150.

Zeithaml, V. A., Berry, L. L., & Parasuraman, A. (1996). The behavioral consequences of service quality. *Journal of Marketing, 60*(2), 31–46.

Customer Relationship Management Issues in the Business-To-Business Context

13

13.1 Overview

Business marketers serve the largest market of all: The dollar transaction volume in the business-to-business (B2B) market is significantly greater than that in business-to-consumer (B2C) markets. Moreover, a B2B customer's level of purchasing activity can be extremely high (Hutt & Speh, 2007). For example, the purchasing department at General Motors (GM) spends more than $125 billion annually on B2B products and services—a sum larger than the gross domestic products of several entire countries, such as Ireland, Portugal, or Greece (Porter, 2002). Some of the most valuable and powerful brands in the world operate mainly in B2B markets, including, for example, Cisco, DuPont, FedEx, Hewlett-Packard, IBM, and Intel.

Unlike the B2C context, a customer in a B2B environment is an organization (company or institution), which means that there are fewer customers. For example, Australia has a population of 20 million people but only 1 million registered businesses. As the statistics imply, business customers make much larger purchases than households, and the organizational buying process is far more complex. Finally, compared with B2C relationships, relationships between buyers and sellers tend to be closer (Buttle, 2009). In general, relationships can be classified as transactional (distant) or collaborative (close). Transactional relationships involve the timely exchange of basic products for highly competitive prices; collabora-

tive relationships describe strong ties built over time, with the intent of achieving mutual benefit (Anderson & Narus, 1991). In a B2B context and in reference to the customer relationship management (CRM) definition we introduced at the beginning of this book, B2B CRM is the strategic process of strengthening relationships with business customers, especially important clients, beyond transactional relationships to better manage the value of these buyer seller relationships. A report by Stanford University and Accenture highlights that companies can increase their market capitalization by 8% or more and earn premiums of 17–26% for their valuation, just by introducing collaborative relationships into their supply chains (Spekman & Carraway, 2006); to build such collaborative relationships, a seller needs a deep understanding of the buyer's internal business and environment, and the communication between partners should be linked to all levels of management, to guarantee extensive information exchange.

CRM AT WORK 13.1

IBM: Understanding the Customer's Business

For some of IBM's *Fortune* 500 customers, account executives act as direct participants in the customer firm's strategy planning sessions. IBM adds value to the relationship by providing specific recommendations about how its products and services can be used to further the firm's competitive advantage. As a relationship with a large account grows and flourishes, a full-time sales team is often created to serve the needs of that customer. This team includes sales, service, and technical specialists who have extensive knowledge of the customer's industry. Some team members have worked exclusively with a single customer organization for years.

Source: Hutt and Speh (2007)

The IBM example in the preceding box shows that the sales force is an important and significant investment for most sellers, because it is entrusted with the seller's most important asset: customers. The sales force is in the unique position of being very close to the customer and thus having the ability to establish long-lasting and strong relationships. Nearly half a company's growth can be ascribed to the competence, organization, and quality of its sales force (Karlöf & Lövingsson, 2005). Thus, *sales force management* (SFM) constitutes one of the most important strategic issues in a B2B CRM context. Due to the decreasing marketing efficiency and effectiveness, as we noted at the start of this book, the task of the sales force is to effectively and efficiently manage relationships with the organization's buyers, to win over and maintain satisfied customers while keeping costs down. The most important question in this context is thus how the sales force can manage buyer–seller relationships, both effectively and efficiently.

To answer this question, we first discuss the construct of *sales force automation* (SFA) as an important subtopic of SFM within the B2B CRM domain. As a transactional tool, SFA describes any information technology applied to a sales situation that is intended to facilitate a repetitive, administrative task and to make it more efficient, especially from the internal perspective of the seller. By completing tasks more efficiently,

salespeople can focus on more value-adding activities for customers and thus increase customer satisfaction, leading to greater customer retention. The effectiveness dimension describes SFA as a tool to build long-lasting relationships with customers. Because a company often needs to build this kind of relationship only with its most valuable, important clients, so called key accounts, we also acknowledge the main elements of *key account management* (KAM) in this chapter. With KAM, the firm allocates the proper activities (from the buyer's, respectively external perspective) to the most promising customers (from the seller's perspective). Finally, we discuss *the shift from goods to services,* including the emergence of *hybrid offerings*, as potential tactics for organizations to lock in customers effectively. Hybrid offerings mainly focus on buyers' demands and needs, which implies an external perspective. These three subtopics of SFM help companies build stronger buyer–seller relationships and better manage the value of their relationships, from both internal and external perspectives. Figure 13.1 outlines the conceptual organization of this chapter accordingly.

13.2   CRM and Sales Force Automation

In the past two decades, SFA tools have been used increasingly to facilitate customer relationship management processes. Due to advanced telecommunication devices, SFA has become more and more important, and the trend seems likely to continue in the future. We therefore begin by describing SFA and illustrating its benefits, as well as the most important conditions and prerequisites facilitating them.

13.2.1 What Is SFA?

The term SFA refers to any information technology applied to a sales situation with the goal of

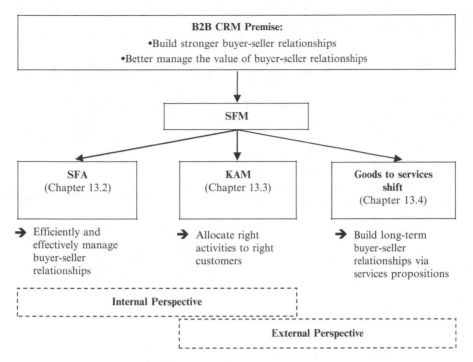

Fig. 13.1 Conceptual organization of the chapter

supporting the sales function. The variety of hard- and software capabilities in SFA technologies mean they can vary in terms of their complexity and the degree to which they should be integrated into the company's organizational infrastructure (Speier & Venkatesh, 2002). Relevant technologies include, for example, electronic data interchange, databases, Internet, spreadsheets, sales forecasting tools, inventory management systems, contact management programs, e-mail programs, graphics and presentation software, laptops, cellular phones, and fax machines (Hunter & Perreault, 2007).

CRM AT WORK 13.2

InvisibleCRM: Bridging the Gap between Business Apps and Productivity Tools

InvisibleCRM is headquartered in San Mateo, California, where its sales and support offices also are located. Development centers operate in Moscow, Russia and in Kiev, Ukraine. InvisibleCRM is a small enterprise with 30 employees; its main application is a suite of products that seamlessly merge back-end applications with Outlook and Windows usages. Thus InvisibleCRM provides a fast gateway to a user's CRM system through MS Outlook. As a synchronization tool for business users, it comprises three products.

First, SalesDesktop offers a CRM Outlook integration. Second, SalesFolder is a document sharing and delivery tool that synchronizes files between a corporate repository and a local subfolder on the user's desktop. Third, SalesAlerts delivers real-time notifications on important changes made in the corporate system.

Source: Moon (2008)

SFA tools are designed specifically to support the seller's organization in its efforts to meet its CRM objectives. A primary topic then is its impact on sales productivity. For example, SFA software capabilities can capture, store, analyze, and distribute customer-related data to

Fig. 13.2 Two
dimensions of SFA benefits

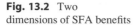

SFA Benefits

SFA Efficiency	SFA Effectiveness

salespeople to make them more efficient. By efficiently completing sales routine tasks, salespeople reallocate their time to more personal contacts with their customers, which leads to more effective buyer–seller relationships (Hunter & Perreault, 2007). It thus becomes evident that the two main dimensions of SFA's benefits are its *efficiency* and *effectiveness* (Fig. 13.2).

13.2.2 SFA Benefits

Salespeople, sales managers, and senior management can derive a lot of benefits from implementing SFA. With SFA tools, salespeople gain timely access to customer, product inventory, and market intelligence information and thus can respond to customer questions more quickly and with better information. The sales force appears more informed, knowledgeable, competent, and responsive than its competing forces; it also enjoys a better customer understanding. Customers perceive that their needs are better catered to and met, leading to improved customer relations through increasing customer satisfaction. Better process accuracy achieved through shorter order cycles, for example, might increase customer satisfaction and sales productivity, which in turn raises the benefits attained by sales managers (Rogers, Stone, & Foss, 2008). The same pattern holds for improved resource allocation. By using SFA tools, the sales force can perform administrative tasks more efficiently and thus spend more time with the customer, engaging in value-adding activities that increase customer satisfaction and improve customer relations. Finally, SFA efficiency and effectiveness, including increased sales productivity and improved customer relations, lead to greater sales revenue for senior management and the firm as a whole. Figure 13.3 summarizes how these different beneficial characteristics are linked and how they contribute to increased sales revenues.

At this point, we also should mention that SFA can increase sales revenue only in certain conditions, as we discuss in the next section.

13.2.3 Conditions for Realizing Benefits

To gain efficiency and effectiveness benefits from employing SFA tools, sales managers and senior management must ensure that the entire sales force actually adopts and uses the SFA technology. A failure in adopting or using these tools represents the biggest barrier to a firm's pursuit of the full range of SFA benefits. Important drivers that enhance *SFA adoption* include the commitment of both top management and immediate supervisors to the technology. Both variables influence SFA adoption individually, whereas the salespeople's perceptions of the alignment between the two commitment variables (called management commitment alignment) influences SFA adoption even more. Therefore, any resources expended to reach such alignment condition are easily justifiable (Cascio, Mariadoss, & Mouri, 2010). The likelihood of adoption also is positively influenced by personal innovativeness (the extent to which a person is quick to adopt innovative ideas compared with others in the system), the perceived usefulness of the new system (the extent to which a person believes use of the system will enhance his or her job performance), overall attitude toward the new system, and compatibility with the existing system (the extent to which the new system fits with the adopter's existing values, experiences, and needs) (Jones, Sundaram, & Chin, 2002). Moreover, the perceived usefulness of the new system and its compatibility with the existing system are influenced by the salesperson's own individual characteristics. Individual perceptions of SFA technology tend to be more positive among younger employees, male employees, and employees who have strong

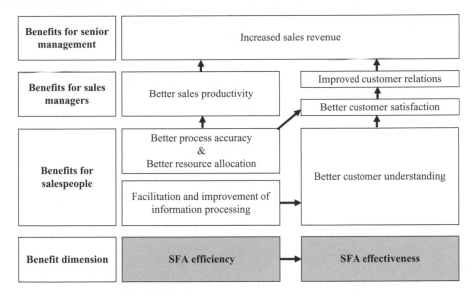

Fig. 13.3 Beneficial characteristics of SFA

computer self-efficacy, as well as those with more computer playfulness tendencies. Organizational characteristics such as management support, perceived voluntariness of the use, and early involvement and participation of the user population also can have positive influences on individual perceptions of SFA technology (Speier & Venkatesh, 2002).

The adoption of SFA technology thus is strongly associated with its usage. The extent of *SFA technology usage* depends on personal innovativeness, attitude toward the new system, and usage-facilitating conditions i.e. the extent to which a person believes she or he has been provided with sufficient resources and external support to use the system (Jones et al., 2002). Furthermore, the extent of use of SFA technology relates positively to a salesperson's degree of market information processing (Park, Kim, Dubinsky, & Lee, 2010).

To guarantee the adoption and usage of SFA technology, the seller's organization should ensure and communicate the commitment and support of top management and supervisors and hire young salespeople who demonstrate, during the interview process, personal innovativeness, a high degree of computer playfulness, and computer self-efficacy. Furthermore, the firm should inform salespeople about the system's features

and benefits, provide continuous support and training, involve salespeople before purchasing and implementing the SFA tools, and provide the sales force with all necessary market information. Table 13.1 summarizes these measures to ensure that the seller receives the full benefits of SFA.

As it has been pointed out in this chapter, a seller can improve customer relations by implementing SFA. But we also must recognize that increased customer satisfaction and improved customer relations are most critical for the most valuable customers of the seller's organization, which leads us to the topic of CRM and key account management.

13.3 CRM and Key Account Management

KAM is one of the most significant trends in B2B marketing practice in recent years. Pressures exerted on suppliers by increasing globalization, customer power, procurement sophistication, complex offerings, and the need to find innovative ways to handle a company's most important customers produced the concept of KAM, with its unique characteristics and steps for successful implementation.

Table 13.1 Seller's benefit conditions checklist

Benefit conditions	Measures
Adoption	
Commitment of top management and supervisors	Ensure and communicate commitment and support
Personal innovativeness	of top management and supervisors
Positive attitude toward new system	Hire salespeople who demonstrate personal innovativeness
Perceived usefulness and compatibility	during the interview process
Individual characteristics	Hire young salespeople with computer playfulness and
Organizational characteristics	computer self-efficacy
Usage	Inform salespeople about the system's features and benefits
Personal innovativeness	Provide continuous support and training
Positive attitude toward new system	Involve salespeople before purchasing and implementing
Facilitating conditions	SFA tools
Market information	Provide the sales force with necessary market information

13.3.1 What Is KAM?

A lot of different terms, such as key account selling, national account management, national account selling, strategic account management, and global account management, can be subsumed under the term KAM. Today, key account management is the most widely used term in research publications (Homburg, Workman, & Jensen, 2002). KAM refers to the performance of additional activities and/or dedication of special personnel to a company's most important customers (Workman, Homburg, & Jensen, 2003). Instead of being transaction-oriented, these additional activities are relationship-oriented and aim to create long-term customer relationships. Additional activities and special personnel offer critical benefits and opportunities for profit enhancement for the seller, along with the benefit enhancements for the buyer (McDonald, Millman, & Rogers, 1997). Thus, for CRM in a B2B context, KAM is a highly relevant topic that cannot be ignored.

13.3.2 Implementation of the KAM Program

To implement a KAM program successfully, a company should follow three key steps: (1) select key accounts, (2) design elements of the KAM program, and (3) advance the KAM program (Fig. 13.4).

13.3.2.1 Step 1: Selection of Key Accounts

The essential step of selecting key accounts is central to the definition of KAM (Workman et al., 2003). Before carrying out the *selection process*, a company must select different *criteria* for distinguishing normal from more important customers (Fig. 13.5).

Selection Criteria
In general, both quantitative (financial) and qualitative (strategic) criteria serve to decide which customer is a key account, and which are just regular accounts.

The quantitative criteria might include:
- Sales volume
- Market share
- Revenues/contribution/profit

Because financial data are quite easy to measure and can address fixed costs, most companies use certain financial "rules" as prime criteria for deciding on the key account status of their customers (Winkelmann, 2006):
- Key accounts must generate 50–60% of the sales volume.
- The Pareto rule identifies key accounts as those 20% of customers that account for 80% of sales volume.
- Key accounts are the top 10 customers.

Yet there are also qualitative criteria to define key accounts; for example:

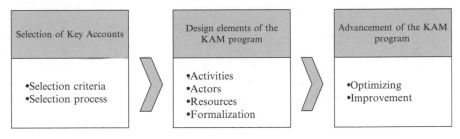

Fig. 13.4 Key steps for successfully implementing a KAM program

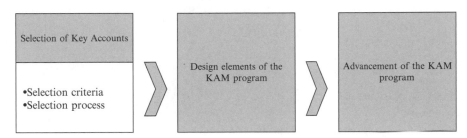

Fig. 13.5 Step 1 of the implementation process

- Image
- Reference potential
- Technology potential and know-how
- Interorganizational and cultural fit

A positive image of the buyer might allow the seller to realize positive spillover effects onto its own image and brands. With a high reference potential, the key account can function as a market multiplier for the seller by positively influencing other important buyers. Furthermore, a high technology potential and know-how in the buyer's organization can offer the seller additional knowledge and thus might be useful for encouraging the development of the seller's organization. In these qualitative criteria, the focus thus is on long-term and interorganizational relationships, as well as on strategic aspects. Table 13.2 summarizes the various (dis)advantages of different types of selection criteria.

Because the buying process in B2B relationships is rather complex, and the buyer–seller relationships seem closer, B2B marketers cannot only focus on quantitative facts but also need to consider qualitative aspects associated with long-term, interorganizational relationships when selecting their key accounts. A mix of quantitative and qualitative criteria allows companies to combine the advantages and minimize the disadvantages of these different measures.

Selection Process

After having chosen the criteria, the company is ready to begin the selection process. A very pragmatic approach first arranges a list of all selection criteria that are relevant for the company, which then need to be prioritized and weighted, from the seller's point of view. Next, the seller evaluates these different criteria for every potential key account. After the evaluation is multiplied by the corresponding weighting of the criterion, the seller can calculate the sum of all points. The higher the final score of a buyer, the more attractive that customer is in terms of key account status (Capon, 2001) (Table 13.3).

CRM AT WORK 13.3

FestoAG: Selecting Key Accounts

Festo is a leading, worldwide supplier of automation technology and the performance leader in industrial training and education programs. Its 15,500 employees globally maintain its portfolio of approximately 30,000 catalogue products, with several hundred thousand variants. Festo's key account selection process contains the following steps:

1. Definition of the most interesting industries (potential).

Table 13.2 (Dis)Advantages of selection criteria

	Advantages	Disadvantages
Quantitative criteria	Relatively easy to measure	Monetary and short-term focused
	Coverage of fixed costs	
Qualitative criteria	Positive spillover effects	Not very easy to measure
	Multiplier function of the buyer	No coverage of fixed costs
	Additional knowledge	
	Long-term and interorganizational focused	
	Strategic focused	

Table 13.3 Example of a selection process

1. Criterion	2. Weighting (W) (%)	3. Evaluation (E)	4. Final Points (W × E)
Sales volume	40	5	2
Market share	5	1	0.05
Image	30	8	2.4
Interorganizational and cultural fit	25	9	2.25
5. Sum (Final Score)	**100**		**6.7**

The evaluation points range from 1 (low) to 10 (high)

2. Searching for the world's biggest companies within the different industries (sales volume).
3. Preparation of a list with the 200 biggest companies with the highest potential.
4. Analysis of attractiveness (sales volume, competitive situation, image, etc.), chances of acquisition, and segmentation (products, industry, etc.) of these 200 companies.
5. Selection and clustering of potential key accounts.
6. Definition of most interesting key accounts.
Source: Klebert (1999)

13.3.2.2 Step 2: Design Elements of the KAM Program

In this section, we discuss the types of decisions the seller should take into account when designing its key account program, namely, what is done, who does it, with whom it is done, and how formalized it is. That is, the elements that must be designed for a KAM program are *activities, actors, resources,* and *formalization* (Fig. 13.6).

Activities refer to interorganizational (external) elements, whereas actors, resources, and formalization describe intraorganizational (internal) elements of a KAM program. Figure 13.7 depicts

their relationships (the following illustrations refer to Homburg, Workman, & Jensen, 2000; Homburg et al., 2002; Workman et al., 2003).

Activities

Regarding the marketing mix, suppliers can offer special activities for their key accounts, such as special pricing, product customization, joint coordination of the workflow, information sharing, or taking over business processes outsourced by the customer. The intensity and proactiveness of these activities distinguish them from those offered to an average customer. Intensity designates the extent to which additional activities get performed for the most important customers, while proactiveness refers to the extent to which the supplier initiates the activities. Proactive activities make the seller more flexible in designing activities that match its own interests and capabilities. Moreover, an intensive, proactive KAM shows the buyer that the supplier is willing to invest in the relationship, which should deepen trust in the key account and strengthen the buyer–seller relationship.

CRM AT WORK 13.4

3M: Activities for Key Accounts

Especially for its key accounts, 3M offers a 2-day event, "Fascination Glue,"

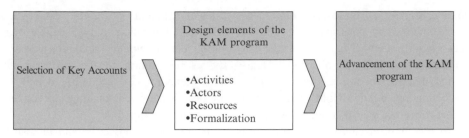

Fig. 13.6 Step 2 of the implementation process

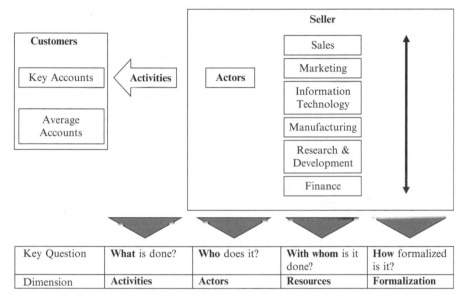

Fig. 13.7 Conceptualization of KAM (Source: Homburg et al., 2002)

which features lectures, discussions, shows, and evening events. Thus 3M not only provides its most important customers with up-to-date information about special topics, trends, innovations, and solutions that 3M can provide but also offers them the promise of building or strengthening networks with other companies, suppliers, and processing plants, as well as with researchers. But only for its strategic key accounts.

Source: http://solutions.3mdeutschland. de/wps/portal/3M/de_DE/Corporate/About/ Info/News/?PC_7_RJH9U5230O8JD0IIJB 82B22072_assetId=1273674110641, 3M, April 7, 2011

Actors

Special actors represent the personal coordination mode of KAM, which entails top management involvement, the use of teams, and key account managers. Top management involvement is the extent to which a company's top management actively participates in KAM. With senior-level involvement in KAM, the firm displays its commitment to kcy accounts, leading to greater involvement and a further strengthening of the buyer–seller relationship. However, key account managers remain the main point of contact for the key account. These managers need specific skills, including integrity, extensive product/service knowledge, communication skills, selling and negotiating skills, and a deep understanding of the buying company's business and environment

(McDonald et al., 1997). Thus, key account managers have to be trained exhaustively in order to fulfill these requirements. The use of teams can ensure a broader set of available skills. Dedicated teams that can coordinate the activities for key accounts preferably should be composed of members from various functions and backgrounds, to guarantee access to different types of resources that can meet the buyer's needs. For example, the key account manager at SAP knows all the contacts linked to each key account, so when new requests arise, the manager can compose a special, task-related team and adjust existing structures to address the specific requirements, (Belz, Müllner, & Zupancic, 2004).

Resources

Successful KAM requires the coordination of activities within the organization. The esprit de corps of the selling center and access to (non) marketing and (non)sales resources represent important assets for building strong, long-lasting buyer–seller relationships. Esprit de corps refers to the extent to which the members of the selling center feel linked to common goals and to other members. Access to (non)marketing and (non) sales resources is the extent to which a key account manager obtains necessary contributions to KAM from (non)marketing and (non)sales groups. Only KAM coordinators with access to such necessary resources can fulfill their organizations' commitments and thus succeed in building strong relationships with buyers.

CRM AT WORK 13.5

Philips: Access to Various Kinds of Resources

By cross-functionally composing its KAM team, Philips guarantees that the key account manager has access to resources from customer support service, production, R&D, marketing, and the sales department.

Source: Belz et al., (2004), p. 155

Formalization

Formalization refers to the extent to which key account handling has been formalized through rules and standard procedures established in the seller's organization. A high degree of formalization leads to bureaucracy and a lack of flexibility in responding to the different needs of heterogeneous key accounts, which is rather unfavorable for establishing effective buyer–seller relationships.

In all then, a proactive and intensive KAM, involving top management, cross-functional teams, and key account managers with special skills, as well as access to (non)marketing and (non)sales resources, plus a low degree of formalization can advance efforts to establish effective buyer–seller relationships.

13.3.2.3 Step 3: Advancement of the KAM Program

After having designed the key elements of a KAM program, the firm needs to advance its program by *optimizing* and continuously *improving* it (Fig. 13.8). The following illustrations refer to Davies and Ryals (2009).

Optimizing

In the optimizing phase, the firm makes significant financial investments to integrate the KAM program throughout the entire organization. All members gain an education in and become engaged with KAM, so the whole culture of the organization adopts a strong KAM orientation. Internal performance measurements fade away, replaced by benchmarking against competitors and reliance on customer feedback. The adaption of internal processes, policies, and IT systems is another primary element in this phase.

Improvement

During the continuous improvement phase, the company becomes increasingly focused and targeted, with fewer and fewer key accounts. To reduce the use or waste of expensive resources, top management becomes less involved. The focus on cost management thus is a main element of this phase.

KAM is never fully implemented but always can be described as an ongoing, continuous, very long-term commitment to improving among the best practice KAM companies.

Fig. 13.8 Step 3 of the implementation process

CRM AT WORK 13.6

Hilti: Best Practices

Hilti is a global leader that provides value-added, top-quality products for professional customers in the construction and building maintenance industries. Hilti's top management is involved in the management of the key accounts, and KAM is integrated throughout the company's overall strategy. In terms of its activities for key accounts, Hilti offers "VIP" solutions that solve specific customer problems in fleet management; the solutions support and maintain a broad composition of electronic tools. Hilti expects much of its key account managers, including extensive experience in international, multicultural environments; absolute fluency in English; demonstrated global, corporate thinking and acting; leadership; motivational abilities; excellent communication; superior negotiation skills; and analytical and interpersonal skills. To achieve its best results, Hilti provides special training to all key account executives, such as presentation and negotiation techniques, teamwork, and the use of analytical and strategic tools.

Source: Belz et al., (2004)

The example of Hilti's best practices in the preceding box shows that additional services represent one method of offering the right activities for the right customers. Therefore, especially in B2B markets, the shift from goods to services is a compelling possibility for establishing mutually beneficial, long-term buyer–seller relationships.

13.4 CRM and the Shift from Goods to Services

Nowadays, many firms combine products with services to create innovative offerings, widely known as hybrid offerings, hybrid solutions, solution selling, or customer solutions. In so doing, they hope to defend their positions in increasingly competitive product markets and increase revenues and cash flows. For example, Xerox sells not just the printers that initially made its name but also offers a consulting service to help customers publish their documents. These hybrid offerings can attract new customer segments and increase demand among existing customers by providing additional, superior value (Shankar, Berry, & Dotzel, 2009), which increases customer loyalty and retention. We therefore describe a typology of services for hybrid offerings and illustrate the advantages and disadvantages of the shift from goods to services. In turn, we offer a set of rules for a successful shift.

CRM AT WORK 13.7

Xerox: Best Practice

Xerox is an industry leader in document solutions and outsourcing services, with decades of experience and 15,000 business professionals spread across 160 countries. It helps companies optimize their printing

Table 13.4 Classification scheme of industrial services for hybrid offerings

		Service recipient	
		Service oriented toward the supplier's good	Service oriented toward the customer's process
Nature of the value proposition	Supplier's promise to perform a deed (input-based)	Product lifecycle services (PLS)	Process support services (PSS)
	Supplier's promise to achieve performance (output-based)	Asset efficiency services (AES)	Process delegation services (PDS)

Source: Based on Ulaga and Reinartz (2011)

infrastructures and streamline their marketing communications and business processes to grow revenue, reduce costs, and operate more efficiently. Xerox specializes in the planning and delivery of the following document management services:

- Managing print services for office, production, and virtual worker sites.
- Consolidating in-house production and commercial printing under a single point of control.
- Improving communication processes and back-office functions associated with creating, capturing, managing, and routing customer, employee, and supplier information.
- Designing, authoring, and translating technical and user documentation.
- Creating personalized, multichannel marketing communications.
- Developing defensible best practices in electronic discovery.
  Source: http://www.xerox.ca/consulting/xerox-global-services/enca.html, "About documents solutions from Xerox Global Services", Xerox, January 28, 2011.

13.4.1 What Are Hybrid Offerings?

Hybrid offerings can be defined as a combination of "one or more goods and one or more services, creating more customer benefits than if the good and service were available separately" (Shankar, Berry, & Dotzel, 2007). There are several types of services a seller can combine with physical goods to form hybrid offerings; the resultant classification contains two dimensions. The first dimension refers to whether the service is

directed at the supplier's good or the customer's process. The second pertains to whether the supplier's service value proposition is input-based, which implies it is grounded in the promise to perform a deed, or output-based, which means it promises to achieve certain performance. In combining these two dimensions, we can derive four categories (Table 13.4) that fundamentally differ in the resources and capabilities needed to develop the hybrid offerings (Ulaga & Reinartz, 2011).

- *Product Lifecycle Services (PLS):* These input-based services are oriented toward the supplier's good. They facilitate the customer's access to the supplier's good and ensure its proper functioning throughout its lifecycle. For example, the installation of a high-voltage circuit breaker is a PLS. In this category, sellers cost-efficiently meet buyers' basic expectations, using standardized services.
- *Asset Efficiency Services (AES):* These services are also oriented toward the supplier's good, but they are output-based. AES are offered to achieve productivity gains from assets invested by customers, such as welding robot software customization. In moving from PLS to AES, firms commit to performance related to asset productivity, and shift from cost-based to value-based pricing for their hybrid offerings.
- *Process Support Services (PSS):* These services that are oriented toward the customer's processes are input-based. They help customers improve their own business processes, tailored to their specific contexts and needs. For example, a lot of industrial gases (e.g., hydrogen, oxygen) are regarded as pure commodities, but by understanding the application of the gases in the buyers'

processes (e.g., food conservation in a meat processing plant), the manufacturer can differentiate itself in the market.

*   *Process Delegation Services (PDS):* Finally, PDS are oriented toward the customer's processes and are output-based. These services perform processes on behalf of the customers, such as tire fleet management for a trucking company. The goods and services are integrated and individually customized. To guarantee this customization, there must be a high degree of interactivity in communication and exchange of information between the buyer and the seller. These characteristics reflect the high degree of complexity of these services.

The promise for services is great, especially for PDS (widely regarded as 'solutions'). BASF Coatings, a best practice example in the field of PDS, offers solutions for automotive manufacturers and supports them in the painting process; thus it generates a transaction volume of €2.3 billion annually (Ahlert & Kawohl, 2008). However, approximately half of all solution sellers manage to realize only modest benefits and one fourth actually lose money (Stanley & Wojcik, 2005). The shift from goods to services is not a simple or innate process; it may pose certain challenges.

13.4.2 Advantages and Disadvantages of the Shift to Hybrid Offerings

In the B2B CRM context, the main benefit of extending products to hybrid offerings for a seller is increased *buyer loyalty*. Because hybrid offerings are more intangible to the customer, they are more difficult to evaluate, which decreases market transparency but increases the buyer's perceived purchase risk. Furthermore, greater interactivity in terms of communication and information exchanges between the buyer and seller that is required in service selling (compared to product selling), especially in PDS, should produce strong, collaborative relationships featuring higher degrees of trust and cooperation. Because the seller has developed an individually customized and integrated solution to solve the buyer's special problem, the seller becomes more important for the buyer, and the buyer becomes depen-

dent or locked in to the relationship. As long as the buyer's needs and requirements are fulfilled, long-term and loyal relationships can be established via selling hybrid offerings, leading to an increase in *customer lifetime value*. Furthermore, the seller might *leverage its resources and knowledge* from product manufacturing to service manufacturing and thus realize synergies that offer cost savings and competitive differentiation advantages in increasingly competitive product markets. These advantages refer to those illustrated in Fang, Palmatier, and Steenkamp (2008).

But in the course of this shift, firms must consider the prevalent potential for *capability risk* (the mentioned disadvantages refer to those illustrated in Fang et al., 2008; Sawhney, Balasubramanian, & Krishnan, 2004). The greater complexity of hybrid offerings (compared with pure product offerings) may cause a seller to lose its strategic focus. The seller has to acquire a lot of organization's resources, capabilities, and competencies from different domains to develop suitable hybrid offerings and meet a buyer's needs and requirements. In this confusing realm, a seller often fails to develop effective hybrid offerings, because it cannot optimally allocate required resources across the different domains or because its existing capabilities and organizational culture do not fit with the required offerings, leading to organizational conflict. This conflict usually harms employees' motivation, effort, and productivity, which can decrease the ability to create value for the buyer. Because the margins of services also tend to be lower than those for products, sellers also face a *financial risk* in transitioning to services. Their intense efforts to gather resources and capabilities, as well as the high level of complexity make it difficult to increase these margins. Moreover, *market risk* is a key concern; it describes the possibility that the buyer does not adopt the service, whether because it does not want to or is not able to do so. For example, if the interactivity in communication and exchange of information between the buyer and the seller fails, the developed hybrid offering may be ineffective and thus not valuable for the buyer, because it does not meet its requirements and needs. Figure 13.9

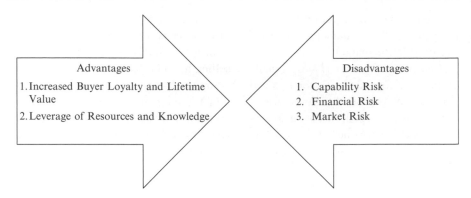

Fig. 13.9   (Dis)Advantages of the shift

summarizes these advantages and disadvantages of shifting an offer from goods to services.

Managers should be well prepared to overcome the possible disadvantages and keep in mind certain aspects that will help them build long-term relationships and realize the advantages of increased customer loyalty and lifetime value, instead of the disadvantages. We thus offer some rules for a successful shift from goods to services, with reference to possible risk types.

13.4.3 Rules for Successful Shifts

In line with our discussion of the disadvantages of the shift from goods to services, the rules for successful shifts aim to reduce or eliminate capability, financial, and market risks (Fig. 13.10).

To *reduce or eliminate capability risk*, especially the loss of strategic focus and organizational conflicts, the seller has several options (Sawhney et al., 2004; Ulaga & Reinartz, 2011):

- Mandate a centralized administration of services, such as putting different services in one location or a separate organization.
- Design services that build on existing product platforms.
- Ensure access to resources, such as data about the installed base product usage and process, product development and manufacturing assets, sales forces and distribution networks, and a field service organization that build the required capabilities.

- Leverage the partner organization's capabilities by acquiring or partnering with a service-cultured company that has key resources, capabilities, and competencies.

To *reduce or eliminate the financial risk*, the seller could, for example, (Sawhney et al., 2004; Shankar et al., 2009):

- Identify the most profitable product/service and combine it with the most commonly bought product/service.
- Use the Internet to link goods and services and thereby lower the total unit costs of the offering.
- Find opportunities to balance the timing and magnitude of cash flows from products and services.
- Perform robust, early, and frequent economic value analyses.

Finally, to *reduce or eliminate market risk*, the seller should (Sawhney et al., 2004):

- Create a service-savvy sales force.
- Offer trial periods, prototypes, and iterations.
- Blueprint according to customer specifications.
- Focus on existing customers and processes and meet their needs and requirements through effective hybrid offerings.

In summary, we note three different types of risks—capability, financial, and market—that limit the advantages of hybrid offerings (i.e., increased customer loyalty and lifetime value), so the seller must reduce or eliminate these risks. For PDS in particular, few firms venture into this area, because of the very sophisticated

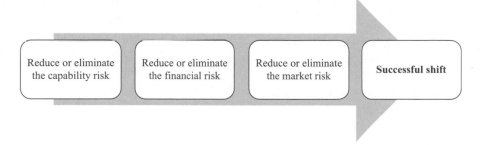

Fig. 13.10 Rules for the successful shift

capabilities required to achieve its benefits without suffering from its risks (Ulaga & Reinartz, 2011). The following box offers a good conceptualization of solutions (or PDS) and their effectiveness.

PDS: Effective Solutions

Tuli, Kohli, and Bharadwaj (2007) define solutions as a set of buyer–seller relationship processes that address buyers' business needs. The processes include:

- Customer requirement definition
- Customization and integration of industrial goods and/or services
- Their development
- Post-deployment customer support.

For the seller, the most important factor is guaranteeing that a buyer adopts the solution and to meet the buyer's needs and requirements through the design of effective solutions. Thus the seller has to know which factors will ensure the success or effectiveness of a solution. Because of the need for interactivity in communication and information exchanges between the buyer and the seller, solution effectiveness depends on specific supplier- and customer-related variables.

Supplier variables:

- *Contingent hierarchy*: Must be multiple and flexible, instead of stable, to develop successful solutions, because it ensures a greater power balance across the supplier's firm units/divisions.

- *Documentation emphasis*: The degree to which supplier employees are required to document the purpose of the solution, individual roles, work performed, and outcomes; it helps manage the complexity of the solution's development and guarantees that the postdeployment support team has access to critical knowledge.

- *Incentive externality*: Describes the extent to which employee incentives are complementary across units and divisions; greater complementarity leads to more effective development and better postdeployment, as well as more shared information across units.

- *Customer interactor stability*: The duration for which salespeople and support staff, or customer interactors, are assigned to the customer; the greater the stability, the stronger the relationship with the customer and the better their understanding of customers' requirements.

- *Process articulation*: The degree to which a supplier firm clearly gives information about the solution development process to employees, such as rules for specifying reporting structures, sharing customer information, and clarifying responsibilities; offers a framework for interaction across units, functions, and customers that can help guarantee the correct definition of customers' requirements and articulation of needs.

Customer variables:

- *Customer adaptiveness*: Refers to the extent to which the customer is able and willing to adapt internal routines and processes to accommodate the supplier's products and/or services; high customer adaptiveness makes it easier to customize and integrate a solution, so the supplier firm can work more effectively.
- *Political counseling*: The degree to which a supplier receives information and guidance about the political landscape facing the customer organization; through political counseling, the supplier firm gains a better understanding of the varying priorities of different stakeholders in the customer firm, leading to a better definition of the customer's requirements, increased customization and integration of goods and/or services, and more effective postdeployment support.
- *Operational counseling*: The degree to which a supplier receives information about the customer's operations, including details about the technical system, business process, and policies; the supplier firm can define the customer's requirements more completely and accurately and can better customize and integrate a solution with such information.

Managers should be aware of any changes and developments, especially in the customer variables involved in adopting particular activities and practices.

Source: Tuli et al., (2007)

13.5 Summary

Over the course of this chapter, we have discussed several CRM-related issues in the B2B context. We first introduced *SFA* as a tool for efficiently and effectively managing buyer–seller relationships by increasing sales productivity and improving customer relations, which should lead

to increased sales revenue. We also pointed out the conditions—namely, SFA adoption and usage by the sales force—and measures that sales managers and senior management can take to guarantee and support the pursuit of the relevant benefits. Furthermore, we noted the promise of *KAM* as a means to allocate the right activities to the right customers. The selection of key accounts, design elements of the KAM program, and advancement of the KAM program constitute three key steps for successfully implementing a KAM program and realizing its goal of creating long-term relationships with the seller's most important and valuable buyers. Finally, acknowledging its actual relevance in B2B markets, we have illustrated the widespread *shift from goods to services,* respectively the shift to *hybrid offerings* as a method to provide the right activities to customers. In addition to defining hybrid offerings and creating a typology of services in hybrid offerings, we outlined the advantages and disadvantages of this shift, as well as some rules for avoiding the risks and realizing the advantages, which in turn should lead to stronger buyer–seller relationships. With this chapter, we therefore have illustrated that with SFA, KAM, and hybrid offerings, a seller can build strong, lasting, valuable buyer–seller relationships and better manage the value of these relationships, which means it can achieve its ultimate goals within a B2B CRM context.

Exercise Questions

1. Describe the benefits of SFA and their linkages.
2. How can sales managers and senior management support SFA adoption and usage by employees?
3. What are the key steps to successfully implementing a KAM program?
4. Explain the advantages and disadvantages of the different criteria for selecting key accounts.
5. Explain which type of hybrid offering Xerox provides to its customers.
6. What are the risks associated with the shift from goods to services?
7. How can the risks of the shift from goods to services be reduced or eliminated?

References

Ahlert, D., & Kawohl, J. (2008). *Best Practices des Solution Sellings* (Projektbericht, Vol. 1). Münster: Westfälische Wilhelms-Universität.

Anderson, J. C., & Narus, J. A. (1991). Partnering as a focused market strategy. *California Management Review, 33*(3), 95–113.

Belz, C., Müllner, M., & Zupancic, D. (2004). *Spitzenleistungen im Key Account Management—Das St. Galler KAM-Konzept.* Frankfurt: Moderne Industrie.

Buttle, F. (2009). *Customer relationship management-concepts and technologies.* Amsterdam et al.: Elsevier.

Capon, N. (2001). *Key account management and planning.* New York et al.: The Free Press.

Cascio, R., Mariadoss, B. J., & Mouri, N. (2010). The impact of management commitment alignment on salespersons' adoption of sales force automation technologies: An empirical investigation. *Industrial Marketing Management, 39*(7), 1088–1096.

Davies, I. A., & Ryals, L. J. (2009). A stage model for transitioning to KAM. *Journal of Marketing Management, 25*(9–10), 1027–1048.

Fang, E., Palmatier, R. W., & Steenkamp, J. E. M. (2008). Effect of service transition strategies on firm value. *Journal of Marketing, 72*(5), 1–14.

Homburg, C., Workman, J. P., & Jensen, O. (2000). Fundamental changes in marketing organization: The movement toward a customer-focused organizational structure. *Journal of the Academy of Marketing Science, 28*(4), 459–478.

Homburg, C., Workman, J. P., & Jensen, O. (2002). A configurational perspective on key account management. *Journal of Marketing, 66*(2), 38–60.

Hunter, G. K., & Perreault, W. D. (2007). Making sales technology effective. *Journal of Marketing, 71*(1), 16–34.

Hutt, M. D., & Speh, T. W. (2007). *Business marketing management: B2B.* Mason, OH: Thomson South-Western.

Jones, E., Sundaram, S., & Chin, W. (2002). Factors leading to sales force automation use: A longitudinal analysis. *Journal of Personal Selling & Sales Management, 22*(3), 145–156.

Karlöf, B., & Lövingsson, F. H. (2005). *The A-Z of management concepts and models.* London: Thorogood.

Klebert, S. (1999). Key Accounts Portfolios—Die Selektion von Schlüsselkunden. *Absatzwirtschaft, 4*, 44–45.

McDonald, M., Millman, T., & Rogers, B. (1997). Key account management: Theory, practice and challenges. *Journal of Marketing Management, 13*(8), 737–757.

Moon, M. (2008). How to increase CRM user adoption—interview with Inna Proshkina of InvisibleCRM. *Journal of Digital Asset Management, 4*(4), 225–233.

Park, J. E., Kim, J., Dubinsky, A. J., & Lee, H. (2010). How does sales force automation influence relationship quality and performance? The mediating roles of learning and selling behaviors. *Industrial marketing management, 39*(7), 1128–1138.

Porter, A. M. (2002). The top 250: Tough measures for tough times. *Purchasing, 132*(7), 31–35; cited in Hutt, M. D., & Speh, T. W. (2007). *Business marketing management: B2B.* Mason, OH: Thomson South-Western.

Rogers, B., Stone, M., & Foss, B. (2008). Integrating the value of salespeople and systems: Adapting the benefits dependency network. *Database Marketing & Customer Strategy Management, 15*(4), 221–232.

Sawhney, M., Balasubramanian, S., & Krishnan, V. V. (2004). Creating growth with services. *MIT Sloan Management Review, 45*(2), 34–43.

Shankar, V., Berry, L. L., & Dotzel, T. (2007, February). Creating and managing hybrid innovations. AMA Winter Educators' Conference, San Diego, CA.

Shankar, V., Berry, L. L., & Dotzel, T. (2009). A practical guide to combining products + services. *Harvard Business Review, 87*(11), 94–99.

Speier, C., & Venkatesh, V. (2002). The hidden minefields in the adoption of sales force automation technologies. *Journal of Marketing, 66*(3), 98–111.

Spekman, R. E., & Carraway, R. (2006). Making the transition to collaborative buyer-seller relationships: An emerging framework. *Industrial Marketing Management, 35*(1), 10–19.

Stanley, J. E., & Wojcik, P. J. (2005). Better B2B selling. *McKinsey Quarterly, 38*(3), 15.

Tuli, K. R., Kohli, A. K., & Bharadwaj, S. G. (2007). Rethinking customer solutions: From product bundles to relational processes. *Journal of Marketing, 71*(3), 1–17.

Ulaga, W., & Reinartz, W. J. (2011). Hybrid offerings: How manufacturing firms combine goods and services successfully. *Journal of Marketing, 75*(6), 5–23.

Winkelmann, P. (2006). *Marketing und Vertrieb–Fundamente für die Marktorientierte Unternehmensführung.* München/Wien: Oldenbourg.

Workman, J. P., Homburg, C., & Jensen, O. (2003). Intraorganizational determinants of key account management effectiveness. *Journal of the Academy of Marketing Science, 31*(1), 3–21.

Customer Privacy Concerns and Privacy Protective Responses

14

14.1 Overview

Companies increasingly collect and use data about their current and potential customers to improve their customer relationship management (CRM), sales, and service effectiveness. By obtaining information on customers' transactions and behaviors, as well as their socio-demographic profiles, companies can better understand their customers' preferences and desires. Thus they build up customer intelligence to enable them to refine their strategic marketing decision making and enhance customer relationships, especially with their most valuable customers. The value of such customer information to companies is clear from Goldman Sachs's valuation of Facebook at $50 billion, largely because the online social network site hosts customer profiles of more than 550 million users worldwide (Sorkin & Craig, 2011). However, companies are also finding a growing reluctance among customers, who prefer not to disclose their personal information or allow tracking of their behaviors out of their concerns for privacy (Wirtz & Lwin, 2009). For example in 2010, many German homeowners protested against the use of images of their houses by Google's online mapping system, Google Street View. As a result, Google had to pixilate about 3% of all affected households in 20 German cities. In a managerial survey by McKinsey & Co.

from 2007, 33% of all respondents named privacy and data security as among the top three issues likely to gain the most public and political attention in the next 5 years (Bonini, Greeny, & Mendonca, 2007). Furthermore, growing governmental regulations related to the gathering and use of personal information are raising new obstacles for companies. Accordingly, this chapter outlines customer privacy concerns and their respective implications for successful customer relationship management.

First, the chapter begins by presenting trends and drivers related to customer privacy concerns. Second, we discuss governmental regulations in a cross-country comparison to reflect the different prepositions that companies face in different markets. Third, the underlying psychological processes and respective customer responses are identified and summarized in a comprehensive conceptual framework that indicates implications for responsible privacy handling policies. We also shed light on the privacy paradox, namely, the relationship between consumers' intention to disclose personal information and their actual personal information disclosure behaviors (Norberg, Horne, & Horne, 2007). Our overall framework depicts the context of customer privacy concerns and the respective consequences and implications for companies, as we show in Fig. 14.1.

V. Kumar and W. Reinartz, *Customer Relationship Management*, Springer Texts in Business and Economics, DOI 10.1007/978-3-642-20110-3_14, © Springer-Verlag Berlin Heidelberg 2012

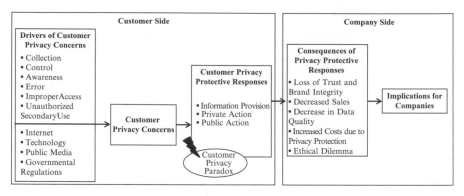

Fig. 14.1 Customer privacy concerns and implications for companies

14.2   Customer Privacy Concerns

14.2.1 Customer Privacy

Definitions of privacy vary broadly depending on the setting and environmental factors. Especially in the context of CRM, the concept of customer privacy often has been merged with data protection, such that privacy represents a form of personal information management (Roznowski, 2003). Customer privacy then can be defined as "the power of the individual to personally control (vis-à-vis other individuals, groups, organizations, etc.) information about one's self," which includes the collection, storage, usage, and release of personal information (Stone, Gueutal, Gardner, & McClure, 1983). If a company's CRM is to foster relationships with current customers and acquire new customers, the firm must ensure a constant flow of up-to-date information about customers' buying habits and individual needs. However, if customers feel they are losing control over their personal information, they will begin to feel concern about their privacy, which can lead to reluctance to disclose any further personal information. This scenario creates serious obstacles for the efficiency of a company's CRM practices. Thus, it is crucial for companies to know how they can positively influence customers' perceptions of the handling of their personal information to reduce privacy concerns. For this purpose, companies must pay attention to the factors that drive customers' privacy concerns.

14.2.2 Drivers of Customer Privacy Concerns

Customer privacy is one of the most important management practice issues. When customers become concerned about their privacy, CRM processes are especially affected, because they rely on a mutual exchange of information between the customer and the company. In the past decade, customers have paid increasing attention to privacy issues as their perceived ability to control access to their personal information has eroded. A customer survey from 2010 revealed greater anxiety about privacy than existed in earlier studies (KPMG, 2010). This increase in customers' privacy concerns can be attributed to different internal, company-related factors, as well as several external conditions we present in Fig. 14.2.

Internal Drivers of Customer Privacy Concerns
Customer privacy concerns arise from different sources, such as the way companies collect personal information *(Collection)*, whether a customer can control the uses made of this information *(Control)*, and the clear understanding of the company's conditions and practices with respect to privacy *(Awareness)*. These primary dimensions determine the extent of customers' privacy concerns. Furthermore, customers' privacy concerns can be fostered if they fear that information is not accurate *(Errors)* or is

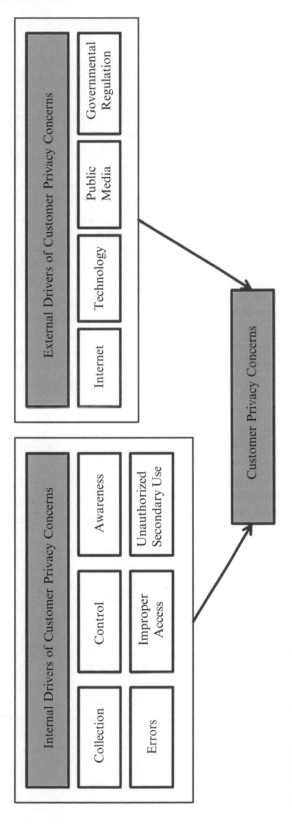

Fig. 14.2 Drivers of customer privacy concerns

accessible *(Improper Access)* to unauthorized entities. Personal information used for reasons not authorized by the customer also can increase privacy concerns *(Unauthorized Secondary Use)* (Malhotra, Kim, & Agarwal, 2004).

Collection

Collection can be defined as "the degree to which a person is concerned about the amount of individual specific data possessed by others relative to the value of benefits received." Thus, collection comprises customer concerns about the amount of and the way in which personal information is collected.

Control

Control refers to a person's degree of "control over personal information as manifested by the existence of voice (i.e., approval, modification) or exit (i.e., opt-out)" (Malhotra et al., 2004). Customers' control over their personal data is exercised through approval, modification, or the right to opt-out or opt-in.

Awareness

Awareness indicates an "understanding of established conditions and actual practices" with respect to a company's information collection. Thus, awareness refers to the extent of transparency with which companies communicate the collection and usage of customer data.

Errors

Errors denote concerns that "protections against both deliberate and accidental errors in the data are not adequate" (Harris, Van Hoye, & Lievens, 2003).

Improper Access

Improper access relates to "concerns that data are readily available to parties not authorized to use it" (Harris et al., 2003).

Unauthorized Secondary Use

Unauthorized secondary use refers to "concerns that information collected by the organization for one purpose will be used by the same organization for a different, unauthorized purposes (inter-

nal use) or given to another party for other purposes (external use)" (Harris et al., 2003).

CRM at Work 14.1

In practical applications, companies can gain insights into their customers' privacy perception of data handling and CRM practices through a customer survey that contains all these constructs. All the items we present here can be measured on seven-point scales anchored by "strongly disagree" and "strongly agree."

Control:

1. Consumer online privacy is really a matter of consumers' right to exercise control and autonomy over decisions about how their information is collected, used, and shared.
2. Consumer control of personal information lies at the heart of consumer privacy.
3. I believe that online privacy is invaded when control is lost or unwillingly reduced as a result of a marketing transaction.

Awareness:

1. Companies seeking information online should disclose the way the data are collected, processed, and used.
2. A good consumer online privacy policy should have a clear and conspicuous disclosure.
3. It is very important to me that I am aware and knowledgeable about how my personal information will be used.

Collection:

1. It usually bothers me when companies ask me for personal information.
2. When companies ask me for personal information, I sometimes think twice before providing it.
3. It bothers me to give personal information to so many companies.
4. I'm concerned that companies are collecting too much personal information about me.

Errors:

1. All the personal information in computer databases should be double-checked for accuracy-no matter how much this costs.
2. Companies should take more steps to make sure that the personal information in their files is accurate.
3. Companies should have better procedures to correct errors in personal information.
4. Companies should devote more time and effort to verifying the accuracy of the personal information in their databases.

Unauthorized Secondary Use:

1. Companies should not use personal information for any purpose unless it has been authorized by the individuals who provided the information.
2. When people give personal information to a company for some reason, the online company should never use the information for any other reason.
3. Companies should never sell the personal information in their computer databases to other companies.
4. Companies should never share personal information with other companies unless it has been authorized by the individuals who provided the information.

Improper Access:

1. Companies should devote more time and effort to preventing unauthorized access to personal information.
2. Computer databases that contain personal information should be protected from unauthorized access—no matter how much it costs.
3. Companies should take more steps to make sure that unauthorized people cannot access personal information in their computers.

Global Information Privacy Concern:

1. All things considered, the Internet would cause serious privacy problems.

2. Compared to others, I am more sensitive about the way companies handle my personal information.
3. To me, it is the most important thing to keep my privacy intact from companies.
4. I believe other people are too much concerned with privacy issues.
5. Compared with other subjects on my mind, personal privacy is very important.
6. I am concerned about threats to my personal privacy today.

Source: Malhotra et al. (2004)

External Drivers of Customer Privacy Concerns

Several key external drivers—namely, the Internet, technological advances, public media coverage, and governmental regulations—further foster customers' privacy concerns. These drivers influence one another and ultimately increase customers' concerns about their privacy.

Internet

In 2000, Bill Gates, the founder and chairman of Microsoft Corp., recognized that "In an era where the internet is increasingly central to our lives at work, at home and at school, it is more important than ever that our industry gives customers the assurance that their information will remain secure, respected and private." (Microsoft, 2000)

Customer privacy has always been a significant issue in marketing, but it has gained even more importance with the advent of the Internet. Correspondingly, research has found that customers have grown even more alert to information privacy issues online, compared with those associated with traditional media (Hoffman, Novak, & Peralta, 1999).

The online environment also offers new and different conditions for companies with respect to their data collection and data processing efforts (Rust, Kannan, & Peng, 2002).

- Customer data collection is rendered relatively cheap and easy to execute.
- By means of cost-efficient data-mining processes, companies gain the opportunity to

develop customer profiles, behavioral profiles, and insights for targeting and discrimi-
nating among their customers.

- The network environment in which the data is
collected and coded facilitates the combination of seemingly disparate customer data to
create complex profiles of customers.

As a result, customer data can be used efficiently and successfully to build and foster customer relationships. Consider a recent example.
In 2010, the Dutch airline KLM launched a CRM
campaign to foster existing passengers' loyalty
(http://surprise.klm.com/). Noting customers'
social media activities, such as posts on Twitter
about upcoming trips, KLM employees selected
small gifts, such as travel guides, and presented
them to the individual customers prior to their
flights (KLM, 2011). Not long after, critics
accused KLM of stalking its customers though,
thus highlighting customers' growing concerns
about their information privacy. Customer privacy concerns are the top reason non-users still
avoid the Internet.

In an online setting, there are different ways to
gather customer information:

- Customers voluntarily enter personal information, such as their name, address, and credit
card number, into databases.
- Information on customers' online behavior is
collected using cookies and click-stream technology without customers' consent.

When browsing the web or making purchases
online, customers must provide certain personal
information to be able to gain access to content
offerings or complete a purchase transaction.
Thus, they face a trade-off between the advantages they receive from providing personal information (e.g., name, address, and credit card
number) and their fear of the threats associated
with sharing such sensitive information. It has
even been argued that it is nearly impossible for
customers to transact on the Internet without
revealing information about themselves that
they might be unwilling to share (Rust et al.,
2002). Massive databases continue to record customers' demographics and past purchase activities.

But what raises customer privacy concerns
even more is the approach that companies use

to track their online behaviors without consent.
The application of behavioral advertising—personalized advertising messages that are based on
customers' prior browsing behavior and online
purchasing patterns—serves as an example. A
customer survey from 2009 revealed that 68%
of U.S. customers "definitely" would not allow
companies to track their online behavior to tailor
advertisements to their interests (Turow, King,
Hoofnagle, Bleakley, & Hennessy, 2009). Yet
the rise of online social media websites, such as
Facebook, MySpace, or Twitter, means that customers voluntarily share personal information,
giving advertisers detailed insights into their
lives, which the companies then can use for customer segmentation and targeting (Kluth, 2008).
Furthermore, concerns about privacy can arise in
relation to potential breaches of confidential customer data. For example, Facebook recently
acknowledged that some of its social networking
applications provided personal information to
marketers, without users' knowledge, leading
the European Commission to call for stronger
protection of Internet users' personal information
(Pfanner, 2010).

In summary, the Internet often represents a
threat to privacy and has the potential to under-
mine a company's marketing performance in the
long run. Thus privacy concerns raised by the
Internet require a lot more attention by companies and their respective CRM departments.

Technology

Different technological innovations have made it
easier for companies to gather, process, and use
customer data to gain a competitive advantage,
but they also have fostered customers' privacy
concerns. The main innovations driving this
development are as follows:

- Mobile and smart phones
- Location-based services
- Radio frequency identification technology

Mobile and smart phones have made their
way into people's daily lives. Their penetration
rates are steadily increasing, with reported
worldwide subscription rates of 90% in 2010
(ITU, 2010). Furthermore, new technologies
and software like smart phones (i.e., mobile

phones with advanced connectivity and computing ability) and *location-based services* have become extremely popular. As a result, people have become comfortable using smart phones to share information about themselves, via mobile applications that access social networks such as Twitter and Facebook.

For example, Foursquare.com gives users the means to report their physical location online, so they can connect with friends or receive coupons (Miller & Wortham, 2010). However, such technological innovations also provide companies with the opportunity to get in touch with customers and offer targeted advertising based on their location, such that the distinction between public and private space seems to be eroding. Customers can no longer depend on the intuitive sense that "If I can see you, you can see me too" but instead feel they are losing control over their personal information. Pleaserobme.com collected posts from Twitter that showed that the posters were somewhere other than home; this initiative attempted to draw attention to customers' "oversharing" of personal information. Furthermore, the initiators wanted to inform people about potential risk associated with the use location-based services, such as criminals misusing customer information to rob empty houses (The Economist, 2010). They received notable attention for this effort, though customers' sensitivity about information privacy in general still seems to be decreasing, considering the mass adoption of smart phones.

Another technological innovation, *radio frequency identification (RFID)*, is increasingly being applied in retail environments and thus fuelling customers' privacy concerns. This item-tagging technology is reliable and relatively inexpensive, does not require a power supply, and can be attached to nearly any item. When exposed to a radio signal, RFID tags send back information, mostly a long number that identifies the object to which they are attached. Thus retailers use RFID to assist customers with their grocery shopping: A store or loyalty card can be fitted with an RFID tag to identify customers on arrival, and then a device on the shopping cart or trolley can monitor everything placed in it, dou-

ble check with past shopping patterns, and nudge customers: "You have just passed the Oriels, which you usually buy here" (The Economist, 2008). But this technology implies a risk of jeopardizing customer privacy and reducing or eliminating purchasing anonymity.

Consider some examples of RFID-related threats (Garfinkel, Juels, & Pappu, 2005):

- **Action threat.** By embedding hidden RFID tags into or on objects and documents, companies are able to infer individual behavior, without the knowledge or consent of the individual engaging in the behavior. For example, in 2003 Walmart equipped cosmetic shelves in one of its stores in Broken Arrow, Oklahoma, with RFID technology to track Max Factor Lipfinity lipsticks being removed from shelves. Then Proctor & Gamble researchers used video monitoring to observe customers' behaviors after they picked up the lipstick. This major violation of customer privacy rights without prior consent became publicly known as the Broken Arrow Affair (Hildner, 2006).

- **Association threat.** A customer's identity can be associated with the item's electronic serial number and, with rich data stored in back-end systems (e.g., from a loyalty program), lead to the creation of comprehensive customer profiles that reveal the customers' brand or item preferences in a specific product category. In contrast to the use of loyalty cards, this type of association can be clandestine and even involuntary. Even if item-level information remains generic, identifying items people wear or carry could associate them with particular events or ideas, such as political rallies.

- **Location threat.** If people carry unique tags attached to the items they purchase, they can be located even after they leave the retail store. This possibility also evokes the danger of unauthorized third-party disclosures.

Technological innovations continue to provide companies with opportunities to gain customer information more easily and at a lower cost and thus better serve their customers and improve their customer relationships. A case in point is the German Metro Group, which rolled out a RFID initiative in its Kaufhof department store in Essen in 2007. Part of this initiative entailed the introduction of smart dressing rooms, which recognize garments via RFID and, on integrated displays, provide customers with useful information, such as price, material, and care instructions. Even such helpful uses of RFID technology can be perceived as intrusive into customers' privacy though and increase concerns about the collection and usage of the obtained information.

Public Media

Public media also play a key role in shaping perceptions of privacy issues. During the past decade, increasing attention in both electronic and print media has focused on privacy issues and actively shaped customers' concerns. Greater media coverage of privacy issues ultimately can increase information privacy concerns. In addition, private consumer groups, such as the Electronic Privacy Information Center (EPIC), report privacy breaches to popular media, heightening customers' attitudes and concerns about privacy issues. A study of mass media coverage of customer privacy issues between 1990 and 2001 across newspapers, consumer magazines, and trade publications revealed that the number of total articles across all three formats increased by 70%, from 2,278 articles in 1990 to 3,876 in 2000. In consumer magazines in particular—which have the greatest impact on customers' privacy perceptions—the number of articles was seven times higher in 2000 than in 1990. Finally, three times as many negative as positive articles were published, which shows how important it is for companies to consider customer privacy issues (Roznowski, 2003). Other recent research shows that actual media coverage of privacy issues, especially through the increased diffusion of social networks, has grown even more. This growth also reflects new conceptualizations of journalism, exemplified by non-professional authors publishing news on blogs that blur the distinction between independent journalism and other information sources (Peltier, Milne, & Phelps, 2009).

Even companies acknowledge the importance of media coverage; Facebook reacted to reports of a customer privacy breach of its social network site only after the problem was prominently covered by *The Wall Street Journal* (The Economist, 2011). Public media in all its forms thus shapes customers' perceptions of information privacy, and newer platforms such as Twitter and social networks can help spread negative news immediately and worldwide, with dramatic potential impacts on companies' bottom lines.

Government Regulation

Government regulation, or the lack thereof, has a powerful impact on customer privacy concerns. A perceived lack of business policy or governmental regulation results in greater privacy concerns (Wirtz, Lwin, & Williams, 2007), and different regulatory approaches to customer privacy, as well as the extent to which governments (mis)use personal information, highlight cross-national differences in privacy concerns. Access to personal information can help governments serve their citizenry better, collect taxes, and enforce laws and regulations. But governments must take a very different position toward personal information than either businesses or individuals. Governments have the power to take and use information without permission; Great Britain maintains a closed-circuit television surveillance system in public and private sectors (e.g., roughly 500,000 cameras are positioned around London) and extensive government and commercial databases. Its police-run DNA database is the largest worldwide. The British government even has plans to track and monitor all 11.7 million children in the country with RFID technology (The Economist, 2007).

The USA Patriot Act, which introduced legislative changes after the September, 11, 2001, attacks in an attempt to prevent terrorism, serves as another example. The surveillance and investigative powers of law enforcement agencies were significantly increased, and agencies such as the Department of Defense received permission to search telephone, e-mail communications, and the medical, financial, and other

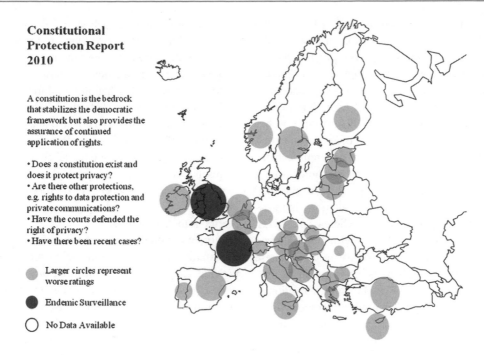

Fig. 14.3 Constitutional protection in Europe (Source: www.privacyinternational.org)

records of U.S. citizens without their consent, which in turn stoked significant privacy concerns (EPIC, 2011).

Privacy International, a human rights group established in 1990 to provide information about surveillance and privacy invasions by governments and corporations, published a comprehensive report on privacy and human rights in Europe in 2010, in which it rated different countries' governments on privacy-related measures, such as privacy enforcement, visual surveillance, and constitutional protection (Privacy International, 2011). The constitutional protection results appear in Fig. 14.3.

With respect to the constitutional protection of privacy, significant differences become apparent even among members of the European Union (EU). Germany has "Significant Protection and Safeguards," but the United Kingdom's rating indicates its "Epidemic Surveillance," due to the lack of a written reference to the right to privacy in its constitution. Even though the EU has established an overall framework of privacy protection for its members, these requirements are rather limited and allow for a

wide margin of enforcement by different governments.

Yet these ratings do not always fully represent customers' concerns about privacy protection in their home countries. Rather, privacy concerns raised by customers (or the media) in a country can demand legislative actions by the government, leading to improved privacy protections (Roznowski, 2003). Germany, with its very concerned customers and high position in the privacy ranking, serves as a good example.

14.3 Regulations to Protect Customer Privacy

The difference between European and U.S. regulation of customer privacy is well-established: In general, information privacy is protected more under European law than U.S. law (despite differences among EU members). Specifically, customer privacy regulations generally reflect two perspectives: *industry self-regulation* or *government-imposed regulation*. These two approaches summarize the difference between the protection frameworks established by the EU and the United States, as well as the extent to which the respective government controls privacy protection. Whereas the EU has adopted a data protection directive that sets strict privacy standards, U.S. privacy protections tend to be left to self-regulation within industries. These approaches represent the differences in their cultural and societal values and thus their different perceptions of customer privacy. For example, from a German viewpoint, the protection of personal dignity (e.g., image, name, reputation) is threatened primarily by the media, whereas in the U.S. mindset, protection of liberty within one's home is threatened primarily by the government. These differences have their roots in the countries' histories. The German privacy law and protection of personality and position within society have emerged as reactions to fascism and the strictly hierarchical society structures of the seventeenth and eighteenth centuries. In contrast, the United States has embraced the principal of a "limited government," which idealizes minimal governmental intervention in personal liberty and the economy, ever since the introduction of the Bill of Rights in 1789 (Whitman, 2004). We therefore present both types of protection frameworks using the United States and Germany as representative examples.

14.3.1 United States: Customer Privacy Protection Based on Industry Self-Regulation

- **U.S. Constitution:** The U.S. Constitution does not explicitly provide citizens a right to privacy, though a limited constitutional right of privacy has been established, according to several provisions in the Bill of Rights.
- **Robinson list:** The U.S. government has established a Do-Not-Call registry for people to register to avoid receiving telemarketing calls. Registration is free, and telephone numbers placed on the registry will remain there permanently, according to the Do-Not-Call Improvement Act of 2007 (National Do Not Call Registry, 2011). Similar approaches also

exist for Germany, such as the Robinson list of the German Direct Marketing Association, though they are not government regulated.
- **FTC:** The main agency protecting U.S. customer privacy also handles violations of the Federal Privacy Act of 1974. The Federal Trade Commission (FTC) also has outlined the Fair Information Practices Principles, a series of reports, guidelines, and model codes that represent widely accepted principles concerning fair information practices (FTC, 2000):

Notice and Awareness
Customers should receive notice of an entity's information practices before being requested to provide any personal information. Without notice, a customer cannot make an informed decision about whether and to what extent to disclose personal information. Moreover, three other principles—choice and consent, access and participation, and enforcement and redress—are meaningful only when a customer has notice of an entity's policies and his or her rights thereto.

Choice and Consent
Choice means giving customers options as to how any personal information collected from them will be used. Specifically, choice relates to secondary uses of information, or those beyond the uses necessary to complete the contemplated transaction. Such secondary uses can be internal, such as placing the customer on the company's mailing list to market additional products or promotions, or external, which implies the transfer of the information to third parties.

Access
Customers have the right to view their personal data and to contest that data's accuracy and completeness. The access process must be timely and relatively inexpensive, and incorrect information should easy to contest, verify, or amend.

Integrity and Security
To ensure data integrity, collectors must take reasonable steps, such as using only reputable sources of data and cross-referencing data

against multiple sources, providing customer access to data, and destroying untimely data or converting it to anonymous forms. Security involves both managerial and technical measures to protect against loss and the unauthorized access, destruction, use, or disclosure of the data.

Enforcement and Redress
Without an enforcement and redress mechanism, even a fair information practice code is merely suggestive; it cannot ensure compliance with core fair information principles. Alternative enforcement approaches include industry self-regulation, legislation that creates private remedies for customers, and/or regulatory schemes enforceable through civil and criminal sanctions. Table I.1 in the Appendix gives an overview of recent FTC settlements related to violations of the fair information practice principles.

Furthermore, the FTC has published a report to protect customer privacy in the online environment. Titled "Protecting Consumer Privacy in an Era of Rapid Change: A Proposed Framework for Businesses and Policymakers," this report includes the FTC's recommendation for the "Do Not Track" mechanism that customers can use to opt out of the collection of information about their Internet activity for the development of targeted advertisements, recognizing: "Industry must do better. For every business, privacy should be a basic consideration—similar to keeping track of costs and revenues, or strategic planning" (FTC, 2010). Although the FTC has been successful enforcing its privacy guidelines in many court cases, it seems not yet to have managed to set a legal precedent to simplify legal enforcement. But analysts predict that a settlement, like the one introduced in the Google Buzz case, which we present in Sect. 14.3.3, could be decisive for inducing change in U.S. privacy practices and strengthening the FTC's position (Gartner, 2011). Thus, the overall extent to which U.S. customers' privacy is protected, in comparison with EU consumers, remains very limited. A lack of governmental legislation and associated privacy concerns push customers to attempt to regain control over their privacy, such as by fabricating false personal information or even refusing to purchase (Wirtz et al., 2007).

This development could be fueled further by media publicity; the U.S. government already is dedicating more attention to the topic of customer privacy and is likely to increase governmental regulation of customer privacy. But whether additional privacy protection laws will reduce customer privacy concerns ultimately depends to a large degree on their enforcement.

14.3.2 Germany: Customer Privacy Protection Based on Governmental Legislation

The German Constitution
Article ten of the Basic Law (as the German Constitution is known) states: "(1) Privacy letters, posts, and telecommunication shall be inviolable. (2) Restrictions may only be ordered pursuant to a statute. Where a restriction serves to protect the free democratic basic order or the existence or security of the Federation, the statute may stipulate that the person affected shall not be informed of such restriction and that recourse to the courts shall be replaced by a review of the case by bodies and auxiliary bodies appointed by Parliament."

Data Protection Law
Germany has one of the strictest data protection laws in the EU. The general purpose of this act is to protect individual rights to avoid impaired privacy. The act covers the collection, processing, and use of personal data by public federal authorities and state administrations and by private bodies that rely on data processing systems or non-automated filing systems for commercial or professional use. Most federal statutes with any impact on personal information or privacy contain references to the Federal Data Protection Act, if they do not carry special sections on the handling of personal data themselves.

The German Teleservices Data Privacy Act
This Act protects customer privacy online and requires explicit user consent before the usage logs of a session may be stored beyond its duration, usage profiles of different services combined, or user profiles constructed in a non-

Table 14.1 Customer privacy protections in the U.S. and Germany

	U.S.	Germany
Cold calling	Allowed (if not on Robinson List)	Forbidden
Contacting prospective clients or customers with unexpected telephone calls		
Unsolicited commercial e-mails	Forbidden	Forbidden
Commercial electronic messages, typically sent out in bulk without any prior request or consent given by the consumer		
Cross-country data transfer (U.S. to Germany and vice versa)	Allowed	Only allowed with Safe Harbor compliance
Transfer of customer-related data to a different country than where it has been collected, such as when consumers make online purchases from sellers located in a different country		
Data transfer to third parties (without consent)	Allowed	Forbidden
Provision of personal data to other companies, such as marketing service providers, without notifying the customer		
Right to opt-out from data collection	Not given	Given
Upon providing their personal information, customers are able to deny any further use of their data		

pseudonymous manner. Websites may not decline service if customers decline to grant approval but instead must abandon these methods or use other legitimate methods in these situations.

Section 7 of the German Unfair Competition Act

Direct marketing issues are addressed by Section 7 of the German Unfair Competition Act. According to its general clause, it is unfair to annoy market players (customers) inappropriately. By default, this rule applies to unwanted advertisements, unsolicited commercial phone calls, marketing methods that use automated calling machines, fax machines or e-mail (spam) received without prior consent, and any direct marketing that cannot be linked to the senders' identity.

Direct marketing via e-mail is not prohibited as spam if

- The organization has received the e-mail address in the context of selling goods or services to the customer.
- The organization uses the e-mail contact for marketing very similar products and services.
- The customer has not opposed the use of e-mail for further direct marketing.
- At the time of the collection and each usage, the company clearly sets out the right to opt-out from direct marketing via e-mail.

- There is no cold calling, which is a violation of the Unfair Competition Law.

As a member of the EU, Germany also has incorporated Article 8 of the European Convention of Human Rights, which protects "the right to respect for private and family life," and the new Charter of Fundamental Rights, which contains articles on both "Respect for Private and Family Life" and "Protection of Personal Data," into its own law (Whitman, 2004). Even despite these comprehensive data protection laws, information privacy remains a vital topic of discussion both for customers and the German government.

Table 14.1 contains an overview of important customer privacy regulation aspects for companies to consider when doing business in the United States or Germany.

14.3.3 Safe Harbor Provision

For multinational companies that operate in, say, the United States and European Union, complying with the requirements of the different privacy protection frameworks in the various markets is especially difficult. As a partial solution, the U.S. Department of Commerce and the European Commission have formulated the "Safe Harbor

Agreement," which prescribes minimum levels of protection for data of European origin. This agreement, approved by the EU in 2000, states that consumers must be notified about the purposes for which the company collects and uses data and given the opportunity to choose whether their data are disclosed to third parties. Companies must protect data from loss, misuse, unauthorized access, disclosure, alteration, or destruction. Furthermore, they must ensure that data are reliable for the intended use, accurate, complete, and current. Individuals have the right to view, correct, amend, or delete their data. To participate in the Safe Harbor Agreement, companies must register with the U.S. Department of Commerce (Zwick & Dholakia, 2001). An up-to-date list of all participants appears at www. export.gov/safeharbor/.

CRM at Work 14.2

Safe Harbor: The Google Buzz Case

Participation in the Safe Harbor Program is voluntarily, but firms must annually self-certify their compliance with the issued requirements to be granted Safe Harbor benefits and be included on the publicly available list of participating organizations. There are seven key principles a company must follow to qualify for the program:

Notice:
Customers must be informed about the purpose of the collection of their data, as well as the usage of the information and how they can contact the organization regarding their data.

Choice:
Customers can choose the disclosure of their data to any third parties.

Onward transfer of data:
If an organization transfers data to a third party, that third party must comply with the Safe Harbor requirements as well.

Access:
Customers should be able to view, amend, or delete their data.

Security:
Organizations must take precautions to protect data from loss or any unauthorized access, disclosure, alteration, and destruction.

Data integrity:
Organizations should ensure that the personal information obtained is relevant for the purpose of its usage, as well as reliable, accurate, complete, and current.

Enforcement:
To ensure adherence to the principles, organizations provide independent recourse mechanisms to deal with complaints, verification procedures to verify the implementation of the commitments, and obligations to solve problems resulting from failure to comply with the framework.

The enforcement of the policies is mainly carried out through private sector self-regulation, but it is also backed up by governmental enforcement activities where needed.

A good case in point is Google Buzz, Google's social-networking service, which violated its customers' privacy several times after its launch in February 2010. In April 2010, privacy commissioners from 10 countries, including Germany, Canada, and the United Kingdom, sent a letter to Google's CEO Eric Schmidt accusing the company of failing "to take adequate account of privacy considerations" when launching Google Buzz. Their approach had no legal consequences and was advisory in nature. In March 2011, the FTC also raised charges against Google, alleging it had violated substantive privacy requirements of the Safe Harbor Framework.

According to the FTC, Google Buzz failed to fulfill the principles of *Choice* and *Notice* by making personal information of their users' public without their consent, for a purpose other than that for which the data were initially collected. The FTC then announced a settlement in April 2011 that required Google to implement a dedicated "privacy by design" program for all future products and services. This program means that Google must obtain opt-in consent for any secondary use of data—a requirement that goes even beyond the required opt-out choice—and undertake biannual, independent privacy audits for the next 20 years. This case of privacy enforcement has set new precedents for any companies dealing with personal data from customers from the Europe and the United States.

Sources: The Economist (2011). Stopped in their Track. March 17, 2011; FTC (2011)

In conclusion, companies must be constantly aware of the different legal requirements they face, in the U.S. or the EU, because staying in compliance with a multitude of privacy laws is tricky business for even the best and most honorable CRM programs. This warning holds true especially for companies operating internationally and for e-retailers that offer their products and services over the Internet. Furthermore, companies must take customer responses to their privacy practices into account, as we discuss in the following section.

14.4 Customer Privacy Protective Responses

Increasing privacy concerns among customers have led to the development of negative attitudes toward CRM practices. The more customers fear that their privacy is endangered, the higher the level of risk they will perceive. Meanwhile, an increase in customers' privacy concerns reduces trust in the company. A high level of risk and a low level of trust in the company together increase customers' intentions to protect their privacy while reducing their willingness to provide any personal information. Furthermore, customers who perceive threats to their privacy respond with defensive actions that may enable

them to regain control over their personal information, such as refusing to purchase.

Many of these responses increase costs for marketers and ultimately reduce the effectiveness of CRM initiatives. Furthermore, this defensive demeanor represents a substantial threat to the development of new forms of information-led marketing. Thus, companies must realize the different ramifications of customer privacy concerns. Our proposed taxonomy of privacy protective responses, in Fig. 14.4, identifies six behavioral responses, classified into three categories: (1) information provision, (2) private action, and (3) public action (Son & Kim, 2008).

Information Provision
If customers are concerned about their information privacy, they sometimes provide falsified personal data (*Misrepresentation*), which threatens the data quality that is so crucial to ensuring efficient CRM (Wirtz et al., 2007). Furthermore, some customers just refuse to give out personal information (*Refusal*). Anonymizer.com, a protective online service, blocks attempts to identify ISP domains, browser settings, surfing histories, and e-mail addresses, thus providing customers with a means to hinder companies from collecting online information. Because CRM relies on customer-provided information as a vital source of data, which then enables accurate relationship-fostering efforts and better targeting of prospective customers, such responses constitute major threats to CRM practices.

Private Action
In addition to information disclosure, concerned customers might take private actions such as boycotts of particular retailers, service providers, or products. For example, online information privacy concerns might lead to information boycotts, such that customers remove their personal information from company databases or online communities (*Removal*).

Online customers also might choose to opt-out and explicitly restrict a website from transferring their data to any third party not directly involved in processing the transaction for which the data were collected.

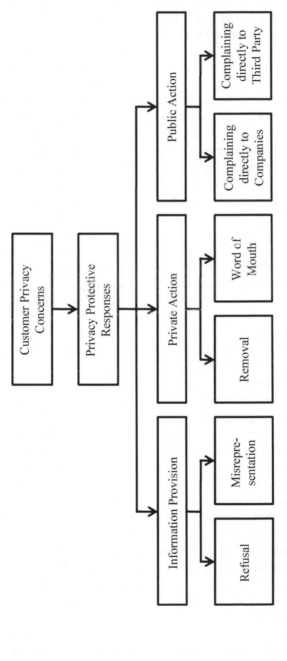

Fig. 14.4 Taxonomy of privacy protective responses (Source: Based on Son and Kim's (2008) taxonomy)

If they perceive a threat to their information privacy, customers often voice negative comments to their friends and relatives (*Negative Word-of-Mouth*). Because a customer's in-group includes like-minded people, companies that are subject to such negative word of mouth lose the chance to recruit new potential customers and bear the potential damage to their reputations.

Public Action

Taking public action is another type of customer response to information privacy concerns: The customer either directly complains to the company (*Complaining Directly to Companies*) or indirectly notifies a third-party organization (*Complaining Indirectly via Third Party*). When customers turn to the company to complain about its handling of their data, the company has the opportunity to respond adequately and even solve the issue, which means it gains a chance to retain customers. If companies do not deal with the complaints adequately though, customers often turn to third-party organizations, such as EPIC and the FTC. In this case, the audience for the complaint is much larger. Unlike private actions, such public actions aim not only to obtain a personal benefit but also to help the general public, because the accused company can no longer violate customers' privacy.

Although customers' privacy protective responses pose a serious constraint on companies' CRM practices, intentions to respond to privacy concerns do not always directly translate into actual behavior—especially when it comes to information disclosure. Many studies have shown that customers often contradict themselves by stating that they would not give out information to a company but then actually do so (KPMG, 2010), the so-called *privacy paradox*.

14.5 Privacy Paradox

The search engine Ask.com learned a valuable lesson when it introduced AskEraser, a feature that promised to let customers turn off tracking of their search history so they could remain anonymous while surfing the Internet. Designed as a response to customers' concerns about the tracking of their online search behavior, AskEraser did not lead to the success that Ask.com had hoped to gain: Its market share remained at only 4.6% of all U.S. searches (compared with Google's nearly 60%), which implied that customers cared little about information privacy. A Pew Internet Study from 2005 also showed that 54% of respondents believed that websites that tracked their behavior invaded their privacy—but 64% of them would offer personal information to access a website. This evidence uniformly points to the privacy paradox, namely, the discrepancy between people's intentions to protect their own privacy and their actual behaviors in the marketplace. This phenomenon also has been observed in research that demonstrates that people claim they are less willing to provide personal information to marketers than they actually provide when a marketer directly requests such information. This gap appears due to the different perceptions of risk and trust that arise in response to intention measures versus actual disclosure settings (Norberg et al., 2007).

Companies must pay close attention to this discrepancy though, especially with respect to their CRM practices. Specifically, CRM managers need a deep understanding of the link between customers' intentions to disclose information and their actual behaviors, to avoid alienating customers and to align their CRM initiatives appropriately and fairly. They especially need to take into account that even if customers give out their personal information, overly intrusive CRM practices can agitate public media, which likely means damage to the company's image. Furthermore, companies should strive to find ways to increase consumers' willingness to share important information voluntarily, such as offering small monetary incentives. Such voluntary sharing of information can enhance the data accuracy and effectiveness of knowledge management systems designed to help organizations interact with customers, as well as maximize the benefits of customer relationships.

14.6   Consequences of Privacy Protective Responses

If customers fear their privacy is being endangered and react with privacy protective responses, several consequences are likely for companies. Especially in the context of CRM practices, companies should be aware of the following potential ramifications (Blattberg, Kim, & Neslin, 2008):

Loss of trust and brand integrity
If breaches of customer privacy become public, customers' privacy concerns increase and lead to a loss of trust in the company. This negative impression can harm a company's brand image and ultimately alter customers' choices and consumption patterns.

Decreased sales
Customer privacy concerns reportedly resulted in estimated losses for e-retailers of $2 billion in 2006 (Gartner, 2006). A recent independent Ponemon Institute research report estimated that a random sample of 90 U.S. companies failed to spend $604.9 million on online behavioral advertising because privacy fears translated into $2.8 billion in unearned sales (Evidon, 2010).

Decrease in data quality
If customers falsify their personal information or refuse to give out any data, data quality becomes threatened and decreases the effectiveness of CRM practices. Limited access to accurate customer data paints a biased picture of the customer and thus decreases the precision of predictive models and targeting initiatives (Wirtz et al., 2007).

Increased costs due to privacy protection
Compliance with stricter privacy rules is estimated to increase the total costs of catalog or online apparel retailers by 3.5–11% (Turner,

2001). This cost applies especially in the United States; the EU privacy protection framework is already very strict.

Ethical dilemma
Collecting data that consumers do not want to be collected places managers in an ethical dilemma. Do they ignore customers' wishes to protect their privacy, and thus increase their chances of economic success, but also run the risk of alienating their most valuable assets?

In summary, privacy concerns pose a real threat to companies practicing CRM. Negligence leads to decreased sales and lower efficiency for their predictive modeling. Moreover, compliance and litigation costs can reduce profitability. Thus companies must carefully balance the benefits of obtaining additional customer information, such as more accurate targeting of their offerings and marketing communications, against the increasing concerns of customer privacy, which can lead to disloyalty and customer churn.

14.7   Implications for Companies

This discussion of customer privacy concerns and their implications reveals that customer privacy is an important topic for companies, to be considered especially in the context of CRM. Consequently, CRM mangers and marketers constantly look for appropriate ways to react to or even prevent customers' privacy concerns. Using a checklist adapted from Harriet Pearson, vice president, security council, and chief privacy officer at IBM, we seek to provide insights into where companies must consider privacy issues, what legal requirements they must take into account, and how they can achieve the successful implementation of responsible privacy protection practices in a CRM context (Pearson, 2007).

Align privacy with strategy
Privacy concerns can translate into negative brand images and harm a company's valuable assets. It is thus especially important for businesses with very valuable brands or that compete

in information-intensive industries (e.g., health care, finance, high-tech) to take the lead when it comes to privacy and data protection.

Look beyond rules to values
Trust perceptions of a company and its CRM practices generally are determined through direct customer–employee contacts. Embedding privacy and security values into corporate cultures thus will yield greater returns than even the most comprehensive set of rules. When values are developed from the bottom up, they tend to be lived, not just recited.

Anticipate issues
It should be someone's job to scan for products or practices, within the business or across the industry, that raise legitimate privacy concerns, and then collaborate with stakeholders to develop reasonable solutions. Firms must be prepared to work across the industry as well as internally. Furthermore, they should think about implementing a third-party certification, such as TRUSTe or the Better Business Bureau, to obtain recognizable privacy seals and thereby signal high privacy standards to customers.

Create accountability
The role of a privacy or security officer is to unite and coordinate efforts across functional silos. All those involved in setting and implementing information policies—the head of human resources, the chief information officer, and the marketing vice president, for example—should participate, but there also must be a single person who is responsible and accountable for privacy efforts.

Do not conflate security and privacy
Getting privacy right in a business context means meeting societal or regulatory expectations for what type of information is collected, how much, with whom it may be shared, how it will be used and protected, and how long it is retained. Resist the temptation to focus solely on data security; firms must be aware of the different legal requirements in different countries in which they operate.

Treat privacy as a social responsibility
In globally connected, information-rich societies, privacy and data protection belong on the corporate citizenship agenda, right alongside the environment, diversity, and other important issues.

Manage your data supply chain
Data handling obligations flow with data that cross corporate or national boundaries. Business ecosystems that include global sources of talent and services need standards for data management that can rationalize an international patchwork of expectations and regulations.

Rely on technology when appropriate
They cannot substitute for leadership, common sense, and good policies, but simple tools (e.g., automated checklists, encryption, audit logs) can do wonders to enable compliance. And emerging capabilities, such as face masking in digital surveillance systems or privacy-preserving data mining, can help resolve conflicts between information use and privacy.

Plan for disaster recovery
No information system is fail-safe. In case of a data loss or breach, a rehearsed response should be in place to address technical, individual, legal, and other needs.

Heed both boomers and millennials
The under-25 crowd is not dismissive of privacy, but it embraces online, collaborative work and play far more than earlier generations. Privacy thinking should span generational norms and expectations. One employee may freely post pictures and personal information online but recoil from having an employer or the government collect a biometric identifier; another may prefer just the opposite.

14.8   Summary

In the present chapter, we discuss the central role of customer privacy concerns in CRM practices. For this purpose, we firstly introduce and define customer privacy in the context of CRM. Thereafter, we identify drivers of customer privacy concerns, both internal and external. Internal drivers hereby advert to company-related operations which evoke customers' fears about the disclosure and handling of their personal information. In this context, the way companies collect personal information *(Collection)*, whether a customer can control the uses made of this information *(Control)*, and the clear understanding of the company's conditions and practices with respect to privacy *(Awareness)* are especially recognizable. In a next step, we identify external drivers which foster customers' privacy concerns, namely Internet, technological advances, public media coverage as well as governmental regulations. We find that the rise of the Web 2.0 and online social networks provides customers with various possibilities to share personal information, thereby opening doors for companies to

collect openly available data about customers. But in this context especially companies' data collection without customers' consent fosters privacy concerns thus posing a risk for efficient CRM practices. Additionally, technological advances, such as RFID technology and location-based services, as well as the coverage of this topic in public media add to customers' increasing fear of losing control over their personal data. Different privacy regulatory frameworks in different countries also affect customers' privacy concerns. Thus in the following, we compare the regulatory frameworks of both the E.U. and the U.S. We find privacy protection in the U.S. to be mainly industry self-regulated. One central role is hereby occupied by the Federal Trade Commission (FTC) which protects customer privacy in the U.S. and handles violations of the Federal Privacy Act. On the other hand, Germany as a member of the E.U. protects

Appendix I (Petlier, Milne, & Phelps, 2009)

Table I.1 Selected settlements in violation of FIP principles

FIP	Company/settlement date	Case
Notice/ awareness	Centurion Financial Benefits (2007)	Consumers were told they were providing information for a $2,000 credit card limit. Instead, they received an application for a scored value/cash card with no line of credit
	Sony BMG (2005)	Sent flawed and overreaching computer program via millions of music CDs that was officially intended to restrict the consumers' use of the music. The program also could report listening habits and installed undisclosed and sometimes hidden files on computers that could expose users to tampering by third parties
	DoubleClick (2002)	Violated state and federal laws by surreptitiously tracking and collecting consumers' personally identifiable data and combining it with information on their web surfing habits
Choice/ consent	Bank of America (2007)	Disclosed consumers' personal, private, and confidential information to third parties without consent
	Gateway Learning Corporation (2004)	Rented personal information, in violation of promises made in its privacy policy statement. After collecting consumers' information, privacy policies were changed to allow sharing of information without prior notice or consent given by customers
	Cartmanager International (2005)	The FTC alleged that CartManager did not adequately inform consumers or merchants that it would collect and rent information and that the company acted knowing that it was contrary to the privacy policies of many merchants

FIP	Company/settlement date	Case
Access	Quicken Loans (2002)	Failed to provide "adverse action" notices in violation of the Fair Credit Reporting Act and failed to comply with the provisions of the Act to notify the consumers when an action was based wholly or partly on their credit report
	Performance Capital Management (2001)	Provided credit bureaus with inaccurate "delinquency dates" for its accounts, resulting in negative information remaining on consumers' credit reports. PCM failed to investigate consumer disputes referred by credit bureaus or notify bureaus when consumers disputed collection accounts
Integrity/ security	Guidance Software (2006)	The FTC charged that failure to take reasonable security measures to protect sensitive customer data contradicted security promises made on the website. This failure allowed hackers to access sensitive credit card information for thousands of consumers
	ChoicePoint Inc. (2006)	Failure to take appropriate security measures to protect sensitive information of tens of millions of customers resulted in fraudulent purchases worth millions of dollars
	Microsoft Corp. (2007)	The FTC alleged that Microsoft did not employ reasonable and appropriate measures to maintain and protect the privacy and confidentiality of consumers' personal information collected through its Passport and Passport Wallet service, including credit card numbers and billing information

customers' privacy by means of different governmental laws and regulations. This has implications for companies such that in Germany it is not allowed to contact customers via telephone (Cold Calling) or email (Unsolicited Emails) without their prior consent. For multinational companies operating in the U.S. and the E.U., it is especially difficult to comply with the requirements of privacy protective frameworks in different markets. For this purpose, the Safe Harbor Provision was introduced which serves as a set of guidelines for the collection and proper handling of customer data. Nevertheless, CRM managers still have to be aware of customers' privacy concerns and the respective protective responses they might face. In this regard, we identify three categories of customers' reactions to privacy concerns, namely the refusal or misrepresentation of information (Information Provision), the removal from the respective company or the spreading of negative word-of-mouth (Private Action) as well as complaining to either the company itself or a third party (Public Action). Although customers' privacy protective responses pose a serious constraint on companies' CRM practices, intentions to respond to privacy concerns do not always directly translate into actual behavior—

especially when it comes to information disclosure. We also discuss this phenomenon, the so-called privacy paradox. In a concluding step, we list potential ramifications for companies of customers' privacy concerns in the context of CRM and give advice on how responsible privacy protection practices can be implemented in a company.

Exercise Questions

1. Please explain the role of public media as a driver of customers' privacy concerns.
2. The U.S. and Germany reflect two different perspectives of customer privacy regulation. Please state and describe both perspectives and explain their historical and cultural origin.
3. Imagine you are the manager of a U.S. company selling apparel over the Internet. What are the main privacy regulations to be kept in mind when selling to a German customer?
4. Please give examples for customers' privacy protective responses and explain the potential consequences for companies.
5. Please explain the phenomenon of the privacy paradox.

Appendix II

European Union
http://ec.europa.eu/justice/policies/privacy/
index_en.htm
www.privacyinternational.org
United States
www.ftc.com
http://www.export.gov/safeharbor/
https://www.donotcall.gov/
Germany
http://www.bfdi.bund.de/EN/Home/homepage_node.html
http://www.robinsonliste.de/
Research/Reports
http://blogs.wsj.com/wtk-mobile/
http://www.digitalcenter.org/

References

Blattberg, R. C., Kim, B. D., & Neslin, S. A. (2008). *Database marketing: Analyzing and managing customers*. New York: Springer.

Bonini, S. M., Greeny, J., & Mendonca, L. T. (2007). *Assessing the impact of societal issues: A McKinsey global survey*. The McKinsey Quarterly (November).

EPIC. (2011). *US Patriot Act*. http://epic.org/privacy/terrorism/usapatriot/#introduction. Accessed September 29, 2011.

Evidon. (2010). *Economic impact of privacy on online behavioral advertising*. http://www.evidon.com/documents/OBA_paper.pdf. Accessed September 29, 2011.

FTC. (2000). *Privacy online: Fair information practices in the electronic marketplace*. http://www.ftc.gov/reports/privacy2000/privacy2000.pdf. Accessed September 29, 2011.

FTC. (2010). *Protecting consumer privacy in an era of rapid change—A proposed framework for businesses and policymakers*. http://www.ftc.gov/os/2010/12/101201privacyreport.pdf. Accessed September 29, 2011.

FTC. (2011). FTC charges deceptive privacy practices in Google's rollout of its buzz social network. http://www.ftc.gov/os/caselist/1023136/110330google-buzzcmpt.pdf. Accessed April 7, 2011.

Garfinkel, S. L., Juels, A., & Pappu, R. (2005). RFID privacy: An overview of problems and proposed solutions. *IEEE Privacy & Security, 3*(3), 34–43.

Gartner. (2006). *Gartner says nearly $2 billion lost in E-commerce sales in 2006 due to security concerns of U.S. adults*. http://www.gartner.com/it/page.jsp?id=498974. Accessed September 29, 2011.

Gartner. (2011). *Google-FTC settlement may have important privacy implications*. http://www.gartner.com/DisplayDocument?id=1620221. Accessed September 29, 2011.

Harris, M. H., Van Hoye, G., & Lievens, F. (2003). Privacy and attitudes towards internet based selection systems: A cross cultural comparison. *International Journal of Selection and Assessment, 11*(2–3), 230–236.

Hildner, L. (2006). Defusing the threat of RFID: Protecting consumer privacy through technology-specific legislation at the state level. *Harvard Civil Rights-Civil Liberties Law Review, 41*(1), 133–176.

Hoffman, D. L., Novak, T. P., & Peralta, M. A. (1999). Building consumer trust in online environments: The case for information privacy. *Communications of the ACM, 42*(4), 80–85.

ITU. (2010). *The world in 2010—ICT facts and figures*. http://www.itu.int/ITU-D/ict/material/FactsFigures2010.pdf. Accessed September 29, 2011.

KLM. (2011). *KLM surprise*. http://surprise.klm.com/. Accessed September 29, 2011.

Kluth, A. (2008). The perils of sharing. *The Economist* (November 19, 2008).

KPMG. (2010). *Consumers & convergence IV*. http://www.kpmg.com/Global/en/IssuesAndInsights/ArticlesPublications/consumers-and-convergence/Documents/Consumers-Convergence-IV-july-2010.pdf. Accessed September 29, 2011.

Malhotra, N. K., Kim, S. S., & Agarwal, J. (2004). Internet Users' information privacy concerns (IUIPC): The construct, the scale, and a causal model. *Information Systems Research, 15*(4), 336–355.

Microsoft. (2000). *Bill Gates opens SafeNet 2000 summit*. http://www.microsoft.com/Presspass/press/2000/dec00/safenetpr.mspx. Accessed September 29, 2011.

Miller, C. C., & Wortham, J. (2010). *Technology aside, most people still decline to be located*. The New York Times (August 29, 2010).

National Do Not Call Registry. (2011). www.donotcall.gov. Accessed September 29, 2011.

Norberg, P. A., Horne, D. R., & Horne, D. A. (2007). The privacy paradox: Personal information disclosure intentions versus behaviors. *Journal of Consumer Affairs, 41*(1), 100–126.

Pearson, H. (2007). Privacy checklist for business. *Harvard Business Review, 86*(10), 123–130.

Peltier, J. W., Milne, G. R., & Phelps, J. E. (2009). Information privacy research: Framework for integrating multiple publics, information channels, and responses. *Journal of Interactive Marketing, 23*(2), 191–205.

Pfanner, E. (2010). E.U. says it will overhaul privacy regulations. *The New York Times* (November 4, 2010).

Privacy International. (2011). *European privacy and human rights*. https://www.privacyinternational.org/ephr. Accessed September 29, 2011.

Roznowski, J. L. (2003). A content analysis of mass media stories surrounding the consumer privacy issue 1990–2001. *Journal of Interactive Marketing, 17*(2), 52–69.

Rust, R. T., Kannan, P. K., & Peng, N. (2002). The customer economics of internet privacy. *Journal of the Academy of Marketing Science, 30*(4), 455–464.

Son, J. Y., & Kim, S. S. (2008). Internet Users' information privacy-protective responses: A taxonomy and nomological model. *MIS Quarterly, 32*(3), 503–529.

Sorkin, A. R., & Craig, S. (2011). Goldman unit passed on earlier facebook investment. *The New York Times* (January 6, 2011).

Stone, E. F., Gueutal, H. G., Gardner, D. G., & McClure, S. (1983). A field experiment comparing information-privacy values, beliefs, and attitudes across several types of organizations. *Journal of Applied Psychology, 68*(3), 459–468.

The Economist. (2007). Information overlord–The public wakes up to the surveillance society. *The Economist* (January 18, 2007).

The Economist. (2008). The science of shopping–The way the brain buys. *The Economist* (December 18, 2008).

The Economist. (2010). Location-based services on mobile phones—Follow me. *The Economist* (March 4, 2010).

The Economist. (2011). Anonymous no more. *The Economist* (March 10, 2011).

Turner, M. A. (2001). *The impact of data restrictions on consumer distance shopping.* White paper, Direct Marketing Association.

Turow, J, King, J, Hoofnagle, C. J., Bleakley, A., & Hennessy, M. (2009). *Americans reject tailored advertising and three activities that enable it.* Working paper, UC Berkeley.

Whitman, J. Q. (2004). The Two western cultures of privacy: Dignity versus liberty. *Yale Law Journal, 113*(6), 1151–1221.

Wirtz, J., & Lwin, M. O. (2009). Regulatory focus theory, trust, and privacy concerns. *Journal of Service Research, 12*(2), 190–207.

Wirtz, J., Lwin, M. O., & Williams, J. D. (2007). Causes and consequences of consumer online privacy concern. *International Journal of Service Industry Management, 18*(4), 326–348.

Zwick, D., & Dholakia, N. (2001). Contrasting European and American approaches to privacy in electronic markets: Property right versus civil right. *Electronic Markets, 11*(2), 116–120.

Part V

Advances in CRM Applications

Applications of CRM in B2B and B2C Scenarios (Part I)

15

15.1 Overview

Delta Airlines had long been operating a customer loyalty program that computed the accumulated frequent-flier reward points solely on the basis of the total number of miles flown by a customer (Kumar & Ramani, 2003). The loyalty program did not differentiate between those customers who pay economy class fares and those who pay business class fares, to fly the same distance. From a profitability viewpoint, this program was misaligned. Delta Airlines' loyalty program was clearly not based on the customer's value to the firm. No wonder, then, this program was recently replaced with one that differentiated between customers paying for different fare classes. Now, a customer flying business class gets 50% more points than does a customer traveling economy class. This new approach recognizes customers who are more profitable to the firm need to be rewarded more.

General Motors revised the redemption scheme on its 10-year-old GM card in 2002. The maximum amount of earnings a customer can redeem toward the purchase or lease of a new GM car, truck, or SUV now depends on the year, make, and model chosen. This move is similar to the one adopted by Delta, in that a customer who spends on a premium product is rewarded more than a customer who purchases a low-end product.

There seems to be two complementary reasons why firms are becoming unabashedly profit-oriented in their approach toward customer rewards programs. First, firms are in a better position, thanks to technology, to record customer actions and ascertain their individual profitability levels. Thus, firms no longer use surrogate measures like unit volume of business, share of wallet, and duration of association to reward their customers. Let us examine the share of wallet measure some firms use to decide on customer-level investments. Share of wallet (SOW) is defined as the ratio of the total customer spending with the firm to the total category spending (the firm plus its competitors) for that customer. It is clear that achieving a large SOW a low-spending client may not be as good as achieving a low SW of a high-spending client. Thus, firms do not need to continue using surrogate measures because the drawbacks inherent in these measures can now be overcome by concentrating directly on individual customer profitability. Second, customers realize they can no longer expect a firm to believe they are special if they are not genuine high-value buyers. Differential treatment of customers is therefore being accepted as a way of life by both firms and customers. However, differential treatment can work for a firm in the long run, only if it has an eye on the future. The challenge for a firm today is to develop an optimal blend of differential

15

levels of treatments such that over every customer's lifetime, the profits earned by the firm are maximized. Not every firm understands how to develop a strategy which balances customer relations and profitability.

The level of sophistication of the adoption of the customer value metric approach into a firm's marketing program could vary. A firm operating a loyalty program can start using the customer value metric to examine whether the customers being rewarded are indeed the profitable ones. It should take corrective action if it finds that such is not the case. At the next level, a firm can begin to observe when its customers are beginning to turn unprofitable. The firm can decide to let go of these customers without wasting further efforts on them. Moving up another level, a firm could determine the factors likely to affect how long a customer is likely to stay profitable. This enables the firm to control and manage the variables necessary to increase a customer's profitability. At the next level, a firm can plan investments in marketing initiatives on the basis of an analysis of expected profits from its customers during a given planning period. A firm can achieve the next level of sophistication by understanding the impact of changing the frequency of its marketing communication elements on the profitability of each customer. In this manner it can allocate its resources optimally across marketing initiatives, by cutting down on wasteful efforts and increasing the frequency of effective efforts, one customer at a time. At the next level, a firm can predict the timing of purchase of each of the products in its portfolio and tailor the communication message around the product likely to be next purchased by a customer. Mathematical models necessary to carry these levels of analyses and predictions have been developed in the CRM literature (Venkatesan & Kumar, 2004a).

15.2   Measuring Customer Profitability

Successful marketing initiatives are contingent upon the firm having a good understanding of how their actions affect customers. This becomes difficult for firms since their customer base is dynamic and involves interplay of several marketing variables such as tenure of the customers with the firm, profitability of the customers, purchase behavior over time, adoption of multiple channels to purchase, and demographic factors governing purchase behavior, among others. With so many inputs making up individual customer profiles how can firms expect to offer effective marking initiatives to attract the largest number of desirable customers?

Management has access to a tool, which takes into account all of these inputs and allows segmentation based on future profitability. The metric is known as Customer Lifetime Value (CLV). By using CLV as the primary planning tool for marketing initiatives, firms can ensure that they only target those customers who have the most future value to the company. From this they can optimize scarce marketing resources and ensure the future profitability of the firm.

Customer Lifetime Value is defined as follows:

> The sum of cumulated future cash flows – discounted using the weighted average cost of capital (WACC) – of a customer over their entire lifetime with the company. Kumar (2008, 2007)

In other words, CLV is a multi-period evaluation of a customer's value to the firm, and it assists managers to allocate resources optimally and develop customer-level marketing strategies.

15.2.1   Computing CLV

To compute CLV, it is essential to consider the setting in which the customer's purchases are being made i.e., contractual and non-contractual. A contractual setting is one where the customers are bounded by a contract such as a cable TV subscription. On the contrary, in a non-contractual setting such as grocery store purchases the customers are not bounded by a contract. The business implication of these two situations is that in a contractual setting, the firm gets *stream revenue* or fixed monthly revenue through the subscription. But, in a non-contractual setting, the stream revenue would be absent. Therefore, these differences will have to be included while computing CLV. To cover both the situations, CLV can be expressed in the following form:

$$CLV_i = \sum_{t=1}^{T} \underbrace{\frac{Base\,GC}{(1+d)^t}}_{\text{Baseline}} + \underbrace{\sum_{t=1}^{T} \frac{\hat{p}(Buy_{it}=1)*\hat{GC}_{it}}{(1+d)^t} - \frac{\hat{MC}_{it}}{(1+d)^t}}_{\text{Augmented CLV}}$$

(15.1)

where, CLV_i = lifetime value for customer i
$\hat{p}(Buy_{it})$ = predicted probability that customer i will purchase additional product(s)/service(s) in time period t
$\hat{GC}_{it}$ = predicted gross contribution margin provided by customer i in time period t
$\hat{MC}_{it}$ = predicted marketing costs directed toward customer i in time period t
t = index for time periods; such as months, quarters, years, etc.
T = marks the end of the calibration or observation time framed = monthly discount factor
Base GC = predicted base monthly gross contribution margin

As is evident from (15.1), this formula can be applied in both the contractual and non-contractual settings. The baseline CLV represents the net present value of the future stream revenue from the customer. The augmented CLV represents the net present value of future cash flows from a customer based on the products/services purchased. In the case of a contractual business setting, the CLV would be the sum of the baseline CLV and the augmented CLV, since the customers will be contributing revenue to the firm by way of their monthly subscription. In the case of a non-contractual setting, the CLV would only be the augmented CLV, since the customer is not contractually obligated to contribute any monthly revenue to the firm. Now, let us look an example that can help us compute CLV in each setting.

Consider the case of Amy, a customer of a mobile phone company. The monthly subscrip-

tion or the base GC provided by Amy is $40. At the end of May, the company wants to know the value Amy is likely to provide to the company in the next 4 months (June, July, August, and Sep-tember). Table 15.1 provides Amy's probability of buying additional services or $\hat{p}(Buy)$ (such as downloads, ringtones, text messaging, etc.) for the next 4 months, her monthly purchase amount, the percentage of margin for each purchase, and the marketing cost incurred by the company in contacting Amy.

Assuming an annual discount rate (r) of 12% (or 1% monthly rate), we can now compute the CLV of Amy for the next 4 months. First, let us compute the CLV of Amy at the end of July using (15.1).

Amy's lifetime value at the end of June

$$= \frac{40}{(1.01)^1} + \frac{(0.55)^*(20^*20\%)}{(1.01)^1} - \frac{5}{(1.01)^1}$$

Therefore, $CLV_{Amy,\,June}$ = $36.9
Similarly, we can compute the value Amy would give to the company at the end of each subsequent month as follows—July: $33.2, August: $32.8, and September: $29.6. A summation of all the 4 months' CLV would yield a value of $132.5. In other words, over the next 4 months Amy would provide $132.5 in value to the company through her subscription and additional purchases.

Table 15.1 can also be used to explain the case of non-contractual purchases. Assume that Table 1 indicates Amy's monthly cappuccino purchases from her nearby café. However, this case will not have the monthly subscription or baseline CLV. Now, let us compute Amy's CLV at the end of July using (15.1).

Table 15.1 Transaction details of Amy

	June	July	August	September
$\hat{p}(Buy)$	0.55	0.50	0.40	0.20
Monthly purchase ($)	20	10	10	15
Profit margin (%)	20	20	20	20
Marketing cost ($)	5	7	7	10

Amy's lifetime value at the end of July

$$= \frac{(0.55)^*(20^*20\%)}{(1.01)^1} - \frac{5}{(1.01)^1}$$

Therefore, $CLV_{Amy, June} = -\$2.7$

In other words, Amy will be costing the café $2.7 in June by receiving marketing communication from the café and by being a part of their customer base. Similarly, we can compute the value Amy would give to the café at the end of each subsequent month as follows—July: −$6.0, August: −$6.0, and September: −$9.0. A summation of all the 4 months' CLV would yield a value of −$23.7. That is, over the next 4 months Amy would cost the café $23.7 in value by being its customer. In other words, the amount spent by the café on marketing to Amy will be more than the revenue contributed by her to the café.

Now that we have learnt the concept of CLV and how to calculate it, we need to clearly understand the factors that drive a profitable relationship with the customer and how they affect CLV. The identification of drivers benefit the firm in (a) providing a better understanding of a profitable customer relationship, and (b) helping managers take proactive measures to maximize a customer's lifetime value.

15.2.2 Drivers of CLV

In order to successfully implement a marketing initiative based on CLV, management must understand the drivers of CLV and know how to measure those drivers. The drivers can be broadly classified into the following categories:

Exchange characteristics: Broadly, exchange characteristics are those variables which affect the customer firm-relationship. Table 15.2 pro-

vides an explanation of the exchange characteristics and its impact on B2B and B2C companies by recent studies.

Customer characteristics: These characteristics refer to the demographic variables such as location of the customer, age, income levels, among others. In a B2B setting, these characteristics include variables such as industry, annual revenue and location of the business. In a B2C setting, these characteristics include variables such as age, gender, spatial income and physical location of the customers.

A clear understanding of the drivers listed above is essential for building and managing profitable customer loyalty. Even as CLV is widely gaining acceptance as a metric to acquire, grow, and retain the right customers, managers often face the challenge of achieving convergence between marketing actions (e.g., contacts across various channels) and CRM. Once the computation of CLV is completed, firms can look forward to maximizing it so as to reap the full benefits of the metric. The rest of this chapter discusses the various strategies that firms can use to maximize customer lifetime value.

The following sections in this chapter discuss several strategies based on empirical studies that demonstrate the importance of the Customer Value Metric in evaluating and monitoring a firm's profitability.

15.3 The Lifetime-Profitability Relationship in a Noncontractual Setting

15.3.1 Background and Objective

A basic tenet of relationship marketing is that firms benefit more from maintaining long-term customer relationships as compared to short-term customer relationships (Reinartz & Kumar, 2000). Convincing conceptual evidence for this argument has been advanced by a number of authors (Sheth & Parvatiyar, 1995). Also, it has been shown that the relationship-marketing payoff to the firm comes only when relationships endure (Bendapudi & Berry, 1997). In a widely quoted HBR article, Reichheld and Sasser state,

Table 15.2 Exchange characteristics and its impact on B2B and B2C firms

Exchange characteristics	What do they mean?	Impact on CLV in a B2B setting (Kumar, Venkatesan, Bohling, & Beckmann, 2008; Venkatesan & Kumar, 2004a, b)	Impact on CLV in a B2C setting (Kumar, Shah & Venkatesan, 2006; Reinartz & Kumar, 2003)
Spending level	Monthly spending level in a given period of time	A high spending level of a customer resulted in a high CLV	When average spending level increased by $10, the likelihood of customer churn decreased by 33%
Cross-buying behavior	Degree to which customers buy products/services from a large number of available categories	A high level of cross-buying behavior resulted in a high CLV	A 15% increase in cross-buying resulted in a 20% increase in CLV
Multi-channel shopping	Degree to which customer shop across multiple channels	NA	A 15% increase in shopping across multiple channels resulted in a 18% increase in CLV
Focused buying	Level of purchases made by a customer within a single category	A heavy instance of customer purchases from within a single category resulted in a lower CLV	A 15% increase in spending in a specific product category resulted in a 14% increase in CLV
Average inter-purchase time	Average number of days between two purchases	Too short or too long inter-purchase time resulted in a lower CLV	CLV tends to be smaller when the inter-purchase time is either too short or too long
Product returns	Number of products the customer returns between two purchase periods	Too few or too many product returns resulted in a lower CLV	Too many or too few returns indicate a low CLV. Moderate amount of returns indicate a high CLV
Relationship benefits	Indicates whether a B2B customer is a premium service member (based on revenue contribution in the previous year)	A premium service member status resulted in a higher CLV	NA
Loyalty instrument	Indicates the status of the B2C customer with the firm	NA	Usage of a loyalty instrument increases the CLV
Frequency of marketing contacts	Number of times a customer is contacted through the various communication channels between two purchase periods	Too few or too many marketing contacts resulted in a lower CLV	Too few or too many marketing contacts have a negative impact on CLV. Moderate level of contacts increases CLV
Bi-directional communication	Ratio of the number of customer-initiated contacts to the total number of customer- and firm-initiated contacts made	Greater the bi-directional communication, greater is the CLV	NA

"Customer defections have a surprisingly powerful impact on the bottom line. As a customer's relationship with the company lengthens, profits rise (Reichheld & Sasser, 1990)."

While anecdotal evidence on the lifetime-profitability relationship seems to be plentiful, Reichheld and Teal's 1996 study seems to be the only well-documented empirical evidence to substantiate the hypothesized positive lifetime-profitability relationship (Reichheld & Teal,

1996). Contrary to the anecdotal evidence that long-life customers are most profitable to the firm, Dowling and Uncles caution, "In short, the contention that loyal customers are always more profitable is a gross oversimplification (Dowling & Uncles, 1997)."

In particular, this study questions the existing contentions that the costs of serving loyal customers are presumably lower, that loyal customers presumably pay higher prices, and that loyal customers presumably spend more with the firm than nonloyal customers. Obviously, the study shows concern with the widespread assumption of a clear-cut positive lifetime-profitability relationship and underlines the importance of a differentiated analysis. Consequently, there seems to be a need for more rigorous empirical evidence on the lifetime-profitability relationship.

Lifetime analyses have typically been conducted in contractual settings (Bolton, 1998; Li, 1995). Examples for this type of relationships are magazine subscriptions, cable service subscriptions, and cellular phone services. In contractual settings, expected revenues can be forecasted fairly accurately and, given a constant usage of the service, one would expect increasing cumulative profits over the customer's lifetime. However, in *noncontractual* settings, the firm must ensure the relationship stays alive because the customer typically splits his category expenses with several firms (Dwyer, 1997). Examples of *noncontractual* settings are department-store purchases or mail-order purchases in the catalog and direct marketing industry.

Catalog marketing involves selling through catalogs mailed to a select list of customers. Consumers can buy almost anything from a catalog. More than 20 billion consumer catalogs are mailed out annually, and the average household receives nearly 200 catalogs a year (Valentino-Devries, 2011). In 2008, U.S. sales revenue attributable to direct marketing was estimated to surpass $2.158 trillion (Direct Marketing Association, 2007). In 2009, direct marketing accounted for 8.3% of total US gross domestic product. Also in 2009, there were 1.4 million direct marketing employees in the US. Their collective sales efforts directly supported 8.4 million other jobs, accounting for a total of 9.9 million US jobs (Direct Marketing Association).

In a noncontractual setting such as the catalog industry, specifically, a customer who starts to purchase in a given time period may then buy repeatedly at some irregular time intervals. If the time intervals are relatively longer, is it wise for the firm to assume this customer is likely to purchase again in the near future, and, if so, to expect him to spend a certain amount of dollars?

This is a necessary element for estimating customer lifetime value. Although duration seems like a simple concept, it can be complicated. The customer portfolios of many companies are composed of a small number of active customers—people who have regular and frequent interactions with the provider—and a large number of inactive customers. Drawing the line is not easy, as inactive customers can become active customers in the future.

In many cases, the actual duration of the relationship is not especially revealing due to normal fluctuations in customer activity over time. For example, direct mail publishers may learn more from the seasonal and life-stage variations in customer buying patterns than from the specific number of years the customer has been in the database. What appears on the surface to be dormancy actually may be a naturally occurring pattern which will trigger purchasing when the next cycle comes around. Different customer segments may exhibit different patterns of attrition, switching, and reactivation (Wyner, 1999). The firm dealing with limited/finite resources must decide when it is appropriate to make contact (through mailing of catalogs or other means) with the customer or stop contacting the customers. Given the cost implications, is it worthwhile to chase the dollars from some customers with longer lifetime duration?

The research takes place in the context of the catalog and direct marketing industry. Given the contradictory statements and sparse empirical evidence available in the literature the main objective of this study is a rigorous and differentiated empirical analysis of the lifetime-profitability relationship in a *noncontractual* context. In order to achieve this objective, we test for the following:

- The strength of the lifetime duration-profitability relationship
- Whether profits increase over time (lifetime profitability pattern)
- Whether the costs of serving long-life customers are actually less
- Whether long-life customers pay higher prices

Once we understand what happens in the marketplace, then we can address *why* it happens that

Fig. 15.1 Lifetime-
profitability association

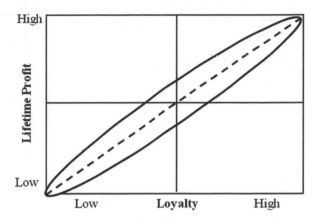

way. As data become available across different situations, empirical generalizations can be advanced. This is important, especially in the noncontractual setting, as the level of uncertainty for a firm is very high. An additional objective is to derive marketing implications from the findings. That is, if distinct lifetime and profitability segments can be delineated, what implications can be derived for a customer management strategy (i.e., tailored communication, early warning indicators, and so on)?

15.3.2 Conceptual Model

Individual customer lifetime profits are modeled as a function of a customer's lifetime duration. Revenue flows over the course of a customer's lifetime, and firm cost is associated with the marketing exchange. We want to investigate the consequences of customer retention namely, profitability.

Customer Lifetime and Firm Profitability

We offer the following four propositions and subsequently test each one of the propositions in anon-contractual scenario.

Proposition 1: The Nature of the Lifetime-Profitability Relationship Is Positive
Ongoing relationships in consumer markets have received substantial attention in recent years (Berry, 1995). The building of strong customer relationships has been suggested as a means for gaining competitive advantage (Reinartz &

Kumar, 2002). The underlying assumption of much of the existing research is that long-term relationships are desirable because they are more profitable for the firm, as compared to short-term relationships. Following this line of reasoning, we would expect a substantial positive association between the duration of a customer-firm relationship and the firm profits derived thereof. (At this point, we are concerned with the sign and strength of the relationship—a one-shot, ex post assessment. In addition, in P_2 we examine the dynamics of the relationship over time) This is true for a contractual case; where there is no repeated cost to entice customers into buying. Figure 15.1 summarizes this situation. In line with the argument, one would expect the majority of relationship outcomes to fall along the diagonal, as shown in Fig. 15.1. In other words, one would expect a substantial positive correlation between the two variables. Thus, an assessment of the numbers of customers falling into each quadrant, along with a simple measure of association between lifetime profits and lifetime duration, would readily yield some insight into the nature of the lifetime-profitability relationship.

A factor that complicates the firm's objective of establishing long-term relationships with its customers is that of intrinsic ability to retain customers. Not all customers want to engage in a long-term relationship with the firm for many possible reasons. For example, in the long-distance telephone service market, many 10-10-xxx companies have emerged. There is no need to sign any contract with the service providers.

Fig. 15.2 Segmentation scheme

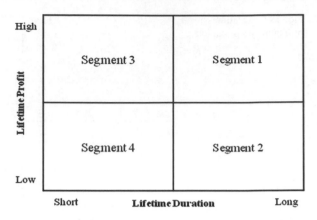

Here, customers use a particular 10-10-xxx company, depending on the quality of service, unit price, and the speed of connection. As discussed before, to retain customers, it is important to satisfy the customers. The satisfaction of customers may come at a significant cost to the company. In a noncontractual case like catalog shopping, a household might have to be sent many catalogs over a period of time before they decide to buy again. Thus, when the costs of satisfying customers exceed the profit margin offered by the customer, the expected positive lifetime profitability relationship need not hold good. Also, some customers may be buying less from a catalog company due to competitive offerings, need for limited spending, or other reasons over a period of time. This forces companies in a noncontractual scenario to look at the spending levels of each of their customers.

Firms should partition their customer base into behaviorally and attitudinally homogenous groups that spend at different levels (see Fig. 15.2) and then estimate the profitability characteristics for each group. This grouping is considered appropriate by many managers in the direct marketing industry as they focus on the revenue generated by each customer over a period of time. Thus, the two dimensions—lifetime duration and revenues—may help managers to make better decisions. Irrespective of the segmentation scheme, conventional wisdom argues for a positive relationship between profitability and time. Although the available evidence suggests a positive lifetime-profitability relationship, it need not be true if the cost of serving the customer is greater than the profit margin

generated by the customer. In fact, there could be many customers who may be receiving catalogs on a regular basis because they bought at least one item in the recent past, even though it may be of lower dollar value.

Proposition 2: Profits Increase over Time. Although a measure of correlation is important and insightful; it presents only a static picture of the lifetime-profitability relationship. While related to proposition 1, the analysis of the *dynamic* aspects of the lifetime profitability relationship yields further important insights. The important difference is that we analyze profits dynamically across time, whereas in proposition 1 we analyze profits in a single lifetime measure across subjects. Recall that we mentioned finding evidence for *increasing* profits per time unit over the length of the customer's tenure. These arguments elm be true for a contractual setting but need not hold good for a noncontractual scenario. In the case of catalog shopping or direct mail offerings, the customer may end up buying once a year and spending a small amount. If this pattern prevails, then the cost of serving this customer can easily exceed the profit margin brought in by the customer. Therefore, profits may not increase over time.

Using the same long distance telephone service example discussed under Proposition 1, there are several instances where the overhead costs of serving long-life customers are higher as compared to the percentage of profit margin offered by the customer. It is necessary for a firm offering the 10-10-xxx service to send monthly bills to all the customers who have started to use their service. Even if a customer does not use the service in a given month, that customer receives a bill. Here, the cost of serving the customer clearly exceeds the profit margin from the customer, and this loss becomes significant for the firm over a period of time and across many such customers. This type of phenomenon occurs in the credit card industry also. Thus, it is not obvious that profit for the firm increases overtime. Therefore, it is worthwhile to test this relationship.

Proposition 3: The Costs of Serving Longer-life Customers are Lower

Another commonly held contention is that long-life customers are less costly to serve than short-life customers. This is possibly true for contractual setting. But, for the broad retail sector, we would hardly expect lower transaction costs for longer-life versus shorter-life customers. For example, there is little reason to believe that transaction costs for a piece of garment in the second purchase encounter with a firm is different from, say, the tenth purchase encounter.

Other costs incurred over the course of a relationship are the costs of the promotional mix directed at each customer. In a noncontractual scenario such as the direct marketing context, promotional costs are typically the largest non-product cost factor in a customer-firm relationship. Following the commonly held contention, we would expect the cost of promotional expenditures per dollar sales revenue is lower for longer-life customers. The reason would be that the promotional mix has a greater efficiency in relation to the longer-life customer. This is possibly due to cumulative effects or a more favorable attitude toward the firm's communication. Thus, we propose that the cost of promoting to a customer) in relation to her revenues) is lower for long-life customers, yet, to our knowledge, there is no empirical evidence in the literature to substantiate this claim. Therefore, it will be interesting to test whether the costs associated with promotional expenditures directed at longer-and shorter-life customers actually differ.

Proposition 4: Longer-life Customers Pay Higher Prices

Previous research (Reichheld & Teal, 1996) has argued that in most industries, existing customers pay effectively higher prices than new ones, even after accounting for possible introductory offers. This would imply that the average price paid by customers and the customer lifetime duration could be positively related.

However, company managers told us that their informal experience suggests a higher value consciousness (i.e., lower average prices paid) for long-term customers. That is, if a customer buys more product units for a given dollar amount, the customer exhibits a higher degree of value consciousness (i.e., wants more "bang for the buck"). If this observation were true, it would contradict the existing evidence. A possible reason for higher value consciousness of long-term customers might be that customers learn over time to trust lower-priced items or brands rather than established name brand products.

Thus, there seems to exist some reasonable evidence for both possibilities. Therefore, instead of proposing a directional effect, we suggest to test this proposition empirically.

15.3.3 Research Methodology

Data

Data from an established U.S. catalog retailer were used for the empirical estimation in this study. The items sold by the firm cover a broad spectrum of general merchandise. The firm's products are offered and can be purchased all year round. The data for this study cover a 3-year window and are recorded on a daily basis. Two key characteristics of this data set are that the customers are tracked from their very first purchase with the firm, and these households have not previously been customers of the company. Consequently, the observations are not left-censored.

A Model for Measuring Customer Lifetime for Noncontractual Relationships

A critical component in our model is customer lifetime duration. The modeling process of a customer's lifetime is contingent on a valid measurement framework that adequately describes the process of *birth, purchase activity,* and *defection*. Toward that end, we empirically implement and extend a procedure previously suggested (Schmittlein & Peterson, 1994). Once the lifetime duration is computed for each customer, we can develop testable propositions dealing with lifetime duration based on conventional wisdom and past literature.

We are using the *negative binomial distribution* (NBD)/Pareto model, which has been proposed and validated in a previous study. The key result of the NBD/Pareto model is an answer to the question: "Which individual customers are most likely to represent active or inactive customers?" This is a nontrivial question because the purchase activity is a random process and the defection is not directly observed. Based on the customer-specific probability of being alive, the model can be used to determine which customers should be deleted from active status. The outcome of the NBD/Pareto model, the probability that a customer with a particular observed transaction history is still alive at time T since trial, is of key interest to our modeling effort.

Given that the outcome of the NBD/Pareto model is a continuous probability estimate, the continuous P(Alive) estimate is transformed into a dichotomous alive/dead measure. Knowing a person's time of birth (when the person became a customer) and given a specified probability level (threshold), we can approximate when a customer is deemed to have left the relationship. The time from birth, t_0, until the date associated with the cut-off threshold, $t_{\text{cut-off}}$, constitutes the lifetime of the customer. Figure 15.3 illustrates the procedure. This procedure allows us to calculate a finite lifetime for each customer, which then can be used for the profitability analysis.

This discussion has been based on the assumptions that the time t_0 when the customer came on file or when she executed the first purchase is known. Given the widespread existence of customers' databases in organizations, this assumption is not difficult to meet.

Establishment of Cut-off Threshold: The choice of cut-off of the P(Alive) threshold c determines the length of the lifetime estimate for each customer. The cut-off threshold that produces the highest percentage of correct classifications is obviously the choice most consistent with the data. In this study, the threshold of 0.5 produces the highest percentage of correct classifications. As a result, for the purpose of the lifetime analysis, we use 0.5 as the cut-off threshold.

Lifetime Estimation: Based on the model and the implementation of the validation process, the final step in the analysis is the calculation of a finite lifetime estimate for each customer. The average lifetime across Cohort 1 is 28.7 months, and the average lifetime across Cohort 2 is 27.9 months (Table 15.3). A cohort is a group of customers who started their relationship at the same point in time (e.g., a particular month or quarter). Cohort 2 consists of customers who started the relationship with the firm 1 month after Cohort 1. The consistency between the two cohorts is very high. In both cohorts, about 60% of the sample has a lifetime less than the observation window. Thus, the available observation window is obviously adequate for describing lifetime purchases of the given sample.

Profit Calculation

Net-present value of profit is calculated on an individual customer basis for the period of 36 months using the following equation:

$$LT\pi_i \sum\nolimits_{t=1}^{36} (CG_{ti} - C_{ti})\left(\frac{1}{1 + 0.125}\right)^t \quad (15.2)$$

where

LT_i = individual net-present lifetime profit for 36 months,

GC_{ti} = gross contribution in month t for customer i,

C_{ti} = mailing cost in month t for customer i, and

0.0125 = monthly discount rate (based on 0.15 rate per year).

The discount rate is set to 15%, which equals U.S. prime rate in 1999 plus 7%. Gross contribution GC_{ti} is calculated from the monthly revenue, which is the total household purchase amount for every month of the observation period. The monthly gross contribution is calculated on average as 30% profit margin of the monthly revenues. This is a rather conservative figure and reflects the firm's managerial judgment. Due to

Fig. 15.3 Illustrative lifetime determination of individual household (Source: Reinartz & Kumar, 2000)

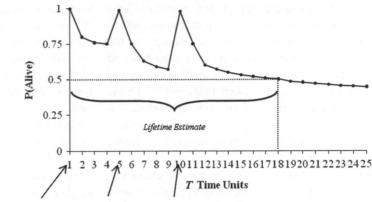

First purchase   Second purchase   Third purchase

Table 15.3 Finite lifetime estimates

	Mean lifetime (months)	Standard deviation	Right-censored (%)	Minimum	Maximum
Cohort 1	28.7	7.8	41.1	11	36
Cohort 2	27.9	7.9	41.7	12	35

the wide assortment the firm offers, the calculation of an average profit seems reasonable. Furthermore, estimates of individual-item direct cost are not available within the firm. The cost component C_{ti} constitutes the total cost of mailing catalogs and solicitations per month and per customer. These costs include catalog production cost, letter shop, and mailing costs. Individual customer mailing costs in the observation window vary between $2.5 and $111.1 for Cohort 1 (mean = $53.3) and $3.3 and $108.5 for Cohort 2 (mean = $57.6). Acquisition costs are not included since the company does not track them on a per-customer basis. Now that lifetime duration and profitability have been computed, we can proceed to test the propositions offered in this study.

Test of the Propositions (The analysis of the test of propositions does not include the acquisitions costs for each customer, as the data are not available. If acquisitions costs were available) they can be easily integrated into the proposed framework. If acquisition costs are somewhat similar across all customers, the findings of the study hold good. For example, the acquisition costs for catalog companies to acquire a customer on the Web are $11, compared to $82 for Internet-only retailers. If acquisition costs are so low for catalog companies, then the variation in

acquisition costs across customers should not affect the results of this study. See: Quick, 2000)

Proposition 1: The Nature of the Lifetime-Profitability Relationship Is Positive

As Fig. 15.2 shows, using *Profit* as the dependent variable, one can segment the customer base with a median split of the independent variables *Lifetime Duration* and *Lifetime Revenues*. Thus, we will employ a median split and create a shorter and a longer *lifetime halt* and higher and lower *revenue half*.

Obviously, we would expect the longer a customer's tenure with the firm and the higher the revenues of a customer, *ceteris paribus*, the more profitable that customer would be in line with the relationship marketing literature, we would expect the customers falling into segment 1 to generate the highest profits. Likewise, customers in Segment 4 would be expected to yield the lowest profits. However, in addition to providing empirical evidence for these expectations, this segmentation scheme lets us test the importance of the off-diagonal segments to the firm. An analysis of the off-diagonal quadrants could provide an answer to an important question. Could we possibly encounter a situation where customers with shorter tenure right actually be more profitable than long-term customers, a claim which runs counter to the theoretical expectations of a relationship perspective? Furthermore, which group of customers is of more interest to the firm, the one that buys heavily for a short period (Segment 3) or the one with small spending but with long-term commitment (Segment 2)? This is a particularly important question in combination with the size of the segments. That is, for example, if the total number of customers in Segment 1 were comparably small, it is imperative for the firm to pay very close attention to the characteristics of their second-most profitable segment. Naturally, the answer to this question is driven by whether revenues and contribution margin are similar or dissimilar.

Proposition 2: Profits Increase over Time

To test the proposition of increasing profits over time, we will (a) examine the profitability evolution visually and (b) analyze the sign of the slope coefficient. If profits were to increase over a customer's tenure, we would expect a positive slope parameter for the same variable. In addition to the linear effect, a dummy variable is included for the first purchase period to reflect the large first month purchase amount. The exact specification of the regression is as follows:

$$\text{Profit}_{ts} = a_s + b_{1s} \times \text{Dummy} + b_{2s} \times t_s + \text{error}$$

where t = month
b_{1s} = regression coefficient
s = segment
Dummy = 1 if first purchase month, else 0

The profit figures are derived for those customers who either have purchase activity in a given month and/or incur cost due to mailings in a given month. The dummy variable was included to achieve a better fit of the estimation because purchases in month 1 were considerably higher for all groups. This higher purchase could be the reflection of the novelty of the situation such as the new vendor, new goods, or new deals. As a result, the estimation better reflects the actual profit pattern beyond month 1.

Proposition 3: The Costs of Serving Long-life Customers are Lower

To test this proposition, we will compute the ratio of promotional costs in a given period over the revenues in the same period. Promotional costs are the total cost of producing and mailing promotions and catalogs, starting with the birth of the customer. This varies for each customer, depending on the purchase transaction history. Within each segment, the mean promotional costs are computed across all households, and then the costs are compared across segments to see if the costs of serving longer-life customers are actually lower.

Proposition 4: Longer-life Customers Pay Higher Prices

We test in our study whether longer-life customers do pay higher prices, as compared to shorter-life customers. Therefore, we will compare the average price paid across products and purchase occasions for each of the four segments. Next, we discuss the findings from the test of propositions.

15.3.4 Empirical Findings

What Is the Nature of the Lifetime-Profitability Relationship?

To test the strength of the lifetime-profitability relationship, the bivariate Pearson correlation between lifetime duration (in months) and lifetime profit ($) is calculated. The correlation coefficient r is 0.175 for Cohort 1 and 0.219 for Cohort 2, which means that only a moderate linear association between lifetime duration and lifetime profits exists. Although a significant positive association (at $\alpha = 0.05$) in line with theoretical expectations clearly exists—overall, it seems weak. Clearly, lifetime duration alone does not explain very well overall lifetime profitability. Furthermore, when segmenting the customers in Cohort 1 using a median split, we find that 2,530 out of 4,202 households fall in the diagonal of Fig. 15.2 (1,322 in the upper right quadrant; 1,208 in the lower left quadrant). That means a very substantive 39.9% of the customers fall into the off-diagonal quadrants.

Thus, the large percentage in the off-diagonal quadrants signals a sizable segment (18.7%) that generates high profits even though the customer

Table 15.4 Tests of propositions—results (Cohort 2 results in parentheses)

	Segment 1					Segment 2				
	1	2	3	4	5	1	2	3	4	5
	Number of customers	Lifetime profit per-customer ($)	Relative profit ($/month)	Mailing cost/sale ratio	Average item price	Number of customers	Lifetime profit per customer ($)	Relative profit ($/month)	Mailing cost/sale ratio	Average item price
Long lifetime	**Segment 1**					**Segment 2**				
	889	50.85	1.43	0.128	47.74	1,332	289.83	8.18	0.063[a]	58.43[b]
	(973)	(55.26)	(1.56)	(0.124)	(48.72)	(1,546)	(322.03)	(9.31)	(0.062)[a]	(58.25)[b]
Short lifetime	**Segment 4**					**Segment 3**				
	1,208	50.49	2.41	0.141	47.97	783	257.96	11.67	0.065	63.54
	(1,504)	(53.67)	(2.67)	(0.143)	(46.80)	(942)	(284.20)	(12.57)	(0.064)	(64.47)
	Low lifetime revenue					High lifetime revenue				

[a]Difference between Segment 1 and Segment 3 is not significant
[b]Difference between Segment 1 and Segment 3 is significant at $\alpha = 0.05$

tenure is short, and another segment (21.2%) that generates low profits even though they exhibit long lifetime. Although our findings moderately support the theoretical predictions from the relationship marketing perspective, additional analyses seem warranted to explain the apparently counterintuitive results. Specifically, we are interested in how much *each segment* con-tributes to overall profits. The goal is to optimally uncover the underlying relationship of lifetime with profitability. Table 15.4 summarizes these results.

Several results in Table 15.4 are remarkable. The first finding is that the average net present lifetime profit per customer is highest for Segment 1 ($289.83). That is, customers who have long lifetimes and generate high revenues represent the most valuable customers to the firm. Of key interest however is the comparison of Segments 2 and 3. Clearly, it can be found for this setting that customers in Segment 3 are, on average, *far* more profitable ($257.96) than customers in Segment 2 ($50.85). The mean profit for segment 3 is significantly (a = 0.01) different from the mean profit of segment 2. In terms of total segment profitability, the short-lived Segment 3 generates 29.2% of the total cohort profits. Thus, while long-term customers in Segment 1 are obviously important to the Firm, short-term customers in Segment 3 are also important because they generate more than a quarter of the total cohort profits.

Thus, this is a case where both long-term customers (Segment 1) *and* short-term customers (Segment 3) constitute the core of the firm's business. Likewise, we find the relationship between lifetime and profits can be far from positive and monotonic. Consequently, an implication for managers is that a firm strategy focusing on relational buyers only as opposed to transactional buyers would clearly be disadvantageous.

Another very interesting outcome of the analysis is that in terms of relative profit (i.e., profit per month), customers in Segment 3 are the *most* attractive of *all* (Table 15.4, Fig. 15.4). Segment 3 customers purchase with high-intensity, thus generating higher profits in a relatively shorter period of time. Thus, in terms of sustaining cash flow, they play a vital role for the firm. The mean

Fig. 15.4 Aggregate profits ($) for short-life segments. Note: Month 1 profits omitted from chart

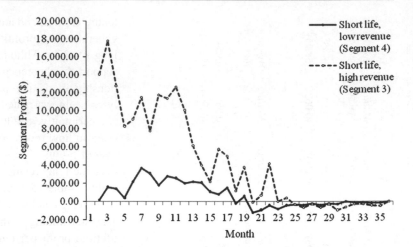

relative profit for each segment is significantly different from the other segment at least at $\alpha = 0.05$ (using the multiple comparison test). The profits per month for longer-life segments are shown in Fig. 15.5, which capture the implications discussed so far.

One needs to speculate on the reasons for this interesting pattern of results. Obviously, Segment 1 customers are the most desirable set for the firm-representing the loyalty effect at its best. These customers' desires are likely to be matched well by the firm's offerings overtime, and they are more likely to be habitual mail-order buyers. For Segment 3 customers (high revenue but short lifetime), we still suspect a good match between offerings and desires, but we assume that their relationship duration is complicated by several moderating factors. For example, consumer factors such as an intrinsic transactional buying behavior, the execution of a limited set of planned purchases, are less of a typical mail-order buyer, or a higher susceptibility to competitor's offers. We suspect that it has less to do with product or service dissatisfaction since they spend at a high level. Dissatisfaction might rather occur for Segment 4, whose customers spend the lowest amount. Although we highlight the speculative nature of these inferences, it seems worthwhile to search for the underlying consumer motivations.

Do Profits Increase Over Time?

To test the proposition of increasing profits over time, we first examine the profitability evolution visually. Figures 15.4 and 15.5 show the lifetime profitability plots for the four segments. A visual inspection of the charts reveals three of the four segments actually exhibit *decreasing profits* over time. Only for Segment 2 (long life, low revenue) we find a slightly positive trend in the profitability evolution.

For a more formal test, we compare the sign and significance of the time coefficient from the regression analysis of profits as a function of time. The results are presented in Table 15.5. With the exception of Segment 2, we generally find that the coefficient for the linear effect has a negative sign, thus highlighting the negative profit trend over time for the three segments. All the coefficients for time are significant at $\alpha = 0.01$.

It is not uncommon that proponents of relationship marketing mention that profits due to loyal customer are higher in each subsequent period. This is typically the case for contractual settings where a firm derives most or all of the business of a customer—for example, for life insurances or health club memberships. However, for noncontractual settings this might be different. For some products and services this is clearly not the case (e.g., there is no reason to believe people bring more and more clothes to their dry cleaner over time).

The theoretical claim is that loyal customers enter a virtual cycle where satisfaction with transactions in previous periods feed not only into loyalty in future periods but also a

Fig. 15.5 Aggregate profits ($) for long-life segments. Note: Month 1 profits omitted from chart

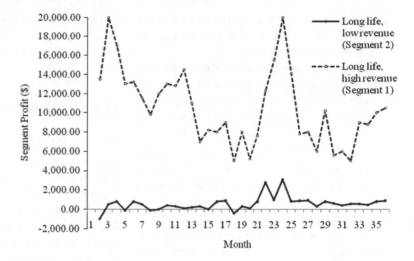

Table 15.5 Regressions results for T = 1–36 months (Cohort 1), validation results in parentheses (Cohort 2)

Segment	Intercept (a)	Dummy coefficient for t = 1 (b1)	Coefficient for t (b2)	R^2
1	12.11 (12.73)	45.77 (46.38)	−0.13 (−0.14)	0.85 (0.85)
2	n.s. (n.s.)	30.24 (30.91)	0.07 (0.071)	0.92 (0.91)
3	19.40 (20.9)	57.85 (58.29)	−0.70 (−9.75)	0.95 (0.94)
4	3.25 (3.69)	29.53 (31.45)	−0.14 (−0.15)	0.94 (0.95)

Notes: All coefficients are significant at $p < 0.01$ except n.s.; *n.s.* not significant

reinforcement and growth in firm profits. The counter forces to this virtual cycle are, for example, variety seeking across firms, customers getting tired of interacting with the same firm, firms' competitive actions, and the fact that no contracts exist. This negative relationship is also possible if the customer contact costs through mailing catalogs are high compared to the potential revenue from the sales realized from each customer.

If costs exceed revenue, then over time, this gap can increase to a point where the negative relationship is prevalent. Obviously, these counter forces are strong enough to block the theoretically existing virtuous cycle, there by leading to decreasing profits overtime. Even for Segment I, the long-life, high-revenue group, the theoretical expectation does not hold. Thus, our finding questions the general claim that loyalty is always desirable to achieve, because we do not find support for the underlying argument (i.e., that profits of long-life customers increase over time). However, loyalty might lead to increased profit over time if there is a forced ongoing relationship, an inertia-driven relationship, or if

cost of maintenance decreases over time at a faster rate than revenue falls off.

Are the Costs of Serving Long-Life Customers Lower?

The objective was to test whether the cost associated with promotional expenditures directed at longer-and shorter-life customers differ. To test this argument, we compute the ratio of promotional costs in a given period over the revenues in the same period for each segment. The segment mean represents the dollar amount promotional cost necessary to sustain a dollar amount of revenue. Results are shown in Table 15.4 for Cohort I and Cohort 2.

The notion that customers with long tenure are associated with lower promotional costs is clearly rejected. The ratio of mailing cost per dollar sales in the longer-life segment (Segment 1) is statistically not different from the mailing cost per dollar sales in the shorter-life segment (Segment 3). This means, in terms of cost efficiency, that Segments 1 and 3 are the most attractive to the firm, although they have very different lifetime properties. Our findings show that the ratio of mailing cost and revenues—which is one measure of efficiency—need not necessarily be lower for long-life customers.

Do long-life Customers Pay Higher Prices?

We wanted to empirically test whether longer-life customers pay, on average, higher or lower prices for their chosen products as compared to customers in the short-life segments. We compute for each transaction the ratio of dollar spending over number of items purchased and average this figure across purchase occasions and customers within segments. Results are shown in Table 15.4 for Cohort I and Cohort 2. The average price per item for segment 3 is significantly ($\alpha = 0.05$) different from (and greater than) that of segment I.

The highest average price paid for a single product item is encountered in Segment 3, the short-life segment. Segment 3 spends, on average, 8.04% (Cohort I) and 10.6% (Cohort 2) more on a single product as compared to Segment I. As a result, our observation of the higher value consciousness of Segment I customers goes counter to the argument that long-life customers are less price-sensitive. It is, in fact, the highly profitable short-term customer who seems to be less sensitive to the product's price. One possible explanation for the behavior of Segment 3 customers could be that these are heavy users of the catalog but not all that brand focused. Thus, they might shop heavily from more retailers and switch more easily for smaller benefits, since for these customers even a small benefit may have a large value. Therefore, the higher spending (average prices paid) by Segment 3 customers may be due to some other benefit sought by them. Thus, our empirical evidence showed four things:

1. A strong linear positive association between lifetime and profits does not necessarily exist.
2. A static and a dynamic lifetime-profit analysis can exhibit a much-differentiated picture: Profitability can occur for the firm from high *and* low lifetime customers. We discovered that, for our case at least, profits do not increase with increasing customer tenure, thereby adding new empirical evidence to the domain.

3. The cost of serving long-life customers is not lower.
4. Long-life customers do not pay higher prices.

15.3.5 Implications

In this study, we showed a context where managers cannot simply equate a long-life customer with increased lifetime spending, with decreasing costs of serving, and with lower price sensitivity. When a firm examines its customer database, it should not be too surprised to find a significant set of customers who transact with the firm for a short while, but in that duration contribute handsomely to the firm's profits. A firm focused purely on rewarding and retaining customers on the basis of how long they have been with the firm may thus miss out on the opportunity to maximize returns from the higher-value, but shorter-lifetime customers. Similarly, rewarding customers simply because they keep coming to your firm for most of their needs and do not conduct much business with your competitors might also not be the shrewdest strategy to adopt in terms of profits.

15.4 Model for Incorporating Customers' Projected Profitability into Lifetime Duration Computation

15.4.1 Background and Objectives

No firm would want to waste its resources by chasing customers who are not likely to be transacting profitably in the future (Reinartz & Kumar, 2003). Deciding when to let go of an unprofitable customer is critical. From a managerial standpoint, it would be extremely desirable to know, at any given time, whether it will be profitable to mail a catalog or send a salesperson to a given customer. If it is profitable, then the manager decides to mail the catalog or initiate a personal contract, otherwise not. Based on this decision metric, it is possible to compute lifetime durations for each customer. Once profitable life-time duration is obtained for each customer, managers are interested in knowing the factors that drive the profitable lifetime duration. In response to this phenomenon, we conducted a study which presents an integrated metric for measuring profitable customer lifetime duration and assessing antecedent factors. The key research tasks were as follows:

- Empirically measure lifetime duration for *noncontractual* customer-firm relationships, incorporating projected profits.
- Understand the structure of profitable rela-tionships and test the factors which impact a customer's profitable lifetime duration.
- Develop managerial implications for building and managing profitable relationship exchanges.

The research took place in the context of the direct marketing industry. Specifically, our research was conducted for one of the leading general merchandise direct marketers (business-to-consumer, or B-to-C, setting) in the United States. Furthermore, we validated the results with a customer sample from a high-technology firm (business-to-business, B-to-B, setting) sell-ing computer hardware and software.

15.4.2 A Dynamic Model of the Antecedents of Profitable Lifetime Duration

In this section, we offer a metric to identify, for each customer, the time periods beyond which they may not be profitable. Toward that end we want to suggest a procedure for estimating the lifetime of customers and implementing this pro-cedure empirically.

Since the model describes and analyzes how and why duration times differ systematically across customers, it is a customer-level analysis. Since our approach exploits longitudinal infor-mation obtained *within* customers, we refer to it as a *dynamic* model. Figure 15.6 details the con-ceptual framework that centers on the, focal con-struct of profitable lifetime duration of customers. *Profitable lifetime duration* is con-ceptualized to be a function of the characteristics of the relationship.

Figure 15.6 not only illustrates how the cur-rent study differs from the previous one, but also shows how the current study incorporates the findings of the previous study in the proposed framework—through the incorporation of reven-ues and cost in measuring lifetime duration. In a nutshell, our research in the last section focuses on the consequences of lifetime duration, while the study in this section focuses on the antece-dents of profitable lifetime duration. Once man-agers understand the important consequences of both longer and shorter lifetime duration (described in the first study), this study tells them how to incorporate those findings when deciding to stop chasing a customer.

The first step involves determining the contri-bution margin expected from each customer in future periods based on the average of the contri-bution margins in the past. The second step is to determine for each future period, the probability that the customer will be alive and will transact with the firm. The third step is to combine these two components. The fourth step is to discount the expected contribution margin in each future period to its *net present value* (NPV) using the cost of capital applicable to the firm. If, in a given month, the cost of additional marketing efforts turns out to be greater than the NPV, we deter-mine that the profitable lifetime duration of the customer has ended.

Although it is useful to know the profitable lifetime duration of each customer to determine when to withdraw marketing efforts directed at that customer, it is also important to understand the antecedents of profitable lifetime duration. This provides a manager with knowledge about the controllable and environmental variables that explain systematic differences in profitable cus-tomer lifetime durations. With this information, a manager is able to focus on appropriate market-ing initiatives likely to improve profitability dur-ing the tenure of every customer. By analyzing and modeling variables for which data are readily available, a firm can determine which factors are significant in affecting customers' profitable life-time durations.

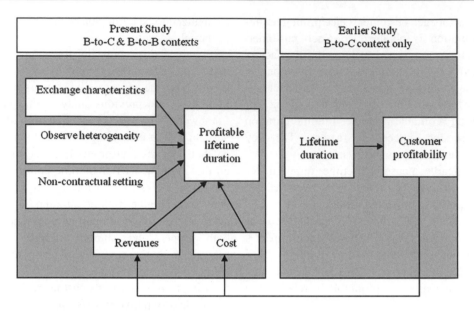

Fig. 15.6 Conceptual model of profitable customer lifetime

The focus of our inquiry is on variables which determine the nature of the customer—firm exchange. Typically, we would need to choose predictor variables of two types to incorporate into the model:

1. *Exchange variables:* Amount purchased, degree of cross-buying, degree of focused buying, interpurchase time, number of product returns, ownership of loyalty instruments, and mailing efforts undertaken by the firm are some variables that can be expected to contribute significantly.

2. *Customer heterogeneity variables:* Location and income of the customer can be expected to add explanatory power to the lifetime duration model

Conceptually,

$$\text{Profitable lifetime duration}$$
$$= f(\text{Exchange characteristics,}$$
$$\text{Customer heterogeneity})$$

Exchange Characteristics: The model provides intuitive explanations for the expected effects of some of these variables. For instance, it is likely that the profitable lifetime duration of a customer is higher for a customer who has spent more than the others and thus has a higher value for the variable *Amount purchased*. Similarly; we can expect a customer who has a tendency to buy across the product line of a firm and therefore exhibits a high *Degree of cross-buying*, should exhibit sustained profitability compared to other customers. Customers who demonstrate a moderate but stable time interval between successive purchases (*Interpurchase time*) are likely to be profitable for a longer duration than customers who have long interpurchase intervals or those who burn out after a rapid series of purchases. Surprisingly, *Number of product returns* can relate positively to profitable lifetime duration, because heavier buyers are also likely to return more merchandise, and a positive experience during the return procedure is likely to boost the buyer-seller relationship.

Customer Heterogeneity: Demographic variables that capture observed customer heterogeneity have been used consistently high response modeling. The main motivation to include these variables is for statistical control purposes, as well as for potential segmentation purposes.

Spatial Location of Consumer: We would expect a higher proportion of long lifetime customers to live in low-density areas as opposed to high-density areas (i.e., cities).

Income: In general, customers with higher incomes are less susceptible to higher price sensitivity (Kumar & Karande, 2000) and are expected to keep buying from the firm for the added convenience,

15.4.3 Research Methodology

The data we use for this research are the same data we used for the study in the last section. The use of the same data set is critical because we are trying to evaluate if our previous findings can be implemented successfully to determine which customers to let go and when to let go. In addition to the data from the two cohorts used in the last study, data from an additional cohort were also used. Thus, we can validate the results across three different sets of customers. Although the data are partiality the same for both studies, the studies have entirely different objectives.

Database: The data are provided by the same U.S. general merchandise catalog retailer, of which the characteristics have been described in the last section. The data for this study also cover a 3-year window and are recorded on a daily basis, the database for the three cohorts consist of a total number of observations of 11,992 households. The sample of households belongs to three different cohorts, the structure of which is depicted in Fig. 15.7.

The customer-firm interaction of Cohort 1 households is tracked for a 36-month time period, the behavior of Cohort 2 households for a 35-month time period, and the behavior of Cohort 3 households for a 34-month time period. The households are sampled randomly from all households that started in January, February, and March 1995, respectively. The number of purchases ranges from 1 to 46 across the sample with a median number of five purchases, the median interpurchase time is 117 days, and the median transaction amount is $91 for each purchase.

15.4.4 Determining Profitable Customer Lifetime Duration

Calculate Net Present Value (NPV) of Expected Contribution Margin (ECM$_{ij}$): Given the nature

of our data (and the data structure in the direct marketing industry in general), managers can easily determine past purchase and spending activity for each customer. Likewise, an estimate of the P(Alive) status, using the NBD/Pareto model, can be obtained for both past and future periods. This allows us to establish the following decision rule: If the sum of the expected discounted future contribution margin were smaller than a currently planned marketing intervention, we would establish the death event for the customer (A managerial consequence would be to stop mailing to that customer, even though this is not our primary concern.) More formally, we compute the estimated future contribution margin:

$$NPV \ of \ ECM_{it}$$
$$= \sum_{n=t+1}^{t+18} P(Alive)_{in} \ x \ AMCM_{it} \left(\frac{1}{1+r}\right)^n$$
$$(15.3)$$

where EC_{it}, is the estimated expected contribution margin for a given month t, $AMCM_{it}$ is the average contribution margin in month t based on all prior purchases since birth (updated dynamically), r is the discount rate (15% on a yearly basis), i is the customer, t is the month for which NPV is estimated, n is the number of months beyond t, and P(Alive)$_{in}$ is the probability that customer i is alive in month n.

For example, the NPV of *expected contribution margin* for customer i in month 18 is calculated as follows: For each month and for each customer, we observe the total purchases in dollars. Then, we multiply the purchase amount by 0.3 to reflect the gross margin. In other words, the *Cost of goods sold* is accounted for, and what we have is gross margin. Next, we subtract the *Cost of actual marketing* efforts (in this case, the cost of catalogs plus the mailing costs) to obtain the monthly contribution margin. If a decision is made at the end of month 18, then we take the average ($AMCM_i$) of months 1–18 by summing up all the 18 contribution margins and dividing the sum by 18.Ifwe are at the end of time period 36, then we take the average (AMCM) of the previous 36 months' contribution margins by

Fig. 15.7 Database
structure for B-to-C setting

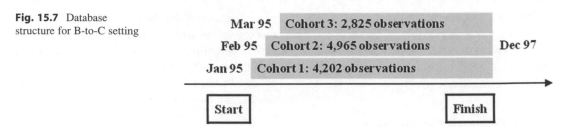

Table 15.6 NBD/PARETO model characteristics and finite lifetime estimates

	Sample size	Pearson correlation of P (Alive)[a]	Mean average percentage error[b]	Mean lifetime (months)	Lifetime standard deviation	Percentage right-censored
Cohort 1	4,202	0.9981	5.83%	29.3	7.5	42.9
Cohort 2	4,965	0.9988	5.22%	28.6	7.7	45.6
Cohort 3	2,825	0.9987	4.75%	27.8	7.2	47.2

[a]Generated from the NBD/pareto estimates of Reinartz and Kumar (2000) and those of the current study, respectively
[b]The P(Alive) of Reinartz and Kumar (2000) and P(Alive) of the current study

summing up all the 36 contribution margins and dividing the sum by 36. Thus, the AMCM estimate is updated monthly—in other words, dynamically modeled and used as a baseline for future purchases (i.e., purchases between t and N). The past purchase level at time t is projected into the future and multiplied monthly with the predicted P(Alive) estimate. It thus endogenously contains the information about the mailing process as well. The future time horizon is limited to 18 months because the associated P(Alive) estimate becomes only marginally different from zero after 18 months. For example, according to the NBD/Pareto model, if a customer hasn't bought in a long time, his probability of being alive is small. Since the predicted P(Alive) for the next 18 months will be even smaller, the net present value of the expected future contribution margin stream will be very low. Thus, having to decide whether to invest in this person (i.e., marketing intervention), chances are that this person would not be deemed as a lucrative future customer—given the cost of mailing.

Decision of Relationship Termination: Formally, if NPV of $ECM_{it} <$ *Cost of mailing*, then the firm would decide to terminate the relationship. Using this decision rule, we establish for every customer at what point he is subjected to the proposed termination policy. The decision rule incorporates the cost of mailings and an average flat contribution margin before mailings of 25% the discount rate is assumed to be 15%.

Calculation of Finite Lifetime Estimate: Based on the decision of relationship termination, the average lifetime across Cohort is 29.3 months, across Cohort 2 is 28.6 months, and across Cohort 3 is 27.8 months (Table 15.6). The consistency between the three cohorts is very high. In all the cohorts, little more than 60% of the samples have a lifetime less than the observation window. Households clearly show variability in lifetime duration. This is evidenced through several factors, such as the wide range between lowest and highest lifetime estimate, the standard deviation of the lifetime estimate, and the relatively small value of s in the NBD/Pareto model.

Thus, we expect considerable scope for exploring the factors that affect lifetime duration. Note that the lifetime duration estimates that incorporate projected profits are different from the one that doesn't incorporate profits.

15.4.5 Analysis

In the proportional hazard model, the hazard rate $h_i(t)$ for individual i is assumed to take this form:

$$h_i(t) = h_0(t)e^{x_{it}\beta} \qquad (15.4)$$

where $h_0(t)$ is the baseline hazard rate and $(X_{it}\beta)$ is the impact of the independent variables. We can estimate the hazard model with the semi-parametric partial likelihood method (Helsen & Schmittlein, 1993).

Variable Operationalization

The criterion variable is the house hold specific estimate of profitable lifetime duration. The time varying variable *Purchase amounts*$_{it}$ enters the model as the monthly spending level ($). The time varying variable *Cross buying*$_{it}$ is operationalized as the number of different departments shopped in, in a given 6-month period. There are a total of 90 different merchandise departments. The *Focus-of-buying* variable is operationalized as a dummy variable. The percentages of customers coded as 1 (buying consistently in one department) are 0.04, 0.05, and 0.04 across the three cohorts. The time varying variable *Average interpurchase time*$_{it}$ is measured in number of days between purchases. AIT_{it}^2 is the square of the AIT_{it} variable. The *Return*$_{it}$ variable is the ratio of returned goods ($ value) to purchased goods ($ value). The *Loyalty instrument* variable is operationalized as a dummy variable, indicating ownership of the corporate charge card. The proportion of customers holding a charge card is 0.39, 0.52, and 0.59 across the three cohorts. The effect of *Mailings*$_{it}$ will be operationalized as a lagged finite exponential decay of past marketing efforts, similar to procedures in advertising-sales relationship literature.

Since the merchandise changes on a continuous basis, the use of a finite decay period seems more realistic than an infinite period. The variable is measured in terms of the number of efforts/mall pieces sent to the customer. The dummy variable *Product category*$_i$ describes whether a buyer predominantly shops in hard goods or in soft goods. The proportion of customers buying predominantly hard goods is 0.50, 0.49, and 0.45 across the three cohorts. The variable *Population density* enters the model as the absolute population number in a given two-digit ZIP code into the model. These numbers were derived from the 2000 U.S. census. The variable *Income* comes from the firm's database and is coded on a scale from 1 to 7, where 1 is a yearly income of lesser than $10.000 and 7 is a yearly income of more than $150,000. The mean rating is 5.19, 4.88, and 5.01 across the three cohorts. Finally, the *Age* variable is measured as the age of the individual in years, calculated from the date of birth information from the database. The mean rating is 34.4, 34.8, and 35.2 years across the three cohorts. A summary of all variables is given in Table 15.7.

The complete model specification is given in (15.5). The hazard of a lifetime event of a household i at time t is given as follows:

$$
\begin{aligned}
h_i(t) = h_0(t)\ \text{EXP}(&\beta 1\ \text{Purchase amount}_{it} \\
&+ \beta 2\ \text{Cross buying}_{it} \\
&+ \beta 3\ \text{Focus of buying}_i \\
&+ \beta 4\ \text{Average Interpurchase Time}_{it} \\
&+ \beta 5\ (\text{Average Interpurchase Time}_{it})^2 \\
&+ \gamma 1\ \text{Returns}_{it} + \gamma 2\ \text{Loyalty instrument}_i \\
&+ \gamma 3\ \text{Mailings}_{it} + \gamma 4\ \text{Product category}_i \\
&+ \delta 1\ \text{Population density}_i + \delta 2\ \text{Income}_i \\
&+ \delta 3\ \text{Age}_i)
\end{aligned}
$$

$$(15.5)$$

15.4.6 Results

The results of the profitable lifetime duration model for the three cohorts are reported in Table 15.8. The table contains the final model parameters, including an interaction term (Returns X Purchase amount).

Effects of Exchange Variables

Purchase Amount: We hypothesized the level of spending for merchandise ($\beta 1$) is positively related to profitable lifetime-duration. We find support for this hypothesis across all three cohorts and across all three models ($p < .01$). Thus, H_i is supported. Due to the strong association between these two measures, it is important to take information on amount of purchases into account when managing profitable lifetime duration.

Table 15.7 Variables for profitable lifetime model

Dependent variable	Measured as	
Profitability lifetime[a]	Months	
Independent variables	**Measured as**	**Hypothesized directional impact on profitable lifetime**
Purchase amount$_{it}$[b]	Monthly spending level ($), moving average over a 6-month period	+
Cross buying$_{it}$	Number of departments shopped in	(+)
Focus of buying$_i$	Dummy: 1 = buys consistently in single dept. only; 0—all other	Nondirectional hypothesis
Average interpurchase time$_{it}$	Number of days	(=) Inverse U-shaped relationship for AIT and AIT2
(Average interpurchase time$_{it}$)^2	(Number of days) 2	(−) Inverse U-shaped relationship for AIT and AIT2
Returns$_{it}$	Proportion of returns (of sales)	(−)
Loyalty instrument$_i$	Ownership of charge card. Dummy variable, 1 = owns card, 0 = no card	(+)
Mailings$_{it}$	Number of mailings sent in last 6 months (=1 season_ since current t, exponential decay, 1 month lag	(+)
Product category$_i$	1 = More than 50% of purchases in softgoods, 0 = more than 50% in purchase of hard goods	No directional hypothesis
Population density	Number of people in the two-digit ZIP code	(−)
Income$_i$	Scale from 1 to 9 where 1 is < $10,000 and 9 is > $150,000	(+)
Age$_i$	Age of individual in years	No directional hypothesis

[a]Subscript$_i$ = variable value does not change over time; subsrcript$_{it}$ = time—varying variable.
[b]Time—varying variables are updated each month

To better understand the relative impact of this variable on the hazard of relationship termination we analyze the risk ratio. From a managerial standpoint, the risk ratio helps in gauging the impact of the drivers of profitable lifetime duration. The risk ratio can be interpreted as the percent change in the hazard for each one-unit increase in the independent variable—controlling for all other independent variables. The risk ratio is calculated as $((\exp(-\beta) - 1) \times 100)$. When the above insight is applied to the purchase amount variable, we observe that a change of only $10 in the monthly spending results in a decrease in the hazard of termination of between 31% and 35%, depending on cohort.

Cross Buying: The degree of buying across departments (β_2) was argued to be positively related to profitable lifetime duration because a broader scope of interaction constitutes a stronger relationship. This contention is supported for all models and for all cohorts in our model ($p < .01$). Apparently, a long customer life is sustained by a higher degree of purchasing *across* departments. Given a certain income, people heed longer time to fill their needs if they purchase across the board rather than in a focused manner. When calculating the risk ratio for this variable, we find that purchases in an additional department are associated with a decreasing hazard of between 59.6% and 72.8%, depending on cohort. Thus, it seems to be extremely desirable for the firm to induce customers to engage in cross-departmental shopping. Hence, H_2 is supported. This is an important finding because the effect of cross-buying on lifetime duration has not yet been documented.

Table 15.8 Coefficients (Std. errors) for profitable lifetime duration model

Independent variable	Parameter	Cohort 1			Cohort 2			Cohort 3		
		Model 1[a]	Model 2	Model 3	Model 1	Model 2	Model 3	Model 1	Model 2	Model 3
Purchase amount$_{it}$[c]	β1	.0497[b] (.00209)	.0360[b] (.00212)	.0354[b] (.00213)	.0486[b] (.00186)	.0373[b] (.00192)	.0364[b] (.00192)	.0433[b] (.00228)	.0341[b] (.00240)	.0324[b] (.00239)
Cross buying$_{it}$	β2	1.389[b] (.0407)	1.293[b] (.0417)	1.276[b] (.0419)	1.226[b] (.0327)	1.172[b] (.0338)	1.154[b] (.0340)	.970[b] (.0346)	.908[b] (.0356)	.912[b] (.0360)
Focus of buying$_i$	β3	−.315[b] (.0647)	−.257[b] (.0660)	−.270[b] (.0662)	−.297[b] (.0624)	−.306[b] (.0630)	−.269[b] (.0632)	−.289[b] (.0841)	−.213[b] (.0862)	−.177 (.0865)
Average interpurchase time$_{it}$	β4	.0121[b] (.000521)	.0133[b] (.000521)	.0127[b] (.000521)	.0146[b] (.000515)	.0153[b] (.000517)	.0147[b] (.00519)	.0171[b] (.000718)	.0178[b] (.000724)	.0171[b] (.000726)
(Average interpurchase time$_{it}$)^2	β5	−8.994 E-6[b] (6.276 E-7)	−9.880 E-6[b] (5.892 E-7)	−9.487 E-6[b] (5.892 E-7)	−.0000121[b] (6.243 E-7)	−.0000123[b] (6.013 E-7)	−.000019[b] (6.046 E-7)	−.0000151[b] (8.912 E-7)	−.0000154[b] (8.660 E-7)	−.0000147[b] (8.747 E-7)
Returns$_{it}$	γ1		−2.214[b] (.222)	−2.050[b] (.226)		−1.690[b] (.214)	−1.557[b] (.215)		−1.323[b] (.320)	−1.323[b] (.320)
Loyalty instrument$_i$	γ2		.666[b] (.0577)	.685[b] (.0577)		.745[b] (.0482)	.753[b] (.0484)		.598[b] (.0618)	.614[b] (.0622)
Mailings$_{it}$	γ3		.00552[b] (.00153)	.00686[b] (.00154)		.00628[b] (.00148)	.00712[b] (.00148)		.00610[b] (.00224)	.00898- (.00229)
Product category$_i$	γ4		−.0278 (.0437)	−.0554 (.0438)		−.0360 (.0414)	−.0476 (.0414)		−.0422 (.0556)	−.0740 (.0558)
Returns$_{it}$ × purchase Amount$_{it}$	γ5		.221[b] (.0188)	.208[b] (.0189)		.148[b] (.0155)	.134[b] (.0155)		.105[b] (.0186)	.0985[b] (.0183)
Population density$_i$	δ1			−3.475 E-8[b] (1.252 E-2)			2.23 E-8[c] (1.196 E-8)			5.305 E-9 (1.584 E-8)
Income$_i$	δ2			.124[b] (.00863)			.111[b] (.00805)			.133[b] (.0104)
Age$_i$	δ3			4.032 E-7 (4.668 E-6)			3.628 E-6 (4.123 E-6)			4.684 E-6 (5.446 E-6)
−2 Log Likelihood		13,728.6	1,337.7	13,126.8	15,678.0	15,200.7	15,004.6	9089.4	8807.7	8639.2
R^2		0.697	0.727	0.743	0.684	0.719	0.730	0.652	0.672	.693

[a]Signs of coefficients have been reversed to reflect effect on lifetime
[b]Significant at 0.01
[c]Significant at 0.05

Focus of Buying: We did not advance a directional hypothesis with respect to focus of buying (β_3) because of conflicting arguments. The empirical test resulted in a negative relationship between focused buying behavior and lifetime duration. Thus, the result is in line with the results of the cross-buying construct—broader buying is generally associated positively with an increase in lifetime duration.

Average Interpurchase Time: AIT (β_4) was hypothesized to be related to profitable customer lifetime duration in an inverse U-shaped fashion. That is, the longest profitable lifetime should be associated with intermediate interpurchase times. We tested for this relationship by introducing a nonlinear term AIT^2 (β_5). We do find support for our hypothesis with both terms being significant at ($p < .01$) and having the hypothesized sign (β_4 positive and β_5 negative). That is, lifetime tends to be shorter when interpurchase times are either very short or very long and lifetime is longest with an intermediate value of *AIT*. Hence, H_3 is supported. Together, the impact of the core exchange variables on profitable lifetime duration is substantial. Between 65.2% and 69.7% of the variance is explained by this group of variables. This once again demonstrates that the exchange variables dominate even in a noncontractual situation.

Returns: Regarding the proportion of returned goods (γ_1), our reasoning assumed a negative association of returns and profitable lifetime. That is, the higher the proportion of returned goods, the lower the associated profitable lifetime duration. Our original results (not shown in Table 15.7) showed the effect was significant at ($p < .01$), but had a positive sign for all three cohorts. Thus, the hypothesis that higher returns were a sign of greater dissatisfaction and therefore would lead to shorter lifetimes was not supported (H_4). A possible explanation for this outcome could be that customers who returned merchandise had a positive encounter with the firm's service representatives, which then might affect their future purchase behavior (Hirschman, 1970). It is interesting to mention that managers told us (upon further inquiry) of their experience, that heavy buyers tend to return proportionately

more. A possible reason for this might be that these buyers are accustomed to the procedures of returning merchandise and are able to do it efficiently. Thus, it might be that these customers see the return process as part of the mail-order buying process. If this effect dominates, then one would expect a positive relationship. Likewise, this would probably mean that as customers spent more with the firm, the effect should become stronger.

To pursue this line of thought, we added post-hoc, an interaction between amount of purchases and the proportion of returns to the model. The final results including the interaction are included in Table 15.7. The interaction turns out to be significant for all three cohorts ($p < .01$). Thus, we find evidence for the conjecture that the degree of returns depends on the degree of spending. Thus, the positive impact on lifetime duration is greatest when the level of dollar purchases and the level of returns are high. Figure 15.8 depicts this situation graphically. Evidence (Clark, Kaminski, & Rink, 1992) has been shown of the impact of positively disconfirming complainants' expectations to achieve (restore) satisfaction. Moreover, the impact of this response seems to be maintained over time. Therefore, we believe, proportionally higher returns might be an indication of this positive disconfirmation. If, for example, the firm has a no-hassle return policy and the customers have come to accept the technical return procedures, greater satisfaction with the exchange can result and therefore greater profitable lifetime duration. Clearly, it would be desirable to have stated satisfaction measures at hand to add additional validity to our results. Similar empirical support for our finding comes from another study (Kesler, 1985) in which Omaha Steaks, a mail-order supplier of high-quality meat, found higher profitability for those customers for which it had quickly resolved complaints.

Loyalty Instrument: Interestingly, the loyalty instrument (γ_2) is significantly related to profitable lifetime duration ($p < .01$). According to our hypothesis, the use of the charge card as a loyalty instrument should lead to a higher lifetime. Thus, in our sample, issuing a charge card appears to be successful as a loyalty instrument because it does seem to be associated with longer customer lifetime. Thus, this is supported. Remember, the findings in literature thus far are not very favorable in terms of loyalty instrument efficiency. However, in this case, it seems at least successful with respect to profitable lifetime duration. Nevertheless, we cannot make a statement about the cost effectiveness of the program. In terms of magnitude of effect, the risk ratio analysis indicates adopting the loyalty instrument is associated with a 45–52% decrease in hazard of relationship termination—substantive amount.

Mailings: The mailing variable (γ_3) was introduced as an important control variable specified as a lagged effect. Recall that mailings and sales are typically not independent in a direct marketing context. The hypothesized effect on lifetime duration was positive. We find a positive significant effect ($p < .01$) for all three cohorts—thus, our decision to control for the variable is correct. Hence, H_6 is supported in that the mailing effort is significantly related to profitable customer lifetime duration.

Product Category: A concern in our modeling effort was that the choice of product category (γ_4) could have a systematic effect on a customer's lifetime. For example, it could be that durable goods (i.e., hard goods) have a potentially long lifetime and thus there is little need for replacement, leading to a potentially shorter customer lifetime. This concern, however, is not substantiated since the parameter γ_4 for the dummy variable is not significant ($p > .1$) for any cohort.

Effects of Observed Heterogeneity

Spatial Location of Customer: It was argued that the spatial location is linked to a customer's tenure with a direct marketer ($\delta 1$) such that the population density is inversely associated with customer lifetime duration. Our results confirm this hypothesis (H_7) for two out of the three cohorts ($p < .05$), thus underlining the need (1) to account for observed heterogeneity in duration modeling, and (2) to demonstrate support for the transaction cost minimization argument.

Income and Age: In terms of the two demographic variables representing income (δ,) and age (δ,), we find that while age does not seem to be related to profitable lifetime duration ($p > .05$), income does ($p < .01$). Our model indicates higher income is associated with longer lifetime. Thus H_8, is supported.

Overall, the information on observed customer heterogeneity adds explanatory power to the duration model, above and beyond the exchange variables. The results are validated in a B-to-B setting. The summary of results is available in Table 15.9.

15.4.7 Technical Appendix: Estimation of P(Alive)

The likelihood of a customer being alive can be computed either through the *method-of-moments* or through *maximum-likelihood* approaches. Due to the computational constraints imposed by the maximum likelihood estimation (MLE), method-of moment estimates have been the method of choice. It has also been shown for the NBD model that the method-of-moments approach and MLE yield approximately the same results (Schmittlein, Morrison, and Colombo, 1987). Thus, there seems to be support in favor of the more manageable method-of moments routine.

Using the likelihood as given in AI, we estimate the four parameters of the NBD/Pareto model (r, α, s, β) with a Fortran routine. The likelihood is:

$$
\begin{aligned}
&lL(r,a,s,\beta)\\
&= \prod_{i=1}^{M} P[X_{i=1} = x_i, t_i, T_i | r, a, s, \beta]
\end{aligned}
\tag{15.6}
$$

with M being a random sample of customers, and customer i made $X_1 = x_i$ purchases in $(0, T_i)$ with the last transaction time at t_i. The resulting MLE parameters are $r = 3.01$, $\alpha = 9.65$, $s = 0.82$ and $\beta = 11.91$ (estimation horizon 30 months). The parameters are quite consistent with the estimates derived by Reinartz and Kumar, who used estimates of $r = 4.24$, $\alpha = 14.95$, $s = 0.93$ and $\beta = 13.85$ (Reinartz & Kumar, 2000). In

Fig. 15.8 Interaction between proportion of returns and purchase amount

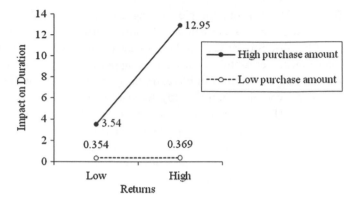

particular, the critical parameters $r/\alpha = 0.312$ and $s/\beta = 0.069$ are similar to Reinartz and Kumar ($r/\alpha = 0.481$ and $s/\beta = 0.069$), resulting in little bias in the P(Alive) estimates (see Table 15.10).Since the results are robust and the computational resources required for MLE are substantially larger, the method-of-moment estimation is preferred.

The model parameters can be explained as follows. The variation across customers in their long-run purchase rate is reflected in the estimate of r only and is independent of α. In other words, the larger the value of the shape parameter r, the more homogeneous is the population of customers in terms of purchase rate. Thus, r can be viewed as an overall inverse measure of the concentration in purchase rates across households. In other words, the larger the value of the shape parameter s, the more homogeneous is the population of customers in terms of dropout rate. The concentration in dropout rates, β, depends on the parameter s only. Overall, the model estimates seem reasonable and show a high degree of face validity and internal consistency. Having calculated the distribution parameters, the characteristic of interest is the probability that a customer with a particular observed transaction history is still alive at time T since trial. Schmittlein, Morrison, and Colombo show this probability depends on the customer's past purchase history (through the number of purchases x) and the time t (since trial) at which the most recent transaction occurred (Schmittlein et al., 1987). The desired probability for $\alpha > \beta$ is given in (15.7) a~ follows:

$$P[\text{Alive}|r,\alpha,s,\beta,x,t,T]$$

$$= \left\{ 1 + \frac{s}{r+x+s} \left[\left(\frac{a+T}{a+t} \right)^{r+x} \left(\frac{\beta+T}{a+t} \right)^{s} \right. \right.$$

$$\times F(a_1 + b_1 + c_1 + (t)) - \left(\frac{\beta+T}{a-t} \right)^{s}$$

$$\left. \left. \times F(a_1 + b_1 + c_1 + (T)) \right] \right\}^{-1}$$

$$(15.7)$$

where $a_1 = r + x + s$, $b_1 = s + 1$, $c_1 = r + x + s + 1$, $z_1(y) = (\alpha - \beta)/(\alpha + y)$, $F(a_1, b_1, c_1, z_1)$ is the Gauss hypergeometric function, $r, \alpha, s, \beta =$ model parameters, $x =$ number of purchases, $t =$ time since trial at which the most recent transaction occurred, and $T =$ time since trial.

It is important to mention that this methodology requires cohorts of customers. Only the cohort analysis yields insight into the dynamic pattern of defection over time, whereas a simple cross-section of customers would not give such insight (because customers are at different stages in their lifecycle).

15.5   Model for Identifying the True Value of a Lost Customer

15.5.1 Conceptual Background

The authors of this study, John B. Hogan, Katherine N. Lemon, and Barak Libai, argue the traditional customer profitability models

Table 15.9 Summary of results

Hypothesis	Description	B-to-C setting	B-to-B setting
H1	Profitable customer lifetime duration is positively related to the customer's spending level	Supported	Supported
H2a	Profitable customer lifetime duration is positively related to the degree of cross-buying behavior exhibited by the customers	Supported	Supported
H2b	Profitable customer lifetime duration is related to the focused buying behavior exhibited by customers	Supported. However, the relationship is negative, indicating that buying only a single department results in shorter lifetime duration	Supported. However, the relationship is negative, indicating that buying in only a single department results in shorter lifetime duration
H3	Profitable customer lifetime duration is inverse U-shaped manner, whereby intermediate AIT is associated with the longed profitable lifetime value	Supported	Partial support. Only the linear term is significant
H4	Profitable customer lifetime duration is inversely related to the proportion of merchandise returned by the customers	Not supported. However, the interaction of returns with purchase amount variable is significant	Not supported. However, the interaction of returns with purchase amount variable is significant
H5	Profitable customer lifetime duration is positively related to the ownership of the company's loyalty instrument (B-to-C) or the availability of line of credit (B-to-B)	Supported	Supported
H6	Profitable customer lifetime duration is positively related to the number of mailing efforts of the company (B-to-C) or the number of contacts (B-to-B)	Supported	Supported
H7	Profitable customer lifetime duration is higher for customers living in areas with lower population density (B-to-C) or business existing in lower population density (B-to-B)	Supported	Not supported
H8	Profitable customer lifetime duration is positively related to the income of the customer (B-to-C) or income of the firm (B-to-B)	Supported	Supported

evaluate customers in isolation from one another and that the effects of social interactions are not accounted for (Hogan, Lemon, & Libai, 2003). Customers are involved in social interactions and they may advocate positive or negative word of mouth about the products and the firm. This, in turn, could influence future prospects to become

customers and existing customers to cease transactions. The exclusion of these indirect social effects could lead to misallocation of scarce marketing resources during the critical early stages of a new product market.

The value of a lost customer depends on whether the customer defects to a competing

Table 15.10 Actual revenues & profits for the selected group of customers based on NBD/PARETO, RFM, and past customer value selection (Cohort 1)

Customer selection based on	Percentage of cohort (selection from top)	Evaluation at 18 months ($)	Evaluation at 30 months ($)
NBD/Pareto with ECM	30 (n = 1,260)	590,452 (123,076)	318,831 (62,991)
	50 (n = 2,101)	756,321 (148,922)	361,125 (61,636)
	70 (n = 2,941)	864,114 (165,735)	380,855 (60,305)
Advanced RFM	30 (n = 1,260)	442,534 (78,555)	140,781 (27,582)
	50 (n = 2,101)	599,100 (99,831)	186,267 (36,380)
	70 (n = 2,941)	687,163 (110,244)	216,798 (42,839)
Past customer value	30 (n = 1,260)	508,997 (86,820)	179,665 (35,916)
	50 (n = 2,101)	648,772 (112,723)	210,860 (41,729)
	70 (n = 2,941)	789,526 (138,124)	225,910 (44,738)

firm or disadopts the product category. Customer defection refers to a situation where a customer leaves one firm and starts transacting with a competing firm. As a consequence, the firm loses direct sales from that customer. In contrast, disadoption occurs when a customer stops purchasing from that product category altogether. This affects the long-term profitability in two ways one is the loss of direct sales and the other is in terms of indirect effects of word of mouth, imitation, and other social effects.

15.5.2 Modeling the Effects of Disadoption on the Value of a Lost Customer

I $\propto$ is the proportion of disadopters in a firm's lost customers, then the value of an average lost customer (VLC) is calculated in (15.8):

$$VLC = VLC_{disadopters} + (1 - \alpha)VLC_{defectors} \quad (15.8)$$

The value of α may vary across firms and markets. The sales effect of slower customer acquisitions caused by the social effects and reduced level of word of mouth is then estimated using the Bass new product growth model. The profit impact of a lost customer is estimated by calculating the difference in the expected profitability of the firm before and after the customer has disadopted. In other words, profit impact of a lost customer = sales estimate from new product

growth model without disadoption—the sales estimate when the customer disadopts after certain time. This takes into account both the direct and indirect effects of disadoption.

15.5.3 The Key Determinants of the Value of a Customer

To study the phenomenon of the lost customer, a Monte Carlo simulation was used in which the key parameters such as external influence (p), internal influence (q), discount rate (r), and disadoption time (t_1) were variable based. The results indicated: (1) the time when customer disadopts has the largest impact on the value of the lost customer, (2) the external influence, p has a negative impact, (3) the internal influence, q has a positive impact on penetration because higher q signifies stronger word of mouth, and (4) discount rate has positive impact on the value of lost customer. The study shows

Table 15.11 Effect of firm & market variables on the value of a lost customer

Parameter		Standardized coefficient	P-Value
p	External influence	−0.432	<0.0001
q	Internal influence	0.147	0.0103
r	Discount rate	0.213	0.0003
t_1	Disadoption time	−0.594	<0.0001

Source: Hogan et al. (2003)

that the earlier a customer disadopts the more money the company loses. This is because at the early stages of a product life cycle, there are only a few adopters to influence the future adoption through word of mouth. Hence, a single disadoption can have larger impact. The effects of various variables on the value of a lost customer are given in Table 15.11.

It is also important to note the value of a lost customer is affected by stages in the product life cycle, the firm's market share, and the rate at which competitors' customers disadopt. This has important managerial implications in terms of spending on customer retention, allocation of retention, and acquisition spending over time, extended return on investment analysis, and managing competitive environment.

15.6 Summary

A study of the lifetime-profitability relationship in a noncontractual setting highlights a concern with the widespread assumption of a clear-cut positive lifetime-profitability relationship and underlines the importance of a differentiated analysis. In the conceptual model, individual customer lifetime profits are modeled as a function of a customer's lifetime duration, revenue flows over the course of a customer's lifetime, and firm cost is associated with the marketing exchange. In a noncontractual scenario such as the direct marketing context, promotional costs are typically the largest nonproduct cost factor in a customer firm relationship. A possible reason for higher value consciousness of long-term customers might be that customers learn over time to trust lower-priced items or brands as much as established-name brand products.

The empirical evidence showed that (1) a strong linear positive association between lifetime and profits does not necessarily exist, (2) profits do not necessarily increase with increasing customer tenure, (3), the cost of serving long-life customers is not lower, and (4) long-life customers do not pay higher prices, However, these factors may have differential impacts in different industries.

The objectives of the second study were (1) to empirically measure lifetime duration for *noncontractual* customer-firm relationships, (2) to incorporate projected profits to the structure of profitable relationships and to identify the antecedents of customer's profitable lifetime duration, and (3) to develop managerial implications for building and managing profitable relationship exchanges. The model first estimated the probability of a customer being alive and then integrated this with the individual lifetime duration. The main drivers of customer's profitable lifetime duration are classified as exchange characteristics and customer heterogeneity. The customer's spending level, cross-buying, focus of buying, average interpurchase time, amount of returns, customer's ownership of loyalty instrument, and the mailing efforts of the company are identified as important exchange characteristics. Spatial location of consumer and his age and income are the important customer heterogeneity factors influencing the profitable lifetime duration.

In the third study, a model is developed for determining the effects of disadoption on the value of a lost customer. This takes into account not only the direct effects of lost sales but also the indirect effects of social effects such as word of mouth. The key determinants of the value of a lost customer are identified as disadoption time, external and internal influence, and the discount rate. The disadoption time is found to have the maximum negative impact on the value-that is, the earlier a customer disadopts, the higher the value of the lost customer.

Customer equity is the aggregation of the expected lifetime values of a firm's entire base of existing customers and the expected future value of newly acquired customers. The NPV objective function required to maximize the customer equity of a firm is related to the cash flow from each customer, the expected interpurchase time, and the cost and frequency of the marketing/communication strategies employed. The objective function is based on a probability model which predicts the interpurchase time of each customer, a panel data model which predicts the cash flows from each customer, and an optimization algorithm which maximizes the profits. By applying an optimization model, a manager can know the extent to which he should use various contact channels. Cross analysis of duration of relationship and customer value obtained on the basis of the NPV maximization objective function indicates not all short-duration customers deliver lower profits, and not all long-duration customers deliver higher profits. Identifying and targeting responsive and profitable customers and deemphasizing efforts on some customers who were not profitable-irrespective of whether they are classified as long-duration or short-duration customers-would be a better approach. Customer value-based approach demonstrated its superiority to the duration of association approach in terms of profitable segmentation of customers.

Purchase sequence model captures the differences in the durations between purchases for different product categories. An individual customer-level profit function is developed to predict customer value. The success of the experiment based on the model demonstrated.

By higher revenue, lower cost of communication, lower number of attempts before a purchase is made, higher profits, and higher ROI for the test group, when compared to the control group, indicates the scope to which the customer value approach offers in improving the quality of marketing decisions.

The acquisition-process is an integral component of the research model. By linking acquisition and the retention process, it is possible to see a complete and unbiased picture of the drivers behind customers election/acquisition, relationship duration, and customer profitability. Also, making the necessary trade-off between offensive processes and defensive processes requires a full specification of the key dimensions of the customer-firm relationship. A more complete model specification addresses the key managerial question of whether the maximization of the respective objective functions as acquisition likelihood, lifetime duration, and customer value would lead to convergent or divergent resource allocation recommendations. This model applies mainly to situations where managers rely mostly

on direct customer communication. Acquisition expenditures will have diminishing marginal associations with customer profitability. Retention expenditures will have diminishing marginal associations with relationship duration and with customer profitability. Highly interpersonal contact channels have a greater association with the likelihood of customer acquisition and relationship duration than less interpersonal contact channels. Though the results are specific to the empirical context, the model can be applied to any environment where acquisition and retention efforts can be separated. Managers can use the proposed integrated framework not only to better understand the drivers of profitability, but also to know how to maximize profitability through optimal allocation of resources.

Exercise Questions

1. How can we measure a customer's worth? What factors typically influence a customer's worth?
2. Discuss the differences in the analysis of customer loyalty between contractual and non contractual settings.
3. In the credit card industry, what drivers of profitable lifetime duration would you expect?
4. Discuss the effect of a lost customer on a firm. How would you capture and quantify this effect?

References

Bendapudi, N., & Berry, L. L. (1997). Customers' motivations for maintaining relationships with service providers. *Journal of Retailing, 73*(1), 15–37.

Berry, L. (1995). Relationship marketing of services growing interest, emerging perspectives. *Journal of the Academy of Marketing Sciences, 23*(4), 236–45.

Bolton, R. N. (1998). A dynamic model of the duration of the customer's relationship with a continuous service provider: The role of satisfaction. *Marketing Science, 7*(Fall), 17–23.

Clark, G. L., Kaminski, P. F., & Rink, D. R. (1992). Consumer complaints: Advice on companies should respond based on an empirical study. *Journal of Consumer Marketing, 9*(3), 5–14.

Direct Marketing Association. (2007). Direct marketing expenditures account for 50% of total advertising expenditures, DMA's 2007 'Power of Direct

Marketing' report unveils. *DMA: Direct marketing association; conferences, seminars, research & articles.* Retrieved October 16, 2007, from http://www.the-dma.org/cgi/disppressrelease?article=1015

Direct Marketing Association. (2009). What is the direct marketing association? *DMA: Direct marketing association; conferences, seminars, research & articles.* Retrieved July 26, 2011, from http://www.the-dma.org/aboutdma/whatisthedma.shtml

Dowling, G. R., & Uncles, M. (1997). Do customer loyalty programs really work? *Sloan Management Review, 38*(4), 78–82.

Dwyer, F. R. (1997). Customer lifetime valuation to support marketing decision making. *Journal of Direct Marketing, 11*(4), 6–13.

Helsen, K., & Schmittlein, D. C. (1993). Analyzing duration times in marketing: Evidence for the effectiveness of hazard rate models. *Marketing Science, 11*(4), 395–414.

Hirschman, A. O. (1970). *Exit loyalty and voice.* Cambridge, MA: Harvard University Press.

Hogan, J. E., Lemon, K. N., & Libai, B. (2003). What is the 'true value of a lost customer? *Journal of Service Research, 5*(3), 196–208.

Kesler, L. (1985, October 17). Steak company welcomes customers' grilling. *Advertising Age, 36*(7).

Kumar, V. (2008a). *Managing customers for profit: Strategies to increase profits and build loyalty.* Upper Saddle River, NJ: Wharton School.

Kumar, V. (2007) "Customer Lifetime Value: The Path to Profitability", NOW Publishers, Inc., The Netherlands.

Kumar, V., & Karande, K. (2000). The effect of retail store environment on retailer performance. *Journal of Business Research, 49*(2), 167–181.

Kumar, V., & Ramani, G. (2003–2004). Taking CLV analysis to the next level: A multistep approach to better understanding customer value. *Journal of Integrated Communications*, 2004, 27–33.

Kumar, V., Shah, D., & Venkatesan, R. (2006). Managing retailer profitability: One customer at a time! *Journal of Retailing, 82*(4), 277–294.

Kumar, V., Venkatesan, R., Bohling, T. R., & Beckmann, D. (2008). The power of CLV: Managing customer lifetime value at IBM. *Marketing Science, 27*(4), 585–599.

Li, S. (1995). Survival analysis. *Marketing Research, 7* (Fall), 17–23.

Quick, R., (2000, April 18). New study finds hope for internet retailers. *Wall Street Journal, A2.*

Reichheld, F. F., & Sasser, W. E. (1990). Zero defections: Quality comes to services. *Harvard Business Review, 68*(5), 105–111.

Reichheld, F. F., & Teal, T. (1996). *The loyalty effect.* Boston: Harvard Business School Press.

Reinartz, W., & Kumar, V. (2000). On the profitability of long-life customers in a non-contractual setting: An empirical investigation and implications for marketing. *Journal of Marketing, 64*(4), 17–32.

Reinartz, W., & Kumar, V. (2002). The mismanagement of customer loyalty. *Harvard Business Review, 80*(7), 86–94.

Reinartz, W., & Kumar, V. (2003). The impact of customer relationship characteristics on profitable lifetime duration. *Journal of Marketing, 67*(1), 77–99.

Schmittlein, D. C., Morrison, D. G., & Colombo, R. (1987). Counting your customers: Who are they and what will they do next? *Management Science, 33*(1), 1–24.

Schmittlein, D. C., & Peterson, R. A. (1994). Customer base analysis: An industrial purchase process application. *Marketing Science, 13*(1), 41–67.

Sheth, J. N., & Parvatiyar, A. (1995). Relationship in consumer markets: Antecedents and consequences. *Journal of the Academy of Marketing Science, 23*(4), 255–271.

Valentino-Devries, J. (2011, April 14). With catalogs, opt-out policies vary. *The Wall Street Journal*, Web. Accessed on July 26, 2011. Accessed at http://online.wsj.com/article/SB10001424052748703841904576256750393074920.html

Venkatesan, R., & Kumar, V. (2004a). A customer life time value framework for customer selection and optimal resource allocation strategy. *Journal of Marketing, 68*(4), 106–125.

Venkatesan, R., & Kumar, V. (2004b). A customer lifetime value framework for customer selection and resource allocation strategy. *Journal of Marketing, 68*(4), 106–125.

Wyner, G. A. (1999). Customer relationship measurement. *Marketing Research: A Magazine of Management and Applications, 11*(2), 39–41.

Applications of CRM in B2B and B2C Scenarios (Part II)

16

16.1 Overview

The ability to know exactly who is going to buy what product and when, and the resources and communication strategy needed to make it happen, will no doubt be on the top of the wish list for CEOs. This ability will help the firm invest on the most profitable customer's at the most appropriate time, and in the most effective way. This will not only avoid overspending or under spending on customers but also increase the revenue and profit from them. However, many companies continue to spend resources on large number of unprofitable customers. They could either be investing on customers who are easy to acquire but are not necessarily profitable or trying to increase the retention rate of all their customers, thereby leading to wastage of limited resources. Allocating resources optimally on an individual customer was not a feasible process before the introduction of the customer value framework. By utilizing the customer value framework, researchers have now devised models to allow customer-level actions.

In this chapter we describe the model for arriving at the optimal resource allocation. This model will help a manager know the extent to which he should use various contact channels to communicate to a customer. A model to predict the purchase sequence is described next. The model addresses questions like: (1) What is the sequence in which a customer is likely to buy multiple products or product categories? and (2) When is the customer expected to buy each product? The third model addresses issues related to allocating resources between acquisition and retention with the objective of maximizing a customer's long-term profitability. It tries to answer questions like: (1) What should be the total budget for acquisition and retention? (2) How much should be spent on customer acquisition and customer retention? and (3) How should these expenditures be allocated between contact channels?

Customer attrition has become a critical concern for many industries, such as telecommunication, retail banking, and insurance. With increased competition, a customer has many more choices of products and services from a number of firms. Coupled with increased choices for consumers, firms are constantly trying to acquire high-value customers from their competitors. As a result, firms find it difficult to retain customers as they easily move from one firm to the other (that is, defect). This chapter discusses a CLV-based strategy to manage customer churn. By answering some important questions faced by managers in retaining customers, the strategy discussed here is also implemented in a telecommunications firm that has borne impressive results for the company in retaining customers.

While a firm's aggregate-level brand value perception continues to influence its bottom line performance, it does not provide the firm with a clear set of guidelines as to how to structure their marketing and brand investment strategies. To design and execute effective brand management strategies, firms need to understand exactly how

V. Kumar and W. Reinartz, *Customer Relationship Management*, Springer Texts in Business and Economics, DOI 10.1007/978-3-642-20110-3_16, © Springer-Verlag Berlin Heidelberg 2012

each of their actions will affect the customer's individual brand value. In this chapter, we forward a framework that firms can use to effectively link Customer Brand Value (CBV) to the Customer Lifetime Value (CLV) metric. The strategies developed using this link help firms better understand and redesign their brand strategies to suit the needs of the individual customer.

Many firms are using metrics such as Customer Lifetime Value to identify their "best" customers and then allocating resources to target these customers with the highest CLV for referral campaigns. However, such programs tend to alienate low and medium-CLV customers because of the lower-level service provided and the differentiated treatment. Therefore, it is important for managers to determine the value of a customer's ability to spread word-of-mouth and make referrals. This chapter introduces and discusses the Customer Referral Value (CRV) metric for profitably managing customer referral behavior. By accounting for the attitudinal behavior of customers and measuring the indirect contribution (referrals or word-of-mouth) made by customers toward the firm's profit, this chapter shows that the CRV metric is the most appropriate metric for designing profitable referral strategies.

16.2 Optimal Resource Allocation Across Marketing and Communication Strategies

Customer equity is the aggregation of the expected lifetime values of a firm's entire base of existing customers and the expected future value of newly acquired customers (Hogan et al., 2002). A firm needs to make trade-offs that reserve strategic resources for the areas in which the expenditures will generate the greatest impact on customer equity (Rust, Lemon, & Narayandas, 2000). The interpurchase time for a customer is influenced by marketing initiatives taken by a firm. A mathematical model for interpurchase time as discussed earlier in this book includes the frequency and nature of marketing and communication efforts. A model to predict the cash flows from each customer can be simultaneously developed. The net present value (NPV) objective function

required to maximize the customer equity of a firm is related to the cash flow from each customer, the expected interpurchase time, and the cost and frequency of the marketing/communication strategies employed. A manager can determine the frequency of each of the available marketing and communication strategies such that the NPV objective function is maximized. An optimization technique can be utilized to accurately arrive at the differential allocation of strategic resources to individual customers across a variety of integrated marketing strategies (Venkatesan & Kumar, 2004). The objective function is thus based on three elements:

- A *probability-based model that predicts the interpurchase time* of each customer, as a function of marketing communication inputs and the customers' past purchase behavior observed over time.
- A *panel data model that predicts the cash flows* from each individual customer, also as a function of marketing communication inputs and the customers' past purchase behavior observed over time.
- An *optimization algorithm that maximizes the profits* from each individual customer by examining the impact of various levels of marketing communication inputs.

By applying an optimization model, a manager can know the extent to which he should use various contact channels. For example, for individual customers, should there be a decrease in face-to-face meetings and an increase in the frequency of direct mailers, or vice versa? Or, for segments of customers, how can total profitability over these segments be maximized? To illustrate the application of the optimal resource allocation procedure, it is useful to look at the results of a real-world situation.

First, it was necessary to establish that the model would do a good job of predicting whether a particular customer would buy in the next 12 months. Based on an analysis of a sample of 324 customers, out of 246 customers the model predicted would buy a product, 225 of them actually bought. Similarly, out of the 78 customers the model predicted would not buy the product, 66 of them did not buy. This suggests

Table 16.1 Effect of firm and market variable on the value of a lost customer

	Actually bought in the next 9 months	Actually did not buy in the next 12 months	Total
Expected to buy in the next 12 months as per the model	N = 225	n = 21	246
Not expected to buy in the next 12 months	N = 12	n = 66	78
Total			**324**

Table 16.2 Comparison of average profits in duration of association approach

	Duration of customer-firm association	
	Short	Long
Average profit per customer	$29,235 (n = 170)	$141,655 (n = 154)

the model had a total accuracy, or hit rate, of 90% (See Table 16.1.)

$$\text{Hit Rate} = 225 + 66 \div 324 = 90\%$$

Given this reassurance, we needed to examine if the customer value approach could eventually lead to an improvement in profits relative to the duration of association approach currently being employed by the firm to select customers and prioritize its marketing action (Duration of association (one of the traditional measures of loyalty) indicates how long a customer has been transacting with the firm).

Table 16.2 shows the results of duration of association approach in terms of the classification of customers and their average profits.

The firm studied would break its customer base into two groups—short-duration customers and long-duration customers. Short-duration customers were those customers who had been transacting with the firm for less than a predetermined cut-off value of years. Consequently, the long-duration customers were the customers who had been transacting with the firm for longer than the cut-off value. From Table 16.2 it seemed as if they were doing the right thing, because the average profits from the short duration group were much lower than the average profits from the long-duration group.

However, across analysis of duration of relationship and customer value, obtained on the basis

of the NPV maximization objective function, indicates not all short-duration customers deliver lower profits, and not all long-duration customers deliver higher profits. A superior approach could be thus adopted by identifying and targeting responsive and profitable customers and by deemphasizing efforts on some customers who were not profitable, irrespective of whether they are classified as long-duration or short-duration customers. Some of the profitable customers had escaped the firm's attention when only the duration of association approach was being followed. Also, the firm was allocating disproportionately higher resources to some long-duration customers in the mistaken belief that the duration of their association with the firm was indicative of their profitability (See Table 16.3.)

The observations in *Cell III* indicate more than 50% of the customers that the firm was chasing in the long-duration segment were actually low-value customers. The observations in *Cell II* indicate the firm was ignoring a sizable set of customers by classifying them as short-duration customers, when indeed they were contributing significantly to profits. Thus, the customer value-based approach demonstrated its superiority to the duration of association approaching terms of profitable segmentation of customers. By using the optimal resource allocation model, we can improve profitability in each of the cells as shown in Fig. 16.1.

The analysis recommends changing the frequency of face-to-face meetings, direct mail, and telesales in each cell to an optimal level, thereby enhancing the effectiveness of the marketing/communication initiatives. By changing over to the optimal frequencies, recommended by the model for face-to-face meetings and direct mail telesales, in each of the four cells, a 10% decrease in overall costs and a 6% increase in overall profits were observed.

Table 16.3 Customer value versus duration of customer-firm relationship

	Shorter duration		Longer duration	
Low customer value	$N = 78$	*Cell I*	$N = 82$	*Cell III*
	Average profit $= \$1,387$		Average profit $= \$1,245$	
High customer value	$N = 92$	*Cell II*	$N = 82$	*Cell IV*
	Average profit $= \$52,976$		Average profit $= \$302,542$	

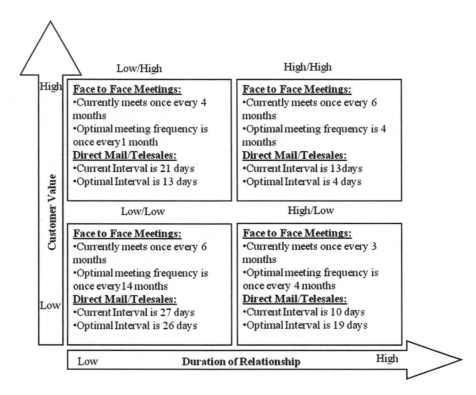

Fig. 16.1 Reallocation of resources based on customer value (All figures have been altered by a constant multiplier for confidentiality reasons)

16.3 Purchase Sequences Analysis: Delivering the Right Message to the Right Customer at the Right Time

In the case of a multiproduct firm, it is important to understand which product in the portfolio is likely to be needed next by a customer. An ideal contact strategy is one where the firm is able to deliver a sales message relevant to the product likely to be purchased in the near future by a customer. The next level is therefore the development of a *purchase sequence model*.

A purchase sequence model (Kumar, Venkatesan, & Reinartz, 2004) addresses three questions:

1. What is the sequence in which a customer is likely to buy multiple products or product categories?
2. When is the customer expected to buy each product?
3. What is the expected revenue from that customer?

This model captures the differences in the durations between purchases for different product categories. The interdependence in purchase

Table 16.4 Change between current year and previous year

	Test group	Control group
Revenue ($)[a]	1,050 (18,130)	1,033 (17,610)
Cost of communications ($)	−750 (3,625)	75 (4,580)
Number of attempts before purchase	−4 (15)	1 (18)
Profits ($)	3,000 (9,080)	637 (6,275)
Return on Investment (%)	5.4 (3.7)	2.2 (2.0)

Note: Number indicates change from base level (previous year). Base level is in parentheses
[a]The reported values are unit values per customer

Table 16.5 Difference in performance between test and control group

	Difference between test and control group
Revenue ($)[a]	537
Cost of communications ($)	−1,780
No. of attempts before purchase	−8
Profits ($)	5,168
Return on investment (%)	4.9

[a]Number indicates change from base level the previous year. Base level is in parentheses. The reported values are unit values per customer

propensities across products is modeled by incorporating cross-product category variables. An individual customer level profit function is developed to predict customer value. To demonstrate such a model delivers superior results in the field, an experiment was set up in the sales department of a high technology B2B vendor, which markets multiple categories of products.

The model was developed for the hardware products of the firm. The model is able to prioritize customers by indicating the propensity to purchase different hardware products for each of its customers. It also predicts the expected profits. Empirical evidence from this experiment suggests profits predicted on the basis of a purchase sequence model are accurate and that using the model results in a greater return on marketing investments. Table 16.4 is an illustration of the improvement for the hardware category, over the previous year, in profits generated by the test group of salespersons who adopted strategies based on the outcome of the purchase sequence model versus the control group of salespersons not provided the predictions given by the model.

As Table 16.4 shows, there is a significant decrease in the cost of communication resulting in a saving of $750 on last year's base of $3,625. In comparison, the control group saw an increase in its cost of communication by $75 on an already high last-year base of $4,580. The test group was able to reduce the average number of attempts before purchase by four, whereas for the test group this number increased by one, compared to the respective figures for last year. Similarly, for the test group, profits were higher and so was ROI.

Table 16.5 provides the difference in performance between the test group and the control group.

We see again during the experiment period, the test group revenue is higher, cost of communication is lower, number of attempts before a purchase is made is lower, profits are higher, and ROI is higher, when compared to the control group. The success of the experiment indicates the scope that the customer value approach offers in improving the quality of marketing decisions.

16.4 The Link Between Acquisition, Retention, and Profitability: Balancing Acquisition and Retention Resources to Maximize Customer Profitability

Measuring, managing, and maximizing customer profitability is not an easy task. From a marketing resource allocation perspective, it requires a

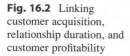
Fig. 16.2 Linking customer acquisition, relationship duration, and customer profitability

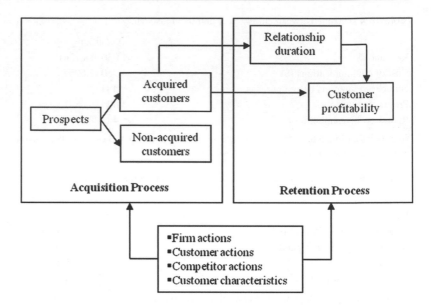

manager to (1) set a budget, (2) balance how much to spend on customer acquisition and customer retention, and (3) determine how the expenditures are allocated between contact channels. The objective is, of course, to maximize a customer's long-term profitability. For example, a manager of a paper company distributes sales force efforts and directs marketing efforts among its set of 350 business customers. The manager also has to constantly juggle how many new prospects should be targeted at a given point in time vis-à-vis the portion of time and effort to be directed to existing customers. In this section, we summarize the findings of a study that examines these questions (Reinartz, Thomas, & Kumar, 2005).

In contrast to most other studies, the acquisition process is an integral component of the research model. The conceptual link between the acquisition and the retention process is important for two reasons. First, only by linking the two, one can see a complete and unbiased picture of the drivers behind customer selection/acquisition, relationship duration, and customer profitability (See Fig. 16.2) (Heckman, 1979).

Prior research has specifically shown that a failure to link acquisition and retention can lead to biased results and incorrect inferences (Thomas, 2001). This is due to the selection

bias resulting from the omission of information on no acquired prospects. Second, offensive processes and defensive processes compete for the same resources. Making the necessary trade-off requires a full specification of the key dimensions of the customer-firm relationship. Thus, a more complete model specification allows us to address a key managerial question: "Does the maximization of the respective objective functions (a.k.a, acquisition likelihood, lifetime duration, and customer value) lead to convergent or divergent resource allocation recommendations?"

It is important to note this model applies mainly to situations where managers mostly rely on direct customer communication, such as via sales force, direct mail, or Internet. This is the case for most B-to-B environments, as well as for many direct marketing contexts.

The interest of this study lies mainly in the impact of (1) amount of spending and (2) contact channel type on three dependent variables: acquisition rate, retention rate, and customer profitability.

As firms increase their acquisition budget, the associated acquisition rate and customer profitability will be less and less responsive (concavity). Even if, for all practical purposes, there were no limits on acquisition expenditure, firms are able to capture only a certain share of the potential targets. We can expect that acquisition expenditures will have diminishing marginal associations with the likelihood of customer acquisition. Also, acquisition expenditures will have diminishing marginal associations with customer profitability. Similarly we can see that increasing retention expenditures will cease to be profitable beyond a certain level. Thus, we can expect retention expenditures will have diminishing marginal associations with relationship duration and with customer profitability.

We would also like to see if the nature of the contact channel affects acquisition and relationship duration. We can expect highly interpersonal contact channels have a greater association with the likelihood of customer acquisition than less interpersonal contact channels. Also, highly interpersonal contact channels have a greater association with relationship duration than less interpersonal contact channels.

At the most simple level, different contact channels may be seen as having independent effects on the respective dependent variables, acquisition, duration, and customer profitability. However a potential interaction effect between channels is likely to exist. For example, one could argue that contacting a prospect via telesales and via direct mail at the same time may have a stronger effect than the sum of the separate effects administered at different points in time. This is due to the mutual reinforcement of the message delivered through the different contact channels at the same time.

The empirical context for this research is the same B-to-B firm as in the previous two examples. The following substantive conclusions emerge from this empirical context:

1. The *amount of investment* in a customer as well as *how it is invested* has an impact on acquisition, retention, and customer profitability.
2. Investments into customer acquisition and retention have diminishing marginal returns.
3. How much is invested in a customer-firm relationship has a larger impact on long-term customer profitability than how the expenditures are invested across communication channels.

Thus, optimizing the amount of relationship investment is of prime importance.

4. The relative effectiveness of highly personalized communication channels is much greater than the less personalized communication channels. However, the relative cost also needs to be taken into account when deciding the communication strategy as it affects the overall profitability.
5. Under spending in acquisition and retention is more detrimental and results in smaller ROIs than overspending.
6. When trading off between allocating expenditures to acquisition versus retention, a suboptimal allocation of retention expenditures will have a larger detrimental impact on long-term customer profitability than suboptimal acquisition expenditures.
7. The customer communication strategy that maximizes long-term customer profitability maximizes neither the acquisition rate nor the relationship duration. Instead, developing a communication strategy to manage long-term customer profitability generally requires a long-term and holistic perspective of the relationship. This perspective tends to give more emphasis to more interpersonal and interactive communications than a limited focus on acquisition.

Although the results are specific to the empirical context, the model can be applied to any environment where acquisition and retention efforts can be separated. Managers can use the proposed integrated framework not only to better understand the drivers of profitability, but also to know how to maximize profitability through optimal allocation of resources.

16.5   Preventing Customer Churn

Customer retention is a crucial function for any organization. When customers churn and end the relationship, it impacts the firm in several ways. First, the firm incurs a loss of revenue from the customers who have defected. Second, the firm loses the opportunity to recover the acquisition

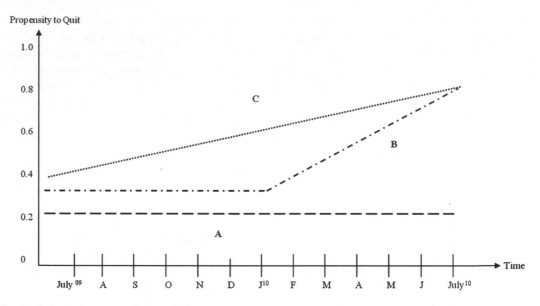

Fig. 16.3 Predicting propensity to quit

cost incurred on the defected customers, thereby increasing the pressure to break even. Third, the firm loses the opportunity to up-sell/cross-sell to customers who have defected, and this loss can be treated as a loss of potential revenue. Fourth, there are some "lost" social effects such as influencing other customers on product/service adoption and a potential negative word-of-mouth. Finally, firms must also invest additional resources to replace those lost customers with new customers, thereby draining the firm's resources already impacted by the loss of customers.

Given these potential problems of losing customers, it is essential for companies to adopt appropriate analytical tools to prevent customer churn. Analytical models (such as Dynamic Churn models) are used to predict future customer behavior and help firms decide which customer/distributor is likely to quit and at what time. These models empower the managers to execute timely, customer-specific marketing interventions that result in an increase in ROI. Some of the strategic questions faced by managers in implementing this strategy are:

• Should we intervene?
• Which customers should we intervene with?
• When do we intervene?

• Through which channel do we intervene?
• What do we offer them?

These critical questions can be answered by building propensity-to-quit models and integrating them with the CLV based models. To decide on the intervention necessity, it is essential on the part of the managers to study customer quitting tendencies. For instance, consider Customer A, Customer B, and Customer C. The predicted propensity-to-quit of the three customers over time (July 2009–July 2010) is illustrated in Fig. 16.3.

As shown in Fig. 16.3, Customer A does not intend to quit and is denoted by a straight line. Though Customer B does not exhibit a quitting tendency initially, he shows an increase in propensity to quit from January 2010. Customer C, represented by a steep curve, shows a strong tendency to quit from early on. Clearly, this indicates that Customers B and C are likely to quit in the near future and they are the customers to be intervened with.

Once the need to intervene and the customers to be intervened with have been decided, firms have to identify when the intervention has to be made. The answer to this question lies with a proactive intervention strategy. That is, the customers who show a strong tendency to quit (in

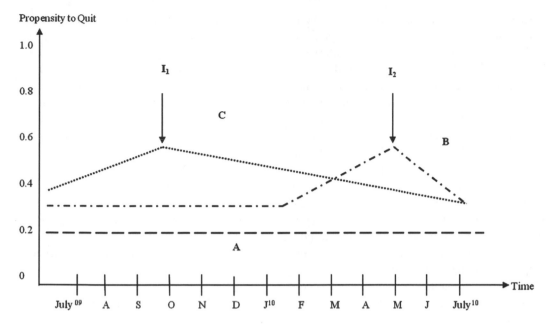

Fig. 16.4 Proactive intervention strategy

this case Customers B and C) should be targeted with intervention offers by the firm. Figure 16.4 shows the time periods in which Customers B and C should be intervened with.

In Fig. 16.4, points I_1 and I_2 denote the intervention points when customers B and C should be intervened and this is followed by a decrease in propensity to quit on the part of the customers. Here, Customer B is being intervened with in May 2010 and Customer C in October 2009. The reason for the time lag between the customer intervention stems from their respective propensities to quit. So, while Customer C is intervened with early on, Customer B can be intervened with at a later stage.

The decision on the channel of intervention and the type of offer through which the intervention is to be made is based on individual customer characteristics. The amount of resources to be spent on each customer is directly linked to the Customer Lifetime Value. If it costs the company $100 per customer to intervene with, it is not prudent to promote to a customer whose CLV is only $50. The company should intervene with an offer that costs less than $50. Thus, proactive intervention strategies help companies to pre-empt customer attrition and thereby increase ROI.

This strategy to prevent customer attrition was tested in a recent study for a telecommunications firm (Kumar & George). The firm first computed the propensity to quit for all its customers using 3 years of transaction and marketing communication data. Then, they created two groups of matched customer pairs who were similar in terms of their propensity to quit and the exchange characteristics such as their revenue contribution to the firm and duration. In other words, the customers in both groups had the same probability of quitting.

The average revenue per customer in both groups was $600 per year. The test group had 2,601 customers and the control group had 2,602 customers. There was no intervention for the control group and this group was used to see the impact of intervention on the test group. For all customers in the test group, however, the firm predicted propensity to quit and identified those customers who are likely to quit.

Based on the CLV of each customer, the firm designed customer-specific intervention strategies for all vulnerable customers. The total cost of intervention for the firm was $40,000 for the test group. The intervention saved 643 customers for the firm. By multiplying the number of customers by the average revenue contribution per customer, the total revenue gain was $385,800 for the group that was intervened. Thus, even after taking into account the cost of intervention, the firm had a net revenue gain of $345,800 by preventing attrition and the return on investment was close to 860% (i.e., the revenue contribution was 8.6 times the investment).

From the above study, it is clear that churn models help firms to identify the customers who are likely to quit, the intervention strategy based on CLV helps to effectively intervene to retain valuable customers. In this regard, targeting profitable prospects is an important planning phase for firms. Accurate customer profiling analysis helps firms implement a solid marketing strategy. Firms should target prospects precisely by choosing segments that match the firm's customer base and channels that match the customer's preferences. Additionally, firms should apply the knowledge gained about the new customers across the entire organization, cultivating customers, synchronizing departments and approaching customers on the one-to-one basis and providing solutions to their needs and wants.

16.6 Customer Brand Value

In our everyday lives, we come across different brands that we use. We perceive some brands as very high and some brands as very low. Why does this happen? Ideally, brands are developed to perform three important roles—(a) to draw new customers to the firm, (b) to remind existing customers about the products/services it offers, and (c) to forge an emotional attachment with its consumers (Rust et al., 2004). When brands start to perform poorly on one or more of these roles, it starts to lose its sheen and falters.

When a brand starts to face such hiccups, the brand manager or the marketing manager, and in some cases the entire corporate board faces some dilemma. Some of these questions include: (a) What do we invest on—building brands or building the customer base? (b) How do we manage the brand? (c) What can we do to renew our relationship with our customers? The single

answer to all these questions is to strengthen the brand and nurture profitable customer relationships simultaneously. How can we achieve this?

We can strengthen a brand by ascertaining and increasing the value a customer provides to the brand. This is value is referred to as CBV. And, we have already seen in the previous section that CLV can help firms in managing customer relationships profitably. Therefore, by establishing a link between CBV and CLV, we can strengthen the brand and build profitable relationships simultaneously. This section provides an approach to determine CBV and also designs an approach that will link CLV and CBV in order to ensure simultaneous growth in brand equity and customer equity.

16.6.1 What Is Customer Brand Value?

The concept of CBV refers to the differential effect of an individual's brand preference on his/her response to the marketing of a brand. It comprises of eight constructs (Kumar, Luo, & Rao, 2008). They are:

1. *Brand knowledge*, which is made up of a customer's awareness of the brand (brand awareness) and a customer's image of the brand (brand image)
2. *Brand attitude*, which is made up of a customer's trust in the brand (brand trust) and a customer's emotional response towards the brand (brand affect)
3. *Brand behavior intention*, which is made up of a customer's intention to purchase a brand (purchase intention) and,
4. *Brand behavior*, which is made up of a customer's repeat-buying behavior (brand loyalty), relationship with other customers of the brand (brand advocacy), and willingness to pay a price premium over other brands (brand price premium behavior)

Based on these eight constructs, it has been found that customers with greater brand value are more likely to engage in activities that result in an increase of customer lifetime value when compared to customers with low brand value. Intuitively, we can understand that an individual customer's brand knowledge, brand attitude and brand behavior intentions affect his/her brand purchase behavior. When this brand purchase behavior of a customer is linked to their lifetime value, a firm can expect to maximize profitability. This brings us to the next question, how do we link CBV and CLV?

16.6.2 Linking Customer Brand Value to Customer Lifetime Value

The link between CBV and CLV is established using customer-level data and advanced modeling techniques. The customer-level data is important to compute CLV and CBV. We have already seen that data for computing CLV can be secured from the customer transaction database within the company. To compute CBV, firms can get information regarding the various components of CBV from survey data. A survey that contains questions pertaining to the eight constructs can yield the firm information that is necessary for computing CBV. Once this information is available, the next step is to estimate how these components affect each other by using sophisticated estimation techniques. The components of CBV are obtained using a ten-point scale from a sample of customers. For the same customers, CLV is computed at that time. Conceptually, the CLV score is modeled as a function of these eight constructs.

16.6.3 What Are the Managerial Benefits of Linking Customer Brand Value to Customer Lifetime Value?

There are three key implications of linking CBV to CLV. They are:

Monitor the overall performance of Customer Brand Value. This linkage can help firms to monitor the overall performance of CBV. Firms can sample a group of existing and potential customers. Then, they can measure their individual brand values. Finally, they can identify the weak components in the individual brand values and come up with different strategies to improve or positively influence them.

Manage brand at the segment level. In order to manage the brand at a segment level, firms can segment customers based on CBV and CLV. This would yield a matrix with four cells, very similar to the "Managing loyalty and profitability simultaneously" strategy of CLV (refer Chap. 15). Here, we can segment high CLV-high CBV customers as "True Loyalists"; high CLV-low CBV customers as "Acquaintances"; low CLV-high CBV as "Poor Patrons"; and low CLV-low CBV customers as "Strangers".

The marketing strategy for "True Loyalists" is to keep building positive brand knowledge and attitude with this segment of customers. For the "Acquaintances" segment, firms should think of other ways to increase their CLV with limited brand investment. With regard to the "Poor Patrons" segment, firms should moderately invest to improve the brand values in this segment. They can encourage cross-buy and add-on selling to increase the customers' CLV values. Finally for the "Strangers" segment, firms should invest moderately on the strangers who have the potential to increase their CLV values.

Manage brand at the individual level. Firms can also manage brands at the individual customer level. We saw in the "Managing loyalty and profitability simultaneously" strategy of CLV that "True friends" are the most valuable asset of a company. Therefore, firms can manage brand at the individual level to make sure that the brand message appeals to this segment of customers. Firms should select a sample of True Friends and constantly monitor their individual knowledge structure, positive brand attitude, purchase intention, and brand behavior. Once the individual decision process is understood, personalized marketing action can be performed to send the right message at the right time so that the individual's CLV and CBV can be simultaneously maximized.

Until now, we have seen how a customer can provide value to a firm through his/her purchases and to a brand through his/her preferences towards the brand. These two sources of value originate directly from the customers. However, a customer can also provide indirect value to a firm through his/her referrals or positive word-of-mouth. The next section discusses the

Customer Referral Value metric, its measurement and strategies to maximize it.

16.7 Customer Referral Value

Many firms now use viral marketing programs to harness the power of word-of-mouth and referrals to acquire new customers. Typically, satisfied customers provide referrals and positive WOM to their friends or associates. Some of these referred customers will have the potential to be profitable customers of the firm. Consequently, a customer's CLV for a firm will not only be the profits they contribute but also the profits resulting from those they influence. This indirect value that a customer brings in through referrals is measured by the CRV metric.

We have seen that the CLV metric is a superior customer value metric over all the conventional metrics. However, the treatment this metric gives to customer satisfaction is not so complete. While it is true that the customer satisfaction information is captured by accounting for customer buying behavior, it does not involve a direct measurement. It is clear that customers can not only contribute value to the firm through their own transactions (direct profits), but they also have an impact on the transactions of other customers through word-of-mouth and referrals (indirect profits) by helping the firm to acquire new customers at lower costs. Therefore, we need a metric such as CRV to determine the value of a customer's ability to spread word-of-mouth and make referrals.

16.7.1 What Is Customer Referral Value?

Customer Referral Value is defined as a customer's expected future referral value with the firm. This metric enables managers to measure and manage each customer based on his ability to generate indirect profit to the firm. This indirect impact on the firm's profit comes through savings in acquisition costs and through the addition of new customers by way of customer referral.

Calculating customer referral value (CRV) is more complex than calculating the lifetime value. Consider a customer, Jane, for whom we will compute the referral value. First, we need to compute the average number of successful referrals she will make after we offer her an incentive to do so through a marketing campaign. As we do for her CLV, we look at Jane's past behavior, but we need to look at a period longer than a month to get enough variance in the number of referrals for proper statistical modeling and predictive accuracy. The time period varies from industry to industry.

Then, we need to estimate the time frame for which our marketing campaign has an impact in generating referrals. In other words, we need to determine the time until which Jane's referrals are actually prompted by our referral incentive. In research studies, it has been found that this time period is about 1 year. That is, referrals made by customers after a referral-incentive marketing campaign can be attributed to that campaign for about a year. Therefore in computing CRV, we count only those referrals that are made within a year.

Then, we need to determine how many of those referrals would have become customers of the firm anyway, even if Jane had not recommended the firm. The reason for determining this is simple. If a new customer, let's call him John, would not have joined without Jane's referral (referred to as a type-one referral), then Jane's referral value should include the value of John's business. However, if John would have become a customer without Jane's referral (referred to as a type-two referral), then, Jane's CRV should include only the savings in acquisition costs for John, since no direct marketing effort was needed to get him. Obtaining this information can be done through surveys by asking a simple question such as: "How likely is it that you would have purchased our product/service without a referral in the next 12 months?"

After collecting this information, we can compute Jane's referral value as the present value of her type-one referrals plus the present value of her type-two referrals. Therefore, if we assume that if John would not have become a customer had Jane not referred him, then, Jane's type-one referral of John is essentially the same as his lifetime customer value—the present value of the difference between John's contribution to margin and the cost of marketing to him, projected over 1 year. Consequently, the value of type-two customers is the present value of the savings in acquisition costs. As with all cost-revenue analyses, if the cost involved in acquiring type-two referrals exceeds the cost of alternative acquisition methods, type-two customers can be a liability for the firm. Therefore, the CRV formula can be expressed as follows:

$$CRV_i = \sum_{t=1}^{T} \sum_{y=1}^{n1} \frac{(A_{ty} - a_{ty} - M_{ty} + ACQ1_{ty})}{(1+r)^t}$$
$$+ \sum_{t=1}^{T} \sum_{y=n1}^{n2} \frac{(ACQ2_{ty})}{(1+r)^t}$$

$$(16.1)$$

Where:

T = the number of periods that will be predicted into the future (e.g. quarters, years)

A_{ty} = the gross margin contributed by customer 'y' who otherwise would not have bought the product

a_{ty} = the cost of the referral for customer 'y'

1 to n1 = the number of customers who would not join without the referral

n2 − n1 = the number of customers who would have joined anyway

M_{ty} = the marketing costs needed to retain the referred customers

$ACQ1_{ty}$ = the savings in acquisition cost from customers who would not join without the referral

$ACQ2_{ty}$ = the savings in acquisition cost from customers who would have joined anyway

In simple terms, (16.1) can also be expressed as follows:

Table 16.6 Tom's referral behavior in a financial services company (semi-annual data)

Number of referrals per period (n_2)	4
Marketing cost per period (M_{ty})	$18
Average gross margin (A_{ty})	$98
Cost of referral (a_{ty})	$40
Acquisition cost savings ($ACQ1_{ty}$ and $ACQ2_{ty}$)	$5
Number of referrals that would have joined anyway ($n_2 - n_1$)	2
Yearly discount rate (r)	15%

Having seen the concept and measurement of CRV, let us actually compute the CRV of a customer from a hypothetical financial services company.

16.7.2 How Can Compute Customer Referral Value Be Computed?

In order to value customers and see how they truly impact the bottom line of the company, let us consider a typical customer—Tom, from a financial services company. Using this customer's referral behavior data from the company, we will compute his referral value (CRV). The data we need to compute the referral value is provided in Table 16.6.

There are four steps involved in the computation of CRV. They are:

Step 1: In the first step, we determine whether customers would have made purchases anyway. As is evident from Table 16.6, Tom refers four customers per period (6 months) and of those four customers, two would have joined anyway. So, n_1 in this case is two and n_2 in this case is four. For the purpose of illustration, we consider here only the value of those customers who were directly referred by Tom and made a purchase. This approach can also be extended to include

$$CRV_i = \frac{Value\ of\ customers\ who\ joined\ because\ of\ referral}{Discount\ rate}$$
$$+ \frac{Value\ of\ customers\ who\ would\ join\ anyway}{Discount\ rate}$$

$$(16.2)$$

the value brought in by customers who were indirectly referred by Tom, wherever applicable.

Step 2: In the second step, we predict the future value of each referred customer. The future value of each referred customer is based on that customer's gross margin per period ($98), marketing cost per period ($18), acquisition cost savings ($5), cost of referral ($40), and discount rate (15% annually).

Step 3: In the third step, we predict the number of referrals generated. The number of referrals predicted for Tom is four per period. Because we are measuring CRV for 1 year, Tom will generate a total of eight referrals.

Step 4: In the final step, we predict the timing of customer referrals. Since, Tom refers four customers per period, in terms of timing this means that four customers are referred in the first half of the year and four customers are referred in the second half of the year.

Applying these steps for the data we have for Tom, we get the following:

For Period 1:

$$CRV_1 = \sum_{y=1}^{n1} \frac{(A_{1y} - a_{1y} - M_{1y} + ACQ1_{1y})}{(1+r)^1}$$

$$+ \sum_{y=n1+1}^{n2} \frac{(ACQ2_{1y})}{(1+r)^1}$$

$$\hspace{10cm} (16.3)$$

$$CRV_1 = \sum_{y=1}^{2} \frac{(\$98 - \$40 - \$18 + \$5)}{(1+0.075)^1}$$

$$+ \sum_{y=3}^{4} \frac{(\$5)}{(1+0.075)^1}$$

$$\approx \$93$$

For Period 2:

$$CRV_2 = \sum_{y=1}^{n1} \frac{(A_{2y} - M_{2y})}{(1+r)^2}$$

$$+ \sum_{y=1}^{n1} \frac{(A_{2y} - a_{2y} - M_{2y} + ACQ1_{2y})}{(1+r)^2}$$

$$+ \sum_{y=n1+1}^{n2} \frac{(ACQ2_{2y})}{(1+r)^2}$$

$$\hspace{10cm} (16.4)$$

$$CRV_2 = \sum_{y=1}^{2} \frac{(\$98 - \$18)}{(1+0.075)^2}$$

$$+ \sum_{y=1}^{2} \frac{(\$98 - \$40 - \$18 + \$5)}{(1+0.075)^2}$$

$$+ \sum_{y=3}^{4} \frac{(\$5)}{(1+0.075)^2}$$

$$\approx 225$$

$$Total\ CRV = CRV_1 + CRV_2 \approx 318$$

Therefore, the total CRV for Tom for 1 year is the sum of CRV_1 and CRV_2, which is around $318. As the results show, the impact grows as time progresses. The main reason for this is the growth of the customer base due to referrals in each period. In period 1, there were only four new customers, whereas in period 2 there were six customers in the value of the CRV (four new customers and two customers from period 1 who bought only because of the referral).

As mentioned already, because this is a conservative estimate of the value of customer referrals (that is, only the direct referrals are used in the CRV), it does not provide a true picture in terms of the number of new customers who have been acquired by the firm and the total value all these new customers are worth to the firm. If we want to see how many new customers came on board over these two periods that stem from the original customer and the value of these new customers, we need to look at both the direct and the indirect referrals (For more information on direct and indirect referrals see Kumar & Bhaskaran, 2010). If each of the customers who were referred during a specific period also made some referrals in subsequent periods, we would see an exponential growth in the total number of new customers who were acquired in the two periods and the total CRV for those customers. Given that CRV also considers the net present value brought in by a customer, one might wonder how CRV is linked with CLV. The following section provides the linkage.

16.7.3 How Can Customer Referral Value Be Linked to Customer Lifetime Value?

Once the CRV of customers has been computed, it is essential for managers to understand the relationship it shares with CLV. Now that we have a measurement for both CLV and CRV, we know the value provided by the actual purchases made by the customer (CLV) and the influence that customer has on other potential customers (CRV). With this information, managers can begin to make decisions about how to treat and market to customers based on the various combinations of whether the customer is low or high on CLV or CRV.

As noted previously, many firms are using CLV as a method for selecting customers for word-of-mouth and referral campaigns. If the customers who rated highly on CLV were the same customers who rated highly on CRV, managers would not need to use both metrics when managing customers. However, because only transactional and demographic data (not attitudinal data) has played an important role in predicting CLV, customers who score highly on CLV are probably not the same as those who are successful at referring new customers. In fact, a recent marketing study found that customers who score high on CRV are not the most valuable customers, as determined by CLV. This study used the transaction and referral behavior data from a telecommu-nications firm to investigate the link between CLV and CRV. The findings of the study are provided in Table 16.7 (Kumar, Petersen, & Leone, 2007).

As is evident from Table 16.7, the top 30% of the customers ranked on the basis of CLV (deciles 1, 2 and 3) have no overlap with the top 30% of customers based on CRV (deciles 5, 6, and 7). This finding provides managers important insights on customer management. If managers ignored the concept of CRV and focused only on CLV, then they would miss out on the positive WOM and the cascading business it would generate. Consequently, if they focused only on CRV and ignored high CLV customers, they would be alienating the most valuable customers for want of positive WOM. Any of these two scenarios can cause much harm to customer growth and, in some cases may even generate negative WOM.

16.7.4 What Are the Managerial Benefits of Linking Customer Referral Value and Customer Lifetime Value?

To show the impact of measuring and managing these two metrics simultaneously, a field study was conducted with the telecommunications firm to see the benefits of measuring and managing CLV and CRV simultaneously.

For the purpose of the field study, a test group and a control group of 9,900 customers each were considered. CLV and CRV were measured for each of the groups. Based on these two values, the customers in both groups were divided into four cells of a 2 × 2 matrix. The cells were segmented on the following basis— high CLV/high CRV, high CLV/low CRV, low CLV/high CRV, and low CLV/low CRV. The cutoff points for the four segments were determined based on the median value for both the CLV and CRV measures. Table 16.8 summarizes these results.

Of the sample of 9,900 customers, the "Misers" and "Champions" segments had 2,079 customers each, and the "Affluents" and "Advocates" segments had 2,871 customers each. These findings also validate the findings presented in Table 16.8

Table 16.7 Customer deciles of CLV and CRV for a telecommunications firm

Deciles (ranked by CLV)	CLV ($) (1 year)	CRV ($) (1 year)
1	**1,933**	40
2	**1,067**	52
3	**633**	90
4	360	750
5	313	**930**
6	230	**1,020**
7	190	**870**
8	160	96
9	137	65
10	120	46

Source: Adapted from Kumar et al. (2007)

Table 16.8 CLV-CRV matrix for a telecommunications firm

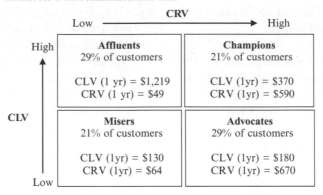

	CRV Low → High	
High ↑ CLV	**Affluents** 29% of customers CLV (1 yr) = $1,219 CRV (1 yr) = $49	**Champions** 21% of customers CLV (1yr) = $370 CRV (1yr) = $590
Low	**Misers** 21% of customers CLV (1yr) = $130 CRV (1yr) = $64	**Advocates** 29% of customers CLV (1yr) = $180 CRV (1yr) = $670

that high CLV and high CRV customers are distinct sets of customers. The results of this measurement of CLV and CRV show that there are distinct sets of customers found in the four different cells based on the large differences in the values for CLV and CRV across the cells. Further, it has to be noted that there exists a significant difference between the customers who are high on the CLV measure and those who are high on the CRV measure. Now, let us consider each of the cells separately.

The *"Affluents"*, or the high CLV/low CRV customers, purchase a lot of products and services for themselves, but they do not refer many new customers to buy products and services. On the contrary, the *"Misers"*, or the low CLV/low CRV customers, do not purchase much or refer many new customers. Their low purchase behavior may be due to frequent brand switching, small SOW or they might be waiting to find out from others whether the product is worth purchasing.

The *"Advocates"*, or the low CLV/high CRV customers, do not exhibit a high purchase behavior for themselves. However, they are actively involved in talking about the product to other customers and encouraging them to buy products. Finally, and true to their name, *"Champions"*, or the high CLV/high CRV customers, are more likely to buy more products/services from the company and talk more about them to other customers.

Given the vast differences between the four cells, the customers in each of the cells should be evaluated differently with respect to their total value to the company and then approached with different types of marketing offers to get the greatest overall value from them. To understand the true value of treating customers differently, the telecommunications firm initiated three different campaigns over the course of 1 year in an effort to migrate customers from low CLV/CRV cells to high CLV/CRV cells. These campaigns were administered to the sample customers from the test group. The control sample did not receive any of these targeted marketing communications. Table 16.9 summarizes these campaigns.

It is clear from Table 16.9 that each of the three campaigns was designed with a different goal in mind. The campaign for the 'Misers' was designed to help the company identify opportunities of building a relationship with them. This campaign not only offered incentives for them to buy more products for their own use, which would increase their CLV, but also offered them incentives to refer new customers, which would increase their CRV. The goal of this campaign was to migrate them toward one of the other three cells ("Affluents", "Advocates", or "Champions"), depending on whether the campaign increased their CLV, their CRV, or both.

The campaign for the "Affluents" was launched to encourage referral behavior using referral incentives, while retaining their CLV at the highest level. And when their referral value increases, it will cause them to migrate toward the "Champions" cell. Additionally, this will also increase the average CLV of the "Champions" cell over time, as the "Affluents" bring their high CLV with them.

Table 16.9 Campaign for "Misers", "Advocates" and "Affluents" for a telecommunications firm

Campaign for "Misers"	Campaign for "Affluents"	Campaign for "Advocates"
Targeted with bundled offers for one or more products	Targeted with emphasis on the referral incentive for both them and the referred customers	Sent personalized direct mail communication that included offers for bundling one or more products
Personalized communication sent via direct mail and followed up with another direct mail piece within a 2-week period	Contacted through a direct mail communication, followed by another direct mail communication within 2 weeks	Follow up communication was sent through direct mail within 2 weeks
Telephone assistance for those customers on questions regarding additional services and the value of obtaining the additional services	Emphasized a $20 incentive for both the referral and the referring customer for signing up for products and/or services	Contacted a sample of these customers via the telephone to answer any questions regarding the additional services and the value of subscribing to multiple products/ services
Value of making referrals was highlighted for these customers and a $20 incentive was offered to them for making a referral		

Similarly, the campaign for the "Advocates" was designed to encourage these customers to spend more while at the same time keeping their CRV at the highest level. The company could potentially gain a higher direct profit from these customers by migrating them to the "Champions" cell.

So, what was the result of all these campaigns? The study tracked the three segments individually and monitored their performance. At the end of 1 year, the company realized impressive results from these campaigns. Table 16.10 presents the results of the campaigns.

From Table 16.10 it is clear that the goal to migrate customers was achieved. After administering the campaign, the number of customers in the "Misers" segment decreased from 21% to 9%. Of the 12% who migrated to other segments, 4% of the customers went to the "Affluents", "Champions" and "Advocates" segments each. The gains from this migration were also substantial. The average CLV of the "Affluents", "Champions" and "Advocates" increased by 185%, 138% and 422% respectively. Additionally, the "Champions" segment also witnessed a 328% increase in its average CRV. In actual numbers, of the original sample of customers from the "Misers" cell (2,079 customers), 396 of them moved toward "Champions" and produced increases of CLV of $71,280 and CRV of $83,160. While these numbers may seem small, this would pro-

duce huge numbers when projected to the entire customer base of the company.

With respect to the "Affluents" segment, nearly 4% of the customers migrated to the "Champions" segment. In value terms, this resulted in a 388% increase in referral value gains. This means that not only is the telecommunications firm increasing its revenue from all its customers, but that the customer base is growing, too. This allows the firm to greatly expand its customer base and find new revenue sources outside of just trying to cross-sell and up-sell to its current customers.

With respect to the "Advocates" segment, nearly 5% of the customers migrated to the "Champions" segment. This resulted in an increase of 61% in its average CLV. In this case, the telecommunications firm has been able to take customers who it would have initially ignored if they were looking only at CLV because of their low CLV and moved them toward the most desirable cell in the 2×2 matrix (those with high CLV and CRV).

It is therefore clear from these findings that the strategy was successful in not only migrating customers toward better cells, but also in moving these customers to cells that have significantly higher CLV, CRV, or both. Now, one might wonder how much it cost the company to run these campaigns, and whether the gains were

Table 16.10 Campaign results for "Misers", "Advocates" and "Affluents"

Segment	Total segment size (%)		% of customers migrated towards (%)			Average customer value before campaign		Average customer value increase after campaign		
	Before campaign	After campaign	Affluents	Champions	Advocates	1 year CLV	1 year CRV	Affluents	Champions	Advocates
Misers	21	9	4	4	4	$130	$64	CLV ↑ to $370	CLV ↑ to $310 CRV ↑ to $274	CLV ↑ to $334
Affluents	29	25	–	4	–	$1,219	$49	–	CLV ↔ at $1,219 CRV ↑ to $239	–
Advocates	29	24	–	5	–	$180	$670	–	CLV ↑ to $290 CRV ↔ at $670	–

Source: Adapted from Kumar et al. (2007)

worthwhile or not. The cost of the three campaigns, which included direct mail, email, and selected telephone calls for the 7,821 customers (customers from the three cells: "Affluents", "Misers", and "Advocates") in the sample, was approximately $31,500. On a per customer basis, this would be nearly $4 per customer. The overall profit obtained through increases in each customer's CLV or CRV from each of the three campaigns was $486,090. Therefore, the overall ROI of the campaign was around 15.5.

As evident in Table 16.10, the ROI from running these three customized campaigns has generated significant gains in profit. It is also important to note that a considerable amount of customization is required to realize such gains. Therefore, while this study cannot be directly applied in another industry, with similar customizations similar gains can be achieved. Now that we have learned about CRV and its link to CLV, let us see the managerial implications of adopting this approach.

16.7.5 What Should the Focus Be on: Customer Referral Value or Customer Lifetime Value?

Companies like Bank of America and Vonage have introduced a value-oriented referral incentive program that rewards both the referral and the referring customer. Bank of America rewards both the referral and the referring customer $25 whenever a referral opens a personal checking account. Similarly, when a business owner opens a business checking account both the referral and the referring customer get $50.

On the other hand, Vonage leverages the social media buzz to reward the referring customer. For every referral that signs up for Vonage service, the referring customer gets 1 month of free service. Similarly, DIRECTV provides $100 to both the referral and the referring customer. This reward is offered in the form of $10 monthly bill credits for 10 consecutive months. These incentives seem to be in proportion to the typical value brought in by each member in the respective referral groups.

Therefore, it is clear that customers who score highly on the CLV measure are not the same customers who score highly on the CRV measure. Further, firms should measure both CLV and CRV to implement marketing campaigns that focus on customers based on both dimensions. A marketing campaign that focuses on both metrics will allow firms to both increase the profitability of each customer and, cash in on the power of positive WOM.

Now the question is how managers can know which campaign to choose—a campaign for CLV or a campaign for CRV? In other words, is there a trade-off when maximizing one versus the other? With information about the objective of the campaign, the stage of the product in its life cycle, the potential number of prospects in the pool, and the nature of competition in the market, managers can decide on the nature of the campaign that will drive revenue and profit.

A CLV campaign would be most appropriate in a situation where the goal is to get users to buy more in a specific category or buy across more categories. Typically, such campaigns happen in competitive markets where it is tough to acquire new customers or in niche markets where the prospect pool is very limited. On the other hand, a CRV campaign would be most appropriate in a situation where the aim is to acquire more customers/prospects through their current customers. This is because, the current customers may already be spending the majority of their budget with the company, and programs to increase cross-selling or up-selling would not yield much success. Of course, the caveat in selecting the choice of customers for CRV campaigns is to be cognizant of the fact that high-CLV customers are not the customers who refer the most. The study explained here shows the importance of measuring the value of a customer's own transactions *and* the value of their impact on the transactions of other customers, and not one or the other in isolation.

It is therefore important to encourage customers to build social networks and provide referral incentives for them to talk to other customers. Strong social networks can also be a source of long-term competitive advantage for both the customers and the firm. This is because, it becomes harder for the competitors to lure away customers who are tightly locked in to their social network, while at the same time consumers in a strong network enjoy ease of information sharing about products and services and the use of common products and services. Therefore, a firm should view its customers as skilled resources and work with them to build strong social networks through which both the firm and the customer can benefit.

16.8 Summary

Customer equity is the aggregation of the expected lifetime values of a firm's entire base of existing customers and the expected future value of newly acquired customers. The NPV objective function required to maximize the customer equity of a firm is related to the cash flow from each customer, the expected interpurchase time, and the cost and frequency of the marketing/communication strategies employed. The objective function is based on a probability model which predicts the interpurchase time of each customer, a panel data model which predicts the cash flows from each customer, and an optimization algorithm which maximizes the profits. By applying an optimization model, a manager can know the extent to which he should use various contact channels. Cross analysis of duration of relationship and customer value obtained on the basis of the NPV maximization objective function indicates not all short-duration customers deliver lower profits, and not all long-duration customers deliver higher profits. Identifying and targeting responsive and profitable customers and deemphasizing efforts on some customers who were not profitable-irrespective of whether they are classified as long-duration or short-duration customers-would be a better approach. Customer value-based approach demonstrated its superiority to the duration of association approach in terms of profitable segmentation of customers.

Purchase sequence model captures the differences in the durations between purchases for different product categories. An individual customer-level profit function is developed to predict customer value. The success of the experiment based on the model demonstrated by higher revenue, lower cost of communication, lower number of attempts before a purchase is made, higher profits, and higher ROI for the test group, when compared to the control group, indicates the scope to which the customer value approach offers in improving the quality of marketing decisions.

The acquisition-process is an integral component of the research model. By linking acquisition and the retention process, it is possible to see a complete and unbiased picture of the drivers behind customers election/acquisition, relationship duration, and customer profitability. Also, making the necessary trade-off between offensive processes and defensive processes requires a full specification of the key dimensions of the customer-firm relationship. A more complete model specification addresses the key managerial question of whether the maximization of the respective objective functions as acquisition likelihood, lifetime duration, and customer value would lead to convergent or divergent resource allocation recommendations. This model applies mainly to situations where managers rely mostly on direct customer communication. Acquisition expenditures will have diminishing marginal associations with customer profitability. Retention expenditures will have diminishing marginal associations with relationship duration and with customer profitability. Highly interpersonal contact channels have a greater association with the likelihood of customer acquisition and relationship duration than less interpersonal contact channels. Though the results are specific to the empirical context, the model can be applied to any environment where acquisition and retention efforts can be separated. Managers can use the proposed integrated framework not only to better understand the drivers of profitability, but also to know how to maximize profitability through optimal allocation of resources.

Reaching out to potential customers with targeted offers has never been easier. Discovering the firm's best target requires extensive customer profiling research. Firms need comprehensive, reliable customer profile information to effectively customize their marketing plans. Targeting specific audience and understanding the demographic characteristics, lifestyle behaviors and purchase preferences that drive customers' buying decisions leads to a successful marketing campaign. The strategy described and illustrated here shows the effect of the customer intervention strategy in a telecom firm. Using the strategy, the firm realized a net revenue gain of $345,000 after accounting for the cost of intervention, and the ROI was close to 860%. This clearly shows that the key to retaining customers is to identify those who are likely to quit and reach them with appropriate messages.

Customer brand value refers to the differential effect of an individual's brand preference on his/ her response to the marketing of a brand. When companies understand the link between CBV and CLV, they can efficiently allocate their resources to generate maximum value. The CBV is influenced by several factors such as brand knowledge, brand attitude, and brand behavior intentions. By establishing a link between these factors to the final customer behavior outcomes, firms can effectively manage the CBV and CLV simultaneously. Additionally, this linkage enables firms to take appropriate corrective measures to simultaneously build both the customer's brand value and lifetime value.

Customer referral value refers to a customer's expected future profits obtained through his referrals. This chapter has shown that it is important for firms to use both CLV and CRV metrics when managing customers. Customers who score high on the CLV metric do not score high on the CRV metric. Therefore, it is important to understand that a customer provides value to the firm either through CLV or CRV—or both. However, customers should be evaluated differently with respect to their total value to the company and then they should be approached with different types of marketing offers catering to maximizing CLV and/or CRV. This allows firms to increase the profitability of each customer and, in turn, increase the number of new customers buying products and services.

Exercise Questions

1. Consider a multiproduct company and discuss the likely sequence in which the average customer would buy these products. Why do you think an average customer may not be the best way to consider this problem?
2. Discuss the relative importance of the customer acquisition and retention processes from the perspective of customer lifetime value.
3. What are the important questions companies should think about in order to develop a successful proactive intervention strategy?
4. Should we invest in building brand value or customer value?
5. "By focusing referral program efforts only on the high value customers, it is possible for companies to increase their CRV." Do you agree with this statement? If not, which customer segment(s) should managers focus on, and why?

References

Heckman, J. J. (1979). Sample selection bias as a specification error. *Econometrica, 47*(1), 153–161.

Hogan, J. E., Lehmann, D. R., Merino, M., Srivastava, R. K., Thomas, J. S., & Verhoef, P. C. (2002). Linking customer assets to financial performance. *Journal of Service Research, 5*(1), 26–38.

Kumar, V., & George, M. Saving customers through timely intervention. *Working Paper,* Georgia State University, Atlanta.

Kumar, V., & Bhaskaran, V. (2010). How influential are the influencers?: Calculating word-of-mouth value of the networked individual. *Working paper*, Georgia State University.

Kumar, V., Luo A., & Rao, V. R. (2008). Linking an individual's brand value to the CLV: An integrated framework. *Working Paper*, Georgia State University.

Kumar, V., Petersen, J. A., & Leone, R. P. (2007). How valuable is word of mouth? *Harvard Business Review, 85*(10), 139–146.

Kumar, V., Venkatesan, R., & Reinartz, W. (2004). A purchase sequence analysis frame work for targeting products, customers and time period. Forthcoming in *Journal of Marketing*.

Reinartz, W., Thomas, J. S., & Kumar, V. (2005). Balancing acquisition and retention resources to maximize customer profitability. *Journal of Marketing, 69*(1), 63–79.

Rust, R. T., Lemon, K. N., & Narayandas, D. (2004). *Customer equity management*. New Jersey: Pearson Education.

Rust, R. T., Zeithaml, V. A., & Lemon, K. N. (2000). *Driving customer equity: How customer lifetime value is reshaping corporate strategy*. New York: The Free Press.

Thomas, J. S. (2001). A methodology for linking customer acquisition to customer retention. *Journal of Marketing Research, 38*(2), 262–268.

Venkatesan, R., & Kumar, V. (2004). A customer lifetime value framework for customer selection and optimal resource allocation strategy. *Journal of Marketing, 68*(4), 106–125.

Future of CRM

17

17.1 Overview

CRM has become an integral function in corporate strategies in recent years as marketing strategies are becoming increasingly customer-centric. From multinational corporations to small businesses, firms of all industries and sizes are investing more resources into CRM and placing a greater emphasis on its role in marketing to their customers. The growth in importance of CRM implementation is exemplified in the case of Zappos, the online shoe retailing phenomenon. Founded in 1999, Zappos has grown to become the internet's largest shoe retailer and was sold to Amazon.com for $1.2 billion in 2009 (Hsieh, 2010).

At Zappos the entire company philosophy starts with customer service and CRM proficiency. By adopting a customer-centric business model that preaches customer satisfaction, and not monetary profit as the day to day goal has been integral in their massive success over the last decade. All newly hired employees including executives are required to participate in a 4-week customer loyalty course in order to have all company members buy into the company concept and mission (Beaudry, 2009). While product and brand loyalty are at an all time low, Zappos has made it its mission to provide customers with the kind of individual attention that is increasingly scarce.

Zappos customer service is intent on knowing everything about their customers' lives. The story of a middle aged woman, Zaz Lamarr, is a great example of the in-depth customer knowledge that Zappos strives to obtain. Lamarr meant to return some shoes to Zappos, but her mother passed away and, naturally, she just did not have the time. Zappos launched an inquiry to find out what was happening to the shoes, and Lamarr informed them that she had not had the time to return them due to these exigent circumstances. Without hesitation, Zappos arranged to have UPS come pick up the shoes before sending her flowers and their deepest condolences (Marco, 2007). All of these new means of gathering and disseminating data are facilitating relationships, and when building customer loyalty, being able to incorporate mutual benefit as the foundation for the relationship can go a long way.

To understand the future of CRM, let us first take a step back and look at where CRM stands right now by summarizing the three different CRM perspectives that were discussed throughout the previous chapters.

The first perspective, *Strategic CRM*, has as an objective to mold the interactions between a firm and its customers in order to maximize CLV for the firm. Firms must be aware that customers vary in their value contributed through their purchases, and therefore strive to shape the customer-firm interaction through acquisition and retention strategies aimed at driving firm profitability. This complex set of customer-oriented activities forms the foundation for a sustainable and inimitable competitive advantage leading to a successful strategic CRM. As

V. Kumar and W. Reinartz, *Customer Relationship Management*, Springer Texts in Business and Economics, DOI 10.1007/978-3-642-20110-3_17, © Springer-Verlag Berlin Heidelberg 2012

discussed in the text (Chaps. 3 and 4), the four integral inputs in a CRM strategy are:

1. A customer-management orientation
2. Integration and alignment of organizational processes
3. Capture of information and alignment of technology
4. Implementation of CRM strategy

The second perspective, *Analytical CRM*, is designed to help firms migrate from relying entirely on traditional marketing metrics to customer-based value metrics. This change has been possible largely due to technological advancements in collecting and mining customer-level data to glean insights regarding customers, markets, products, and processes. This data mining process is essential to providing businesses the ability to make informed, knowledge driven strategic business decisions in order to predict future trends and behaviors.

The third perspective, *Operational CRM*, is gaining significant traction among firms due to changes with respect to (1) consumers, (2) marketplaces, (3) technology, and (4) marketing functions.

1. With respect to consumers, factors such as increasing customer diversity, time scarcity, value consciousness, intolerance for low service levels, information availability and technological aptitude, and decrease in loyalty have contributed to constantly changing customer profiles. These changes in customer profiles have significantly impacted consumer power and choice, and thereby profits for businesses.
2. The global marketplace has changed significantly over the past few decades due to increased globalization, and the growth in the services economy and advancements in technology. These catalysts have been the root cause for intensified competition for customers, market segmentation, and product/service differentiation in the marketplace. As a consequence of these trends, a good product is no longer sufficient to compete and harder to differentiate in a world of high product standards. Due to this, companies are focusing more on enduring commercial relationships

through behavioral and purchase histories in order to customize products and services. This shift to a customer-centric model has underlined the importance of Customer Relationship Management for companies in their market positioning.

3. The supply and demand of data storage technology has changed dramatically, with the former getting cheaper despite increasing in quality, and the latter experiencing an explosive growth in data that is available for storage. This is due to the growth in online visits by consumers, which consequently increases the amount of transactions, web log files, and applications. All of the above increases have provided firms with revolutionary opportunities to inform themselves regarding customer behavior and attitudes. Having said that, the real value in this opportunity exists in firms' ability to manage, analyze, and apply such a mass of insight and information to drive profits for the companies.
4. The nature and methods of marketing communications are experiencing prominent changes, with direct and interactive media outpacing traditional mass marketing techniques due to their ability to customize and adapt to increasingly segmented and demanding consumers.

Having reviewed the various CRM perspectives and how businesses have transformed over the years, it is clear that marketing has had a significant role in the transformation. As we look ahead, there are some developments that we expect would bring in the next wave of transformation into the marketing realm. This chapter discusses some of the developments that are already making considerable headway in the business world.

17.2 Social CRM

One of the newest and fastest growing forms of CRM is Social CRM. The emergence of the social web has been the focal point and the catalyst for the growth of Social CRM. With the emergence of peer-to-peer networks, conversations no longer have boundaries and limitations. These networks are increasingly influencing how customers interact with each other and how businesses use the social media tools to manage customer relationships. We provide here a review of the popular social media channels and their influence in CRM activities.

17.2.1 Popular Social Media Channels

17.2.1.1 Blogs

The blogosphere has become a key influencer in designing marketing strategies and tactics over the last half decade Marketing News, 2009. According to San Francisco-based Technorati, the number of blogs has increased from an estimated 300,000 in 2003 to over 112 million in 2008. From Fortune 500 marketers to small business retailers, the blogosphere has become a key marketing platform to improve efficiency in communications, customer service, and brand marketing. Technorati research has shown that four out of five bloggers post attitudinal product or brand reviews, showing a clear need for marketers to listen to the peer-to-peer conversations and respond accordingly. Furthermore, given the importance of blogs in consumer decision-making (through product and brand reviews) it is an important medium that marketers can channel favorably to promote their products, services, or brands. As a result, U.S companies' use of blogs as a means for marketing is projected to rise from 34% in 2010 to 43% in 2012, in various sectors such as media, B2B firms, academic institutions, and even government institutions (Verna, 2010).

As a recent development, micro-blogging sites such as Twitter are becoming an important channel of communication for companies to interact with customer groups. Many companies such as General Motors, H&R Block, and Kodak are using Twitter as the primary communication portal for customer service, and the feedback has helped to turn around their company image and improve CRM initiatives.

17.2.1.2 E-Mail

E-mail has remained one of the most used forms of direct marketing. According to the Direct Marketing Association, $600 million was spent on commercial e-mail in 2008 yielding an average ROI of $45.06 for every dollar spent. Although that ROI figure has dropped from previous years, it continues to be one of the most cost-effective marketing tools. Given the recent economic downturn, the cost-effective nature of E-mail marketing has made it increasingly attractive as marketers strive to communicate with and cater to their customers at a low cost.

In addition, a study performed by Experian Simmons Research in September 2010 revealed that e-mail has the highest frequency out of all click marketing formats (emarketer, 2011a). Apart from the timing and accessibility of these e-mails, customizing these automated e-mails based on the recipient's interests and activities is a key component to a high success rate. For instance, XM Satellite Radio has recently been sending out e-mails to customers and prospective customers alike with radio "guides" that inform the recipients of all of XM radio's upcoming programming. On the other hand, recent research performed by the Participatory Marketing Network revealed that Generation Y consumers (those born between 1980 and 1995) prefer direct communication with their retailers about products and services.

17.2.1.3 Social Networking Platforms

Social networking platforms have been the hottest topic of discussion for marketers in the past few years. Substantial growth over the past 5 years has made social networking one of the most lucrative and high potential marketing and CRM tools. The market research firm, eMarketer estimated that advertising revenues on social networking platforms would reach nearly $6 billion worldwide in 2011, a 71.6% increase compared to 2010. In a survey conducted by the office services firm Regus, it was found that 47% of businesses have engaged successfully in the use of social networking for customer acquisition in 2011 (a 7% rise from 2010) (emarketer,

2011b). According to the study, while companies in developing countries experienced revenue growth regardless of using social networks for business acquisitions (probably due to overall economic growth), there appears to be a direct positive correlation between the use of social networking for acquisition and the growth in revenue.

Identifying and targeting micro-segments of consumers, starting dialogs with consumers, and building brand awareness are all benefits that firms can profit from by establishing and managing their presence on one of these platforms. Companies such as Papa John's, RedBull, and Target have used Facebook as a means of creating a new portal into their "world". While Papa John's engages in free give-aways for "liking", RedBull has essentially transposed their website onto their Facebook page, and Target has used their page as a platform for promoting their CSR efforts. All the three companies have used distinctly unique approaches, with the same common goal of raising and improving brand awareness.

17.2.1.4 Podcasts and Internet Radio

The use of podcasts has been on the rise in recent years, with eMarketer anticipating 37.6 million Americans to download podcasts on a monthly basis by 2013. They also estimate about 37.5% of internet users above the age of 12 to engage in the usage of internet radio or podcasts (Phillips, 2011). Research from Arbitron/Edison and internet radio ad network TargetSpot has uncovered interesting results with regards to the rise of Pandora and other online radio stations. On the one hand, Pandora provides demographic details on the individual listener since users have to fill out an information form when registering, which can be very useful to marketers in segmenting and customizing their messages on an individual basis. On the other hand, a rise in internet radio listening seems to have coincided with a rise in over the air radio listening, and subsequently, a rise in ad expenditures through this medium. Until there are clear signs of online radio stations replacing the traditional radio medium, marketers will be hesitant to go with the lower volume

and unknown option. Another difficulty that marketers are encountering with podcasts is being able to sift through the hundreds of millions of podcasts and internet radio outlets and determine which ones will best help them communicate with their target markets.

17.2.1.5 Mobile Applications

Recent research performed by mobile analytics firm Flurry has revealed that mobile applications are now gaining a greater share of users' time commitment than the web is. According to U.S based market research firm World Mobile Applications Market, the mobile application market was valued at nearly $7 billion in 2010 and is expected to be worth $25 billion by 2015. These impressive growth rates and market valuations hold significant marketing opportunities for companies such as Apple, Android, Windows Mobile, and Blackberry that provide mobile applications (Perez, 2011).

While the increasing number of mobile applications allows marketers to cater to specific customer segments with targeted mobile applications, it also poses a challenge for marketers to constantly update the applications, and in some cases replace them with more relevant offerings, to make the marketing efforts worthwhile. This condition has ensured that companies are not only developing applications designed to provide utility to their target market, but also creating niche applications for specific customer groups. For instance, Coca-Cola offers several free applications such as a digital "spin the bottle" application and a "magic coke" application, meant to emulate a Magic Eight Ball. Nike offers a "Nike Training Club" application, allowing users to create their own workouts and schedules with a built in point system that grades the users based on if they accomplish their initial goals.

17.2.1.6 Widgets

Widgets have been generating a lot of buzz in the marketing community. Although widgets are growing in popularity and garnering a lot of attention and usage from a consumer standpoint, companies are still reluctant to spend money on marketing through this up and coming medium.

According to eMarketer, spending more than doubled from $15 million in 2007 to $40 million in 2008, but is still not a preferred marketing tool. In addition to the skepticism regarding the profitability of widgets as a marketing tool, there is also a growing concern of widgets experiencing "application burnout", as well as some marketers anticipating widgets to be more of a fad than a mainstay (Williamson, 2008). However, despite the wariness of some to explore widgets as a means for marketing to target markets, some companies have already used them yielding successful results. The Center for Disease Control and Prevention created a "peanut recall" widget that alerted consumers of all products known to have had any traces of salmonella during the U.S peanut scare in 2009. Other companies such as Pizza Hut, Proctor & Gamble, and Barclaycard have used widgets to communicate with their consumers.

17.2.1.7   Viral Videos

Viral Videos have emerged as a user-driven method of communicating. The goal for marketers in approaching viral videos is to create something that they believe will be shared by the viewer with the rest of his or her network. Sites such as Youtube and Vimeo are a testament to the fast growing nature and high potential of this communication outlet. Although viral videos exhibit the potential for marketing and promotion, marketers have not yet established a benchmark for success, with some even suggesting that viral videos are still supplemental to TV. Opposition to the latter claim suggests that viral video is growing in tandem with the mainstream media channels and is now vying for share from TV viewership. In a 2009 survey conducted by FEED, a California—based marketing agency, approximately 35% of the firms surveyed intend to increase their viral video budgets by at least 25%, with another 25% increasing their budgets by 50% (FEED Company, 2008).

Many brands are using viral videos as a way of strengthening brand awareness and brand association. Dos Equis, the Heineken owned beer company, launched a viral video campaign based upon the exploits of their new spokesman "The Most Interesting Man in the World". The massive success of this campaign brought the commercial to the mainstream and into the TV market, which has led to a substantial rise in revenue for the brand. In 2007, Diet Dr. Pepper used self-made Youtube star Tay Zonday to feature in a new viral video promoting a new beverage. By backpacking on the success of an already existing viral video star, Dr. Pepper was able to garner over a million hits on the video within 2 weeks.

17.2.1.8   Social Coupons

Social coupons, or online daily deal sites such as Groupon and LivingSocial, have sky-rocketed over the last few years creating a new customer acquisition method for businesses and a new product/brand research portal for consumers. The success of these deal sites is undeniable— the Wall Street Journal estimates that the industry leader Groupon's upcoming IPO could value it up to $20 billion (Das & Fowler, 2011). The effectiveness of these coupons lies within their ability to acquire new customers for businesses due to unparalleled deals, which customers can then easily share with friends.

Although coupon clippings are still the most common method of couponing, the digital coupon is growing at an exponential rate, with eMarketer estimating that nearly half of all online consumers will use a digital coupon in 2011. The recent rise success of these deal sites can be attributed to the recession, which has prompted consumers to find maximum value for their dollar. Also, as consumers become savvier and spend more time researching products online, they are exposed to these sites and promotional offers. From corner restaurants to big corporations, everyone is finding a way to use the social coupon craze to further their customer acquisition success rate.

17.2.2   Consumer-to-Consumer Interaction: A New Marketing Portal

With Social Media outlets garnering more traffic every day, consumer-to-consumer conversations concerning products and services are becoming a new marketing portal. Rather than engaging in direct B2C marketing strategies, firms are beginning to insert themselves into conversations that are already happening between consumers. The conversations that firms used to have to start are already going on, at greater frequency and with more valuable information. The conversations on social media portals and forums provide consumers the freedom and accessibility to view, discuss, and judge products and services. This setup has provided consumers the ability to formulate opinions on products on their own terms, and influence their peers in their buying decisions

With the advent and subsequent proliferation of social technologies and tools, consumers are not only able to access information on the web, but also share information using a multitude of web technologies amongst their network of fellow users on any scale, and any frequency. This has enabled consumers to actively engage and participate in the development and marketing process of products and services. Additionally, the ability of consumers to access information on their own terms, evaluate products independently, and influence purchase decisions of other users has brought them a new level of autonomy and a sense of "ownership/control" over the products. In other words, we are gradually witnessing a change in the way companies used to know and understand the purchasing habits and the elements of consumer behavior.

The rate of diffusion pertaining to product - related web content has increased manifold. The constantly increasing volume, as well as the vast array of channels through which the information is processed and shared amongst consumer is proving to be difficult for companies to keep track of the content. Additionally, the concept of owning customers, let alone products, is dissipating as consumer-based communities are taking charge. "The Power is with the Consumer," says A.G Lafley, Chief Executive at the Procter and Gamble Company. "Marketers and retailers are scrambling to keep up with her". Consumers are beginning in a very real sense to own our brands and participate in their creation. We need to learn to begin to let go". An example of handing over the brand to the customer can be found

in the case of Mini USA, a branch of BMW North America. Of the 40,000 Minis sold every year, around 60% of them are customized, a sign that managing director James L. McDowell says is proof of the lack of control they have over both brand and customer. In response to this, Mini USA encourages their customers to customize their cars, noticing that some customers have even dressed their cars up for Halloween (Elliot, 2006).

In light of the increasing popularity of these social media tools and their impact on B2C CRM, companies must adapt their CRM strategies as well as their philosophies of control over products and customers. The first step for companies in re-assessing Social CRM strategies is to acknowledge that it may not be possible to have complete control on the web-based content related to them. Rather, companies must be constantly participate in the online communities and adapt their offerings accordingly. According to Adam Sarner, a research director at Gartner, "This doesn't mean that you give them everything like they own it. If you aren't prepared that they'll take some of the control, then don't have the community. And if you can't handle harsh responses, you shouldn't ask questions in the first place. Don't ever, ever, ever ask if your product is good or bad if you aren't prepared to hear the answer and take the consequences of hearing 'It sucks.'" The overall idea behind this philosophy is that to engage in Social CRM and be effective, companies must accept the changing realities of consumers (McKay, 2009).

17.2.2.1 Listening as a First Step

In establishing this new infrastructure for Social CRM, companies must establish a starting point. Given the high degree of consumer generated information, the most logical first step is a simple one: Listen. Being able to utilize information collected on customers begins with listening, and through that, identifying the best strategies in addressing customer demands, concerns, and wants. With marketing and customer communications taking on a whole new perspective, the increasingly active role of the consumer is changing the nature of business altogether.

Firms that do not recognize these market trends and successfully implement them into new CRM strategies must be prepared to face the consequences (Wright, 2006).

In the "Retail Customer Satisfaction Study 2006", conducted by Toronto-based consulting firm Verde and the Jay H. Baker Retailing Initiative at UPenn's Wharton Business school, results showed that although only 6% of dissatisfied customers expressed their feelings directly to the retail company, upwards of 31% communicated their feelings with other customers. "Even though these shoppers don't share their pain with the store, they do share their pain with other people, apparently quite a *few* other people," says Stephen J. Hoch, professor of marketing at Wharton. Furthermore, almost half of those involved in the study confessed to having not gone to a particular store because of hearing about someone else's negative word-of-mouth. This trend is exacerbated by word-of-mouth embellishment, in which each time the story is retold the events and details become more exaggerated and incriminating for the store. As Paula Courtney, President of the Verde Group, explains, "As people tell the story the negativity is embellished and grows. For example, the first time the story is told, it might be about a customer service representative who was rude. By the time the third or fourth person hears the story, the customer service representative becomes verbally abusive. To make a story worth telling, there has to be some entertainment value, a shock value. Storytelling hurts retailers and entertains consumers" (Knowledge@Wharton, 2006).

There are also companies that are engaging in proactive Social CRM strategies revolving around listening to customers. Radian6, a social media monitoring and engagement company, has received acclaim for its ability to listen to online conversations. Their Listening Stations, On-Site Training, lay down valuable frameworks for companies to process, analyze, and respond to customer conversations. Nielsen Online is another example of basing Social CRM strategies on listening; their BuzzMetrics have received overwhelming positive feedback regarding its Brand Monitoring, Brand Connections & Customer Relations, and Brand Campaign Planning and Management (McKay, 2009). Companies such as Dell and WholeFoods are even integrating their own listening-interacting strategies on Social Media platforms, rather than achieving these solutions outside the company via consulting or outsourcing. In both of these examples, the companies opened Twitter accounts and established them as customer communication portals that provided superior service, information, and value to the customer, as well as being a great way to integrate them into the peer-to-peer conversations and gather data on their target audience.

JetBlue's implementation of a Twitter account for Customer Service has created a huge buzz in the airline community due to its innovative nature. JetBlue's Twitter account is accessible for any airport or airline related query, ranging from looking for a wheelchair for airport transportation to being able to reschedule and rebook flights. One particular experience involved a JetBlue passenger experiencing a weather induced flight cancellation. After numerous unsuccessful attempts with JetBlue's 800 number (largely due to the mass flight cancellations in response to inclement weather), the passenger decided to tweet his frustrations with JetBlue and the overall situation. What he received next came as a surprise, as JetBlue's Customer Service Twitter account asked if he could Direct Message them his confirmation number. After sending the number, this passenger received a courteous message less than 15 min later with a complete rebooking and a sincere apology. Due to severe weather, the passenger experienced cancellations several more times and every time he received quick, efficient, and personalized treatment from a Twitter based customer service representative. Here was the chronology of Twitter DM between the customer and JetBlue's Customer Service representatives:

1. Customer Tweet: Complaint on his own account
   Response: Direct Message request for Confirmation Number
2. Customer DM to JetBlue thanking them
   Response: "You're welcome. Happy Holidays! ^kb"

3. Customer flight cancelled again, tweet to Jet-Blue

Response: "Man, you have had a rough day! We're on it. ^kb"

2nd Response: "You just got the last seat on that flight! Confirmation has been emailed (again). Let us know if we can help in any other way. ^kb"

4. Customer flight cancelled again, tweet to Jet-Blue

Response: "We're working very hard to take care of our customers. I will sleep when everyone has been taken care of. Smiles. ^kb," replied the JetBlue Twitter rep.

JetBlue Twitter Customer Service sends new flight information

5. Additional, voluntary Customer Service:

"Are you okay on the return flight? ^co"

"As a token of our appreciation for your patience during last week's snowstorm when we canceled your flight, please accept 10,000 TrueBlue points which you can apply toward future travel to any Jet-Blue destination." (Murillo, 2011).

As it turns out, this customer is a well followed blogger and shared his story with countless followers, who in turn, passed it on through their peer-to-peer network. From the JetBlue's response, it is easy to note the importance of customer management, and a key factor that impacted these processes: listening to customers.

17.2.2.2 Mutual Purpose and Transparency

A key issue today in the implementation of Social CRM is that most companies find it difficult to define their purpose for engaging in it, for themselves or for the customers. For successful utilization of Social Media tools, it is essential to define (within certain parameters) the "mutual purpose" that states the incentives for both the customers and the company (Tsai, 2009).

The entire model of interactive social media tools is based around voluntary interaction between different parties. In creating accounts on Twitter, Facebook, and other social platforms, there must be value adding activity for both the company and the customer, otherwise it serves no purpose. Given the high volume of web pages, applications, and users, just "being on" social networks will no longer be enough. Therefore, identifying this "mutual purpose" is essentially the activity of understanding why the company is actually going onto this social network, and how it will positively affect them and their customers alike.

Frank Eliason of Comcast and his Twitter Customer Service account encompass the mind-set that is required in successful Social CRM implementation. Along with a team of 10 representatives, Eliason saw an opportunity for Social CRM that could better serve their target audience who were already talking about them. People had been voicing their displeasure and issues that they had encountered as customers of Comcast, only they were doing so on vast online social platforms that were going unnoticed by Comcast. This untapped source provided Eliason with the idea of being able to directly address customer queries on a personal level, while also gathering valuable data on their customer groups.

Eliason chose to focus on Twitter and the millions of searchable micro blogs in order to proactively engage in customer conversations to help solve the issues being tweeted, blogged, and shared by millions of customers. By approaching customers in a proactive, candid, and positive manner (ignoring insults and dead end criticisms) Eliason became a personality among his followers and within the Twitter community. Soon, the media caught on to this innovative way of communicating with each individual customer, one based off of proactively reaching out to customers who were already talking about Comcast.

Perhaps the most intriguing and important facet of this strategy was encompassed by Eliason himself when he said, "I never thought I'd become famous on three words: Can I help?" This embodies how basic and how essential mutual purpose and listening arc as a foundation for Social CRM. Eliason clearly defined that there was a gap in communication between Comcast and its customer groups which was negatively impacting customer service. Rather than building a broad presence on Twitter, Eliason realized that the people who were complaining about various aspects of Comcast were already identifiable, and were in need for answers to their questions and concerns. The mutual purpose existed in customers' need for answers, and Comcast's need to reach out to a large customer base and learn about them (Weier, 2009).

Given the high volume of information available to customers, transparency and relevancy are becoming key drivers to the successful diffusion of information and the retention of customers. Customers are becoming less inclined to respond to marketing communication, advertisements, or any kind of information source that would appear to have vested interest as the driving force behind it. Users are ignoring these marketing vehicles more now because they are willing and able to gather information and discern the important from the not-so-important on their own.

It is therefore important to stress authenticity, transparency, and relevancy in order to stay involved in the customers process of obtaining information. This trend is ushering in a new wave of marketing that is in sync with the consumer needs. Rather than performing a corporate pitch, companies need to engage in a closer, more meaningful discussion with their customers. It is through the latter that companies will be able to gain the confidence of their customers, help identify the value of their customers, and serve their needs in a more targeted fashion.

In this regard, it is important for companies to understand that customers now want and feel entitled to closely interact and engage with the brand, a trend that is growing at an exponential rate as the Millenials become the drivers of the market. Social media platforms should be used as access points for these discussions to take place, and then be funneled into a relevant activity for marketers. It is about putting a true and honest face to the brand, one that is candid and whose purpose is not to sell, but rather to inform. Numerous companies are engaging in this type of behavior, including H&R Block, Ford, Southwest Airlines, Dell, Popeyes, DunkinDonuts, and Samsung. By participating in various forms of social engagement, these companies are putting a face to their brands. In the case of automaker Hyundai's "Think Tank", that face is often that of a top executive. Hyundai launched this community that holds live chat sessions with some of the company's most important executives, including CEO and President John Krafcik. Having access to key decision makers within the organization gave customers a sense of importance, as well as establishing transparency, truth value, and "not hiding" Hyundai's image.

17.2.3 Social CRM Strategies: How to do it?

17.2.3.1 Social Strategies: Not Social Tools

Perhaps one of the easiest mistakes to make when establishing a Social CRM strategy is to focus on the available tools rather than creating an adaptable social platform. Although there are some apparent mainstays within the Social Media industry (at least for now) such as Facebook, Twitter, and LinkedIn, reality suggests that social tools evolve and change constantly. Thus, establishing a sustainable Social CRM strategy based on existing specific tools is a recipe for being left behind. In essence, disposable applications are exactly that, but social computing and interaction are constantly flourishing and becoming more and more essential. The underlying concept and strategy is therefore more important than the short-term implementation (Lager, 2009).

17.2.3.2 Implementation: Task-Specific

Going from "We're on Facebook" to "We're on Facebook, in order to achieve _____, which we will accomplish by _____", is a jump that many companies are yet to take. Questions such as "What problems are you trying to fix? How does this platform address these problems? How does this fit into your overall CRM strategy?" would evoke only general and vague responses from companies. As mentioned earlier, it is no longer good enough to just be a website, profile, or account on these Social Media platforms.

Companies such as Comcast and JetBlue are great examples of utilizing a social media tool because of a need or for a purpose, rather than just because "they probably should".

The issue that many companies are facing is that Social CRM, along with many of the social media channels within it, is in the infant stage of its life cycle. Further given that there are very few recognized and recommended approaches to implement Social CRM, companies usually take the lead of other companies because "everyone else is going social". Although it may seem slightly hazardous and undefined, trial and error has proven to be a successful method for some companies to design and implement successful Social CRM strategies. As Justin Goldsborough, social media manager for telecommunications provider Sprint says, "I've learned more by doing and trying things, and that's why we've had more success at Sprint". As noted by Anthony Lye, Senior Vice President of Oracle CRM, companies can also adapt proven and successful Social CRM strategies and technologies used other companies to match their existing goals (McKay, 2009). Being a fast follower of available strategies currently in usage can also be a great way of integrating a social CRM strategy into the overall company strategy.

17.2.4 Sentiment Analysis

One of the most talked about and interesting trends within Social CRM is the growth of analytics and text analysis. With an increasing number of consumers taking to consumers now willingly talking more than ever on public platforms, the World Wide Web is filled with all the information and data that companies have always wanted from their customers. Consumers want to be heard, and that is why social tools such as Twitter, Facebook, and other platforms in the blogosphere and social networking hold a unique value. Twitter, for example, enables companies to sort information shared by demography, topic of interest, or any other preferred criterion.

Companies are now beginning to see the value of these sites and are constantly listening to what

consumers have to share about their experiences with the products, services and brands. To correctly discern the meaning of the information shared by the consumers, companies are now turning towards sentiment analysis that helps them uncover the intended meaning behind consumer opinions and reviews. Companies such as Best Buy, Viacom, Paramount Pictures, Cisco Systems, and Intuit are using sentiment analysis to improve CRM strategies and provide more targeted offerings.

In May of 2009, the ticket-selling agency StubHub used an innovative online sentiment monitoring technology developed by San Francisco based ScoutLabs. They ticket agency took this measure following a rain delay in a New York Yankees vs. Boston Red Sox game at Fenway Park. The rain delay seemingly coincided with a rise in negative sentiment, which upon further review, arose from the company's inclement weather policy for refunds. The negative sentiment seemed to be a result of StubHub's refusal to provide fans with refunds on the basis that the game had already gone underway. However, after using ScoutLab's technology and seeing the negative impact it would have on their brand image, StubHub proceeded to offer discounts and credit awards to those fans in attendance. Furthermore, this entire saga has led to StubHub re-evaluating its refund policy in situations with bad weather. All of these improvements stemmed from the use of ScoutLab's sentiment analysis technology (Wright, 2009).

One of the fastest growing technologies for automated sentiment analysis is text analytics. This tool collects text data on consumer insights not only from web platforms such as the social media, but also from news articles or information databases. The text analytics provides an objective summary of consumer reactions and responses to a particular company, product, or service. The market for text analytics is expected to double from $499 million in 2011 to almost $1 billion in 2014, according to a report by Forrester Research (King, 2011).

Other forms of text analytics solutions offered by companies such as Attensity, ClearForest, Content Analyst, SPSS, Inxight, and Lexalytics are being harnessed by different companies, with each solution providing a unique competitive advantage. For instance, Lexalytics recently launched a web-based application for media relations called MediaVantage which enables a firm to implement automated sentiment analysis of blogs, social media platforms, and any other user feedback over the web in multiple languages.

17.2.5 A Final Word on Social CRM

For the consumers, social media has turned the web from a predominantly communication medium to a medium that encourages collaboration, creation and sharing of information on their own terms. Enabling consumers to express their feelings with regards to a company and their product or service is something that companies have been trying to facilitate for years. With this invaluable insight, companies can now leverage the analytical capabilities of social CRM to understand and uncover the various facets of consumer decision making.

From the above discussion it is clear that in this new digital age, the expansion and popularity of social media is not only increasing the engagement level of consumers, but also reducing the communication gap between consumers and companies in the B2C, B2B, and C2C markets. These social interactions are becoming critical to business operations as formal marketing communication methods are slowly being reconsidered, and novel social media approaches are receiving constant attention.

17.3   Global CRM (GCRM)

Global CRM is defined as "The strategic application of the processes and practices of CRM by firms operating in multiple countries, or by firms serving customers who span multiple countries" (Kumar, Sunder, & Ramaseshan, 2011; Ramaseshan, Bejou, Jain, Mason, & Pancras, 2006). This definition suggests that firm and customer level

differences impact a firm's cross-cultural and cross-national success. At the firm level, these differences include integral components such as production, operations, product portfolio, and firm size. On a customer level, key measures such as customer expectations, drivers of satisfaction, loyalty, and profitability all contribute to the degree of success a firm has in GCRM implementation. Additional recent perspectives on CRM systems suggest that the consumer-centric view could grow among companies as a result of goodwill (Endacott, 2004). This perspective has changed, however, with companies now identifying CRM as a vehicle for profitability on a global scale.

The basis of understanding GCRM begins with understanding the general trends of globalization. As innovative technologies continue to spawn, facilitating rapid and constant company-consumer interaction across oceans and continents, the relationship elements between a company and its customers undergo changes. This is particularly true with regards to CRM, as globalization has stressed the importance of having a defined and systematic GCRM strategy in order to adapt to dynamic and widespread customer bases.

17.3.1 Informational Technology Needs

Global CRM as a concept is evolving at an accelerated rate due to the introduction of new innovative technologies. Software as a Service (SaaS) has particularly impacted GCRM models and has become a motor for growth and progress within the marketing field. Worldwide cloud services revenue is forecast to reach $68.3 billion in 2010, a 16.6% increase from 2009 revenue of $58.6 billion, according to Gartner, Inc. The industry is poised for strong growth through 2014, when worldwide cloud services revenue is projected to reach $148.8 billion. Gartner also estimates that, over the course of the next 5 years, enterprises will spend $112 billion cumulatively on software as a service (SaaS), platform as a service (PaaS), and infrastructure as a service (IaaS), combined (Gartner, 2010).

Following the growth of GCRM, multinational enterprises are beginning to implement and build SaaS models in order to integrate customer and company level data across various geographic regions. This phenomenon is accelerating the growth of smaller service firms such as Salesforce.com, and will continue to do so as SaaS requirements for companies become increasingly diverse and specialized.

The room for improvement in SaaS implementation, however, is fairly prominent. The global CRM practices are known to report lower costs in attracting and retaining customers, increasing employee productivity and call center efficiency, as well as creating more accurate sales forecasting for increased customer sales and satisfaction. As firms aim to establish an international presence through off-shoring business processes, foreign direct investment (FDI), and other expansion methods, global CRM practices can be implemented to facilitate the above mentioned processes.

One company using a SaaS solution is the ambulance group, First Med. By choosing the cloud as there automated model, they were able to reduce turnaround time from the output to mailing of statements in their billing system. This SaaS solution allows First Med to directly transfer information from its billing system to the SaaS platform. "We don't need another software," said Matt Ellis, the company's accounts receivable manager. "We simply upload straight from our system and everything's right there." All that is required is for the statements to be uploaded onto the SaaS platform, at which point First Med employees access them on a web interface. Additional advantages from the SaaS software include, tracking capabilities of the process as well as mail production at the SaaS facility (Berard, 2011).

17.3.2 Global Diffusion

17.3.2.1 Regional and National Heterogeneity

Although the growth of GCRM is often categorized in the functional, industrial, and regional aspects, the regional aspect of GCRM has had the most success and holds great promise for the future. National and regional heterogeneity have become important players in determining the outcomes of CRM implementation. The constant advances in communications and technology have accentuated the blurring of national boundaries, thereby accelerating the global diffusion of CRM as well as allowing firms to operate within and outside of specific geographic regions. Owing to variations in worldwide growth trends, the type of business clients, and cultural environments, companies face a series of challenges on designing and implementing business and marketing strategies. Global CRM systems and practices can help managers to understand and align with their partners and clients from all regions, thereby facilitating the process of making informed decisions and adapting appropriately to the economic, cultural, and political climates of each area of business.

17.3.2.2 Applying It As a Firm

Being able to implement a successful Global CRM system and strategy involves starting from the top and allowing for a trickledown effect to occur. Developing a uniform outlook on GCRM strategy is essential to then being able to adapt it and implement it on a regional or national level. The difficulty in this process exists in being able to find a middle ground between the region/country -specific needs across the board and the global requirements of the strategy without losing sight of the customer-centric strategy of CRM practices.

There is no completely uniform GCRM solution. Industry, customer type, region and other variables must all be accounted for as they change by country or region in order to maximize the effectiveness of the GCRM practice. An example of being successful in this practice is that of U.S electronics retailer Best Buy. The firm successfully adopted a customer centric model, beginning with a $50 million investment to obtain, process, and analyze customer-level data before eventually using this information to change the hierarchical structure of the company. By orienting the salespeople towards the customer instead of towards the product, Best Buy was able to better serve its customers across the board and was able to streamline and funnel their marketing strategy directly to them. This example illustrates a definitive need for firms to prioritize Global, and yet adaptable, CRM strategies in order to maintain a customer-centric outlook.

As shown in the example of Best Buy, a GCRM program has a certain methodology and different requirements that must be fulfilled in order to have sustainable and effective implementation. Finding the balance between focusing on the local or global scale is often mismanaged, leading to disastrous results in particular regions or the eventual collapse of the global strategy due to unmanageable segmentation. Therefore, developing a CRM strategy at the highest level of management, but leaving room for needed adaptability is crucial to the delivery of the program and practice. This ensures that local customers' particular needs are met and accounted for, while also alleviating the company from risking sever deviation from its global standards. Much like with Social CRM, engaging in any form of GCRM prior to strategizing for the long term. The big picture should show local CRM practices integrated into a globally managed one.

Global CRM serves to build and maintain relationships with customers that span multiple countries and is an integral part of the overall global business strategy that aids in the paradigm shift from product centricity to customer centricity. Firms that have implemented GCRM can leverage their integrated database to segment regional and global market and target the most profitable segment(s) as well as individual customers with the right product offer at the right time regardless of their geographical location, thereby fulfilling customer centric strategy. Global CRM also enables firms to have more effective data analytics and more accurate forecasts about global, regional, and individual market trends. New products or innovations do not usually diffuse simultaneously (sprinkler strategy) throughout several countries because of different economic, political, or cultural conditions; rather, they sequentially spread (waterfall

strategy) from one country to another (Kalish, Mahajan, and Muller 1995). Thus, GCRM provides a firm with learning benefits as it applies the knowledge it gains from one country to another.

17.4 Database CRM

17.4.1 Introduction

A database is a collection of information pertaining to customer interactions with the company that can be subsequently used for various marketing activities. Chapter 8 discussed, in detail, the various types, benefits, and uses of databases. Many businesses use these lists in order to better understand their customers whilst differentiating each individual customer based on these statistical findings. Using this information that they have on current customers, businesses can therefore target prospective customers and preemptively build profiles and cater to their individual wants and needs from the beginning. These CRM databases and consulting products provide companies with the ability to store and keep track of information on customers, their purchasing habits, and all of the nuances within their feedbacks and behaviors that have an impact on the buyer-seller relationship. For many years, companies handled all of this information with a physical storage space containing the database(s), resulting in high costs and restrictions with regards to off-site accessibility to the system. As mentioned in the GCRM section, global practices are becoming more and more common (and necessary), resulting in the need for more cost-efficient digital platforms for using, accessing and constantly updating the databases.

17.4.2 Cloud Computing

The development of cloud computing has allowed for more accessible and customizable implementation of CRM practices. It offers large organizations the luxury of disseminating all applications, data, and products within the

CRM strategy to the members within the organization who should require it. As the fastest growing method for data storing, cloud computing provides a unique advantage for CRM, in that the previous physical and organizational restrictions no longer exist. Providing businesses the opportunity to install, use, and share CRM related applications on a web platform allows for remote access and real time updating in order to keep up with the dynamic and evolving nature of databases.

The adaptability and customization capabilities of these applications have made for a more effective CRM tool for each individual employee. Employees are now able to access all of customer data and information on a point-and-click interface, which adapts according to each employee's specific requirements or preferences. Another advantage of housing CRM data with the cloud is that there is no longer a need to allocate massive amounts of server capacity for hypothetical outcomes as a preventative measure. Instead, cloud computing scales up and down as demand dictates, eliminating the need for housing endless preparations for various outcomes. Through this automated and customizable platform, companies are able to cut out the manpower and additional costs that are associated with physical databases such as upfront investments in hardware, housing, and maintenance costs. Through this switch, companies are gaining ground in CRM data-processing as a more cost-effective and flexible solution that houses the same security and confidentiality, all while maximizing users' ability to access and share applications at will.

Many large corporations such as Google, IBM, and Amazon have not only integrated cloud computing into their business infrastructure, but have also made it a cornerstone of their CRM strategy and its everyday functionality. IBM's launch of their Smart Cloud Services has paved the way for a new way of company thinking. "Rethink IT. Reinvent business" is an apt slogan for a company that is offering a wide range of innovative cloud-based solutions such as SaaS, IaaS, PaaS, Cloud Security, Development, and Testing. Many of these services have the goal of creating capacities for their customers to process business software within data hubs. Furthermore, IBM is projecting these cloud computing services to account for 5% of company revenues by 2015, a total of $7 billion (Ricadela & Hoffmann, 2011). Google and IBM are also utilizing Cloud Computing, for various reasons such as improving maintenance times, streamlining processes, and improving employees' productivity and performance by repositioning their focus to the tasks rather than the software issues that need solving in order to accomplish that task.

As one of the world's leading technology organizations for the past few decades, IBM's switch to cloud computing stemmed from issues that many organizations today are still facing. IBM was experiencing issues on all fronts—starting with having too many platforms hosting their various departments, to using applications that became incompatible with the introduction of new software and systems (some applications upgraded while others remained stagnant). To address these issues, IBM turned to Siebel (a CRM Solution software provider) to create an integrated company-wide CRM solution platform that would provide a single source for customer and marketplace data.

These cloud computing based CRM applications can be applied easily and are economical without any infrastructure or maintenance obstacles. In today's age, business software must be readily adaptable for accessing and processing data in relation to market changes and increasing profits. Being able to familiarize employees quicker with the newest apps grants them the ability to focus more on the work itself: helping, understanding, and serving customers.

The implementation of cloud computing has been growing at an exponential rate, with IDC research forecasting a threefold increase in cloud-related expenditures by 2013 (for a total of $44.2 billion). This industry, expected to surpass $140 billion by 2014, is growing across company boundaries, with midsize companies beginning to embrace these strategies in addition to the major multinational corporations already profiting from the cloud's CRM solutions (Modavi, 2010).

17.4.3 Privacy Issues and Concerns

The rise of cloud computing and database information management has led to questions and concerns from businesses and consumers alike regarding the privacy and security of the content. The accessibility of these web-based platforms is simultaneously the root cause of concern for issues such as identity theft and individual privacy. Privacy Rights Clearinghouse, a nonprofit organization for customer information and consumer advocacy reports that since 2005, more than 500 million sensitive records from 2,610 data breaches have been breached. This alarming statistic explains the cause for concern to safeguard privacy and control the personal information on web-based platforms (Privacy Rights Clearinghouse, 2010).

Users are questioning the levels of regulation and privacy that go into the processes involved in collecting information on consumers and online transactions as they are becoming increasingly wary of these methods. Online companies are now placing "cookies" into users' computers, enabling them to garner personal information on the user without their consent or awareness. The practice of placing files called "cookies" and Web bugs by online companies in the user's computer during a visit is quite common. The cookies acquire the information while the user is visiting a particular site and create a pathway for them to continue to systematically retrieve information on this user. Information such as purchase history, advertisement responses, and other online activity can all be gathered in these processes.

Therefore, while several precautions are advised by privacy rights associations, the key to reduce the risk due to fraud lies in closely guarding personal information such as Social Security number (SSN), financial information, and driver's license number among others pieces personally identifiable information for any fraudulent transactions, and monitoring credit history regularly. At the same time, online marketers and researchers will have to reassure customers and participants that their personal information is secure by not only closely guarding the information, but also put in place recourses for consumers in the event of a data breach.

17.5   Summary

Within all of the growing trends in CRM, there is still a great deal of unchartered territory that experts and companies are striving to understand. Within the trends of social CRM, GCRM, and cloud computing, there are intricacies and channels that have yet to be fully tested and understood.

Social networking is changing the way people live, and its effect on the consumer world has had a clear impact that is altering the B2C world. However, the same cannot be said for social media's impact on B2B, where the new channels and methods of communication between parties are barely causing a single ripple within the larger network (Lager, 2009). What this stems from is a hesitancy to move away from sound and tested strategies in favor of the unknown. Because B2B transactions tend to have larger implications than individual B2C relationships, the risk is higher for failure. That does not indicate that social media and social CRM cannot penetrate the infrastructure of B2B networks. There are already subtle examples of these tools having their use within B2B transactions. The BlackBerry Pearl, for example, is a social tool that is directly marketed to professionals with the purpose of facilitating communication processes in their business environment. Although this is on an individual scale, and one could treat these individuals as consumers, the reason for which these people are using this product is to gain from the competitive advantages it provides in the business world.

In conclusion, CRM is undergoing significant changes. With recent developments in speed, reliability, and spread of information channels such as social media have made the concept of CRM fascinating for academicians and practitioners. It has grown tremendously from a predominantly database concept operating at the aggregate level to one that can be customized for individual customers and applied to areas across the world.

Its ubiquity can be felt from daily, routine activities to specialized marketing campaigns, all made possible by the power of data and customer information. The advancements in CRM have also given rise to issues and concerns such as identity thefts, privacy right violations, cyber stalking, and many more. As soon as one crime is brought under control, another crime, bigger and much larger in size, comes up. Despite these contrasting sides, CRM continues to provide a viable option for information for marketers and consumers alike.

References

Beaudry, J. E. (2009). *Zappos milestone: Customer service*. Retrieved May 4, 2009, from www.about.zappos.com

Berard, J. M. (2011). *SaaS brings big-company efficiency to document delivery*. Retrieved January 27, 2011, from www.enterprisecioforum.com

Das, A., & Fowler, G. (2011). Groupon to gauge limits of IPO mania. *The Wall Street Journal Digital Network*. Retrieved June 3, 2011, from www.online.wsj.com

Elliot, S. (2006). *Letting customers control marketing: Priceless*. Retrieved October 9, 2006, from www.nytimes.com

emarketer. (2011a). *10 best practices for email marketing*. Retrieved May 2011, from www.emarketer.com

emarketer. (2011b). *Social media marketing brings new revenues, customers*. Retrieved June 24, 2011, from www.emarketer.com

Endacott, R. W. J. (2004). Consumers and CRM: A national and global perspective. *Journal of Consumer Marketing, 21*(3), 183–189.

FEED Company. (2008). *Viral video marketing: The agency perspective*. Retrieved August 18, 2011, from http://www.feedcompany.com/wp-content/uploads/Feed_Company_Viral_Video_Marketing_Survey.pdf

Gartner. (2010). *Gartner says worldwide cloud services market to surpass $68 billion in 2010*. Press Release. Retrieved June 22, 2010, from, http://www.gartner.com/it/page.jsp?id=1389313

Hsieh, T. (2010). *Why I sold Zappos*. Retrieved June 1, 2010, from www.inc.com

King, R. (2011). *Sentiment analysis gives companies insight into consumer opinion*. Retrieved March 1, 2011, from www.businessweek.com

Kalish, S., Mahajan V., Muller E. (1995). Waterfall and Sprinkler New-Product Strategies in Competitive Global Markets. International Journal of Research in Marketing 12, 105–119.

Knowledge@Wharton. (2006). *Beware of dissatisfied customers: They like to blab*. Retrieved March 8, 2006, from www.wharton.upenn.edu

Kumar, V., Sunder, S., & Ramaseshan, B. (2011). Analyzing the diffusion of global customer relationship management: A cross-regional modeling framework. *Journal of International Marketing, 19*(1), 23–39.

Lager, M. (2009). Sales and social media: No one's social (yet). *CRM Magazine, 13*(6), 29–33.

Marco, M. (2007). *Zappos sends you flowers*. Retrieved October 17, 2007, from www.consumerist.com

Marketing News. (2009). Marketing news' digital handbook. *Marketing News*, March 4, 2009.

McKay, L. (2009). Strategy and social media: Everything's social (now). *CRM Magazine, 13*(6), 24–28.

Modavi, J. (2010). *CRM consulting in the age of cloud computing*. Retrieved April 23, 2010, from AllThingsCRM.com

Murillo, A. (2011). *One awesome customer experience: How JetBlue's Twitter Saved the day*. Retrieved January 24, 2011, from www.theetailblog.com

Perez, S. (2011). *Mobile app market: $25 billion by 2015*. Retrieved January 18, 2011, from www.readwriteweb.com

Phillips, L. (2011). *The internet radio audience: Personalized, mobile, and targetable*. Retrieved May 2011, from www.emarketer.com

Privacy Rights Clearinghouse. (2010). *500 million sensitive records breached since 2005*. Retrieved August 23, 2011, from https://www.privacyrights.org/500-million-records-breached

Ramaseshan, B., Bejou, D., Jain, S. C., Mason, C., & Pancras, J. (2006). Issues and perspectives in global customer relationship management. *Journal of Service Research, 9*(2), 195–207.

Ricadela, A., & Hoffmann, K. (2011). *IBM aims to make cloud computing more palatable to companies*. Retrieved April 7, 2011, from www.bloomberg.com

Tsai, J. (2009). Marketing and social media: Everyone's social (already). *CRM Magazine, 13*(6), 34–38.

Verna, P. (2010). *Corporate blogging: Media and marketing firms drive growth*. Retrieved October 2010, from www.emarketer.com

Weier, M. (2009). *Comcast's Twitter team coaching SalesForce.com*. Retrieved March 25, 2009, from www.informationweek.com

Williamson, D. A. (2008). *Web widgets and applications: Destination unknown*. Retrieved February 2008, from www.emarketer.com

Wright, J. (2006). *Blog marketing: The revolutionary new way to increase sales, build your brand, and get exceptional results*. New York: McGraw-Hill.

Wright, A. (2009). *Mining the web for feelings, not facts*. Retrieved August 23, 2009, from www.nytimes.com

Index

Printing: Ten Brink, Meppel, The Netherlands
Binding: Stürtz, Würzburg, Germany